MONEY OF THE MASSES

Series: MONETARY HISTORY OF INDIA

This series aims to present thematic volumes on various aspects of the monetary history of India, covering the entire period for which written documentation is available, i.e. from *c.* 1300 onwards. It also aims to reassert the importance of the use of numismatic sources in historiography and that of archival sources in numismatography by presenting comprehensive readers, comprising select academic contributions along with the contemporary archival records on select themes.

Series Editor: SANJAY GARG

OTHER TITLES IN THE SERIES

a. *Monetary Foundations of the Raj,* ed. Sanjay Garg (2019)
b. *The Raj and the Rajas: Money and Coinage in Colonial India,* ed. Sanjay Garg (2022)
c. *Fiscal History of India* [tentative title], ed. Bazil Sheikh
d. *Paper Currency in India* [tentative title], ed. Bazil Sheikh

Monetary History of India

SERIES EDITOR: SANJAY GARG

MONEY of the MASSES

Copper Coin Production and Circulation in India 1500-1900

Edited by

JAN LUCASSEN

MANOHAR
2026

First published 2026
First eBook edition 2026

ISBN 978-93-6080-667-5 (hardbound)
ISBN 978-93-6080-181-6 (eBook)

Published by
Ajay Kumar Jain *for*
Manohar Publishers & Distributors
4753/23 Ansari Road, Daryaganj,
New Delhi 110 002

Cover design by Manoj Kumar

Typeset by Ravi Shanker, Delhi 110095

Printed and bound in India

Contents

Illustrations

Figures

Plates

Maps

Tables

Introduction to the Series

Themes dealing with history and numismatics have rarely been integrated in the mainstream historiography of India. For Mughal India, a beginning was indeed made to bridge this gulf (*The Imperial Monetary System of Mughal India*, 1987). Sadly, this noteworthy initiative had no takers amongst historians and numismatists dealing with post-Mughal and colonial India.

While excellent studies, both in the fields of economic, social and political history of India as well as on the contemporary coinage, its production technologies, and mint administration have appeared over the last one and a half centuries, seldom have these two streams intermingled or even intersected. Likewise, the enormous historical material available in the form of official records, personal narratives, and other contemporary accounts as well as in the archives of the British East India Company and later the Crown's representative government in India remains largely untapped in the numismatic writings dealing with this period.

Though a beginning to fill this vacuum was made with the publication of *The Coins of the Bengal Presidency* (Stevens 2012) and *The Sikka and the Raj* (Garg 2013), many more studies are needed to evolve a better understanding of the monetary history of India.

This proposed series, therefore, seeks to fill this vacuum by presenting comprehensive readers on the monetary history of India, covering the entire period for which written documentation is available (both from Indian and colonial authorities), i.e. from *c*. 1300 CE onwards. The individual volumes in this series would be a mix of the published and unpublished research papers as well as the archival sources on different topics ranging, from coinage and paper currency management, to coinage production and circulation, and its effects on financial health of the State, as well as the symbiotic relationship between currency and fiscal management, international trade and overall economy of a nation, to name a few. The actual ratio between the published studies and unpublished documentary sources would, however, vary in each volume and where necessary, translations of non-English sources would be provided. A fresh introduction would integrate these selections into the overall theme. A comprehensive bibliography-cum-list for further readings would be appended to each of these volumes so as to make them a veritable reference tool.

SANJAY GARG

Preface

My interest in the socio-economic history of India emerged rather late in my career. Asked to join the International Institute of Social History (IISH) in Amsterdam in 1988, to set up a separate research department, I had to select a central topic of interest. Opting for global labour history in the long term, I had to find ways of assembling a team of specialists covering the most important parts of the world. One of them was Willem van Schendel, professor in Modern Asian History, first at the Erasmus University Rotterdam and later at the University of Amsterdam. To get me more acquainted with his field of expertise he invited me to a congress at Bangalore in March 1995, my first encounter with India. Almost immediately this sparked my interest in the possibility of making comparisons between European and Indian labour history.

Initially, I concentrated on the work of brickmakers, about whom I had already collected a lot of information about Early Modern and Modern Europe. It turned out that similar information for this interesting and large occupational group was available for India from the mid-nineteenth century until now. After several extended visits and interviews at a dozen or so brick kilns, especially in north India but also around Hyderabad, I wanted to research their history. This led me to the rich sources of the National Archives (NAI) in New Delhi, in particular the extensive series of the Public Works Department, but most of all the Military Board Proceedings and its predecessor. They enabled me to study in more detail the labour organization of brickmakers engaged in the building of the Ganges canal. It also brought me to another group of workers, those employed in the late eighteenth century by the Ichhapur (Bengal) gunpowder manufactory – one of the largest industrial establishments in the world at the time.

My growing interest in the payment of wages to these workers opened up many more avenues at the crossroads of labour and monetary history, about which I published, amongst other things, a series of articles together with Jan Lingen. A final result of my annual visits to the NAI from 1999 onwards was the collection of wage data. Together with my colleagues Pim de Zwart, Paulo Teodoro de Matos and Hélder Carvalhal, I was able to reconstruct a long series starting in the early sixteenth century, by combining data available at the NAI in New Delhi and archives kept at The Hague and Lisbon. This has culminated in a series of articles and book chapters over the last twenty years.

After so many years of archival research and active engagement with Indian colleagues, it is probably time to publish my more encompassing ideas about long-term developments. Recently, I summarized them in my *The Story of Work: A New History of Humankind* (2021) but this volume on such a crucial issue as wage payments outside the more widely studied North Atlantic offers a second chance to do so.

Gouda, the Netherlands JAN LUCASSEN
13 May 2024

Acknowledgements

My primary debt is to the authors and publishers who have contributed to Part I of this volume. They are:

Frank Perlin, 'Changes in Production and Circulation of Money in Seventeenth and Eighteenth-century India: An Essay on Monetization before Colonial Occupation', in Sanjay Subrahmanyam (ed.), *Money and the Market in India 1100–1700* (Delhi: Oxford University Press, 1994), 276–308 [originally published in E. van Cauwenberghe and F. Irsigler (eds.), *Minting, Monetary Circulation and Exchange Rates* (*Trierer Historische Forschungen* VII, 1984, 323-60; *Akten des 8th International Economic History Congress, Section C7, Budapest 1982*)].

Jan Lucassen, 'Deep Monetization, Commercialization and Proletarianization. Possible Links, India 1200–1900', in Sabyasachi Bhattacharya (ed.), *Towards a New History of Work* (New Delhi: Tulika Books in association with Association of Indian Labour Historians, V.V. Giri National Labour Institute, 2014), 17-55.

Jan Lucassen, 'Labour and Deep Monetization in Eurasia, 1000–1900', in Karin Hofmeester and Pim de Zwart (eds.), *Colonialism, Institutional Change, and Shifts in Global Labour Relations* (Amsterdam: Amsterdam University Press, 2018a), 327-60.

Jan Lucassen, 'Deep Monetization in Eurasia in the Long Run', in Bert van der Speck and Bas van Leeuwen (eds.), *Money, Currency and Crisis: In Search of Trust 2000 BC to AD 2000* (London: Routledge, 2018b), 55-101.

Irfan Habib, 'The Price Regulations of 'Ala'uddin Khalji: A Defence of Zia' Barani', in Sanjay Subrahmanyam (ed.), *Money and the Market in India 1100–1700* (Delhi: Oxford University Press, 1994), 85–111 [Originally published in *The Indian Economic and Social History Review* 21: 1 (1984), 393-414.

Najaf Haider, 'Structure and Movement of Wages in the Mughal Empire, 1500–1700', in Jan Lucassen (ed.), *Wages and Currency: Global Comparisons from Antiquity to the Twentieth Century* (Bern: Peter Lang, 2007), 293-321.

Prakash, Om, 'Long Distance Trade, Coinage and Wages in India, 1600–1960', in Jan Lucassen (ed.), *Wages and Currency. Global Comparisons from Antiquity to the Twentieth Century* (Bern: Peter Lang, 2007), 323-48.

Jan Lingen and Jan Lucassen, 'Coin Circulation in the Bihar Fortress of Barharia, 1771'.

This study has never been published before.

Jan Lingen and Jan Lucassen, 'Warfare and Coin Circulation: Two Lacs of Bharatpur and Bindrabund Rupees and 15 Bags of Copper Pyce, Captured at Dig on Christmas Eve 1804', *Numismatic Digest* 36–7 (2012–13), 157-81 [published Spring 2014; a slightly revised version with the same title in *Journal of the Oriental Numismatic Society* 218 (Winter 2014), 24-132].

Jan Lingen and Jan Lucassen, 'Copper Circulation in Northern India in 1830', *Numismatic Digest* 34-5 (2010–11), 148-83.

Jan Lingen and Jan Lucassen: '*Pucka* Pice in Fathepur District 1839: The Wide and Long-lasting Circulation of Awadh's Coppers', *Journal of the Oriental Numismatic Society* 247 (Spring 2022), 9-15.

Jan Lingen and Jan Lucassen: 'The "*Mansúri*" or "*Munsooree Paisa*" and its Use: Combining the Numismatic and Social History of India, *c.* 1830–1900', in *Numismatic Digest* 31 (2007), 187-220.

Jan Lucassen, 'The Logistics of Wage Payments: Changing Patterns in Northern India in the 1840s', in Jan Lucassen (ed.), *Wages and Currency: Global Comparisons from Antiquity to the Twentieth Century* (Bern: Peter Lang, 2007), 349-90.

My thanks go firstly to Dr. Sanjay Garg, former Deputy Director of the National Archives of India (NAI) at New Delhi. He has assisted me in my research at his wonderful institute for more than twenty years. Moreover, he has stimulated me to compose this volume and, together with his wife, Roohi, has always welcomed me in the friendliest way. The staff of the NAI Reading Room have also been very helpful over the years, in particular the kind Mrs. Jaya Ravindran. In addition to the introduction to Indian history by Willem van Schendel, also Jan Breman must also be mentioned. In the same year that I visited India for the first time, a conference took place at the International Institute of Social History (IISH) (26-28 October 1995), entitled 'South Asian Labour: Linkages Global and Local', which, one year later, led to the foundation of the Indian Labour Studies Association with its lively annual conferences under the unsurpassed leadership and inspiration of the learned and kind Prof. Sabyasacchi Bhattacharya (JNU). He, together with Rana Behal, Prabhu Mohapatra, Chitra Joshi, and other active members of the Association, has always encouraged me to publish the results of my research. These colleagues and friends, alongside my colleagues at the IISH in Amsterdam, as well as those engaged more particularly in the study of wages (Radhika Seshan, Najaf Haider, Dhiraj Kumar Nite, Pim de Zwart, Paulo Teodoro de Matos, and Hélder Carvalhal) have broadened my view on Indian history in a global context. The IISH is also deserving of a special mention for facilitating so many archival trips to India, Anna Yeadell's expert and creative language editing, Annelieke Vries' clear maps (I.1, I.2, 1.1, 8.1, 10.1, 12.1 and 13.1), and all the help received from my dear colleague Aad Blok.

As for monetary and numismatic history, apart from Sanjay Garg, I must make special mention of Jan Lingen, who unreservedly shared his enormous knowledge of Indian coins with me and with whom I published a number of articles. Having already named the NAI and the IISH, a special word of thanks goes to a third institution, the M.S. Merian – R. Tagore International Centre of Advanced Studies, which offered me a fellowship that enabled me a longer stay in Delhi. I also thank the copyright holders of the studies reprinted in this volume for their kind permission.

Last but not least, without the hospitality of Dr. Prita Trehan in Delhi and the enduring support of my life mate Lieske Vorst, this work would never have been possible.

Gouda, the Netherlands JAN LUCASSEN
13 May 2024

Abbreviations

AH	Hijri year
BCE	Before the Current Era (BC)
CE	Current Era (AD)
DML	deep monetization level
g	grams
Gvt Rs	(British Indian) government rupees
IESHR	*Indian Economic and Social History Review*
i.n.o.	in the name of
JESHO	*Journal of the Economic and Social History of the Orient*
JONS	*Journal of the Oriental Numismatic Society*
kg/kgs	kilogram(s)
KM	*Krause – Mishler* (coin catalogues)
NAI	National Archives of India, New Delhi
MB/MBP	Military Board (Proceedings)
ONS-NL	*Oriental Numismatic Society Newsletter*
R/Rs	rupee(s)
RY/ry	Regnal year
SACPM	*South Asian Coins and Paper Money* (2013)
SaR/SaRs	sicca rupee(s)
st. rs.	Sonat Rupees
VS	Vikram Samvat year

Introduction

1. The Significance of Studying the Money of the Masses, Especially in India, 1500-1900

Even with the rise of electronic payments, for the contemporary reader, spending and receiving currencies in all their forms for the exchange of goods and services, including labour, remains a given. More generally, a monetized society using coins, paper money and, recently, 'plastic money' (cards and electronic payment devices), is also seen as a sign of 'modernity'. In contrast, in this view, barter or the exchange of services and labour efforts without material payments is a sign of primitivity, backwardness, or retardation. Whatever the terminology used, fluctuations and modifications in the circulation of the means of exchange are intimately linked to the character of society as a whole. In particular, the 'money of the masses', i.e. the means of exchange used to pay out wage labourers, in this volume mostly copper coins.

In order to understand a society and its past working population, it is therefore useful to know more about developments in the circulation of coins: were they scarce or amply available, does scarcity reflect a lack of demand or of supply, which transactions precisely were copper, silver, and gold coins (and later, paper money) used? Moreover, who decided on their production and distribution? And, lastly, how do all these issues reflect more fundamental societal change, especially with respect to the masses of the working poor?

This volume discusses these questions in relation to India over the past five centuries, up until the dominance of modern, mechanized coin production and circulation.

Why India?

The need to study these questions for India has to do with one of the most fruitful debates in world history over the last decades: the 'Great Divergence' debate. It questions the long-held idea that, for millennia, society in the 'West' (the North Atlantic) has been fundamentally superior to those in the 'Rest' of the old world. This story pretends that the West, rooted in Classical Antiquity and Christianity, gave birth to the Renaissance and Enlightenment, the Industrial Revolution, and modern superior levels of welfare.[1] Against this dominant idea, the American sinologist Kenneth Pomeranz posited that not only the West but also Ming China, Mughal India and the Ottoman Empire made major achievements in the sixteenth and seventeenth centuries. This is in sharp contrast to what happened in the nineteenth and a greater part of the twentieth century when the West undoubtedly gained economic, military, and political dominance. Pomeranz thus reformulated the whole debate by asking when these initially equally successful societies started to diverge and why. When and why did the European growth spurt occur, and at what point did Asia begin to lag behind: in the seventeenth century or already before? In the eighteenth century or even later?

Thus far, the Great Divergence debate has taught us that the classical premise of Europe's intrinsic advantage from the beginning of its 'Great Discoveries', or even earlier, is no longer tenable. But is has also revealed how difficult it is to make a meaningful comparison of the economic achievements of Western Europe, China, India, and other contemporaneous civilizations. This is especially true for a comparison of the societies and the institutions behind these achievements.

Indian history has received very little attention in the Great Divergence debate compared to Great Britain and China.[2] This is a pity for at least two reasons. First, omitting from the equation a subcontinent, home to one of the world's greatest and most successful polities in the sixteenth and seventeenth centuries is inadmissible. But second and foremost, because of the special nature of Indian society given its caste system. In its purest economic form, i.e. the strict inheritability of professions and occupations, this puts severe constraints on social mobility (geographical as well as occupational) and, as such, it provides an interesting variable in the great laboratory of experiences offered by global history in general and by global labour history in particular.

Part of the Great Divergence debate circles around indicators of (economic) performance, like the ready availability of raw materials, especially combustible fuel (think of the role of coal in the Industrial Revolution) and human capital, resulting in welfare levels. A ready proxy for these levels is found in wage data.[3] Indeed, the combination of daily food prices and real wage levels provide much of the new evidence in the Great Divergence debate.

The first attempts to produce wage data in order to say something about welfare levels in India are more than a century old. The British colonial servant William Harrison Moreland had already formulated such questions in 1923, receiving critical comments from Indian professor of economy Brij Narain six years later.[4] After a long silence, the debate was revived in the 1990s by Prasannan Parthasarathi, Sashi Sivramkrishna, Roman Studer and others, but because of the paucity of data no consensus was possible. It is only recently that the discussion has been given fresh impetus by the addition of archival data from English, Dutch and Portuguese sources beginning in the early sixteenth century. The latest article on this topic concludes 'that the Great Divergence between western Europe and India goes back at least to 1500', but with two important caveats: 'the gap narrows substantially between roughly 1550 and 1650, because of dropping real wages in north-western Europe and, initially, rising ones in India'.[5] At the same time, the authors observe 'diverging developments within Europe, the so-called Little Divergence, between Northwest and the South, in particular the Iberian Peninsula. Only from 1800 onwards dropping living standards in India started to diverge substantially from those in Southern Europe (as did those in Japan)'. Despite their great step forward (from a few dozen to thousands of observations), the authors remain hesitant to come up with explanations for these divergent and convergent welfare levels in different parts of Eurasia.

The debate continues with the input of new archival evidence (also, befittingly, from vernacular language sources including Persian), but also by viewing the results from a fresh perspective. Thus, questions arise about the size and composition of the Indian working-class household, the capacity of its members to contribute to household income and, of course, the flexibility of the Indian labour market and social and occupational mobility.[6]

Because of all the uncertainties related to long-term real wage development studies, additional and alternative approaches are much-needed. Fortunately, as this volume tries to demonstrate, such an alternative is available in the form of written sources combined with information from other historical disciplines. In particular, archaeology and its subfield numismatics are useful here to provide an escape route from often inadequate archival sources. This route via the 'deep monetization' approach, is followed in this volume.

Archaeology, numismatics, and deep monetization

The degree to which interpersonal exchange is expressed in money value, or to which currency plays a role in this exchange, is called monetization. It has drawn the attention of economists and historians (although less in the framework of the Great Divergence debate) because it is generally considered a crucial step in economic development.[7] Also for India, where a debate has been waged between authors (like B.R. Ambedkar) who date this process in the British period and historians from the Aligarh School (like Irfan Habib, Shireen Moosvi and Najaf Haider), who date it much earlier, at least from the Mughal Empire. Others like Sanjay Subrahmanyam, John Deyell and Frank Perlin, have underlined the importance of monetization levels for the assessment of economic performance, and – without explicitly referring to it – for resolving the Great Divergence debate.[8]

The huge advantage of these kinds of monetary and numismatic studies is that they look for evidence not only in archives and libraries, where it is mainly limited to more recent centuries but also in museums. Especially for the Mughal Empire and its predecessors, museum coin collections have been investigated with a view to coming up with proxies for the frequency of mintage in the past. Simply put, these archaeological objects are counted and tabulated based on the supposition that the more frequently a certain type of coin (or year / mint house) occurs in such collections, the more were produced in the past. And vice versa.

For a meaningful interpretation, it is necessary to distinguish between different types of coins performing different socio-economic functions. For example, wealthy individuals mainly used gold coins for savings in the form of hoarding as well as for rare – due to the risk – transfers of huge sums of money.[9] Big silver coins are apt for seasonal payments, e.g. land taxes and other rents, but also for the payment of medium sums of money in commerce. Small fractions of silver, but mainly copper coins, are the common person's means of exchange, used for the payment of wages, and for their subsequent purchases in the marketplace and shops. Together with cowrie shells they also serve as small changes. The central role of wage payments and the labour market must be underlined here, as it is not at all obvious to most social, economic, and monetary historians, let alone archaeologists and numismatists. Too often, sweeping statements are made about low-value coins as primarily 'small change and used for the payment of very small purchases, alms and of insignificant services', in this case by the eminent Portuguese historian Vitorino Magelhães Godinho (1918-2011), while at the same time being well aware of the significance of wage labour.[10]

As will be worked out below, because of this specific socio-economic payment function, small change informs us about the frequency and nature of daily monetary transactions. We must rely on archaeological evidence to know how many small-value coins were put into circulation because detailed written sources on production appear only very late in history. For India, they are sparsely available for the late eighteenth century, and somewhat better for the nineteenth century, in particular for the so-called Presidency Mints of Calcutta, Bombay and Madras; however, there is no information available about, e.g. the quite significant mint output of the state of Hyderabad until 1949. We only have complete mint production figures for independent India. Luckily, the main raw material used for producing small change, i.e. copper ore, was largely imported from abroad. Thus, international trade statistics from the fifteenth to the eighteenth centuries offer indications for the actual conversion of copper into copper coins.

We cannot do without archaeology here, but how do we translate finds of old coins into historical production figures? This question will be discussed below, resulting in estimated production figures for small coins, and therefore for deep monetization levels in India during the centuries covered by this book.

The role of wage labour and the explanatory power of the deep monetization concept

Apart from this reconstruction of deep monetization figures, we must ask ourselves what happened after the striking of the coins and their leaving the mint house: how were they put into circulation, who used them and for what kind of transactions? To answer these questions, we have to turn from archaeology to history again. Written sources are available, mainly from the second half of the eighteenth century, which enable us to envisage the daily practice of small coin transactions and, in particular, the first step in the chain: the paying out of wages. And the related question of how many Indians had to rely – partially or fully – on wages for their income.

This is a rich story, directly linked with labour relations and social relations more generally. It also enables us to see wage workers in action: which coins did they accept, and which did they refuse? And what did they do when they did not agree with the coins they received? Did they protest or just accept the means of exchange they were given, or the conditions imposed by the vendors in shops and at the market, or by the money changers? The last category, the 'shroffs' (*sarrafs* in Arabic), who changed denominations of different compositions deserve special attention. For wage workers, it was crucial which exchange rate the shroffs used in converting specific silver units, mainly rupees and their fractions, into coppers, but also, especially in the north-east, coppers into cowries. And vice versa, of course. For the modern reader, who is used to exclusively fiduciary money, where there is no relation whatsoever between the material (metal / paper / plastic) value of the currency and its exchange value, 100 paise make one rupee, or, for that matter, 100 pennies make one pound and 100 cents make one dollar or one euro. That, however, is a fixed exchange rate, which can only be maintained and enforced if there is a strong central authority to guarantee the entire process of building a fiduciary currency. To a certain extent, this may already have been true for the heydays of the Mughal Empire; it was certainly the case for British India, albeit it occurred gradually in the nineteenth century and even later. In the intermediate nearly two centuries it certainly was not. Most Indian wage workers between 1500 and 1900 were well aware of fluctuations in the exchange rate between silver (and sometimes gold) and copper, and between copper and cowries. And they acted accordingly.

Leading questions and structure of this volume

The full story of small change circulation or deep monetization, including the behaviour of workers, offers a mirror image of the socio-economic history of a country. And this also goes for India and, for that matter, India's place in a wider global context, including the Great Divergence debate.

The following topics will be worked out in the various parts of this introduction. Chapter 2 of this introduction provides a brief outline of the monetary history of India and especially of the process of deep monetization, from its beginning 2,500 years ago until now. This will put the core period of this book, 1500-1900, into perspective for the reader. In Chapter 3, the production of small change takes centre stage. Based on conceptual and methodological considerations, sources of information on raw materials (mining and importation of copper, but also imports of non-metallic small currency objects) and the actual minting will be reviewed. This is necessary in order to reconstruct the total production of small change in the long run. In Chapter 4, we turn from production to circulation; that is, from the more economic to the more social aspects, in particular the behaviour of wage workers. Chapter 5 of the introduction summarizes the general quantitative and qualitative developments between 1500 and 1900, as well their implications for our view of Indian history as a whole in a global context and (in the Outlook) of India's specific social structure. Finally, the introduction concludes with an introduction to the next parts of this volume: the Studies and the Records.

Fortunately, the series Monetary History of India in which this book appears, enables the reprint of important earlier studies in the field (in Part I, the Studies) as well as the publication of archival documents (in Part II, the Records). The selection made here illustrates and, at the same time, underpins the view developed in the introduction. The four Appendices to this introduction have a similar function, albeit they are of a more quantitative nature. The usual bibliography, a list of contributors to Part I (the Studies) and an index close the book.

2. 2,500 Years of Coin Production and Circulation in India

Coinage in north India – including coinage of small denominations – goes back 2,500 years. Its use is therefore as old as that in the Eastern Mediterranean or China. India, like Asia Minor and the classical Greek world, had been practising a multi-denominational and multi-metal currency system since the mid-first millennium BCE.[11] The Chinese authorities meanwhile organized their coinage differently by producing only small copper 'cash' coins until the end of the nineteenth century. In order to frame more broadly the developments in the four centuries between 1500 and 1900 – the core period of this volume – it is useful to give a bird's eye view of the main monetary developments over the last two-and-a-half millennia.

A kick-start: 500 BCE-400 CE

Although there were certainly contacts between West and South Asia around 500 BCE – think of Indian mercenaries in Persian armies – most likely the introduction of coins in north India at the time occurred largely independently.[12] Certainly, the totally divergent form they took in these two parts of Asia points in that direction: mostly punch-marked or cast and often rectangular coins in the Indian subcontinent as opposed to the die-struck and mostly round coins in the Eastern Mediterranean. In the course of the fifth century BCE, India shifted from the original large silver coins (the 'bent-bar' siglos of 5.5 gram) to smaller fractions up to a twentieth and a fortieth of a siglos (0.10-0.15 gram). Also significant was the introduction everywhere of copper coins alongside the silver series.[13]

Some rare texts from the early years of the Maurya Empire (*c.* 321-185 BCE), and in particular the *Arthashastra*, provide information about the way coins were used. Despite major problems in dating this information (between its earliest known version from the third century BCE to 500 years later), the classification of workers in this text may be directly linked to the usage of small change. The *Arthashastra* distinguishes between slaves, bonded labourers, unpaid labourers who worked in lieu of paying a tax or fine, casual labourers working for wages, piece-rate workers, individuals working for a regular wage (all of them tenured servants) and the self-employed. Paying their wages and spending of these in the market apparently posed no serious problem.

Besides the silver *karshapana* of 3.5 gram and its three fractions (the smallest, of 1/8 *pana*, weighed 0.44 gram), there were also four copper fractions ranging from 1/16 down to 1/128 *pana*. As the *Arthashastra* suggests, based on the fact that the lowest paid state servants received a cash wage of 5 *pana* per month, the hourly wage must have been about 1/40 *pana*. Consequently, the smallest copper fraction equalled one-third of an hour's work. At the other end of the scale, the highest-paid bureaucrats received 800 times more.

In this first period of a market economy and of deep monetization in South Asia, central states such as the Maurya Empire, the Indo-Greek states, the Kushana and, finally, the Gupta Empires were dominant in northern and central India. There were also times in between when apparently the economy and monetization were well developed, but more decentralized, i.e. organized by cities, city states, guilds or 'tribes'. Common to all these polities is a virtually uninterrupted period of nearly a thousand years during which small change was abundantly available, foremost in the north, but increasingly also in the centre, and only to a lesser extent in the south. Unfortunately, other detailed information about its usage, of the kind provided in the *Arthashastra* is lacking, so for this long period as a whole we have to content ourselves with this, thankfully rich, image.

Demonetization 400-1200

Deep monetization, as described here, came to an end in South Asia around 400 CE, remarkably, in the same period as in Western Europe.[14] This tendency to market contraction started with the Gupta dynasty and may well be related to its revival of Hinduism (and the demise of Buddhism) with the concomitant extension of the caste system. Although the origins of this rigid hierarchical system of social segregation may be traced back to an earlier period, it now became dominant and severely restricted professional mobility and social mobility at large. This must have had a limiting effect on the functioning of the labour market and, for more than half a millennium, we can notice a process of large-scale demonetization. Although the Guptas are famous for their exquisite gold coins and also continued to mint silver ones, new small denomination coinage, and especially copper coins, almost completely vanished. Of course, over this long period and in such a large subcontinent, certain series can be identified (like in early medieval[15] Europe with its great regional variety), but both their overall scarcity and poor craftmanship compared to the coins struck in the centuries before and after are noteworthy. The isolated evidence of the usage of cowries is intriguing (see para 3d of this introduction) but does not change this assertion. India not only became a subcontinent 'without silver', as famously formulated by John Deyell, but the circulation of non-precious metal coins also became much less important.[16]

India 1200-1500

Muslim invaders from the west initiated a return of the market and of a ubiquitous and technically highly qualified coinage, including the production of small fractions.[17] From the eighth century, it spread, tentatively initially, in the extreme west (Sind) and, from the late twelfth century, across north India, with the successful Delhi Sultanate and, subsequently, with other sultanates over the entire subcontinent. An important, seemingly autonomous phenomenon in the south, including Ceylon, is the deep monetization of the Chola Empire in the eleventh and twelfth centuries by way of a prolific copper coinage. This was followed, albeit to a lesser extent, by other dynasties, including the Pandyas and Vijayanagara.[18]

Quantification of coin production in India is difficult and, accepting many uncertainties, it is only possible from around 1200 onwards.[19] As in Europe, however, the initial jump in Indian deep monetization levels (DML) is already visible in the Middle Ages. No doubt, there was an initial acceleration of the circulation of small-value coinage (copper, billon and silver coins weighing less than 5 gram) in the period from 1275 to the mid-fourteenth century. Because these denominations amount to daily rather than hourly wage levels, we must speak of, in this case, medium rather than deep monetization in north India by 1300.

Especially during the reign of Alauddin Muhammad Khalji, Delhi Sultan 1296-1316, in addition to gold and silver coins, a huge number of two- and six-*gani* billon coins were put into circulation.[20] Annual wages for unskilled workers (servants) were then ten to 12 *tankas*, or 1⅓ to 1⅗ *jitals* per day, whereas for skilled workers, like weavers and tailors, they were 2-3 *jitals*. Given that, according to the famous mint-master Thakkura Pheru, the basis of the system was the one *gani-jital*, Alauddin's *dugani* (a two-*gani* coin containing 8 per cent silver) and a six-*gani* coin with 25 per cent silver roughly equalled the wages for between one and three days' work. This makes the circulation of copper *paikas* of ¼ *jitals* and its fractions, which gradually replaced one-*jital* pieces much more interesting for our DML criteria. However, these coins did not occur in such large numbers as the billon pieces.

Firoz Shah, Delhi Sultan (1351-88), made a new attempt to ensure enough small change by increasing copper coin output, in particular the number of half and quarter *jital* coins.[21] Firoz Shah's court historian, Shams Siraj Afif, summed up the policy:

> The thought crossed Firoz Shah's august mind that if poor people bought something from the market and a balance in half or quarter *jital* was left of the amount paid, the shopkeeper would not have the quarter change. If the buyer let it go, he would lose money. If he demanded it from the shopkeeper how could he be paid when no such coin existed? In the end, the balance due to the buyer would be left with the shopkeeper. For these reasons, the transaction between the buyer and the seller would drag unnecessarily. Sultan Firoz Shah gave orders for the striking of a half *jital* coin called *adh* [literally 'half'] and a quarter *jital* coin called *paika*.[22]

Somewhat later, numismatic evidence for north and central India suggests a second acceleration between 1425-50 and 1525, decades for which little qualitative information is available to clarify why this occurred.

India 1500-1800/50

Because this period is at the heart of this volume and will receive ample attention hereafter, only a few remarks will suffice here. First, the successful political unification under the Mughals extended their empire roughly to a size seen only once earlier, under the Mauryas, and only once later, under the British from the 1850s onwards. This extension had major economic and monetary implications. To mention a few, improvements to the infrastructure and the (temporal) improvement of the standard of living and – as will be explained later – of the monetary system, initially under the Suri dynasty.

Second, the changed relations with the world outside the peninsula proper. Until this time, links with the outside world depended on land routes and sea routes within the Indian Ocean and to the east up to the South China Sea. Following the arrival of the Portuguese, the land routes to the north-west and, somewhat later, the Red Sea route experienced serious competition from the sea route around the Cape of Good Hope. This eventually resulted in the subjugation of India to a foreign power between 1757 and 1849, which would last until 1947, once again with major economic, monetary, and also social implications.[23] These gradually became perceptible in the late eighteenth century. On the other hand, there was much continuity in the trade within the Indian Ocean and the land trade with Central Asia, including the importation of slaves from East Africa and the exportation of slaves to the north. What was new was the exportation of slaves by Europeans, e.g. the Dutch, from southern India to Indonesia.[24]

Because the financing of international trade does not find a logical place in the rest of the text, it is important to understand here that not only did the levels and nature of deep monetization change in this period, but also large-scale financial transactions. As in Europe, big merchants and governments preferred written instruments over the movement of large sums of precious metal. The same functions of bills of exchange that developed in Western Europe in the thirteenth century were performed by so-called *hundis* in India.[25] When exactly *hundis* became important instruments of payment in India is not clear, but they certainly were in use in the sixteenth century.[26] The 'book money' payment method was also being used, i.e. by assignment on merchants' bank accounts. A rather late example of this is available for Ahmedabad where, because of the scarcity of the rupee in 1780/1, merchants resorted to transfers into each other's books as a method of mutual payment. This was called 'dealing in a(u)nt'.[27] These written transfers were impossible, however, where the balance of trade was unequal. Because Europe had few trade goods to offer in exchange for Indian spices, textiles, and more 'oriental' luxuries, it had to pay in cash silver and gold, much in demand in India where it could not be mined. In these centuries of revived intercontinental trade, therefore, large-scale shipment of precious metals (and of copper, as we will see below) still played an important role in the trade between India and Europe, and also in the Indo-Chinese trade.

India 1800/50-1947

The consolidation of British India after the Third Maratha War (1817-19), and the subjugation of the Sikhs in 1849 enabled the new masters to impose a uniform system, although a few indirectly ruled states, the largest of which was Hyderabad, were allowed to continue their own coinage. This process has been studied in detail by authors such as Sanjay Garg and Paul Stevens, and will also receive attention in the chapters hereafter. The centralized colonial bureaucracy enables us to come up with better estimates for the DML, which compares favourably with Europe, i.e. monetary transactions using small change must have occurred as frequently in India as in the then most prosperous parts of the world. What was new was the introduction, in the 1820s, of paper money for large transactions in economic centres, as is clear from the mostly high nominal value of the fractions put into circulation by the government and by private banks. The lowest was five rupees – a very good monthly wage for an ordinary worker at the time.[28]

India 1947-now

For the common man and woman, India's Independence did not bring major changes in the monetary system, with a few exceptions: first, the omission of the portrait of the British king (proclaimed emperor of India 1877-1947); then the introduction of decimal coinage in 1957; and, third, the limitation of coinage to non-precious metals (with the exception of commemorative coins starting in 1969). Due to price inflation, we are also able to observe the issuing of small denominations of paper money, down to one rupee (in emergency situations like the Second World War they had even been smaller). The same phenomenon caused the ousting of coins from daily use in the twenty-first century. Finally, in 2016, in an attempt to curb tax evasion and black money, the Government of India demonetized of all high-value banknotes

(Rs. 500 and 1,000), which forced the population to open bank accounts, thus diminishing substantially cash payments, which are now increasingly superseded by plastic money, thereby heralding the end to a 2,500-year tradition in the foreseeable future.

3. Production[29]

Historians have engaged with the problems surrounding long-term trends of deep monetization in various ways, both theoretically and practically. These will be reviewed here, starting with concepts, theories and sources, focussing on India in para 3a. There then follow three paragraphs on the logistics of deep monetization, from ore to minting: para 3b on copper mining in India; para 3c on copper imports; and para 3d on the imports of non-metal currencies. The actual production, both the technical and organizational side dealt with briefly) as well as my estimate of India's small coin production and supply in the long run follows in para 3e. The social implications of these results are the topic of Chapter 4.

3a. Concepts, Theories and Sources

Questions relating to the (deep) monetization of India have developed along two different historiographical traditions. One is more conceptual and theoretical and will be discussed here briefly before going deeper into the other, more empirical aspects.

For obvious reasons, historians of Classical Antiquity and of the early Middle Ages in Western Europe have been the forerunners in this field.[30] They were also inspired by anthropologists who studied non-European societies with different monetary systems. Deep monetization denotes the usage of coins deep into society until reaching a large mass of the population. Its implications, in economic terms the permeation of the market economy, are obvious. Its social implications have been interpreted by historians in two diametrically opposite ways.[31] Perhaps, best known is the pessimistic interpretation, which, in the Marxist tradition, stresses the increasing dependency of especially wage labourers, but also small producers or more powerful employers and tradesmen on coin usage. But there is also an optimistic take on this with a long pedigree, best known from the work of the German philosopher Georg Simmel. According to this view, being paid for services or goods in currency provides freedom to choose how to spend the earnings, and therefore provides freedom from employers or big merchants. As will be shown in Chapter 5 of this introduction, there is no real contradiction between these two views and both apply to the Indian case, although in a highly specific way.

More formally, a few years ago I proposed a concrete yardstick to measure deep monetization levels in such a way as to enable comparisons through time and space. We can speak of a specific geographical unit in a specific time period as 'deeply monetized' when a substantial stock of currencies per capita is in circulation, consisting of denominations equaling the value of one hour or less of waged work. Substantial, in this case, means a per capita stock equal to between five and ten times the prevailing hourly wage.[32]

For India, Shailendra Bhandare has used this term in a numismatic article of 2008, much inspired by Frank Perlin who, without using this concept, had already called attention to this phenomenon in his PhD thesis, submitted in 1983. He found many signs of a vibrant monetary economy in his studies of eighteenth-century Maharashtra, which he contrasted with the negative and derogatory view of the British colonizers, but also with the presumed golden age under the great Mughal emperors.

His emphasis is on coin production more generally, which includes copper. He observes 'a marked decline in quality of crafting' by the late seventeenth century, resulting in a 'gimcrack appearance'.[33] Surprisingly, he does not blame this loss of craft skills among mint personnel on economic decline. Quite the opposite, Perlin stresses the substantial and growing demand for low-denomination means of exchange:

> [L]ow-quality monies, such as the extraordinarily crude coppers which became especially abundant towards the end of the eighteenth century, were more than likely to have functioned, as in Central India, in the captive coin markets [...] where financiers and traders were directly involved in making advances to large numbers of humble producers of market-

destined crops and textiles, or at the more humble and profuse levels of urban circulation: thus the iron, tutenag and lead issues of eighteenth-century Surat, Goa and Bombay, respectively; the cheap copper 'cash' put out in the urban entrepots of Southern India; the cowries which circulated among urban and rural producers in Bengal.

This type of small-value and poorly executed coins was produced simultaneously with two different silver currencies: poor quality silver coins for regional trade and good quality silver coins for long-distance commerce.[34]

Research, using the definition of deep monetization as presented here, requires data for specific geographical and time units on low-value coin production, wage levels, and population size. The available sources for such research will be reviewed next.

Written sources

For most of the period covered by this book, archaeological sources are more important for quantitative reconstructions of long-term trends than written sources. That is because written sources on the production and circulation of coins, and in particular copper coins, in India are rare. There are still a few extant from before the seventeenth century, from the later period of the Sultanates and the early Mughal period. Data become more abundant for the period 1850 to 1900, when, with the help of modern machinery, the British became successful in monopolizing coin production and, consequently, its circulation.[35] My own archival research has concentrated on the colonial period between the mid-eighteenth and the late nineteenth centuries. In particular, three series kept in the National Archives of India in New Delhi have proven to be helpful.[36]

The oldest systematic collection of written information on coin production is the papers of the Mint Committee set up in 1792 at Fort William in Calcutta to offer advice to the Governor-General.[37] Its papers for the period 1792-1820 are invaluable because all other relevant archival series start later.[38] In fact, these papers go back even further in time as they contain a precious set of answers on coin circulation from a dozen district collectors, dating from 1787.

Unfortunately, the papers from the 1820s have been lost and the series resumes only in the 1830s.

That is also the decade when another series starts that is important for our topic: this time by the Foreign Department. Foreign, in this case, not only means countries outside British India but also, primarily, 'princely states', i.e. Indian states under indirect British rule. This indirect but very real power was realized by the Governor-General's (based at Fort William in Calcutta and representing the East India Company until 1858 and the British Crown until 1947) appointment of British colonial 'residents' at princely courts. As his representatives, they reported on many aspects of princely rule, including one of the important *regalia*, i.e. the right of coinage. Thanks to good indexes, it is possible to trace and study many relevant documents between 1830 and 1902 regarding 'native' coinage and coin circulation, including copper coins.

Less easily accessible, but not to be dismissed, is the series 'Residencies, their predecessor and successor bodies (1756-1954)'. The indexing of the several 'Agencies' in which the residencies were clustered is very uneven but has yielded some informative documents, especially from the Central India Agency and Hyderabad Residency, mainly from the 1840s onwards.

Finally, a number of civil servants, both Indian and colonial, have made their own useful observations on contemporary coin circulation, most explicitly William Wilfrid Webb (1858-1911), who wrote a small monograph on the currencies of the Hindu States of Rajputana (Preface dated Dublin, 10 May 1893).[39]

The records of mint masters or state officials that have survived (rather sporadically) pose their own problems of interpretation. Apart from the many metrological pitfalls, we have to understand who exactly took the initiative to mint coins, under what conditions this was done, and, subsequently, who was responsible for the distribution of the coins. As already said, coin production was one of the *regalia*: the bundle of exclusive rights held by the sovereign. The sovereign, however, was dependent on the availability of the usual metals out of which coins are made (as a rule, gold, silver, and copper), either from mines at home or through foreign trade. Besides, sovereigns often did not take the initiative of minting coins but rather left this to the public, in particular to merchants – who were subject to paying the required taxes (called *seigniorage*) and obeying his instructions to the mint masters. Mint masters had to operate within this legal framework, and this was checked by the warden, appointed by the sovereign, and occasionally by the *essayeur,* who had to check the fineness of samples from the production, which were collected systematically. Merchants were mostly interested in having the metals they brought to the mint reminted into large gold and silver trade coins, which they could use in interregional trade. Apart from collecting *seigniorage* taxes, sovereigns could also try to make short-term profits through debasements, as is well documented for the later Delhi sultans.

Finally, all that has been said certainly applies to gold and silver coins, but not necessarily to copper coins, and certainly not to non-metallic currency like cowries. Here, we have to envisage private initiatives outside the state. Especially for the nineteenth century, private production of copper coins, similar to those issued by the princely states, is well documented (see many examples in Parts I and II of this volume).

Related to the introduction of uniform, Western-style coins in the Bengal Presidency in 1830, the government became interested in the possibilities of extending them to larger parts of India. This resulted in regional reports on coin production and coin circulation in newly subjugated regions and the still semi-autonomous Princely States. In 1831, the Bengal Presidency ordered enquiries into the state of the currency in the western provinces, i.e. north India under direct British rule, situated west of Bihar, Bengal, and Orissa. These were actually made by local officers in the following year, and their collated answers were sent by the Sudder Board of Revenue to the Government on 4 September 1832.[40]

There is no comprehensive written or published overview of Indian mints available before *c.* 1870, so we must collect our information from every nook and corner. However, in order to achieve a uniform currency throughout India, the British government in Calcutta had to convince the Indian princes to give up their coinage rights and to close their mints or assimilate their coinage with that of British India. For that purpose, the Finance Department asked the Foreign Department in 1868 to provide a complete and detailed overview of all the mints in the princely states and their production.[41]

On the occasion of the Native Coinage Act of 28 March 1876, a second enquiry was undertaken into the state of the coinage in the various states.[42] For the, in the meantime, substantially reduced number of mints of Indian princes, supplementary information is available for the production years 1871/2 to 1875/6,[43] and for the 1880s[44] and 1890s (esp. coin circulation related to the replacement of Indian princely states coins by British Indian or 'Government' coins). This is also the time of the first estimates of the total money supply (see Part 1: Studies, No. 13, Table 13.1 in this volume).[45]

Archaeological sources

Luckily, apart from surviving written records on the coin production and circulation that are the backbone of this study, a range of supplementary archaeological evidence is available to historians. Among other information (e.g. iconographic, political, linguistic), it enables us to estimate and guestimate long-term fluctuations. The main methods applied in this field are so-called die studies and the analysis of coin finds, museum collections and the frequency of coin types found in the collectors' market.[46]

'Die studies' can broadly indicate how many coins of a certain type were produced by closely comparing surviving coins and establishing the number of different dies that were used in the production of a coin. On the condition that enough specimens of the same type are available, this is possible for the period in which each steel die was cut out manually, causing minor differences between them. Because the lifetime of upper- and lower-dies differ substantially, it is possible to reconstruct the number of dies used subsequently. Assuming an average number of coins struck per upper and lower die, the total production for such a type can be estimated.

Another relatively new approach is the chemical analysis of coins. For the Netherlands, for example, this has provided clues to the geographical origin of copper ores, used for minting coins in the Early Modern period.[47] Such technical studies are particularly useful for providing clues to coin production before the later Middle Ages.

If documented properly, metal coins found by archaeologists and amateurs can help us to explain how money was used. Indeed, documentation about the finding circumstances is crucial here. Coins may be discovered together as hoards or otherwise as stray finds.[48] Hoards are concentrations of larger numbers of coins, clearly buried together in the ground or basements, walls, etc. They may be interpreted as savings, unrecovered because of the sudden death of the owner, but also more generally because of calamities like war. In the latter case, they may have been hidden by private persons but also by beleaguered armies in fortresses.[49] Those who have to hide coins have an understandable predilection for gold or, rather, silver, as these represent more value per weight.[50] For the study of the money of the masses, stray finds, therefore, tell us more about the general usage of mostly, low-value coins. The restricted and unsystematic recording of stray finds in India puts severe limits on this method for our purpose.

The present occurrence of old coins in museums (and sometimes also in private collections) has been used by a number of historians to study the spread and frequency of coinage. There is a long tradition of studying historical trends based on such analysis of (published catalogues of) museum collections, mainly of gold and silver specimens.[51] Some long-term insights acquired by this method will be discussed below.

The majority of coin finds do not end up in public but in private collections by way of a vibrant collectors' market. Although the precise origin of coins that are for sale, as a rule, remains obscure, this market is rather transparent and increasingly so by way of online information on prevailing prices for direct buying and selling as well as for prices realized at auctions. Average prices, as published in collectors' catalogues, serve as guidelines for those interested in acquiring these material testimonies of history. At the same time, they may also be used as indicators of original production and circulation figures.[52] In combination with written sources, this archaeological source will be used in this study, as worked out below in Appendices 1-3. Before presenting the analysis of this source in para 3f, the logistics of deep monetization deserve special attention as a kind of circumstantial evidence.

3b. Copper Mining in India

The raw material from which small coins were made in India was mainly copper (along with, but only to a very limited extent, lead, tin, or alloys of such metals). Its availability and the way it was processed in the mint houses also impacted the final circulation of small coins. The copper used to produce coins had two sources of origin in India. In the period 1500-1900, locally mined ores were not sufficiently available, and so the mints largely depended on the importation of foreign copper. This was even more important because, apparently, copper was re-minted far less than the more precious silver and certainly gold. Only rarely do we hear about the reminting of old coins circulating locally. According to Willis, copper coins in India were hardly reminted 'as the cost would have been prohibitive relative to the value of the coin, and thus surviving dam coins were commonly quite worn'.[53] More frequently, we find complaints about the difficulties experienced in reworking old supplies into new coins. It certainly would have happened more often than we know, but, as a rule, locally mined copper ore and, most of all, imported copper bars were used to produce new coins.

In the centuries studied here, copper ore for producing coins was mined in the west of India, roughly eastern Rajasthan, in the north, bordering on Nepal (and also in Nepal itself) and in the south-east near Nellore. The main copper mining areas listed by Abul Fazl in his *Ain-i Akbari* in the 1590s are Narnaul, Bairat, and Alwar for mining in the suba Agra and, a few hundred kilometres southward, Chittorgarh in the adjacent suba Ajmer.[54]

Rajasthan

In the Aravalli range in Narnaul Sarkar (Rajasthan), the copper mining belt of Khetri, stretching 12 km north towards Singhana, catered for the mint at Narnaul, established in 1543/4, and for

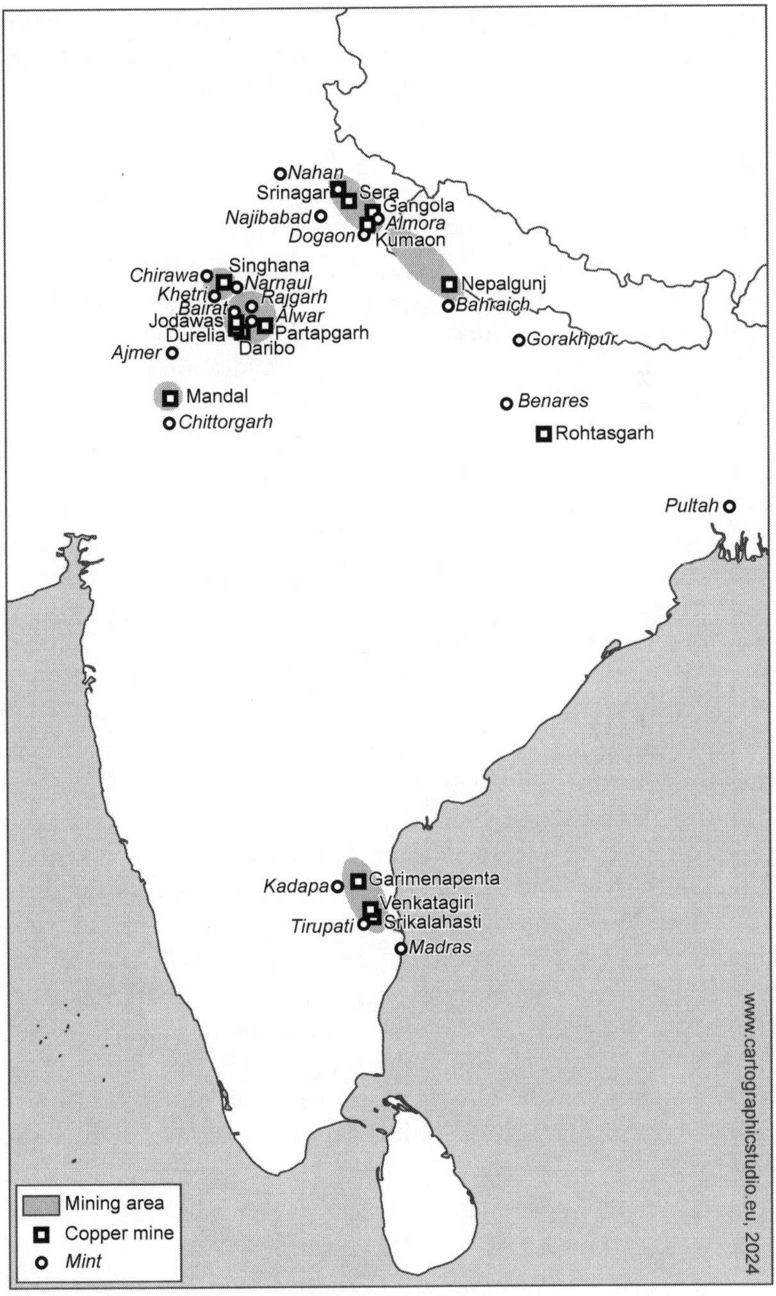

MAP I.1: COPPER MINING AREAS IN INDIA, 1500-1900

sixty years continuously the most important mint for copper dams under the reign of Akbar.[55] Apparently, it lost its prominence after 1605, to disappear as a Mughal mint by the end of that century. Only in the third quarter of the nineteenth century did these mines reappear in the colonial reports, when they were exploited in a semi-official way, catering for local mints not only at Khetri but also at nearby Chirawa.[56]

Less than 100 km south of the Khetri copper belt are two other mines mentioned in the *Ain-i Akbari*: Bairat and Alwar, both in Alwar Sarkar. This is one coherent belt some 40 km southwest of Alwar. From there, initially, the mint at Alwar drew its copper, shifting around 1570 to Bairat, nearer to the mines.[57] In total, these two important Mughal copper mints were active for a century, beginning (like Narnaul) under the Suris in the 1540s and becoming less important in the 1640s, only to peter out later in that century. Later, like the Khetri belt, it saw a revival, but in a different way.[58] In this case, official state mines at Durelia, Partabgarh, Jodawas, and Debra / Daribo supplied the Alwar State mint at Rajgarh regularly for another century, starting in 1772. This mint is situated just east of the mines and, therefore much nearer to it than the capital city of Alwar.

The third group of copper mines in Rajasthan mentioned in the *Ain-i Akbari* is situated at or near Mandal, 66 km north of Chittorgarh and 125 km south of Ajmer. The mint at Ajmer (also called Salimabad) was established nearly twenty years later than those at Narnaul and Alwar. Ajmer produced coppers for forty years from 1561/2 through 1600/1, although not without interruption.[59] In the period 1590-1600, Chittorgarh (also called Akbarpur) emerged. Just as we saw with Alwar / Bairat, transportation costs of the copper ore may have mattered and no later revival is known.[60] Apparently, the supply from this copper belt was much more limited than from the two northern ones, of which the Alwar-Bairat-Rajgarh succession of mints appears to have been the most enduring.

The North

Another copper belt was situated in the north, roughly in the western half of Nepal and the adjacent border regions of India. It supplied copper for some mints immediately south of it. The earliest evidence regards the Mughal mints at Bahraich for which coppers are known from 1558/9 through 1585/6[61] and, partially parallel, at Dogaon from 1561/2 through 1604/5 and again sporadically around 1640.[62] Even more clearly than with the shifts of mints from Alwar to Bairat and from Ajmer to Chittorgarh, we observe here a change in mint production most likely dictated by the transportation costs of the copper ore. Originally, Bahraich prevailed as the Sarkar's headquarters, only to be surpassed by Dogaon, which was much nearer to the Nepalese copper transported from Nepalgunj down to Nanpara. No later products from these two mints are known and it is only in the eighteenth and early nineteenth centuries that we hear again about the importation of copper from these hills. We now find three northern mints using such copper; in chronological order: Gorakhpur; Najibabad; and John Prinsep's private mint at Pultah.[63]

In a long report, written in 1787, about the mint at Benares, which started the minting of copper pice in 1740/1, it is stated that, early on, the demand for such small change was met by the mint at Gorakhpur.[64] It used copper called 'Lungeree', brought from the 'Northern Hills', no doubt directly north in Nepal. This mint (called Muazzamabad) was long-established, founded in 1566/7, but it was not very active. We only know of a few years of issue under Akbar, and even less thereafter (resp. 1566/7-1579/80, 1603/4-1605/6, 1668/70, 1712/3 and 1763/4-1776/7). So, strangely, the pice alluded to in the report about Benares cannot easily be identified.[65]

Much more successful was the mint at Najibabad, a town founded in the 1740s by Najib ad-Dawlah (died 1770). Its paisas, named *nujeeb khannees* after him, were coined out of Srinagar copper between 1762/3 and 1800, and increasingly in great numbers, for originally 'the territories of the chief in question, which comprehended only the north-western portion of Rohilcund, but extended generally over the whole of that province and far beyond its precincts'. In the same letter, from 1804, it is also stated that, previously, 'there were no coined pice in any part of Rohilcund. The then copper currency consisted of oval pieces of that metal called Muddha Sahees, which had neither letter nor figure of any kind stamped upon them but were supposed to weigh 18 maushes or 290 grains avoirdupois'.[66]

The copper belt referred to here, and already mentioned in the *Ain*, is to be found in the Kumaon hills. Without a doubt, copper was exported from the Kumaon to the south, but it was also minted locally at Almora, Srinagar and Nahan, all active between 1770 and 1816 before being closed by the new masters.[67] Immediately after ousting Nepal from this region, the British wanted to know its mining potential.[68] In 1815, the Calcutta assay master had to analyse several specimens of copper ore from the Serah and Gongola mines. Their location is not specified, but they must have been in the eastern Kumaon hills, not far from the Nepalese border. According to his letter of 24 December 1815, the quality of these specimens was unimpressive, the best one being from Gongolea, but considered of much lesser quality than the copper ore from Nellore (see below). Moreover, the Kumaon suffered from serious deforestation as a consequence of smelting ores. Many improvement plans were made, but none of these materialized.[69]

Unfortunately, even more vague than the preceding information is the origin of the copper ore, used by John Prinsep (1748-1830) for his mint at Pultah (now Palta) between 1781 and 1783 (see Appendix 2).[70] From his correspondence in early 1780, with the government in Calcutta, we only learn that the mines for which he had been granted a concession were situated 'under and near the hills of Rotas Gurr' (Rohtas Garh 150 km south-west of Patna and in the district of Munger under the collector of Boglepur). His expectations about the quantity and quality of the ore were probably too optimistic because the next year he was already mixing his own with English and Japanese copper. No other information is available about these mines, so we can conclude that they were of limited significance for the minting of copper coins.

The South

A copper belt located near Nellore is not mentioned by the *Ain*, because, at the moment this text was being composed, this place was situated outside the Mughal Empire. We learn of it from the geological reports made by the British from the late eighteenth century onwards.[71] They found several deserted mine pits in an area 36 miles north-west of Nellore and at an equal distance inland from the Coromandel Coast. Places mentioned here include Agricondalah near Innaconda, and Gurumanipenta (also written as Gurumani or Garipenta), and, south of Nellore, Srikalahasti, and Venkatagiri. The reports of experts like Benjamin Heyne (who – like John Prinsep in Bengal earlier on – also proposed to mint copper coins[72]), C.A. Kerr and Thomas John Newbold, who inspected this region personally between 1800 and 1840, as well as of James Prinsep, praise the high quality of the ores as well as its availability in the valleys and, nearer to the sea, the abundance of forest wood for smelting, but also – and most interesting for us – the extension of these antique works. Kerr describes the deserted Bungheral Metta Mines, which he discovered and cleared in about 1835, as immense tanks covering several hundred square feet and about 45 feet deep, from which galleries extended into the rocks.[73] A few years later, Newbold added that these mines are the most extensive of all for which 'an immensity of labour' must have been performed 'by the ancient miners […] a tank has literally been cut in the solid rock, and for the most part, through a dead country'. Regarding the population of this district, Newbold remarks that it 'is of an industrious character; that of Gurumanipenta, which place may be considered as the capital of the mining area contains chiefly natives of the Upér caste, whose business it is to dig wells and tanks'.[74]

When exactly the Vellore copper mines were active remains vague. Newbold heard from 'the most respectable natives' that they went back to the days of the Vijayanagara Empire and that, after its demise, successor states, including the Mughals and Haider Ali and Tipu Sultan continued to exploit them.[75] The observation by several of these authors that, in the early nineteenth century, the region was barren and virtually without trees may also indicate extensive smelting activities early on.

The next step, i.e. how to link the Nellore copper belt to actual mints in the period treated in this volume, is a rather difficult one. There was certainly a rich production of copper coins in Southern India, but – apart from Venkatagiri – the mints listed in the specialized and very detailed overviews by Michael Mitchiner are located far away from the copper mines.[76] Only two other mints might qualify, the nearest of which was Kadapa, roughly 100 km upstream of the River Penner, where, between *c.* 1750 and 1790, copper coins were minted in large numbers by the Nawab of Arcot.[77]

At a greater distance, and southwards, is Madras, where the Mughal mint Machilipatnam started its activities under Aurangzeb in the 1660s, becoming very productive from the 1690s until the British took over in the 1770s, continuing to mint the same type of paisa for a while.[78] The main question is whether the transport costs in these two cases were prohibitive, not least because, as we will see in the next paragraph, the Machilipatnam mint received its copper from Japan. It is also possible that the Nellore copper belt had no significance at all for the production of copper coins in southern India but instead was important for the fabrication of kitchen utensils, guns or other armoury.

Contrary to what the influential Braudel and many after him thought, as demonstrated here amply, India had copper mines.[79] This inventory of copper has demonstrated that some mints in Rajasthan, and in the north near the Nepalese border, used locally mined raw material. Nevertheless, this must have been a small proportion of the total production of copper coins in the entire peninsula. In 1780, even the optimistic entrepreneur John Prinsep compared the average annual copper imports by the EIC alone of 11,106.20 maunds with his own Rotas mines' production of only 2,000 maunds per annum.[80] So, demand clearly outstripped the production of small indigenous mines, certainly when – as we will see – this demand grew quickly under the Suri dynasty. We must therefore look for foreign sources, and, bearing in mind the important transport costs, for the origins of overseas copper bars or sheets.

3c. Copper Imports

Certainly, not all copper imports were meant to be minted. Household utensils like vessels, but also guns for the army, accoutrements for cavalrymen and many more useful objects, including religious statues, were made from copper or bronze. At the end of the eighteenth century, a new demand emerged for the coppering of ship's bottoms. Nevertheless, copper imports can inform us about fluctuations in copper coin production. This will become clear from a systematic review of overseas imports via the Red Sea (and the Persian Gulf), via the Cape and Portugal, from Japan and, finally, via and from England.[81]

Via the Red Sea

Information about copper flowing via the Near and Middle East to India is haphazard, but this source was by no means unimportant. The Romans exported copper to India via the Red Sea and, in the eleventh century, so did Italian (from Italy proper and those trading from Egypt) and Egyptian merchants. They exchanged copper, lead and textiles for Indian spices and dyes.[82] In the fifteenth century, the average Venetian import of pepper from India via Alexandria increased from 230,000 kg around 1400 to nearly 400,000 kg around 1500. In the same period, imports of ginger increased more than tenfold from 22,000 to 250,000 kg. In return, apart from precious metals, goods, including copper, served to balance this trade with ports like Calicut (Kozhikode). This became possible following the opening up of new, rich copper mines in Central Europe and in the Balkans and Anatolia. There, mines were active in the north of Anatolia at Kastamonu (conquered by the Ottomans in 1459) and in the south in the Isaurian Taurus mountains. For the minting of their fulus, the Mamluks of Egypt and Syria became dependent on copper traded by the Venetians, which amounted to between 500,000 and 1,000,000 kg of this metal per annum around 1500. It came primarily from Kastamonu (381.6 ton in 1507). Part of this, but we do not know how much, was re-exported to India, also as Mamluk copper coins, where their value was much greater.

Although the Portuguese sought to outcompete Muslim merchants trading between Egypt and India, there is plenty of evidence that they did not succeed and that, among other goods, copper continued to reach western India via that route.[83] This was reported for Diu in 1523 and three years later the Portuguese took three ships, whose cargo contained, among other things, 58.8 ton of copper. In 1548, Goa complained that every year 50 to 60 ships plied the waters between the Red Sea and western India with merchandise like copper. In 1557, a similar complaint pointed especially to Cambay where the affluence of copper depressed prices to such an extent that it profoundly impacted Portuguese competition. The Ottoman military successes in the Red Sea and beyond in the subsequent decades boosted spice exports from India to Egypt and beyond. There is no doubt that Central European and possibly also Turkish copper flowed, via Venice, in exchange. On the other hand, the Ottoman authorities considered the strategic value of copper to be very high. Consequently, exports of Central European and Turkish copper to Alexandria (18.1 ton in the late sixteenth century via Venice) could only reach India by way of illegal re-exportation.

Given India's copper famine, there is no reason to believe that – because of European competition, explained hereafter – the copper supply from and via the Near and Middle East to India dried up completely later on.[84] Unfortunately, until the mid-eighteenth century we have no information to substantiate this. In 1759/60, the VOC re-exported 12 ton of old Persian copper (i.e. copper previously imported from Persia) to Bengal, and no less than 100 ton in the following year. That proved to be too much and, ultimately, it was sold at discounted prices in 1762.[85]

Thanks to another, later source, we know that this Persian copper was, in fact, Turkish. In the 1790s, the copper mines of Diyarbakir in eastern Anatolia yielded 250,000 attaree maunds (or about 750,000 kg[86]) per year, of which 16,000 (48,000 kg) were exported to India in 1791 via Mosul and Basra, increasing to 70,000 (210,000 kg) in 1796.[87] I have no earlier information about the Diyarbakir copper belt, but, based on the fact that Jean Aubin makes no mention of copper in his detailed description of the trade relations of Hormuz in the early sixteenth century, it is clear that the Diyarbakir-Euphrates connection was established later on.[88] Moreover, in the sixteenth century, the Ottoman state had forbidden the export of copper. Only after the peace treaty between the Safavids and Ottomans in 1555 did the regular export of Turkish copper via the Persian Gulf become feasible.[89] But equally so via the Red Sea, which seems to have been preferred. Furthermore, the Dutch East India Company's (VOC) importation of Japanese copper into Persia from the 1620s until the 1720s, via Basra and Masqat, reveals not only a dearth of copper in Persia at this time, but also the increasing importance of Japan in the context of India's eternal hunger for this crucial resource.[90] It is likely that Turkish copper was used for export to India in the 1790s. It certainly gained importance in the early nineteenth century, when the annual export of Turkish copper, refined at Diyarbakir and exported via Basra, amounted to 750,000 kg.[91]

Portugal

Given India's hunger for copper predating the Great Discoveries, we do not have to wonder whether copper figured prominently among the products that the Portuguese used to trade with the subcontinent. Compared to Venetian copper exports to Egypt, worth 34,000 ducats a year, the Portuguese exports of copper to India soon after were valued at 39,000 ducats. At 16 ducats per quintal ('old weight' 51.4 kg) this means over 100,000 kg.[92] The shipwreck of the Portuguese ship *Bom Jesus*, bound for India and lost between 1525 and 1538 near Namibia, contained *c.* 20 metric ton of copper ingots, and this can be considered low for ships of that period. The annual average of Portuguese copper exports to India in the first quarter of the century exceeded 200,000 kg and it may also have continued to be important later in the century.[93]

Its importance becomes clear from Duarte Barbosa's description of Chaul [Cheul] in 1514:

> A large quantity of copper is sold in this place of Cheul, and at a high price, for it is worth twenty ducats the hundredweight, or more, because in the interior money is made of it, and it is also made throughout the country for cooking-pots [...] which coper [...] is brought to this place by the Malabar merchants, who get it from the factories of the King of Portugal; and they get more of it by the way of Mekkah, which comes there from Diu.[94]

The Indian demand for copper in the fifteenth and sixteenth centuries was, indeed, substantial, in particular for coining copper coins (as Barbosa emphasizes) in the sultanates of Gujarat and Ahmadnagar, both of which were producing large quantities of copper coins in various fractions.[95]

This great copper hunger stimulated Indian merchants to buy the metal from the Portuguese. According to one of them, Malik Gopi, in 1513, Gujarat expended nearly 4 million kg annually, two thirds of which was destined for the port of Cambay and one third for Diu.[96] To put this into perspective, let us suppose for a moment that half of this amount was spent in falus coins weighing 10 gram, this would enable an output of 40 million pieces.

The Portuguese also used this European copper themselves, for example 94 metric ton per year at Goa between 1518 and 1521 and 188 metric ton at Diu in 1525. Part of this was re-exported to their settlements along the Indian west coast, South-East Asia and beyond.[97] The local Portuguese mints would also have used it. The mint at Goa dates already from 1510, Cochin from 1524 or earlier (although copper coinage only from 1544), Bassein 1611, Daman 1611, Chaul 1646 and Diu 1684 – in addition to Malacca 1511 (mainly tin coinage) and Ceylon 1598.[98]

However popular Portuguese copper became after 1500, this information also shows that most of it must have originated elsewhere, locally, from the Levant but probably also via the Persian route. Following the stabilization or even decline of Portuguese shipping to Asia, India must have been continuously interested in other sources.[99]

TABLE I.1: PORTUGUESE COPPER EXPORTS TO INDIA AND COINAGE IN LUSO-INDIAN MINTS, 1502-9

Year of departure	*Ton*	*Details*	*Copper coinage*
1502		1502-18 Cochin received nearly 2,900 ton or annually on average *c.* 175 ton	
1503		1503-21 Goa, Calicut, Cananore, Coulão received 1206.6 ton or an annual average of *c.* 65 ton, *c.* 50 of which for Goa	
1504	146.5		
1505	205.6-235		
1509	107.8		
1510			Lisbon for Goa 5.88 ton
1511			Goa 352.2 kg; Lisbon's capacity for Goa was 35.3 ton per annum
1513	235		Goa 44.2 ton
1514			Cochin
1516	147.7		
1517			Copper minting at Goa: 5/6 in bazarucos (leais) and 1/6 in pequeninos fractions
1518	118		
1525/6	470		
1528		Stock at Cochin: 334.9 ton	
1537-8	Annually 352.5		Goa before 1542: 88.1 ton annually
1542-5			Goa: annually 27.2 to 27.2 ton (1544/5 in 48 weeks 126.9 ton, May-September 1545 24.7 ton)

(Contd.)

1545-50	Annual estimate 323.1-440.6	1543/4 new mint of Cochin with an annual capacity of *c.* 325 ton
1558	25.7	
1559		All copper from Portugal to be coined

Sources: Vieira 2018, 125-36; Magelhães Godinho 1969, 403-17 (idem 404, fn. 4 for the etymology of *bazaruco*; also, Gerson da Cunha 1880, 91).

The situation changed radically after 1550. Copper prices in Portugal rose sixfold and the minting of copper coins in the capital Lisbon came to a virtual standstill between 1580 and 1640.[100] Because of rising copper prices in Portugal, by 1560 the heyday of copper exports to the country's settlements on the Indian coast was over, following decades in which the Goa mint had produced twice as many copper coins as the Lisbon mint achieved for homeland consumption.[101] This ratio also indicates what was really happening: Goan copper coins were being re-exported beyond the colony to be reminted into Suri and later Mughal copper coins.

Another sign of the difficulties emerged in 1577 as copper started to be mixed with the much cheaper tin from Malacca (then also a Portuguese settlement) for use as mint material at Goa and Cochin – this particular Luso-Indian habit would continue for centuries. At the end of the sixteenth century, Chinese copper, bought by the Portuguese in their settlement of Macao, provided a brief respite.[102] In 1583, for the first time the Goa mint house produced copper bazarucos from Chinese copper and, in 1588, the intention was to mint 41.1 ton of copper into bazarucos there. The trade became so brisk that, in 1592, one author stated that the Estado da India could easily import 235 ton of copper from China. Unfortunately, we have no information regarding copper imports from overseas by the Portuguese for later years.[103]

Because of the cheapness and availability of Chinese copper in those years, the Portuguese could not resist the temptation to make enormous profits by valuing their bazarucos far above the copper and production price. In 1582, for example, they valued the bazaruco at 42.75 cruzados per quintal or 165 per cent above the original purchasing price of the copper at 16.5 cruzados. As a consequence, social unrest emerged in their settlements and these overpriced coppers immediately left the Portuguese territories – according to the Portuguese sources they went to nearby Indian mints where they were used for making the counterfeits that were flooding the Goan market.[104] It is very possible, however, that most of these bazarucos (or, more likely, unminted Chinese copper bars, immediately after landing at Goa) reached Mughal mints for recoinage into dams or fractions. For these reasons, as well as because of an important demand from the military, and an increased internal Chinese demand for casting cash coins, the coinage of copper bazarucos at Goa stopped in 1606. The Dutch blockades of Goa in 1604, 1607, and 1608 would also have played a role. Tutenag (a Tamil word) or crude zinc, also imported from China, now became the preferred metal for coining the bazarucos.

In 1612, Francisco Pais, estimated the Estado da India's annual demand from China at 176.3 ton, one third of which was for casting guns and two thirds or 117.5 ton for striking bazarucos, primarily to pay out wages.[105] This ratio is remarkable in view of the heavy military-commercial rivalry between the Portuguese and their fresh competitors in Asia from Holland. However, Chinese copper was hardly available anymore. Instead, Japan became the new supplier, but only gradually and for all kinds of reasons its significance for India was only firmly established after some decades.

Japan

Japanese copper mining and minting started in the eighth century, but did not meet its internal needs. So, from *c.* 1150 to 1550, this country supplied itself with Chinese copper cash. Gradually, its production grew and when Ming China forbade the export of copper in the fifteenth century, Japan was even able to export copper to China and Vietnam. From 1604 to 1635, a brisk Japanese foreign trade involved 356 ships (more than ten per year), half to China and half to South-East Asia, carrying with them mainly silver but also copper cash. Vietnam was an important destination, where European (Portuguese and Dutch) also traders stepped in.

From the 1630s, the trade with Japan was dominated by the Dutch and the Chinese while the Portuguese could only maintain a fairly constant low-level trade.[106]

In 1641, the VOC was the only European power to acquire exclusive trading rights with Decima in Japan, a situation that lasted until 1859 – alongside contingents from China, Korea, Ryukyu, and the Ainu people. Copper was one of the main Japanese products shipped after that year by the Dutch to South-East and South Asia. Thus, from 1645 until far into the eighteenth century, the Dutch were the main suppliers of Japanese copper to India. This much-desired product also reached India indirectly, mainly via China through ports in South-East Asia. After their expulsion from Japan in 1633-9, this was the only way for the Portuguese to acquire Japanese copper, primarily meant to make guns and cannons in defence of the Estado da India against the Dutch. According to Stephen, in the seventeenth century, 100,000 picos Chinese weight or no less than 6,100,000 kg were imported via Macao and Manilla. He does not mention how many vessels and how many years it took to ship this enormous amount (cf. the Dutch annual exports of 225,000 kg for 1646-55) but, if this figure is correct, it must have been many ships and, given their low frequency, at least during several decades.[107]

The Dutch portion has been studied in detail by Ryuto Shimada and Gujarat by Ghulam Nadri.[108] Their research provides a detailed reconstruction of India's consumption of Japanese copper between 1650 and 1800 and a glimpse of its usage for minting coins. The first Dutch ships arrived in Japan in 1609, and returned with copper, but initially silver was much more important. More-over, the Japanese government prohibited the export of copper between 1637 and 1646 to enhance the issuing of a new copper coin. Hence, the 1650s saw the beginning of 'the golden age of Japanese copper exports', coinciding with a substantial extension of copper mining. By the late 1670s, Japan had become the largest copper-producing and exporting country in the world.[109]

The VOC exported the copper from Decima, in Nagasaki, to Malacca (only until 1710) and Batavia, from where it was re-shipped to other ports in South and South-East Asia, and sometimes even to Europe (e.g. during the Danish-Swedish War, 1658-60 and the Third Anglo-Dutch War, 1672-9, with their great demand for guns). From 1747 to 1752, part of the copper was occasionally shipped directly from Decima to South Asia, leaving Batavia aside.

Between 1645 and 1715, the VOC exported initially around 450,000 Dutch pounds (225,000 kg) per year, which increased quickly to 10 lakh kg per year. Between 1715 and 1780, the volume shrank again to 5 lakh kg per year and to even less after that. In the later seventeenth century, half of this amount had India as its destination, where Gujarat, Coromandel and Bengal were most important, followed by Malabar and, further away, Ceylon. Shimada makes the intriguing remark that 'this regional ranking reflected the export trends in cotton textiles from each region to the VOC, suggesting that copper imports to South Asia were intricately connected to Indian textile exports'.[110] In the eighteenth century, the Indian share in the Dutch Japanese copper exports from Nagasaki / Decima increased to 90 per cent. In sum, India received roughly 5 lakh kg per year from this source between the late seventeenth and the late eighteenth century. The distribution over South Asia is shown in Table I.2.

By examining the imports of Japanese copper in more detail, by subregions of India (which is mainly possible for the eighteenth century), its relation with copper coinage can be established more firmly, even to the extent that, as Shimada concludes and despite severe critics, we can readily accept Frank Perlin's hypothesis 'that almost all the [imported] copper was used at mints'.[111] The following discussion relates to the VOC copper supply and its final destinations of Bengal, North Coromandel, South Coromandel, the Fishery Coast, Malabar and Gujarat.

Japanese copper for Bengal[112]

The earliest figures for Bengal that I have found are for the years 1679-84, when the VOC factories at Hugli, Balasore, Kasim Bazar, Dhaka, and Patna together imported 2,483,472 ponds (or 1,227,000 kg, which is an average of 250,000 kg per year).[113] In

TABLE I.2. QUANTITIES OF JAPANESE COPPER RE-SHIPPED FROM MALACCA AND BATAVIA TO INDIA (AMSTERDAM POUND AT 0.495 KG), 1677-1790/1

Period	*Bengal*		*Coromandel*		*Ceylon (incl. the Fishery Coast)*		*Malabar*		*Gujarat*		
	A	*B*	*A*	*B*	*A*	*B*	*A*	*B*	*A*	*B*	*C*
1677	110		320		90		650		390		
1696	400		360		240		0		560		
1700/4	322	451	657	721	344	69	129	44	431	2,011	1,232
1705/9	203	250	524	813	197	231	13	38	336	1,487	2,013
1710/14	309	875	105	487	241	163	36	63	438		1,573
1715/19	381	300	419	838	133	265	65	130	125		1,272
1720/4	250	1,255	250	1,250	205	1,025	168	837	141		877
1725/9	260	1,300	527	2,633	208	1,038	16	79	101		540
1730/4	240	1,200	418	2,088	160	800	68	338	59		309
1735/9	179	715	650	2,600	218	870	31	125	108		604
1740/4	212	735	673	2,019	67	200	33	100	117		362
1745/9	135	270	723	330	45	90	70	140	30		542
1750/4	147	166	667	1,317	127	380	78	234	235		506
1755/9	263	1,150	408	1,631	44	175	70	278	255		1,311
1760/4	120	600	597	2,985	36	180	140	700	370		1,155

1765/9	275	1,377	430	2,150	39	195	68	340	138		875
1770/4	185	1,825	370	1,650	109	545	149	747	119		729
1775/9	300	1,500	280	1,400	70	350	134	670	210		916
1780/4	70	350	145	725	160	800	183	913	30		145
1785/9		745		875		250		200			1,179
1790/1											122

Source: Shimada 2006, 18 (A, my estimates from graph for shipments via Malacca only), 20 (A), 200-4 (B), but note the inconsistencies in his data; Nadri 2009, 213-15 (Gujarat C; no data available for 1724, 1742 and 1744).

the early eighteenth century, this annual average had dropped to 150,000 kg per year, and later in the century to 100,000 kg. Most of it was auctioned at the Dutch settlement of Chinsura, north of Calcutta, and initially also smaller quantities at Patna, Dhaka, and Kasim Bazar (Balasore is no longer mentioned). Because there were no copper mints in Bengal it was shipped upstream from Chinsura to the Benares mint and even beyond to Gorakhpur. The important Benaras mint produced some 50,000 kg of copper coins per year in the 1770s and 1780s, and was therefore good for half of the VOC copper supply auctioned at Chinsura. No doubt other mints west of Benares also drew copper via this route, but further details are lacking.

Japanese copper for North Coromandel[114]

The first Japanese copper onboard VOC ships already arrived in Coromandel in 1614 and three years later it was sold for a favourable price at Masulipatnam.[115] Little information is available for the rest of this century, except for 1684, when the VOC factories at Paliakate, Golconda, Bimlipatam, Negapatnam, Tegnapatnam, Porto Novo, and Sadras together sold an impressive 2,279,528 pound (1,126,000 kg). For some years, in the last days of the Qutb Shahs, the kingdom of Golconda bought a major share of this.[116] In 1681/2, it acquired 1,178,916 pound; in 1683/4 it bought almost 2.3 million pound of copper (resp. 0.6 and 1.1 million kg) and in the following year, a native merchant called Zierum Chodenda, signed a contract with the VOC for 1.5 million pounds annually, mainly for the coinage of 'nevels'. Unfortunately for this merchant, Golconda was captured in 1687 by the Mughals, which led to the loss of his credit and, consequently, his bankruptcy, but also to the Company starting a lawsuit against its servants at Golconda.[117] Despite this, the VOC expected – initially too optimistically – to increase its sales. Later, this may have become true as the new rulers continued the copper mint at Hyderabad, now named Farkhanda Bunyad.

In the eighteenth century, Coromandel never imported less than 150,000 kg annually; in the 1740s it was twice as much. If we add the copper imports for nearby Ceylon, part of which also ended up in India (good for 50,000 in the 1700s to 100,000 in the 1720s only to drop to 30,000 in the 1740s and later), this part of India consumed a rough 200,000 kg of Japanese copper per year.

The VOC disembarked most of its copper on this part of the Coromandel Coast, at its settlement of Masulipatnam and smaller portions at Jagannathapuram, where it had its own gun factory, and at Bimlipatam (Bheemunipatnam). Their own mint only produced gold coins, so we must look elsewhere for the destination of the copper (apart from the special case of the gun factory in the 1750/60s). Originally, it would have been the kingdom of Golconda and its successor Hyderabad in general, but in two cases a more direct link can be seen between the VOC supply and the minting of copper coins. The Mughal mint at Masulipatnam, named Machhlipatan (Bandar), bought nearly the total supply, auctioned locally, between 1727 and 1740, and its British successor from 1753 until 1803 almost certainly did the same. Interestingly, over a number of years, the British minted similar coppers at Visakhapatnam, just south of the VOC settlement at Bimlipatam, where part of the VOC copper was also sold.

Japanese copper for South Coromandel[118]

The Dutch exploited their own mint at Pulicat (or Paliakate) from the beginning of their settlement there in 1610 and, notably, after 1647 when they produced substantial quantities of undated 'kasjes' weighing 1.7 gram. This cannot explain the substantial annual supplies of copper it received, however, and certainly not the much bigger supplies for the VOC settlement at Sadras, both via Negapatnam. Most likely, this copper was bought by the British for minting coppers at Madras (half way between Pulicat and Sadras) in 1679-85 and 1740, the nearby and short-lived Mughal mint at Mylapur (1704/5), the mints of Arcot and Vellore (directly upstream of the Palar River from Sadras), and possibly other copper coin production centres.

The main VOC port in this part of India was Negapatnam, where all the copper was disembarked initially. Part of it was re-exported to Pulicat and Sadras, as we just have seen, but also to Porto Novo, from where it may have provisioned the French mint at Pondicherry (which was briefly Dutch from 1693 to 1698, during which they struck *kasjes* there), the Danish at Tranquebar and maybe other mints as well, like those at Salem or Karur. In the same way, the VOC settlement of Kunimedu may have provided copper for the mint at Gingee in the early eighteenth century. Moreover, the VOC had its own copper mint at Negapatnam, which was briefly active between 1662 and 1695 (partially for Ceylon).

We, therefore, have to think of other destinations; first, the important and age-old mints of Madurai (closed in 1843), Tanjore and Palani (closed 1799), and, in the eighteenth century, also those at Pudokkotai and Sivaganga (both started in 1729 and closed in resp. 1799 and 1843) and Trichy (Tiruchirappalli, 1744-1843). As virtually all the coppers produced in these places are undated, it is impossible to be more precise about the relation between the Negapatnam supplies and actual copper coin production. Nevertheless, we can get an impression of the order of magnitude in the mid-eighteenth century by supposing that the 200,000 kg produced per year were divided over 20 mints nearby or in the hinterlands of the dozen or so VOC settlements along the Coromandel Coast. This would amount to 10,000 kg per mint, which would be good for 5 million *kasus* with an average weight of 2 gram. Such an impressive issue of small copper coins would certainly make sense for such an important textile region at the time, employing numerous spinners and weavers.

Japanese copper for the Fishery Coast opposite Ceylon

The relationship between the Dutch settlements at Ceylon (most importantly Jaffna on its northern tip) and the opposite so-called Fishery Coast was so close that we can see it as one economic unit. The Fishery Coast settlements did not coin themselves but must have transshipped substantial amounts to inland mints. The VOC post at Kilakkarai may have provided the mint of Ramnad, for example, which was active throughout the seventeenth and eighteenth centuries. The same may be true for the VOC port of

Tuticorin and, though less significant, those of Manapadda and Comorin, which supplied the highly productive copper mint of Tirunelveli in the Poligar region.

Japanese copper for Malabar[119]

The imports to Cochin, the headquarters of the VOC on the Malabar Coast, were dominant in the 1670s (about 300,000 kg per year in 1677, but nothing in 1678[120]), dropping in the eighteenth century to 50,000 kg per year, small amounts of which were reshipped in the early part of that century to Cannanore and an even smaller quantity to Quilon (Kollam). Currently, I have no explanation for this substantial drop. Because the copper issues of Dutch Cochin were insignificant, and this port even imported Dutch *duiten* after 1724 (already 2.3 million pieces in 1753/4 alone) virtually all of this copper must have been transported to mints in the hinterland. The main candidates here are the Wodeyar dynasty mints at Mysore. Their issues of small, largely (until 1746) undated copper *kasus* in the Kongu Plain is impressive, starting from the sixteenth century and ending between 1780 and 1799 with the multidenominational elephant-type series of Haidar Ali and Tipu Sultan. To this can be added the copper *kasus* of Travancore and some other places along the coast of Kerala.

Japanese copper for Gujarat

All VOC copper destined for Gujarat was disembarked and auctioned at Surat.[121] The earliest reports about VOC imports of copper date from 1629, when 996 piculs (about 60,000 kg) were sent to Surat.[122] Quantities grew quickly in the second half of the century until the 1780s (and possibly the 1790s, although we have scant data) to 400,000 kg per year. These numbers fluctuated drastically in the eighteenth century, from annual averages of 150,000 kg in 1700/19 they dropped to only 50,000 kg in 1720/54, recovering to 125,000 in 1755/64 and again in 1785/9. There was another severe slump in between with only 65,000 kg per year from 1765 to 1779 (and even less in the ensuing years of the

Fourth Anglo-Dutch War). To this were added other imports by sea, both shipments by local Surat traders who bought Japanese copper directly in Batavia and shipments from Persia (from the 1750s) and increasingly from Europe from the 1770s onwards (see Table I.3).[123]

TABLE I.3. SURAT SALES OF VOC COPPER, ANNUAL AVERAGES IN AMSTERDAM POND AT 0.495 KG, PER FIVE-YEAR PERIODS, 1629-1791

	Average annual Surat sales in ponds	*Remarks*
1629	59,640	Only this year
1635		The first recorded appearance of VOC imports of Japanese copper in Surat (Moreland 1923b, 184)
1645	34,378	Only this year
1646-50	39,974	1649 missing
1651-5	151,253	
1656-60	272,168	
1661-5	408,493	
1666-70	326,930	1669 missing
1671-5	545,534	
1676-80	660,267	
1681-4	808,320	Only 4 years available
1685-95		No published data
1696	560,000	Only this year [my estimate]
1697-9		No published data
1700-4	308,095	Only 4 years available
1705-9	402,613	1705 no copper imports
1710-14	314,673	
1715-19	254,428	
1720-4	219,258	Average of 4 years (data for 1724 not available)
1725-9	108,072	1726 and 1729 no copper imports
1730-4	61,850	1730 no copper imports

1735-9	120,834	1736 no copper imports
1740-4	120,719	Average of 3 years (data for 1742 and 1744 not available)
1745-9	108,470	
1750-4	101,126	1753 no copper imports
1755-9	262,226	
1760-4	231,037	
1765-9	175,009	1768 and 1769 no copper imports
1770-4	145,706	1774 no copper imports
1775-9	183,152	
1780-4	28,932	Because of Fourth Anglo-Dutch War only copper imports in 1784 (144,660 kg)
1785-9	235,743	
1790-1	121,516	Only 1 year

Sources: Glamann 1953, 64-5; Glamann 1981, 175; Shimada 2006, 18 (my estimate from his graph for 1696/8); Nadri 2009, 213-15.

Overall, these are impressive quantities, which raises the question of what they were used for. Surat had a Mughal mint from the end of the sixteenth century, initially only minting silver, and from 1656 (regnal year 29 of Shah Jahan) until the mid-eighteenth century also copper coins.[124] This is also the time when VOC imports were important. We do not have coin production figures until late in the eighteenth century, however. In the last three years of the eighteenth century, they amounted to 1,500 maunds per year for the Surat mint, which at 17 kg per maund makes more than 25,000 kg (see Appendix 2). It is noteworthy that, in certain years, Dutch VOC officials secured the right from the Mughal Governor, Safdar Khan, to coin Japanese copper into paisas at the Surat mint. In the late 1740s and in 1750 this was done by Jan Schreuder.[125]

This leaves enough room in the years of abundant copper imports to supply other customers, including mints in that part of India. As we have seen, some were provided with copper mined in Rajasthan – albeit partially and to a diminishing degree – but most were dependent on copper imports. We can think of the following destinations: to the south Bombay and the Deccan, in the immediate surroundings and, further inland, Broach, Baroda, Ahmedabad and others (the Holkar, Sindhia, Gaekwad, and Pawar – Dhar and Dewas – states) as well as to the west the mints on the Saurashtra Peninsula (Kutch, Nawanagar). We have more precise information to substantiate this around the middle of the century, when the VOC thought of selling 500,000 kg in the Deccan.[126] It also disposed of some of its copper through subordinate factories at Kutch, Danda Rajapuri, and Bassein. In the latter place, for instance, the Dutch Commissioner H. Kronenbergh thought that he could sell 300,000 kg in 1754/5.[127] Caravan transports of copper from India's west coast, via Nasik, confirm this impression.[128]

European copper from and via England

For a long time, the English only occasionally shipped small quantities of Japanese copper to India, acquired in Chinese ports or from Chinese merchants in South-East Asia. This increased when their factory at Canton opened in 1715.[129] But it was only in the second half of the eighteenth century that this supply venue became important for India. Official British exports of copper to India only started in 1731, but even then much of this was re-exported from Sweden, Spain and its colonies and Northern Africa.[130] Volumes imported by the East India Company only started to rise in the second half of the eighteenth century: to Madras from 100 ton in the 1750s to 200 ton in the 1760s, and to Calcutta from 100 ton in the 1730s to 300 ton in the 1770s (Table I.4).[131] Not only did copper exports from England start relatively late, but for a long time the quality of this copper for minting was considered to be far below that of Japan. It, therefore, does not serve our purpose to draw conclusions from copper imports from Europe for the output of copper coins for the earlier period before, say, 1800. Nevertheless, it is safe to say that the flagged VOC imports of Japanese copper in the late eighteenth century were more than compensated for by the British ones, and these were only to increase in the next century.

TABLE I.4. EUROPEAN COPPER SHIPPED BY THE EIC TO INDIA, IN BRITISH POUND AT 0.4536 KG, 1730-99

Period	*Bengal*	*Madras*	*Bombay*	*Total EIC*	
				British lbs	*Million kg*
1730/4	689,950	113,400	117,606	920,956	0,418
1735/9	1,785,370	134,400	401,484	2,321,254	1,053
1740/4	4,093,112	222,015	306,124	4,621,251	2,096
1745/9	733,527	318,392	380,787	1,432,706	0,650
1750/4	3,022,999	807,815	1,502,921	5,333,735	2,419
1755/9	3,489,902	2,271,156	2,172,967	7,934,025	3,599
1760/4	3,320,589	1,825,939	4,520,372	9,666,900	4,385
1765/9	3,290,061	2,721,707	3,030,782	9,042,550	4,102
1770/4	3,585,555	2,872,841	4,795,533	11,253,929	5,105
1775/9	11,426,975	5,473,661	4,761,962	21,662,598	9,826
1780/4	6,732,236	3,846,992	3,420,488	13,999,716	6,350
1785/9	5,299,689	3,934,043	6,370,299	15,604,031	7,078
1790/4	6,969,100	3,069,424	4,615,236	14,653,760	6,647
1795/9	6,626,627	3,775,899	4,063,491	14,466,017	6,562

Source: Shimada 2006, 205-6.

Summary: The availability of copper for minting coins

Copper can be used for many purposes, civil and military, but the main purpose in India, especially before industrial applications such as sheathing ships, seems to have been minting coins. Apart from a limited inland availability of copper ore, which could supply only a handful of mints in Rajasthan and along the Nepalese border, the bulk of copper used for minting therefore had to be imported. Consequently, imports of copper can help us understand fluctuations in minting coins.

Subsequently, imports via the Red Sea, from Portugal, from Japan, and, starting in the last decades of the eighteenth century, from England (from England proper and from other European countries) – at that time supplemented by imports from Turkey via Persia – were indispensable for the production of copper coins.

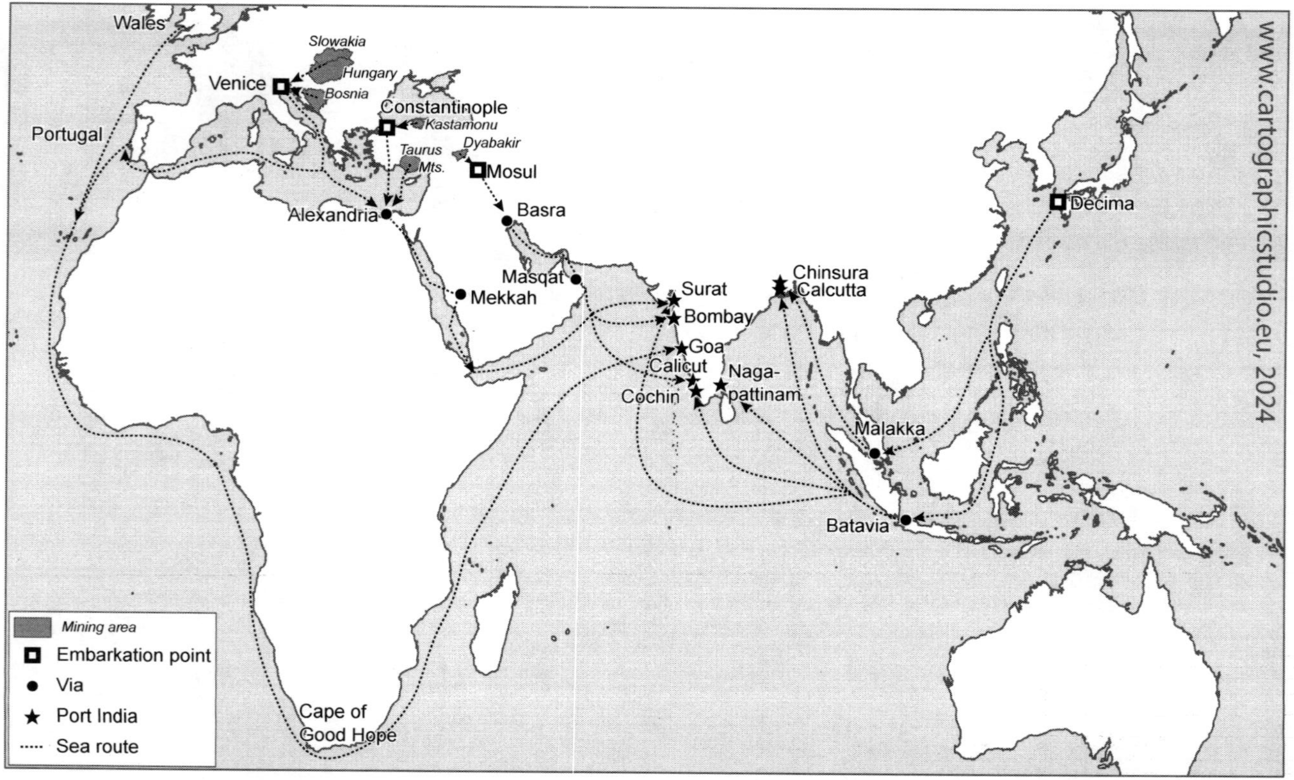

MAP I.2: EMBARKATION POINTS FOR FOREIGN COPPER AND POSSIBLE LINKS WITH MINT HOUSES, 1500-1800

There seems to have been an abundance of foreign copper available for India via the Red Sea and the Cape of Good, in particular from the 1520s until 1605.

Half a century of low imports was to follow at a time when Portuguese supplies had not yet been replaced by Dutch ones, and when the Ottomans frustrated copper exports via the Red Sea. After that, the imports grew quickly, to levels that were sufficient for a healthy copper coin provision by Indian mint houses. It may be no coincidence that the problems with copper imports coincided with the substantially diminishing production figures of Indian mints in the decades between the 1610s and the 1660s. International price levels therefore certainly matter, particularly in the seventeenth century.[132] Whereas the Dutch bought their copper in Japan in the 1650s at 10-11 tael per picol, the price had risen to 12.4 in 1665/6 and to 12.7 in 1670. Though later it fell again to 11.9 from 1676 and 1691, prices remained high overall in the eighteenth century (12.36 in 1700 and 12.8 in 1701 with a climax of 14.84 in 1716). These fluctuations must have been one of the reasons for the Mughal currency reforms in the early 1660s.

3d. The Imports of Non-Metal Small Currencies

At the lower end of the scale, non-metallic, uncoined currencies were also used as small change; specifically, bitter almonds in parts of western India and cowries in especially Bengal and Orissa. In both cases, production proper did not take place in the Indian subcontinent. Bitter, non-edible almonds in the nut, called *badams*, were imported from Persia, while cowries were primarily collected on the beaches of the Maldive Islands. From there, they were shipped to ports in India, especially to Balasore and later Calcutta, from where they were distributed over north-eastern India. In a description of the currency of Malwa Province *c.* 1800, we find a clear explanation for why metal currencies were insufficient for the smooth functioning of the economy: 'Besides pice there are cowries (a shell coin) and these again are subdivided into fractional parts, which form a nominal money, quite essential in countries where both labour and the common articles of subsistence are so cheap, and the standard coin comparatively high.'[133] Because of the complementarity of copper and cowries for small change our figures, which are based only on the production of small-value coins, underestimate deep monetization levels as a whole.

Our best source for bitter almond nuts is Tavernier in the 1660s, according to whom this fruit was imported from the Lar Desert in Persia into Gujarat via Hormuz:[134]

> They grow in dry and arid places among rocks, the tree that produces them closely resembling our broom. These almonds are called badam, and so bitter [...] that there is no need to fear that children will amuse themselves by eating them. [...] In those years when the trees do not bear, the price of this sort is very much raised in that country; and the money changers know how to make profit.

Exactly when this type of currency was introduced is unknown, but the earliest reference for Gujarat dates from the early 1500s, whereas price quotations are restricted to seventeenth-century South and Central Gujarat, and its port city and capital Surat in particular. It is like the *badam* lost its currency function in the eighteenth century.

The area of distribution of cowries was much larger than that of almonds, it covers a much longer time period and it will have involved many more people.[135] Bin Yang, who devotes an entire chapter to the history of cowrie use in India, from prehistoric times onwards, makes an important distinction between their function as valued objects and their monetary use. He dates their use as currency to the late seventh century and possibly even a few centuries earlier. All his evidence, until the introduction of large silver coins by the sultans of Bengal, pertains to large sums transmitted in trade and especially land revenue payments. At the time, copper money did not circulate in Bengal and Orissa, and it is also unlikely that cowries functioned as a substitute.

The first mention of cowries being used as small cash in this part of India dates from the fourteenth century. Unfortunately, this and similar early reports are not very specific, and only the Portuguese Tomé Pires, in 1511, is clear in explaining that the silver tanka (then 11 gram of high-grade silver) was worth 8,960 cowries, which could be divided into seven cahons (1,280 cowries), whereas the cahon could be divided into 16 pon (80 cowries). Arithmetically unrelated to this series is the calaim (448 cowries), but here we reach solid ground with respect to its purchasing power because with this *calaim* one could buy a good chicken.[136] Good chickens, however, are not among the daily, and not even among the weekly necessities of life. Finally, in the next century, several European travellers inform us about the daily use of cowries, most clearly Thomas Bowrey, visiting East Orissa in the 1660s. Rather condescendingly, he writes:

> I have often been to their villages, and where they have been more than 20 families of them, they could not all change one Rupee into Cowries, whereby to pay for a little milke or fish (or else wee had of them) in the currant moneys of this Kingdome and Orixa and Arackan, and withal soe ignorant that they know not Silver from Tootanagga [...] Cowries (all the moneys knowne to the ignorant Ourias) are small shells, brought from the Islands of Malldiva.[137]

Concretely, daily payments with low-value cowries, indispensable for exchange facilities, are described for early nineteenth-century Assam. There, moneychangers, called *potdars*, visited the markets. They were:

> ... a very numerous class, but many of them, having no shop, sit in the open air with heaps of cowries placed before them. In the more rural tracts, the money changer goes to market with a bag of cowries on his head; if a rich man, with a loaded ox, which, if strong, may carry to the value of 150 rupees. All the early time of the market, he sells cowries for silver to the people, and in the evening the various hucksters bring back their cowries and exchange them for silver, paying a batta [interest premium] in exchange each way to the potdar.[138]

The ubiquity of cowries in northeastern India can also be illustrated by the widely accepted conventions about how to count them and how to designate specific quantities – simply put, multiplication rather than dividing coins into their fractions. Three systems have dominated the market, partially subsequently, partially next to each other (see Tables I.5-I.7).

From its original circulation in coastal Bengal and Orissa, where the cowries were landed from the Maldive Islands, they spread upriver, westwards, where they are mentioned already in the late sixteenth century in Jaunpur, north of Benares.[139] There, in 1571, cowries were used not instead of copper coins but as fractions of copper. Specifically, they were used when rural construction workers had to make customary payments of four cowries for every copper coin in their wage packet to the superintendent overseeing the building of a bridge. Another author describes himself as a boy selling cowries in Jaunpur. Less than a century later, Tavernier finds them even further upstream at Agra. The same author also mentions the export of cowries from the Maldives to Golconda, immediately south of Orissa, as well as to Bijapur. In the latter case, we must consider another sea route because Bijapur is situated on the west coast and thus much nearer to the Maldives than the Bay of Bengal.[140] In central-north India, cowries as small change are reported in Malwa, Delhi and Awadh. In the early 1850s, the mint of Lucknow issued a copper half *falus* coin with a value of 12 [*gonda*], quarters with the cypher 6 and an eighth *falus* with the cypher 3.[141]

All evidence points, however, to the overwhelming currency function of cowries in Orissa and Bengal. According to Lindsay in the 1770s: 'This cowrie, or shell, is well known in every part of Bengal, and used in the purchase of the smallest articles of life by the lower ranks of society, and they answer all the purposes of commerce.' Some of the most detailed information has been collected by him for Sylhet in north-eastern Bengal, which he calls 'the poorer country and more suitable for the purchase of the smaller article of traffic in lieu of copper currency'. At the same time, all the land revenue taxes in Sylhet, amounting to Rs. 250,000, were collected by him in cowries, or the enormous number of 1.3 billion shells, which all had to be shipped to Dacca where they were sold at auction.[142]

The general drop in the price of cowries in the second half of the seventeenth century may have stopped a further extension. The British refusal to accept cowries for the payment of land revenues in 1805 heralded their slow demise.[144] An official enquiry, managed from Calcutta, into the desired supply of newly coined

TABLE I.5: DENOMINATIONS OF COWRIE SHELLS IN INDIA IN THE SIXTEENTH AND SEVENTEENTH CENTURIES

Cowrie	*Ganda*	*Bodi/budi*	*Pan/pana/ pun/pund*	*Kahon/ kahan*
4	1			
20	5	1		
80	20	4	1	
1,280	320	64	16	1

Sources: Garg 2007, 250, 254 (instead of budi also kakini, and instead of kahon also drama); cf. De 1952, 6; Haider 2015, 99.

TABLE I.6: DENOMINATIONS OF COWRIE SHELLS IN INDIA IN THE EIGHTEENTH AND EARLY NINETEENTH CENTURIES

Cowrie	*Gunda*	*Pun/pund*	*Cawn*	*Rupee*	
4	1				
80	20	1			
1,280	320	16	1		
5,120	1,280	64	4	1	
40,960	10,240	512	32	8	1

Sources: Yang 2019, 57, 64; cf. Garg 2007, 250 (in 1755 at Calcutta 48 to 50 pund per Arcot rupee); See Part 1: Studies, No. 13 in this volume for the Awadh system described in a Dutch source.

TABLE I.7: MULTIPLES OF COWRIES AND CONVERSION TABLE INTO COPPER PICE, C. 1800 IN DELHI AND MALWA

	Gunda	*Dumrie / damri*					
		1	*2 (chhedaum)*	*3 (tundumrie)*	*4 (adillah)*	*5*	*8*
Cowries	4	12	24	36	48	60	96
Gundas	1	3	6	9	12	15	24
Pice		⅛	¼	⅜	½	¾ (paon pice)	1

Sources: Malcolm 1822, 478-9 (his equation 'the punj dumrie, or five dumries to the paon pice, or three quarter pice' is problematic); cf. NAI, MBP, 22 June 1819, 817 (in May 1819 the exchange rate fluctuated heavily in Delhi from 2 to 3.5 'dumurees' per rupee.There are numerous examples in the sources, but it is not that easy to come up with precise information.[143] Two questions are raised: one on the shifting geographical area in which this medium of exchange was current, the other on quantities imported.

copper coins among the districts provides us with information about the geographical extension of the cowries at that moment (Table I.8).

In general, we might conclude that not only Calcutta and its immediate surroundings, but also urbanized districts like Chittagong and districts along the Hugli and Ganga rivers demanded copper pice, and this demand increases if we go to the west, from Murshidabad in Bengal via Bihar to Benares in eastern UP. The Council of Patna remarked in 1773 that 'exchange of cowries is not so common [in Bihar] as in Bengal' and therefore wished 'to coin annas and pice'. If not, 'the latter would become very dear and enhance to the poor the price of all kinds of provisions'.[145] For Bengal proper, the rule seems to be: the further away from the sea and the Hugli and Ganga rivers, the more widespread the usage of cowries for small change.

Around Cuttack in Orissa, i.e. adjacent to Midnapore district in the south-west of Bengal, cowries were also popular until well into the nineteenth century. In 1814, no less than 27.5 per cent of the total currency value in circulation was composed of cowries, in contrast to 10 per cent of copper, 60 per cent of silver and 2.5 per cent of gold coins.[146]

Apart from the isolated records about Golconda and Bijapur (Lindsay in the 1770s explicitly states that they were not 'found either on the opposite coast of Malabar or Coromandel'[148]), I consider the occurrence of cowries up to Agra and Delhi as the widest extension, and primarily as an addition to and not a replacement for copper currency in the riverine parts of north India. In Orissa and Bengal proper, cowries provided a complete alternative to copper currencies, as the 1805 enquiry shows, and later, to a decreasing degree, until cowries stopped functioning as such around 1900.

Moving from geography to trade, Table I.9 presents some stray data on the importation of cowries, their quantities and their price. We do not have systematic trade statistics for cowries, but occasional data may afford us an idea of the quantities involved. However, drawing further conclusions from shipments is more difficult as there was not one type of cowries, but instead a number of varieties, each fetching different prices, as exempli-

TABLE I.8: AMOUNT OF PICE REQUIRED FOR CIRCULATION IN THE DISTRICTS OF BENGAL, 1808

District	*Amount required*		*Remarks*
	in rupees	*in pice*	
Bhaugbhon [Bhagalpur?]	30,000:0	1,920,000	
Burdwan	781:4	50,000	
Chittagong	50,000:0	3,200,000	
Dingapoor [Dinajpur]	2,000:0	228,000	
Jessore	6,250:0	400,000	
Moorshedabad [Murshidabad]	22,000:0	1,408,000	
Mymensing	400:0	25,600	
Purneah [Purnia]	1,562:4	100,000	
Rungpore [Rangpur]	10,000:0	640,000	
24 Pergannahs [Parganas]	1,000:0	64,000	
Sarum [Saran]	52,000:0	3,328,000	
Shahabad	30,000:0	1.920,000	
Tirhoot [Tirhut]	36,000:0	2.304,000	
Hidgellie [Hijuli]	5,000:0	320,000	
Benares	700,000:0	44,800,000	
SUBTOTAL	946,993:8	60,607,560	
Sylhet	0		Report wanting
Beerbhoom [Birbhum]	0		Copper coin not current / not in circulation in this district
Dacca [Dhaka]	0		
Nuddea [Nadia]	0		
Rajeihahye [Rajshahi]	0		
Tipperah [Tripura]	0		
Midnapore	0		

Source: Stevens 2012, 264-5. The interpretation of the placenames between [ ] is mine.[148]

fied by two ships carrying 30 ton of cowries in 1769. The EIC Warehouse in Bombay stipulated that they should be 'the cheapest procurable'. In this case, and another a year later, we find no less than four different types with their own price notations.

In terms of the circulation of non-metallic currencies, we can

TABLE I.9: COWRIE PRICES IN BOMBAY (RS. PER SURAT CANDY AT 355 KG), 1769-70

	1769/70	*1770*
Maldive cowries	60	
Maldive cowries excl. broken shells and stones, but incl. dead shells		28
Patta cowries	25	
Joanna cowries	20	

Sources: http://www.psindiancoins.com/unzipped/Europe/Bombay after Bombay Consultations, IOR P/341/32, 1769, p. 661 (29 September 1769) and idem 33, 1770, p. 517 (26 October 1770); Nadri 2009, xxi (1 candy = 784 pounds avoirdupois).

conclude that Bengal and Orissa were a copperless part of India before about 1800, but this does not exclude them from deep monetization as, here, cowries took the place of copper. Quantification is impossible, however. Cowries spread over riverine north India in the seventeenth century, possibly because of the diminishing production of copper coins. But they were not a replacement for copper; rather, they were a supplementary source for deep monetization. The same may be true for the circulation of *badams* in Gujarat. This supplementary function may have lasted until the early nineteenth century in Bihar and Awadh. Consequently, the increased copper coin production by the British in the nineteenth century does not necessarily imply a process of deep monetization in Bengal and Orissa but rather the substitution of cowries with copper coins. This process extended from Calcutta to more inland parts of Bengal, with the last iteration possibly in Sylhet.

3e. Minting Small Currencies: How and How Many?

This is not the place to examine minting techniques in any detail. That has been done by various authors already, with a focus on the differences between traditional hand-striking techniques and mechanization. This was started by the British at the end of the eighteenth century with the introduction of laminating machines,

machines for the cutting of blanks, the screw press and, finally, the application of steam power.[149] Whereas an increase in production before mechanization depended on the number of coiners employed, now, gradually, investment in mechanization became decisive. Apart from this, the typical labour history dimension remains a vast unexplored terrain with many sources available from especially the late eighteenth century onwards. A few remarks will suffice here. Most important is the initiative to coin, from which follows considerations as to which denominations precisely. To paraphrase Najaf Haider:

> The mint operated on the principle of open coinage i.e. suppliers could obtain coins on payment of minting costs (brassage) and an imperial tax (seigniorage). [It] was controlled by the state but the market governed its production. For this control, purity of silver and gold mattered most, next the right text and finally the weight of the main coins, the silver rupee and the gold mohur. According to the *Ain* the brassage per unit of value was higher for the 1/8th rupee (7.95 per cent) than for the quarter and half (2.88 per cent) and whole rupee (2.3 per cent). The seigniorage for full denomination was the same (5 per cent) for both metals but we do not have any information about the seigniorage charged on fractional pieces. In all likelihood the premium (in terms of metal weight) was higher for the fractional piece to safeguard its usage.[150]

Both the state and individual entrepreneurs could take the initiative to coin, but it is impossible to say something more general about the continually shifting balance between these two actors, in particular regarding the coinage of coppers. Much more is known about silver, and, in this regard, merchants seem to have been far more important than governments.[151] Driven by the possibility of making profits, silver seems to have offered more chances than copper and, as a general rule, governments stepped in where public demand for small change was not met, for whatever reason, by private parties. This certainly applies to small states with a limited number of civil servants. Only large and powerful states like the Mughal Empire, between *c.* 1550 and 1700 and British India after *c.* 1850, were able and willing to take the actual coinage into their own hands.

Moreover, there was more chance of making a profit minting

bigger rather than smaller coins. That is the main reason why, in India, fractions of the rupee were struck much less than whole rupees or similar coins. The earliest example known to me comes from the VOC settlement at Negapatnam, on the Coromandel Coast, in 1694. Although pertaining to coins meant for Dutch Ceylon, the minting costs of copper give us an impression of the economics involved (Table I.10).

TABLE I.10: MINTING COSTS OF COPPER COINS IN PAGODAS PER BAHAR (480-500 AMSTERDAM POUND OR C. 242 KG) OF COPPER, NEGAPATNAM, 1694

	Minting duit (1/8 stuiver), stuiver, dubbeltje	*Minting only stuiver (1/20 guilder) and dubbeltje*
Mint workers' wages	15.0	14.0
Charcoal	2.5	2.5
Loss of 12 pond of copper	1.5	1.5
Total processing costs	19.0	18.0
Raw materials (copper bars)	48.0	48.0
Total production costs	67.0	66.0
Market value of total production 8,778 stuivers	88.0	88.0
Gross profit	21.0	22.0

Source: Prakash 1987, 186-7 (wages, charcoal and production loss of copper).

Assuming (a) that here we are talking about 480 Dutch pounds or 237 kg of copper with a yield of 8,778 stuivers of 27 gram each; and (b) a copper price of 50 Dutch guilders per 100 Dutch pounds, or the costs of 240 guilders per one bahar of copper; and, finally (c) that the pagoda was valued at about 5 guilders, the result may have been a very handsome gross profit of 24 per cent, and even more if the production was restricted to only the largest size coppers. Remarkably, there is no mention of taxation in this source, so the net profits must have been lower, possibly half.[152]

A grey zone is occupied by private mints, more or less recognized – or at least condoned – by small polities. They did not make coins of their own design, but rather imitations of popular coins of neighbouring states. We know of their existence from the complaints of mighty neighbours who feared disruption of their own coin circulation. In reality, it looks as if the success of these 'counterfeiters' was much more due to the lack of official mints, unable to react to a growing demand from the common people. It is no coincidence that we see this happening predominantly in the second and third quarter of the nineteenth century. These were the years when the gap between the pretensions of the colonial state to take care of a healthy coin circulation did not correspond with actual coin production and distribution across the subcontinent by the presidency mints of Calcutta, Bombay and Madras. Some telling examples are included in the Studies and Records section of this volume.[153]

It is only around 1880 that we find reliable circulation numbers for coins in the entire peninsula, including the small ones equalling a daily wage of one anna (1/16 rupee) or less, as explained more extensively below in paragraph 4a. (We must caveat this with the fact that these estimates only relate to those parts of the subcontinent that were directly under British rule). However, as argued in Appendix 1, there is an alternative available to reconstruct long-term tendencies in deep monetization. On the basis of a data set of all types of small coins struck from 1500 to 1947 whose actual rarity (expressed in a market price for collectors) is known, we can get an impression of the increases and decreases in small coin production. What the implications of this reconstruction are will be explained later. For now, we will just observe what the trends are and whether this enables us to subdivide the four centuries in this book into meaningful sub-periods.

Instead of presenting the number of new coin types per half century (see Appendix 1), we can regroup them into sub-periods according to important changes in the frequency of new types (see Table I.11).

If we then attribute weights according to rarity to the various types, using the method explained in Appendix 1, we obtain an idea of fluctuations over time in the total production of small coins (see Figure I.1).

TABLE I.11: AVERAGE NUMBER OF NEW TYPES OF SMALL DENOMINATION COINS PER YEAR, INDIA 1500-1947

Years	*Average number of new coin types per year*
1500-41	6.3
1542-1605	12.4
1605-99	4.1
1700-49	6.3
1750-99	12.4
1800-80	11.8
1881-1947	4.5

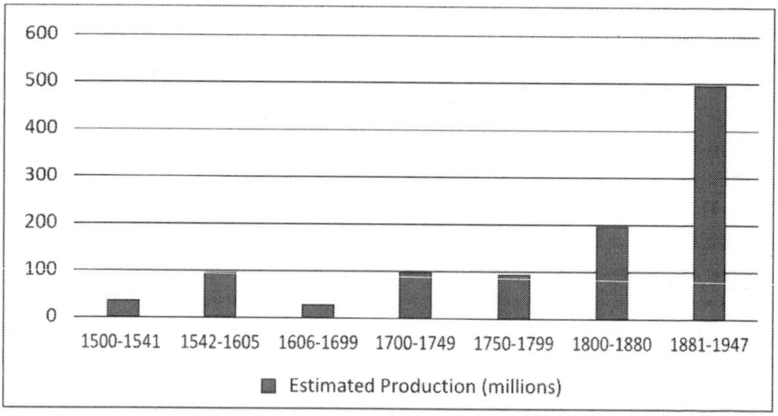

FIG. I.1: ESTIMATE OF ANNUAL NUMBER OF SMALL DENOMINATION COINS STRUCK PER SUBPERIOD, 1500-1947

It should be stressed that this graph depends on a number of suppositions (see Appendix 1) and therefore should be interpreted cautiously. Nevertheless, I believe that if not the absolute production figures, then certainly the trends it represents can be trusted.

A comparison with the results for the distribution of coin types per half century (see Figure I.2 in Appendix 1) offers an explanation for the apparent anomaly of the strongly decreasing number of *new coin types* in the late colonial period. The graph above shows that this is more than fully compensated for by the *absolute number of coins struck per type*. To give an example, during the reign of King George V, the Calcutta and Bombay mints poured out millions of coins of the same unchanged types year after year.

How do we explain these fluctuations in the production of small coins? To a certain extent, the preceding chapter on the availability of overseas copper already provides part of the answer. The upsurge in the 1540s was made possible by the combined imports via the Red Sea and the new route via the Cape of Good Hope. But copper supply as such is not enough, there should also be a demand for small coins and this was rising under the Suris and under the first Mughals. The second upward trend in the course of the eighteenth century was certainly facilitated by the combined import possibilities from Japan and England. In between, the downward trend in the seventeenth century can be linked to import fluctuations – and in particular to the failing of copper imports from Europe via the Cape. At the same time, the Japanese alternative was not yet strong enough.

We can immediately tackle one obvious determinant of the demand side, i.e. population developments. To what extent can they explain the fluctuations? Alas, the historical demography of India is still in its infancy. Following the latest overview by Tim Dyson, with all its uncertainties (see Table I.12), it is possible to arrive at the deep monetization level per capita.

We can now discuss possible explanations for upward and downward trends in terms of population change; in other words, deep monetization levels per capita. Focusing on the turning points on which Figure I.1 is based, let us start with the brisk production increase in the 1540s, which continued under Akbar until his death in 1605. It is likely that this coincided with and was possibly connected to population growth in the same period. At the same time the estimated 50 per cent population growth in the sixteenth century was far less than the increase in small coin production between 1542 and 1605. Apparently, the per capita demand for small coins in those years increased substantially, suggesting the growing importance of wage labour. The increase in real wages around the same time also points in that direction.

TABLE I.12: INHABITANTS OF THE INDIAN SUBCONTINENT, 640-1941

	Inhabitants (millions) [best guess]	*Remarks*
640	[58]	Minimal 30; maximal 86
1000	[77]	
1500	[80]	My extrapolation
1595	[125]	Minimal 116; maximal 145
1700	[150]	My extrapolation
1800	[187]	Minimal 159; maximal 207
1821	[200]	Maximal 220
1871	255	
1881	257	
1891	282	
1901	285	
1911	303	
1921	306	
1941	389	

Source: Dyson 2018, 44-5, 68-71, 88-91, 114-17, 125, 173.

All these developments might have been influenced externally by increased international connections and internally by the successful institutional innovations of the Suris and early Mughals.

The spectacularly receding production numbers in the seventeenth century, and in particular during the first half of the reign of Jahangir (1605-27) and, subsequently, Shah Jahan (1628-58) cannot be explained by demographic decline; indeed, the contrary may be true. Of course, the lack of new coins does not mean that the old coins vanished, so the huge numbers struck under the Suris, and under the first three Mughals, remained in circulation. They may even have become more frequently available for small payments because of the simultaneous increase in silver imports in India from about 1600 and the subsequent replacement of copper by silver coins in payments of revenue.[154] At the same time, it is also possible that, especially in northern riverine India, cowries replaced copper coins for small purchases (see paragraph 3d). The interplay of all these factors is hard to measure, but it is too early to conclude that the failing production of small coins in the seventeenth century put so much pressure on labour relations that it caused de-proletarianization, though this cannot be excluded without further research.

The partial production recovery in the eighteenth century, together with slow population growth, will not have changed the situation described for the seventeenth century substantially. The coppers in circulation may have become more worn and the popularity of cowries in part of the country will not have diminished. A real increase of the per capita deep monetization level (DML) took place in the nineteenth century, when a doubling of small coin production between 1800 and 1880 was by no means matched by population growth of perhaps 40 per cent. We may suppose that the availability of small coins reached the same levels as in the late sixteenth century – or even more, if we take into account the usage of copper under Akbar, where the abundant silver was later used instead. As demonstrated elsewhere (see below paragraph 4a and Studies, No. 4 in this volume), this put India at similar deep monetization levels to most countries in Western Europe.

The increased production figures for the late colonial period (1880-1947) again far exceed population growth and, consequently, suggest increased DMLs. By implication, proletarianization, already substantive for ages as we have seen, must have increased, although a small part of the explanation may also be found in the vanishing of the last cowries from the marketplaces and shops in north-eastern India. A comparison between estimated production figures for the two last sub-periods (1800-80 and 1880-1947), as shown in Figure I.1 above, and new coin types (Figure I.2 in Appendix 1) also points to an interesting political phenomenon. The contrasting movements, and especially the drop in coin types in the last period, combined with the explosion of total production figures, were the result of the sustained efforts of the British to suppress minting by Indian states, as amply shown by Sanjay Garg.[155]

In order to gain a better understanding of the demand side, let us now turn in the next chapter of this introduction from the more economic-monetary historical approach to the social aspects, i.e. to the usage and the actual users of small change.

4. Circulation

Coin production in a modern state is principally meant for circulation within its own borders. This applied much less in the past, especially before the mid-nineteenth century, also in India. However, for the subcontinent as a whole (but not for individual states, as we will see), export of coins was unimportant and certainly of small coins. This implies that the total production of small coins, as reconstructed above, also circulated on the subcontinent. A few exceptions that prove the rule deserve a mention here. In 1685, the Portuguese exported copper bazarucos from Goa to Mozambique (Records, No. 1 in this volume).[156] This African colony had no coins of its own before 1725 and therefore this cargo is also remarkable because, according to conventional wisdom, sub-Saharan Africa did not use coin at all at the time. Instead, the Portuguese used to export beads, witness a report Cesar Frederic, a merchant of Venice 1563:

> The Portuguese trade all the way from Chaul along the coast of India, and to Melinda in Ethiopia, in the land of Cafraria, on which coast are many good ports belonging to the Moors. To these the Portuguese carry a very low-priced cotton cloth, and many paternosters, or beads made of paltry glass, which are manufactured at Chaul, and from thence they carry back to India many elephants' teeth, slaves, called Kafrs or Caffers, with some amber and gold.[157]

Another exception are some commissions performed by the Calcutta Mint for Pulau Penang, Bencoolen and Mauritius with its slave economy.[158]

The first issue to be addressed here is how the main actors, merchants and governments were able to measure demand in such a proper way (see paragraph 4a). Having produced coins, it was an art in itself to distribute the coins and to get them accepted (paragraph 4b). Money changers or shroffs played an important role in the circulation of coins (paragraph 4c). On this basis, we can better understand the problems experienced by workers in receiving their wages and in spending these wages in exchange for their daily necessities (paragraphs 4d and 4e).

4a. Measuring Demand

The reconstruction of the output of small coins may be difficult; obtaining an impression of the demand is even more complicated. Of course, we may suppose that there is a relation between the output and the demand, but it is also important to know in what way the contemporary suppliers (both governments and merchants) determined the demand and how they responded to it. Because of the decentralized organization of coin production, it is rare to find relevant information like the very early one where Firoz Shah (1351-88) ordered the issuing of small change because the ordinary people needed it (See Part 1: Studies, No. 5 in this volume). Occasionally, we find considerations and estimates by governmental bodies about how many coins of a specific denomination are needed, and, from the 1880s, even estimates about the total stock from which, of course, the future need can be derived – given a certain replacement rate.

On the whole, the government set the rules of minting and taxed it, but the initiative to actually mint metal into coin was left to merchants (see paragraph 3e). The detail of the minting regulations and the necessary enforcement of these rules depended on the power of the state. From its beginnings, the Mughal Empire, adopting the Suri innovations of AH 950 (1543/4), was able to maintain a centralized monetary system for the most of India from the mid-sixteenth until the mid-eighteenth century, whereas the situation beyond its territory, in southern India, was much more diffuse and, to a larger extent, determined directly by the merchant communities.[159] From Akbar until Aurangzeb, and a few of his successors, central mints enabled merchants to have gold, silver and copper coins of a high and stable quality, manufactured at a reasonable charge, allowing them a decent profit.

For the common man, a high- and stable-quality copper coin meant, in the first place, a stable exchange rate, at least for the foreseeable future. This provided certainty regarding the purchasing power of his wage and his living standard. Akbar's system determined the value of the copper dam, weighing 20 gram at 1/40 part of the silver rupee (and, by extension, of its fractions, mainly of 1/2, 1/4, and 1/8 dam; occasionally, tankas or double dams were also coined). Rising copper versus silver prices on the world market in the early period of Aurangzeb's reign (1663/4) forced him to reduce the official weight of the copper dam, now generally called paisa, from ca. 20 to 13 gram (two-thirds of the standard weight), without, however, changing the exchange rate of 40 paisa to the unaltered silver rupee. The maintenance of this official exchange rate must have at least softened market fluctuations.[160]

With the waning central power in the course of the eighteenth century, exchange rates became much more variable and, equally unavoidable, the standard weight of the paisa was reduced. Due to both factors, from the mid-eighteenth century, the actual exchange rate of the circulating coppers depended on many local circumstances. Instead of government taking the lead as before, town governments now became followers by publishing at regular intervals the exchange rates of coppers as part of the general list of recommended market prices. These public lists are called the *neriq*, documented for many places until far into the nineteenth century.[161] In Mandsaur (Mundissore in Malwa) and the more southern Sailana and Ratlam, *c.* 1800, new copper to silver exchange rates were assessed every two to three months, undoubtedly by the community of shroffs, and probably also published officially.[162]

This changing situation, from *c.* 1750, of varying and sometimes even volatile exchange rates of copper coins may already have been the rule in the decentralized south much earlier, in fact for nearly the entire period covered by this book. The lack of silver money there meant that the exchange rate between gold and copper was what mattered. Like much later in the north, market forces, de facto the guild of the shroffs and its individual members, took these important decisions.

How should we imagine this market process of market decision-making on exchange rates and on whether or not to bring copper to the mint for minting paisas (in the north) or cash (in the south), or other commonly accepted copper money? In this regard, it is good to distinguish between short-term and long-term decisions to mint a certain coin type, which, to a certain extent, coincides with the distinction between implicit and explicit arguments. We have hardly any detailed information about the considerations of Indian merchants in this respect, but a few more or less similar cases of their English counterparts may be illustrative.

The first case regards work on the fortifications of Fort William at Calcutta in 1757. In October of that year, the Committee of Works wrote: 'it will be extremely troublesome and inconvenient to pay the cowleys, labourers and bricklayers, to be employed on the fortifications in cowries'. Therefore, they recommended 'that copper, brass or tutenague tickets may be stampt of different values for the payment of those people, which shall be taken back at the value stamp'd on the respective tickets'. This idea was approved by the government and Mr. Frankland, the mint master of Calcutta, was ordered to mint such 'tickets', of which we know of copper 2, 3, 6 pice and one anna pieces.[163]

In 1774, the initiative to strike copper one and two anna pieces came from the postmaster at Patna, designated as Azimabad. It is possible that they were issued in order to pay for sending letters, but they may also have had a wider circulation.[164] We know much more about the third example, the series of copper coins of half, quarter, one-eighth and one-sixteenth anna minted by John Prinsep (1748-1830) at Pultah, north of Calcutta, in 1780/1.[165] Having acquired rights for mining copper (see paragraph 3b) he looked for possibilities to process the ores himself. The best way, so this young British entrepreneur thought, was to mint coins and he got the permission from the government to go ahead. In the extensive correspondence between Prinsep and the authorities in Calcutta, we find that these issues were partially meant to replace old and worn copper coins and cowries, and that they would be of 'much public utility' in Bengal, Bihar and Orissa (the three provinces).[166]

In Europe, at the end of the eighteenth century, attempts were made to determine exactly the demand for specific denominations of coins (see Part 1: Studies, No. 4 in this volume) and it is not difficult to find records with plannings of specific issues for those parts of India ruled by the British. This innovation was greatly enhanced by the establishment of so-called Mint Committees, comprising important and expert civil servants to assist the government in determining the demand, rather than it be the sole responsibility of the mint master. The Mint Committee, appointed by Lord Cornwallis in May 1792 was mainly concerned with silver and gold currency, but was also instructed to 'enquire into the state of the copper coinage' (point 4).[167]

An important indicator for the decision taken by the Mint Committees of Benares and Calcutta to mint new copper coins was the supply available in the treasury.[168] The Mint Committee of Benares was very active and many of its records have been preserved and partially published.[169] In 1808, the amount of (copper) pice required for circulation in that district was estimated at Rs. 700,000.[170] The district, then still undivided, most likely identical with the later Benares 'Division', with over five million inhabitants according to the 1901 census. Given an average population growth of 40 per cent in nineteenth-century India, the number of inhabitants may have been some 3.7 million in 1808, ten per cent of whom lived in Benares city. The per capita copper coin circulation thus amounted to 0.2 rupees or 3 annas or 15 pice. Given that the daily wage of a labourer was four pice,[171] this would imply that, with a DML of four, the district as a whole was on the verge of deep monetization.

The earliest known reliable and detailed figures of the total money supply for India as a whole date from around 1880 (see Part I: Studies, No. 13 in this volume). As has been stressed before in this introduction, the experts who made this reconstruction of coin circulation in India remarked that gold coins were only used for hoarding, export or were melted down for ornaments. Silver coins were used to pay rents and taxes, and for petty trade transactions.[172] At the end of the nineteenth century, silver coins played a much greater role in India than in Europe. In the words of an old India hand in 1892: 'the whole trade of India [...] is now conducted by the actual transfer of coin from hand to hand, except in the Presidency towns, and some of the large up-country towns, and even there you will see at the present-day men paying their debts, by bringing in bags of rupees, rupees in thousands'. Throughout his entire life, however, the ordinary man would have seen only the lowest possible denominations, in general meaning copper coins. Most surprisingly, these copper coins, with an estimated value of 48.1 million rupees – or a fifth of a rupee (three annas) per capita – expressed in hourly wages of a quarter of an anna, resulted in a DML of no less than 12.[173]

This comparatively high level warrants some qualification. Wages outside agriculture may have been slightly higher than a quarter of an anna, and working days may have been longer than eight hours; even so, the result would be a per capita copper circulation of more than five times the hourly wage. Furthermore, the actual circulation of copper coinage is likely to have been higher, because the estimates probably exclude both copper coins produced before 1862 – the first coinage under the British Crown – and the numerous humble 'native coins' that continued to circulate. Nevertheless, there are other reasons to conclude that the idea that India was already deeply monetized by 1880 may be not too far off the mark. Moreover, the proportion of wage labourers was not very different from contemporaneous outcomes for European countries (see paragraph 4d below).[174]

4b. Distribution

Most modern states claim the monopoly over producing their own national currency and to keep its internal circulation in check. Even today, however, that is an ideal rather than reality for many countries. Some states do not have a currency at all (e.g. Ecuador, officially since 1999 when it adopted the US$), some allow or condone the wide circulation of foreign currencies like the US dollar, the euro (or earlier on the deutsche mark) or the pound sterling. Conversely, the countries or groups of countries concerned (in this example the USA, the EU resp. Germany, or Britain) produce currencies for a wider usage than internally. The circulation of 'greenbacks' worldwide is a telling example.

This was no different in the past. The circulation of Spanish and Spanish-American dollars worldwide and of Dutch gold and big silver coins in Asia in the seventeenth and eighteenth centuries are well-known examples, but there are many more, also in Indian history. It is therefore necessary to ask what the geographical distribution of each type of coin was: did it coincide with the territory of the state that had authorized its production, or only part of it; or was it also used beyond its political boundaries? Apart from archival sources, travelogues, etc., archaeological finds (see above) can tell us about the relation between production and distribution sites. It is not possible to elaborate on this theme here, except for occasional examples, which can be found in Appendix 2.

Logistically, we may distinguish between the following stages: putting minted coins into circulation; importing coins and non-metal currencies; and accepting these coins. Loud and clear proclamation in public of the issue of new coins seems to have been the rule. In early 1510, the Portuguese in Goa assembled a meeting of all Muslim and Hindu merchants where:

> it was fit to make it public by proclamation being read to the people throughout the city, *as was the native custom*, [...] to take the royal flag, trumpets and kettle drums, to assemble all the men in the fleet [...] went with this multitude of people all around the city; proclaimed the minting of the coinage, and at each proclamation that was made scattered quantities in handfuls of the new money over the heads of the crowds, which were naturally very great, and eager to catch as many pieces as they could [...] The people were very much pleased with the money, and from that day henceforward they began to trade with their merchandise.[175]

Proclamations could also be printed, like when John Prinsep's new series of copper coins had to be advertised in Calcutta in 1781 (see Records, Nos. 2 and 23 in this volume). From this time, regular English-language newspapers were published in India in which authorities could announce new currency regulations, i.e. Hicky's *Bengal Gazette* (1780-2), the *India Gazette* (from 1780), and the *Calcutta Gazette* (from 1784). See Records, No. 4 in this volume.

In reality, putting new coins into circulation and getting the public to accept them is less simple than it looks. Also, for strong-handed authorities like the British. This is – to give but one example – vividly illustrated by the great difficulties they experienced in 1831 when introducing the new quarter annas in the Bombay Presidency.[176] One reason for the issues was the lower intrinsic value in relation to the nominal value of the new quarter annas compared to the old, already circulating copper coins. This was immediately noticed by the shroffs and the public in general, which made the new coins very unattractive. Only by offering a premium for the old currency 'if brought to the mint in sums of a certain amount before the expiration of two months, after which the old coin was to be received only at its metallic value' did the operation ultimately succeed. In hindsight, the East India Company (EIC) in London disapproved 'of the several instances in which the new currency was forced upon the humbler dependents of Government in the discharge of a portion of their pay and allowances. Such attempts should not under any circumstances have been made and their obvious inexpediency is aggravated by the certainty that they must always prove abortive.'[177]

The circulation of coins may be imagined in its most simple form as follows: states collect revenues in order to pay their servants, especially the military, who spend coins in the market to buy food, produced as a surplus (after deducting their own consumption) by the peasants and farmers, who subsequently pay revenues.[178] The state, being the single largest employer of waged workers, primarily soldiers, could start the process by paying their wages and salaries.

This way, predominantly silver coins come full circle, if only because of the prohibitive cost of transporting the much heavier copper coins from the base to the centre and back. The circulation of copper coins was probably much more intense if only travelling short distances. Unlike the case of silver and gold coins, the acceptance of small change does not depend primarily on its metal content, i.e. on the market price of precious metals, but rather on political and also geographical conditions. Political, because the value of non-precious metal coins depends only partially on the price of the metal they contain, but also, or even more, on the political power of the issuing polity to guarantee or enforce their acceptance. And power is strongly related to reliability, as exemplified by the following description of the copper coin issuing states of Malwa at the beginning of the nineteenth century:

> With respect to the copper coinage, it scarcely merits notice, being fluctuating in its value, and confined in its circulation [...] both its stamp, its size, and established value, are continually changed by the ruling officers for the purpose of illicit profit. Accepting therefore the Oojein, Indore, Kotah and Bhopaul Pice, which have some character, the copper circulation of most places is confined to its own immediate district or town.[179]

Geographical conditions play an obvious role because of the fact that coin circulation involves costs. Although the common expression 'coin circulation' suggests that coins have feet or, like a perpetuum mobile, wheels so as to roll on their own, every coin is carried by a human being or his pack animal, boat or other means of conveyance. Not only from the mint to the region of circulation (which may have been far away, especially after the concentration of British Indian mints from the second quarter of the nineteenth century onwards), but also within the region where its circulation is accepted.[180] Neglecting these transportation costs and other logistics involved could have grave consequences, as attested by the precocious and near-simultaneous closure of the British mints at Benares in 1830, Pune in 1834 and Saugor in 1835.[181] The subsequent penury of small change in central India made private minting extremely attractive (see Records, No, 28 in this volume). The underestimation of logistics also meant the much slower penetration of 'Company' mints in India than the government in Calcutta and the Board of Directors in London had expected (see Part 1: Studies, No. 13 in this volume).

Another consequence of the transport costs of coins and, in particular, the bulky coppers minted by small mints, was their geographically limited circulation from the issuer, via wage labourer, to shopkeeper, market huckster and, finally, shroff, who initiated a new circulation round. The action radius of such coins may be envisaged in terms of a few days by foot.

4c. Exchange of Small Currencies: The Function of the Shroff

Given the norm of simultaneous circulation of pure metal currencies, variations in exchange rates were unavoidable, despite any attempts at assigning nominal values. De facto, before the British introduced it, the notion of fiduciary coins was absent in India (for currency more broadly, the Hundi system with its fluctuating exchange rates and based exclusively on trust, was an exception). Money changers, or shroffs or *sarrafs*, were therefore indispensable. In 1870, J.P. Stratton explained this very clearly:

PLATE I.1: MONEY CHANGER IN GOA, *c.* 1540

An anonymous 16th century Portuguese illustration from the *Códice Casanatense*, depicting a 'xarafo', or money changer from the Sultanate of Gujarat. Among his Indian clients in the crowd are also a woman and a few Portuguese men. The inscription reads: *Xarafo whom we call money changer of the Kingdom of Cambay.*

Source: Códice Casatanense in the Casanata Library (Rome). Image courtesy: Wikimedia Commons (https://commons.wikimedia.org/wiki/File:Codice_Casanatense_Moneychanger_of_Gujarat.jpg)

Among natives, and a fortiori those of Native Territory, copper pice are looked on less as money or as furnishing a standard of value, than as a common market commodity, the value of which itself varies from day to day in the Bazaar, and is expressed by the number (in Bazaar language the number per Rupees of 'Gundahs' each of 4 pice, or as 'Tukas' each of two pice) procurable per rupee. In fact native Narikhs or price current usually contain the rate of pice just as they give that of any other articles, which is the more needful as, besides the market variation of every kind, some of the sorts vary among themselves in weight, so that it appears these native pice cannot all have been designed exactly one quarter of an anna as in our currency (see Records, No. 32 in this volume; cf. Studies, Nos. 3, 9, 10, 13 in this volume).

Apart from arbitrage, they also performed the function of 'decentralized assayers' of individual pieces. In the sources, the discussion is dominated by how big their space for manipulation was, and also what their link with mint masters and minting personnel was. Firstly, we have to differentiate between higher and lower echelons of shroffs. At the top of the pyramid were real bankers, performing national and even international functions, whereas at the bottom we find small shopkeepers dealing with the exchange of small sums of cowries and copper, and copper and silver.

The family history of the Sah family of Benares, who identified as both bankers and shroffs, provides us with an example of the higher echelons.[182] In the last quarter of the eighteenth century, part of their activities included paying the British Indian troops, in particular in the Mysore wars. They used both bills of exchange (hundis) and bullion. They were also involved in the minting of coins and in exchange operations, albeit exclusively of precious metals. Nowhere in their history is copper mentioned. The same type of money dealer is known from the seventeenth century, as described by Om Prakash (see Part 1: Studies, No. 7 in this volume). One of their main dealings was the conversion of imported silver coins and bullion from abroad (from America via Europe via the Philippines, or Japan) into Mughal silver rupees and gold mohurs, and of old and worn silver coins into newly minted 'sicca' ones. Most famous among them was the house of the Jagat Seths in Murshidabad.

Bills of exchange were most important for moving large sums over long distances without actually moving precious metals, but smaller sums could also be transferred this way. Among wage labourers, substantial numbers worked far away from their families, i.e. most soldiers. John Malcolm describes this for Bengali soldiers posted in the province of Malwa: 'a great number of the natives of the Company's Provinces [Bengal] are in service, or have become inhabitants of Malwa: these continually require remittances for the support of their families, and have usually recourse of petty shroffs, who engage for increased profits, to pay them at the place of residence'.[183] We should not be misled by the term 'petty', as the same author remarks about the moneylenders or *sahukars*: 'Sahokars in their accounts have no lower fractions than a quarter of an anna: Bunniahs or Bazar men enter dumries [a measure for cowrie shells, see Table I.7 above], and all the lesser fractions in their accounts.'[184]

The main shroffs may have been as influential as their equivalents in contemporaneous Europe, but we know far too little about the economic and political power of the minor ones. However, it is important to know that they did not work on their own, rather they were organized locally, probably into kinds of trade guilds (see Part 1: Studies, No. 7 and Records, No. 14 in this volume). This enhanced their influence substantially. In 1810, for example, the Madras government felt compelled to form an official 'Establishment of Shroffs' at the presidency. 'If you can't beat them, join them', must have been the thinking. However, this concession had its price. With an annual expense of the enormous sum of 240 pagodas, this institution voluntarily agreed to reduce exchange rates between silver and copper currencies and to standardize them. This may have helped for a while in Madras, but not permanently and not everywhere.

Twenty years later, an engineer in-charge of the building and maintenance of irrigation canals north of Delhi, having been sent there from Calcutta with boxes full of silver rupees, was confronted by workers who wanted to be paid in exactly specified local copper coinage (see Part 1: Studies, No. 10 in this volume). Thus, he was compelled to exchange his silver into copper; he complained about the shroffs that 'the price of *pice* is always raised when my works commence'. He even planned to go directly to the mint masters, who he found out made the coins, but his masters in Calcutta frustrated this plan by ordering him to use the newly minted official colonial coins instead. The creative engineer lost his case, notwithstanding his reply that: 'The supply of pice ordered up will be utterly useless to me on the works without a special regulation of Government making the pice of the Calcutta mint the only legal copper coin throughout the Companies' territories. The pice in question cannot be introduced by an individual and will only subject me to infinite trouble and annoyance as no one will willingly take pay from me in a coin not in general currency'. Again and again, until the late nineteenth century, ordinary Indians refused to accept fiduciary money.

To what extent village shroffs also cooperated on a regional scale is unknown, but must not be excluded. Already *c.* 1666 (coincidentally or not only a few years after the reduction of the exchange rate of the copper dam) a French traveller writes that a village in India may indeed be very small if it had no money changer (see Part 1: Studies, No. 6 in this volume). In 1776, Rangamati in Bengal, a purely rural marketplace of 256 houses, had thirteen shops, including three dealers in cowries and two shroffs.[185] Given that the operations of these small village shroffs depended on colleagues higher up in the hierarchy, it seems unavoidable that they, too, were part of an organization of kinds.

4d. The Payment of Wages

Labour relations

Remuneration for the performance of work could take many forms.[186] It could be done in a reciprocal way in which the service by one person was balanced by that of another. That is the basis of work done within the household, but in India, it could also take place at the level of a village. This is the so-called *jajmani* system in which village artisans were entitled to a share of the harvest of the farmers for whom it was necessary to mend and make ploughs, carts, and other utensils. Village priests could also be remunerated that way. Although unique, this kind of *jajmani* exchange applied to only a small portion of the occupational population. By far the most work was performed for the market, either by small producers like peasants, artisans or merchants or by wage earners. Those market producers in the centuries studied here depended on currencies to be received and, subsequently, paid out in exchange for their food and other necessities.

Apart from the household producers already mentioned – mainly spouses, children and other inhabiting relatives of peasants and artisans – one other category was also excluded from receiving and paying currency, i.e. slaves. This category is often forgotten in the socio-economic history of India, although it certainly existed.[187] Moreover, definition questions, partially historical but also partially related to contemporary political discussions about 'untouchables', obscure our understanding of this specific type of labour relation. Its proportion of the total population of India is difficult to determine because of a lack of serious historical research and due to regional and temporal fluctuations before the formal abolishment of slavery in the mid-nineteenth century, but certainly in the south, and maybe also in Bengal, it may have reached ten per cent.

Early studies were done in the wake of the British abolition movement and some of its results have been blamed for a colonial and racist bias with a tendency to exaggerate the extension of the phenomenon. An older study on Bengal between 1772 and 1843 (the official abolition of slavery in British India; in some of the native states this happened later, e.g. in Travancore in 1853) distinguishes between domestic and agrestic slavery. The latter was by far the most important group. In 1841, their total number was estimated at over 4 million persons or a staggering ten per cent of the population.[188] Rajat Datta writes emphatically that there was hardly any unpaid slave or corvée labour in Bengal's agriculture in the eighteenth century; this contrasts with Bihar where, at the time, zamindars exploited their *muttazadah* (Muslim slaves) and *kahar* (Hindu slaves).[189] In the south of the continent, slaves may also have constituted 10 per cent of the population.[190]

PLATE I.2: MONEY CHANGER IN JAIPUR, *c.* 1948

Source: © Fondation Henri Cartier-Bresson/Magnum Photos/ANP. Used by Permission.

For our topic, it is important to note at this point that slaves could be paid partially in cash, and, at the same time, that wage workers could be paid partly in cash and partly in kind (see below). Before embarking on these important questions, which have a direct impact on DMLs, let us first briefly discuss the composition of the paid labour force.

Despite all the uncertainties, it is nevertheless safe to say that the majority of the working population was, in principle, available for the labour market. The earliest possible quantitative reconstruction of labour relations in a larger region of India so far demonstrates this for the Deccan in the 1820s (Table I.13).[191]

In this case, out of a working population of about 1.8 million men and women, more than 700,000 were dependent on wages and the majority of the nearly as many self-employed (mostly small peasants) and their working dependents earned part of their income doing wage work. We find the same picture for Goa around 1850.

The question for this important part of the population, then, is how frequent and in what way these wages were paid out, what customs prevailed and what happened when conflicts arose about the way wage payments were handled. It goes without saying that, apart from the remuneration of domestic servants, soldiers and sailors payment in kind is hardly possible in cities. Therefore, a preliminary question for determining DMLs regards the urbanization rate. A famous estimate by Irfan Habib puts it at some 15 per cent in the seventeenth century, which compares favourably with only 10 per cent according to the census of 1901.[192] Some important caveats are in place here. First, there was an urban-rural continuum with a highly developed countryside around cities, in particular where the cottage industry was thriving, such as in eighteenth-century south India. This also stimulated a free labour market in general.[193]

Second, it would be a mistake to think of the rural population as mainly consisting of self-producing farmers who depended solely on the sale of their produce and were therefore operating outside of the labour market. On the contrary, many if not most rural households were also active outside agriculture. In order

TABLE I.13: PRIMARY LABOUR RELATIONS OF THE TOTAL POPULATION (x1000) OF THE DECCAN IN THE 1820s

Status	*Population*		
	Male	*Female*	*Total*
Not working	385	374	759
Dependent kin producers for the household	0	218	218
Redistributive labourers (*jajmani*), heads of household	86	0	86
Dependent kin producers of the redistributive labourers (*jajmani*)	63	124	187
Self-employed, heads of household	248	0	248
Dependent kin producers of the self-employed	213	114	327
Wage labourers, heads of household	193	0	193
Dependent kin producers of the wage labourers	142	279	421
Wage labourers for the polity	28	0	28
Dependent kin producers of wage labourers for the polity	28	37	65
Total	1387	1146	2534

Source: Lucassen in Lucassen and Seshan 2022, 213 (improved and slightly revised figures: https://datasets.iisg.amsterdam/dataset.xhtml?persistentId= hdl: 10622/5RVUII)

to supply the important weaving sector, for example, most rural women spent part of their time spinning. A telling example of the diversity of occupations of heads of household in the countryside is available for two Bengali villages in the later eighteenth century: Rangamati near Murshidabad and Sibpur on the western bank of the Hugli River (Table I.14).

As Table I.13 for the Deccan already shows, the variety of income sources is substantially greater than even the most refined tabulation of the occupations of heads of households suggests, because virtually all other members of the household contributed as much as possible to the common income, except for the small leisured class.

Third, a substantive part of the labour force in these centuries consisted of paid soldiers or mercenaries as they are sometimes

TABLE I.14: PROFESSIONS/ OCCUPATIONS OF HEADS OF HOUSEHOLD IN TWO BENGALI VILLAGES, 1771, 1791

Professions / occupations	*Rangamati 1771*	*Sibpur 1791*
Agriculturalists	101	150
Silkworm breeders	22	
Officials	33	
Brahmins, physicians, *kyasthas*		86
Craftsmen	15	35
People engaged in commerce	3	27
Fishermen and fishmongers	7	91
Milkmen	17	4
People engaged in textile	10	26
Coolies	22	
Other and unknown	26	
Total	256	419

Source: Datta 2000, 189-91.[194]

called. In peacetime, they might spend their time in barracks in or near cities but when on campaign that is impossible and it is therefore useless to speak, in this case, of either an urban or rural labour force. For deep monetization, however, it is important that the majority originated in the countryside and continued to maintain links with it, including transmissions of part of their pay. Much of this 'marketized violence' took place in the winter slack, providing extra income for many small peasants and rural proletarians. In times of extensive warfare, like during the expansion of the Mughal Empire and its demise mainly by the Marathas and the imperialist subjugation of the peninsula by the British commanding an Indian army, paid employment was widely stimulated.[195]

Modalities of payment

For the main sections of the working population, just described, I will try to delineate the proportion between payment in kind and in cash and other modalities of compensation: for the slaves, the artisans, the sharecroppers, the wage labourers and the military.

From south India in the nineteenth century, we know that slaves received their remuneration mostly in kind, mainly in the form of rice in the south, some other edibles and a minimum of cloth, but also small sums of money. The proportions are unknown before 1800, but afterwards, the cash component started to grow.[196]

Artisans received their remuneration in principle after finishing and delivering a piece of work, which would involve larger sums and therefore also larger denominations than wage earners. In reality, however, they could not live without advances, paid out at regular intervals, which boiled down to piece wages. Undoubtedly, the most important sector, weaving, was organized entirely like this. In Bengal, middlemen between the textile merchants and the weavers paid out the advance, called *dadni* or *dadan*. This was necessary to bridge the time between the beginning and end of making a standard piece of cloth, which could take half a year. After the EIC took over the role of the most important merchant, the independence of the weavers, who had previously bought their own yarn, was severely diminished, which may have made them even more dependent on regular advance payments.[197] Advances may have been paid out once a month or even more frequently. One of the reasons to pay the weavers in instalments and small sums was the 'fear that they shall spend the money on food and deliver no cloths or run away to another place'.[198] Spinners, as a rule women preferably working in the rainy season, were also paid piece rates by way of cash advances.[199]

Although percentages are difficult to give for our period, it is clear that most agricultural work in India was done by small peasants who contracted with large landowners or tenant farmers as sharecroppers. Big estates, exclusively run with the help of agricultural workers or slaves, were only a minority, and so was the small independent farmer working his own plot (held in property or tenancy). Only a few groups, especially the Jats in the northwest can be qualified as independent farmers, tilling their lands mainly using household labour.[200] Apart from sharecropping, their income was derived from exploiting a small garden plot meant for daily consumption of vegetables, seasonal work on land sub-let by landowners to big peasants and from cottage industry, mainly spinning by women, as we have seen. Apart from the garden plot, all other income-gaining activities involved cash payments in return for work performed.

Sharecroppers' usage of coins in their main occupation, tilling the soil, basically took two different forms. First, the landowner or his tenant farmer could provide seed, implements of husbandry and daily maintenance at the start of the season, sell the whole produce of the harvest and pay out the sharecropper between 40-60 per cent, according to the initial agreement – after deducting the initial disbursements plus interest, of course.[201] Second, instead of the sale of the total produce by the landowner (or his tenant farmer) the sharecropper could receive 40-60 per cent of the harvest (again after deduction of disbursements plus rent) in order to sell it on the market himself. This is not the place to discuss the different kinds of exploitation and oppression to which the sharecropper was exposed during this process, but it is important to underline how cash-dependent both forms were, in contrast to the more conventional and now antiquated interpretations of sharecropping in eighteenth-century north India, as a system of mutual protection and interdependence in a 'cash-strapped' society.[202]

Besides sharecroppers, there were agricultural workers who, as we have seen, could be paid out both in kind and in cash. A preliminary question relates to the proportion of wages paid out in kind and not in currencies of any kind. Like in Europe in the same period, payments in kind did happen, although they were far less important than payment in money, as our reconstruction of money circulation indicates. Even for the twentieth century, it is difficult to provide a reliable overview of the extent to which wages were paid out in kind. It is simply impossible for the earlier period. Let us instead see what the circumstances were, under which one prevails over the other.[203] Clearly, they matter greatly in times of highly fluctuating grain prices. If paid out in kind, the agricultural labourer is saved from market vicissitudes, but in times of high grain prices employers often shift to cash payments, and vice versa.

Wage work outside agriculture depended fully on cash payments in cities and, apparently, to a great extent, also in the countryside, as most historical wage studies from 1500 onwards demonstrate. In Portuguese settlements on the west coast of India, we see already a working labour market at the beginning of the sixteenth century, where the labour force for the rebuilding of the fortress of Diu in 1547 was recruited from as far as Bassein (200 km away by ship), Chaul (400 km) and Goa (750 km).[204] A second example of temporal long-distance labour migration is provided by the Ichhapur gunpowder manufactury in the 1790s, which drew yearly workers from Chittagong (700 km across the sea), Midnapur (*c.* 150 km) and Burdwan (over 100 km). Similarly the great infrastructural works like canal and railway building in the nineteenth century.[205]

Little information is available for the frequency of wage payments, but monthly or fortnightly seems to have been the rule.[206] By implication, wage workers did not obtain much credit from shopkeepers. We may suppose that, like in Europe, upon payment, the worker or his wife had to pay off their debts at the local shop and that for the rest of the month there was not much cash left over. From that moment, new debts were built up with the shopkeepers or market vendors, with whom a close and rather fixed relation will have existed. At the Ichhapur gunpowder manufactory, a very formal system existed for the workers to bridge the month. The director wrote in 1796:

> Every man receives upon his arrival a billet of credit, on a moody [grocer], to whom a previous advance of money has been made. Of course, the Agent [director of the factory] suffers the loss of all those whose fears [of casualties with handling gunpowder] prompt them to abscond before the manufacture commences. Now I […] undertake at [my] own charge and risk to supply with provisions at the lowest rates all the people who may assemble from six weeks before to five weeks after the annual opening of the season, on the prospect of recovering the amounts on the respective paydays of every month.[207]

Five years later, in a letter to the Military Board (his superiors at Fort William), he underlines the importance of the credit lines between the factory, the shops, and the workers by complaining that he is still waiting for his advances for May and June, necessary to pay the workforce at the end of that season. This puts him in an impossible position because 'it will not be in my power to discharge the people without paying them as the moodies' shops would be immediately shut against them and they would be left to starve'.[208]

A report on Calcutta's criminal statistics from 1798 makes clear how this dependency on shopkeepers was more important in urban than in rural areas.[209] In this big city, which already had one million inhabitants, between 18,000 and 24,000 'causes' of dispute were recorded annually. These were mainly financial disputes between inhabitants, nearly three-quarters of which were decided by so-called commissioners in favour of the plaintiffs. The majority of plaintiffs and defenders appeared in court in person. The reporter has made the effort to take a sample of 2,500 cases and concludes: 'The principal cause for actions is Balance of Accounts. For a better understanding of the nature of this plaint, it may be expedient to mention, that the lower classes of natives, generally deposit their money with a shopkeeper who supplies them with whatever necessaries they require, and also acts as their banker, in paying any cash, they may occasionally want for other purposes.'

In order to make this more concrete for his readers in East India House in London, he provides the detailed budget of a Hindu family in Calcutta for one month between 13 December 1797 and 10 January 1798. His source is the bookkeeping of the grocer-cum-banker, the results of which he checks with the head of household, who confirms the correctness of the figures. The household consists of 'two men, three women and one child at the breast', which should be interpreted as a married couple with their daughter, son, and daughter-in-law with a baby. One of the men, we may assume the head of household, earns Rs. 4 per mensem as an examiner in a warehouse. The other, probably his son, earns on average Rs. 5 as a bricklayer, as a rule working at piece rates. I will forego here the highly interesting details of this budget, which comprises no less than 31 separate items, but the key conclusion is that out of a total monthly household income of Rs. 9, the shopkeeper provides Rs. 5:10:9, of which 2 maunds and 20 seers of rice, costing Rs. 2. A second important conclusion is that the women do not contribute to the cash income. This is in stark contrast to their sisters in the countryside, who sometimes earn more than their husbands. Apart from different job opportunities in cities and the countryside, caste prejudice against female outdoor work may also have played a role.[210]

The fact that the two men hand over most of their money to their preferred shopkeeper every month has important implications according to our criminal reporter: 'If the proprietor has at any time a balance due to him from the shopkeeper of 8 or 10 rupees and is desirous of drawing the whole amount out of his hands, he is generally under the necessity of applying to the Court of Requests to enforce the payment. On the other hand, if the shopkeeper advances money on account of sickness, expense of marriage &ca he is in like manner obliged to institute an action before he recovers the amount.'

It is likely that this mutual dependency of wage earners and shopkeepers applied mostly to the regularly employed and paid wage workers and artisans in big cities – in short, the majority of the urban population – whereas the really poor, dependent on casual work and irregular earnings, as well as the seasonal immigrants, would not have had this form of credit, and would therefore have had to pay each time they purchased something in a shop or at the market place.

Records about the amount of money, which workers received, are indispensable for standard of living studies (and thus the backbone of the Great Divergence Debate, see paragraph 1 above) and, luckily, they are gradually becoming more available. In contrast, those mentioning the exact coins in which workers' wages were paid out are extremely rare. This notwithstanding, there are good reasons to suppose that the coins in which workers were paid will have been mainly coppers (and in Bengal cowries, see paragraph 3d). The maintenance work on the Western Jumna Canal in 1848/9 is such a rare case for which we have the details of actual wage payments (see Part 1: Studies, Nos. 12 and 13 in this volume). Here, gang bosses were paid out in copper pice coins, which had been exchanged locally 'on the road'. Similarly, workers on the same canal in 1830 and on the Grand Trunk Road at Fatehpur in

1839 received copper pice (see Part 1: Studies, Nos. 10 and 11 in this volume).

Where large sums had to be paid out at once, it is likely that, initially, they were sent as silver rupee pieces in order to avoid unnecessary transport costs (the same sum in silver being less weighty in silver than in copper), which were subsequently converted locally into coppers. This was probably also the case when the director of the Ichhapur gunpowder manufactory addressed the Military Board on 17 January with the following request:

> I am now in advance for people and different articles about Sicca Rupees 4,000. I request the Board will be pleased to apply to Government for an advance of Rs. 20,000, and I hope they will be pleased to make it a rule that I shall always be allowed a certain proportion in silver for the pay of the people, which amounts to Rs. 4,500 per mensem.[211]

The numerous soldiers and sailors were a category of wage workers with their own particularities. Their pay was partially in coin, but partially also in kind. Like domestic servants, they lived in and therefore their remuneration included food and lodging. The rest seems to have been paid out either in silver rupees or in copper coins or, most likely, in both. Evidence for payment in silver is available for the British troops in Patna in 1771, who were very keen to receive rupees minted at Patna, apparently instead of similar ones minted at Murshidabad. Not that the soldiers themselves could see the difference, but the shroffs where they wanted to change these rupees did or pretended to do so and offered less coppers for the Murshidabad than for the Patna rupees. No wonder that the shopkeepers followed suit. In the end, the protests of the troops were successful and their pay was maintained in the highest valued sicca rupees from Patna.[212] In addition to silver, soldiers were also paid directly in copper coin. This becomes clear from the booty found in besieged fortresses after their surrender, where, apart from silver (and occasionally gold mohurs) big amounts of copper coins were also found, without doubt also meant to pay the troops (see Part 1: Studies, Nos. 8 and 9 in this volume). On the rare occasions when gold was used to pay soldiers, it immediately caused a major protest (see below).

An interesting aspect of the payment of soldiers and sailors is the remittance of part of their pay to the household members left behind, which often was stipulated meticulously. By showing the relevant document of this agreement, the spouses of men sent far away, e.g. on duty from Bengal to the Mysore wars, or even further overseas to Bencoolen on Sumatra, they were entitled to receive this part of the income before their husband's return.[213]

Workers' agency

As we have seen on some occasions already, workers were not simply victims of economic fluctuations or evil actors like the shroffs. Against this one-sided view, we should consider a few more examples of workers' agency.[214]

When the copper content of the dam was reduced by a third in 1663, the reaction of the workers in Ahmedabad was clear:

> The administrator of buildings, gardens and other workshops of Ahmedabad City represented to the Celestial Court that [...] workers have declined to accept the new coins in place of the old, saying that the difference between them is in the order of 10:15. When the intelligence of this matter reached the August Presence [Emperor Aurangzeb], an order was issued to the finance minister of the province [of Gujarat] that, in the ratio 10:15, the daily wages should be paid at the rate of one and a half tanka instead of one tanka.[215]

This fits in a more general picture of workers' collective protest for which we have examples from the seventeenth century onwards. Here, the wage levels, the specific mix of payment in kind and in cash and other secondary labour conditions were at stake. In 1678, the Madras boatmen protested against the level of their piece wages, but also against the exchange rate for the fanams in which their wages were paid against the pagoda. In 1706, the washermen of the same place undertook collective action for better rates as well for a fairer and more transparent way to convert cash wages into rice provisions.[216]

Such reactions, demonstrating that labour was paid in cash as well as illustrating the agency of the receivers, are demonstrated by a few more examples from the end of that century. The first dates from 1797, when the spouses of Bengal artillery soldiers fighting overseas in the Mysore war, against the Tipu Sultan, vehemently but successfully protested against the mode of payment of their husbands' salaries. They protested loudly against attempts to pay them in gold as soon as they found out that, as a result, they would receive less copper money from the money changers.[217] In addition, from the 1790s, and also from Bengal, we have the consistent collective action of the thousands of seasonal workers employed by the Ichhapur gunpowder manufactury, who were largely successful in gaining better pay and, most of all, better secondary labour conditions, including a pension scheme for victims of work accidents.

Much more common than collective actions are private strategies to ensure one's income.[218] In the above-mentioned 1798 report on criminal statistics, the sample of 2,500 causes of disputes explicitly lists 39 regarding 'work done', 144 regarding 'wages due to servants', and 12 regarding 'wages due to prostitutes', or 8 per cent of the total. Supposing an average of 20,000 such court cases per year, this would mean wage workers – including at least 100 women – were involved 1,600 times per year. This is not to mention the many more frequent disputes – as stressed by the reporter – relating to the delivery of goods and money lending.[219]

The following examples of collective wage actions date from the 1840s, when the seasonal brickworkers employed on the Ganges canal consistently and successfully waged several strikes. Nearly simultaneously, we find collective actions against malpractices in wage payments by the navies who maintained and repaired the Sonipat division of the Western Jumna Canal, north of Delhi, in 1849 (see above). And let us not forget the troops receiving 'the great bulk of disbursements' and who 'it is well known, are exceedingly sensitive on any point connected with their pay'.[220]

Many more were to follow, but here we enter the realm of modern labour history, which is beyond the scope of this volume. Here, it is important to note that, also in the period 1500-1900, payment and payment modalities mattered for the workers and that, on a number of occasions at least, they tried to redress the worsening of labour conditions. Often with success.

4e. Day-to-Day Spending of Small Currencies[221]

The most difficult topic to research is the day-to-day practices of those who depended on small denomination coins. Here, the examples are scarce and quantitative data is absent. A great step forward could be made by mapping the extension of and the fluctuations in marketplaces and shops for the common man. That they abounded is clear from the literature, but how to draw conclusions about the frequency of payments and their modalities is still unclear. Rajat Datta made an exemplary start for rural Bengal between 1760 and 1800, but much more is needed for a total overview, which would enable us to make linkages with deep monetization studies. Datta draws important conclusions about a spectacular proliferation of markets between *c.* 1770 and 1810, which must have stimulated the demand for small change, initially mostly cowries perhaps, but increasingly also coppers, as the issues of John Prinsep, followed by those of the Presidency mints illustrate.[222]

The importance of retail may be illustrated by reverting to Rangamati 1771, of which we have just seen the diversity of occupations. For its 256 households (see Table I.14) there were already three local shops, one *moodi* or grocer and two *dokandars* or shopkeepers. But that was not all as their services were supplemented by a periodic, probably weekly market (*haat*) with three grocers, one tobacconist, one carpenter, two widows (we do not know what they sold) and one general provisioner. No wonder that this same market also counted no less than three cowrie shops and two shroffs.[223] Here, we see deep monetization in full swing in the countryside. This apparent oversupply of retail services also had a practical reason. Workers had to do their shopping very frequently as there was not enough storage room to preserve food properly in their modest dwellings. Therefore, as is testified for Ichhapur, they had to go 'at least twice a day' to the *moodi* shop, located immediately outside the factory premises. Similarly, due to 'their poverty', the 'daily labourer and working artist' in the province of Benares were obliged 'to take their pay daily'.[224]

From all that has been said, it is clear that the common man usually disposed of only a few coins at the time. Of course, those few coins poor Indians did have in their possession were kept carefully. Hindu men carried their money in knots made in the upper margin of the loincloth or *dhoti*, which is tucked at the waist.[225] More specifically, it was crucial not to mix up different denominations by mistake. A solution was to tie coins of one specific denomination in separate corners of a piece of cloth, like a sari or *dhoti*. This has been attested for India as late as the 1950s.[226] This way of keeping small change without a purse or wallet is documented in detail for countrymen on pilgrimage in Moscow 1914, using four different edges of the cloth for each denomination of copper kopek coins.[227] Of course, rich people and moneylenders had purses. In UP, moneylenders even held a ceremony called *thaili ki munh khulai*, or 'opening the string of the purse', during which the borrower, on receiving a loan, had to pay a fee (by way of an immediate deduction of one anna per rupee, or about 6 per cent; this was in addition to the interest).[228]

Taboos in the handling of coins

Like every exchange of goods or messages between human beings, also the usage of (small) coins is not neutral. In particular, this had implications in caste-dominated India for the exchange between members of different castes. In order to understand the situation in the centuries between 1500 and 1900 more properly, we need to take a long-running jump like the one made in Chapter 2 of this introduction.

Briefly, in the period 500 BCE-400 CE, the marketization and monetization of (north) India did not diverge substantially from what happened at the same time in Western Asia and Europe, on the one hand, and in China on the other. It is only under the Guptas that the caste ideology – the origins of which are much older – finally prevailed, which logically coincides with the demonetization of the subcontinent.[229] Nevertheless, exceptions are possible. Rich Paraiyas who had become untouchable in south India as late as the Chola and Vijayanagara empires were still allowed to have their donations to Hindu temples recorded in inscriptions – notwithstanding the opinion of influential authors that they were denied the possibility of paying the penalty of a crime by fines, 'for these are dirty people among men, so their wealth is inherently dirty'. According to the same logic, only Brahmans were qualified to receive gifts, whereas Shudras were qualified as neither receivers nor givers.[230]

A novel situation emerges with the reintroduction of the market economy and (deep) monetization by the Muslim invasions and the expansion of Muslim societal norms from, say, 1200. This expansion of Islam to the east, into a largely Hindu subcontinent (sometimes called 'the second Islamic wave', designating the Islamization from the thirteenth century onwards,[231]) brought with it a need for Brahman theologians to come to terms with it. In the words of Aktor: expanding trade and urbanization increased the dependence on unskilled manual labour as well as on Shudra artisans, which 'necessitated both interaction and segregation at the same time'.[232]

The regressive reaction is best represented by men like Gopinatha in the fourteenth century.[233] Going against the new Muslim masters (in his case the Bahmanis), he urged for strict observation of caste rules. However, those authors who follow him from the sixteenth century onwards, insert all kinds of modifications to reconcile the strict classical principles of cast hierarchy and cast relations with the new reality. This creates theological and ritual space for the entrepreneurial castes, including craftsmen and the money men (especially at Benares) – a logical reaction without formally dissenting from the right principles.

Here, we reach the topic of this volume, if only because of the very practical day-to-day necessity of cash payments to be made between members of different castes, in particular the payment of cash wages by employers higher up in the hierarchy to the muscle-using and sweating mass below.[234] The concrete question is, how do you pay wages to an untouchable (or lower caste person in general) without physical contact? How do you exchange coins anyway between members of different castes considering that any physical contact is, by definition, a source of impurity?

The earliest encompassing description of social relations in the south, made by Francis Buchanan around 1800, leaves no doubt about the wide extension of slavery, but also of social segregation between all workers and their employers. Just how prevalent the imposition of physical distance was within this system is illustrated by the so-called Niadis or Nayadis, those designated the lowest kinds of slaves in Malabar, who were 'so impure, that even a[nother] slave will not touch them'. Consequently, if somebody wanted to give them some food out of compassion, this food was deposited at a clear distance.[235]

As to the remuneration of slaves, it seems that the main solution was to provide it nearly exclusively in kind, mainly rice and some minimal cloth, which could be deposited by intermediaries at a safe distance without the risk of pollution. Part of the rice could then be exchanged by the unlucky in shops for other necessities. Equally, supervision could be done at a distance if the farmer hired a servant to superintend his slaves.[236] Low caste workers, however, seem to have received part of their wage in kind, part in cash, but Buchanan provides no concrete descriptions of how this was done.

A century later, Edgar Thurston and Kadambi Rangachari summarized most of the ethnographic descriptions available at the time, supplemented by their own observations, in a multi-volume work on the castes and tribes of southern India. Here, we find more details of what Francis Buchanan had attested with respect to rural agricultural labourers, now no longer formally slaves.[237] The rules about maintaining a physical distance to untouchables were not only general but also very detailed. The Malayalam-speaking caste of (former, but de facto still) agricultural slaves – Cheruman – were not allowed to approach a Brahman village or temple or tank, had to stand at a distance of 30 feet from a person of a superior caste and had to warn others loudly on the public road and to leave it to prevent the pollution of those others. The Pulayas in the south of Cochin State had to stand at a distance of 90 feet from Brahmans, 64 from Nayars 'and this distance diminishes towards the lower castes.'[238] Such precisely stipulated distance rules were easily extrapolated to the 300 feet determined for the Nayadis, in the south, at the very bottom of the prevailing societal hierarchy of the labouring poor.

Payment in kind, mostly food, is easier to achieve at a distance than payment in cash, even if occasional.[239] We have no concrete examples regarding cash payments, but the way alms were given probably tells us enough. We read about the Cherumans in Palghat, for example, that they might sit 'with a dirty piece of cloth spread on the roadside, and yelling in a shrill voice, 'Ambrane, Ambrane, give me some pice, and throw them on the cloth'. In this same *taluk*, they were forbidden, even in 1900, from entering the bazar.[240] So, spending these few pice directly was also impossible and almost certainly necessitated an intermediary.[241] The Nayadis, clamouring for charity 'will follow at a respectful distance, for miles together, any person walking, driving, or boating. If anything is given to them, it must be laid down, and, after the person offering it has proceeded a sufficient distance, the recipient comes timidly forward, and removes it.'[242]

In the north, where Muslim culture was much more influential, marketization and (deep) monetization tipped the balance towards integration rather than segregation, to use the terminology of Aktor again. This is not to deny the importance of caste distinctions among the Hindus (and to a much lesser extent, the Muslims[243]) in the north, but the practical consequences for the exchange of cash coins were much less severe than in the south. Possible pollution via food and water was a great concern, but, as we have seen, distance rules like those in the south were virtually non-existent.[244] No wonder that we find no traces of impediments to cash payments in the records there (see Part 1: Studies, Nos. 8-12 in this volume).

Yet, it is possible that subtle distinctions were made in the way coins were handed over depending on who paid whom. In the early nineteenth century, it was said about the Dom, one of Bengal's outcasts, that 'whenever an eclipse of the sun or the moon occurs, each Hindu householder places at his door a few copper paisa, which are regarded as the perquisite of the Dom.'[245] Usually, payments, including payments of wages, were straightforward, but it is possible that corporal contact was avoided even then, although thus far the evidence is very thin. A series of photos of a Hindu bania, sitting in his grocery and moneylending shop in Thal in the North-West Frontier Province (now Pakistan) in 1946, shows him dealing with a Sikh client. One photo shows the banian writing in his ledger and holding up his left hand while his client throws coins into it from a distance of about 10 centimetres (see Plate I.3).[246] This interpretation is supported by a contemporaneous observation of a domestic servant, being offered food by her mistress, while the latter avoided touching the former.[247]

5. Conclusions and Outlook

In this last section of the introduction, three topics deserve special attention. First, there is a summary of the development of deep monetization of India in the long run. Second, an international comparison is provided, in particular in the framework of the Great Divergence, as introduced in Section 1. Finally, an outlook offers perspectives on further research.

5a. General Trends in Deep Monetization 1500-1900[248]

Some conclusions were already drawn in para 3e about long-term trends in coin production. Here, I want to combine them with other aspects of India's social and economic history, as touched upon in this introduction.

A great leap forward towards the deep monetization of the Indian subcontinent was realized under the short-lived Suri dynasty in Delhi (1538-54), succeeded by Akbar, the great Mughal Emperor, from 1556 to 1605. Billon (low-base silver) coins were replaced by copper 'dams' (initially called paisas), as well as fractions of half down to one-tenth of a paisa. Whole and half dams were struck in immense quantities in many different mints over successive years. Especially the half dams and lower fractions may be considered as small change (smaller fractions were also made, but far less frequently). As craftsmen earned two dams per

PLATE I.3: HINDU BANIA, SITTING IN HIS GROCERY AND MONEYLENDING SHOP IN THAL (NOW PAKISTAN) IN 1946, DEALING WITH A SIKH CLIENT

Source: © Margaret Bourke-White/The LIFE Picture Collection/Shutterstock. Used by Permission.

day or more, this suggests that a paisa equalled two to four hours of work for craftsmen, and half a dam, one to two hours.[249] Not only our reconstruction of the growth of the DMLs, but also the number of copper coins in Akbar's probate inventory demonstrates this success. This would yield a DML of between six and twelve. One of the reasons for this unexpectedly high figure may be the lack of small silver coins, which caused copper ones to be used instead.[250] This partial replacement of silver by copper notwithstanding, deep monetization must have made an impressive jump in the second half of the sixteenth century anyway.

The picture in the seventeenth and eighteenth centuries becomes less clear. The production of new copper coins in the seventeenth century decreased. This does not mean that actual circulation decreased because old coins stayed in circulation, albeit the total stock gradually diminished due to wear and tear (see Appendix 1). Possibly, this was compensated for, to a certain extent, by the usage of cowries and bitter almond nuts, as well as by small fractions made out of the growing supply of American silver.[251] On the other hand, nominal wages rose, as a consequence of which prevailing copper coins (paisas) equalled hourly wages more than ever before. According to the VOC merchant Francisco Pelsaert, in the years 1620-7, artisans in Surat and Agra earned five to six takas (or paisa to the value of a thirtieth of a rupee) per day.[252] As other wage data for the seventeenth century suggests, this entailed a substantial increase under Akbar's successors, but prices rose as quickly. The consequences become clear from Pelsaert's comments:

> They know little of the taste of meat. For their monotonous daily food they have nothing but a little kitchery, made of green pulse mixed with rice, which is cooked with water over a little fire until the moisture has evaporated, and eaten hot with butter in the evening; in the daytime they munch a little parched pulse or other grain, which they say suffices for their lean stomach.[253]

Copper coin production in India was heavily dependent on Japanese and European imports. Although production figures for Indian and Nepalese copper mines are scarce, we know enough about copper imports now to consider them supportive of our statistically based conclusions about long-term trends in DMLs (see Appendix 1). Moreover, thanks to mass importation of copper from overseas, India underwent a first phase of deep monetization in the sixteenth century, although it could barely be maintained in the seventeenth century when increasingly worn coppers must have dominated circulation.

This would slowly change in the eighteenth and, definitively, in the nineteenth century, when, again, copper coin production increased more quickly than population growth. Initially, this was the work of Indian princely mint houses, only gradually taken over by mints under direct British control. The growing demand for small coins must have come mainly from a growth of wage dependency, triggering an immediate response by regional Indian mints. Soon afterwards, the British wanted to replace these with their own coins, first completely in Indian (Persian) script, later with the addition of Latin script. In 1847, the collector of the Delhi district wrote that he needed '50,000 rupees worth for the use of his district to replace the native pyce. The double pyce or half anna pieces are in no demand and are not taken willingly by the sepoys. I therefore beg that in the future dispatches of copper coin may include only the single pyce of which 64 go to the Rupee.'[254] These and similar efforts at replacement only became successful in the third quarter of the nineteenth century, and, even then, a number of 'native' mint houses remained active, some of them up until India's Independence in 1947. This story demonstrates that the British institutions in India were weaker than the superpower of the day wished for.

5b. International Comparisons

After a first step in the fourteenth century, north India is very likely to have been deeply monetized already in the sixteenth century. Notwithstanding possible dips in the seventeenth and eighteenth centuries, it was certainly back to similar levels in the early nineteenth century, which goes for the entire subcontinent around

1880. These are unexpected results for a subcontinent that is rarely considered as a candidate for serious economic development.

Although research in this field is still lacking, the ubiquity of paid labour (both independent and waged) and the insistence of wage workers for payment in specific types of small change is remarkable. This not only points to much greater agency of Indian wage labourers than expected, but also to small circulation circuits per type of coin before the mid-nineteenth century. Political disunity may offer one explanation, but that is not very convincing if compared with equally departmentalized Europe at the same time. Coin production might have been prolific, but, at the same time, state institutions in India hardly ever seem to have taken responsibility for checking or determining exchange ratios between silver and copper. This was left to market forces. This fostered an enormous amount of power held by the intermediate layer of money changers, in particular after the British tried to impose fiduciary copper coin exchange rates. Consequently, workers tried to avoid exchange costs by insisting on specific coins being used for their wage payments.

In sum, precise data are lacking for India, but trends are certainly visible. Clear steps towards deep monetization were set in the late Middle Ages, but it was only in the second half of the sixteenth century that India reached DMLs comparable to other well-developed parts of Eurasia. Maybe these could not be fully sustained in the centuries afterwards, but a new increase might have led to DMLs of ten in the nineteenth century. We may speculate why these levels are so surprisingly high, given our understanding of India's economic performance. One reason might be, as already suggested, that proletarianization and commodification had become more widespread than expected. Another might be the underdevelopment of credit for the poorly paid.[255]

This conclusion has major implications for India's place in the Great Divergence debate as it places India at a deep monetization level on a par with the other great civilizations in this comparison. Thus, I fully agree with Sanjay Subrahmanyam who critically opposed the view that, before the deployment of British colonialism, India was a non-market society. In his words:

> In the context of colonial India, [the] hypothesis [of forced commercialization] was used to argue that commercialization was forced on the peasantry by a variety of means – some subtle and some more explicitly coercive in nature. An older 'moral economy'- an economy underpinned by a set of mutually reinforcing and relatively ideal customs, say *jajmani*, was thus replaced by the market.[256]

Instead, India in the centuries researched here was by all means a market society with a full-fledged labour market, and thus fully comparable with other developed parts of Eurasia.

The comparison of welfare across Europe and Asia suggests, however, a rather low performance of India when compared to most parts of North-Western Europe. At some points in time it comes close to the welfare levels prevailing in Southern Europe, but most of the time India's income levels mostly resemble those of East Asia.[257] Although the details of this type of research are beyond the reach of this study, the explanation for these differences across Eurasia points to differences in social structures, which probably matter and are related to the themes discussed here, as will be touched upon in the outlook.

5c. Outlook

It has not escaped my notice – to borrow a famous expression[258] – that the specific role and development of deep monetization in the long run that I have postulated here, has immediate implications for our view on the historical development of India's caste system.

If we accept (see Chapter 2 of this introduction) that the full expansion of the caste system coincided with or even, logically, was connected to the long period of demonetization from the Guptas onwards until the advent of the Delhi and other sultanates, what are the implications of the return of the market economy afterwards? What has the re-introduction of small change from, say, 1200 onwards and its blossoming from 1540 onwards meant for this caste construction, which, for so long, functioned mainly outside the market economy? The first part of the answer is the refutation of antiquated notions about the 'traditional' or 'pre-modern' Indian society before the advent of 'imperialism' or 'capitalism'. As already said, only a very limited importance may be attributed to the often invoked *jajmani* system, meaning a cashless exchange of services or labour between members of different castes within a rural village. If that had reigned universally in our period, there would have been almost no demand for small change. Consequently, the cashless *jajmani* system outside the market can only have covered a small part of all exchanges of the labouring poor.

Instead, if we consider Indian society between 1500 and 1900 as deeply monetized as Western Europe (and likely also as the Far East), the demand for small coins must have originated mainly from workers, earning their wages in the countryside, not least because urbanization rates were still low. In the first place, agricultural workers, alongside cottage workers and the numerous soldiers, were generally subsumed as peasants, but, like all peasants worldwide, were obliged to look for all possible ways to supplement the paltry income from their small tenant farm or garden.

In this light, it seems unavoidable to conclude that what I would like to dub 'the second deep monetization' of India (the first took place between 500 BCE to 400 CE) from the 1540s onwards has only been possible in reaction to a quickly expanding labour market. It should also be emphasized that this took place in the framework of an already fully developed caste system, which – crucially – suggests that this very system was apt to adjust to the payment of wages between employers of a generally higher caste and workers from a lower caste.[259]

Finally, this adaptation to the market of a basically non-market societal system, forces us to fundamentally rethink the implications of monetization.[260] It follows that a market economy with an important role for the payment of wages does not only provide liberty in a positive sense, as underlined by a number of thinkers (see paragraph 3a).[261] Apparently, deep monetization is also capable of underlining, or even reinforcing, existing deep social cleavages between market parties – most of all between employers and workers. This is possible because by quitting obligations by way of payment, the economic link between two market parties is finished. At the same time, money can liberate people from obligations and stress the impersonality of human relations, and for that matter social distance, as emphasized between members of different castes. We might call this the social fossilizing capacity of deep monetization.

In sum, India's historical experience demonstrates that money may also confirm and emphasize distance. To what extent these two dimensions of monetization – the liberating and the fossilizing one – apply in a specific society seems to be a fruitful field of research for world historians, including those interested in the labouring poor in India's caste society.[262]

NOTES

1. Lucassen 2021, 245-8; Lucassen and Seshan 2022, 2-9; recently Lally 2024, 175-8.
2. More extensive in Lucassen and Seshan 2022, 2-9.
3. Other indicators used by historians and social scientists are literacy, numeracy, and gender equality, see Lucassen 2021; cf. Drèze and Sen 2013; Van Zanden et al. 2014.
4. More details about the historiography of historical wage studies in India in Lucassen and Seshan 2022, 2-7; Carvalhal, Lucassen and De Zwart 2023.
5. Carvalhal, Lucassen and De Zwart 2023, Carvalhal and Lucassen 2025.
6. Carvalhal and Lucassen 2025. See also Haider 2007 (see Part I: Studies, No. 7 in this volume).
7. Lucassen 2014 (see Part I: Studies, No. 2 in this volume).
8. Subrahmanyam 1994; Deyell 1976, 1987, 1990, Deyell and Mukherjee 2019 (on p. 207 he prefers 'coin based monetary system' over 'monetization'); Perlin 1983, 1987, 1993, 1994 (see Part I: Studies, No. 1 in this volume). Most authors are vague about what exactly they mean by monetization, see e.g. Stephen 2009, 62 where he remarks already about the Cholas before 1350: 'The economy became more monetized with a greater volume of money in circulation. This money economy even penetrated the peasant villages'. He even concludes: 'The first capitalist state was that of the Cholas, which also happened to be the Indian power to establish numerous merchant settlement colonies in the regions of South East Asia and East Asia' (Idem 65); Mathew 2016, 304-12 suggests that the arrival of the Portuguese has stimulated the 'monetization of economy'; Nadri 2009, 104: 'by the end of the sixteenth century the economy [of India] was substantially monetized'; Lally 2024, 181-2 (he also uses 'the cash nexus' as a kind of equivalent); Parthasarathi 2016, 18; Bayly 1998, 213 ('increasing monetization […] under the post-Mughal 'successor' regimes').

9. Spufford 2008; Lucassen 2014 (see Part I: Studies, No. 2 in this volume).
10. Magelhães Godinho 1969, 371 (quotation), 409-10 (copper coins used for paying wages).
11. Ray 2006. For (partial) historical overviews see also Perlin 1994 (see Part I: Studies, No. 1 in this volume); Habib 1994 (see Part I: Studies, No. 5 in this volume); Lucassen 2014 (see Part I: Studies, No. 2 in this volume); Lucassen 2018A (see Part I: Studies, No. 3 in this volume) and Lucassen 2018A (see Part I: Studies, No. 4 in this volume).
12. This section mostly after Lucassen 2021, 125-6, 143-8 and 159-60, with the necessary references. Subsequently, Pieper 2021 has appeared with a slightly different take on the 'originality' of the earliest Indian coins, but not on its dating.
13. For *mashaka*s, the smallest silver denominations of one *rati*, varying between 0.09 and 0.16 gram, see Mitchiner 1978, 546-7 and Pieper 2021, 47-8 who dates them as Mauryan and post-Mauryan.
14. A fresh view on this period in Western Europe is provided by Naismyth 2023 who makes the important point that, even under circumstances when coins had become scarce or even absent, people 'continued to think with money', ibid. 392). It would be interesting to investigate this also for India.
15. There is a difference between the usage of the term 'medieval', indicating the period 1200-1750 for most Indian historians (Haider 2015, 86) and the period 500-1500 (followed by the Early Modern period 1500-1800 and the Modern period from 1800 onwards) for most other historians. I will follow the latter convention in this book in order to enhance international, intercontinental and cross-cultural comparisons (see also Lucassen 2021). Haider (ibid.) subdivides the medieval period according to the ethnic origin of the most important reigning dynasties between Turkish (1206-1450), Afghan (1451-1526 and 1540-55) and Mughal (1526-40 and 1555-1757).
16. Especially Deyell 1990 and 2017; Richards 1983, 184-5; Stein 2010, 105-29; Palat 2015: 122-30, 161, 171-5; Deyell and Mukherjee 2019. No modern comprehensive catalogue is available for the coinage in South Asia between 400 and 1000/1100, but already Mitchiner 1978 and 1979 and, most recently, especially Pieper 2021 testify to this phenomenon of coin scarcity after 400. Although Pieper does not cover the prolific Indo-Greek and Indo-Scythian coinage, already some 84 per cent of his overview deals with the period before 400 CE, leaving 16 per cent for the centuries between 400 and 700/1000.
17. Richards 1983 emphasizes that the conquest also involved a substantial outflow of precious metals.
18. See Stephen 2009, 43-72 and Seshan 2024, 63-8 for the Tamil (including the Chola) economy before the arrival of the Portuguese; Lucassen 2021, 159, 177-8, 186; for a catalogue, see Mitchiner 1979, 121-46 (his low price quotations suggest mass production of Chola coppers); for the rare wage data, see Lucassen and Seshan 2022, 8 and Stephen 1997, 192-5.

19. Lucassen 2014 (see Part I: Studies, No. 2 in this volume).
20. Ibid.; Habib 1994 (see Part I: Studies, No. 5 in this volume); Haider 2011 and 2015.
21. Haider 2015, 90.
22. Haider 2015, 90. For the actual coins meant, see Goron and Goenka 2001, 66. For frequency estimates, see Lucassen 2018b (see Part I: Studies, No. 4 in this volume).
23. Seshan 2024. For increased labour intensity see Lucassen 2021, 212-21.
24. Stephen 2009, 194-7; Lucassen 2021, 276-9; Van Rossum et al. 2020.
25. Perlin 1994, 294-7 (see Part I: Studies, No. 1 in this volume). For Europe, see Spufford 1988, 254-9 and 2002, 34-43.
26. Perlin 1987, 280-7; Prakash 2004, 405-9; Prakash 2007 (see Part I: Studies, No. 7 in this volume); Chaudhury 2015, 68-95.
27. Stevens 2019, 263.
28. Lucassen and Zuijderduijn 2014. For India, paper money issues are catalogued *in South Asian Coins and Paper Money* (henceforth *SACPM*) 2013, 502-44. Only the Bank of Hindostan in the 1820s issued four-rupee notes (ibid., 530) and from the First World War smaller denominations were issued because of a scarcity of metal coins, cf. Prakash 2007 (see Part I: Studies, No. 7 in this volume); Lucassen 2014 (see Part I: Studies, No. 2 in this volume); Lucassen 2018a (see Part I: Studies, No. 3 in this volume).
29. This section has been inspired by Zuijderduijn, Stapel and Lucassen 2018.
30. A more extensive historiography in Lucassen 2014, 2018a and 2018b (See Part I: Studies, Nos. 2, 3 and 4 in this volume). See further Perlin 1994, 309-16 (see Part I: Studies, No. 1 in this volume); Habib 1994 (see Part I: Studies, No. 5 in this volume); Lucassen 2007 (see Part I: Studies, No. 13 in this volume). For theoretical reflections on the usage of coins, see also Blanchard Vol. II, 2001, 602-66, Haddad and Araújo 2022, and Naismith 2023.
31. More extensively in Lucassen 2018b (see Part I: Studies, No. 4 in this volume). For the pessimistic Marxist view see e.g. the GDR-version in Fengler, Gierow and Unger 1977, 234, where they state that the introduction of coins has fundamentally contributed to the deepening of class oppositions. A completely different approach emphasizes the ritual function of coins, see Naismith 2023, 85-91, and Parthasarathi 2016 for South India around 1800.
32. Lucassen 2018b, 57-8 (see Part I: Studies, No. 4 in this volume).
33. Perlin 1994, 287-8 (see Part I: Studies, No. 1 in this volume). For earlier versions of this argument, see Perlin 1987, 299-301, preceded by Perlin 1983, 45-7.
34. See Part II: Records No. 30 in this volume; also NAI, Foreign, Political Proceedings 7 April 1848, No. 218 on the difference between the hali rupee and the Company's rupee.
35. Garg 2022.
36. For my selection of telling documents, see Part II, Records in this volume. Their counterparts at the British Library have been studied by Paul Stevens

2012, 2019 and his indiancoins.com for more. See also Appendix 2. For my own research in the British Library, see especially Lucassen 2007 (see Part I: Studies, No. 13 in this volume).

37. Garg 2019, 85-6, where Edgar Thurston already in 1893 stated that earlier records have been lost.
38. NAI, Financial, Mint Committee, subdivided into index volumes, proceedings volumes, and correspondence volumes.
39. See Record, No. 31 in this volume; for the report on the mint of Marwar in the 1880s in *The Official Gazette*, published in Hindi by Musahib Alah and Munshi Deviprasad, see Lingen 2012, 184-207; Webb 1893. Webb's obituary is to be found in *The Times*, 22 November 1911, Issue 39749, p. 11. For the actual functioning of an Indian mint with manual labour, see Part II: Records, No. 11 in this volume.
40. Garg 2020, 498-9.
41. Garg 2022, 64-5, 68, fn 49-53, 90-3, 97-8, fn. 70-87, 149-67, fn. 32-90, 304-452, referring to NAI, Foreign Department, Finance Branch, 'A' Proceedings, July 1868, nos. 11-13; October 1868, nos. 17, 20; July 1869, nos. 1-2; November 1870, nos. 2-27; May 1871, nos. 5, 11; June 1871, no. 14; August 1871, no. 51; May 1872, no. 10; June 1872, nos. 15-24; September 1872, no. 1; October 1873, nos. 1-12; April 1876, nos. 9, 14; March 1880, no. 47; NAI, Financial Department, Mint and Currency Branch, 'A' Proceedings, July 1874, nos. 6-13, September 1875, nos. 1-2 'B' Proceedings, August 1874, no. 6.
42. Garg 2022, liv-lvi, 69-102, 453-587.
43. Ibid., lv, 588-601.
44. Ibid., lv-lvi, 602-14.
45. Ibid., lvi-lviii, 615-757.
46. Lucassen 2014, 2018b (see Part I: Studies, Nos. 2 and 4 in this volume); ; Haddad and Araüjo 2022.
47. See for die studies e.g. Stahl 2000, 387-90; De Callataij 2011; Yossif 2015, 233-72; Naismith 2023; 50-3; For India Rahman 2005, 52-3, Deyell 2010, 97-8; Cf. also see Part I: Studies, No. 2 in this volume. For chemical analysis of copper, see Pelsdonk 2023.
48. In the Indian context where hoards must be reported officially, finders, or dealers and collectors who buy from them, want to evade this obligation for various reasons. They have an interest in not providing information or rather in providing deceptive information about discovery circumstances. This problem is raised time and again in many numismatic articles.
49. Apart from archaeological finds, hoards can also be reported in written sources (so-called paper hoards, see Perlin 1987, 265, 339-40; Lingen and Lucassen 2014, 2025 (see Part I: Studies, No. 9 and 8 in this volume).
50. For exceptions to this rule, see Gerson da Cunha 1880, 79-80 (in 1855, a hoard of 1,000 coppers from 1545-1548) and Deyell 1987, 48-58 (two hoards of Akbari dams). Also, Deyell in Habib 1987.

51. Hasan 1969 and 1994; Deyell 1976 and 1987; Moosvi 1980 and 1987; Perlin 1987, 240-1, 343ff.; Perlin 1993, 239; Subrahmanyam 1994b, 204; Hussain 2017, 131-53; Lucassen 2014 (see Part I: Studies, No. 2 in this volume).
52. Lucassen, 2014 (see Part I: Studies, No. 2 in this volume).
53. Willis 2024, 79. A rare example of recoinage for political reasons (Portuguese Goa reminting coins of the Adil Shahs) in Gerson da Cunha 1880, 9-11.
54. Prinsep 1835, 581-4; Habib 1986, 12, 16, 20, 32, 104 (and maps 0B, 3B, 4B, 5B, 6B, 7B, 8B, 13B); Deyell 1987, 58-60; Grout 1995. See the map in Lingen and Lucassen 2007 (see Part I: Studies, No. 12 in this volume; see also see Part I: Studies, Nos. 8 and 13 in this volume). I will leave out the history of copper mining in India in later times (for some regions in Rajasthan discussed here, see e.g. the Lok Sabha debates, 6 September 1960, written answers, 7143).
55. Deyell 1987, 21, 22, 32, 36, 39, 47, 51, 53, 54, 56 and Goron and Goenka 2001, 104, The importance of Narnaul mint until the reign of Shah Jahan is clear from the long series of production years of dams and also *nisfis* in combination with the low price in the actual collectors' market (see *SACPM* 2013, 23, 26-7, 40, 54, 72). Willis 2024, 81 notes that the copper ores from northern Rajasthan were found mixed with traces of gold and iron; hence, some of the coins made from them are magnetic.
56. Lingen and Lucassen 2007, 206-8 (see Part I: Studies, No. 12 in this volume), and Appendix 2 to this introduction. Until 1869 'Surajghar and Charana in Khetri' were the official mints of Jaipur, but further information is lacking, see Webb 1893, 74, 81-2 (Prinsep 1858 mentions a copper coin from Bairat weighing 252 grain).
57. Deyell 1987, 59, Goron and Goenka 2001, 102, 117-18, and *SACPM* 2013, 23-7, 40, 53-4, 71 give more or less uninterrupted production years from 1543/4 through 1569/70 for Alwar coppers (with a short revival around 1615) and (apart from the single year 1563/4) from 1569/70 through 1638/9 for Bairat. Unfortunately, the copper paisas struck at the Bairat mint under Aurangzeb bear no date, so we do not know when that mint, and, for that matter, its mining district was closed.
58. Lingen and Lucassen 2007 (see Part I: Studies, No. 12 in this volume); *SACPM* 2013, 231-3. A lack of evidence means we do not know whether these mines also supplied the nearby Jaipur copper mint, which was very active from the 1760s onwards, see *SACPM* 2013, 318-25.
59. *SACPM* 2013, 15, 21, 24. The lower collectors' value of the Chitor dams compared to the Ajmer ones suggests a higher production by the former mint and therefore a competitive advantage.
60. *SACPM* 2013, 17, 25.
61. Ibid., 21, 23, 25.
62. Ibid., 23, 25, 27, 54.
63. Possibly, other mints south of the Himalayas also used copper from there. What, for example is the origin of 'Kodaleah' copper minted at Benares

1779-87 (see Part II: Records, No. 3 in this volume)? Apart from copper ore, Nepalese copper coins were also exported to north India, e.g. NAI, Finance, Letters from Secretary Mint Committee to Governor-General, January 1817-November 1818, pp. 335-6 (copper coin from Nepal 1817 to be prohibited). See also Nepal in Appendix 2.

64. See Part II: Records, No. 3 in this volume.
65. Appendix 2 and Part I: Studies, Nos. 2 and 8 in this volume.
66. NAI, Finance, Mint Committee Proceedings, 1804-5, pp. 25-6 (Archibald Seton to Secretary to Government in the Department of the Ceded provinces, Mint Committee Bareilly 26 January 1804). See Part I: Studies, No. 6 in this volume
67. *SACPM* 2013, 167-8.
68. NAI, Finance Committee Proceedings, 1 January 1816, no. 64, pp. 175-7; Grout 1995, 55-6.
69. Grout 1995, 46, 55, 59.
70. Ibid., 36-42, 52, 259-61; Stevens 2012, 108-19; Besides, many letters on this subject in NAI, Home Department Public Original Consultations 29 November 1780, 29 January, 8 February, 6 March, 2 April, 7 May, 31 May, 24 September (see Part II: Records, No. 2 in this volume) 1781, 14 June, 28 June, 8 September, 4 October 1784, 3 January, 10 February, 20 June, 15 September, 3 November 1785.
71. Grout 1995, 60-5, 321.
72. Ibid., 322.
73. Prinsep 1835, 577; Newbold 1843, 149. Grout 1995, 318, 322 on the restricted possibilities of employing Indian peasants in mines.
74. Newbold 1843, 160.
75. Newbold 1843, 158.
76. Mitchiner 1998.
77. *SACPM* 2013, 233.
78. Appendix 2.
79. Grout 1995, 38 quoting Braudel 1973, 338.
80. Stevens 2012: 112. Prinsep may have exaggerated his own production.
81. Perlin 1994, 283-4 was one of the first historians to stress this (see Part I: Studies, No. 1 in this volume; also Nos. 8, 12, and 13).
82. Ashtor 1976, 196-7, 305, 325, 328-9; Blanchard III, 2005, 1495-1524; It is possible that the Diyabakir copper mentioned below is identical to the 'Constantinople' copper that, already in the 1330s, was shipped in particular by the Genoese from the Black Sea via Constantinople to i.e. Alexandria. Blanchard is unable to be more precise about its origin other than 'from the northern Armenian mines on the Kurdestan border' (ibid., 1515-19, 1523; p. 1516 'whose source still remains shrouded in history'). This might imply that the ore in those times was transported northwards overland to the Black Sea instead of – as later – via the Euphrates to the Persian Gulf; Mathew

2010, 285; Mathew 2016, 26, 42 (in the fourteenth century even the Chinese exported copper to Malabar); Vieira 2018, 111, 155-6.

83. Vieira 2018, 135.
84. In Classical Antiquity, Persia itself did not have important copper mines. Instead, it imported copper from Southern Georgia in the Caucasus (this stopped in the early Middle Ages) and Central Asia (Blanchard I, 2001, 16; Kuparadze, Pataridze, and Kerestedjian 2008).
85. Shimada 2006, 126.
86. If this refers to maund Tabreez, used for weighing copper at the customs house of Bandar Abbas, this equals about 3 kg (6.75 pounds avoirdupoix), see Lockyer 1711, 229.
87. NAI, Home Department, Original Consultation 31 July 1797, No. 2 (see Part II: Records, No. 10 in this volume); Cf. Grout 1995, 39.
88. Aubin 2000, 287-415; copper even went in the opposite direction, see Mathew 2016, 195.
89. Sahillioglu 1983, 279. Ibid. 288-9 for tri-metallism, incl. copper during 1687-91.
90. Glamann 1981, 170, 173; Shimada 2006, 20-1, 24, 43, 77, 84 and 126 (Dutch attempts in 1759 to buy copper in Persia in the eighteenth century met with meagre success), 200-03. This hypothesis is reinforced by the rapid increase in imports of Turkish copper by the British between 1792 and 1800 (Shimada 2006, 71). For the late start of Persian copper exports, see also Glamann 1981, 167.
91. Urquhart 1833, 177-8, citing figures of 20 years earlier; Brant 1836 suggests a very poor state of contemporaneous copper mining in East Anatolia.
92. Mathew 2016, 154-5; Thomas 2018, 59-61, 71-6, 84-7.
93. Mathew 2016, 198-203, 208-10, 213, 221-7, 238, 246 (on the late sixteenth century).
94. Gerson da Cunha 1876, 33.
95. Goron and Goenka 2001.
96. Aubin 2000, 234; Thomas 2018, 72; Goron and Goenka 2001, 350 (map), 367 (main mints Mustafabad, Ahmedabad and Diu), 373/9, 383/6; Mathew 2016, 195 makes a different conversion of the quintal, resulting in 2,098,360 kg; Vieira 2018, 112 calculates it at 1,762.6 to 2.350 ton.
97. Mathew 2016, 154-5, 159, 194-203.
98. Ibid., 226-7, 304-12 (cf. The Manuel Romanos Collection 1996 and Appendix 2 s.v. Diu and Goa).
99. Although the numbers of ships leaving Portugal declined after the first decades of the sixteenth century – from an annual average of around 10 to 5 and even 1-2 after 1630, their average tonnage increased from 400 to 600. See Magelhães Godinho 1993. On the earlier Luso-Indian monetary history, see idem 1969, 403-17, much supplemented and brought up to date by Vieira 2018.

100. Magelhães Godinho 1969, 377-8. For copper prices, see also Brennig 1983, 489-90, 495.
101. Magelhães Godinho 1969, 407.
102. Vieira 2018, 139-51.
103. Two isolated communications without due references to copper imports from elsewhere still need to be explored. According to Stephen 2009, 317, the Portuguese also imported copper 'to the Tamil coast from Manilla and Macao via Mexico and Peru'. And according to Arasaratnam 1991, 153, before the Dutch imported copper from Japan it was brought from Burma and Siam to the Coromandel Coast (cf. Blanchard Vol. III, 1562-1572 who only mentions in South-East Asia as a source of copper).
104. Vieira 2018, 147-9.
105. Ibid., 144; cf. Carvalhal, Lucassen and De Zwart 2023.
106. Glamann 1981; Yamamura and Kamika 1983; Whitmore 1983; Shimada 2006, 24-8, 94-5; Vieira 2018, 151-4; Lucassen 2021, 201-3, 206-10. For Indian copper markets, see also see Part II: Records, No. 12 in this volume.
107. Stephen 2009, 252-3, 333 (a pico is 61 kg); idem 155, 158, 161, 165-7, 216-19, 236, 241 for the handful of Portuguese ships per year plying the waters between South and South-East Asia. There is also reason to doubt the value of this figure because of the rather insignificant copper export from Japan to Manilla between 1599 and 1610, for which data are available, see Hesselink 2015, 491, 507-8. On the other hand, around 1700 there was also a substantial re-export of Japanese copper from Malacca, Ayutthaya, and other ports to South Asia (mainly Madras) by non-Dutch merchants (Shimada 2006, 23-8).
108. Shimada 2006; Nadri 2009; see also Eiji 2013.
109. Shimada 2006, 12.
110. Ibid., 18. This also implies that the imported copper was used to strike copper coins, used for paying the spinners and weavers.
111. Shimada 2006, 114.
112. Ibid., 87-90, 115-28; for river shipping, see Jha 2013, Ch. 6; for the Benares and Gorakhpur mints, see Appendix 2.
113. Glamann 1953, 51.
114. For Coromandel and Ceylon, see Perlin 1993, 261-6; Shimada 2006, 18-21, 41-2, 87-92, 98, 107-17, 121-5; for Masulipatnam and Visakhapatnam, see Appendix 2; for VOC coinage at Paliakate, see Scholten 1951, 133-7 and Passon 2022, 86-96; for all other mints mentioned here, see Mitchiner 1998.
115. Glamann 1981, 169.
116. Ibid. 1953, 53, 66; Glamann 1981, 177; Goron and Goenka 2001, 342; *SACPM* 2013, 70-1, 165-6.
117. Glamann 1953, 66-7.
118. For the mint of Paliakate, see Scholten 1951, 133-7, 141, 147; for Negapatnam, see idem 138-42. Cf. Passon 2022, 86-96.

119. Shimada 2006, 41, 87-9, 92, 98, 115-17; Scholten 1951, 143-5; Passon 2022, 86-96; for the Indian mints, see Mitchiner 1998, I, 222-43, II, 256-7, 261-2.
120. Glamann 1953, 55 (in 1677, Malabar received one third of all the quotas from Malacca and Batavia).
121. Shimada 2006, 87-9, 92-3, 115-17; Nadri 2009.
122. Glamann 1981, 173; idem 1953, 62 also mentions imports in 1635 (see Table I.3 below).
123. Nadri 2009, 105 gives one example from 1765 (6,000 pounds of bar copper from Batavia to Bombay). Idem 109-11 for imports from Europe, mainly by the English, but occasionally also by Swedish, Danish and Ostend companies. In 1680, two (probably Danish) ships brought 900 pikols (63,000 kg) to their settlement at Tranquebar and one English ship transported 300 pikol from Macao to Bengal (Glamann 1953, 33; clearly 1880 is an error).
124. *SACPM* 2013, 53 (a ¼ and a ½ dam of that year). For later years, see idem 69-72, 96, 102, 106 (for the period 1713-19), 113, (for 1719), 115 (for 1719), 117 (only 1728 and 1731). In the late seventeenth century, Pieter van Dam (1939, 54) makes the important remark that the minters at Surat wanted to coin copper coins only when there was no silver left to be minted. Being paid piece wages, they obviously earned less for working copper than silver.
125. Nadri 2009, 183, fn. 71 (this issue is not in *SACPM* 2013, 133-4).
126. Ibid., 110, 184, fn. 80 (similarly, in 1762, they proposed to sell about 700,000 pounds).
127. Ibid., 110, 184, fn. 81.
128. Perlin 1993, 241, 267-9 (55,285 kg in 1762/3, 159,008 in 1775/6, 2,128 in 1781/2, 460,619 in 1785/6, 74,707 in 1790/1, 328,229 in 1791/2, 96,372 in 1792/3, and 314,959 in 1794/5).
129. Glamann 1953, 79.
130. Grout 1995, 38.
131. Shimada 2006, 66-80, 107-28. For the ratio between Indian and foreign copper, see Prinsep, who, in 1780, contrasted average annual copper imports (for four years) of 11,106.20 maunds with Rotas mines' production of only 2,000 maunds per annum (Stevens 2012: 112). Additionally, in 1753, Swedish merchants imported 120,000 pounds of copper (Nadri 2009, 109, 183 fn 70). Other figures for the English imports: 1761 EIC 400,000 pounds unsold at Bombay, so sent to Surat (idem, 109, 183 fn 72); 1762 EIC 100,000 pound from Europe (idem, 109, 183 fn 72). Due to the war, and, probably, the decreasing mining production in Cornwall, English copper exports to India fell substantially in the early 1800s (Grout 1990, 5). See also Bhattacharya 1969, 121 and Perlin 1993, 262-6.
132. Glamann 1953, 72.
133. Malcolm 1822, 478-9. It is not clear to me what exactly this author means by 'nominal' (cf. his next sentences: 'All the money below the half pice, except the cowrie, is nominal. The nominal anna, or sixteenth part of a rupee, exists in Malwa and in other Provinces').

134. Haider 2015, 102-3; Perlin 1993, 141-6, Garg 2007, 246-8.
135. Yang 2019, 40-72, 174-7; cf. Magelhães Godinho 1969, 389-91; Perlin 1993, 270-1; Prakash 2007 (see Part I: Studies, No. 7 in this volume); Lucassen 2007 (see Part I: Studies, No. 13 in this volume); Garg 2007, 249, 253-4. For the monetary function of cowries in Bengal from the ninth century onwards, see also Deyell and Mukherjee 2019.
136. Yang 2019, 49, 51-2. He quotes one earlier ratio between silver and cowries: in the 1330s, cowries were still cheaper at more than 11,520 cowries to the silver tanka (then 10.9 gram).
137. Ibid., 52-3.
138. Ibid; the exchange rate of the cowries changes under the influence of transport costs According to Tavernier, near the sea coast one paisa is given for up to 80 cowries but at Agra only 50 to 55 (Haider 2015, 102).
139. Haider 2015, 101-2; Hussain 2017, 119; Yang 2019, 56. The copper *flus* in this source must be the Jaunpur falus of 4.5 gram, struck in great quantities less than one century earlier (Goron and Goenka 2001, 348; the much devalued and rare falus struck after the Lodi conquest seems to be a less likely candidate). If we apply to this the exchange rate (idem, 101) of 80 cowries per paisa (or dam of 20 gram), this supervision recognition would boil down to 1-2 per cent of workers' wages. If, however, it refers to the twice as heavy coppers minted by Humayun at the Jaunpur mint (Hussain 20017, 145, Plate 5) the percentage would rise from 2 to 4 per cent.
140. Yang 2019, 56, 68 (here he even mentions Kashmir, adding 'This, however, needs further study'; cf. Garg 2007, 253). Garg 2007, 253, 260, fn. 3 also suggests Patan in Gujarat as a place of destination in the seventeenth century.
141. Lingen and Lucassen 2022 (see Part I: Studies, No. 11 in this volume).
142. Yang 2019, 60-7. For the situation around 1770, see Part II: Records, No. 6 in this volume.
143. Hogendorn and Johnson 1986; Lucassen 2007a; Stevens 2012: passim; Haider 2015; Yang 2019.
144. Haider 2015, 100-1. His exchange tables of cowries per rupee and per paisa seem to contain many outliers, but the trend is clear, including that of a cheapening in the nineteenth century. Additionally, cf. Yang 2019, 53, 57 (3,200 cowries per rupee in the 1660s and against 2,560 cowries per rupee in 1703), 61-2, where he links the devaluation of the cowries to the loss of their significance for the transatlantic slave trade.
145. Datta 1978, 186-7. Maybe the issue of the so-called 'post office tickets' at Patna in 1774 is related to this (*SACPM* 2013, 429).
146. Shimada 2006, 123 after De 1952; for the central position of the nearby seaport of Balasore in the international cowrie trade, see Yang 2019, 173-4.
147. Yang 2019, 63; Garg 2007, 254. Two specific references for Gujarat: 1638 and 1666 (Haider 2015, 100-1). Besides, India's west coast served as transit ports for the cowrie export to Africa.

148. Regarding the requirements for Bihar, it is reported: 'Cannot ascertain the extent of copper in circulation'. For three districts both the amount in rupees and pice is given, from which follows that, in this table, 64 pice equals one rupee. For Sylhet, it is safe to assume that only cowries were current there (Yang 2019, 60-7; Garg 2007a); In 1880, 5,309 equalled a rupee, which meant 332 to the anna and 28 to the pie (Lucassen 2007, 362: See Part I: Studies, No. 13 in this volume). In Cooch Behar, in 1841, a government agent writes: 'Myself and people were put to much inconvenience by the people of the country everywhere refusing to take Company's rupees or pice, the only coins current being Narrainnee Rupees, and French Arcots, and the small purchases being all made with cowries' (NAI, Foreign Department 1840-9, Coinage 162. Cooch Behar Raja denied the privilege of coinage, 5 April 1841 / 162-3 / PC).
149. Perlin 1993; Idem 1994 (see Part I: Studies, No. 1 in this volume); Haider 2007 (see Part I: Studies, No. 6 in this volume); Garg 2007; Stevens 2012, 2019; Lucassen 2014 (see Part I: Studies, No. 2 in this volume).
150. Haider 2015, 87, 98.
151. Prakash 1987, 1994, 2004
152. For these assumptions, see Scholten 1951, 138-42; Martin 1987, 90-1 (copper minting profits according to the Ain), 97; Lingen in *Encyclopedie 1986-2002* s.v. Negapatnam, and Shimada 2007, 117.
153. See Part I: Studies, Nos. 10-13 and see Part II: Records, No. 32 in this volume.
154. E.g. Habib 1987, 153 (in Rajasthan, the copper component in the revenue collections fell from about a third in 1677 to about one eighth in 1688). For the wear and tear of coins, see Appendix 1, and Velde 2013.
155. Garg 2019, 2022.
156. Only one type of coins really qualifies for this shipment. See *SACPM* 2015, 402 (KM2) for the years 1668-82. The first coins struck for Mozambique date from 1706, all copper but rather rare nowadays, so probably struck in limited numbers. For Mozambique in the sixteen-seventeenth centuries, Magelhães Godinho 1969, 384-5 mentions currency in the form of bars or ingots, viz one measuring 10 × 5 cm. valued at 1 tanga or 60 reis, another of 2 tangas or pondos and cakes, as well as beads and cowries. The coppers from Diu mentioned in this document can therefore be situated between the cowries and beads on the one hand and the one tanga bars on the other.
157. Gerson da Cunha 1876, 3.
158. E.g. for Mauritius 1817-18, see NAI, Finance, Mint Committee proceedings 7 January 1817, pp. 2-3; idem 1819-23, First part, No. 25 (2 February 1819), Third Part, No. 66 (15 September 1821), Fifth Part, Nos. 116 and 121 (5 January 1822); idem 1821-3 (6 and 20 July 1821).
159. Deyell 1987; Martin 1987; Prakash 1987; Prakash (see Part I: Studies, No. 7 in this volume); Haider 2007 (see Part I: Studies, No. 6 in this volume).

160. Habib 1987, 140, 149-50 (the copper: silver ratio 1583-1750); Haider 2015, 96-7. Dams of the old weight of 20 gram were still struck alongside, albeit irregularly, e.g. by Shah Jahan II in Akbarabad 1719 or later at Elichpur.
161. Cf. Datta 2000, 200 ('the prices which the vendors generally regulated on their own', confirmed by the official seal of the market supervisor, the daroga-i-bazaar); cf. Jain 1929, 41.
162. Malcolm 1822, 478.
163. Stevens 2012, 7-8, 21-3; Sengupta 2016. Remarkably, Datta 1978, 204 mentions a similar demand in the same year from the engineer in charge of the construction of the fort of Berhampore.
164. *SACPM* 2013, 429.
165. Stevens 2012, 108-39; see also see Part II: Records, Nos. 2 and 8 in this volume.
166. Stevens 2012, 113-15.
167. Datta 1978, 195. See Part II: Records, No. 6 in this volume for a first overview, based on an earlier enquiry by the Board of Revenue. See also Part II: Records, No. 12 in this volume, which shows how inventive some collectors were in their approach to this new problem (e.g. by consulting 'intelligent natives'), in particular J. Sherburne, collector of Birbhum (Bengal). The earliest known estimates for total coin circulation come from the Carnatic in 1775 (Garg 2019, 211).
168. See many examples in Stevens 2012.
169. Stevens 2012: 264-5, 319-23, 336-42, 355-67, 378-9, 488; *Imperial Gazetteer of India* 1908 for information on Benares Division, District and City.
170. Stevens 2012: 264-5 in fact gives a figure of 700,000 lakhs or 70,000,000,000 units (1 lakh = 100,000). Supposing these units stand for coins, this would result in 20,000 pice coins per capita, which is impossible. The data for the districts of Burdwan, Jessore and Purneah also clearly show that the units meant must be rupees.
171. Stevens 2012: 321 (in a report from 1786).
172. *Report of the Committee* 1893 for all quotations. For details, see Part I: Studies 4 in this volume.
173. Strictly speaking, the small proportion of the coppers consisting of half anna pieces has to be deducted, as this coin exceeds the hourly wage level.
174. Lucassen 2018b (see Part I: Studies, No. 4 in this volume); Lucassen and Stapel, 'Shifts', Table 23. For Europe, see cross-sections 1900 for Italy, Spain, and the Netherlands at https://collab.iisg.nl/web/labourrelations.
175. Gerson da Cunha 1880, 9 [my emphasis].
176. Stevens 2019, 245-59.
177. Stevens 2019, 257-8; Lucassen 2007 (see Part I: Studies, No. 13 in this volume).
178. Admirably illustrated for three central provinces of the Mughal Empire by Blake 1987 (although by writing about sums in dams he suggests that

coppers were making this long journey); and by Richards 1987, based on archival evidence from Khandesh.

179. Malcolm 1822, 478.
180. Manzar 2021, 244, fn. 453 (transport costs of Rs. 8,000 per camel over 19 days; Rs. 30 from Agra to Benares). For transportation risks, see also Haider 2007 (see Part I: Studies, No. 6 in this volume) and Lucassen 2007 (see Part I: Studies, No. 13, and also see Part II: Records, Nos. 18, 19, 24 in this volume.
181. Stevens 2012, 379-80, 491-2 and idem 2019, 301.
182. Sah and Sah 2007. For banking houses and shroffs, see also Jain 1929; Bhattacharya 1969, Ch. IV; Perlin 1987; idem 1993, 278-81; Schwecke 2022; Willis 2024, 110-19.
183. Malcolm 1822, 485.
184. Ibid., 479.
185. Datta 2000, 207-8.
186. Lucassen 2021; cf. Lucassen 2007 (see Part I: Studies, No. 13 in this volume).
187. See the following recent studies that include references to earlier ones: Van Rossum et al. 2020, Lucassen 2021, Ekama, Hellman and Van Rossum 2022, Lucassen and Seshan 2022, 11-13; Lally 2024, 193-5.
188. Chattopadhyay 1977, 66; cf. Raychaudhuri 1969, 196-7; Datta 1978, 67-73; Datta 2000, 194, 266.
189. Datta 2000, 159-61; cf. Habib 2014, 142-3, who does not consider slavery in the Mughal Empire to be very important.
190. Kumar 1992, Chs 3-4. She uses both the terms slave and (34-48) and the overarching term 'agrestic servitude'; Buchanan 1807 provides many telling details.
191. Such reconstructions are necessary to understand the actual labour relations and social relations in general. This also goes for the census period (for India from 1870), which gives a distorted picture of what people really do for a living, see William Crooke's early warning: 'The statistics do not fully illustrate this condition of things, because even when a man derives his support mainly or largely from some other employment, he is wont to return at the census his traditional trade industry. Thus, the man whose loom is quite insufficient to provide food for his family will call himself a weaver, although much of his earnings will be derived from cultivation or day labour' (Crooke 1907, 130, 161; cf. Bayly 1998, 99, 122-26). Cf. Matos and Lucassen 2020.
192. Habib 2014, 84.
193. Lally 2024, 135-46, 190-3.
194. I have corrected the number of agriculturalists for Sibpur because the number of 106 given by Datta is not consistent with the rest of his text.
195. Lally 2024, 230-2, 235-8; cf. Kolff 1990; Alavi 1995, 132-5, 182-5; Gommans 1993, 2003).

196. Examples in Buchanan 1807 and Kumar 1992; cf. Paul 2022, 204. The earliest example known to me of a slave receiving cash dates from 1743 (Van Rossum et al. 2020, 183: a female domestic slave in Cochin receiving 4 fanams per month).
197. Chaudhury 2020, 38-40, 145-7, 179-80; advances may have been paid out once a month (idem 225, fn. 15); Chakraborty 2025, Ch. 5. For artisans, also outside the textile industry, see Prakash 2007 (see Part I: Studies, No. 7 in this volume) and Manzar 2021.
198. Chaudhury 2020 225, fn. 15 (per month); Gupta 1984, 157-8.
199. Chaudhury 2020, 42-5, 228-9; cf. Lucassen 2021.
200. This is my reading of important monographs on Indian agricultural history like Habib 2014, Kumar 1991 and Datta 2000 (explicitly for Bengal 187-113). Lally 2024 seems to be in line with this. For the Jats, see Crooke 1897, 222-4, 288-90; 346-52; Idem 1907, 92-4, 158-60; cf. Amin 2005.
201. Datta 2000, 218-20.
202. Datta 2000, 107, quoting the well-known historian Chris A. Bayly.
203. Lucassen and Seshan 2022, 28; De Matos and Lucassen 2020. Chakraborty 2025 gives examples of in kind payment in 1670, but also of refusal of such practices in 1771.
204. Carvalhal, Lucassen and De Zwart 2023.
205. Lucassen 2012, 46-9; Idem 2006. See also Haider 2007 for construction workers in the sixteenth century (see Part I: Studies, No. 6 in this volume).
206. Lucassen and Seshan 2022, 28-9. Cf. Sengupta 2016, 240-1 for daily payments; Robb 2000 for wage payment practices, including deductions by intermediaries.
207. Lucassen 2012, 255.
208. NAI, MBP, 14 August 1801, p. 2551 (letter by John Farquhar to MB, Banky Bazar, 13 August 1801).
209. British Library, IOR, Home/Misc/420, 301-30 (First Statistical Report on Judicial System and Police, Fort William 1798). Cf. Carvalhal and Lucassen 2025 (forthcoming).
210. Cf. Francis Buchanan-Hamilton about Bihar in 1811/12 (Royal Asiatic Society, London, GB 891 FBH, Vol. 2, Book 4, 121: 'Notwithstanding the extreme jealousy of the men, the women of the day labourers make almost as much as the men, as they are employed to weed and transplant rice, receiving the same allowances as men, and they assist in the harvest. People of high cast, although they will work on their own farms at every labour except holding the plough, will not hire themselves as day labourers, but poor people of the cultivating tribes (*chasas*) or artificers do not consider this employment as at all disgraceful, and by its means many small farmers gain a part of their subsistence.' See also Carvalhal and Lucassen 2025.
211. NAI, MBP, 18 January 1796, pp. 3557-8.
212. Stevens 2012, 185-9.

213. E.g. NAI, MBP 20 November 1793, 162-4; 4 April 1796, 4698-9; 30 May 1796, 435; 25 October 1799, 2697.
214. Lucassen 2021; for India, see also Lucassen 2006 and 2012 ; Robb 2000; Sengupta 2016.
215. Haider 2007, 311 (see Part I: Studies, No. 6 in this volume).
216. Seshan 2022, 103-5. For early examples of collective action see also Chakraborty 2025.
217. Lucassen 2007 (see Part I: Studies, No. 13 in this volume). For the payment logistics of troops, see Lingen and Lucassen 2014 (see Part I: Studies, Nos. 8 and 9 and see Part II: Records, No. 8 in this volume).
218. In general, see Lucassen 2021, 186-91 and passim.
219. See note 209.
220. NAI, Financial Department, Proceedings Financial papers 28 May 1847, no. 29 (C. Grant, accountant North-Western Provinces to A. Shakespear, Asst. Secy to the Govt in the Financial Dept NWPs Agra, Agra, 17 April 1847).
221. I refrain here from the more ceremonial usage of coins, e.g. at weddings and successions to the throne. For everyday practice, see also Felten 2022.
222. Datta 2000, Ch. 4. For the Deccan, see Lucassen 2022, 207 (sellers at the market of Goreh in the Deccan, 1826).
223. Datta 2000, 190.
224. Lucassen 2012, 255, esp. see Part II: Records, No. 12 in this volume.
225. Amin 2005, 102.
226. Friendly communication from Dr. Prita Trehan regarding a domestic servant using her sari this way in Jabalpur in the early 1950s, and most recently regarding an old man in New Delhi, tucking Rs. 30,000 away in his *dhoti*.
227. 'The old ladies took a handkerchief out of the pocket of their underskirts, in the points of which they had knotted their money. In one point were the one kopeck pieces, in another those of two, in yet another those of five. Then it took some time for the pilgrim women to untie the stiff knots with their teeth, after which, with a thrifty look, they counted out their money. In their haste, they often made a mistake and unbuttoned the wrong point. Then, they would pull the knot back together with their teeth and start picking loose the next one.' Translation from the Dutch edition of Paustovskij 1976, 25, cf. also 22 (the 'copper' and 'silver' tram line), 23 (exchange of copper, silver, and paper money), 40-7 (use of money), 57 (work satisfaction).
228. Jain 1929, 105. For an illustration of purses, see Bayly 1999, 42 and Plate 13.1 in Part I: Studies, No. 13 in this volume.
229. Lucassen 2021, 143-8, 159-60, 172-3, (mainly after Jha 2018 and 2020) and Olivelle and Davis 2018. Cf. Aktor 2002, 251: 'Not only do the untouchable categories proliferate, the complex of avoidances is also extended during the medieval period (from about sixth century CE)'.

230. I would like to thank Mikael Aktor for his assistance in understanding this complex. See Aktor 2008 (quoting Hanumanthan 1979, 157-9) and idem 2002, 2018a and b.
231. Lombard 2000.
232. Aktor 2002, 246. See also Aktor 2018a and b.
233. O'Hanlin, Hidas and Kiss, 2015. For Gopinatha's reaction to Bahmani rule: idem 107.
234. Maybe it is not too much of a speculation to suppose that the classical Brahminical counterreaction was more successful in the south than in the north, because Muslim influences reached South India later. Consequently, there it could be more effective than in the north.
235. Buchanan 1807 II, 413-15. On Buchanan, Thurston, Crooke and other British (proto-) ethnographers, see Bayly 1998, Ch. 3.
236. Buchanan 1807 II, 370-4.
237. Thurston 1906, 450-5; Thurston and Rangachari 1909, esp. II, 15 (s.v. Chandala), 45-91 (s.v. Cheruman); V, 274-83 (s.v. Nayadi); VI, 77-119 (s.v. Paraiyan); VII, 19-27 (Thanda Pulayan). It may be relevant to know that Rangachari was of a modest social background.
238. Thurston and Rangachari 1909, II, 52.
239. Ibid., V, 276 (the Nayadis receive copper coins for gum from the mattipal tree, used as incense).
240. Ibid., II, 51-52 (after Appadorai Iyer 1900, 365-70; idem V, 275 about the Nayadis).
241. Thurston and Rangachari 1909, VII, 25 (in Cochin, a temple servant as intermediary for Thanda Pulayan, depositing coconuts and coins on a stone, a quarter of a mile distant from the priest in the temple).
242. Ibid., V, 274.
243. Crooke 1907, 152 about the Punjab: 'The bulk of the population being Mohammedan, the absence of caste restrictions permits a considerable amount of co-operation in the matter of food and cooking'; cf. Bayly 1998, 198.
244. Cf. Crooke 1907, 112-14, 117, 120, 124-5; Randeria 1990/1 only gives a few examples for Gujarat (308: untouchable priests and genealogists 'say that acceptance even of money from cremation ground attendants would pollute them irremediably'). Manzar 2021, 156 points to the implications for strangers who could travel much more easily in the north, with its many *sarais*, than in the south.
245. Wise 2016, 321 (originally 1883 and quoting H.H. Wilson 1828/32).
246. https://www.oldindianphotos.in/2012/11/life-work-and-family-of-india.html. This coincides with a friendly communication from Shailendra Bhandare: 'In Maharashtra it was customary to 'drop' anything from above and not exchange it 'hand-to-hand' to maintain ritual purity of the parties. I would also imagine that if something like a pile of money was received from an *A-varna* (as opposed to *Sa-varna*) person, it would be subjected to

a purification ritual, like sprinkling of water.' See also the promotion film 'The Story of Indian Tea' (Assam, 1917), which shows a European planter throwing coins to his workers on pay day (available on YouTube).

247. Friendly communication from Dr Rana Behal about his youth in Amritsar and the 'Bhangan' (low caste) woman who came daily to clean the toilet, for which she was paid normally and whom the children also were told to respect. After completing her task and having taken a bath at home, she would come back 'and my mother would give her food in her hands without touching her'.
248. See Part I: Studies, Nos. 3 and 4 in this volume; cf. also Deyell and Mukherjee 2019, Deyell 2017, and Chakraborty 2025.
249. Lucassen 2018b (see Part I: Studies, No. 4 in this volume).
250. See also hereafter the discussion of considerably deep monetization levels for China. For the low production of silver rupee fractions, see Prakash 2007, 337 (see Part I: Studies, No. 7 in this volume) and Habib 1987, 145 ('It would therefore seem that everything that an ordinary person might buy in an ordinary North Indian city during Akbar's reign would have its price fixed in copper money. Only luxury and export items would need payment in rupees'). See Haider 2015, 93-4, for a different view. For wear and tear see Velde 2013.
251. Habib 1987, 158-164; Haider 2015, 98-103; Willis 2024.
252. Kolff and Van Santen 1979, 309 (wage), 311 (servants 3-4 rupees per month, which at 30 paisa per rupee would mean 3-4 paisa per day) and 117 (exchange rate); cf. much less favourable exchange rates of 57-8 dam/paisa per rupee in these years: Prakash, 2007, 343 (see Part I: Studies, No. 7 in this volume).
253. Kolff and Van Santen 1979, 309; Haider 2015, 91 (quoting the English translation by Moreland and Geyl). See also De Zwart and Lucassen 2020.
254. NAI, Financial Department, Proceedings Financial Papers 10 December 1847, no. 235 (C. Grant, accountant North-Western Provinces to J. Thornton, Secy to the Govt NWPs Agra, Agra 11 November 1847).
255. See MBP, 21 March 1820, 5109-10: non-resident labourers in Allahabad enjoy 'no credit and are obliged to pay on the spot for their food'.
256. Lucassen and Seshan 2022, 11, quoting Subrahmanyam 1994, 8-11, 55; cf. Chakraborty 2025.
257. For the latest results of real wage studies, see De Matos and Lucassen 2019; De Zwart and Lucassen 2020; Carvalhal, De Matos and Lucassen 2022; Carvalhal, Lucassen and De Zwart 2023 and Carvalhal and Lucassen 2025 (forthcoming).
258. Cf. James D. Watson and Francis H.C. Crick at the end of their one-page article on the double helix in *Nature* 1953: 'It has not escaped our notice that the specific pairing we have postulated immediately suggests a possible copying mechanism for the genetic material.'

259. Bayly 1999 argues that the caste system even expanded in the period she studies, i.e. from the eighteenth century onwards, although she devotes relatively little attention to the labouring poor. For caste, see also Haider 2007 (see Part I: Studies, No. 6 in this volume); Also Chakraborty 2025, who emphasizes the high occupational mobility among low-caste wage workers in pre- and early-colonial Bengal and Bihar.
260. As also propagated by Parry and Bloch 1989; cf. Carrier 2022.
261. Cf. also Randeria 1990/91, 308: 'money is not a neutral medium of prestation […] Unlike Simmel's characterization of it, money is neither impersonal nor anonymous in the context of gift exchange in India'. For another comment on Simmel, partially in line with mine, see Banerjee 2000.
262. A similar contradiction in market institutions is noted by McCants 2024 (esp. 147), who makes a distinction between 'immoral guise' and 'the possibility of achieving well-being under capitalism'.

APPENDICES

Appendix 1: Description of the Database of Coin Types, Small Denominations India 1500-1947

The starting point of any analysis of coin circulation in India between 1500 and 1900 is a reconstruction of all coin types produced in this long period and falling within the definition of small change. As explained in the introduction of this book and more amply in Part I, Studies, Nos. 2 and 4 in this volume, the criteria are denominations equal to one day's wage or less of an unskilled male worker, which, in this case, implies denominations of 1 anna (1/16 rupee) or less. Collecting all types that qualify from the main coin catalogues results in a database containing [3,839] types of 'small' coins. For virtually all these types, consistent data on their rarity in the actual coin market are available.

The requirement of consistency of type selection and of rarity indicators means that only a limited number of reference works has been selected in full recognition of the fact that more detailed and more recent research may distinguish more types and sub-types and may also differ in the assessment of rarity of a type. This database, however, does not pretend to be an exhaustive type of catalogue, nor a guide for collectors. Such a goal would far exceed the aim of this overview (the reconstruction of general trends in deep monetization), but it would also be a project in its own right.[1] My aim is to reconstruct the production of small change in India between 1500 and 1947, nothing more, nothing less. Most

[1] A simple comparison of the different catalogues per polity makes this immediately clear. To give but one example of the Awadh coppers: the listings in *SACPM* 2013, Kapoor and Master 2018, and the continually updated website www.zeno.ru are nearly completely overlapping as to types, but at the same time show a number of differences regarding precise dates of issue. The continuous updating of the ZENO website, however useful, does not produce many new coin

types [3,055] have been published in *South Asian Coins and Paper Money* (*SACPM*) 2013, which lists all coin types, starting for most regions in the second half of the sixteenth century. For the missing types, from 1500 onwards, this had to be supplemented by Goron and Goenka 2001 for the Delhi sultanate and other great Muslim states as well as by Mitchiner 1998 for southern India, all in all resulting in a database containing [3,839] coin types in total. The rarity indications of the different reference works (see Table I.15) turned out to be highly consistent and therefore could be unified into one.

TABLE I.15: CORRELATION OF RARITY CLASSIFICATIONS OF SMALL DENOMINATION COINS OF INDIA, 1500-1947, IN DIFFERENT CATALOGUES, 1500-1947

Goron and Goenka 2001, xvi	*Price for preservation grade 'fine' in* SACPM *2013 (in US$) and Mitchiner 1998 (price in Pound Sterling)*	*Database*
CC (very common)	0-10	CC
C (common)	11-15	C
S (scarce)	16-25	S
R (rare)	26-50	R
RR (very rare)	51-100	RR
RRR (extremely rare)	101-500	RRR
	501 and more	RRRR

The following columns are to be found in the database:

A. State / polity
B. Source 1: *SACPM* 2013 (generally referring to KM#, which stands for Krause-Mishler, the most common reference used for Indian coin types after 1500; sometimes also to Y##, which stands for the older, Yeoman catalogue. The texts in Part I of

types, certainly not after 1500, and certainly not the common ones that matter most in this study (friendly information from Sanjay Garg).

this volume also feature references to Bruce, a later editor of the Krause-Mishler catalogues)

C. ruler
D. first year of rule CE
E. last year of rule CE
F. mint place
G. denomination
H. metal
I. weight (in grams) minimum
J. weight (in grams) maximum
K. first year of striking
L. last year of striking
M. known number of years struck
N. first year CE
O. last year CE
P. market price in US$ (for Mitchiner 1998 in pound sterling) in preservation grade 'fine' for most common date or year of this type (in a few cases not in *KM* / *SACPM*, but estimated by me)
Q. technique (hand or machine made)
R. Source 2 (other catalogues than *SACPM* 2013 as under B)
S. Source 2: amount minted
T. Source 2: rarity index
U. Source 2: market price (as explained sub P)
V. Source 3 (other catalogues than those listed under B and R)
W. Source 3: estimated market price
X. remarks

Two weaknesses of this database must be mentioned. A minor one is that a number of types are missing. This is minor because, after virtually two centuries of serious collectioning and description of Indian coins, discoveries of new types are without exception rarities. For that reason, they cannot influence the results of my approach substantially. More serious is the imprecise dating of [about one hundred] coin types of southernmost India pre-1800. However, as Table I.16 shows, it makes little difference for the long-run analysis whether we classify a coin type per half century according to the first or the last year mentioned in the catalogues

TABLE I.16: DATING OF COIN TYPES PER HALF CENTURY ACCORDING TO THE FIRST OR LAST KNOWN YEAR OF ISSUE, 1500-1947

	1500-49	*1550-99*	*1600-49*	*1650-99*	*1700-49*	*1750-99*	*1800-49*	*1850-99*	*1900-47*	*Total*
First year of issue	449	529	303	168	309	621	623	528	202	3,732
Last year of issue	438	480	281	203	239	657	654	567	246	3,765

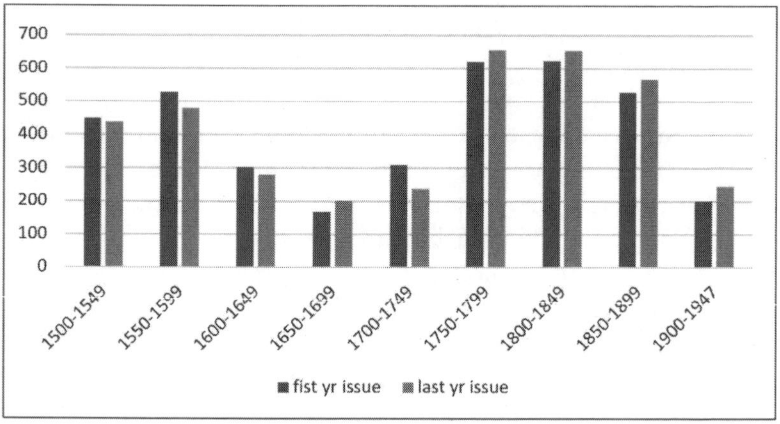

FIG. I.2: NUMBER OF SMALL DENOMINATION COIN TYPES PER 50-YEAR PERIOD, INDIA, 1500-1947

In 304 cases, production figures per type are also available, partially in the works cited, partially in archival sources or in specialized works. All these production figures have been collected in the database and more extensively explained in Appendix 2 under their respective mints. They have been summarized in Appendix 3 and this enables us to determine the relation between the price per coin type in the collectors' market and actual production. This relationship turns out to be quite strong – at least, strong enough to take the market price as a proxy for the original production and circulation figures. My aim is not to use this proxy for estimates of absolute production, but instead as a reliable indicator of long-term trends in the usage of small coins (see Chapter 3e in the main text of the Introduction). Finally, let me reiterate the warning, already mentioned in the introduction, that production does not equal circulation as – nevertheless wear and tear – old coins continue to be used for decades, and sometimes for centuries.[2]

[2] For a more detailed statistical analysis, see Lucassen and Stapel 2026 (forthcoming). John Deyell 2010, 97 put the 'half-life' of coins in circulation at twenty years. For a more extensive research of eighteenth and nineteenth-century European and American silver and gold coins see Velde 2013. In the Netherlands in the nineteenth century the 'half-life' of copper coins was thirty years (Lucassen 2014, 91). Roughly we may assume that at the end of a fifty-year period half of the coins brought into circulation will have been lost, and this certainly applies to copper coins.

Appendix 2: Mints Producing Small Denominations, India, 1500-1947

The aim of this appendix is to provide an overview of Indian mints (in addition to European mints in Birmingham-Soho, and Lisbon as far as producing exclusively for parts of India) coining small denominations since 1500, listed in the database made for this volume (see Appendix 1). Specifically, it contains published and unpublished records that provide information about the production of small denomination coins as described in Appendix 1. It is by no means a full overview of all mints as known from private and public collections and as published in catalogues, auction and sale lists, and on the website of the Oriental Numismatic Society (https://www.zeno.ru/).

Where necessary, short lemmata for states are also included, especially where there are more mints per state or where the connection between state and mint is not obvious at first sight. In those cases, the circulation per state is also included.

There are innumerable variations in the spelling of geographical names in the sources. As a rule, the current spelling of place names is given first (with the exception of Benares, Bombay, Calcutta, and Madras); this is followed by the historical name between (), especially in cases where the mint's name appears on the coin. For the rest, spelling variants are only included in order to prevent any confusion. They are separated by an oblique.

This list contains the following information:

- Historical and – when necessary – actual names of mint places (together with the polities to which they belong and geographical coordinates);
- Period when active, in particular in producing small value coins and the metals used;

- Reference to the database via *KM#* (the catalogue listing, used as explained in Appendix 1);
- References to written sources.

Abu

Suri mint.
Goron and Goenka 2001, 14, 92.

Achalpur

See Elichpur.

Agra (Akbarabad Mustaqir al-Khalifat)

Mughal and Maratha mint, coining silver and copper. British conquest 19 October 1803, after which it continued coining rupees as part of the 'Conquered and Ceded Provinces' until 1805 (AH 1219/RY 47 and AH 2020/RY 47) and copper pice in the name of Muhammad Akbar II until 1806 or later (1834: 9.59 grams, 1/60 rupee, current in the Agra district).

Prinsep 1834, 51; Maheshwari and Wiggins 1989, 133-6; Stevens in Garg 2022, 235-6; *SACPM* 2013, 182.

Ahmadnagar

See Farrukhabad.

Ahmadpur

Bahawalpur mint (mainly rupees 1794-1869; coppers c. 1800).
SACPM 2013, 248-50.

Ahmedabad

Founded 1411 and capital of Gujarat State, 1572/3-1757 part of the Mughal Empire (with a Maratha interruption 1752-5), of the Marathas 1757-1802, and of Baroda 1802-17 (coining rupees and fractions; mint closed 1780/1-1805/6), after which ceded to the British, coining 1817-35. Production:

TABLE I.17: COIN PRODUCTION, AHMEDABAD, 1817/18–1833/4

Denominations		*Weight*	*Period*	*Remarks*
⅓ mohur	gold	3.07-3.10	AH 1249 (1833/4)	
Rupee	silver	11.43-11.78	AH 1233/4, 1236, 1239, 1241/4, 1248/51 (1817-35/6)	minted 1,264,490 (Dec 1817-June 1818)
½ rupee	silver	5.76-5.84	AH 123x., 1242/4, 1248/9 (1826/7-1833/4)	
¼ rupee	silver	2.83	AH 1243 (1827/8)	
⅛ rupee	silver	1.44-1.46	AH 1244, 1248 (1828/9-1832/3)	
Pice [*KM*#46]	copper	7.33-7.94	AH 1233/6 (1817-1820/1)	Mintage of copper pice at 1/64 rupee 1817/18: 100 maunds of copper*
½ pice [*KM* -]	copper		AH 1234 (1817/18)	See above

Note: *1832 exchange rate 68 = 60 new Bombay quarter anna. The production of 100 maunds of copper (*c.* 3,700 kg) in only one year, 1817/18, would equal roughly half a million pieces.

Maheshwari and Wiggins 1989, 38-41; Goron and Goenka 2001, 365; Stevens 2019, 260-8; Bhandare in Garg 2022, 107-8; Stevens in Garg 2022, 169-76, 188-9, fn 1-19, 191-2, 202; www.psindiancoins; *SACPM* 2013, 174-89, 252.

Ahmednagar (Nagar)

Mint belonging to the Ahmadnagar Shahs and later to the Marathas in the Deccan, coining copper paisas. After the British conquest in 1817/18, it was provisionally maintained as 'transitional', coining (together with Nasik) an average of 205,000 Chandore rupees annually from 1823/4 to 1833/4, but plans for pice 1820 probably not materialized.

Maheshwari and Wiggins 1989, 37; Goron and Goenka 2001,

323-31; Stevens in Garg 2022, 202, 213-16; *SACPM* 2013, 15, 147, 180.

Ajmer (Ajmir Dar ul Khair, Salimabad)

Mint belonging to the Mughals, the Marathas, and Gwalior State.

Maheshwari and Wiggins 1989, 136-9; *SACPM* 2013, 15, 19, 286.

Akbarabad

Bharatpur mint (mainly rupees and fractions 1761-73; paisa 1787).

SACPM 2013, 260-4. See also Agra.

Akbarnagar

See Rajmahal.

Akbarpur

See Chittor.

Akbarpur Tanda

Mughal mint.

Garg/ Hodivala 2014, 168-72; *SACPM* 2013, 15-16.

Akulkote

Jagheerdar of Satara State. 1869 no mint as British Indian coinage was the chief medium of exchange.

Garg 2022, 316, 356.

Allahabad

Originally a Mughal mint until the late eighteenth century. Awadh mint 1722-58; 1774-1801 (mainly rupees; copper falus *c.* 1780/90). Allahabad was ceded to the British in 1798 (the fortress) and 1801 (the district). It continued coining rupees 1802-5 as part of the 'Conquered and Ceded Provinces'. Plans to coin 3,000,000 copper pice (weighing 1½ rupees) did not materialize (1834: 9.14 grams).

TABLE I.18: RUPEE PRODUCTION, ALLAHABAD, 1802-6

Period	*Date*	*Amount*		*Remarks*
		Shumshary type	*Lucknow type*	
May-December 1802	AH 1216	128,179	124,283:2:6	
January-April 1803		66,664	100,637:8:6	
May-June 1803	AH 1218		225,758:5:9	
Until May 1804			?	below standard
1806			?	unauthorized
Total		194,843	min 450,000	

Sources: Prinsep 1834, 51; Kapoor and Master 2018, xxii-xxxiv; Garg 2022, 499; Stevens in Garg 2022, 235, 237-40.

Almora

Copper mint 1770-1816 (1834: 5.38 grams).

SACPM 2013, 167-8; Prinsep 1834, 51; See Introduction, 3b in this volume.

Alwar/ Ulwur

Mint belonging to the Delhi Sultans, the Suris, the Mughals, and Alwar State, 1869-70, with three mints at Rajgarh (since 1772. See Rajgarh (1)), Durelia, Jodhawas, coining silver rupees and copper pice; 1877 silver rupees from the Calcutta mint and agreed to abstain from coining silver in its own mint for thirty years. Also, circulation [perhaps apart from its own coins] of Bheelari rupees, originally from Bheelara in Mewar and circulating (apart from in Sirohie state) among 'the Bheel and Grassia tribes on the border'. Also, in general circulation in this state is the dhubboo ('a roughly stamped copper coin [...] from Marwar, struck at Joudpore and Pallee [...] the average rate being about 40 dhubboos to the Imperial rupee, making 2½ dhubboos equal to one anna'). Prior to 1871, old state rupee (81/96 tolas or 11 mashas 3 ratis) coined; 1876 annual silver production 300,000 rupees. Closure of state mint in 1877 and subsequent coinage produced by British mints. 1883-

6 annually supplied with British Indian copper coin at nominal value of Rs. 20,000 per year. 1894 old state rupees only 1/1000 of total circulation.

Webb 1893, 109-15; Goron and Goenka 2001, 13, 92; Lingen and Lucassen 2007 (see Part I: Studies, No. 12 in this volume); Lucassen 2007, 378-82 (see Part I: Studies, No. 13 in this volume); Neogy in Garg 2022, 163; Garg 2022, 51-2, 76, 335, 387-9, 407, 558-60, 607, 659; *SACPM* 2013, 16, 231-3.

Amaravati

Mint belonging to the Bhonsla Rajas of Nagpur.

Kulkarni 1990, 23; *SACPM* 2013, 186.

Amber

Jaipur State mint (silver and copper) before moving to Jaipur city in 1728. See also Jaipur.

Garg 2020, 396; *SACPM* 2013, 318-25.

Amirkot/ Sherkot

Mughal mint.

Garg / Hodivala 2014, 84-5; *SACPM* 2013, 19.

Amjhira

See Rajgarh (2).

Amritsar/ Umritsur

Mughal and later Sikh State mint.

Garg 2022, 508-9; *SACPM* 2013, 206-10.

Angria

State in the Konkan with five mints 1830/1-2 (two at Cusba Apta, one each at Mouza Kopur, Mouza Dar Pulee, Mouza Gowan), coining copper dubhoos, imitations of the Bombay double pice (*KM*#200), 1832 total value Rs. 55,000, if 1/50 rupee 2,750,000 pieces.

Stevens 2019, 242-5; Stevens in Garg 2022, 230-3; *SACPM* 2013, 433.

Anhirwala Patan

See Patan.

Arcot/ Arkad

Vijayanagar, Arcot State, French India, and EIC mint.
Mitchiner 1998, II, 229-40; *SACPM* 2013, 233-5, 373-95, 439.

Arunadri

See Tiruvannamalai.

Asafabad

See Bareli.

Assam

State with its own silver and gold mintage since the mid-seventeenth century at Garhgoan and from 1707 at Rangpur, including fractions of 1/8 and 1/16 rupee since the mid-eighteenth century and even of 1/32 around 1800. In 1834, the British sought to replace the locally minted 'Rajmohree and Narayanee currencies' with the new Farrukhabad rupee into Assam and the north-eastern parts of Rangpur, and in September 1834 they sent Rs. 455,500 (original request in July was for Rs. 700,000).

TABLE I.19: COINS SENT FROM CALCUTTA TO ASSAM, SEPTEMBER 1834 (FARRUKHABAD RUPEES)

	Whole in tale	*Half in tale*	*quarter in tale*	*2 annas in tale*	*copper in Rs*	*Total*
N.E. Rangpur	20,000	40,000	80,000	10,000	10,000	70,000
South Central Assam		20,000	60,000			25,000
North Central Assam		95,000	200,000	20,000		100,000

Upper Assam		50,000	48,000			37,000
Lower Assam: Gowhatty		20,000	400,000			200,000
Lower Assam: six pargunnahs		24,000	48,000			24,000
Total pieces	20,000	429,000	836,000	20,000		
Total rupees	20,000	214,500	209,000	2,500	10,000	456,000

Sources: NAI, Foreign Department, Political Proceedings 18 September 1834, No. 29, pp. 530-2 (letter from Accountant General to the Deputy Secretary to Govt in the Poll Dept, Fort William, 11 September 1834; obvious mistakes in the additions in the original); *SACPM* 2013, 148-58.

Astagram

The Foujdar of Astagram was the destination of the minting machinery from Mysore (including the stamps from Mysore and Nagar) after the abolition of that mint in 1833. Not known as a mint in its own right.

NAI, Foreign Department, Political Consultations, 2 August 1833, No. 36 (letter from the Resident to the Acting Secretary for the Affairs of Mysore Bangalore, Mysore Residency, 8 July 1833).

Attock (Atak Benares)

Mughal mint. Now in Pakistan.

SACPM 2013, 17.

Aurangabad (Khujista Bunyad)

One of the two official mints, active in 1843 in Hyderabad (mainly rupees and fractions 1762-1847; copper 1798-1804, 1841).

SACPM 2013, 301-2. See also Hyderabad.

Aurangnagar

See Mulher.

Ausa / Owsa

Mughal mint.

SACPM 2013, 16.

Awadh / Oudh (Khitta)

Suri, Mughal, and Awadh State mint, virtually independent from the Mughal Empire since the 1770s. Lost one third of its territory to the British in 1802. In 1819, stylized a kingdom until 1858. Mints at Allahabad, Anupnagar Kasganj, Anupnagar Shahbad, Anwala, Asafabad, Awadh (Akhtarnagar Awadh), Banaras (Muhammadabad Banaras), Bareli (Bareli Qasbah, Bareli Qitah, Asafabad Bareli), Bisauli (Asafnagar), Etawa, Faizabad (Akhtarnagar Awadh), Jhansi (Balwantnagar Jhansi), Kanauj (Shahabad Qanauj), Kora, Lakhnau (also named Muhammadabad Banaras), Gorakhpur (Muazzamabad), Muradabad, Najibabad, Shujatnagar. Three different copper coins in 1834: Lucknow old or Muchheesahy / Nuwabsahee of 12.64 gram and 1/47 rupee, Lucknow new or Shershahy of 11.99 grams and 1/46 rupee (both 'current in Oudh and Kanouj to Mynpoooree') and the 1806 coppers of 18.44 gram or 1/26.5 rupee. Introduction in 1841 of the Company's rupee to pay the troops, etc. In 1847, circulation of Shumshere Sahee rupees, issued every year after the Mohurrum.

Prinsep 1834, 52; Goron and Goenka 2001, 92; Bhandare in Garg 2022, 109-12; Garg 2022, 505-6; Kapoor and Master 2018; *SACPM* 2013, 16, 235-47.

Awadh (Akhtarnagar Awadh)

See Faizabad.

Azamnagar

See Belgaum.

Azimabad

See Patna.

Bagalkot / Bagrekotta

Maratha mint in the Deccan coining Bagulkota rupees until 1817/18 when taken by the British (coining rupees with the fixed date 1819 and very sparsely ditto half rupees); 1833 closed.

Maheshwari and Wiggins 1989, 44-6; Stevens 2019, 269-73; Stevens in Garg 2022, 194-200; *SACPM* 2013, 174, 178-9, 182, 189.

Bahadurgarh

Mughal mint.
SACPM 2013, 16.

Bahawalpur

Bahawalpur State mint. Now in Pakistan. Mints at Ahmadpur, Bahawalpur, and Khanpur (coining rupees 1838-69; coppers 1780-1940). No longer in production in 1869 and 1870 (rupee) mint not to be reopened.

TABLE I.20: RUPEE CIRCULATION, BAHAWALPUR, 1894

Designation	*(Probable) mint*	*Weight (mashas: ratis)*	*Value*	*Proportion in circulation*
British Indian	Calcutta, Bombay			
Bahareal Khani	Bahawalpur	9:00	Rs. 0:10:0	
Ahmad Puri	Ahmadpur	7:10	Rs. 0:09:3	very limited
Fatteh Khani	Khanpur	10:07	Rs. 0:13:3	

Sources: Garg 2022, 10, 350, 524, 669; Neogy in Garg 2022, 159; *SACPM* 2013, 248-50.

Bahraich

Mughal mint.
Garg/ Hodivala 2014, 38, 47; *SACPM* 2013, 16.

Bairata

Mughal mint.
SACPM 2013, 16.

Bajrangarh (Jaynagar)

State mint (*c.* 1816 independent coinage of gold, silver, and copper) and of Gwalior from 1818; 1847 its Bujrumghuree rupees circulating in Gwalior, Indore, and adjacent regions (*KM*#12/17). 1861 coinage of Phoolsahee rupees suppressed by the prince, and instead coinage of Chandoree rupees introduced (actively in 1863, together with Esaghur and Bhilsa); 1870 combined output of Bajrangarh and Esaghur is Rs. 35,000 annually; circulation in these three districts of Gwalior; 1894 the Bajrangad rupee still circulating in Gwalior state.

NAI, Residences, Central India Agency 51, Agent Governor-General Bandlecund to Secretary to Government of India with the Governor-General Simla, Jhansie, 27 May 1847; idem 813, 1863 report on the coinage of native states (letter Political Agent at Gwalior to Agent Governor-General for CI Indore, Camp Khokhra, 21 December 1863); Lingen and Wiggins 1978, 22-3; Garg 2022, 77, 319, 372, 439, 446, 539, 549, 705; Bhandare in Garg 2022, 112-13; *SACPM* 2013, 250, 285, 291, 295-7 (there only Bhilsa, apparently including Bajrangarh and Isagarh).

Bakkar / Bhakkar

Mughal mint.

SACPM 2013, 16.

Bakori / Buncoree

Orchha mint. By 1871 there had been 20 years or more extensive coinage of counterfeit copper coin, especially Pootlie Shaie, Nowabee, or Muchlee Shaie (old Lucknow coin), Tirsolee of Nagpoor, and Bala Shahi of Jalaun.

Garg 2022, 580.

Balapur / Balapur Birar

Mughal mint.

Garg / Hodivala 2014, 87; *SACPM* 2013, 16.

Balhari

Mysore State mint, probably identical with Mysore Town.

SACPM 2013, 191.

Bangalore / Bengaluru

Mysore State mint. See also Magadi.
SACPM 2013, 191.

Bankot / Fort Victoria

Mint in the Southern Konkan, 1817 coining 'bad light pice', exported to Malabar. 1820/1 the demand for the estimated 650,000 inhabitants and for 'the export of copper pice being a common mode of remittance by sea during the fair season' (Bombay Consultations, IOR P/411/40, p. 115, 15 September 1820. Letter from the Collector in the Southern Concan Mr. Pelly to Mr. Chief Secretary Warden, dated 4 September 1820). Especially recommended was the half pice, 'because the inferior classes of inhabitants who are the greatest consumers of trifling retail articles, are always sure to suffer by the lowest denomination of coin in a country, being of comparatively high value, since scarcely anything they buy is charged lower than the smallest current coin – and probably would not be charged much higher, even if its intrinsic value were far less. The numbers have been selected from the convenience they afford of each of them dividing by the annas in a rupee, without a remainder' (Bombay Consultations, IOR P/411/40, p. 67, 12 July 1820. Letter from the Collector in the Southern Concan Mr Pelly to Bombay, dated 30 June 1820, as quoted in www.psindiancoins.com). This resulted in a plan to coin ½ pice (*KM* #225), pice (*KM* #226) and 2 pice (or ½ anna; *KM* #228), proposed in three equal batches of Rs. 25,000, totalling Rs. 75,000, which at 1/64 Ankosee Chinchoree rupee equals 3,200,000 half, 1,600,000 whole and 800,000 double pice. The contractor proposes 'for every Ankosee Chinchoree rupee received I engage to deliver one tola of copper in pice, or in English weight, seventeen ounces one quarter Avoirdupois'. The final contract, however, mentions half the value (Rs. 37,500 or 4,800,000 pieces) in half pice and the other half in whole pice (2,400,000 pieces), omitting the double pice. In 1824, and again in 1826 and 1827, they were partially exported to Surat (Rs. 20,000) and Broach Rs. 15,000). Imitated in 1828/9 at Rahimatpur.

Stevens 2019, 278-8; www.psindiancoins.com; *SACPM* 2013, 432-3.

Banswara

State. 1868-69 Durbar mint in Banswara, coining silver Salum Sahee rupees and 1870 only copper Luchmun Shahi pice, weighing 7 masas and 1/80 of a Salum Sahee or Udaipur rupee (value 5/32 British anna). 1894 circulation of mostly Salim Shahi rupees (500,000, rate 100 Government Rs. = 125 Salim Shahi, coined at Pertabgarh); other rupees: Citori (15.5 annas Salim Shahi), Indore Hali (19 annas Salim Shahi), Babashi (17.5 annas Salim Shahi), also government Rs.

Webb 1893, 33-4; Garg 2022, 76, 82, 335, 374, 378-80, 401, 433-4, 552, 682; *SACPM* 2013, 250-1.

Bareli (Bareli Qasbah, Bareli Qitah, Asafabad Bareli)

Mughal, Rohilla, and Awadh State mint. Part of the 'Conquered and Ceded Provinces' since 1801, it continued coining rupees until 1805.

TABLE I.21: RUPEE PRODUCTION, BARELI, 1801-5

Period	*Corresponding* AH *date on coins*	*Value in Rs.*
1801-2	1216	?
March-December 1802	1216/17	1,201,235
1803	1217/18	1,023,761
1804	1218/19	2,000,235
January-August 1805	1219/20	2,500,585
Total		> 6,725,816

Note: Production in 1834 of a paisa of 9.65 grams, 1/40 rupee.
Sources: Prinsep 1834, 51; Kapoor and Master 2018, xxii-xxxiv; Stevens in Garg 2022, 235, 239-43; *SACPM* 2013, 16, 204, 235-7.

Baria / Devgarh Baria

State in Bombay Presidency. 1869-70 mint at Baria, established 'by the tacit permission of the Political Agent', manually coining copper Kuttaris pice (90-5 per British Indian rupee) and ½ pice (thick copper pieces, irregular in form; total annual outturn of both Rs. 250); current only within the state limits. See Rewa Kantha.

Garg 2022, 76, 87, 320, 334, 356-9, 531-2; not in *SACPM* 2013.

Barmawal

Sailana Feudatory State Barmawal mint.

SACPM 2013, 379.

Baroda / Vadodara (Daulatabad)

Mint belonging to the Gujarat Sultans and later of Baroda State, coinage. Mint from 1790/1 gold, rupees and fractions, and coppers (1811-93); 1869 one mint at Baroda, manually coining silver Baroda rupees (annual outturn Rs. 7,500,000) and copper Baroda pice; 1894 silver circulation in Baroda State, the Mahi Kantha, and Rewa Kantha states (total 3,241 square miles).

TABLE I.22: SILVER COIN CIRCULATION, BARODA 1894

Type of rupees	*Specifications*	*Baroda State*	*Outside Baroda*
Babashai	weight old 177.5 and new 176; fineness 79.6-80	30,000,000	20,000,000
Siccai	weight 176.5-177; fineness 86-86.4	10,000,000	10,000,000
British Indian	weight 180	10,000,000	
Total		50,000,000	

Note: Baroda also minted for Lunavada.
Sources: Goron and Goenka 2001, 350, 356; Stevens in Garg 2022, 181; Garg 2022, 33-4, 58, 76, 334, 356-9, 530, 574, 642-3, 660, 666, 674; *SACPM* 2013, 251-60, 360.

Basoda

Gwalior mint (rupees and fractions *c.* 1800, 1822/3, early 1830s-1861), suppressed 1861 by the prince.

NAI, Foreign Department, Political Consultations, 4 November 1831. No. 33; NAI, Residences, Central India Agency 813,

1863 report on the coinage of native states (letter Political Agent at Gwalior to Agent Governor-General for CI Indore, Camp Khokhra, 21 December 1863); Lingen and Wiggins 1978, 24-5; *SACPM* 2013, 289, 293, 296.

Bassein / Vasai

Portuguese India mint.

SACPM 2013, 399.

Bednore

See Haidarnagar.

Bela / Las Bela

Bela State mint. Now in Pakistan.

SACPM 2013, 260.

Belgaum (Azamnagar)

Maratha mint in the Deccan until the British conquest in 1817/19. Mint reopened in 1821, coining the old types, including the Shahapur rupee (weighing 11.21 grams and half rupee, previously coined in the town of that name), only with new date of 1821.

Maheshwari and Wiggins 1989, 49-50; Stevens 2019, 269-73; Stevens in Garg 2022, 194-201. Not in *SACPM* 2013.

Benares / Varanasi (Muhammadabad Banaras; Varanasi)

Mughal and later Awadh State mint (1733-75 mainly rupees; also golden ashrafis) and, from 1775, British Indian mint, coining gold, silver, and copper. According to Barlow, the Benares mint was first established in the fifteenth year of the reign of Muhammad Shah (AH 1145 or 1732/3) and ceded to the East India Company in the seventeenth year of the reign of Shah Alam II (CE 1776). Several debasements of the Benares rupee resulted in different types of rupees in circulation, necessitating continuous exchange operations. Barlow Report, p. 96 (in ink / p. 100 in pencil).

TABLE I.23: RUPEE PRODUCTION, BENARES, 1763-86.

Name	*Shah Aulum regnal year*	*Rs.*
Called thomkâ ghur shashees, 'thomka' signifying small, and Gogurshah the king's name prior to his accession to the throne	5	2,921,148
Called chowrah or broad Ghurshashee to distinguish them from the thomka or small one, which Sujah ud Dowlah, following Lord Clive's wishes, ordered to be discontinued.	9	855,624
	10	1,865,873
	11	
	12	1,577,380
		1,240,980
Called jhardar due to a mark or branch stamped on the coin.	13	1,646,190
	14	1,186,684
Called phooldar (bearing a flower) as it had a lolas stamped on it.	15	1,456,387
	16	1,044,486
Sicca rupees of the same weight and fineness and that ought to pass at the same value. They are also distinguished by the appellation mulchlydar, based on a fish head stamped on the coin.	17	1,693,421
	18	1,078,012
	19	988,188
	20	965,757
	21	447,180
	22	669,764
	23	2,209,544
	24	252,614
	25	1,784,178
	26	1,350,330
	27	1,144,804
	28	49,370

TABLE I.24: COPPER COIN PRODUCTION, BENARES, 1775-1830

Year	*Coin type*	*Maunds of copper*	*Rupee value*	*Tale*
1775/6	'mudhooshahee pice' 10.06 gr copper *KM*#15			2,307,500
1776/7				11,421,250
1777/8				4,858,000
1778/9				319,500
1779/80				94,250
1780/81				1,865,150
1781/2, 1782		2,232		2,854,300
1782/3, 1783		Nd		Nd
1783/4, 1784		128		2,737,500
1784/5, 1785		0		27,056,950
1785/6, 1786		Nd		5,690,750
1786/7, 1787		Nd		384,800
Subtotal 1775-87				59,589,950
				Annual average 5,417,268
1788	Idem *KM*#16	755		
1789		580		
1790		Nd		
1791		Nd		
1792		0		
1793		377		
1794		369		
1795		71		
1796		203		
1797		Nd		
1798		0		
1799		Nd		
1800		148		
1801		0		
1802		0		
1803		175		

1804		59			
1805		0			
1806		0			
Subtotal 1788-1806		Min 2,737		Min $8,367,009	
1806/07, 1807	*KM*#A54 (1/2 pice);	126	110,000	**7,040,000	
1808	*KM*#25 (pice 6.2 gr copper); *KM*#A55 (2 pice)	*20	1,280,000 pice = Rs. 20,000	½ pice 1 pice 2 pice	20,000 320,000 400,000
1806-08		*128	130,000	If in 1 pice	8,320,000
1815-20	*KM*#27.1/3		593,657	**Total 54.206.528 Annual average 6,022,948	
1820-23			253,320		
1823-26	*KM*#28-30		89,000	**Total 34.634.432 Annual average 4,947,776	
1826/27		***94,322	74,161		
1827/28			214,267		
1828/29			78,336		
1829/30			85,399		
Subtotal 1815-1830			1,388,140	**88.840.960	

Notes: Cf. slightly different numbers in Part II: Records, No. 3 in this volume.
*1806-8 128 maunds in total, so perhaps these 20 maunds of copper for 1808 should actually be read as 2.
**At 64 pice per rupee.
***August 1826-May 1827.
$This is the weight of produced copper coins. The minimum production (because data for four years are missing) is estimated as follows: 1 Calcutta maund = 82.4 lb = 30.755 kg, and 1 pice = 10.06 g; consequently, a maximum 3,057 pieces of this type could be coined out of 1 maund of copper.
1834 production of trisooly paisa of 6.36 gram and 1/64 rupee by Regulation X of 1809, also Regulation VII of 1814.
Sources: NAI, Finance, Mint Committee Proceedings 1792 May-August, Proceedings, 26 June 1792, pp. 75-180 (Report on the Benares Mint by G. H. Barlow, August 1787 (see also Part I: Studies, No. 8 and Part II: Records, No. 3 in this volume); Prinsep 1834, 21-2, 51; Stevens 2012, 264-5, 304-411, 488; Kapoor and Master 2018, xxii-xxxiv; Bhandare in Garg 2022, 105; *SACPM* 2013, 421-2.

Bengmars

Assam State mint, situated east of Ranipur.
SACPM 2013, 157.

Berar

Mughal mint.
SACPM 2013, 16.

Bharatpur / Bhurtpore (Brij Indrapur)

State-run mint, established at the enclave of Bindraban by the British. Mints also located at Akbarabad, Bharatpur (Braj Indrapur), Deeg, and Kumber: copper coin of 17.82 grams, 1/32 rupee. Government rupee introduced in 1858, during the minority of Maharaja Jaswant Singh (born 1851, reign 1853-93); 1871 only one mint reported at Bharatpur, rarely used, coining only Rs. 3,000 in silver Bhurtpoor rupees annually (due to a gross fraud c. 1865); circulated in Bharatpur territory; 1871/2 British complaints that 'copper coins, purporting to be struck at Gwalior, and bearing the name of the Ex-King of Delhi, Bahadur Shah II, have, for years past, been issued: a practice which is objectionable'; production *c.* 550,000 'double pice' and 1,450,000 single 'kutcha pice'.

TABLE I.25: COIN PRODUCTION, BHARATPUR, 1872/3-1875/6 (GOVT Rs.)

	1872-3		*1873-4*		*1874-5*		*1875-6*	
	amt	*value*	*amt*	*value*	*amt*	*value*	*amt*	*value*
gold	0		0		0		0	
silver	694,380	716,080	53,126	54,786	?	?	8,331	8,591
copper	0		0		0		0	

Note: Value in native coins converted into Government rupees.

TABLE I.26: COPPER COIN PRODUCTION, BHARATPUR, 1884-91

Samvat Era	CE	*Takas* (KM#*101)*
1941	1884	784,254
1942	1885	3,925,178
1943	1886	1,000,732
1944	1887	27,736
1945-8	1888-92	0
Total		5,737,900
Annual average		1,434,475

Sources: Prinsep 1834, 51; Webb 1893, 125-9; Lingen and Lucassen 2012/13 (see Part I: Studies, No. 9 in this volume); Garg 2022, 45-8, 76, 335, 453, 509, 564-5, 587, 598; Bhandare in Garg 2022, 118-19; Neogy in Garg 2022, 163; *SACPM* 2013, 260-4, 294 (#45 of Gwalior).

Bharuch / Broach

Mint from 1748/54 by permission of the emperor; British from 1772-82, including Jambusir, a few miles north of the port town (see there for the British mint 1772-82: production figures of silver at Broach for each year 1787-1803 in Board's Collections, 19 December 1806. IOR, F/4/1016. Bombay Consultations, Letter from the Collector at Broach to Government dated 31 October 1814, IOR P/411/35, p. 103; cf. Lingen and Wiggins 1978, 29-30). 1782-1803 it moved to Gwalior (only paisas). From the second British occupation until 1831 mintage was resumed of silver rupees (not distinguishable from the Scindia issues of Gwalior), half rupees, and possibly even smaller fractions, as well as two types of pice (1/64 rupee; 139 grain 15 dwt).

TABLE I.27: COIN PRODUCTION, BHARUCH, 1803-30 (Rs.)

	Rupee and half rupee	*Pice type 1*	*Pice type 2, probably KM#200 of Bombay Presidency*
	silver, total in Rs		*copper, total in Rs*
1803	959,686:0		
1804	1,469,700:0		

(Contd.)

1805	1,837,597:0		
1806	355,686:0		
1807	662,228:2		
1808	0		
1809	24,283:0		
Total	5,309,180:2		
annual average	884,863		
prior to 1824		X	
1824			7,000
1827			15,000
1828			10.000
1829			10,000
1830			25,000
Subtotal 1824-30			67,000 = 4,288,000 pieces
Annual average			857,600 pieces

Sources: Lingen and Wiggins 1978, 29-30; Stevens in Garg 2022, 176-82, 192-3; *SACPM* 2013, 272, 286-91, 433.

Bhavnagar / Bhaunagar

State mint coining pice (1759/60, 1825, 1831), also circulating in the Ahmedabad Collectorate. In or before 1870, this state abolished its mint in exchange for Rs. 2,793 per year.

Stevens 2019, 236-42; Stevens in Garg 2022, 224-9; Garg 2022, 327; *SACPM* 2013, 264.

Bhilsa (Alamgirpur)

Gwalior mint, established *c.* 1750/70; 1834 copper coin 14.58 grams; 1833 Bilshow rupees, coined at the Bhilsa mint, current in the Saugor and Nerbudda territories; 1847 coinage of Bhelsa rupees; provisionally suspended its work until 1861, when permission to mint was obtained from the Gwalior Durbar; 1869-70 manually coining silver Chandoree rupees (like Isagarh and Bhilsa, also from 1861); 1870 annual output Rs. 200,000, current throughout the Gwalior territory.

TABLE I.28 SIVER COIN PRODUCTION, BHILSA, 1870 AND 1891-1900

	Dating			KM#	*Production*	
Reported production year	KM *dating*		*AH / RY conversion in CE*		*In tolas (rounded off)*	*In tale*
	AH	*Regnal year*				
1870	-	25	1867/8	#23.1/2, 29 (1/8 rupee), 24.1/2, 30 (1/4 rupee); 25, 26, 31 (1/2 rupee); 28, 32 (rupee)		200,000
1891	1310	34	1892	#245 (rupee)	169,023	
		35	1893			
1892	1311	34	1893		302,376	
		35	1893			
		36	1894			
1893 Jan/Jun	1312	34	1894		92,774	
1893 Jul/Sep		35	1894		391,618	
1893 Oct/Dec		36	1895		85,113	
1894	1313	37	1895/6		254,929	
1895	1313	38	1896/7		79,560	
1896-1900					0	

Sources: NAI, Foreign Department, 108-9, Governor-General's minute on question of egalization in value and weight of the rupees, 18 July 1833 (Coins in circulation in the Saugor and Nerbudda territories by D. Presgrave, Assay Master, Saugor 3 January 1833); NAI, Residences, Central India Agency 51, Agent Governor-General Bandlecund to Secretary to Government of India with the Governor-General Simla, Jhansie 27 May 1847; idem 813, 1863 report on the coinage of native states (letter Political Agent at Gwalior to Agent Governor-General for CI Indore, Camp Khokhra 21 December 1863); idem 839 Pt. III / 1900-2, Particulars regarding Native State mints in central India to which Act 1876 does not apply; Prinsep 1834, 51 (Bhilsa and possibly also Bishennath); Lingen and Wiggins 1978, 26-8; Garg 2022, 77, 334, 369, 372, 439, 446, 549; *SACPM* 2013, 285, 291, 295-7 (for *KM#* and dating; in 1870 only Bhilsa, apparently including Bajrangharh and Isagarh; different interpretation of dating and mint).

Bhilwara / Bheelwarra

1834 copper coin of 19.89 grams; 1869-70 Durbar mint of Mewar, coining only copper pice; previously also Bheelaree rupees, circulating 1870 in Sirohi State and among the Bhil and Grassia tribes on the border of Alwar; 1870 negotiations about closure on foot.

Prinsep 1834, 51 (Bhilara); Garg 2022, 335, 376, 388-9, 400; *SACPM* 2013, 363-4.

Bhinda / Bheendur

1869-70 subsidiary or jageerdar's mint of Mewar. Coining only copper pice, the Bhindriya paisa, from 1799/1827; 1870 abolition recommended.

Webb 1893, 16-17; Garg 2022, 79, 82, 310-11, 319, 335, 373, 376, 401, 433-4; *SACPM* 2013, 365.

Bhingar (Burhanabad)

Ahmadnagar State and Mughal mint.

Goron and Goenka 2001, 323-31; *SACPM* 2013, 17, 147-8.

Bhopal

Bhopal State mint. 1834 copper coin 14.58 grams; 1833 Bhowpall rupees, coined at the ditto mint, current in the Saugor and Nerbudda territories; 1847 coinage Bhopalee rupees; 1870 'About 2,000,000 rupees exchange hands annually amongst all classes, Government, mercantile, and agricultural. [...] The Bhopal coin is current in the territory itself and to the distance of 100 miles beyond, in the states of Rajghur, Nursinghur, and Kilchepore'. Mint at Bhopal established *c.* 1770 under Faiz Muhammad Khan; 1,870 manually coining silver rupees ('each coin is separately made and separately impressed'); annual outturn Rs. 1,200,000; no gold coinage. 1871 plans to modernize silver rupee coinage. Coinage 1873/4 to 1875/6 Bhopal rupees and fractions ⅛, ¼ and ½ (*KM*#7-14; value in native coins converted into government rupees).

TABLE I.29: SILVER COIN PRODUCTION, BHOPAL, 1873/4-1875/6 (BHOPAL Rs.)

	1873-4	*1874-5*	*1875-6*
	Value	*Value*	*Value*
Silver	436,480	636,354	775,145

Notes: 1882 introduction of the British Indian pice in Narsingarh State to replace the current Barari pice (meant are the copper pies, ¼, and ½ annas and annas, struck until 1891/2)
1893 circulation and annual demand 3,000,000 million rupees; total production until that date estimated by the Bhopal Durbar at 15,000,000 rupees. Mint closed by 1894.

TABLE I.30: SILVER COIN CIRCULATION, BHOPAL, 1894

Circulation: Rupees	*Region*	*Weight*	*Alloy*	*Amount*
Bhopali	11 named places	11/12 tola	155/192 copper; 7/64 silver	90 per cent
British Indian				10 per cent
Hali (from Indore)		11/12 tola	329/384 silver, 23/384 copper	comparatively inconsiderable

TABLE I.31: SILVER COIN DEMAND, BHOPAL, 10 NOVEMBER 1897 (GOVT Rs.)

Polity	*Details*	*Demand in British Indian rupees*
Bhopal State	here only the Bhopal rupee current	3,600,000
Narsingarh	lesser states adjoining Bhopal, where the Bhopali rupee was current (in addition to Narsingarh, British Indian, and hali rupees)	500,000
Rajgarh		800,000
Maksudangarh		20,000
Sutiala		10,000
Agency	British Agency at Bhopal	5,000,000
		9,930,000

TABLE I.32 SILVER COIN EXCHANGE, BHOPAL, 1898 (Rs.)

	Exchanged at the rate of 124 Bhopali = 100 British Indian	
Before 1898	7,400,000	
Early 1898	6,944,000	
Total 4 March 1898	14,344,000	Besides a demand for Rs. 45,000 worth of small silver coins

Sources: NAI, Foreign Department, 108-9, Governor-General's minute on question of equalization in value and weight of the rupees, 18 July 1833 (Coins in circulation in the Saugor and Nerbudda territories by D. Presgrave, Assay Master, Saugor 3 January 1833); NAI, Residences, Central India Agency 51, Agent Governor-General Bandlecund to Secretary to Government of India with the Governor-General Simla, Jhansie 27 May 1847; idem 842 Pt. III/ 1894-8 Printed correspondence regarding the closing of Bhopal State mints of the currency arrangements in Bhopal (1898 exchange – and smelting – of Bhopali rupees for British Indian rupees); Prinsep 1834, 51; Garg 2022, 60-1, 68-9, 76, 334, 365-6, 537-8, 582-7, 597-9, 686, 754; *SACPM* 2013, 265-6.

Bhore

Mint in the capital of Punt Suchen State in the Deccan. Coining pice until *c.* 1829; British decided to abolish it in 1831.

Stevens 2019, 233-6; Stevens in Garg 2022, 221; not in *SACPM* 2013.

Bhugsara

Gwalior mint. 1847 coinage of Innukshahee rupees, circulating in Gwalior, Indore, and adjacent regions.

NAI, Residences, Central India Agency 51, Agent Governor-General Bandlecund to Secretary to Government of India with the Governor-General Simla, Jhansie, 27 May 1847; not in *SACPM* 2013.

Bhuj

Mint at Kutch since samvat 1810, originally coining only silver. 1869 coining gold mohurs, silver rupees, copper trunbias, dokras, etc, manufacturing by means of iron rollers, presses, etc.; 1870 no regular output.

TABLE I.33: SILVER COIN PRODUCTION, BHUJ, 1872/3-1874/5 (GOVT Rs.)

KM *Y#16.1*	*1872-3*	*1873-4*	*1874-5*
Value in British Indian rupees	228,127	235,998	149,041

Sources: Garg 2022, 78, 333, 356-9, 598; *SACPM* 2013, 354. See also Kutch.

Biana

Suri mint.

Goron and Goenka 2001, 92.

Bidar

Bidar State mint.

Goron and Goenka 2001, 320-2; *SACPM* 2013, 159.

Bijapur

Bijapur State and Mughal mint.

Goron and Goenka 2001, 312-19; *SACPM* 2013, 16, 159-61.

Bikaner

State. Mint from 1759; c. 1824 own mint building; 1847 coining Gujsahee rupees (*KM* 32); 1869 one mint at Bikaner, coining silver rupees (*KM*#42-5, apparently with fixed date vs 1916).

TABLE I.34: RUPEE COIN PRODUCTION, BIKANER, 1863-8

Samvat	CE	*Annual output (Rs)*
1920	1863	332,482
1921	1864	458,208
1922	1865	321,830
1923	1866	441,841
1924	1867	275,899

(Contd.)

1925	1868	122,946
Total		1,953,206
Annual average 1863-68		325,534

Notes: Copper coins from ore, mined at Durelia and Jodhawas; additionally, there is an unworked copper mine at Debra. 'The copper is not melted.' Weight of early copper pice, called 'Guj Sahee pice' (*KM*#5), 'Soorut Sahee pice' (*KM*#13/14), and 'Ratan Sahee pice' (*KM*#20/2) was 14 masas. Now only 'Sirdar Sahee pice' (*KM*#34, 41, 50) coined, weight 7 masas and valued at 1/53 of the Bikaner rupee weight 10 masas, value 1.03 of government rupee).
1872/3 to 1875/6 coinage of Bikaner rupees (*KM*#51/4) value in native coins converted into government rupees.

TABLE I.35: SILVER COIN PRODUCTION, BIKANER, 1872/3-1875/6 (GOVT Rs.)

Bikaner rupees	*1872-3*		*1873-4*		*1874-5*		*1875-6*	
	Amt	*Value Govt Rs.*	*Amt*	*Value Govt Rs.*	*Amt*	*Value Govt Rs.*	*Amt*	*Value Govt Rs.*
Rupee fractions*	511	266	43,656	22,540	74,236	38,328		
Rupees	28,385	28,385	57,531	57,181	241,424	239,923	325,854	319,298

Note: * My interpretation: The difference between, apparently, fractions of rupees (*KM*#53/3: resp. ⅛, ¼ and ½ and whole rupees (*KM*#54). Ed.

TABLE I.36: SILVER COIN PRODUCTION, BIKANER, 1868-1890 (Rs.)

Samvat	CE	*Rupees*	*8 anna*	*4 anna*	*2 anna*
1943	1886	44,342			
1944	1887	60,798	3,966		
1945	1888	29,602			
1946	1889	171,740	3,774	588	
1947	1890	24,350		21,020	184 (=1,472 pieces)

Note: KM#62-5; Webb 1893, 63, probably all in rupee value, not in tale.
In 1893, copper for paisas (coined 1889, *KM*#61) is procured from Calcutta.
Sources: NAI, Residences, Central India Agency 51, Agent Governor-General Bandlecund to Secretary to Government of India with the Governor-General Simla, Jhansie 27 May 1847; Webb 1893, 55-63; Garg 2022, 53-4, 76, 335, 389-90, 392-5, 404, 556-7, 597, 652, 741; *SACPM* 2013, 267-70.

Bindha / Bhindar

Mewar (Udaipur) State mint.

SACPM 2013, 365.

Bindraban

See Vrindavan and Bharatpur.

Birmingham

Matthew Boulton at Birmingham-Soho struck copper coins for the Bombay Presidency in 1791, 1794 and 1804, and for the Madras Presidency in 1794, 1797, 1803 and 1808. Ralph Heaton & Sons, Birmingham (UK) occasionally struck copper coins for the EIC and Pudokkottai.

Selgin 2008, 117-18; Symons 2009, 88-90, 93-7, 210; *SACPM* 2013, 374, 437, 442-5, 448-9; See also Soho and Tables I.51 and I.115 below.

Bishennath

See Bhilsa.

Bombay (Mumbai)

British 1665-1947. Bombay mint from 1672, initially coining European type denominations and, in addition, Mughal type silver and gold types 1688-94, 1717-78, and again at the new steam-driven mint (under the name Surat) 1832-5.

Here, production figures are collected, first for tin/zinc (until 1773) and then for copper coins (until 1831); no specific data are available for the lower denomination silver coins of $^{1}/_{16}$, $^{1}/_{12}$, and ⅛ rupee.

For tin /zinc

1673 tinny or buzerook (*KM*#130, 1.56 gram; buzerook is derived from the Portuguese *bazaruco*) out of 2,500 Surat maunds of tin, or (at 17 kg per Surat maund) over 20 million tinnys (Stevens

2019, 30). Demonetized 1677 because too light and melted down.

1716 forty maunds of tin coined into buzerooks (*KM*#155, 1.65 gram), or over 400,000.

1724 circulation of Rs. 40,000 of tin pice or duccanees (*KM*#156.1 and earlier) or over 3 million pieces of 13.6 gram or half that number if 2 pice (mixture unknown; Stevens 2019, 77), half of which to be remelted.

TABLE I.37: TIN OR ZINC COIN PRODUCTION, BOMBAY 1741 (Rs.)

Date	*Tin in maunds: seers*	*Price in Rs. per maund*	*Tin in Rs: anna: raes*	*Tale*	*Net gain in Rs. (=20 per cent)*
Feb 1741 (order)			200:0:00		
Jun 1741 (production)	227:26	7:8	1,707:4:88		
	500:00	6:10	2,207:8:00		
After Jun 1741	500:00	6:10	2,207:8:00		
Total	1,227:26			>1.5mio if one pice	3,841

Sources: KM#156.1-156.2; Stevens 2019, 77-8.

1754 tin or zinc pice (*KM*#156.2 and 157.1): 1000-1500 maunds needed (Stevens 2019, 79).

1757 zinc quarter (*KM*#170) and ½ pice (*KM*#171) for Rs. 10,000 (mixture unknown; Stevens 2019, 80-1).

1769 (*KM*#156.2, 13.16 gram) for Rs. 20,000, at Rs. 8 per Surat maund, or 2,500 maunds, or more than 3 million pieces (Stevens 2019, 80-1).

1771 offer to coin tin/zinc pice (*KM*#156.1-157.1) for Rs. 30,000 at Rs. 7:4 per Surat maund, 4,138 maunds, or over 5 million pieces of 13.6 gram or half that number if 2 pice (mixture unknown; Stevens 2019, 81).

1773 value of (tin/zinc and copper) pice reduced from 1/80 to 1/100 rupee (Stevens 2019, 81-3). 1774 superfluous zinc to be sold at Rs. 3:10 / Surat maund, but 1775 yielding Rs. 4:0:50 (Stevens 2019, 83-4).

For copper

1672/3 copperoons (*KM*#131-3, 136) December 1673: 1000 Surat maunds of copper, or (at 1,205 duganees per maund) 1,205,000 copperoons / duganees (Stevens 2019, 21, 26). 1674 1500 more chests of copper ordered by sea (originating from England as well as Japan via Bantam).

1676 arrival of 329 plates of Barbary copper, but their use was discontinued because one third was lost in melting and, consequently, they had to wait for the expected Japanese copper bars.

1697 Feb-Mar copperoons (probably *KM*#172 and 149) minted from 46 and later 37 cwt, in total 83 cwt (or 4,216.4 kg which makes 3,088,938 full pice of 13.65 gram or 6,177,875 half pice of 6.75 gram).

1728 out of Persian 'goz' (bought at 1/72 rupee) coppers (*KM*#A173, 173, A165 and 165) to be coined at Rs. 20:8 per Surat maund.

1748 pice (*KM*#150): 220 Surat maunds of old copper, or (at 1,476 pice per maund) 324,720 pice; valued at Rs. 28:4:64 per Surat maund) (Stevens 2019, 79).

1749 pice (*KM*#150, 173, 167): 75 maunds of (probably Persian) copper, or (at 1,476 pice per maund) 110,700 pice (Stevens 2019, 69, 72).

1773 whole, half, and quarter balemark pice (*KM*#155, 187, 188): plan 5 Oct 1773 to coin for Rs. 20,000, out of which Rs. 10,000 to 12,000, or (at 80 pice per rupee) 800,000 to 960,000 pice, were to be ready 26 November 1773 (Stevens 2019, 72-3).

1775 order for balemark pice (*KM*#188): Rs. 20,000, or (at 80 pice per rupee) 1,600,000 pice (Stevens 2019, 74).

1784 single pice (*KM*#150?): 200 maunds (half of which Japanese copper), or (at 1,476 pice per maund / 100 per rupee) 295, 200 pice (Stevens 2019, 74).

1775-84 a total of Surat maunds 6,067:35 seer coined: 15 pice 'a sum more than double what is required for the currency of this island, Salsette and Carana', and therefore 1/3 or 2,000 maunds to be purchased and to be 'defaced and sold as lump copper' (or about 8,956,368 pice at 1,476 pice per maund) valued at Rs. 199,570:0:33

(or about 45 pice per rupee, which is nearly the rate of 49 in 1802; this requires further explanation (Stevens 2019, 74-5, 139-40.

1788 countermarked pice (*KM*#190-191): minimum Rs. 3537: 2:50, or 353,700 pieces at 100 pice to the rupee (Stevens 2019, 75-6).

1792 old pice (7,314 avoirdupuis grains per rupee = pice types coined until 1749?) now replaced by new pice (10,000 avoirdupuis grains per rupee = *KM*#150, 151, 151a 189; 1/50 rupee). 1797 copper coin of 13.74 grams, 1/40 rupee, and, according to Prinsep, marked '48 to one rupee 4 VEIC and arms'; 1802 introduction of these new pice denominations made of Japan copper according to the following specifications (Stevens 2019, 139-40; www.psindiancoins.com).

TABLE I.38: COPPER COIN PRODUCTION COSTS, BOMBAY, 1802-29 (Rs.)

Proposed denominations	*¼ p*	*½ p*	*1 p*	*1½ p*	*2 p*	*4 p (anna)*
Production period	1816-25	1802-29	1802-29	?	1802-29	1802-16
KM#	219	197	198	?	199	201
Reas	1	2	4	6	8	16
Per maund old			980			
Per maund proposed			1,200			
Production costs per rupee old			23:3			
Production costs per rupee proposed			24			
Weight old in grains			200			
Weight proposed in grains			164			

Note: 1 Bombay maund = 28 lb =196,000 grains (as 1 avoirdupuis = 7,000 grains)

TABLE I.39: COPPER COIN PRODUCTION, BOMBAY, 1802-29

Year	¼ p	½ p	1 p	2p	4p	All denominations	
						Rs	Whole pice equivalent
1802		X	X	X	X		?
1803			4,445,909	X	555,739	104,201	5,210,050
1804			X	X	X		?
1805/7							0
1808		X	X	X			?
1809			X	X		6,795	339,750
1810		X	X	X		61,151 [= 375 Surat maunds]	3,057,550 [10,000 / day]
1811/12							0
1813 Jan-Feb		X	X	X		112,217	5,610,850
1814						9,486	474,300
1815		X	X			See 1814	
1816	X	X	X	X	X	25,000	1,250,000
1817							0
1818		X	X	X		500,000 needed	[25,000,000]
1819		X	X	X		57,603	2,880,150
1809/19						277,357	13,867,850
							17,179,650 [actually ½, 1, 2 pice, so proportionately more ½ pice coined than 1 and 2 pice]
1820							0

(Contd.)

1821	X				258,385	16,536,640
1822/4						0
1825	X	X	X	X		?
1826		X	X	X		?
1827		X	X	X		?
1828			X	X		?
1829		X	X	X		?

Notes: 1 Bombay maund (40 seers) = 28 lbs avoirdupois; 1 Bombay seer (Stevens 2019, 144/6); Prinsep 1834, 58: 1804/5-1832/3 total amount of copper coins (not differentiated by denominations), produced at Benares: Rs. 1,390,140.

Quarter annas 1830-3 (*KM*#231.1) whose Jan-Dec 1831 production was valued at Rs. 141,100 or 9,030,400 pieces. In October 1831, a great demand for silver money means the production of copper coins will take 3-4 years to deliver (Stevens 2019, 229-30, 245-59). February 1832 production capacity of the new mint more than 100,000 per day (www.psindiancoins.com).

Sources: Stevens 2019, 139-46, 152-53, 163, 183, 193; www.psindiancoins.com.

TABLE I.40: COPPER COIN CIRCULATION, BOMBAY PRESIDENCY, 1788

Region	*Copper coin in circulation (in rupees)*
Bombay	100,000
Salsette and Carabjah	25,000
Tellicherry	10,000
	135,000

Without the later-acquired provinces of Malabar and Canara (Stevens 2019, 360). Estimated supply of copper coins needed in 1813: Rs. 64,000 per annum.

TABLE I.41: COPPER COIN CIRCULATION, BOMBAY PRESIDENCY, 1817

Collectorates	*In rupees*	*In tale*
Bombay	50,000	3,200,000
Surat	50,000	3,200,000
Broach	50,000	3,200,000
Kaira (incl. Dholara)	50,000	3,200,000
	200,000	12,800,000

Source: www.psindiancoins.com

Estimated supply of copper coins needed in 1818 'for circulation in the newly extended districts of this government': Rs. 500,000, yielding a profit of Rs. 250,000 (www.psindiancoins.com). For later production figures of all-India low denominations from 1835 onwards by the Bombay mint, see Calcutta. For minting of coins for Goa 1871-88, see there.

Prinsep 1834, 51, 58; Stevens 2019; Stevens in Garg 2022, 171-2; www.psindiancoins.com; *SACPM* 2013, 430-8.

Braj Indrapur

See Bharatpur.

Broach

See Bharuch.

Budaon/ Budaun

Delhi Sultans' and Mughal mint.

Goron and Goenka 2001, 13; *SACPM* 2013, 17.

Budhanadih

Suri mint.

Goron and Goenka 2013, 92.

Bumori

Mint in Orchha (near Mow Ranipur). 1870 counterfeiting Nagpur pice, which were distributed by Mow merchants to the Jhansi district.

NAI, Residences, Central India Agency 818 / 1870-5, letter Political Agent for Bundelkhand to the Agent Governor-General for Central India Indore, Nowgong, 31 October 1870 (for details, see Gerowli, below).

Bundi

State mint under Akbar from c. 1570. 1834 copper coin of 17.75 grams, 1/32 rupee. 1847 its Boondeka rupees (*KM* C#30a) were also circulating in Gwalior, Indore, and adjacent territories. 1869-70 one mint at Bundi, coining a few gold mohurs (*KM* Y#A7), and annually 100,000 Hali (also Ram Shahee; *KM* Y#6) rupees (15¼ annas British Indian money) and 2,500 Suniya rupees (*KM* Y#6a; 14¼ annas British Indian money), in total *c.* Rs. 100,000 in silver rupees (Garg 2022, 335, 410), or Rs. 20,000 (ibid., 417, 565). Also copper 'Boondee' pice, weighing one tola five masas each, or about 28 to the pound (*KM* Y#3: takkas, 1/28 rupee, weighing 17.15 to 17.65 grams) and paisas (*KM* Y#2, 1/48 rupee, weighing 10.6 to 10.7 grams). Average annual output 10,000 pice. Average annual income derived by the state (including restamping) Rs. 10,000. 1870 retention of the mint recommended.

TABLE I.42: COIN PRODUCTION, BUNDI, 1872/3-1875/6 (GOVT Rs.)

	1872-3		*1873-4*		*1874-5*		*1875-6*	
	Amt	*Value*	*Amt*	*Value*	*Amt*	*Value*	*Amt*	*Value*
Gold (*KM* Y#A7)	15	249					10	175
Silver (*KM* Y#5/6)	100,700	97,190	35,880	34,313	40,680	39,060	60,500	58,343
Copper (*KM* Y#3)	15,000	570						

TABLE I.43: SILVER COIN CIRCULATION, BUNDI, 1894 (GOVT Rs.)

Rupees	*Weight*	*Alloy*	*Amount*
Ram Shahi (Y#9)	23/4 tola	5.9	1,500,000
Kattar Shahi (Y#9a)	11/12 tola	1.7	1,500,000
Gyara Sunna (for presents)	45/8 tola	11.1	400,000
British Indian (proportion 2 government to 16 Bundi rupees			

Sources: NAI, Residences, Central India Agency 51, Agent Governor-General Bandlecund to Secretary to Government of India with the Governor-General Simla, Jhansie 27 May 1847; Prinsep 1834, 51; Webb 1893, 85-8; Garg 2022, 76, 81, 314, 323, 335, 411, 416-18, 429, 565-6, 570, 595-9, 683; Neogy in Garg 2022, 159; *SACPM* 2013, 272-6.

Bupas

Jaipur mint. Long since relinquished by 1870.
Garg 2020, 396; not in *SACPM* 2013.

Burhanabad

See Bhingar.

Calcutta (Kolkata)

British Indian mint 1757-1947, originally mainly coining silver and gold, but occasionally also copper: in 1757 copper 'monetary tickets' (Stevens 2012, 7-8, 21-3, 162; Sengupta 2016, 240-3), annas in 1763/4 and 1774/5, and also ½ annas in the latter year (Stevens 2012, 84-5, 103). Regular copper coin production only started in 1795, initially still in moderate numbers. Weight reductions 1796, 1809, and standard weight 1817 and 1831, also in Prinsep 1834.

TABLE I.44: COPPER COIN PRODUCTION, CALCUTTA, 1795-6

Denomination	*Production year*	*Identification*	*Tale*	*Value in whole pice*
½ pice RY37 (1795)	1795	*KM*#50; St4.30	642,992	321,496
Pice RY37 (1795)	1795	*KM*#52; St4.28	363,000	363,000
½ pice RY37 (1795)	1796	*KM*#51; St4.31	605,000	302,500
Pice RY37 (1795)	1796	*KM#53; St4.29*	1,226,000	1,226,000
Total value in full pice				2,212,996
Total value in rupees				34,578

Source: Stevens 2012, 168, 179.

TABLE I.45: COPPER PICE PRODUCTION, CALCUTTA, 1800-1

Denomination	*Production year*	*Identification*	*Tale*	*Value in rupees*
Pice RY37	Dec 1800 May 1801 Oct 1801	*KM*# - (possibly included in *KM*#53); St6.25 [issued 1802]		
Total amount			640,000	
Total value in rupees				10,000

Source: Stevens 2012, 261, 298-9.

TABLE I.46: COPPER COIN PRODUCTION, CALCUTTA, 1807-9

Denomination	*Production year*	*Identification*	*Tale*	*Value*	
				In whole pice	*In Rs.*
½ pice RY37 (= quarter Benares pice)	1807/9	*KM*#A54; St 7.183	400,000	200,000	
Pice (= half Benares pice)	1807/9	*KM*#25; St 7.181	320,000	320,000	
2 pice (= whole Benares pice)	1807/9	*KM*#A55; St 7.179	400,000	800,000	
Subtotal 1807/9				1,320,000	20,620
Pice RY37	1809*	*KM*#56; St 6.26	10,157,696	10,157,696	158,714
Total					179,334

Notes: Stevens 2012, 263, 298-9, 336, 402-4: deducted from totals for 1795-1807: Rs. 223,912 minus Rs. 44,578 = Rs. 179,000 for 1807/9 minus the Benares type totalling Rs. 20,620 = Rs. 158,714 left for the new pyce 1809.

*The data for 1809 in this table can be made consistent with those for 1808 to 1810 by supposing that these 10,157,696 pice have to be subsumed under the 41 million pice produced in 1808/9 and 1809/10. Materially, however, the possible discrepancies do not really matter as the main conclusion is that, in these years, tens of millions of copper pice of the type *KM*#56 / St 6.26 were minted at Calcutta.

TABLE I.47: COPPER PICE PRODUCTION, CALCUTTA, 1808/9-1825/6

Denomination	*Production year*	*Identification*	*Tale*	*Value in rupees*
Pice RY37	1808/9	*KM*#56; St 6.26	23,976,218	
	1809/10		17,246,049	
	1810/11		22,395,298	
	1813/14		11,777,016	
	1814/15		299,400	
Subtotal			75,693,981	

Pice RY37	1817/18	KM#55; St 6.27	6,841,000	
	1818/19		302,600	
	1820/1		5,672,300	
	1821/2		6,108,550	
	1823/4		864,400	
	1824/5		3,103,000	
	1825/6		2,650,000	
Subtotal 1813/14 to 1825/6			37,618,266	587,785
Pice RY37	1828/29	*KM#54*; St 6.28	17,625,088	105,192
	1829/30			170,200

Sources: Stevens 2012, 266, 269, 298-299, 488; cf. Prinsep 1834, 57. Cf. Copper coin production January 1801-December 1813: SaRs 1,099,170:5:6 (Prinsep 1834, 57).

TABLE I.48: COPPER COIN PRODUCTION, CALCUTTA, 1830/1-1832/3

Denomination	*Production year*	*Identification*	*Tale (tentative)*	*Value in rupees*
pice RY37 [1/64 rupee]	1830/1	*KM#57*; St 9.27	23,976,218	402,116
pie [1/192 rupee]	1831/2	*KM#58*; St 9.31	108,943,872	567,416
½ anna [1/32 rupee]	1832/3	*KM#59*; St 9.28/9.29	8,607,237	268,976

Sources: Stevens 2012, 488, 527, 529, 538-540; my tentative attribution of denominations to production years. Cf. Copper coin production 1825/6-1832/3: SaRs 1,611,461:1:6 (Prinsep 1834, 57).

TABLE I.49: COPPER COIN PRODUCTION, CALCUTTA, BOMBAY, AND MADRAS, 1835

Denomination	*Year*	*Mint*	*Tale*	*KM*		*SW*	
				#	*Market value (quality fine)*	*#*	*Rarity*
¼ anna	1835	C	186,529,741	446.1	2	1.86	C
		B	36,766,900	446.1	2	1.87	C
		M	755,059,377	446.2	2	1.98	C
½ anna	1835	B	8,658,092	447.1	5	1.79	C
		M	95,202,278	447.1	5	1.83	C

Note: For all Tables I.49 to I.57: C = Calcutta; B = Bombay; M = Madras.

TABLE I.50: COPPER 1/12 AND ½ ANNA, AND SILVER 2 ANNA COIN PRODUCTION, CALCUTTA, BOMBAY, AND MADRAS, 1841-8

Denomination	*Year*	*Mint*	*Tale*	*KM*		*SW*	
				#	*Market value (quality fine)*	*#*	*Rarity*
1/12 anna	1848	C	14,380,924	445.0	10	2.61	C
½ anna	1845	C	17,160,010	447.1	25	2.59/ 2.60	C
2 anna (silver)	1841	C	8,385,077	459.2	25	2.50	C
		B	11,430,800	459.1	25	2.53	C
		M	10,503,600	459.3	30	2.55	C

TABLE I.51: COPPER ½ PICE AND ¼ ANNA, AND SILVER 2 ANNA COIN PRODUCTION, CALCUTTA, BOMBAY, MADRAS, AND BIRMINGHAM-SOHO, 1841-58

Denomination	*Year*	*Tale*	*KM*		*SW*	
			#	*Market value fine*	*#*	*Rarity*
½ pice	1853	62,408,000	464.0	5	3.84	C
¼ anna	1857	47,040,000	463.1	30	3.74	C
	1858	62,720,000	463.1	4	3.77	C
		172,480,000	463.2	4	3.80	C

2 annas (silver)	[1841]	43,002,080	460.2	20	3.62	C
		8,427,040	460.3	20	3.66	C
		26,930,380	460.4	20	3.68	C

TABLE I.52: COPPER (ALL DENOMINATIONS), AND SILVER 2 ANNA COIN PRODUCTION, CALCUTTA, BOMBAY, AND MADRAS, 1862-76

Denomination	*Year*	*Mint*	*Tale*	*KM*		*SW*	
				#	*Market value fine*	*#*	*Rarity*
1⁄12 anna	1862	C	2,501,952	465	1.25	4.184	N
		B	2,999,380	465	1.25	4.189	N
		M	40,487,040	465	1.25	4.190	C
	1874	C	4,819,200	465	200.00	5.57	N
		B	2,960,448	465	200.00	5.58	R
	1875	C	4,646,400	465	1.25	5.59	N
		B	part of 3,067,584, say 1,533,792	465	1.25	5.61	R
	1876	C	20,318,400	465	1.25	5.62	N
		B	part of 3,067,584, say 1,533,792	465	1.25	5.63	R
½ pice	1862	C	96,842,826	466	3.00	4.179	CN
		M	6,400,000	466	3.00	4.181	SR
¼ anna	1862	C	99,504,000	467	3.00	4.165	C
			10,654,000	467	5.00	4.166	C
		B	32,148,715	467	1.00	4.170	C
			2,365,568	467	150.00	4.171	C
		M	186,227,000	467	1.00	4.172	C
	1874	C	44,678,400	467	2.00	5.48	C
	1875	C	36,236,800	467	2.00	5.49	C
		B	14,493,504	467	2.00	5.52	C
	1876	C	43,580,800	467	2.00	5.53	C
		B	3,360,000	467	2.00	5.54	C

(Contd.)

½ anna	1862	C	7,235,886	468	10.00	4.151	R
		B	4,802,496	468	10.00	4.158	R
		M	66,514,56	468	5.00	4.159	N
	1875	C	1,145,600	468	300.00	5.45	R
	1876	C	2,291,200	468	20.00	5.47	R
2 annas (silver)	1862	C	29,653,000	469	10.00	4.144	C
		B	21,037,000	469	10.00	4.147	C
		M	4,202,000	469	10.00	4.149	C
	1874	C	5,689,600	469	30.00	5.36	N
		B	9,508,000	469	30.00	5.37	N
	1875	C	6,512,160	469	20.00	5.39	N
		B	1,712,000	469	20.00	5.41	S
	1876	C	10,504,400	469	200.00	5.42	N
		B	3,911,400	469	300.00	5.43	N

TABLE I.53: COPPER 1/12 ANNA PRODUCTION, CALCUTTA, AND BOMBAY, 1877-1901

Year	*Mint*	*Tale*	*KM #488 market value fine*	*SW*	
				#	*Rarity*
1877	C	5,880,000	1.25	6.610	C
	B	1,551,360	1.25	6.612	N
1878	C	5,524,800	1.25	6.614	C
1881	B	2,953,536	1.25	6.616	R?
1882	C	4,344,000	1.25	6.617	C
1883	C	9,840,000	1.25	6.618	C
	B	4,794,432	1.25	6.620	C
1884	B	8,073,600	1.25	6.621	C
1885	C	4,783,126	1.25	6.623	C
1886	C	18,663,046	1.25	6.624	C
	B	5,783,424	1.25	6.626	C
1887	C	8,724,222	1.25	6.627	C
	B	8.,241,600	1.25	6.628	C
1888	C	4,662,320	1.25	6.629	C
	B	2,142,750	1.25	6.630	C

1889	C	7,601,850	1.25	6.631	C
	B	5,660,160	1.25	6.632	C
1890	C	21,732,075	1.25	6.633	C
1891	C	17,306,015	1.25	6.635	C
1892	C	13,792,52	1.25	6.640	C
1893	C	10,034,076	1.25	6.644	C
1894	C	18,391,524	1.25	6.648	C
1895	C	15,207,753	1.25	6.651	C
1896	C	921,600	1.25	6.655	C
1897	C	20,822,400	1.25	6.659	C
1898	C	13,881,600	1.25	6.663	C
1899	C	10,056,000	1.25	6.667	C
1901	C	21,345,354	1.25	6.672	C

TABLE I.54: COPPER ½ PICE PRODUCTION, CALCUTTA, 1877-1901

Year	*Mint*	*Tale*	*KM #484 market value fine*	*SW*	
				#	*Rarity*
1885	C	6,205,840	15	6.561	C
1886	C	7,733,430	4	6.562	C
1887	C	6,464,053	4	6.563	C
1888	C	3,190,351	15	6.564	C
1889	C	7,587,200	4	6.565	C
1890	C	3,504,000	4	6.566	C
1891	C	5,139,262	4	6.568	C
1892	C	4,774,338	4	6.572	C
1893	C	7,004,800	4	6.576	C
1894	C	7,776,882	4	6.580	C
1895	C	9,873,826	4	6.583	C
1896	C	6,113,374	4	6.587	C
1897	C	8,483,515	4	6.591	C
1898	C	12,940,403	4	6.595	C
1899	C	7,936,000	4	6.599	C

(Contd.)

1900	C	5,219,900	4	6.603	C
1901	C	16,056,900	4	6.606	C

TABLE I.55: COPPER ¼ ANNA PRODUCTION, CALCUTTA, AND BOMBAY, 1877-1901

Year	*Mint*	*Tale*	*KM #486 market value fine*	*SW*	
				#	*Rarity*
1877	C	65,209,600	2	6.486	C
	B	9,320,128	2	6.488	C
1878	C	40,812,800	2	6.490	R
1879	C	43,072,000	10	6.492	R
1880	C	12,835,200	10	6.494	S
1882	C	52,291,200	2	6.495	C
	B	12,408,960	2	6.496	S
1883	C	57,571,200	2	6.497	C
	B	12,442,752	2	6.498	C
1884	C	43,195,790	2	6.499	C
	B	16,844,800	2	6.500	C
1885	C	36,699,482	2	6.502	C
1886	C	36,120,514	2	6.503	C
	B	14,389,888	2	6.504	C
1887	C	59,060,219	2	6.505	C
	B	26,204,800	2	6.506	C
1888	C	34,531,157	2	6.507	C
	B	8,293,408	2	6.508	C
1889	C	88,559,359	2	6.509	C
	B	19,109,856	2	6.510	C
1890	C	82,908,762	2	6.511	C
1891	C	86,076,747	2	6.513	C
1892	C	68,131,253	2	6.519	C
1893	C	76,038,400	2	6.523	C
1894	C	45,744,400	2	6.527	C

1895	C	35,743,600	2	6.530	C
1896	C	109,852,800	2	6.534	C
1897	C	82,288,000	2	6.538	C
1898	C	12,118,400	40	6.542	C
1899	C	36,896,000	2	6.546	C
1900	C	30,534,240	2	6.550	C
1901	C	136,090,726	2	6.554	C

TABLE I.56: COPPER ½ ANNA PRODUCTION, CALCUTTA, AND BOMBAY, 1877

Year	*Mint*	*Tale*	*KM #487 market value fine*	*SW*	
				#	*Rarity*
1877	C	3,584,000	20	6.458	S
	B	3,454,141	20	6.461	S

TABLE I.57 SILVER 2 ANNA PRODUCTION, CALCUTTA, AND BOMBAY, 1877-1901

Year	*Mint*	*Tale*	*KM #488 market value fine*	*SW*	
				#	*Rarity*
1877	C	3,574,560	20	6.347	C
	B	2,214,720	20	6.353	C
1878	C	3,993,520	40	6.354	C
1879	C	3,541,040	40	6.358	C
1880	C	2,539,200	200	6.360	C
1881	C	4,399,680	40	6.361	C
	B	2,448,880	40	6.363	C
1882	C	14,359,680	20	6.366	C
	B	2,628,880	20	6.367	C
1883	C	2,736,400	30	6.373	C
	B	4,000,000	30	6.374	C
1884	C	7,200,000	20	6.378	C
	B	2,000,000	20	6.379	C

(Contd.)

1885	C	1,335,440	20	6.386	C
	B	2,262,240	20	6.387	C
1886	C	10,346,320	10	6.390	C
	B	3,154,720	10	6.391	C
1887	C	13,927,280	10	6.392	C
	B	3,282,560	10	6.393	C
1888	C	9,306,640	10	6.394	C
	B	8,038,960	10	6.396	C
1889	C	1,077,120	10	6.397	C
	B	5,894,800	10	6.398	C
1890	C	9,836,320	10	6.399	C
	B	7,789,840	10	6.401	C
1891	C	8,620,880	10	6.406	C
	B	4,229,680	10	6.409	C
1892	C	6,971,440	10	6.414	C
	B	9,347,200	10	6.417	C
1893	C	8,002,720	10	6.421	C
	B	8,037,000	10	6.424	C
1894	C	2,460,800	10	6.427	C
	B	2,679,000	10	6.429	C
1895	C	9,668,320	10	6.430	C
1896	C	6,616,080	10	6.431	C
	B	8,234,720	10	6.434	C
1897	C	12,103,040	10	6.436	C
	B	8,040,856	10	6.439	C
1898	C	4,011,120	10	6.441	C
	B	1,588,480	10	6.442	N
1900	C	1,704,592	10	6.446	N
	B	6,103,024	10	6.448	C
1901	C	8,904,130	10	8.452	C
	B	1,705,880	10	8.453	N

Sources: Prinsep 1834, 51, 57; Stevens 2012; www.psindiancoins; *SACPM* 2013, 421-9, 448-68.

Cambay

See Khambhat.

Candeish

See Khandesh.

Chakan (Mominabad Chakan)

Maratha mint.
Maheshwari and Wiggins 1989, 54-5; *SACPM* 2013, 181.

Chamba

Chamba State mint.
SACPM 2013, 277-8.

Champanir (Muhammadabad)

Gujarat Sultanate mint.
Goron and Goenka 2001, 356.

Chanderi

Malwa Sultanate mint.
Goron and Goenka 2001, 452.

Chandor (Jafarabad)

Maratha mint.
Maheshwari and Wiggins 1989, 55-7; *SACPM* 2013, 174, 181-8.

Chandore / Chandwad

See Nasik.

Chaul (Murtadabad)

Ahmadabad Shahs' and Portuguese Indian mint.
Goron and Goenka 2001, 324; *SACPM* 2013, 147-9, 399.

Chennai

See Madras.

Chhachrauli

Mughal mint and, later, of the Sikh State of Kalsia, and, *c.* 1800 and in the 1820s and early 1830s, north of Dadupur. See also Kalsia.

Lingen and Lucassen 2010/11 (see Part I: Studies, No. 10 in this volume); *SACPM* 2013, 139, 341.

Chhatarpur/ Chutterpore

State in Bundelkhand. Closure in 1818 ordered by the British who gave permission to coin their money at Saugar; 1833 Chutterpore rupees circulating in the Saugor and Nerbudda territories; 1834 coinage going on; 1845 coining Chutturpooree rupees (probably C#15); 1847 mint 'at work merely by [British] sufferance' and Chutterpore rupees circulating in Gwalior, Indore, and adjacent regions; 1851 copper coinage (possibly *KM*#2), but suppressed by the British, which is then appealed; 1855 currency deficiencies since suppression of coinage; 1869-70 formerly had its mint manually coining silver rupee; its production had long ceased but coinage still largely circulating.

NAI, Residencies, Central Indian Agency 811 /1849-62, copy letter 123 of 1855 by Political Assistant for Bundelkhand and Rewa to Agent General for Central India Indore, Nogade, 30 November 1855; copy letter 358 of 1859/60 by Accountant NWP to Commissioner of Jhansie DN at Jhansie, Agra, 23 May 1859; idem 1726 / 1863, no. 51 Agent Governor-General Bandlecund to Secretary to Government of India with the Governor-General Simla, Jhansie, 27 May 1847; NAI, Foreign Department. Currency of Native States, Governor-General's minute on question of equalization in value and weight of the rupees, 18 July 1839/ 108-09/ PC; Garg 2022, xliii, 81, 316, 370, 501, 503-4; Neogy in Garg 2022, 152, 166; *SACPM* 2013, 278.

Chhota Udaipur

State in Bombay Presidency. 1869-70 one mint at Chhota Udaipur, only established in later period 'by the tacit permission of the Political Agent', coining manually thick copper Oodeypoorie pice (at 1/64 British Indian rupee; average annual outturn Rs. 400; *KM* Y#1, possibly including *KM* Y#2.1, 2.2); current only within the state limits. See Rewa Kantha. Garg 2022, 77, 87, 320, 334, 356-9, 532; *SACPM* 2013, 278-9.

Chikkaballapur

Avati Chiefs' mint.
Mitchiner 1989, I, 247.

Chiknayakanhalli

Hagalavadi Chiefs' mint.
Mitchiner 1989, I, 246-7.

Chinapattam

Mughal mint in Madras Town.
SACPM 2013, 17.

Chittor (Akbarpur)

Mughal and Mewar State mint since *c.* 1750. 1847 coining Chittore rupees (*KM* C#26), circulating in Gwalior, Indore, and adjacent territories; 1869-70 coining silver Suroop Sahee rupees (introduced by the late Maharana; *KM* Y#5); negotiations about closure).

NAI, Residencies, Central Indian Agency, 1726/ 1863, no. 51, Agent Governor-General Bandlecund to Secretary to Government of India with the Governor-General Simla, Jhansie, 27 May 1847; Garg 2022, 79, 319, 335, 373, 376, 400-1; *SACPM* 2013, 17, 362-3.

Chitradurga

Mint belonging to the Nayakas of Chitradurga.
Mitchiner 1989, I, 214-15.

Chunar

Suri and Mughal mint.

Goron and Goenka 2001, 29; *SACPM* 2013, 7.

Churawa / Charama

Place in Khetri state, a feudatory of Jaipur State, with many small mints. The Churawa mint discontinued in 1860; however, thirteen active mints in 1868, coining, in addition to Jaipur pice, short-weight counterfeit pice of Gwalior, Jaipur, Bharatpur, Bikaner, and other princely states for circulation at Agra, Mathura, Ajmer, etc. (including Shahpura). 1869 permanently closed.

Lucassen 2007, 369, 380, 382; Garg 2022, 74, 396, 424, 514-16; Neogy in Garg 2022, 154-6; not in *SACPM* 2013.

Cis-Sutlej states

Faridkot (https://en.wikipedia.org/wiki/Faridkot_State),
Jind (https://en.wikipedia.org/wiki/Jind_State, see Jind),
Kaithal (https://en.wikipedia.org/wiki/Kaithal),
Maler Kotla (https://en.wikipedia.org/wiki/Malerkotla_State, see Malerkotla),
Patiala (https://en.wikipedia.org/wiki/Patiala_State, see Patiala),
Thanesar (https://en.wikipedia.org/wiki/Thanesar); 1870 only coined occasionally.
Garg 2022, 320; Neogy in Garg 2022, 161; *SACPM* 2013, 283, 332, 341, 360-2, 371-3.

Cochin

See Kochi.

Cooch Behar

State. Treaty with the British 1772 to coin Narainy rupees (*KM*#127, 133, 141); 1834 valued at 34/100 Farruckabad rupee. Restricted by the British in 1776, 1795, and 1800; consequently, 1814 output only 12,000, as Holi presents. 1841 coinage of Narainee currency (*KM*#151) forbidden by the British. The Narainies, introduced around 1500, were used in Rangpur (Bengal), Bihar, Bhutan, Tibet, Mymensing, Assam, and Nepal, passing as equal to Sicca rupees. Circulation in 1864 was less than Rs. 600,000 in Cooch Behar, plus Rs. 1,500,000 to 3,500,000 imitations, coined in Bhutan.

NAI, Foreign Department 5 April 1841/ 162-3 /PC 162, Governor-General's Agent N.E. Frontier, Diary of Proceedings 4-10 March 1841; Garg 2022, li-lii, 284-300; *SACPM* 2013, 161-4.

Coorg

State mint at the capital Mercara.

SACPM 2013, 279.

Cuddalore / Tegnapatnam (Fort St. David)

EIC mint.

SACPM 2013, 440.

Cuddapah

Arcot and Mysore mint.

SACPM 2013, 195, 233.

Cusba Apta

In Angria State (Konkan), at 5 koss from Panvel. Two mints, established in July and September 1831, coining copper dubhoos (value Rs. 13,000, if at 1/50 rupee 650,000) until 1832; imitations of the Bombay double balemark pice issued 1802-31 (most likely *KM*#200).

Stevens 2019, 242-5; Stevens in Garg 2022, 230-4; not in *SACPM* 2013, 433.

Cuttack

See Katak.

Dalipnagar

See Datia.

Daman/ Damaõ

Portuguese India mint.
SACPM 2013, 400-1.

Dar al-Darb

See Faridpur.

Dar al-Sultanat

See Golconda.

Daryapur

Hyderabad Feudatory Elichpur mint.
SACPM 2013, 309.

Datia

Datia State mint in Bundelkhand. British ordered the closure of the mint at Dalipnagar in 1818 and granted permission to coin their money at Saugar; 1845 coining Duttia rupees (*KM* C#38); 1859 mint tolerated by the British; 1869-70 no coin manufactured for many years, or, at any rate, since the mutiny.

1894 no mint. Circulation mainly Raja Shahi rupees, also in various parganas, including the Bala Shahi of Jalaun, the Nana Shahi, and the Raja Shahi.

Garg 2022, 81, 316, 370, 501, 503-4, 690; Bhandare in Garg 2022, 115-16; Neogy in Garg 2022, 152, 154, 166; *SACPM* 2013, 279-82.

Daulatabad / Deogiri

Ahmadnagar State, Mughal, and Hyderabad State mint.
Goron and Goenka 2001, 325; *SACPM* 2013, 17, 147-8, 300.

Daulatabad

See Baroda.

Daulatgarh

Bhopal State mint.
SACPM 2013, 264.

Delhi (Shergarh, Shahjahanabad)

Mint belonging to the Delhi Sultans, the Suris, and the Mughals (from Humayun onwards; since AH 1048 or 1638/9 with the epithet Dar ul-Khalifat); after the British conquest of 11 September 1803, it was part of the 'Conquered and Ceded Provinces' and continued coining copper (*KM*#770/771). Also coined paisas until 1818, 11.15 grams, valued at 1/44 to 1/60 Rupee in 1834, and silver, in great numbers from 1806-15 and only rarely until 1842, mainly for ceremonial purposes. Plans, including detailed estimates, in 1826, and for a copper mint, in 1829, did not materialize. Production 1812-18:

TABLE I.58: GOLD AND SILVER COIN PRODUCTION, DELHI 1812-18

	Gold mohurs (KM#781) amount	*Silver rupees (KM#777) amount*	*Net revenue Rs.*
1812			20,000
June 1816-May 1817	457	78,148:12	
June 1817-28 May 1818	41	59,323:12	

Note: 1833 Delhi rupees still circulating in the Saugor and Nerbudda territories.
Sources: NAI, Foreign Department, 108-9, Governor-General's minute on question of eqalization in value and weight of the rupees, 18 July 1833 (Coins in circulation in the Saugor and Nerbudda territories by D. Presgrave, Assay Master, Saugor, 3 January 1833); Prinsep 1834, 51; Goron and Goenka 2001, 86-134; Lingen and Lucassen 2012/13 and 2010/11 (see Part I: Studies, Nos. 9 and 10 in this volume); Garg 2022, 16, 34, 385, 682; Stevens in Garg 2022, 235-6, 243-8; *SACPM* 2013, 17, 145-6, 271 (for Vrindavan).

Deogav / Devgadh / Deola

Partabgarh State mint.
Garg/ Hodivala 2014, 105-10; *SACPM* 2013, 373-4.

Deogiri

See Daulatabad.

Dera Ghazi Khan

Sikh State Dera mint.
SACPM 2013, 217.

Dera Ismail Khan

Sikh State Derajat mint.
SACPM 2013, 217.

Deryabad

Pergunnah in Awadh; 1827 coining counterfeit rupees in five different villages for Benares.

NAI, Foreign Department, Documents (see Part II: Records, No. 17 in this volume).

Devgarh Baria

See Baria.

Devogarh

Mughal and Gond State mint.
Garg / Hodivala 2014, 105-10; *SACPM* 2013, 166-7.

Dewas

State mint (with a junior and a senior branch). 1894 circulation in junior branch 900,000 to 1,000,000 rupees of all denominations (Halis from Indore and Ujjain, Guman Shahi, and Salim Shahi).
Garg 2022, 697-9; *SACPM* 2013, 281.

Dhabol / Dabul

Bijapur Sultanate mint.
Goron and Goenka 2001, 314; *SACPM* 2013, 159-61.

Dhaka / Dacca (Jahangirnagar)

Mughal and, from 1765, EIC mint. Now in Bangladesh.

Stevens 2012, 183-218, 238-43; Garg 2022, 291-2; *SACPM* 2013, 17, 281, 421.

Dhar

State mint. 1863 Dhar pice (*KM*6) equivalent to three British government pice.

NAI, Residencies, Central Indian Agency, 813, 1863, No. 111, 2nd Asst Agnt GGCI and Offg Supt Dhar to 1st Asst Agnt GGCI, Dhar, 22 June 1863; *SACPM* 2013, 281-2.

Dharwad / Dharwar (Nasirabad, Khurshed Sawad)

Mughal mint, named Nasirabad, passed on to the Marathas and Mysore, and in 1817/18 to the EIC, who employed the mint with an annual average production of 266,000 rupees between 1823/4 and 1833/4. Reported as having no mint in 1869-70.

Maheshwari and Wiggins 1989, 59-60; Mitchiner 1989, I, 235; Garg 2022, xlvii, 80; Stevens in Garg 2022, 194-200, 235; *SACPM* 2013, 190-203.

Dholara / Bandar Dholara

British mint in Kaira collectorate; *c.* 1810/11 coining copper pice. Production of pice at 1/64 rupee 1810: 419 maunds of copper; 1811/12: 330:11.25 maunds of copper, value Rs. 11,343:2:37 at 64 per rupee yielding 725,990 pieces.

Stevens 2019, 273-7; Stevens in Garg 2022, 228-9; www.psindiancoins; not in *SACPM* 2013.

Dholpur

State mint with branches at Gohad and Dholpur (from 1804). 1847 coining Dhoulpore rupees, circulating in Gwalior, Indore, and adjacent territories; 1857 new rupee mint established (Tamancha Sahee rupees); 1870 coining of silver rupees, small output, no more than about Rs. 10,000 annually (probably *KM*#C12c); circulating in the state and also in Gwalior and Patiala. 1894 average circulation of the British Indian rupee: 2,200,000 per annum.

Webb 1893, 133-5; Garg 2022, 32-3, 132, 134, 136, 144, 335, 408, 509, 561, 653; *SACPM* 2013, 282-3.

Dig / Deeg (Mahe Indrapur)

Bharatpur State mint from 1763 until 1806/37 and from *c.* 1870 to 1878, when finally closed.

Webb 1893, 126; Lingen and Lucassen 2012/13 (see Part I: Studies, Nos. 8 and 9 in this volume); Bhandare in Garg 2022, 119; *SACPM* 2013, 260-4.

Dilshahabad

Mughal and Hyderabad Feudatory State Narayanpet mint.

SACPM 2013, 17, 310.

Dindigul (Khaliqabad)

Mysore mint.

Mitchiner 1998, I, 235; *SACPM* 2013, 191.

Diu

Gujarat Sultanate and Portuguese India (1684-1859) mint.

Goron and Goenka 2001, 350, 356-73; Ferraro Vaz and Correia de Sousa 1980; *SACPM* 2013, 401-4.

Dogaon / Dukam / Dukampur

Mughal mint in Bahraich district but not identifiable with modern place (cf. map in *SACPM* 2013, 14: just north of Bahraich).

Garg / Hodivala 2014, 32, 37-8, 40, 44, 47, 167, 173, 176, 178, 197, 201-2, 229; *SACPM* 2013, 17.

Dohad

Gwalior State mint.

SACPM 2013, 285.

Dowdee

Gwalior mint. 1834 coining Shivaji pyce for circulation in Pune.

See Part II: Records, No. 28 in this volume; Lingen and Wiggins 1978, 37-8 (there Dohad / Devada); *SACPM* 2013, 294-5.

Dukam / Dukampur

See Dogaon.

Dungarpur

State. In 1868 it was recorded that some sixty years ago the mint coined old Chittore, Tursooleea, and Putreesereea rupees, after which the mint closed. Again, coining copper pice 1860/1, but silver coinage postponed and no gold coinage. 1869-70 no mint in operation, although it was asserting the right to coin silver and copper coins; 1870 diverging opinions on reopening of mint. 1894 no mint, but currency from Mewar (the old Udaipuri rupee, 10 mashas, fineness 85 per cent) in addition to a small amount of government rupee. Emergency copper paisa coinage 1944.

Webb 1893, 29-30; Garg 2022, 80, 82-3, 335, 374, 380, 402, 552-3, 710; Neogy in Garg 2022, 159, 161, 433-4, 692; *SACPM* 2013, 283.

Durelia

Mint in Alwar. 1849 coining takkas; still active 1869-70.

Lingen and Lucassen 2007 (see Part I: Studies, No. 12 in this volume); Lucassen 2007, 369, 378, 381 (see Part I: Studies, No. 13 in this volume); Garg 2022, 76; not in *SACPM* 2013.

Elichpur / Achalpur

Mughal and Hyderabad Feudatory State Elichpur mint.

SACPM 2013, 17, 309.

Etawah / Itawa

Mughal and Maratha / Rohilla mint coining rupees. Awadh mint

1775-93 (rupees), abolished many years before 1801 when ceded by Awadh to the British.

Maheshwari and Wiggins 1989, 141-4; Kapoor and Master 2018, xxii-xxxiv; Stevens in Garg 2022, 235, 249; *SACPM* 2013, 17, 174-83.

Faizabad (Akhtarnagar Awadh)

Awadh mint 1722-45 (mainly rupees; also golden ashrafis).

Kapoor and Master 2018, xxii-xxxiv.

Faiz Hiṣar

See Gooty.

Falta

See Pultah.

Faridpur (Fathabad, Dar al-Harb)

Mint belonging to the Bengal Sultans.

Goron and Goenka 2001, 143.

Farkhanda Bunyad

See Hyderabad.

Farrukhabad (Ahmadnagar)

Mint belonging to the Mughals, of the Bangash Nawab of Farrukhabad, and, in 1802, as an EIC mint, it continued coining as part of the 'Conquered and Ceded Provinces'. New mint built in 1805 to produce new-style silver and copper coins by way of the gradual introduction of 'a mold for casting the plates of metal, a laminating engine and rollers for giving the plate its uniform and exact thickness, and a steel trepan to shape and cut off the planchet at one and the same time'. Full mechanization in 1810. Output of silver coins:

TABLE I.59: SILVER COIN PRODUCTION, FARRUKHABAD, 1802-23/4

	Rs	*Remarks*	
1802 June-December	557,670	monthly 80,000; AH 1217	
1803 January-September	1,057,334	monthly 110,000; AH 1217/18	
1803 October	50,154	AH 1218	
1803 November	104,189	AH 1218	
1803 December	175,100	AH 1218	
1803 total	1,386,777	monthly 115,565; AH 1218/19	
1804 January	135,467	AH 1218	
1804 February	318,087	AH 1218	
1804 March	151,120	AH 1218	
1804 total	2,658,719	monthly 221,560; AH 1218/19	
1805 January-June	2,036,284	monthly 339,381; AH 1219/20; die repair [= replacement] necessary after hammering 8,000-1,000; daily production 15,000	
1805 October-1806 May		mint actually at Futy Ghur	
1806 June-1807 July		handmade rupees	
1807 August		partially machine made 'new' rupees	
1807/8	3,398,877	monthly 283,240	
1808/9	5,553,341	monthly 462,778	
1810		fully machine-made 'new' rupees	
		government	*individuals*
1813	6,807,150	1,861,795	4,945,355
1814	3,033,694	2,385,843	647,851
1815	2,694,464	2,543,247	151,217
1816	3,420,300	2,764,656	655,644
1817	7,818,455	5,875,424	1,943,031
1818	5,190,208	2,890,168	2,190,208
1820/1	5,489,573	2,030,507	3,459,066

(Contd.)

1821/2	5,424,899	2,714,092	2,710,807
1822/3	974,519	794,043	180,476
1823/4 (Jan-Apr)	47,251	41,612	5,639

Note: 1805 proposal to coin copper pice (18.8 or 16.1 gram; same size as rupee) and half pice (same size as half rupee) not put into practice. Regulation XXI of 1816: copper paisa of 6.48 gram, 1/64 rupee. Copper coin production 1804/5-1832/3 Rs. 755,594:12. Mint closed in 1824 and equipment sent to Sagar.
Sources: Prinsep 1834, 51, 58; Stevens 2012, 443-69; Stevens in Garg 2022, 235, 242, 245-6, 250, 253-75; *SACPM* 2013, 17, 164, 425-6.

Farrukhi / Feroke

Mysore mint.
Mitchiner 1989, I, 235; Mitchiner 1998, II, 245; *SACPM* 2013, 191.

Farrukhyab Hisar

Mysore mint.
Mitchiner 1989, I, 235; Mitchiner 1998, II, 245; *SACPM* 2013, 191.

Fathabad

See Faridpur.

Fathpur

Mughal mint.
SACPM 2013, 17.

Firoznagar

See Yadgir.

Gagraun

Kotah mint (see there).
Webb 1893, 91-4; not in *SACPM* 2013.

Gangkok / Tuk Khani / Pachay Khani

Capital and Sikkim mint.
SACPM 2013, 218.

Garhgaon

Capital and Assam State mint until 1707, coining silver.
SACPM 2013, 148-58.

Gaur / Gauda / Gour

See Lakhnauti.

Gerowli / Kurrara Gurowlee

Jagir in Bundelkhand; 1851 one copper mint active, but suppressed by the British. By 1871, it had been more informally active for twenty years, but coined extensively.
Garg 2022, xliii, 504, 580; Neogy in Garg 2022, 152; see Part II: Records, No. 32 in this volume.

Gingee

Vijayanagar mint.
Mitchiner 1998, I, 178, 210-12.

Goa

Portuguese mint 1510-1869 (gold, silver, copper, and tin after which coins for Goa were minted at Bombay (1871-88) and Lisbon (1901-61). Production figures of copper leales for Goa 1510-11: 14 quintals, from which about 200,000 copper 2 reis coins (probably 'cepaicas' averaging 3.7 grams) could be made according to the contract.

TABLE I.60: COPPER COIN PRODUCTION, GOA, 1773-1801

	Annual production in arrobas de cobre (at 32 lbs or 14.5 kgs)	*Coin types (KM#)*
1773	3,564	A119, 120, 121, 122, 123, 125, 126, 135, 143
1774		120, 122, 123, 126, 135, 155, 157
1776	74,434	A119, 122, 123, 125, 135, 143
1777	23,278	165, 166, 167, 168, 169, 170, 171

(Contd.)

1781		198
1786	8,429	165, 166, 167, 168, 169, 170, 171
1787		196, 197, 198
1789	6,667	
1796	25,600	
1800	19,200	
1801	6,420	

Source: Gerson da Cunha 1880, 119-20.

TABLE I.61: COPPER COIN PRODUCTION, GOA, 1805-28

	Annual production in arrobas de cobre (at 32 lbs or 14.5 kgs)	*Coin types (KM#)*
1805	6,678	209, 210, 211, 212, 213, 214, 215, 216, 217, 224, 225, 226, 227, 228, 229, 230, 231, 232, 233, 234, 263
1807	672	
1810	3,828	
1812	966	
1813	400	
1814	3,015	
1815	5,394	
1816	27,293	
1817	25,205	
1818	3,100	
1820	1,530	
1823	2,720	
1824	4,033	
1825	6,404	
1826	1,320	
1827	8,086	
1828	22,160	

Source: Ferraro Vaz and Correia de Souza 1980, 595.

TABLE I.62: COPPER COIN PRODUCTION, GOA, 1845-56

	Annual production in arrobas de cobre (at 32 lbs or 14.5 kgs)	*Value*	*Coin types KM#*
		Xerafins:tgs:reis	
1845	42	2,899:2:35	257, 258, 259, 260, 261
1846	28	1,876:0:00	257, 258, 259, 260
1847	10	873:2:30	258, 260
1848	5	337:1:16	257, 258, 259, 260, 262
1849	0	0	260
1850	59	3,989:3:42	265, 266
1851	70	4,770:2:28	
1852	199	13,418:3:00	
1853	54	3,639:4:15	
1854	45	3,064:1:12	
1855	0	0	
1856	9	775:2:45	

Source: Gerson da Cunha 1880, 119-20. *NB*. I have omitted a column with conversions to English weights that seems to contain many errors.

TABLE I.63: COIN PRODUCTION, BOMBAY MINT FOR GOA, 1871-86

Denomination	*Period struck*	*Dates known*	*Production*		*Lowest KM price in fine*
			Total	*Annual average*	
3 reis	1871	1	52,080	52,080	60
5 reis	1871	1	50,900	50,900	60
10 reis	1871	1	51,075	51,075	60
¼ tanga (15 reis)	1871	1	50,664	50,664	35
½ tanga (30 reis)	1871	1	50,063	50,063	35
tanga (60 reis)	1861	1	50,004	50,004	35
⅛ tanga	1881-86	3	12,396,800	4,132,267	25
¼ tanga (15 reis)	1881-88	4	7,242,800	1,810,700	5
⅛ rupia (oitavo; silver)	1881	1	901,688	901,688	300

Sources: Gerson da Cunha 1880, 118-20 (slightly different figures for 1871; 1880-1: 4 lakhs of rupees coined at the Calcutta mint; the rest at Bombay); Ferraro Vaz and Correia de Souza 1980, 595; Gomes 1996; Romanos Collection 1996; *SACPM* 2013, 399-421; Mathew 2016, 315.

Gobindpur

Mughal mint.

Garg / Hodivala 2014, 159-60; *SACPM* 2013, 17.

Gohad

Dholpur State mint.

SACPM 2013, 282-3.

Golconda (Dar al-Sultanat, Muhammadnagar)

Mint near Hyderabad Town belonging to the Golconda Shahs and the Mughals.

Goron and Goenka 2001, 334; *SACPM* 2013, 17, 165-6.

Gooty / Guti (Faiz Hisar)

Mysore and Maratha mint.

Maheshwari and Wiggins 1989, 177; Mitchiner 1998, I, 235; *SACPM* 2013, 176-7, 191.

Gorakhpur (Muazzamabad)

Mughal mint, under Akbar, coining damris, nisfis, and dams during 1566/7-1579/80 and again 1603/4-1605/6, and falus under Aurangzeb 1669/70 and Jahandar 1712/13. Awadh mint but with the title of Shah Alam II 1768/9-1776/7, initially coining silver and gold, but 1763/4-1790/1 only copper paisas; production of copper paisas AH 1190 (1776/7): 2,920,000. Imitations are known from Benares and other mints. Prinsep 1834, 51: 12.05 gram, 1/26-1/36 rupee or 1/530 pusseree (5 seers) at Gazipur and 'entire Bengal', current in 'Benares district, former standard pysa.'

Prinsep 1834, 51; Kapoor and Master 2018, xxxiv, 8, 33, 70; *SACPM* 2013, 17-18, 21-7, 72, 102, 139, 238; supplementary data from zeno.ru; see Part I: Studies, No. 8 in this volume.

Gour / Gaur / Gauda

See Lakhnauti.

Gulshanabad

See Nasik.

Gurramkonda (Zafarabad)

Mysore mint.

Mitchiner 1998, I, 235; *SACPM* 2013, 191.

Gwalior

Mint belonging to the Suris, Mughals, and Gwalior State governed by the Sindhia (Scindia) Maharajas and a capital at Ujjain; 1803 treaty with the British. 1834, according to Prinsep, it was coining the 'Gwalior old, marked Mahomed Akber Shah', 9.46 grams, 1/62 rupee. Ten mints at work in Gwalior State in 1847; this was reduced to six 1869-70 (Lashkar since 1811, Bhilsa, Bajrungarh, Isagarh, Ujjain, Jhansi); 1870 contemplated the introduction of machinery for a new mint.

Coinage 1872/3 to 1875/6 of copper (paisa at *c.* 71/5 rupee as in Lashkar 1870) and silver (value in native coins converted into government rupees; no straightforward identification possible):

TABLE I.64: COIN PRODUCTION, GWALIOR, 1872/3-1875/6

	1872-3	*1873-4*	*1874-5*	*1875-6*
Silver	1,200,000	1,200,000	1,200,000	1,200,000
Copper (*KM*#232?)		150,000		

Note: 1847 coins circulating in Gwalior, Indore, etc.
Sources: See Part I: Records, No. 30 in this volume; Prinsep 1834, 51-2; Lingen and Wiggins 1978, esp. 41-8; Garg 2022, 77, 372, 539-47, 596-9, 704-6; Neogy in Garg 2022, 161; *SACPM* 2013, 284-300.

Hafizabad

Mughal mint.

SACPM 2013, 17.

Haidarnagar / Bednore

Mysore mint.

Mitchiner 1998, I, 216-17, 235; *SACPM* 2013, 191.

Hampi

See Vijayanagar.

Haridwar

Maratha mint.

Maheshwari and Wiggins 1989, 155-7; *SACPM* 2013, 180.

Hasanabad

Mughal mint. Possibly identical with Hasanabad, north-east of Agra.

SACPM 2013, 139 (paisa AH 1177, 'uncertain mint. Possibly a mint for Awadh or Rohilkhand').

Hathras

Mughal and later Awadh mint, coining rupees and possibly also copper pice until taken by the British in 1801. Possibly continued the coinage of silver and copper for some time as part of the 'Conquered and Ceded Provinces'. The circulation of the latter recorded in 1832 as 'Hatras pysa coined by Rajah Dyaram', on average 1/45 rupee (fluctuating from 36 to 46) current at Hatras, Surswe, Moorsawn c.s., and at Coel at a discount. 1834: Hatras copper of 18.14 grams, 1/34 rupee, current in Nagpur. The Munsoory pysa (1/64 to 1/66 rupee) and Nuwabee pysa (1/53 to 1/54 rupee) were also current in this state.

Prinsep 1834, 52; Lingen and Lucassen 2007, 217 (see Part I: Studies, No. 12 in this volume); Stevens 2012, 412, 471; Stevens in Garg 2022, 235, 249-50; *SACPM* 2013, 17, 235, 238, 240.

Hinganghat

Mint belonging to the Bhonsla Marathas.

SACPM 2013, 186-7.

Hisar / Hisar Firoza

Suri and Mughal mint.

Goron and Goenka 2001, 92; *SACPM* 2013, 17.

Husaingarh

Mughal Mint.

SACPM 2013, 138.

Hyderabad (Farkhanda Bunyad)

Mint belonging to the Golconda Shahs, Mughals, and Hyderabad State. In 1843, the Nizam has 10 million silver rupees in Golconda Fort and 8 million rupees in golden ashrafis at his Hyderabad palace. 1843-7 British attempt to homogenize its currency; mints at i.a. Hyderabad and Aurangabad. Circa 1850, 'several mints in different parts of the country' in addition to the state mint; 1869 mint within the walls of the capital city Hyderabad, manufacture of silver rupees by hand, when fully operational output is Rs. 1,500,000 per mensem or 18,000,000 per annum, but mint seldom at work for more than four to six months at a time.

TABLE I.65: SILVER COIN PRODUCTION, HYDERABAD, 1871/2-1874/5 (GOVT Rs.)

	1871-2		*1872-3*		*1873-4*		*1874-5*	
	Amt	*Value*	*Amt*	*Value*	*Amt*	*Value*	*Amt*	*Value*
Silver	93,563	80,032	11,993	10,259	67,136	57,427	9,638	38,334*

Note: *This must be a mistake (possibly 8,334).

In 1894, it is believed that, in ordinary times, there are between 2,000,000 and 2,500,000 Hali sicca rupees (weight 11 mashas = 10 mashas pure silver and 1 masha alloy) and between 100,000 to 150,000 British Indian rupees in circulation in Hyderabad and the suburbs. The mint sometimes produced gold mohurs. 1895 proposal to coin 300,000 Hali sicca rupees for Hyderabad at the Bombay mint. See also Golconda.

NAI, Foreign Department, 18 Nov 1843, pp. 80-1; 87-102/ PC (Political Proceedings, vol. no. 959, 18-25 November 1843); Goron and Goenka 2001, 334; Garg 2022, 77, 337-41, 505, 512-13, 522-3, 598, 647-50, 723; *SACPM* 2013, 17, 300-10.

Ikkeri

Keladi Nayaka mint.
Mitchiner 1998, I, 216-17.

Imphal

See Manipur.

Indore

State ruled by the Holkar Maharajas and it also had a mint from *c.* 1770. Under British control from 1818. Indore Hali rupees used to pay British Indian troops in 1836. 1834: Indore copper of 7.45 grams, current 'in Malwa generally'. Production figures 1837/8 to 1845/6 of Hali rupees (for all production figures that follow: *KM*#76 and its fractions *KM*#71, 72, 73), necessary for the opium trade as opium contracts between the state, the merchants, and the farmers are made in this currency, growing quickly in the 1840s (103¾ Hali rupees = 100 Company's rupees).

TABLE I.66: HALI RUPEE PRODUCTION, INDORE, 1837/8-1845/6

Years	*Hali rupees*
1837-8	382,152
1838-9	177,481
1839-40	102,497
1840-1	145,500
1840-1 [*SIC*]	120,102
1841-2	195,987
1842-3	659,809
1843-4	663,883
1844-5	1,343,265
1845-6	1,101,460

1869-70 one mint at Indore, coining silver rupees; for early description, see Malcolm 1822; introduction of machinery by 'an experienced Englishman from the Bombay mint' *c.* 1858/60, but 'never put in working order', 'still [1870] is desirous of putting an

English plant in operation'; capacity 25,000-30,000 rupees per day, but easily increased according to demand; average annual production in six years 1864-9: Rs. 2,124,625:1 (or daily average of Rs. 6,177:8); 1874 average annual coinage of 2,125,000 silver rupees and a maximum limitation of 2,500,000 (or Rs. 10,000 at a ½ per cent profit) considered; 1875 offers the suspension of its minting rights for 99 years and a compensation of Rs. 20,000 per annum; negotiations undecided.

TABLE I.67: HALI RUPEE PRODUCTION, INDORE, 1872/3-1875/6 (GOVT Rs.)

1872-3	*1873-4*	*1874-5*	*1875-6*
7,005,086	4,089,761	706,577	1,433,126

TABLE I.68: RUPEE PRODUCTION, INDORE, 1891-1900 (INDORE TOLAS)

Year	*Quarter*	*From new silver*	*From old silver*	*Total*
1891		3,637,712:10	nil	3,637,712:10
1892		3,443,494:02	nil	3,443,494:02
1893	Jan-Mar	1,224,209:03	nil	1,224,209:03
	Apr-Jun	1,878.563:06	nil	1,878.563:06
	Jul-Sep	8,204:02	nil	8,204:02
	Oct-Dec	7,149:06	nil	7,149:06
1894		1,687,817:02	nil	1,687,817:02
1895		360,083:11	65,553:10	425,637;05
1896		4,162,722:10	56,392:07	4,219,115;01
1897		1,105,947:10	60,621:10	1,166,569:04
1898		nil	76,991:03	76,991:03
1899		46,739:11	44,928:01	91,667:12
1900		?	?	?

Note: Indore rupees of 172.17 grains or 11 mashas; identical with *KM*#44 with its fractions *KM*#41, 42; production expressed in Indore tolas of 165 grains.

1894 mint still coining Hali rupees to a limited extent, circulating together with government rupees. Circulation of silver rupees in this state: 50,000,000 Hali rupees and 2,000,000 to 2,500,000 government rupees, in addition to 12,500,000 [1/4 of Indore Hali] Ujjain Hali Sicca. All to be exchanged in silver British Indian silver rupees and currency notes (proposal for 5,000,000 in notes of different values, from Rs. 1,000 to Rs. 50 each). The Indore Hali also circulated outside the state (2/5 of Dhar rupee circulation, 1/5 ditto Gwalior, 2/5 Barwani, 1/10 in Ali Rajpur).

NAI Foreign Department Political Consultations, 7 November 1836, No. 57 (Resident to Secretary Government of India, Indore Residency, 8 September 1836, No. 63); NAI, Residences, Central India Agency 839 Pt. III / 1900-2, Particulars regarding Native State mints in Central India to which 1876 Act does not apply; idem 1901 Printed Correspondence, Proposed introduction of British currency into the Indore State; See Part I: Records, No. 30 in this volume; Malcolm 1822, 478-9; Prinsep 1834, 52; Garg 2022, 77, 91-2, 334, 361-5, 462-95, 500, 534-7, 584, 596, 687, 693, 696; Neogy in Garg 2022, 161, 164; *SACPM* 2013, 310-18.

Isagarh / Esagad

Gwalior mint, coining silver from 1794 and copper from 1824. From 1861, coining (together with Bajrangarh and Bhilsa) silver Chandoreee rupees; combined output of Bajrangarh and Esaghur was Rs. 35,000 annually; circulation in these three districts of Gwalior; 1894 the Esagad rupee still circulating in Gwalior State.

NAI, Residences, Central India Agency 813, 1863 report on the coinage of native states (letter Political Agent at Gwalior to Agent Governor-General for CI Indore, Camp Khokhra, 21 December 1863); Lingen and Wiggins 1978, 49-51; Garg 2022, 77, 439, 446, 539, 549, 705; *SACPM* 2013, 284-300.

Jafarabad

See Chandor.

Jagadhri

Mint north of Delhi, coining coppers around 1830.

Lingen and Lucassen 2010/11 (see Part I: Studies, No. 10 in this volume). See also Chhachrauli and Kalsia.

Jaipur (Sawai Jaipur, Sawai Madhupur)

Jaipur State mint, founded *c.* 1748 for silver and copper from *c.* 1760. Treaty with the British 1818. 1834 coppers of 18.14 grams, 1/32.5 rupee, current in 'Agra and Jypore districts'. Formerly also mints at Mahdupur (in 1847 its rupees were circulating in Gwalior, Indore, and adjacent territories), Jeekur, Bupas, and other places ('have most of them long since been relinquished'); 'at Surujghur and Churawa, of Khetree' (discontinued 1860). Mint at Jaipur (no machinery; 30 shops within a fortified quadrangle; each shop with three men, able to produce 600 blanks a day, which results in a total capacity of 15,000 blanks), coining gold mohurs (recently 300,000 mohurs and 1870 150,000 to 200,000 mohurs), and silver Charshahee rupees (recently 2,500,000-3,000,000 and 1870 1,000,000-1,500,000 rupees). Copper mint, also founded 1728, but 1870 'though still existing, has not been worked for many years, owing to the depreciation in the value of the Jeypore copper money'.

TABLE I.69: COIN PRODUCTION, JAIPUR, 1872/3-1875/6

Coinage of gold mohurs (KM#125), silver rupees and fractions (KM#111, 115, 119), and copper new paisa (KM#105) 1872/3 to 1875/6	*1872-73*		*1873-74*		*1874-75*		*1875-76*	
	Amt	*Value*	*Amt*	*Value*	*Amt*	*Value*	*Amt*	*Value*
Gold (value in Govt Rs.)	145,312	2,433,976	50,522	846,243	38,666	647,656	22,508	377,009

(Contd.)

Silver (value in Jaipur Rs.)	477,629	477,629	906,799	906,979	1,022,866	1,022,866	472,214	472,214
Copper (value in Jaipur Rs.)	6,250,326	97,661	220,461	3,445	1,403,234	21,925	110	2

Note: 1894 the Jharshahi rupee (11/12 tola and fineness with copper alloy of 2 13/32%) circulation amounts approximately to 23,000,000. See also Amber.
Sources: Webb 1893, 71-82; Garg 2022, 50-1, 74, 77, 335, 395-8, 405-6, 424, 510, 558, 594-9, 653; *SACPM* 2013, 318-25.

Jaisalmer

Jaisalmer State mint, established in 1756, coining rupees. 1869-70 one mint at Jaisalmer, coining mainly silver rupees; 'average annual outturn of late years Rs. 200,000 (most likely *KM*#34), but for the time because of the famine quite inactive'. Coinage 1872/3 to 1875/6 Jaisalmer rupees and fractions (the devalued Akhey Sahee rupee weighing 152 grains of pure silver and 16 of alloy, or even worse, resulting in a purity of c. 90 per cent, or *c.* 9.8 grams of pure silver against 165 grains of the British Indian Rupee; *KM*#7, 8, 9, 5.1, 5.2; value in native coins converted into government rupees, which makes it unlikely that amount equals value):

TABLE I.70: SILVER COIN PRODUCTION, JAISALMER, 1872/3-1875/6 (GOVT Rs.)

	1872-3		*1873-4*		*1874-5*		*1875-6*	
	Amt	*Value*	*Amt*	*Value*	*Amt*	*Value*	*Amt*	*Value*
Silver	12,500	12,500	61,000	61,000	210,000	210,000	136,120	136,120

Purportedly copper coinage of 'dodia' in sv 1716 (1660) and sv 1893 (1836) but without date (*KM* C#4, there dated 1660-1863, probably a mistake), 'forty of these small pieces go to the anna, they are used instead of kauris'. 1894 circulation of the Akheshai rupee (500,000-600,000, consisting of 5 per cent old rupees with 7.5 per cent alloy and the new ones, coined for 10 years, with 2.6

per cent alloy and weighing 9/10 tola) 92 per cent of the entire currency and the British Indian rupee 8 per cent.

Webb 1893, 103-6; Garg 2022, 54-5, 77, 335, 385-7, 403, 555-6, 597, 654; *SACPM* 2013, 325-7.

Jalalpur / Jalalpur Sharif

Mughal mint (now in Pakistan)

SACPM 2013, 17.

Jalaun

State in Bundelkhand. Maratha mint, coining rupees and fractions, and also copper takkas; British ordered the closure of the mint in 1818 and they permitted the coining of their money at Saugar; despite this, coinage still occurring in 1834 (copper Bala Shahi, 16.40 grams, 1/40 rupee, current in Bundelkhand, Kalpi, and Sagar).

See Part II: Records, No. 32 in this volume; Prinsep 1834, 51-2; Maheshwari and Wiggins 1989, 107-11; Garg 2022, 503; Neogy in Garg 2022, 166; *SACPM* 2013, 174-83.

Jallandar

Mughal mint.

SACPM 2013, 18.

Jambusir

EIC mint 1772-82, a few miles north of Broach.

Stevens in Garg 2022, 176-7, 192; Not in *SACPM* 2013.

Jamgaon

Place near Ahmednagar. Gwalior mint, established 1793 by Mahadji Scindia, active until 1802, no copper production 1802 to 1830/1, after which resumed ('when the coiners having returned to their village, the mint was again brought into operation'); minting for the Hoozoor stopped 1834, but that for the Mamlutdar, who resided at Scindia's court, still active in that year.

NAI, Foreign Department, Political Proceedings, 13 September 1831, 3-5 and 19 June 1834, 61-6, Scindia's compliance with the order for the suppression of the Jamgaon mint; Lingen and Wiggins 1978, 52; not in *SACPM* 2013.

Jammu

Jammu and Kashmir mint, coining silver rupees and copper cash.

Garg 2022, 353-4; *SACPM* 2013, 169-70, 343-4.

Janjira

State in Bombay Presidency. Closure of mint ordered in 1834, 'but [1870] it appears to have been surreptitiously kept up'; 1870 manually coining gold mohurs, silver rupees (Rs. 1,000 per year), and copper pice (1/80 British Indian rupee; *KM*#28): 'the coinage of copper money has been carried on here for some considerable time back. The custom is to give a bar of copper to Dhamoo Kasar, Tambut, who with six others are employed by the Nawab to make the pice [...] this coin is made here at the rate of an average 3 rupees worth a day' (if working 250 days per year as suggested by Perlin 1987, 355 this would mean an average annual production of 60,000 pieces); to be suppressed and not to be reopened.

Garg 2022, 78, 120-1, 314, 334, 354-5, 360-1, 529; Neogy in Garg 2022, 153, 159; *SACPM* 2013, 328.

Jaora / Jowrah

State mint, 1863 coining copper paisa, 1/24-1/26 for the British Indian rupee; 1869-70 manually coining copper paisa, formerly 14 mashas in weight, but now reduced to 9 or 10 mashas, equal to 1/64 of a government rupee (total production of Ratlam, Jowrah, and Syllana coppers equals S.S. Rs. 30,000).

TABLE I.71: COPPER COIN PRODUCTION, JAORA, 1872/3-1875/6 (GOVT Rs.)

	1872-3		*1873-4*		*1874-5*		*1875-6*	
	Amt	*Value*	*Amt*	*Value*	*Amt*	*Value*	*Amt*	*Value*
Copper	800,000	12,121	850,000	13,281	856,000	13,806	860,000	13,870

Note: 1894 circulation of 1,000,000 Salim Shahi rupees from Pertabgarh and 50,000 government rupees 'to a certain extent'.
Sources: NAI, Residencies, Central India Agency, 813/ 1863, Political Assistant in Malwa to 1st Assistant Governor-General for Central India Indore, 25 June 1863, no. 95; Garg 2022, 78, 367, 538-9, 594-99, 69; *SACPM* 2013, 328-9.

Jaunpur

Mint belonging to the Delhi Sultans, the Suris, and the Mughals. See also Nusratabad.

Goron and Goenka 2001, 13, 92; *SACPM* 2013, 18.

Jawad

Mewar State and Gwalior State mint.

SACPM 2013, 285, 362.

Jeekur

Jaipur mint. Long since relinquished by 1870.

Garg 2020, 396; not in Webb 1893, 74; not in *SACPM* 2013.

Jhabua

State with copper mint 1863-81. Specimens known undated and with dates vs 1903-7 (1846-50) and 1920-36 (1863-79); two denominations (9-11.5 and 13-16.5 grams); nearly all overstruck or restruck on copper coins of neighbouring States of Dhar and Ratlam and also of Sailana and Mughal ones.

NAI, Residencies, Central India Agency, 813/1863, Bheel Agent & Political Assistant to 1st Assistant Governor-General for central India, Sirdarpoor, 22 June 1863, no. 93; Bhatt 1975; *SACPM* 2013, 329-30.

Jhalawar

State; a dependency of Kotah till 1837. From 1837, coinage of silver and copper. 1869-70 two mints, coining Muddun Sahee rupees and copper pice, one at Jhalra Patun (the capital) and one at Shahabad (production unknown, but much less than at the capital); 1870 retaining of the mint recommended. Copper pice minted 1837-57 (*KM* C#21) and from 1857 every year (*KM* Y#1-2; 1891 'from plates of copper obtained from Bombay'). 1894 circulation of the Jhalawar rupee (15/16 tola and 1.75 per cent per cent alloy; circulates also through central India and the neighbouring states of Rajputana) 66 per cent, the Kotah rupee 10 per cent, the Ujjain rupee 9 per cent, the Bundi rupee 6 per cent, the British Indian rupee 5 per cent, the Salim Shahi rupee 4 per cent.

Webb 1893, 97-100; Garg 2022, 78, 81, 311, 314-15, 335, 409, 421-3, 429, 563-4, 597-9, 655; Neogy in Garg 2022, 159; *SACPM* 2013, 330-2.

Jhalra Patun

Capital of Jhalawar since its independence from Kotah in 1838; it had a mint from 1801, when still under Kotah; 1870 annually coining Rs. 200,000 to 300,000 in silver Muddun Sahee rupees and copper pice (weighing 18 masha, or 1/27 pound, or 1/48 rupee); more in detail: output for the ten years, ending sumbut 1924 (1867/8): New rupees (*KM* Y#6.1 and fractions #3.1 and #3.2) Rs. 4,257,447 and pice (*KM* Y#2) from 178,448 lbs copper. Clear profit to the state in ten years (including restamping and probably also Shahabad) Rs. 27,572.

TABLE I.72: COIN PRODUCTION, JHALRA PATUN, 1872/3-1875/6 (GOVT Rs.)

	1872-3		*1873-4*		*1874-5*		*1875-6*	
	Amt	*Value*	*Amt*	*Value*	*Amt*	*Value*	*Amt*	*Value*
Silver	252,418	257,677	370,087	377,797	11,745	11,900	195,574	199,645
Copper							381,450	

Sources: Webb 1893, 91-4; Garg 2022, 78, 311, 335, 421-3, 563-4, 597-9; *SACPM* 2013, 330-2.

Jhansi (Balwantnagar)

State in Bundelkhand. Coinage of silver and copper by the Marathas. British ordered closure of the mint in 1818 and permitted the coining of their money at Saugar; 1834 coining going on, copper coin called 'Jhansi/ Taree/ Tehree' of *c.* 16.85 grams, 1/43 rupee and 'current in Bundelkhund'. 1851 copper mints active in two villages but suppressed by the British; from 1861, part of Gwalior (in exchange by the British Indian government), coining from 1865 silver Nanasahee rupees (1865/6 annual outturn 500,000; afterwards hardly any) and copper Bala Sahee pice (copper mint closed since 1865).

1870 counterfeit copper from Mow and traded at Raneepoor. More generally about these counterfeits (for which, see also Tori Futtehpoor, dependency of Orchha, Buncoree Orcha, Sursair Allypoor, and Kurrara Gurowlee): 'these copper coins, which are merely lumps of copper, some of which bear a stamp, sell for the merely value of the metal, and that the price varies with the rise and fall in the market value of copper [...] the great difficulty in the circulation of Government pice in this district is principally owing to the fact that in the Native States the value of our currency is not recognized [...] The regulation price of Government pice is three times the intrinsic value of copper at its present market rate'; 1894 the Jhansi Nana Shahi rupee still circulating in Gwalior State. For details of the pre-1870 counterfeit coppers, see Gerowli.

Prinsep 1834, 52; Lingen and Wiggins 1978, 57-8; Maheshwari and Wiggins 1989, 115-21; Garg 2022, xliii, 77, 424 (to be read Jhansie instead of Hansi), 440, 503-4, 549-50, 579-82, 705; Neogy in Garg 2022, 152, 166; *SACPM* 2013, 174-84, 284-300.

Jind

Cis-Sutlej State with silver and copper mint since c. 1770. 1869 coining silver Jheendeea rupees, only current within the state. 1894 circulation of British Indian rupees only.

Garg 2022, 78, 346-7, 343, 350, 372, 524-6, 669; *SACPM* 2013, 332.

Jodhawas

Circa 1840-70 mint in Alwar, coining takkas from locally mined copper.

Lingen and Lucassen 2007 (see Part I: Studies, No. 12 in this volume); Lucassen 2007, 369, 378, 381 (see Part I: Studies, No. 13 in this volume); Garg 2022, 76; not in *SACPM* 2013.

Jodhpur / Marwar

Mughal and Marwar (Jodhpur) State mint, 1751-1947, coining gold mohurs and silver rupees; but also coppers circulating generally in Alwar state ('a roughly stamped copper coin [...] from Marwar, struck at Joudpore and Pallee [...] the average rate being about 40 dhubboos to the Imperial rupee, making 2½ dhubboos equal to one anna').

TABLE I.73: COIN PRODUCTION, JODHPUR 1872/3-1875/6 (GOVT Rs.)

	1872-3		*1873-4*		*1874-5*		*1875-6*	
	Amt	*Value*	*Amt*	*Value*	*Amt*	*Value*	*Amt*	*Value*
Gold	2,706	41,943	1,180	18,290	1,068	16,554	2,018	31,279
Silver	269,779	278,209	58,938	60,781	37,573	38,747	122,430	126,256
Copper	20,233	1,012	12,582	629	10,962	548		

Note: According to Enquiry by the Government of Bombay 1884. NB Copper takkas are meant (*KM*#71, Lingen #J.08.01/3) 1872/3 to 1875/6).

TABLE I.74: COIN PRODUCTION, JODHPUR, 1873-83

CE (*VS*)	*Value in Jodhpur rupees: annas*			*Amount of copper takkas*	*Known VS dates (Lingen 2012, 122-3, #J10.01 and #J10.02)*
	Gold	*Silver*	*Copper*		
1873 (1930)	1,179:08	59:943:00	167:00	4,008	VS [19]30 (#J10.01)
1874 (1931)	1,068:04	37,573:08	6,137:25	147,312	
1875 (1932)	2,018:00	127,532:00	0	0	
1876 (1933)	8,985:04	77,300:08	0	0	
1877 (1934)	8,751:08	71,394:08	0	0	
1878 (1935)	6,945:04	64,811:00	2,295:00	54,216	vs [193]5 inverted (#J10.01)
1879 (1936)	14,468:04	61,558:00	63,058:25	1,513,416	
1880 (1937)	12,232:12	58,997:08	151,457:25	3,634,992	vs [193]7 inverted (#J10.01)
1881 (1938)	18,686:12	37,508:00	208,501:00	5,004,024	
1882 (1939)	15,684:04	58,317:08	61,241:00	1,469,784	vs [19]37 inverted (#J10.01)
1883 (1940)	18,647:08	59,776:12	105,608:00	2,534,592	vs 1940 (#J10.02)

According to the Official Gazette of Marwar. NB Copper takkas are meant (1/24 Jodhpur rupee: *KM*#72, Lingen J.10.01-J10.02).

For vs 1940, it is possible that, here, we must add the quantity, equal to Rs. 600, given for Nagaur.

TABLE I.75: COPPER TAKKA PRODUCTION, JODHPUR, 1884/5-1891/2

CE (VS)	*Value in Rs*	*Amount of copper takkas*	*Known VS dates (Lingen 2012, 123, #J10.02 and #J10.03)*
1884/5 (1941)	425,802	10,219,248	VS 1941 (#J10.02)
1885/6 (1942)	4,886	117,264	VS 1942 (#J10.02 and J10.0/3)
1886/7 (1943)	not ascertained		VS 1943 (#J10.03)
1887/8 (1944)	11,147	267,528	only a pie (#J10.05)
1888/9 (1945)	418,725	10,049,400	VS 1945 (#J10.02)
1889/90 (1946)	no return		VS 1946 (#J10.02)
1890/1 (1947)	16,714	401,136	VS 1947 (#J10.02)
1891/2 (1948)	no data		VS 1948 (#J10.02)

Note: Webb 1893, 49 (who provides also the silver and gold coin production, which is omitted here). NB Copper takkas (*KM*#72; Lingen J10.2/3).
Sources: Webb 1893, 37-52; Lingen 2012, 205-7; Garg 2022, 51, 78, 381-5, 388-9, 553-5, 594-9; *SACPM* 2013, 18, 332-9.

Jowrah

See Jaora.

Junagadh

Junagadh State mint. 1869 manually coining silver korees (kori *KM*#23 and ½ kori *KM*#13; 1860-3/4: 3,700,104 pieces) and copper dokras (hammered copper dokdos coined 1823-1909); these coins only current in the state. 1894 circulation of silver Dewanshai kori (2/5 tola; 5/8 fineness) and ½ kori; the proportion of half koris to koris current in the state appears to be approximately 4 per cent to 5 per cent.

Garg 2022, 356-9, 530, 660-1; *SACPM* 2013, 339-41.

Kadapa

See Cuddapah.

Kadri

Mysore mint.
SACPM 2013, 197.

Kalat

Kalat State mint. Now in Pakistan.
SACPM 2013, 341.

Kalayani / Kallian / Basavakalyan

Hyderabad Feudatory State of Elichpur mint.
SACPM 2013, 309-10.

Kalikut / Calicut / Khozhikode

Mysore mint.
Mitchiner 1989, I, 235; *SACPM* 2013, 191.

Kalpi

Suri and Mughal mint.
Goron and Goenka 2001, 92; *SACPM* 2013, 18.

Kalsia

Kalsia State mint. 1869 the ancestors of the present Sirdar struck silver and copper coins, similar to those of Jagadhri; 1870 mint not to be reopened; 1894 only British Indian rupees in circulation. See also Chhachrauli.

Garg 2022, 349-50, 670; Neogy in Garg 2022, 159; *SACPM* 2013, 341; See also Jagadhri.

Kannauj / Qanauj (Shahgarh Qanauj, Shergarh)

Suri and Mughal mint.
Goron and Goenka 2001, 93; Garg / Hodivala 2014, 117-22; *SACPM* 2013, 19.

Kanpur

Mint for counterfeit Lucknow pice around 1870. For details, see Gerowli.

Karanja

Hyderabad Feudatory State of Elichpur mint.
SACPM 2013, 309.

Karauli (Sawai Jaipur)

Karauli State mint, founded by Maharaja Gopal Singh *c.* 1780. 1834 copper coins of 18.21 grams, 1/36 rupee, current in Delhi and Karauli. 1869 coining no gold, but silver rupees and copper pice (2,660 to the maund, 18 mashas each, and ordinarily 1/44, but now 1/52 rupee); 1869 average annual output Rs. 85,000 with a state profit of Rs. 405 (supposedly only silver; *KM*#44.2):

TABLE I.76: COIN (SILVER AND POSSIBLY ALSO COPPER) PRODUCTION, KARAULI, 1867-69

Year Samvat	*Amount coined (Rs.)*	*Balance profit to state (Rs.)*
1924	18,596	5
1925	149,247	810
Half year 1926	43,760	198
Total	211,603	1,031
Average per year	84,641	405

TABLE I.77: COIN (SILVER AND COPPER) PRODUCTION, KARAULI, 1872/3-1875/6 (GOVT Rs.)

	1872-3	*1873-4*	*1874-5*	*1875-6*
	Amount	*Amount*	*Amount*	*Amount*
Silver	1,207	31,200	49,980	29,024
Copper	81,302			

Note: Silver (most likely also *KM*#44.2) and copper (possibly *KM*#51).

TABLE I.78: COIN PRODUCTION, KARAULI, 1885-90 (GOVT Rs.)

Samvat (CE)	*Silver rupee (KM#70), 170 grains*	*Copper takka (KM#51), 280 grains, 1/2660 maund*	
	Weight (maunds:seers)	*Weight (maunds:seers)*	*Tale*
1942 (1885)	0:24.75	1,512:08	
1943 (1886)	1:01.00	1,273:25	
1944 (1887)	15:22.50	135:23	
1945 (1888)	13:04.00	0	
1946 (1889)	18:25.75	0	
1947 (1890)	9:30.75	0	
Subtotal		2,920:00	7,767,200
Annual average			2,589,067

Note: 1894 circulation of 1,000,000 Karauli rupees (15/16 tola or 11.25 mashas; fineness 96.2) and 250,000 government rupees.
Sources: Prinsep 1834, 52; Webb 1893, 119-22; Garg 2022, 54, 78, 335, 390-1, 405, 557-8, 598, 600, 683; *SACPM* 2013, 341-3.

Karikal

French India mint.
SACPM 2013, 395.

Karur

Mint under the Nawabs of Arcot, 1734-44.
Mitchiner 1998, II, 233-4, 236; cf. *SACPM* 2018, 233-5.

Kashmir

Kashmir State mint at Shrinagar for the Kashmir Sultans and the Mughals since 1371; 1847 Sikh mint, coining silver rupees; 1869 formerly several mints, but now only at Srinagar and Jammu.

TABLE I.79: RUPEE PRODUCTION, KASHMIR, 1872/3-1875/6

	1872-3		1873-4		1874-5		1875-6	
	Amt	*Value*	*Amt*	*Value*	*Amt*	*Value*	*Amt*	*Value*
Silver *KM*#Y16b			450,069	281,293	319,453	199,658	332,969	208,106

Note: 1894 Circulation of chilkia/ chilkis (= 10 annas British Indian) and khams (= 8 annas British Indian). In addition to British Indian two, four, and eight anna coins, 'there being no State small silver coins' (in fact there was a small circulation of ⅛, ¼ and ½ rupee fractions), British Indian copper was also current (½ paisa, paisa, ½ anna, and anna) alongside State copper coin (at the rate of ⅛ anna). Total circulation: Rs. 5,811,087 were received into the State treasuries during vs 1950 (1893) and Rs. 7,784,746 were paid out, while in that year the cash balance of the state was Rs. 2,076,000, of which 193,000 British Indian rupees.
Sources: Goron and Goenka 2001, 466; Garg 2022, 78, 83, 320, 333, 351-4, 508-9, 528-9, 598, 644-5, 650, 680-1; Neogy in Garg 2022, 160-1; *SACPM* 2013, 343-5.

Katak / Cuttack / Katak Benares

Mughal and Maratha mint. Now in Pakistan.
SACPM 2013, 18, 186-7.

Kaveripak / Cauvereepauk

Mughal mint.
Garg / Hodivala 2014, 62-4; *SACPM* 2013, 70.

Khairabad

Mughal mint.
SACPM 2013, 18.

Khairpur

State in Sindh (now Pakistan). 1894 no mint, but its older Khairpuri challan or Sahrabi rupees (weight 31/32 tola; fineness of old ones 13-14/16 and new ones 13/15) still circulating currently in the bazaars, mainly of the Shikarpur district, in total 8,000 to 10,000.
Garg 2022, 679-80; not in *SACPM* 2013.

Khaliqabad

See Dindigul.

Khambat / Cambay

Mughals and later Khambat State mint. 1869 one mint at Cambay, manually coining silver rupees; average annual output in ten years Rs. 100,000; current only within state limits, in addition to copper falus, ½ paisa, and paisa coins.

TABLE I.80: RUPEE PRODUCTION, KHAMBAT, 1872/3-1875/6 (GOVT Rs.)

Rupees (KM#Y1)	*1872-3*	*1873-4*	*1874-5*	*1875-6*
	Value	*Value*	*Value*	*Value*
Silver	20,234	38,560	98,603	261,243

Note: 1894 circulation of Cambay rupee (92/96 tola; fineness 70/96 pure silver and 22/96 alloy). Total circulation: Rs. 200,000 British Indian, Rs. 300,000 Babasahi or Gaikwar coins, Rs. 1,000,000 Cambay coins.
Sources: Garg 2022, 77, 334, 356-9, 533, 598; *SACPM* 2013, 18, 276-7.

Khanpur

Mint of Bahawalpur. Now in Pakistan.
SACPM 2013, 248-50.

Khetri

Feudatory of Jaipur State, housing 19 mints, c. 1868-70 coining counterfeit pice of several neighbouring states from locally won copper ore. First mentioned in 1834 with reference to coppers of 16.33 grams. See also Churawa and Surajgarh.

Prinsep 1834, 52; Webb 1893, 81-2; Lingen and Lucassen 2007 (see Part I: Studies, No. 12 in this volume); Lucassen 2007, 369, 380-2 (see Part I: Studies, No. 13 in this volume); Garg 2022, xliii-xliv, liv, 73, 95, 301, 310, 396, 424, 514-18, 587; Neogy in Garg 2022, 154-6; not in *SACPM* 2013.

Khitta

See Awadh.

Khujista Bunyad

See Aurangabad.

Khurshed Sawad

See Dharwad.

Kishangarh

Kishangarh State mint, two or three hundred years old; 1853 or 1863 coining 1,000 gold mohurs (*KM* Y#A1) and annually 5,000-8,000 silver rupees (*KM* Y#1.1, 1.2); 1870 Rs. 25,000 annually in silver rupees (*KM* Y#1.1, 1.2); circulating in Kishangarh State. 1886 contracted out the striking of the copper coinage (*KM* C#24, 25) for a sum of Rs. 3,000 per annum. Stopped because of contractors' malpractice. 1894 circulation of Chobbannia (also called Chaubisania) rupees (67/72 tola and 18.75 per cent alloy) is estimated at 2,500,000, ten years later at 2,000,000.

NAI, Residencies, Jaipur Agency S. No. 105, File No. 4 / 1902-15; Webb 1893, 67-8; Garg 2022, 55, 78, 335, 398-9, 407, 560-1, 612, 654; *SACPM* 2013, 345-6.

Kitturu

Mint in the southern Deccan. 1821 coining (in addition to Shahpur itself) Shahpoor rupees, abolished by the Bombay government in 1823.

Maheshwari and Wiggins 1989, 64; Stevens in Garg 2022, 195-7; not in *SACPM* 2013.

Kochi / Cochin

Mint for Portuguese India, Dutch India (VOC), and Kochi State. 1869 one mint at Kochi, producing silver fanams: single poottens at 10 pies (*KM*#5) and double poottens at 1 anna 10 pies (*KM*#6); last coinage 1857-8; 1870 only coined occasionally.

Garg 2022, 77, 342; Neogy in Garg 2022, 161, 341-2; *SACPM* 2013, 279, 397-400; Scholten 1950; Passon 2022.

Kolhapur

Kolhapur State mint in Southern Maratha country. Abolished by the British 1823; 1869-70 reported as having abandoned coining since the mid-century; 1870 not to be reopened. See also Shahapur.

Maheshwari and Wiggins 1989, 64-6; Garg 2022, 23, 80-1; Neogy in Garg 2022, 153, 159; Stevens in Garg 2022, 197; *SACPM* 2013, 346-7.

Kolkata

See Calcutta.

Kora

Awadh mint 1727-95 (mainly rupees but also golden ashrafis and copper falus in 1780).

Kapoor and Master 2018, xxii-xxxiv.

Kotah

State. 1838 loses Jhalawar, which then becomes independent, including the mint at Jhalra Patun, established for Kotah in 1801. Mint privilege *c.* 1715 but only in operation by permission of Emperor Mahomed Shah (1719-48). 1834 square copper coins of 17.82 grams, 1/34 rupee, current in Kotah, Ajmer, etc. and average silver coinage at three mints (Kotah, Jhalra Patun, and Gagraun) of 3,500,000 per year. 1869-70 one mint at Nandgaon, coining gold, silver, and copper pice (1 tolah 6 mashas; value 1/3 anna); 1870 retaining of the mint recommended.

TABLE I.81: COIN PRODUCTION, KOTAH, 1859/60-1868/9 (Rs.)

	Denominations coined					Gross state income
	Rupee KM Y#6	*8 anna KM Y#5*	*4 anna KM Y#4*	*2 anna KM Y#3*	*Takka KM Y#2*	
1859/60						10,404
1860/1						16,574
1861/2						3,358
1862/3						9,865
1863/4						10,321
1864/5	8,051,064	5,174	1,940	384	49,680	8,723
1865/6						12,570
1866/7						9,198
1867/8						10,582
1868/9						9,908
Average 1864-8 (Rs.)	1,610,213	1,035	388	77	9,936	
Ibid. (tale)	1,610,213	2,070	1,552	616	476,928	

Note: Gross state income, without deduction of establishment (Rs. 453 per mensem).

TABLE I.82: SILVER COIN PRODUCTION, KOTAH, 1872/3-1875/6 (GOVT Rs.)

	1872-3	*1873-4*	*1874-5*	*1875-6*
	Value	*Value*	*Value*	*Value*
Silver	1,606,357	1,625,223	1,619,625	1,263,312

Notes: 1894 circulation of Kotah Hali rupee (11 mashas 5 ratis British Indian weight; alloy 100 silver and 2⅛ alloy) 2,500,000 or 92 per cent, British Indian rupees 6 per cent, Madan Shahi rupees (from Jhalawar and Bundi) 2 per cent per cent.
Sources: Prinsep 1834, 52; Webb 1893, 91-4; Garg 2022, 78, 311, 335, 408-9, 418-20, 561-3, 597, 655-6; Neogy in Garg 2022, 159; *SACPM* 2013, 347-9.

Kotlah

See Maler Kotlah.

Kuchaman / Koochawun

This mint was originally at Ajmer but moved to Kuchaman when Ajmer was taken by the Marathas. 1870 Jageerdar's mint, belonging to the Thakoor of Kuchaman, subject to Marwar (Jodhpur), coining only Kuchaman rupees and its fractions of ¼ and ½ (average mint revenue estimated at Rs. 8,000 per year).

TABLE I.83: SILVER COIN PRODUCTION, KUCHAMAN, 1872/3-1875/6 (GOVT Rs.)

	1872-3		*1873-4*		*1874-5*		*1875-6*	
	Amt	*Value*	*Amt*	*Value*	*Amt*	*Value*	*Amt*	*Value*
Silver	162,339	121,754	98,449	73,837	182,764	137,073	215,354	161,515

Sources: Webb 1893, 49-52; Lingen 2012, 174-181; Garg 2022, 79, 309-12, 385, 402, 430-2, 553-5, 597; *SACPM* 2013, 339.

Kurrara Gurowlee

See Gerowli

Kutch / Cutch

State. Minting right, allegedly obtained from Muzaffar Shah III of Gujarat. Minting since about SE 1810 = 1753); 1869-70 mint at Bhuj, coining gold mohurs, silver rupees, copper trunbias, dokras, etc. but 'no regular outturn'; its currency circulates in Kutch and its dependency Wagur 1888-94. Hand struck until 1927, subsequently machine struck until 1928.

TABLE I.84: COPPER COIN PRODUCTION, KUTCH 1883/4-1885/6

Denomination	*Identification KM*	*1883/4*	*1884/5*	*1885/6*
Trambiyo (½ dokdo)	Y#30-30.1	?	1,530	0
Dokdo	Y#31-31.1	?	116,391	0
Dinglo (1½ dokda)	Y#32-32.3	?	243,399	47,952
Dhabu (3 dokda)	Y#33	?	812	31,143

(Contd.)

Total in tale	?	362,132	79,095
Rupees equivalent	?	5,328	1,818
Expenditure in striking (Rs.)	?	4,071	1,079
Profit (Rs.)	5,741	1,257	739

TABLE I.85: SILVER KORI PRODUCTION, KUTCH, 1883/4–1885/6

Denomination	*Identification KM*	*1883/4*	*1884/5*	*1885/6*
Kori (total in tale)	Y#35		22,814	22,811
Total in gadianas (alloyed silver)			18,127	17,583
Rupees equivalent				6,018
Expenditure in striking (Rs.)				5,897
Profit (Rs.)		887		121

TABLE I.86: SILVER 2½ AND 5 KORI PRODUCTION, KUTCH, 1883/4-1885/6

Denomination	*Identification KM*	*1883/4 (5½ months active)*	*1884/5*	*1885/6*
2½ kori (total in tale)	Y#36			0
5 kori (total in tale)	Y#37.4			36,603
Total big silver in tale			555,256	36,603
Total in gadianas (alloyed silver)		914,173	1,272,423	84,212
Purchase of silver gadianas	1,284,244	866,844	1,284,244	
Rupees equivalent			732,527	48,288
Expenditure in striking (Rs.)			667,947	45,154
Profit (Rs.)		67,293	64,580	3,134

Sources: Information, received from Jan Lingen (from typed and printed annual reports on the State of Kutch in the Ahmedabad Archives); Bright 1975; Garg 2022, 78, 333, 356-9, 530, 672-3; *SACPM* 2013, 349-58.

Lahore

Mint belonging to the Suris, Mughals, Marathas, and Sikh State. Now in Pakistan.

Maheshwari and Wiggins 1989, 157-60; Goron and Goenka 2001, 92; Garg 2022, 508-9; *SACPM* 2013, 18, 179, 206-17.

Lakhnau / Lucknow (Muhammadabad Banaras)

Awadh mint 1775-1858 (mainly rupees and its fractions, incl. ⅛ rupee between 1781 and 1854, and 1⁄16 rupee 1800-53; also golden ashrafis and its fractions; copper 2 falus 1793, falus 1780-1853, ½ falus 1852-53, ¼ falus 1853-55, ⅛ falus 1853).

Kapoor and Master 2018, xxii-xxxiv; *SACPM* 2013, 235-47.

Lakhnauti / Gour / Gaur / Gauda

Bengal Sultans' mint.

Goron and Goenka 2001, 144.

Lashkar

Apparently, from its foundation in 1811, this Gwalior mint was situated in two different buildings, one in the heart of Lashkar city (so-called Lashkar-A), and the other in the Cantonment (Lashkar-B). Lashkar-A coined the silver Gwalior rupee (about Rs. 200,000 in 1870) and the Gwalior pice (most likely *KM*#75); annual output of about 10,000.

Lashkar-B, coined gold mohurs (2,000 annually), silver Chandoree rupees, silver Gwalior rupees (combined output about Rs. 200,000; 'an expert coiner can turn out Rs. 500 diem'), copper Maharaj Sahee pice ('bears a Persian inscription, which is not legible, so most likely *KM*#2331/72), the Gwalior rupee (average annual output 15,000), and Gwalior pice (again, most likely *KM*#75).

TABLE I.87: SILVER COIN PRODUCTION, LASHKAR, 1870, 1891-1900

Dating				*Identification*	*Production*	
Year for which production reported	*KM dating* AH	*KM dating* *Regnal year*	AH / RY *conversion in* CE		*In tolas (rounded off)*	*In rupees*
1870	-	27	1869	*KM*#149 (1/4 rupee); #150 (1/2 rupee); #152 (rupee)		200,000
1891	1309	33	1892	#244 (rupee)	51,958	
1892	13xx	34	1893		655,647	
1893 Jul/Sep					238,816	
1894					11,774	
1895-1900					0	

Sources: NAI, Residences, Central India Agency 813, 1863 Report on the coinage of native states (letter Political Agent at Gwalior to Agent Governor-General for CI Indore, Camp Khokhra, 21 December 1863); idem 839 Pt. III / 1900-2, Particulars regarding Native State mints in central India to which 1876 Act does not apply; Garg 2022, 77, 371-3, 441-7, 539-47; Lingen and Wiggins 1978, 59-73; *SACPM* 2013, 285-99 (my interpretation of dating and mint is different. Ed.).

Leh

Ladakh Kingdom mint.
SACPM 2013, 359-60.

Lisbon

Mint coining for Goa 1901-61. See there.

Loharu

Jaipur State. In 1850, Loharu has 52 mints, employed by local blacksmiths (lohars) and run by Marwaris, coining (from imported copper) coins of thirteen different denominations for Jaipur. After 18 months, all production ceased in 1852. 1868 eight mints reopened, 'which passed the coin in British bazars, even as far off as Calcutta'. 1869 reopening permitted.

1871 mint closed, but successful appeal to the Chief Court of Punjab, 'which reversed the decision and returned all the confiscated coin, on the ground that, as the coin did not purport to resemble anything but what they really were, they were not counterfeit'.

Lucassen 2007, 369 (see Part I: Studies, No. 13 in this volume); Garg 2022, xliv, 166, fn. 56, 577-9; not in *SACPM* 2013.

Lohgarh

Hyderabad Feudatory Elichpur mint.

SACPM 2013, 309.

Lucknow

See Awadh and Lakhnau.

Lunavada / Loonawarrah

State in Bombay Presidency. 1869 mint at Lunavada, only established latterly 'by the tacit permission of the Political Agent', coining manually thick copper Lunawari pice (irregular in form, called 'Loonawarris'; at 80-7 per British Indian rupee; average annual output Rs. 400); current only within the state limits. See also Baroda and Rewa Kantha.

Garg 2022, 78, 87, 320, 334, 356-9, 532; *SACPM* 2013, 360.

Machilipatnam

See Masulipatnam.

Madras (Chennai)

Mughal mint (Santhome of) Mylapur (1704-5). There was also a British mint at Fort St. David active (with interruptions) from 1643 to 1947, including coppers from 1660 onwards. Copper cash production 1679 (probably *KM*#287): 128,000 pieces; 1682-5 138,400 cash pieces (also *KM*#287?) and 345,600 (treble) cash pieces (possibly *KM*#284); 30 April 1740 copper cash coins of about 22.6 troy grains (0.648 grams): '4 candies of copper coined into cash produce 619,020 at 80 cash a fanam and 18 fanams a pagoda' (*KM*#378?); mechanization 1807.

TABLE I.88: COIN PRODUCTION, MADRAS, APRIL 1807-MARCH 1808

Denomination (with weight Proclamation 22 August 1807)	*Metal*	*Year on coin*	*KM#*	*KM weight*	*Tale*
1 fanam	silver	ND (1807) ND (1808)	335,336,337 349	0.92	599,852
2 annas	silver	ND (1808)	405, 406	1,48	22
⅛ rupee	silver	ND	399?	1,51	20,022
2½ cash	copper	ND (1807)	309	1,21	561,622
5 cash (2,42125)	copper	ND (1807)	324	2,41	1,216,822
10 cash (4,8425)	copper	ND (1807)	326	4,83	2,127,922 (plus 600,668 = 2,728,690)
20 cash (9,685)	copper	ND (1807)	328	9,65	3,016,822
40 cash (19,37)	copper	ND (1807)	331.1	19,31	514,922 (plus 131,045 = 645,967)
¼ dub (2,58)	copper	ND (1807)	325	2,57	407,022
½ dub (5,67)	copper	1807	327	5,15	388,272
		1808	345?	4,75	
1 dub (11,34)	copper	ND (1807)	330	10,31	79,222
		1808	346?	10,00	
		1808	347?	9,90	
2 dub (22,68)	copper	ND (1807)	331.1/3?	19,31	2,722 (plus 678 = 3,400)
Regulating dub	copper	1807, 1808	329	7,56	118,272

Note: Minimum number in brackets, struck outside of this period as becomes clear from a comparison with the number in stock on 6 June 1808.

TABLE I.89: SILVER COIN PRODUCTION, MADRAS, 1807-8

Denomination	*Year on coin*	*KM#*	*KM weight*	*Tale 1807-1813*	*Tale new coins from 1813*
1 fanam (silver; ceased 1812)	ND (1807)	335, 336, 337	0.92	1,931,764	0
	ND (1808)	349			
2 fanam (silver; ceased 1812)	ND (1807)	338, 339, 340, 341	1,85	7,333,437	0
	ND (1808)	350			
2 annas (silver)	ND (1808)	405	1,48	64,558	0
⅛ rupee (silver)	ND (1808)	406		20,046	0
	AH1172/6?	408?, 412?	1,51	0	56,019

TABLE I.90: SILVER COIN PRODUCTION, MADRAS, APRIL 1820-MARCH 1821, MAY 1826-OCTOBER 1827, AND 1818/19-1835

Denomination	*Frozen date on coin*	*KM#*	*KM weight*	*Tale 1820/1*	*Tale 1826/7*	*1818/19-1835*
1 anna (silver)	AH1172/6	411	0.73	32,000	2,864,000	Rs. 1,800,000 = 288,000,000 annas or 144,000,000 double annas
2 annas (silver)	AH1172/6	408, 412	1.51	814,000	5,809,000	

Notes: Partially overlapping with the numbers for 1807/8, as reported 12 December 1814.
The Madras 1808 'three fuloos, or one fullum khoord or little fanam' of 7.78 grams listed by Prinsep. For copper coin production at the Madras mint from 1835 until the closure of the Madras mint on 14 August 1869, see Calcutta.
Sources: www.psindiancoins.com; Prinsep 1834, 52; Stephen 2009, 253-5, 273-91; *SACPM* 2013, 70-1 (Mylapore); idem 439-48 (Madras).

Madhupur

Jaipur mint, coining silver and copper. Long since relinquished by 1870.

Garg 2020, 396; *SACPM* 2013, 318-22.

Madurai / Madura

Vijayanagar, Madurai State, and Arcot mint.
Mitchiner 1998, II, 183; *SACPM* 2013, 171, 234.

Magadi

Mint belonging to Kempe Gowda, the Vijayanagar Governor who developed Bangalore.
Mitchiner 1998, I, 248.

Mahé

French India mint.
SACPM 2013, 395.

Mahe Indrapur

See Dig.

Maheshwar

Indore State mint.
SACPM 2013, 311.

Mahi Kantha

Agency encompassing a number of small states in the Bombay Presidency. 1869-70 no more mint and not to be reopened; 1894 no mints.
Garg 2022, 80; Neogy in Garg 2022, 159, 674-8.

Mailapur / Mylapore

Mughal mint, part of Madras.
SACPM 2013, 18.

Makrai

State. Coining counterfeit copper coins. 1846 Raja Devi Shah in Salari village. Official copper pice 1886-1920.

NAI, Residencies, Central India Agency, Indore vernacular; *SACPM* 2013, 360.

Malerkotla / Maler Kotla

Cis-Sutlej State in the Punjab with mint since *c.* 1770. 1869 coining roughly 100,00 silver Kotlah rupees per annum, circulating widely in neighbouring states; 1894 Kotla rupee (11/12 tola, of which silver 65/96 tola; value 11 to 13 annas) chiefly for gifts on the occasion of funerals and weddings. 1908/9 also copper.

Garg 2022, 78, 348-9, 527, 670; *SACPM* 2013, 360-2.

Malharnagar

Indore State mint.

SACPM 2013, 311.

Malot

Suri mint.

Goron and Goenka 2001, 92.

Malpur

Mughal mint.

SACPM 2013, 18.

Mandasor

Gwalior State mint

SACPM 2013, 285.

Mandu (Shadiabad)

Mint belonging to the Malwa Sultans and the Mughals.

Goron and Goenka 2001, 425; *SACPM* 2013, 18.

Mangarh / Mankot

Mughal mint.

Garg / Hodivala 2014, 66-9; *SACPM* 2018, 18.

Manikepur

Mughal mint.

SACPM 2013, 18.

Manipur

State, capital Imphal. In 1869, British Indian and Burmese rupees, 8, 4, and 2 anna pieces in circulation; no circulation of copper and the introduction 'some years ago by the late Dr. Dillon' of pice 'in lieu of the bell-metal coin of the country […] failed utterly […] Copper coins are looked upon with suspicion, their value not being recognized'.

Garg 2022, 518-19; Neogy in Garg 2022, 159; *SACPM* 2013, 172-3.

Marwar (Jodhpur)

State with coinage since 1761. 1834 coining of the Marwar copper of 21.38 grams. In 1870, five mints, viz., four Durbar mints (Jodhpur, Pali, Sujat, Nagore) and one Jageerdar's mint, belonging to the Thakoor of Koochawun, subject to Jodhpur, coining only Koochawun rupees; also a copper mint at Merta. All four Durbar mints coin identical gold Jodhpur mohurs and silver Bijey Sahee rupees; total annual output of all five mints when trade was brisk Rs. 1,000,000-1,200,000, but in 1870 the mints stood (almost) idle, except for the conversion of Akhey Sahee rupees from Jaisalmer into Bijey Sahee rupees; but (formerly?) also coppers circulating generally in Alwar state ('a roughly stamped copper coin […] from Marwar, struck at Joudpore and Pallee […] the average rate being about 40 dhubboos to the Imperial rupee, making 2½ dhubboos equal to one anna').

TABLE I.91: SILVER COIN CIRCULATION, MARWAR, 1894

Rupee	*Specification (tolas and percentage of alloy)*	*Amount*	*Percentage of circulation*
Bijey Shahi	40/41 tolas; alloy 4.5	7,000,000	
British Indian		3,000,000	15

Iktis Sindha coined at Kachawan	38/41 tolas; alloy 35.5		
Akheshahi of Jaisalmer	77/82 tolas; alloy new 2.6; old 7.5		
Chandori	38/41 tolas; alloy 40⅝		
Jharshahi of Jaipur	40/41 tolas; 2.5		
Others			
Total		10,000,000	100

Sources: Prinsep 1834, 52; Lingen 2012; Garg 2022, 78, 309-10, 335, 380-5, 388-9, 402-3, 656-7; *SACPM* 2013, 332-9.

Masudabad

See Najafgarh.

Masulipatnam / Machilipatnam (Bandar)

Mughal and EIC mint, established by Aurangzeb, buying copper from the VOC, for which volume figures are available for the period 1727-40, which can be directly linked to the numismatic data.

TABLE I.92: COPPER PURCHASES AND COPPER COIN PRODUCTION, MASULIPATNAM, 1727/8–1739/40

	Purchase of copper from the VOC by the mint (Dutch pounds)	*Dates (AH plus regnal year of Muhammad Shah) on copper coins of Machhillipatan*	
		Paisa, 13.00-13.87 grams (KM#430.5) AH/RY	*½ dam, 13.00-13.87 grams (KM#429.1)* AH/RY
1727/8	115,200	1140/10 and 11	
1728/9	96,000	1141/10 and 11	1141/11
1729/30	115,200	1142/11 and 12	1142/11 and 12
1730/1	106,080	1143/12	1143/13
1731/2	105,600	1144/14	1144/14
1732/3	96,000	1145/14 and 15	

(Contd.)

1733/4 (data for 5 months missing)	67,200		1146/16
1734/5	111,360	1147/17	1147/17
1735/6	115,200	1148/17 and 18	1148/17 and 18
1736/7	115,200	1149/19	1149/18 and 19
1737/8	117,440	1150/19	1150/19
1738/9	110,960	1151/21	1151/20
1739/40 (data for 4 months missing)	80,640	1152/21 and 22	1152/22

Sources: Shimada 2006, 115; *SACPM* 2013, 117-18.

The paisas are valued in the preservation quality 'fine' at US$10 and the ½ dams at US $20, which suggests that, annually, twice as many paisas were coined as ½ dams. Thus, 80 per cent of the, on average, 50,000 kg (the total amount of Japanese copper) would be spent on paisas and 20 per cent on half dams (40,000 kg divided by 13.5 grams makes about 3 million paisas and 10,000 kg divided by 6.7 gram makes about 1.5 million half dams). 1759 British, minting copper coins of the long series of the previous type (*KM*#D450 for the half paisa and *KM*#E450.2 and *KM*#655 for the paisa, *c.* 13.3 grams) for the Madras Presidency of the EIC until 1808. As there is no way to distinguish between the paisas, called dubs by the British (*KM*#387 weighing 13-14 grams) and those minted by them at Masulipatnam and at Visakhapatnam, available production data have been combined in Table I.93.

TABLE I.93: COPPER COIN PRODUCTION, MASULIPATNAM AND VISAKHAPATNAM, 1753–1803/4

Denomination (KM# under Mughals or EIC, Madras)	*CE*	*AH/RY*	*Production data*			
			Masulipatnam		*Visakhapatnam,*	
			Candies	*Tale*	*Candies*	*Tale*
Paisa (MugE450.2)	1753	1168/1			60	777,600*

(MugE450.2)	1756		10	129,600*		
½ paisa (MugD450)	1758/9	1172/x				
Paisa (MugE450.2)	1759/60	1173/5				
Dub (Mad386)	1760/1	1174/1		?		
Dub (Mad386)	1761/2	1175/4		?		
Paisa (MugE450.2)	1761/2	1175/7				
Dub (Mad386)	1766/7	1180/9		?		
Dub (Mad386)	1772/3	1186/16		?		
Paisa (Mug655)	1773/4	1187/18?	250/300 (request)	3,564,000*		
Paisa (Mug655)	1774/5	1188/xx			60	777,600*
½ dub (Mad385); dub (Mad386)	1775/6	1189/20		?		
Dub (Mad386)	1775/6	1189/25		?		
Paisa (Mug655)	1777/8	1191/xx	100	1,293,343*		
Dub (Mad386)				?		
Paisa (Mug655)	1779/80	1193				
Paisa (Mug655)	1780/1	1195				
Dub (Mad386)	1798/9	1213/xx		?		
Dub (Mad386)	1799/1800	1214/xx		?		

(Contd.)

Paisa (Mug655)	1801	1195?			28 candies, 13 maunds, 13 annas	371,952* 502,250**
Paisa (Mug655)	1802	1195?	>50	>648,000*		
dub (Mad387)	1803/4	1218		?		

Notes: *At 12,960 dubs per candy at the rate in 1773; **at 17,500 dubs per candy as proposed at the rate in 1797.
Sources: www.psindiancoins.com; SACPM 2013, 18, 70-2, 95-6, 105-6, 117-18, 133-4, 139, 439-40 (here named Macchlipattan); Shimada 2006; Scholten 1950; Passon 2022.

Mathura / Muttra

See Vrindavan.

Meerut / Mirath

Mughal mint.
SACPM 2013, 18.

Mercara

See Coorg.

Merta

Marwar mint, coining copper takkas 1787/8-1838 and 1864-71.
Lingen 2012, 30, 81-2; *SACPM* 2013, 139-40 (wrong attribution).

Mewar / Udaipur

State, together with Pertabgarh covering 25,000 square miles where the coinage of Udaipur and Pertabgarh have currency. 1834 the Meywar copper of 2.20 grams, or 1/370 rupee; possibly also the 'Nugur pysa' of 'Sopoor' (Shahpur?) of 11.21-11.40 grams, 'so called by the Natives' (marked 'Nugur 5221', device a rude elephant, some have 'Pun, Putun' or 'Zurb-i-putun'). 1869-70 four Durbar mints: Udaipur, Umrara / Umarda (coining dhingla paisas), Chittor (coining the trisulia paisas), Bhilwara (coining the Bhilwarra paisas), and two Jageerdar's mints (Soolumber and Bhinda); 1870 three subordinate mints (Saloomber, Bhina, Shahpoora); suppression of the mint considered difficult.

TABLE I.94: SILVER COIN CIRCULATION, MEWAR, 1894

Rupees from state mint	*Specification (tolas and percentage of fineness)*	*Output Udaipur mint last 10 years*	*% of circulation*
Old Udaipuri, coined until 1846	5/6 tolas; fineness 75		12
Chittori, coined until 1846	5/6 tolas; fineness 75		10
Sarup Shahi, introduced by Maharana Swarup Singhji (*KM* Y#11)	6.25 higher value than the preceding rupees; fineness 80	2,266,181	75
Chandori for presentations	5/6 tolas; fineness 60	64,303	3
Total			100
Salim Shahi current in the Sadri district, adjoining Pertabgarh		?	
Government		?	5% of local coin

Note: 1894 Mewar provides Shahpura with currency.
Sources: Prinsep 1834, 52; Webb 1893, 2-19; Garg 2022, 44, 79, 82, 310, 335, 375-7, 400-1, 657-8, 684; Neogy in Garg 2022, 159; *SACPM* 2013, 362-5.

Mirath

See Meerut.

Mominabad

See Chakan.

Mouza Dar Pulee / Dapewlee

Mint in Angria State (Konkan), at 1.5 kos from Panvel. Mint established in September 1831, coining until 1832 copper dubhoos (value Rs. 2,000, if at 1/50 rupee 100,000), imitations of the Bombay double balemark pice, issued 1802-31 (*KM*#200).

Stevens 2019, 242-5; Stevens in Garg 2022, 230-4; *SACPM* 2013, 433.

Mouza Gowan / Gonhan

Mint in Angria State (Konkan), at 4 kos from Panvel. Mint, established in August 1831, coining until 1832 copper dubhoos (value Rs. 10,000, if at 1/50 rupee 500,000), imitations of the Bombay double balemark pice, issued 1802-31 (*KM*#200).

Stevens 2019, 242-5; Stevens in Garg 2022, 230-4; *SACPM* 2013, 433.

Mouza Kopur / Coper

Mint in Angria State (Konkan), at 1 kos from Panvel. Two mints, established in August 1830, coining until 1832 copper dubhoos (value Rs. 30,000, if at 1/50 rupee 1,500,000), imitations of the Bombay double balemark pice, issued 1802-31 (*KM*#200).

Stevens 2019, 242-5; Stevens in Garg 2022, 230-4; *SACPM* 2013, 433.

Mow

Boondelkund mint, Jhansie, British Territory. 1871 in and around Mow in Jhansie; production of counterfeit coin, especially old Lucknow coin for the Central Provinces.

Garg 2022, 579.

Muazzamabad

See Gorakhpur.

Mudhol

Mint in southern Maratha country, closed by the British in or before 1823.

Maheshwari and Wiggins 1989, 70; Stevens in Garg 2022, 197; not in *SACPM* 2013.

Muhammadabad

See Udaipur.

Muhammadabad

See Champanir.

Muhammadabad Benares

See Lakhnau.

Muhammadnagur

See Golconda.

Muhiabad

See Pune.

Mulher (Aurangnagar)

Mughal and Maratha mint.

Maheshwari and Wiggins 1989, 72-4; *SACPM* 2013, 18.

Multan

Mughal and Sikh mint. Now in Pakistan.

SACPM 2013, 207.

Mumbai

See Bombay.

Muminabad

See Vrindavan.

Muradabad

Mughal and Rohilla mint.

SACPM 2013, 18, 204.

Murshidabad

Mughal and EIC (Bengal Presidency) mint. French India also coined an anna bearing the mint name Murshidabad.

Stevens 2012, Chapter 5; *SACPM* 2013, 18, 395, 426-9.

Murtadabad

See Chaul.

Mustafabad

Mint belonging to the Gujarat Sultans.

Goron and Goenka 2001, 356.

Mysore (Nazarbar)

Mysore State mint. No mint of any kind in 1869; 1870 mint not to be reopened.

Garg 2022, 222, 333; Neogy in Garg 2022, 159; *SACPM* 2013, 190-203, 365-7.

Nabha

State. Mint established under Sikh rule at Nabha. 1869 coining gold mohurs only occasionally, and silver Nabah rupees, current in neighbouring markets, but not to any great extent. 1894 State rupees (weight 11.25 mashas, of which 5.5 ratis is alloy) are only used on ceremonial occasions. Also gold mohurs.

Garg 2022, 79, 347-48, 526-7, 669; *SACPM* 2013, 367-8.

Nagar / Nuggur

Mysore mint until 1810 (gold, rupees and fractions 1782-1810; copper 1783-99). Stamps sent up to Astagram 1833.

NAI, Foreign Department, Political Consultations, 2 August 1833, No. 36 (letter from the Resident to the Acting Secretary for the Affairs of Mysore Bangalore, Mysore Residency, 8 July 1833); cf. *SACPM* 2013, 195-203, 366.

Nagar

See Ahmadnagar

Nagaur / Nagor

Marwar (Jodhpur) Darbar mint. 1754-1888 coining silver rupees, copper paisas (dating uncertain), and takkas.

TABLE I.95: SILVER COINAGE, NAGAUR, 1872/3-1875/6 (GOVT Rs.)

	1872-3		*1873-4*		*1874-5*		*1875-6*	
	Amount	*Value*	*Amount*	*Value*	*Amount*	*Value*	*Amount*	*Value*
Silver	4,850 ½	5,002	4,185	4,316	2,111	2,177	2,626	2,708

Note: Production of copper takkas in Samvat 1940 (1883, uncertain which type unless struck with Jodhpur dies that have a star added: *KM#72*): Rs. 600 value or 14,400 (at 24 takkas per rupee). In this case, the Nagaur production must be added to that of Jodhpur.

Sources: Lingen 2012, 30, 44, 54-5, 70, 83-4, 97, 114, 205; Garg 2022, 78, 381-5, 597; *SACPM* 2013, 336.

Nagpur

Bhonsla State mint at Nagpur until annexation by the British in 1853. Coinage of silver rupees, capacity of 30 rupees in one minute, maximum per day 25,000.

TABLE I.96: RUPEE COINAGE, NAGPUR, 1831/2-1840/1

Nagpoor fuslee year	*Rupees*
1247 (1831/2)	1,247,034
1248	1,018,987
1249	468,115
1250	546,308
1251	580,652
1252	1,347,234
1253	1,059,200
1254	820,055

(Contd.)

1255	1,586,292
1256 (1840/1)	1,805,594

Note: 1834 'Near Nagpoor' the 'Hadewa' copper of 19.18 grams and the 'Jubulpoor' copper of 16.85 gram, 1/32.5 rupee, current in the Nerbudda Valley. Capacity of the copper mint in 1847: 32,004 pice per day or Rs. 508 worth of pice: 'Copper was only coined when the scarcity of pice became so great as to be felt as a serious evil. Three times within the last few years the Raja had been urged by the British authorities to coin more pice, the scarcity being grievously felt by the men of the Subsidiary Force. 91,000 rupees' worth had been coined in consequence of this representation within the last six, but only very little within the last three years. The intrinsic value was 1.63 of a rupee, but owing to the scarcity the current value often was 1.57 and 1.56 of a Rupee'. At 1/60 rupee this would mean a production *c.* 5,460,000 pice (*KM*#46). The mint was closed soon afterwards.
Sources: Prinsep 1834, 51; Garg 2022, 64, 73, 507-8; *SACPM* 2013, 186-8.

Nahan

Gurkha Kingdom mint in the Sirmur region.

SACPM 2013, 168.

Nahtarnagar

Arcot State mint.

SACPM 2013, 233-35.

Najafgarh / Masudabad

Mughal mint near Delhi.

SACPM 2013, 139.

Najibabad

Mughal, Rohilla, Awadh, and Sikh mint. From 1783 to 1803 also coining copper falus. Sikh feudatory state mint coining paisas, rupees, and imitations, possibly also as part of the 'Conquered and Ceded Provinces'. 1834 copper coin of 15.75 grams, 1/40 rupee, current in 'Barelly and Rohilkhund').

Prinsep 1834, 52; Lingen and Lucassen 2010/11 (see Part I: Studies, Nos. 8 and 10 in this volume); Kapoor and Master 2018, xxii-xxxiv; Stevens in Garg 2022, 235; *SACPM* 2013, 19, 134, 204, 206, 218.

Nandgoan

Kotah mint between 1869 and 1870, coining gold and silver and copper pice, weighing one tola, six masha or about 27 to the pound (*KMY*#2, takka weighing on average 17.4 grams) value 1/3 anna (or 1/48 rupee); annual output Rs. 200,000 (also given as 300,000 to 400,000), current over Kotah State.

TABLE I.97: COIN PRODUCTION, NANDGAON, 1865-70

	Output over five years (c. 1865-69 probably in rupees)
Rupees (*KMY*#6)	8,051,064
8 anna pieces (*KMY*#5)	5,174
4 anna pieces (*KMY*#4)	1,940
2 anna pieces (*KMY*#3)	384
pice pieces (probably takkas of 1/48 rupee, *KMY*#2)	49,680

TABLE I.98: STATE INCOME FROM THE SILVER MINT, KOTAH, 1859/60-1868/9

	Income derived by the state from the mint in Kotah currency
1859/60	10,404:9:0
1860/1	16,574:3:9
1861/2	3,358:8:3
1862/3	9,865:6:3
1863/4	10,321:2:0
1864/5	8,723:9:3
1865/6	12,570:5:9
1866/7	9,198:6:3
1867/8	10,582:11:3
1868/9	9,908:2:3
	'The profit which the State derives from the mint averages about 8 lakhs [Rs. 800,000] a year' (*SIC*, p. 563)

Note: 1870 retaining of the mint recommended.
Sources: Garg 2022, 78, 311, 335, 408-9, 418-20, 561-3; Neogy in Garg 2022, 159; *SACPM* 2013, 347-9.

Narnaul / Narnol

Suri and Mughal mint.

Goron and Goenka 2001, 92; *SACPM* 2013, 19.

Narsingharh

Bhopal Feudatory Narsingharh mint.

SACPM 2013, 267.

Narwar

State, since 1805 under Gwalior. 1834 'Nurwur' copper of 6.93 grams, current in the 'Nerbudda Territories'.

Prinsep 1834, 52; *SACPM* 2013, 284-300, 368-9.

Nasik / Gulshanabad

Mughal mint from around 1700, later (1750-1818) under the Marathas, and subsequently under the British, who closed it in 1833. There was also a mint at Chandore (also called Chandwad), producing under the same name.

TABLE I.99: SILVER COIN PRODUCTION, NASIK AND CHANDORE, 1818/19-1833/4

Year	*Nasik*				*Chandore/Chandwad*	
	Jaripataka rupee KM #324	*½ rupee* KM #165	*¼ rupee* KM #115	*⅛ rupee*	*Chandore rupee*	*pice*
1234 (1818/19)	X					
1235 (1819/20)	X	X				
1236 (1820/1)	X	X	X	X		
1237 (1821/2)	X					
1244 (1828/9)	X					
1247 (1831/2)	69,383				183,928	Rs. 27,050
1248 (1832/3)	X					

1249 (1833/4)	X		annual average 1823/4-1833/4 together with Ahmednuggur 205,000

Note: Mainly Nasik rupees, called 'Jaripatakas'.
The Chandore rupee denotes a coin, also known from other mints in the first half of the nineteenth century, e.g. Gwalior, Udaipur, and Indore).
Sources: NAI, Foreign Department, Public Consultations (PC) 18 July 1833/ 108-9 (Governor-General's minute on question of equalization in value and weight of the rupees); idem PC 19 June 1834/ 61-6 (Scindia's compliance with the order for the suppression of the mint at Jamgaon); Maheshwari and Wiggins 1989, 75-9; Stevens in Garg 2022, 209-13, 216; *SACPM* 2013, 174-90.

Nasirabad

See Dharwad.

Nawanagar

Nawanagar State area 3,160 square miles. 1869 Nawanagar mint manually coining gold mohurs, but mainly silver 1 koree and ½ korees (1,405,918 korees average annual output, probably all silver denominations in total), also copper.

TABLE I.100: COIN PRODUCTION, NAWANAGAR, 1869-1874/5 (GOVT Rs.)

	*1869**	*1871-7*		*1872-3*		*1873-4*		*1874-5*	
	Value	*Amt*	*Value*	*Amt*	*Value*	*Amt*	*Value*	*Amt*	*Value*
Gold		**							
Silver	1,405,918					311,417	84,941	290,720	82,110
Copper		499,501**	18,348	20,800	558				

Note: *Annual average around this year; **including gold.

The gold coins may be identified as *KM*#11 and 12; the silver coins as *KM*#9 and 10; the copper coins as pieces of 3 dokda dated vs1928 (or 1871; *KM*#17). 1894 circulation of its own silver koris (12/29 tolas; fineness 7/12), in addition to panchias (5 kori; 16/29 tolas and pure silver) and ardhias (2½ kori; 35/58 tolas and pure silver); government rupees 25 per cent of total circulation.
Sources: Garg 2022, 79, 356-9, 530-1, 598-601, 662; *SACPM* 2013, 369-70.

Nazarbar

See Mysore.

Negapatnam / Negapattinam

Mint for Dutch India.

See Introduction, 3c; *SACPM* 2013, 397-8; Scholten 1950; Passon 2022.

Nepal

Independent State, not included in this study, but important for providing coins for parts of northern India. Exportation of Nepalese copper coins to neighbouring parts of India. Circulation of Nepali pice in northern Tirhut in 1792. 1834 two types: one of 13.41 grams 'current in the Turaee', and a pysa, called 'Behadur Sahy' (coined and current in Nipal) of 10.63 grams, 1/80 rupee. 1869 copper coin manufactured in the country, but no production figures available.

TABLE I.101: SILVER COIN PRODUCTION, NEPAL 1872/3-1875/6 (GOVT Rs.)

	1872-3	*1873-4*	*1874-5*	*1875-6*
Silver	642,086	697,383	488,208	442,141

Sources: Prinsep 1834, 27-8, 52; Rhodes et al. 1989; Garg 2022, 518, 598; See Part I: Studies, No. 8 and Part II: Records, No. 3 in this volume.

Nusratabad (Fathpur)

Mughal mint, probably identical with Jaunpur.

Garg / Hodivala 2014, 96-8; *SACPM* 2013, 19.

Orchha

State, capital Taheri / Tehri. The right to mint included when the rajah received the title of Mehinder and the insignia of the Order of the Fish from Delhi; 1818 coinage ordered to be stopped; 1826 silver coinage discontinued; 1845 coining Gujasahee rupees; 1848 daily output 2,500-3,000 Gujasahee rupees; annual earnings for the rajah in 1859 Rs. 45,000. In 1870, it was reported that 'it has been an understood custom, of old standing, to make from time-to-time Balasahi, as well as Gujjasahi pice': possibly identical to the 'Gokoola or Gundasahy' of 6.48 grams, 1/70 rupee, 'Current from Muttra to Mynpooree' as mentioned by Prinsep. The latest dated copper paisas from AH 1282/42 (probably 1865/6, *KM* C#25) and AH-/48 (possibly 1871/2, *KM* C#48). In addition, a centre of counterfeit copper coinage (of Pootlie shaie, Nowabee or Muchlee Shaie of Lucknow, Tirsoolee of Nagpoor, and Bala shaie of Jaloun) at Tehri, Tori Futtehpoor (a dependency of Orchha), and Buncoree Orchha. Having been at work since the mutiny, and tolerated by the British, by 1870 it is inactive; coinage 1872-75 of Rs. 60,000 silver money. Mint closed in 1894 but Gaja Shahi still the most common rupee in circulation and 'used over a large tract of country [in Bundelkhand] for wedding purposes', of which 100,000 in circulation in Kanadhiana State. 1896-1902 still limited numbers of silver money struck for the Besant festival 'to change the year' (1896: Rs. 1,000, 1897: Rs. 4,765, 1898: Rs. 5,200; 1899: Rs. 19,607:5; 1900: Rs. 23,000; 1901: Rs. 26,867:15:9; 1902: Rs. 20,407:12).

NAI, Residencies, Central India Agency 818/ 1870-75, Political Agent for Bundelkhand to the Agent Governor-General for Central India Indore, Nowgong, 31 October 1870; idem 839 Pt. II/ 1895-7 and 839 Pt. III/ 1900-2 Particulars regarding Native State mints in Central India to which 1876 Act does not apply; Prinsep 1834, 51; Garg 2022, xliii, lx, 81, 316, 370, 501-4, 579-80, 690, 703; Neogy in Garg 2022, 153-4; *SACPM* 2013, 370-1.

Owsa

See Ausa.

Pachay Khani

See Gangkok.

Palani

Town mint under Madurai and Mysore in the seventeenth and eighteenth centuries.

Mitchiner 1998, II, 222-3; cf. *SACPM* 2018, 171-2.

Pali

1869-70 Durbar mint of Marwar (Jodhpur), coining silver rupees; but formerly also coppers circulating generally in Alwar state ('a roughly stamped copper coin [...] from Marwar, struck at Joudpore and Pallee [...] the average rate being about 40 dhubboos to the Imperial rupee, making 2½ dhubboos equal to one anna').

TABLE I.102: COIN PRODUCTION, PALI 1872/3-1875/6 (GOVT Rs.)

	1872-3		*1873-4*		*1874-5*		*1875-6*		*1883*
	Amt	*Value*	*Amt*	*Value*	*Amt*	*Value*	*Amt*	*Value*	*Value*
Silver	470,004	484,692	472,283	487,042	349,543	360,466	783,924	808,421	474,152
Copper*									849,683

Note: *This refers to takkas, catalogued as Lingen P.06.01/04 (*KM*#12.2, 13, 14.2); at 40 takkas per rupee the production of vs 1940 (1883), valued at Rs. 849,683:4, would have resulted in 33,987,320 takka pieces.

Sources: Garg 2022, 78, 381-5, 388-9, 597; Lingen 2012, 77-9, 205; *SACPM* 2013, 333-4.

Paliakate / Pulicat

Dutch India mint.

Introduction, 3c; *SACPM* 2013, 397-8; Scholten 1950; Passon 2022.

Panna

Panna State mint in Bundelkhand, coining copper paisas and silver rupees. 1834 the 'Kukurety' of 16.33 grams, 1/40 to 1/48 rupee, which 'bears a device, resembling a Hanooman' circulating in Panna in Bundelkhand. Possibly still active in 1859, but 1869-70 reported to have ceased many years ago.

NAI, Residencies, Central India Agency 811/ 1859-62, Regarding mints in petty native states; Prinsep 1834, 52; Garg 2022, 81, 316, 370; *SACPM* 2013, 371.

Panvel

Angria State. Mints near Panvel 1831-2, see Cusba Apta, Mouza Kopur, Mouza Dar Pulee, Mouza Gowan.

Garg 2022, 230.

Parenda

Mint belonging to the Ahmadnagar Shahs.

Goron and Goenka 2013, 325.

Patan / Anhirwala Patan / Shahr Patan

Mughal mint.

Garg / Hodivala 2014, 156, 418; *SACPM* 2013, 19.

Patan

See Srirangapatnam

Pathankot

Sikh mint.

SACPM 2013, 209.

Patiala

State. Mint since sv 1820 (*c.* 1770); 1834 copper 'Putiala (Rajasahy)' of *c.* 11 grams and current in 'Putiala, Delhi, etc.' recorded 1851; 1869 mint at Patiala, manual (with ten blacksmiths and two coiners) production capacity 2,000 coins per diem, coining gold mohurs and silver Raja Shahee rupees, no copper, but considers coining it.

TABLE I.103: SILVER COIN CIRCULATION, PATIALA, 1894

Rupee	*Weight*	*Fineness*	*Amount*	*Proportion in circulation*
Government	11 mashas, 6 ratis	7.5 ratis copper	?	1/3
Rajeshahi	11 mashas, 1 rati	10 mashas, 5 ratis pure silver; 3.5 ratis copper		2/3
Kotla (for marriages, etc.)	11 mashas (as compared with the above two types sold at a discount of 27 per cent		?	

Sources: Prinsep 1834, 52; Garg 2022, 26, 79, 87, 333, 344-50, 524-6, 561, 578, 598, 600, 668; *SACPM* 2013, 371-3.

Patna (Azimabad)

Mughal mint. British Indian 1765-96, coining gold and silver (including ⅛ and 1/16 rupees), rarely coppers (only copper post office tickets 1774 are known; John Prinsep may have coined at Patna in 1781; pice trial 1794); 1834 'Patna old' copper coin 'of native fabrication', 15.55 grams, *c.* 1/32 rupee and Patna copper coins 1817.

Prinsep 1834, 52; Stevens 2012, 84-5, 114, 183, 220-2, 228; 237; Stevens in Garg 2022, 257-8; *SACPM* 2013, 19, 117, 429.

Penukonda

Vijayanagar mint.

Mitchiner 1998, I, 202-7.

Peshawar

Mughal and Sikh mint. Now in Pakistan.

SACPM 2013, 19, 210.

Phaltan

Copper mint near Pune, belonging – like Watar – to the Nimbalkur (a local Maratha clan). British want it to be stopped 1831, but continued until 1836.

Maheshwari and Wiggins 1989, 82; Stevens 2019, 235; Stevens in Garg 2022, 221; not in *SACPM* 2013.

Pondicherry

French and temporarily also Dutch India mint.

SACPM 2013, 395-8.

Porbandar

State, 561 square miles. 1869-70 mint at Porbandar, manually coining ¼, ½, and 1 silver koris (*KM* C#36-8), and copper (*KM#* C#30-3); these coins only current in this state; *c.* 1870 introduction of British Indian coinage.

TABLE I.104: SILVER COIN PRODUCTION, PORBANDAR, 1872/3-1875/6 (GOVT Rs.)

	Annual average (c. 1869-70)	*1872-4*		*1874-5*		*1875-6*	
	Amt	*Amt*	*Value*	*Amt*	*Value*	*Amt*	*Value*
Silver	565,614	?	?	945,877	356,935	585,715	216,731

Sources: Garg 2022, 79, 356-9, 530-1, 598; Neogy in Garg 2022, 164; *SACPM* 2013, 373.

Pratapgarh / Pertabgarh

State in Rajasthan. Mint opened in 1784, recognized by the British in 1804 and 1818; attempts 1821-5 fail to improve the quality of the Salimsahee rupee and also, ultimately, to close this mint; 1868 not coining gold although permitted, now coining silver rupees; 'Formerly there was also a mint at Pertabghur for copper pice, but it has not been working for a long time past.' Minting Salim Shahi rupees and its fractions ½, ¼, and ⅛ with increasing degree of alloy until 1858 and a new one in 1870.

TABLE I.105 SILVER COIN PRODUCTION, PRATAPGARH, 1872/3-1875/6 (GOVT Rs.)

	1872-4		*1875-6*		*1894*
	Amt	*Amt*	*Value*	*Value*	*Value*
Silver	?	?	16,797	12,114	?

Notes: Copper paisas vs 1936-53 (1878-96). 1894 circulation of 1,500,000 Salim Shahi (11.25 mashas each; also called Paintalis Suna) rupees, currently minted; NB. also 500,000 in Banswara 1,000,000 in Jaora, 20,000,000 in Rutlam, and 500,000 in Sitamau, in addition to Dungarpur, Sailana, Jhabua, etc. Also, three outdated Salim Shahi rupees (Untees Suna, Macdonald Shahi, Patriwala) and 25,000-30,000 British Kaldar (i.e. Government) rupees.
Sources: Webb 1893, 23-6; Garg 2022, 79, 82, 317-18, 335, 373, 377-8, 496-7, 552, 598, 682-3, 691-2; Neogy in Garg 2022, 150-3, 401; *SACPM* 2013, 373-4.

Pudukkottai

Mint belonging to the rajahs of Pudokkottai as dependency of the Thanjavur Marathas, and of Pudokkottai State. 1869 mint at Pudukkottai, coining copper amman cash (*KM*#4; 5 amman cash = 3 pice = ¾ anna, so 1 amman cash equals 1/320 rupee); 1870 only coining occasionally and, from 1886, coinage ordered from Birmingham, subsequently Calcutta (*KM*#6 until 1947).

TABLE I.106 COPPER COIN PRODUCTION, PUDOKKOTAI, 1872/3-1875/6 (GOVT Rs.)

	1872-3		*1873-4*		*1874-6*	
	Amt	*Value*	*Amt*	*Value*	*Amt*	*Value*
Copper	0	0	362,560	1,133	0	0

Sources: Mitchiner 1998, II, 208-9; Garg 2022, 80, 342, 601; Bhandare in Garg 2022, 128; Neogy in Garg 2022, 161; *SACPM* 2013, 203, 374.

Pulicat

See Paliakate

Pultah

Place on the East bank of the Hugli River, just north of Barackpur, where John Prinsep (1748-1830) exploited several enterprises in the 1780s, including a factory, a bazar, the ferry toll in the Grand Trunk Road, and a copper coin factory between 1781 and 1783 (based on archival evidence, cited in Lucassen 2012, cf. Stevens 2012, 114, who – following Pridmore – is mistaken in tentatively locating this mint at Falta, south of Calcutta, or even near the copper mines of Rohtas). It issued pieces of $\frac{1}{16}$, ⅛, ¼, and ½ anna. The total production of these four denominations between 29 November 1781 and 31 October 1783 has possibly amounted to only half of what was intended by the original concession. Although not all available information is consistent, we may assume that in total 6 million pieces would have been struck if only one anna pieces had been made. Taking into account that actually four different denominations (1, ½, ¼, and ⅛ anna) have been made, we may guess that roughly on average slightly more than 3 million of each have been produced by Prinsep.

Prinsep 1834, 51; Lucassen 2012, 23-5; Stevens 2012, 108-39, 163; *SACPM* 2013, 424. See also Part II: Records, Nos. 2 and 8 in this volume).

Pune / Poona (Muhiabad)

Mughal mint from Aurangzeb (mint name Muhiabad urf Pune), followed by the Marathas, minting rupees (Hali Sicca, Ankusi, Pharasi Sicca, 1760-1818), including fractions down to ⅛ rupee; in 1830 also pice (AH 1240, indistinguishable from those minted at Satara; see also there and the British).

TABLE I.107: KNOWN YEARS OF SILVER COINS, PUNE, 1822-34

	Known years AH	CE
ankushi rupee	1232-44	1822-34
ankushi ½ rupee	1233, 1238, 1241, 1242	1823, 1828, 1831, 1832
ankushi ¼ rupee	1233, 1237, 1241, 1242	1823, 1827, 1831, 1832
ankushi ⅛ rupee	1234, 1240	1824, 1830
hali sicca rupee	1230-44	1820-34
hali sicca ½ rupee	1233, 1236	1823, 1826
hali sicca ¼ rupee	1230, 1238	1823, 1826
Pice *KM#72*	1230-5, 1237-40	1820-5, 1827-30.

Note: all (AH 1230, 1237, 1238) wrongly attributed in *KM* to Satara.
Sources: Maheshwari and Wiggins 1989, 83-9; Stevens 2019, 233-4; Stevens in Garg 2022, 202-9, 217-18, 220-4, 229; *SACPM* 2013, 19, 188.

Purandar

Maratha mint.

SACPM 2013, 177. Not in Maheshwari and Wiggins 1989.

Purenda / Parenda

Mughal mint.

Garg / Hodivala 2014, 74; *SACPM* 2013, 19.

Qanauj

See Kannauj.

Radhanpur

Radhanpur State mint in Kathiawar, under British control 1813. In 1869, coining gold mohurs, ¼, ½, and 1 silver rupees (average annual output Rs. 250,000, all denominations in total), and copper pice (*KM#3*; average annual output Rs. 10,000, or – supposing 64 per rupee – 640,000 pieces); current only within the state limits. 1894 coining silver Jorawar Sui rupees, which dominate the circulation in this state and frontier towns.

Garg 2022, 56, 80, 334, 356-9, 665; *SACPM* 2013, 374-5.

Rahimatpur

Maratha and EIC (Bombay Presidency) mint. Copper pice production 1828/9 (*KM#227*), imitations of Bankot pice.

Maheshwari and Wiggins 1989, 90; Stevens 2019, 302-3; www.psindiancoins.com; *SACPM* 2013, 433.

Raisen / Raisen Qila

Suri mint.

Goron and Goenka 2001, 93.

Rajgarh (1)

Mint in Alwar State, established 1772; 1870 average annual coinage, based on production figures (value in Rs.) for VS 1913-25 (1856-68/ AH 1273-85) in silver Rs. 125,000 and in pice Rs. 217,000 (according to an estimate in 1869 resp. Rs. 125,000 and 225,00).

TABLE I.108: RUPEE COIN PRODUCTION, RAJGARH IN ALWAR, 1856-68

VS	*CE*	*Ulwur rupees (KM#37)*	*Pice (1/36 rupee: KM#35.1)*	*Profit to the state*	*Remarks*
1913	1856	105,787	179,136	1,931	
1914	1857	212,730	165,528	2,948	
1915	1858	126,595	149\,416	1,582	
1916	1859	125,018	245,088	2,683	
1917	1860	240,270	253,656	4,090	
1918	1861	35,265	275,760	8,094	
1919	1862	104,321	230,400	3,791	
1920	1863	?	?	?	mint leased out, hence no returns
1921	1864	200,967	170,136	6,248	
1922	1865	215,036	209,952	5,876	
1923	1866	?	?	?	mint leased out for six months

(Contd.)

1924	1867	0	227,548	1,949	
1925	1868	0	290,844	2,598	
Total		1,365,988	2,590,464	36,790	
Annual average		124,180	217,340	3,344	apparently supposing eleven production years for silver and profits, but twelve for copper, whereas data for both for only cover nine years

Sources: Webb 1893, 110-15; Lingen and Lucassen 2007, 201-12 (see Part I: Studies, No. 12 in this volume); Lucassen 2007, 369, 380 (see Part I: Studies, No. 13 in this volume); Garg 2022, 52, 76, 335, 387-9, 406, 558-60; *SACPM* 2013, 231-3.

Rajgarh (2)

State in central India. Mint in Amjhira near Bhopal. 1834 copper coin of 17.75 grams, 1/36 rupee. Mint coining copper coins in 1863. 1894 not coining money, circulation mainly Bhopali rupees, in which revenue paid; also government and other rupees (Hali rupees of Jhalrapatan and of Indore, Mir Khan Shahi rupees, and Chandori rupees from Gwalior).

NAI, Residences, Central Indian Agency, 813/ 1863, Report on the coinage of native states; Prinsep 1834, 52; Garg 2022, 687, 754; not in *SACPM* 2013.

Rajmahal (Akbarnagar)

Mughal mint established by Akbar, also coining copper dams. Most important mint in Bengal in the seventeenth and first part of the eighteenth century; still minting a copper coin of 7.06 grams in 1834, recorded as being 'coined at Rajmahal'.

Prinsep 1834, 52; Prakash 1987, 174-82; Perlin 1993, 258-9; Garg / Hodivala 2014, 91-4, 133; *SACPM* 2013, 71-77, 89, 96-7, 102-3, 107, 115, 121, 130, 134.

Rajod

Gwalior State mint.

SACPM 2013, 285.

Ramnad / Ramnathapuram

Mint of the Sethupatis of Ramnad, feudatories of the Banas, later Nayakas of Madurai, succeeded by the Nawabs of Arcot, *c.* 1450-1792

Mitchiner 1998, II, 178-9, 224-5, 241; not in *SACPM* 2018.

Rampur

See Sunth.

Rampura

Rampura State mint.

SACPM 2013, 376.

Ramudpoor

Mint in an Eenam village in the Meritch Territoree, probably belonging to Holkar (Indore). Since 1832, its pyce were circulating in Pune.

NAI, Foreign Department, Public Correspondence, 31 December 1834 / 12 (Letter Principal Collector to Secretary to Government, Pune, 17 September 1834 (see Part II: Records, No. 28 in this volume).

Rangpur

See Assam.

Ranipur

Town in Bundelkand, Jhansie Division. In 1871, called a great mart for the Central provinces for the purchase of counterfeit copper coin, especially old Lucknow coin.

Garg 2022, 579.

Ratlam

Ratlam State mint abolished by the British 1825; 1845 attempts to reopen it fail, but reportedly open in 1863 coining paisas, valued at 1/24 to 1/26 Government rupee; 1869-70 manually coining copper paisa of 8 mashas in weight or 1/64 Government rupee (total production of Ratlam, Jowrah, and Syllana coppers equals S.S. Rs. 30,000, of which some 13,000 for Joara and maybe 6,000 for Sailana, leaving some 11,000 for Ratlam or roughly 650,000 pieces for *KM*#21); 1894 circulation of 20,000,000 Salim Shahi rupees, coined at Pertabgarh.

NAI, Residences, Central Indian Agency, 813/ 1863, Report on the coinage of native states; Garg 2022, xliii, 80, 334, 367, 496-8, 538, 691-2; Neogy in Garg 2022, 151-2; *SACPM* 2013, 376-7.

Rewa

Rewa State mint in Bundelkhand / Baghelkhand 'under the present Chief's father' [a reference to Viswanath Singh, 1835-43]. As reported in 1869/70, coining silver rupees and copper pice (*KM*#24, 26, and 27 in 1849 and earlier), but no longer kept up; 1870 mint not to be reopened.

Stevens 2012, 492; Garg 2022, 43, 81, 316, 370; Bhandare in Garg 2022, 114-16; Neogy in Garg 2022, 159; *SACPM* 2013, 377-8.

Rewa Kantha

Political Agency encompassing 1870 four petty states with their mints, viz., Baria, Chhota Udaipur, Lunavada, and Sunth; 1834 copper 'Rewasahy, device a kind of Nagaree one' of 14.26 grams, 1/46 rupee. 1870 'The states in question derive a pecuniary advantage from the coinage of their own copper money. The intrinsic value of the British copper coin is, I believe, only one-halve of its value as the legal tender, and that of the Native copper coin is even less in proportion. The States, moreover, call in their copper coins every third year to be re-stamped, receiving them at

72 for the Syasaee Rupee and re-issuing them at 64, deficiencies in the currency being supplied with new coins. The working of this process is generally farmed out to a contractor. The ryots, as a rule, prefer the local currency; they lose by it, it is true, but they do not understand this, and they would rather have 72 paisa of the local currency for the Syasaee Rupee than 56 of the Government currency, as their dealings being in a very small way, they consider that the former go further than the latter. The loss by the suppression of the local currency must fall either on the State or on the ryots. Whatever precaution we might take, the former would be certain not to be the loser, and if the local coin were declared to be no longer a legal tender, the copper coin in the possession of the ryots would not fetch as bullion more than 6 annas in the rupee. There being no Government Treasury attached to this Agency, there are no facilities for the introduction of the Government coinage, so as to reach the pockets of the ryots. Many copper local coins of various denominations are in circulation within the States under notice. They are all of lower value than the Government currency, and by their means commodities can be purchased in more infinitesimal quantities; they are, therefore, more suited to the wants of the bulks of the inhabitants, many of whom are miserably poor, and live from hand to mouth. [...]'. 1872 introduction of the British Indian copper coinage on the understanding that no more coin should be issued by the states from their own mints. 1894 the Baroda silver rupee (59/60 tola; 177 grains) is commonly current in the bazaars of each state. 1894 currency in Shihasai: the Godhra Treasury, some 50,000 rupees, 'or about half the total cash in hand – is kept uselessly locked up in the shape of Shihasai coin' without the possibility of conversion into government coin. See also separately Baria, Chhota Udaipur, Lunavada, and Sunth.

Prinsep 1834, 52; Neogy in Garg 2022, 163; Garg 2022, 332, 336, 573-6, 666, 737-9.

Sagar / Saugor (Ravishnagar Sagar)

Maratha mint since 1779, coining silver and copper. Conquered by the British in 1818. 1834 ancient square copper paisa of Sagar district, called 'Nazir Shah (son of Ghias-ud-din Shah)' of 8.49

grams. Under the Bengal Presidency a new mint built in 1824, coining silver and copper.

TABLE I.109: COPPER COIN PRODUCTION, SAGAR, 1827/8-1832/3

Milled trisul pice (KM#A65, 71 and 72)	*In Rupees*	*In Tale*
1827/8	6,898	
1828/9		
1829/30	82,700	
1830/1	40,828	
1831/2	73,207	
1832/3	79,755	
Total	283,388	18,136,832
Annual average		3,627,366

Sources: Prinsep 1834, 25, 52, 58; Maheshwari and Wiggins 1989, 122-7; Stevens 2012, 479-8; Stevens in Garg 2022, 236; *SACPM* 2013, 175, 425.

Saharanpur

Mughal and 1788-1803 Maratha mint, coining rupees and extensively copper. Ceded to the British in 1803. It continued coining rupees, dated AH 1218-20 (1803-5/6), and possibly also coppers, as part of the 'Conquered and Ceded Provinces'. 1834 copper 'Suharunpoor / Aulumshahy' of 16.52 grams.

Prinsep 1834, 52; Maheshwari and Wiggins 1989, 162-72; Stevens in Garg 2022, 235, 250; *SACPM* 2013, 19, 188.

Sahrind

See Sarhind.

Sailana

Sailana State mint, probably resulting from the division of the Rutlam and Sailana territories. In 1869-70 mint at Sailana, manually coining copper: 'Has no coinage of its own, but generally stamps false copper coins of other states of less than the legal standard. Is the general resort of dealers in false copper coinage.

Owing to the Rutlam mint having for the last few years ceased to issue false coins, the out turn of this mint has greatly increased' (total production of Ratlam, Jowrah, and Syailana coppers equals S.S. Rs. 30,000).

TABLE I.110: COPPER COIN PRODUCTION, SAILANA, 1872/3-1875/6 (GOVT Rs.)

	1872-3		*1873-4*		*1874-5*		*1875-6*	
	Amt	*Value*	*Amt*	*Value*	*Amt*	*Value*	*Amt*	*Value*
Copper	432,000	6,171	601,094	8,839	1,306,222	18,913	1,260,000	18,260

Note: Annual average production for the paisa (*KM#5*) 1872-75 is 899, 829 pieces. 1894 circulation of Salim Shahi rupees coined at Pertabgarh.
Sources: Garg 2022, 80, 94, 368, 539, 599, 692; *SACPM* 2013, 378-9.

Sakkarai Kotai / Sakkar Kot

Mysore State mint.
SACPM 2013, 200.

Sakkhar

Mughal mint.
SACPM 2013, 72.

Salamabad

See Satyamangalam.

Salari

Mint where 1846 Raja Debi Shah of Makrai makes counterfeit coins.

NAI, Residences, Central India Agency, Indore Vernacular F40/ 1846.

Salem

Mint under the Hoysala, Kongu Cheras and Vijayanagar, *c.*1300-1800

Mitchiner 1998, II, 24-33, 58-9, 151, 155-8, 221, 241, 243; not in *SACPM* 2018.

Salimabad

See Ajmer.

Salumba / Salumbar / Soolumber

Subsidiary or jageerdar's Mewar Feudatory Salumba State mint. 1879-70 coining only copper pice (the padam sahi paisa, also called salumba dhingla from 1804/48 to 1870) from locally mined very fine copper ore; 1870 suppression of the mint recommended, but considered difficult.

Webb 1893, 16; Garg 2022, 79, 82, 310-11, 335, 373, 376, 401; Neogy in Garg 2022, 159; *SACPM* 2013, 365.

Sambhal

Suri and Mughal mint.

Goron and Goenka 2001, 92; *SACPM* 2013, 19.

Samthar / Sumpthur

State in Bundelkhand. British ordered closure of the mint in 1818 and permitted coining of their money at Saugar.

Garg 2022, 503; Neogy in Garg 2022, 152, 166, n. 41.

Sant and Santrampur

See Sunth.

Sarhind / Sahrind

Mughal mint.

Garg / Hodivala 2014, 115-17; *SACPM* 2013, 19.

Sarkunda Bunyad

See Secunderabad.

Sashti / Sasti

Maratha mint, located in Chandrapur district of Maharashtra.
SACPM 2013, 175, 186; not in Maheshwari and Wiggins 1989.

Satara

Deccan. Maratha mint coining in 1830 copper pice (AH 1240, *KM*#72), indistinguishable from those of Pune. Continued under the British, who took the Deccan in 1818, until 1831. 1869-70 no mint; 1870 mint not to be reopened.

Maheshwari and Wiggins 1989, 93-4; Stevens 2019, 233-6; Garg 2022, 80; Neogy in Garg 2022, 159; Stevens in Garg 2022, 220-4; *SACPM* 2013, 188.

Satyamangalam / Sathi (Salimabad)

Mysore State mint.
Mitchiner 1998, I, 191, 235.

Sawai Jaipur / Sawai Madhupur

See Jaipur and Karauli.

Sawantwadi / Sawant Waree

Mint at Wadi of the Marathas and of Sawantwadi State, abolished by the British 1845; by 1870 it had been closed for twenty years and was not to be reopened.

Maheshwari and Wiggins 1989, 100-2; Garg 2022, 73, 80, 315, 320, 329, 355, 533; Neogy in Garg 2022, 153, 159, 161; *SACPM* 2013, 175.

Secunderabad / Sikanderabad (Sarkunda Bunyad)

Hyderabad State mint.
SACPM 2013, 302.

Seronje

See Sironj

Shadiabad

See Mandu.

Shahabad

Durbar mint of Jhalawar State (dating 'from former times' and ascribed to the 'Nurwur dynasty'). 1869-70 coining silver rupees, comparatively small output; 1870 abolishment recommended.

Garg 2022, 78, 81, 311, 314-15, 335.

Shahapur / Sholapur

Maratha mint near Belgaum in the Deccan, coining copper pice until 1817/18 when abolished by the British. See also Belgaum.

Maheshwari and Wiggins 1989, 94; Stevens in Garg 2022, xlvii, 194-202; not in *SACPM* 2013.

Shahjahanabad

See Delhi.

Shahpur / Shahpura

Mewar Feudatory State Shahpur(a) mint, also holding an estate in the Ajmere district, directly from the British government. 1675 mint privilege from Aurangzeb and coining since 1760/85: gold, silver (the Gyarsanah, Ageeara Sahee, or Igarahsanah rupee with fractions ½ and ¼), and coppers (the Madho Shaii in the period 1827-45). Prinsep 1834 mentions the Madhosahy of 17.50 grams, 1/35 to 1/40 rupee as the 'chief currency of Allahabad and the Doab, formerly of Benares and Mirzapore'; in addition to the Chikna of 15.55 grams, 1/30 to 1/32 rupee as 'the Madhosahy worn smooth' and circulating 'throughout Banda' and under the name Chulun in the Doab.

TABLE I.111: RUPEE COIN PRODUCTION, SHAHPUR, 1858/9-1866/7

Samvat (CE)	*Output in Rs.*	*State income*
1915 (1858/9)	31,826	
1923 (1865/6)	20,611	
1924 (1866/7)	18,130	
Total in ten years*	70,567	674:10:9 Shahpura currency 442:12:0 government currency

Notes: Mainly rupees, only few gold mohurs.
Copper 'Madho Shahee' pice of 8 masas (*KM*#10), coined only until 1836. 'They are in circulation in the capital, but their tender is confined to the sale and purchase of cotton and thread, and the payment of town dues. In all other dealings, and in the villages of the state, Chirawa pice (a currency imported from Bhawana of Hansi [Jhansi?] and Khetree of Jeypore) are used'. This may be identical to the 'Chinawa' of 12.31 grams mentioned by Prinsep. Closure of the mint recommended by the British; 1871 not approved by the Governor-General, expected to die a natural death. 1894 no state mint any more, currency obtained from Mewar.
*The text gives eleven years (p. 424), but also '27 years since the mutiny' (p. 566), which probably should be read as '2.7 years'.

TABLE I.112: RUPEE CIRCULATION, SHAHPUR, 1894

Rupees	*Weight*	*Alloy*	*Amount*
Chittori (rupee of Mewar)	80/96 tola	25.8	1,000,000
Gyara Sunna (older than Chittori)	45/48 tola	37.7	60,000
British Indian			100,000
Total			1,160,000

Sources: Prinsep 1834, 51-2; Webb 1893, 17-19; Garg 2022, 65, 80, 82, 87, 310-11, 315, 319, 329-36, 373-7, 411-14, 423-5, 449, 452, 517, 551, 566-70, 572, 684; Neogy in Garg 2022, 158, 163; *SACPM* 2013, 365, 379.

Shahr Patan

See Patan.

Sheopur

Gwalior State mint.
SACPM 2013, 285.

Shergarh

See Delhi and Kannauj.

Sherkot

Mughal mint.

Garg / Hodivala 2014, 85; *SACPM* 2013, 19.

Sherpur

Mughal mint, possibly identical with Ghazipur.

Garg / Hodivala 2014, 32, 40, 44; *SACPM* 2013, 19.

Sholapur / Solapur

Mughal and Maratha mint.

Maheshwari and Wiggins 1989, 94; *SACPM* 2013, 19, 180, 186.

Shorapur

Hyderabad Feudatory Shorapur mint.

SACPM 2013, 310.

Srinagar

Kashmir Sultanate, Mughal, and State mint. In 1869, manual production capacity of silver Srinuggur rupees Rs. 1,159,920 annually (or 3,222 melting, but 10,000 to 15,000 hammering capacity per day), fluctuating output; also coining copper pice. 1895 old coin (Chilki rupees, valuated at 10 annas and the great bulk of the currency) now in the mint: Rs. 350,000.

Goron and Goenka 2001, 463-84; Garg 2022, 78, 333, 351-4, 740-1; Neogy in Garg 2022, 160-1; *SACPM* 2013, 19, 343-5.

Sikh

State. Prior to 1839 a multitude of mints coining the Pooranah rupee (1785-1813), the Chulnee rupee (1813-23), and the Chitta rupee (1823-47). From 1839, only two mints left, at Lahore and Amritsar, coining gold, silver and copper. 1847 British suggestions for improvements, including in Jallandar and Kashmir. See also Chhachrauli, Dera, and Najibabad.

Garg 2022, 508-9; *SACPM* 2013, 206-18.

Sikkim

See Gangkok.

Sindh

State. 1869 no mints and circulation of only British Indian coins. See also Khairpur.

Garg 2022, 81, 355, 533, 679-80; not in *SACPM* 2013.

Sirohi

State in Rajputana with mint coining coppers. Active 1847, but not in 1863 and 1870.

Garg 2022, 83, 391-3, 404, 557; Neogy in Garg 2022, 159, 161; *SACPM* 2013, 379.

Sironj / Seronje

Mughal mint and, 1736-1817, Maratha mint coining silver. After 1817 to Tonk, minting silver rupees, current in Seronje (1,000 square miles) and pice (containing 16 mashas of copper or 1/56 rupee; *KM* Y#3).

TABLE I.113: RUPEE PRODUCTION, SIRONJ, 1866/7-1870

	Paisa pieces
1866/7	29,400
1867/8	12,656
1868/69 (January-August)	125,776
Total	167,832
Annual average 1866-9	55,944
Annual average 1865-70	54,700

TABLE I.114: RUPEE PRODUCTION, SIRONJ, 1870-1875/6 (GOVT Rs.)

	1865-70	*1870*	*1872-3*	*1873-4*	*1874-5*	*1875-6*
Tonk rupees (*KM* Y#2,4,5,6)	*Annual average*	*Value*	*Value*	*Value*	*Value*	*Value*
Silver	20,000-25,000	20,000	?	234,193	20,133	84,283

Note: 1894 circulation of silver rupees: 40 per cent Bilharee rupees (5/16 tolas; fineness 84.37, 800,000) and 60 per cent British Indian (1,200,000) rupees.
Sources: Maheshwari and Wiggins 1989, 127-8; Garg 2022, 81, 324-5, 334-5, 366, 408, 425-7, 538, 561; *SACPM* 2013, 19, 179, 380-2.

Sitamau

Sitamau State mint in Western Malwa, coining copper pice. In 1894, circulation of 500,000 Salim Shahi rupees of Pertabgarh, 25,000 Government rupees in addition to Hali rupees from Indore and Ujjain.

Garg 2022, 692; *SACPM* 2013, 379-80.

Sivaganga

Sivaganga State mint.

Mitchiner 1998, II, 225-6; *SACPM* 2013, 219.

Sohagpur

Conquered by the British in the Third Maratha war (1817-19) and its mint soon closed.

Stevens in Garg 2022, 236; not in *SACPM* 2013.

Soho

Occasionally, the EIC commissioned this private mint in Birmingham to provide copper coins for India.

TABLE I.115: SHIPMENT FROM THE BIRMINGHAM-SOHO MINT IN 1791 OF BOMBAY PRESIDENCY COPPERS DATED 1791 AND 1794

Denomination	*KM#*	*Tons:hundredweights: quarters:pounds shipped*	*Tale*	*Value in Rs.*
½ pice 1791	192		7,903,280	39,516
1 pice 1791	193		5,472,740	54,727
1½ pice 1791	195		2,690,351	40,359
2 pice 1791	196		1,174,630	23,493
1791		10:14:2:13.5		*158,095
All denominations 1791-4		50		
Demand 1802				100,000
1 and 2 pice 1804	205, 206			?

Notes: Only part of the production with these dates.
*This is inconsistent with Rs. 70,592:2:57 sent from England 1791-4, as reported in 1802.

In 1803, three denominations were coined for the Madras Presidency: 5 cash (*KM#* 316, 317), 10 cash (*KM#*319), and 20 cash (*KM#*321), to the total weight of 160 candies or 1,814.4 kg (or expressed in 10 cash coins of 6.47 grams equal to 280.433 pieces).

For Bombay 1804, copper coin of 12.96 grams, 1/50 rupee. Device, arms, and scales, 'Adul'; for Madras 1803, XX cash piece of 11.66 grams.
Sources: Prinsep 1834, 51-2; Stevens 2019, 253-60; Mason 2009; *SACPM* 2013, 437-38. See also Birmingham in this appendix.

Sojat

Durbar mint of Marwar (Jodhpur) State, 1869-70 coining silver rupees and copper takkas.

TABLE I.116: COIN PRODUCTION, SOJAT, 1872/3-1875/6 (GOVT Rs.)

	1872-3		*1873-4*		*1874-5*		*1875-6*		*1883*
	Amt	*Value*	*Amt*	*Value*	*Amt*	*Value*	*Amt*	*Value*	*Value*
Silver	*28,201*	*29,082*	*37,830*	*39,012*	*36,152*	*37,282*	*18,741*	*19,327*	*9,840*
Copper*									173,574: 4:1

Note: *A reference to takkas, catalogued as Lingen S.06.01. 04/08 (*KM*#12.3, 14.1); at 24 takkas per rupee the production of vs 1940 (1883) would have resulted in 4,165,783 takka pieces.
Sources: Garg 2022, 78, 381-5, 597; Lingen 2012, 79-81, 205; *SACPM* 2013, 333-4.

Solapur

See Sholapur.

Srinagar in Bundelkhand

Maratha mint.

Maheshwari and Wiggins 1989, 128; *SACPM* 2013, 175.

Srinagar in Garwal

Gurkha Kingdom mint.

SACPM 2013, 167-8.

Srinagar in Kashmir

See Shrinagar.

Srivangapatnam / Seringapatam (Patan)

Mysore State mint.

Mitchiner 1998, I, 235; *SACPM* 2013, 191.

Sunth / Sant

State in Bombay Presidency, capital Rampur. In 1869, mint at Santarampur, only established latterly 'by the tacit permission of the Political Agent', coining manually thick copper 'rampuri(ah)s' at 90-5 per British Indian rupee; average annual output Rs. 175 (or some 16,000 pieces annually, most likely paisas, weighing *c.* 8.5 grams, *KM*#4-9); current only within the state limits. See Rewa Kantha.

Garg 2022, 80, 87, 320, 334, 356-9, 532; *SACPM* 2013, 380.

Surajgarh

Jaipur Feudatory Khetri State mint, discontinued in 1860; 1868 has nineteen mints, coining, in addition to Jaipur pice, short-weight counterfeit pice of Gwalior, Jaipur, Bharatpur, Bikaner, and other princely states for circulation at Agra, Mathura, Ajmer, etc.; 1869 closed permanently.

Garg 2022, 154-6, 166, fn. 50-63, 377-8, 396, 514-15; not in *SACPM* 2013.

Surat

Mughal mint. British from 1800; they continued coining gold, silver, and copper (type uncertain; *SACPM* 2013 lists only silver issues of Surat).

TABLE I.117: COIN PRODUCTION, SURAT, 1797-1800

	Unit	*1 May 1797- 30 April 1798*	*1798-9*	*1799 - 8 November 1800*	*Medium of 3 years*
Gold (small pieces)	unknown	657:01	420:00	677:06	584:13
Silver	Rupees (rounded off)	39,200	1,375,635	694,911	703,249
Copper 1/1200 maund (Khoondeh/ Khoordar alamhuree for adjacent villages)	Maunds (whole)	1,461:24	1,608:10	1,495:34	1,498:24
Copper 1/1600 maund (for the town)					

Source: www.psindiancoins.com (Extracts from IOR and others for Bombay).

TABLE I.118: COIN PRODUCTION, SURAT, 1800-28

	1800-2	*1802-3*	*1803-12*	*1 May 1812-28 February 1813*	*1813-15*	*1818 and 28*
Mohur gold				272 mohurs		0
Panchia gold						
Rupee gold						
Rupee silver				40,000		
½ rupee						
¼ rupee						
⅛ rupee						
Pice	?	Rs. 18,000 ?		Rs. 20,000	110 Surat maunds of lead needed as alloy for copper pice	number unknown

Note: In 1869-70 no mint; 1870 mint not to be reopened.
Sources: Perlin 1987, 351-2; 1993, 247; Stevens 2019, 313-15; Garg 2022, 80; Neogy in Garg 2022, 159, 169; Stevens in Garg 2022, 182-8, 193; www.psindiancoins.com; *SACPM* 2013, 19, 140, 144, 396-7.

Sursair Allypoor

Place in Bundelkhand. By 1871, twenty or more years extensive coinage of counterfeit copper coin, especially Pootlie Shaie, Nowabee or Muchlee Shaie (old Lucknow coin), Tirsolee of Nagpoor, and Bala Shaie of Jaloun.

Garg 2022, 580; for details, see Gerowli above.

Taheri / Tehri

Capital and Orchha state mint (Tikamgarh from 1887). See Orchha.

Tanjore / Thanjavur

Vijayanagar mint of the Nayakas of Tanjore and of the Nawabs of Arcot.

Mitchiner 1998, I, 212-13; II, 207-9; *SACPM* 2013, 219, 235.

Tegnapatnam (Fort St. Davis)

See Cuddalore.

Thanjavur

See Tanjore.

Tinnevelly / Tirunnelveli

Mint belonging to the Kings and Polygars of Tinnevelly and of the Nawabs of Arcot.

Mitchiner 1998, II, 213-16, 226-9; *SACPM* 2013, 219, 235.

Tiruvannamalai (Arunadri)

Mint of a semi-autonomous town in the Vijayanagar Empire.

Mitchiner 1998, I, 198-200; II, 189, 191, 237.

Tonk

Tonk State mint, from 1817 a British protectorate. In 1869-70, coining silver rupees; 1870 retention of the mint recommended; 1869-70 there is also a mint at Sironj, its retention recommended.

TABLE I.119: RUPEE CIRCULATION, TONK, 1894

Rupees	*Region*	*Weight*	*Alloy*	*Amount*
Chauhar Shahi, coined in Tonk	Tonk and Aligarh	181/192 tola	9.9	500,000
Mahomed Khani, coined in Tonk	Sironj	91/96 tola	4.39	250,000
Goman Shahi	Chabra (limited)			100,000
Shah Alam Shahi	Nimbahera (limited)			100,000
Ujjain	P/Tarawa			300,000

(Contd.)

Government	perganas Chabra and Nimbahera	900,000 (or 8:14)
Total		2,150,000

Note: 1894 Tonk-Sironj circulation of mainly Chaman Shahee, rupees (received for revenue), government and Bhopali rupees.
Sources: NAI, Foreign Department, 839 Pt. III/ 1900-2, Particulars regarding Native State mints in Central India to which 1876 Act does not apply; Garg 2022, 57, 80-81, 335, 408, 561, 683-4, 687; Neogy in Garg 2022, 159; *SACPM* 2013, 380-3.

Tori Futtehpoor

Dependency of Orchha. By 1871, 20 or more years extensive coinage of counterfeit copper coin, especially Pootlie Shaie, Nowabee or Muchlee Shaie (old Lucknow coin), Tirsolee of Nagpoor, and Bala Shaie of Jaloun. See also Gerowli.

Garg 2022, 580.

Tranquebar

Danish India mint.

SACPM 2013, 387-93.

Travancore

State. 1869 mint at Travancore, coining 96,556 silver fanams (also called panaurs; each at Rs. 0:2:2:96) in a small machine, and, by hand, silver chukrams or chakras (each at Rs. 0:0:0:6:74) and copper cash (each at Rs. 0:0:0:42) at Rs. 2,223:2:8, current in Travancore and Cochin, an area of about 9,000 square miles.

TABLE I.120: COIN PRODUCTION, TRAVANCORE, 1869

		KM#	*Pieces*	*Rs:anna:pice*
Fanam (panaur)	silver	24.1, 24.2	96,556	13,551:11:06
Chukrum	silver	21, A20	1,168,847	41:012:02:11
Cash	copper	20	1,013,481	2,223:02:08
Total				56,786:15:25

Note: consequently 456 cash = 28.5 chukram = 1 rupee, or 16 cash = 1 chukram.

TABLE I.121: COIN PRODUCTION, TRAVANCORE, 1872/3-1875/6 (GOVT Rs.)

	1871-2		*1872-3*		*1873-4*		*1874-5*	
	Amt	*Value*	*Amt*	*Value*	*Amt*	*Value*	*Amt*	*Value*
Silver chukram *KM*#21, A20	1,318,540	28,296	1,271,233	3,726	0	0	2,368,423	6,339
Copper cash *KM*#20					1,804,400	3,957		

Note: Total amount of chukrams produced 1871-4 is 4,958,196 or, on average, 1,652,732 annually. 1895 British Indian rupee = 28.5 chukrams.
Sources: Garg 2022, 80, 333, 342, 523-4, 600, 741; *SACPM* 2013, 383-6.

Trichy / Tiruchirapalli (Nathanagar / Nahtarnagar)

Mint under the Nawabs of Arcot and the EIC, 1744-1843.
Mitchiner 1998, II, 234-6, 246-8; cf. *SACPM* 2018, 233-5.

Tukkhani

See Gangkok.

Tuticorin

Dutch India mint.
SACPM 2013, 397-8; Scholten 1950; Passon 2022.

Udaipur (Muhammadabad)

Mughal and Mewar State mint. In 1834, mintage of copper 'Oodypoor' of 4.21 grams and 1/160 rupee. 1869-70 Durbar mint of Mewar, coining gold mohurs, silver rupees (Udaipur rupees, and 1868-69 500,000 Suroop [= Salum?] Sahee rupees), and copper pice (at a village called Umrara, 3 kos from the city; *KM* C#27); modernization of the mint considered.

TABLE I.122: COIN PRODUCTION 1872/3-1875/6 (GOVT Rs.)

	1872-3		*1873-4*		*1874-5*		*1875-6*	
	Amt	*Value*	*Amt*	*Value*	*Amt*	*Value*	*Amt*	*Value*
Gold			100	637	325	2,072		
Silver	363,245	266,511	892,571	654,831	95,298	69,919	102,676	75,266
Copper	51,207	256			179,543	898	176,438	882

Note: 1894: last ten years output of 2,266,181 Sarup Shahi rupees and 64,303 Chandori rupees.
Sources: Prinsep 1834, 52; Webb 1893, 2-19; Garg 2022, 27, 44, 79, 82, 128, 335, 374-7, 380, 400, 435, 550-2, 595-600, 657, 675; *SACPM* 2013, 20, 362.

Ujjain / Ujjainpur

Mint belonging to the Malwa Sultans, the Mughals, and Gwalior State. 1870 coining silver rupees (named 'Halee', value then virtually similar to the Indore Hali rupee; later higher); output last five years Rs. 1,000,000 or average annual output Rs. 200,000 (but from 6 June 1869 to 5 March 1870 bullion to the value of Rs. 328,776); 'Copper has not been coined for the last eight years, the reason is said to be that British copper coins circulate freely in Oojein and of these there is a constant and regular supply which supplements the stock of local coin and thus renders the supply ample for the wants of the country.'

TABLE I.123: SILVER COIN PRODUCTION, UJJAIN, 1870, 1891-1900

Dating				*KM#*	*Production*		
Year for which production reported	*AH*	*Regnal year*	*AH / RY conversion in CE*		*In tolas silver (rounded off)*		*In rupees*
					old	*new*	
1870	-	23	1865/6	#238 (rupee RY 9)			200,000
	-	29	1887/88	#239 (1/16	?		
1891	-	31	1889/90	rupee); 240 (1/8	0	133,034	
1892	-	32	1890/91	rupee);	0	66,787	

1893 Jul/Sep	13xx	33	1891/92	241 (¼	530,962	7,388
1893 Oct/ Dec				rupee);	299,460	
1894	1310	34	1892/93	242 (½ rupee);	1,252,930	5,859
1895	1311	35	1893/94	243	1,077,450	8,890
1896	1312	36	1894/95	(rupee)	1,451,213	44,967
1897	1313	37	1895/96		1,100,693	18,712
1898	1314	38	1896/97		170,129	0
1899					0	13,473
1900					0	0

Sources: NAI, Residences, Central India Agency 813/ 1863: Report on the coinage of native states (letter Political Agent at Gwalior to Agent Governor-General for CI Indore, Camp Khokhra, 21 December 1863); idem 839 Pt. II/ 1895-7 and Pt. III/ 1900-2, Particulars regarding Native State mints in central India to which 1876 Act does not apply; Lingen and Wiggins 1978, 90-7; Goron and Goenka 2001, 425; Garg 2022, 77, 334, 364, 368-9, 437-8, 501, 547-8, 702-5; *SACPM* 2013, 20, 285-98 (for *KM#* and dating; different interpretation of dating and mint).

Umrara

1869-70 Durbar mint of Mewar, coining copper pice. See Udaipur.
Webb 1893, Garg 2022, 79, 376.

Urdu / Urdu Zafar Qarin

Migrating Mughal mint.
Garg / Hodivala 2014, 30, 43; *SACPM* 2013, 20.

Vadodara

See Baroda.

Vaphgaon

Maratha mint.
Maheshwari and Wiggins 1989, 98-9; *SACPM* 2013, 180.

Varanasi

See Benares.

Vasai

See Bassein.

Vathar

Mint in the Deccan, belonging – like Phultun – to the Nimbalkur (a Maratha clan). 1831 the British want to stop its production.

Maheshwari and Wiggins 1989, 103; Stevens 2019, 235; Stevens in Garg 2022, 221.

Vellore

Mint of the Vijayanagar Empire and of successor states, including the Marathas.

Maheshwari and Wiggins 1989, 187; Mitchiner 1998, I, 210; II, 186.

Venkatagiri

Maratha mint belonging to the Ghorpade Chiefs of Gooty.

SACPM 2013, 176-7.

Vijayanagar / Hampi

Mint and capital of the Vijayanagar Empire.

Mitchiner 1998, I, 158-213; *SACPM* 2013, 229.

Visakhapatnam

Madras Presidency mint from 1753 to 1801, coining the same type of copper coins as Masulipatnam; see there for production figures 1753-1801 (Table I.93).

www.psindiancoins.com; Introduction 3c.

Vrindavan / Brindaban (Islamabad, Muminabad)

Maratha mint coining rupees and pice. Gifted by the British to Bharatpur, and copying Bharatpur rupees, coined 1858-9 with Queen Victoria's portrait. 1834 three types of copper Muttra (Mathura / Islamabad) coins, current in 'Agra, Muttra, Bindrabun, etc.': Muttra old 9.53 grams and 1/46.5 rupee, Muttra new 8.75 grams and 1/68 rupee, Muttra double 17.50 grams and 1/34 rupee.

Prinsep 1834, 52; Maheshwari and Wiggins 1989, 147-54; Lingen and Lucassen 2012/13 (see Part I: Studies, No. 9 in this volume); Garg 2022, 48; Bhandare 2022, 119; *SACPM* 2013, 139, 270-2.

Wadi

See Sawantwadi.

Wani

Hyderabad Feudatory Ellichpur mint.

SACPM 2013, 309.

Yadgir (Firoznagar)

Mughal mint.

Garg / Hodivala 2014, 153-4; *SACPM* 2013, 17.

Zafarabad (1) Jafarabad / Zafarnagar

Mughal mint.

Garg / Hodivala 2014, 126; *SACPM* 2013, 20.

Zafarabad (2)

See Gurramkonda.

Appendix 3: The Relation between Production Figures and Rarity, Small Denominations India 1500-1947

In Appendix 3, all the production figures of small coins given and commented on in Appendix 2 are, as far as possible, combined with rarity indications as contained in the database and as explained in Appendix 1. An exception is made for the data regarding the mints of Bombay, Calcutta, and Madras 1860-1901, for which both production and collectors' value have already been provided in full in Appendix 2.

On this basis, extrapolations have been made in the main text (Chapter 3e, Table I.11 and Figure I.1; see also Appendix 1) for coin types for which such data are not available.

Key to Table I.124

1. Mint as given in Appendix 2; for the central mints 1835-58: B = Bombay; C = Calcutta, M = Madras, S = Soho.
2. Coin type in *South Asian Coins and Paper Money* (*SACPM*) 2013 (as a rule *KM#*, other classifications indicated), as identified in Appendix 2. If the attribution is not certain this has been indicated under 8. (Remarks).
3. First year (simplified for Hijra / HA conversion to the earliest corresponding CE year) for which production data are available; ND means no date, and FD means 'frozen date'.
4. Last year idem.
5. Metal: c(opper), s(ilver).
6. Production figures per coin type per year if available; where this information is unavailable for coin types, known to have been produced over more than one year this is impossible, as has been indicated in the remarks.

7. Rarity: Price in US $ for 'fine' in *SACPM* 2013. Where more prices are given per coin type the minimum (mean) will be given; moreover, outliers have been omitted.
8. Remarks for elucidation (especially denomination and number of years for which production figures are available) and on the reliability of the information. This information will be worked out in function of the analysis of the statistical trends.

TABLE I.124: PRODUCTION FIGURES AND RARITY PER COIN TYPE (ONLY SMALL DENOMINATIONS)

1	*2*	*3*	*4*	*5*	*6*	*7*	*8*
Mint	*Type*	*Period*			*Production*	*Rarity*	*Remarks*
Ahmeda-bad	46	1817	1821	C	500,000	20	Paisa ND with title of Shah Alam 1759-1806; identification uncertain; production known for only 1 year in this period
Bankot	225	1820	1821	C	2,400,000	85	Half pice; average of production of 4,800,000 for 2 years
	226	1820	1821	C	1,200,000	75	Whole pice; average of production of 2,400,000 for 2 years
Bharatpur	101	1884	1887	C	1,434,475	6	Takka; average of production of 5,737,000 for 4 years (15 dates known)

(Contd.)

Bharuch	200	1824	1830	C	857,300	30	Paisa; identification uncertain; average of production of 4,288,000 for 5 years (10 dates known)
Bikaṇer	62	1887	1887	S	1,472	200	2 annas
Bundi	Y#3	1869	1869	C	10,000	10	Takka (27 dates known)
		1872	1872	C	15,000	10	
Madras	287	1679	1679	C	128,000	18	Identification of these cash, dated (16)78 uncertain
		1682	1685	C	138,400		
	284	1682	1685	C	345,000	45	Identification of this treble cash ND uncertain
	378/9	1740	1740	C	619,020	50	Identification of this cash ND (two types) uncertain
	335/7, 349	1807	1808	S	599,852	100	Fanam ND (four types); number in stock
		1807	1813		275,966		Idem, total production 1,931,764, or possible annual average for 7 years
	338/41, 350	1807	1813	S	1,047,634	140	2 fanam ND (five types); total production 7,333,437,

						or possible annual average for 7 years
405/6	1807	1807	S	22	500	2 anna ND (two types)
	1807	1813		12,086		Idem, total production 84,604, or possible annual average for 7 years
399	1807	1807	S	20,022	35	⅛ rupee FD; identification uncertain
408, 412	1807	1813	S	56,019	35	⅛ rupee FD; identification uncertain
309	1807	1807	C	561,622	200	2.5 cash ND
324	1807	1807	C	1,216,822	80	5 cash ND
326	1807	1807	C	2,728,690	80	10 cash ND
328	1807	1807	C	3,016,822	100	20 cash ND
331.1	1807	1807	C	645,967	250	40 cash ND
325	1807	1807	C	407,022	30	¼ dub ND
327	1807	1807	C	388,272	175	½ dub
					75	Idem, if *KM*#345 dated 1808 is included
330	1807	1807	C	79,222	750	Dub ND
					80	Idem, if *KM*#346/7 (two types, dated 1808 are included)

(Contd.)

331.2/3	1807	1807	C	3,400	550	2 dub (two types ND); identification uncertain
329	1807	1808	C	59,136	300	Regulating dub; average of production of 118,272 for 2 dates
411, 423	1820	1826	S	1,448,000	12	1 anna (two types FD); average of production of 32,000 in 1820 and 2,864,000 in 1826
408, 412	1820	1820	S	3,311,500	35	2 annas (two types FD); average of production of 814,000 in 1820 and 5,809,000 in 1826
411, 423, 408, 412	1818	1835	C	16,000,000	12	1 and 2 annas together (four types ND) Rs. 1,800,000, expressed in only 288 mio annas, or 16 mio on average for 18 years
				8,000,000	35	Idem if expressed in only 144 mio double annas, or 8 mio on average for 18 years

Chhota Udaipur	Y#1	1869	1869	C	25,600	20	Paisa, annual average; possibly including *KM* Y#2.1/2, all same date
Delhi	700	1771	1805	C		10	
Goa (Bombay mint)	301	1871	1871	C	52,080	60	3 reis
	302	1871	1871	C	50,900	60	5 reis
	303	1871	1871	C	51,075	60	10 reis
	304	1871	1871	C	50,664	35	15 reis
	305	1871	1871	C	50,063	35	30 reis
	306	1871	1871	C	50,004	35	60 reis
	307	1881	1886	C	4,132,267	25	⅛ tanga; average of production of 12,396,800 for all 3 years
	308	1881	1888	C	1,810,700	5	¼ tanga; average of 7,242,800 for all 5 years
	309	1881	1881	S	901,688	300	⅛ rupia
Gorakhpur	A106	1776	1776	C	2,920,000	15	Paisa
Gwalior	232	1873	1873	C	10,800,000	10	Paisa, dated 1861, 1864, 1875, 1878; identification uncertain; supposedly *c.* 1/72nd rupee
Jaipur	105	1872	1874	C	2,624,674	6	New paisa; average of production of 7,874,021 for 3 years (production of 110 pieces

(Contd.)

							in 1875/6 omitted) out of 8 dates
Janjira	28	1870	1870	C	60,000	10	Paisa; annual average, supposing 250 days production per year
Jaora	2-4	1872	1875	C	841,500	3	Paisa ND (three types); Identification imprecise; annual average
Jhalawar	Y#2	1875	1875	C	381,450	5	Double paisa; 19 dates known
Jodhpur	71	1872	1874	C	14,592	6	Takka; average of production of 43,777 for 3 years
	72	1873	1890	C	2,724,378	6	Takka; average of production of 35,416,920 for 13 years; possibly the production of 14,400 pieces at Nagaur to be added
Karauli	51	1872	1872	C	84,614	3.75	Takka; attribution uncertain
		1885	1887	C	2,589,067		average production of 7,767,200 in 3 years out of 6 dates known

Kishan-garh	C#25	1886	1886	C	150,000	2	Takka ND, supposedly 1/50th rupee; identification not certain; possibly including C#24
Calcutta	50	1795	1795	C	642,992	70	½ pice
	52	1795	1795	C	363,000	10	Pice
	51	1796	1796	C	605,000	70	½ pice
	53	1796	1796	C	1,226,000	10	Pice (possibly 640,000 for 1800/1 to be added)
	A54	1807	1809	C	400,000	30	½ pice FD
	25	1807	1809	C	320,000	20	Pice FD
	A55	1807	1809	C	400,000	35	2 pice FD
	56	1808	1815	C	12,615,663	10	Pice FD; average of 75,693,981 in 6 production years
	55	1817	1825	C	3,648,836	10	Pice FD; average of 25,541,850 in 7 production years
	54	1828	1829	C	8,812,544	20	Pice FD; average of 17,625,088 in 2 production years
	57	1830	1830	C	23,976,218	7	Pice ND; estimated distribution between pice, pie and ½ anna

(Contd.)

	58	1831	1831	C	108,943,872	4	Pie ND; idem
	59	1832	1832	C	8,607,237	15	½ anna ND; idem
C	446.1	1835	1835	C	186,529,741	2	¼ anna
B	446.1	1835	1835	C	36,766,900	2	¼ anna
M	446.2	1835	1835	C	755,059,377	2	¼ anna
B	447.1	1835	1835	C	8,658,092	5	½ anna
M	447.1	1835	1835	C	95,202,278	5	½ anna
C	445	1848	1848	C	14,380,924	10	1/12 anna
C	447.1	1845	1845	C	17,160,010	25	½ anna
C	459.2	1841	1841	S	8,385,077	25	2 anna
B	459.1	1841	1841	S	11,430,800	25	
M	459.3	1841	1841	S	10,503,600	30	
C	464	1853	1853	C	62,408,000	5	½ pice
S	463.1	1857	1857	C	47,040,000	30	¼ anna
S	463.1	1858	1858	C	62,720,000	4	
S	463.2	1858	1858	C	172,480,000	4	
C	460.2	1841	1841	S	43,002,080	20	2 annas
B	460.3	1841	1841	S	8,427,040	20	
M	460.4	1841	1841	S	26,930,380	20	
B/C/M							For 1862-1901, see Appendix 2
Kotah	Y#3	1864	1868	S	616	40	⅛ rupee, but in *KM* only years given from 1879
Kotah	Y#2	1864	1868	C	476,928	4	Takka (18 dates known for this type)
Kutch	Y#30/ 30.1	1884	1884	C	1,530	3	½ Dokdo (4 dates known for this type)
Kutch	Y#31/ 31.1	1884	1884	C	116,391	3	Dokdo; (4 dates known for this type)

Kutch	Y#32/ 32.1	1884	1885	C	145,676	3	1.5 Dokda; average of production of 291,351 for 2 years (6 dates known for this type)
Kutch	Y#33	1884	1885	C	15,976	7	3 dokda; average of production of 31,955 for 2 years (5 dates known for this type)
Lashkar	75	1870	1870	C	720,000	10	Identification not certain; average output of mint Lashkar A, but missing that of Lashkar B (10 dates known for this type)
Lashkar	233	1870	1870	C	1,080,000	10	Identification not certain; Lashkar B average output (6 dates known for this type)
Visakha-patnam	E450.2	1753	1753	C	777,600	100	Paisa (7 dates known for this type)
Masulipat-nam	E450.2	1756	1756	C	129,600	100	Paisa (7 dates known for this type)
Masulipat-nam	655	1773	1773	C	3,564,000	20	Paisa (4 dates known for this type); request

Visakha-patnam	655	1774	1774		777,600	20	Paisa (4 dates known for this type)
Masulipat-nam	655	1777	1777	C	1,293,343	20	Paisa (4 dates known for this type)
Visakha-patnam	655	1801	1801		502,250	20	Paisa (4 dates known for this type; proposed rate)
Masulipat-nam	655	1802	1802	C	648,000	20	Paisa (4 dates known for this type; minimum; proposed rate)
Bombay (Mumbai)	130	1673	1673	T	27,000,000	125	Tinny; soon remelted
Bombay	155	1716	1716	T	400,000	250	Tinny
Bombay	156.1	1741	1741	T	1,500,000	950	Pice (5 dates known for this type)
Bombay	156.2	1769	1769	T	3,000,000	925	Pice
Bombay	131-133	1672	1673	C	602,500	75	Pice, average of 1,205,000 for 2 years
Bombay	150	1748	1748	C	324,720	80	Pice (12 dates known for this type)
Bombay	150, 167	1748	1748	C	110,700	80	Pice (13 dates known for these two types)
Bombay	188	1775	1775	C	1,600,000	30	Pice (2 dates known for this type)

Bombay	150	1784	1784	C	295,200	80	Pice, attribution uncertain (12 dates known for this type)
Bombay	150	1775	1784	C	895,637	80	Pice; annual average for total of 8,956,368 in 10 years (only one date known)
Bombay	198	1803	1803	C	4,445,909	25	Pice (16 dates known for this type)
Bombay	201	1803	1803	C	555,739	130	4 pice (4 dates known for this type)
Bombay	231.1	1831	1831	C	9,030,400	90	¼ anna (2 dates known for this type)
Nagpur	64	1841	1847	C	1,820,000	4	Paisa ND; Average of total production of 5,460,000 in 3 years (very irregular over 6 years 1841-7, mainly 1841-3)
Nandgaon	Y#3	1865	1869	S	614	40	2 anna; average of total 3,072 in 5 years (11 dates known)
Nandgaon	Y#2	1865	1869	C	476,928	4	takka; average of total 3,072 in 5 years (18 dates known)

(Contd.)

Nawa-nagar	17	1872	1872	C	20,800	15	3 dokda
Pali	12.2, 13, 14.2	1883	1883	C	33,987,320	6	Takka; for these three types (by *KM* valued at $10, 6 and 6) 9 dates known
Pudduk-kottai	4	1873	1873	C	362,560	11	Amman cash ND
Radhan-pur	3	1869	1869	C	540,000	6	Paisa ND, annual average
Rajgarh (Alwar)	35.1	1856	1868	C	217,340	4	Takka; average of 12 years (8 dates known)
Ratlam	21	1869	1869	C	650,000	20	Paisa ND
Sagar	A65, 71, 72	1827	1832	C	3,627,366	10	Trisul pice ND; average of 18,136,832 in 5 years; price for the cheapest variant
Sailana	5	1872	1875	C	899,829	1.50	Paisa ND; average of 3,599,316 in 4 years
Sironj	Y#3	1865	1870	C	54,700	7.50	Paisa; average of 5 years (6 dates known)
Sojat	12.3, 14.1	1883	1883	C	4,165,783	6	Takka ND; price for the cheapest variant
Sunth	5-9	1869	1869	C	16,000	7	Paisa undated, 6 types with prices $7-12

Travan-core	24.1, 24.2	1869	1869	S	96,556	40	Fanam ND
Travan-core	21, A20	1869	1869	S	1,168,847	3	Chukram; ND price for the cheapest variant
Travan-core	21, A20	1871	1875	S	1,652,732	3	Chukram; ND average of 4,958,196 for 3 years
Travan-core	20	1869	1869	C	1,168,847	2	Cash ND
Travan-core	20	1873	1873	C	1,804,400	2	Cash ND
Benares (Varanasi)	15	1775	1787	C	5,417,268	8	Pice; average of 59,589,950 for 11 years; 4 dates known
Benares	A54	1808	1808	C	320,000	830	½ pice
Benares	25	1808	1808	C	320,000	20	Pice
Benares	A55	1808	1808	C	400,000	35	2 pice
Benares	27.1, 27.2, 27.3	1815	1823	C	6,022,948	5	Pice ND; average of 54,206,528 for 9 years
Benares	28, 29, 30	1823	1829	C	4,947,776	6	Pice ND; average of 34,634,432 for 7 years

Appendix 4: Metrology and Designation/ Nomenclature of Small Denominations, India 1500-1947

As a rule, before the nineteenth century, the coins of this period bear no indication of their value or exchange rate. However, in the sources we encounter many different designations (see also Part I: Studies, No. 12 in this volume on the enigmatic *mansuri paisa*) – too many to treat here systematically. Luckily, Najaf Haider has done a great job explaining and systematically simplifying the different names of Indian coins per metal and sub-period. I basically follow his system, leaving out the silver rupee and its division into 16 annas and, notably, by converting the insular British system of troy grains into the internationally accepted grams (1 troy grain = 0.06479891, or simplified 0.065 gram). Haider's work goes back, in particular, to that of Irfan Habib, who has provided useful overviews of weight and monetary systems from *c.* 1500 to 1800.[3]

Generally, the well-known modern catalogue of Indian coins *SACPM* 2013 (*South Asian Coins and Paper Money*) provides a good overview of all denominations struck in the subcontinent from about 1550 onwards, although it is poor and sometimes even misleading as to the historical nomenclature of specific non-precious metal fractions and their exchange rate.

[3] Haider 2015, 93-6. See also Godinho 1969, 339-68, esp. for the sixteenth century and Manzar 2021, 397-404 for the seventeenth; Habib 2014, 432-49. See also Perlin 1993, 230-2 (standard conversions and exchange rates).

4.1 Copper

Starting point are the copper coins of the Delhi Sultans until 1540 (see Table I.125).

TABLE I.125: COPPER COINS OF THE DELHI SULTANS, 1215-1540

Designation	*13th/ 14th century*			*15th century*
	Weight (grams)	*Exchange rate*		*Weight (grams)*
		In gani	*In silver tanka of 11.04 grams*	
Paika	4.68	4	240	9.36
Adhva	2.34	8	480	4.68
*Sara visva**	1.17	16	960	2.34
*Visva**	0.94	20	1,920	1.17

Note: *The generic term for the smallest copper fractions was *adli,* which may even have been used for the half *paika.*
Sources: Haider 2015, 95; for actual weight and many other variations, see Goron and Goenka 2001, xvi-xvii, 35-88.

For the copper coins of other sultanates in India (to name the most important after 1500 those of the Deccan, Bijapur, Bidar, Ahmadnagar, Golkonda, Gujarat, Malwa, and Kashmir), I refer to Goron and Goenka 2001. A completely new monetary system was introduced early in the Suri dynasty (1538-55) with a heavy copper coin of *c.* 20 gram. It was called a paisa and, later, under Akbar, it was called *dam,* as the 40th part of the silver rupee.

Besides, Babur and Humayun issued copper *bahlolis,* weighing between 7.63 and 9.20 gram. These were named after the coins of Bahlul Lodi (1451-88), the Sultan of Delhi, whose weight standard they followed.[4]

In the 1660s, the weight of the copper coins was reduced by one third. See Table I.19.

The loss of central power by the Mughals from the mid-eight-

[4] I thank Dr. Sanjay Garg for this information. See also Goron & Goenka 2001, 85-86; Rahman 2005, 45-47, 51, 98-101.

eenth century caused a decentralization of minting authorities and, consequently, a greater variety in the weight of the paisa and its fractions was gradually seen. In the sources, we now generally now *paisa* or *pice* for the single coppers, varying between 5 and 10 grams and *takka* or *tanka* for the double coppers, varying between 15 and 20 grams. In southern India, the generic term *cash* is used for small copper coins, weighing a few gram.

TABLE I.126: COPPER COINS OF THE SURIS AND THE MUGHALS, 1540-1800

Designation	*Weight (grams)*		*In paisa*	*Exchange rate*	
	1540-1665	*1665-1800*		*In rupees*	*In annas*
Takka	42,00		½	20	1.25
Paisa/ dam	21,00	14,00	1	40	2.50
Adhela	10.50	7,00	2	80	5
Paula	5.25	3,50	8	160	10
Damri	2.62	1,75	16	320	20

Sources: Haider 2015, 96-8; for actual weight and many other variations of the Suri coinage, see Goron and Goenka 2001, 89-134.

The British colonizers had to adapt to the existing local currencies, which implies that, until 1835, the three presidencies (Bengal, Bombay, Madras) used and minted different denominational systems. From 1835 until 1947, in the parts of India under direct British rule, and after India's independence from 1947 until 1957, a uniform system was maintained, based on the *rupee*, divided into 16 *annas*. Apart from the gold *mohur*, equal to 15 silver rupees at the top of the pyramid, these annas were subdivided into copper coins of four different denominations: the ½ *anna*, the ¼ *anna* or *pice*, the ½ *pice* or ⅛*th anna*, and, finally, the *pie* or $^1/_{12}$ anna. Independent states (the last was the Sikh kingdom, conquered in 1849) and indirectly ruled states maintained their own monetary systems and designations until unification with and integration into independent India, despite unification attempts by the British, which were only partially successful (see extensively in Garg 2019 and 2022).

Other colonial powers also had to adapt to local conditions, but they did it in their own way. In particular, the Portuguese colonial monetary system diverges from all the others.

4.2 Billon

Billon coins, containing more copper than silver, were minted until the early sixteenth century and continued to circulate even later when the billon *tankas* weighing *c.* 9-9.5 grams and struck by the Lodis were probably worth two of the new copper *paisas* of the Suris.

TABLE I.127: BILLON COINS, DELHI SULTANS, 1290-1390.

Designation		*Denomination in gani*	*Standard weight*	*Silver content (per cent)*	*Exchange rate per silver tanka of 11.04 grams*
Generic					
Jital	*Yakgani*	1	3.68	5.00	60
	Dugani	2		9.75-8.00	30
	Chaugani	4		16.39	15
	Shashgani	6		25.57-24.79	10
	Hashtgani	8		33.14	7.5
	Baragani	12	5.52		5
	Chaubisgani	24	11.04		2.5
	Artalisgani	48	22.08		1.25

Source: Haider 2015, 95; for actual weight and many other variations, see Goron and Goenka 2001, 35-74 (the silver content of the *dugani* and the *shashgani* was diminished in this century).

4.3 Silver

Because of the remarkable stability of the silver rupee from the sixteenth until the early nineteenth century, and the maintenance of its subdivision into 16 annas, the silver section of the denominational system is far less complicated that the copper and billon ones. This also goes for the $1/16$ and even smaller fractions of the rupee that are part of the database made for this study. Nevertheless, in the far south, such as Travancore, and in certain parts of the north (especially on the Saurashtra peninsula), decentralization of political power induced quite divergent silver denominations.

PART I: STUDIES

Theory, Historiography Methods

1

Changes in Production and Circulation of Money in Seventeenth and Eighteenth Century India: An Essay on Monetization before Colonial Occupation

FRANK PERLIN

I. Long-term Contexts

The Task and its Problems

Between the late and early nineteenth centuries a series of profound changes affected India's monetary history. The first has been well charted and concerns the introduction of a controlled and universal value system within Mughal dominions in the course of the late sixteenth and early seventeenth centuries. This formed part of a much broader and longer term movement of increased money-use and piecemeal standardization in different parts of the subcontinent, a development which has so far gained much less attention, but which seems to have been common to other parts of Asia, as well as to the much better-known case of Europe. As for the rest – the history of money from about the last quarter of the seventeenth century, and especially of the later eighteenth century – much less is known, assumptions legion, and there is little discussion or research.[1]

In what follows, I shall try to interpret the monetary events of the eighteenth century, treating them as aspects of a broader continuum running from the sixteenth century to the eve of colonial conquest and embracing the whole subcontinent. Naturally, there were periods of crisis and regression in this long period, regional disparities and areas of marked economic decline, but for the most part we are not in a position to interpret or even identify such reversions and inequalities, and it is arguably a first essential task to draw the outlines of the broader continuity in which, in my view, they formed part.

A major historiographical problem consists of the long established tendency to treat the last pre-colonial centuries in terms of a small number of massive discontinuities, each reversing the trend of previous developments. The first, of course, was the rise and maintenance of Mughal hegemony, the second its collapse, and the third the colonial occupation of the subcontinent which brought the old order to a close. Most major questions of India's economic history are dominated by the brief and brilliant presence of the Mughals, and monetary history is no exception. The centralization and organization of the Mughal state have seemed to make it a grand exception, the byword for an eccentric, but brief case of advance and development, or alternatively standing for developments in the subcontinent at large. As a result, India's neglected century is not the seventeenth – as it is the case for Europe – but the eighteenth, the first viewed as the Golden Age of Mughal power and the second as the period of its dissembling, the condition and prelude to colonial occupation. This eighteenth century downcycle is apparently reflected in chaotic monetary conditions, the evidence for which lies in a marked fall in quality of fabrication, a weakening of centralized control over minting and currency management, and typological confusion and individualism in mint turn-out. These in turn are parts of a closed circle in which general economic decline seems the natural consequence of the political decentralization and military conflicts of the eighteenth century. We could say that the ideological spectre that stalks this history is one inherited from the colonial period itself, in which centralization and scale appear synonymous with development and order.

But I shall argue that the eighteenth century ushers in one of the most interesting changes in India's monetary history, changes bearing close comparison with those affecting other parts of the world during the same period, and partly heralded by earlier developments in the seventeenth century. In order to present the argument, however, it is essential to confront a second and most important problem concerning the seventeenth and eighteenth centuries: the need to understand and larger monetary sphere of productions and exchanges embracing the whole subcontinent (of which Mughal uniformity formed only part). Once one contextualizes Mughal history, even given the large measure of ignorance that renders this task so difficult and hazardous, the events of the eighteenth century may be seen to compose a late and vigorous phase of a longer development instead of a negative print of the brilliant tones of the earlier period. It must be added, thirdly, that this treatment of monetary order and change is simply an important part of a more general reinterpretation of late pre-colonial history.

Moreover, the tasks of synthesis and reinterpretation are even more serious than indicated so far. An essential aspect of India's monetary history is the large international context, especially as concerns supply of monetary media from overseas, but also, more generally, the overall growth of commercial exchanges and increasing European intervention in Asia. Historians have already argued about the importance of supplies in connection with the much disputed problem of price inflation in Mughal India; however, contextualization is more fundamental, involving a much broader set of influences and changes, associated with the general development of commercial capital itself, thus with a network of independent market and production relationships on an international scale. As we shall see, these developments decisively affect monetary relationships in the eighteenth century.

In contrast, in the early nineteenth century, the new colonial regime brings the old monetary order to a close, ushers in a severe economic contraction, and imposes a monetary system of the European type. The major monetary transition takes place in the first decades of the nineteenth century (after the East India Company gains a dominant political position in the subcontinent). In the late eighteenth century, however, there is a complex period in which indigenous economic developments occur simultaneously with the first phase of economic (and political) subordination in the subcontinent, a movement transcending political and colonial frontiers, but yet to be adequately understood or even described.

In the following sections I shall hazard a schematic view of the broad and long-term changes occurring from the late sixteenth century onwards in order to provide a sufficient framework for the discussion in Part II of the central problem concerning this paper, the eighteenth century. In the eighteenth century, the questions of monetary unity and fragmentation become especially serious and fascinating issues.

Monetization and its Background

Although long-term social growth can be observed from at least the thirteenth century, it is from the sixteenth century that the signs of change accumulate in a marked manner. These changes affect the size, pace and scope of urban life, commercial transactions, manufactures, population and agrarian settlement. Manufactures, for example, have a long export-oriented history (besides supplying internal markets), but appear in the seventeenth and eighteenth centuries to adapt to the changing character of international demand. Thus, this is also the period of the inroads of European maritime traders and trading institutions (the Companies), and of a broader international trading system, into the Asian trading nexus, the implications of both remaining a matter of debate. Most important for our subject, these changes are paralleled by a long process of 'institutional' monetization affecting the all important sphere of agricultural taxation and rent, and influencing most, possibly all of the subcontinent; again these developments have visible beginnings in the thirteenth century but become especially notable from the late sixteenth century.

Now, these changes in the form and content of taxation and rents – depending upon a long process of survey and valuation of agricultural lands – form part of a broader set of interdependent changes. On the one hand, alterations in currency organization and production and supply of money match the new demands for money levied upon peasant labour throughout the subcontinent. On the other hand, with the complexifying of the administrative apparati of tax and rent collection, there develops a nexus of private financial organizations extending over the whole subcontinent and which, by the eighteenth century, reach into the most remote villages. Production and circulation of money, these financial institutions, trade and agrarian taxation form central part of a complex set of interdependent relationships about which we have only outline impressions. But putting all these elements together, we may argue that they furnish the infrastructure of demand, which, in the course of the next century and a half, on coast and in hinterland, provided relatively high prices for imported monetary media and stimulated vigorous trading in them.

As for the more limited period of the eighteenth century, I shall argue that continued monetization was associated with an increased density of local economic activity and money use, affecting regions well beyond the more commercialized areas of the subcontinent, such as Bengal and Gujarat. Put briefly, the strictly monetary changes of the eighteenth century were marked by increased use of money among broad sections of the population, for wages, loans and market exchanges. Correspondingly, monetary management and production became more flexible and responsive to commercial and popular needs (the 'weakening of centralized controls', mentioned above), factoring coins in a manner admirably suited to the major changes in commodity production and marketing occurring during this period. The corollary is that the relationship between political organization and monetary history in late pre-colonial India constitutes a much more problematic question than generally accepted in the historiography.

Regional Differences in Monetary Order and Long-term Trends

Discussion of long-term monetary developments in the last pre-colonial centuries is hindered by three serious problems. The first concerns the scarcity of information on broad and important aspects of monetary history, especially as concerns the Deccan and southern India (zones 2 and 3 on map 1.1, p. 324). Secondly, India formed an international arena of contending states in its own right, one in which political frontiers and administrative organizations were highly mobile. Finally, even with respect to monetary organization by itself, different monetary orders are found operating simultaneously in the subcontinent, not necessarily coinciding with political frontiers. The tendency to limit attention to Mughal monetary history (as if it stood for the whole subcontinent) has resulted[2] in a remarkable scarcity of syntheses and long-term treatments.

On a broad and schematic level, the most obvious contrast in monetary organization can be characterized as follows. Generally speaking, north and south constituted zones based respectively on circulation of silver and gold, with the 'intermediate' states of the Deccan gradually shifting in the course of the seventeenth century from gold to silver. By the start of the eighteenth century this transition seems almost complete, while in the south, where gold remains an important medium of circulation, a mixed trimetallic system takes form later in the same century. This much is well known; but what is the significance of this transition? It is informative to try and reconstruct a more complex and long-term set of developments, of which the shift from gold to silver is a part.

In the Mughal north of the subcontinent, and on the eve of the changes concerning us – that is to say before the 1590s – it was copper which in fact formed the dominant metal used both for minting and as a measure of accounting value (although, of course, silver coin was also minted prior to the '90s). Agricultural taxation was levied in copper dams, while Mughal mints produced a relatively large number of copper coins in these years.[3]

Only in the last years of the sixteenth century did silver emerge as the dominant currency medium, partly replacing copper in circulation and as a medium of value, and coming to dominate mint output. This change, together with the advance southwards of the Mughal silver rupee currency system was routed in what seem to have been contingent historical factors: a ready and increasing overseas supply of the metal, Mughal administrative and monetary reforms, and the great period of Mughal military conquest and expansion. However, it is also clear that the advance of silver was accompanied by more fundamental changes of economy and monetary organization.

The dominance of copper lasted longer in the states of the Deccan (intermediary zone 2 on map 1.1, p. 324), together with gold in denominations found all over peninsula India at this time (zones 2 and 3), the pagoda or hon (and its fraction, the fanum). The latter seems not to have been minted in important quantities in the Deccan itself, although found in circulation and forming a unit of account. In two Deccan states in the seventeenth century, the Ahmadnagar Sultanate and that of the Marathas (roughly contiguous with the western part of Maharashtra, today) agricultural taxation was demanded largely in copper, but also partly in gold hons as well as in kind. Moreover, in Golconda gold seems to have been an increasingly vital medium of commercial transactions. It is likely, in the case of Golconda, that a net trading surplus with the ports and towns of southern India (where even the East India Companies established their own mints to produce means of payment for goods purchased in the hinterland), and, in the case of Maharashtra, the flow of booty, tributes and taxation from conquered territories to the south, led to imports of most of the gold coin entering circulation in these regions.

In the south, by contrast, gold formed the basic coining medium, while copper according to one authority, was minted in 'restricted' quantities. The evidence for this qualification is not given but is probably based upon number of finds; while it must be considered debatable the question nevertheless will not affect the following argument.

The question to be focused upon, at this point, is what happens to copper in the long-term all over the subcontinent, irrespective of chronological variations between one region and another. In the course of the later seventeenth century, copper coin seems to become abundant as a subsidiary to the precious metals, a transformation of function which is of vital significance when interpreted in the light of the broader economic changes discussed above, thus as evidence of a more deep seated change in the 'socio-logy' of money-use. Before proceeding to this question we need to look more closely at the major zonal systems themselves. The northern system has been charted in considerable detail by Habib and his students and consists of the establishment in the late sixteenth and early seventeenth centuries of a unified currency order throughout Mughal territories. Mughal coins were remarkable for their standard weighting, their high and consistent pure metal content, and their production in a fluctuating number of officially controlled mints spread through the empire. Like all Indian monetary systems it was characterized by what has been called an 'open' or 'free'-access system of minting, in which persons possessing specie or bullion could ostensibly deliver it for minting on payment of factoring costs and seigneurage.[4] All such inputs were coined in this way, without attempts to control the stock of circulating coin. Exchanges between types of coin and monetary medium were allowed to find their own levels in the market. In sum, Indian currencies were not subject to the centrally operated manipulations and instabilities characterizing European systems.

These last properties also characterized the southern zone, where, nevertheless, currencies were less centralized, being produced by a number of different regimes. Denominations varied in weight and purity, but were essentially of the same general type (notably gold pagodas and fanums), and they may together be thought of as a single set of exchange-adjusted units composing a single, general currency system. The longer perspective in the south, say from the early sixteenth century on, was also marked by the increasing standardization of types and weights.

Production of Coin in Terms of International Supply of Raw Materials

To what extent were India's currency systems, together with the gradual and overall process of monetization, dependent upon supplies of raw materials from overseas? The actual relationship between quantities of imports and existing stocks is highly obscure, and indeed disputed, but it is possible to show that minting itself was closely linked to supplies from beyond the subcontinent. Major mints were often located in or close to the ports and towns through which monetary media entered the subcontinent. Lahore and Quetta, for example, were situated close to the overland route bringing silver from Persia and the Middle East (a major commercial route in its own right); ports and river towns such as Surat, Rajmahal, Murshidabad and Dacca, and a string of mints around the southern peninsula, are further examples. Moreover, in the seventeenth century, Surat issues were found widely distributed within the heartland of the Mughal Empire in the north.[5] Many other indications could be added (some of which will appear below), not least the high priority set by various authorities on encouraging such imports. Let us look at these monetary materials in turn.

Habib has recently suggested that the bulk of India's 'large influx of gold', in the early modern period, derived from America, West Africa and Japan. To these we can add a variety of other Asian sources, distributed through Malacca, and a major gold producing region in East Africa.[6] It is indeed already apparent in the sixteenth century that the ports of southern India provided traders with vigorous markets for Asian and African gold, and that the most of this was minted. Records of the East India Companies in the seventeenth century, for example, describe the conversion of imported gold into coin, both for internal circulation and as means of payment in the hinterland (the Companies soon establishing their own mints to produce coins of local type, such as pagodas and fanums, for this purpose). On the other hand, copper was exceptional in being mined within the subcontinent, both in Rajasthan and Nepal, important Mughal mints being situated on the routes connecting these mines with the central positions of the Empire (for example, Narnol). Nevertheless, from the early seventeenth century indigenous copper seems to have been in increasingly short supply, and between the sixteenth and the end of the eighteenth centuries, European and Japanese copper becomes one of the structural mainstays of Portuguese, Dutch and English trade in Asia (as well as being one of their most profitable commodities); it is now evident that substantial amounts of the metal were imported into India over this long period and subsequently minted, and these imports seem to have formed the basis for increased copper circulation. Other monetary media, such as silver and cauris, had no Indian sources, other than existing stocks; thus the vast Mughal output of new silver coin that commenced in the 1590s depended almost entirely upon imported Japanese and especially American supplies. The latter came overland up to the middle of the seventeenth century and also by sea, via the Pacific as well as the Cape of Good Hope.

Finally, there is the question of the non-metallic media, which came to dominate small exchanges in the seventeenth century. These also derived only from external sources, cauris from the Maldives and badam from Persia, the first exchanged and re-exchanged in the ports of the Indies and Indian Ocean, sold in Indian ports for internal use, and eventually leaking, partly through entrepots in Europe, into the expanding African/Atlantic slave trade where cauris formed an essential means of payment. Thus imports of a variety of media, from diverse overseas sources, formed the raw materials of India's highly monetized economies.

A qualification needs to be made for the much disputed question of hoarding and dehoarding. Indianists have long rightly relegated hoarding from its ubiquitous role as an explain – all for India's substantial and continuous import of precious metals, although it continues to appear in works of a comparative nature, for example in those of Ardant, Nolte and Wallerstein.[7] However, dehoarding is also cited as a possible source of the raw materials necessary for the conversion to silver in the Mughal Empire, thereby deflating the role of imports. Dehoarding may indeed explain certain short-term aspects of these changes, but the fact remains that we know very little about the actual practice of hoarding in early modem India (it acts simply as an exogenous explanation for awkward problems), its role in monetary economies is disputed (the very term 'hoarding' begs the question of its function), and it is necessary to widen the framework of explanation so that demand for precious metals can be linked to infrastructural aspects of the subcontinental economies themselves. As we have seen, these imports also included humbler monetary media such as copper, cauris and *badam* (leaving aside more occasional metals such as tin and lead) and these were much less likely to have been stocked in considerable quantities. It is also clear that silver, like copper, generally fetched prices which made their long-distance trade profitable, while imports were encouraged, and sometimes even enforced in certain branches of trade by the Mughal authorities themselves. Moreover, as already mentioned above, such imports were quickly fed into the great coin factories set-up in the major ports and nearby capitals, most notably seventeenth century Surat (Gujarat) and early eighteenth century Murshidabad (Bengal).

This broad-based and long-term import of coinage media implicates some central questions about what is taking place in the subcontinent during the period concerned, not least with respect to continuities transcending the political decline of the Mughal Empire. The import of silver has already given rise to a substantial debate on inflation with both its Hamiltonian and populationist phases. This cannot be dealt with in this essay, but it is worth suggesting that a more interesting question concerns the structure of demand that brought these media into the subcontinent, and which surely lies behind the relatively stable and high prices paid for them. In the following sections we shall attempt to link this question to changes in production and factoring of money.

II. Changes in Mint Production and Growth of a Mass Market for Coin

A Problem of Transition

The changing character of seventeenth century demand is reflected in the differing fortunes of cauris and minted copper, namely in the gradual development of a mass market for money.

In the northern zone, in the early seventeenth century, copper rapidly, but temporarily declined as a major minting metal, being partly replaced by non-metallic media such as cauris and *badam*. Cauris were observed by traders as popular exchange media in most parts of the subcontinent, except in the special monetary zone of Gujarat, where another non-metallic medium, *badam*, circulated. By the end of the seventeenth century, copper (which by no means disappeared from circulation and which continued to be imported for monetary purposes) again reappeared in substantial quantities as a major monetary metal, but for sub-rupee and sub-pagoda denominations. The reasons for this temporary and partial eclipse probably lay in the high value of copper at the end of the sixteenth century and in the difficult transition of the mint from production of high quality, crafted coinages to the more flexible factoring of coins suitable for increased commercial and popular consumption. The indications available suggest that imports of non-mintable media expanded considerably during this period. What is especially notable is that cauri and *badam* circulated in the most commercial and urbanized parts of the subcontinent, as well as in the rural hinterlands, and that later, in the eighteenth century, when copper had already largely replaced them elsewhere (or, as in Surat, had become the major sub-precious metallic payments medium above baser and non-metallic monies), cauris survived and even grew in importance in what by then had become the most precocious manufacturing region of the subcontinent, Bengal.

As for copper, evidence of increasing consumption of copper for monetary purposes appears towards the end of the seventeenth century. For example, at the same time that export-oriented textile manufactures grew in importance in coastal Golconda, local merchants undertook contracts for huge purchases of Japanese copper chiefly for minting.[8]

Similarly, in the 1670s, the East India Company mint at Bombay commenced production of crudely crafted copper coins, not only for use by its own merchants or for circulation within the port itself, but for sales in the Deccan hinterland and territories to the south, which were then providing profitable markets for copper coin.

The implications of these and many other cases, is that the general expansion of cauri-use, and the partial and temporary disappearance of copper, can be viewed together as complementary symptoms and responses to growing markets for monetary media, to problems of supplying copper in sufficient quantities in the early seventeenth century to meet the changing structure of demand, and to difficulties in production of coin within the mint (costs of production having to be reduced if copper was to fulfil its role as subsidiary or substitute money). If it can be shown that the relative price of copper declined over the long term (despite its behaviour on international markets), its increasing use as a payments medium for large numbers of humble producers of crops and textiles in town and countryside. and for urban circulation among the broad mass of urban dwellers, can be explained. In Bengal, in contrast, where prices of foodstuffs and labour were unusually low until late in the eighteenth century, cauris prevailed as the main subsidiary to silver.

Nevertheless, it is the contrast between the late sixteenth and late eighteenth centuries which presents the most interesting and difficult problems with respect to changing money-use and growth of a mass market for coin. A contemporary gazetteer proudly describes the carefully controlled, highly skilled craftsmen of the early Mughal mint. Despite the fundamental reforms of the 1590s, which increased demand and output of silver, techniques of production do not appear to have altered in the decades immediately following. By the late seventeenth century, however, many of the new copper coins show a marked decline in quality of crafting, and this is also true of silver rupees, though to a more modest extent. East India Company coppers, for example, betray a frequently gimcrack appearance at the same time as Company officials complained about the technical difficulties of producing large numbers of coins at sufficiently low cost for popular usage. Correspondingly, silver coin often lacks the degree of care put into cutting and die design in the earlier period, although retaining reliable silver content. A typical bottleneck factor in the transition of the mint to heightened levels of output lay in the scarcity and cost of skilled personnel. The European trading companies, for example, set up mints to produce hammered coins of local type (attempts to use machinery in the late seventeenth century were soon abandoned), but it is notable that personnel were scarce and expensive, while those that were available were often insufficiently skilled, the companies even attempting to import their own specialists, although with indifferent results. These mints were precursors of the low quality coin factories which increasingly came to characterize the eighteenth century.

In short, decline in crafting formed one of the responses to the growth of a mass market for coin, allowing less skilled personnel to be employed, output to be simplified and increased, and copper to be brought back into production on a large scale.[9] In Europe's more centrally controlled currency orders the authorities commenced a long and difficult transition to mechanized production, ostensibly for similar reasons.

Results of Transition in the Eighteenth Century

By the eighteenth century, it is clear that we can no longer treat production of money in terms of the relatively homogeneous and undifferentiated payments media which had earlier characterized the Mughal north but which had unfortunately formed the typological standard of comparison in most of the secondary literature (surely because it most resembles the ideal of European currency systems). The eighteenth century, long treated in terms of political and economic decline, is better understood in terms of an increasingly complex, differentiated and localized type of economy in which large numbers of urban and rural producers became more involved in money-use. On the one hand, penetration by the European companies took on a new and monopolistic character, and the export-orientation of substantial sectors of both urban and cottage textile manufacturing increased. In addition, however, the inhabitants of relatively remote regions also came to participate to an unprecedented degree in the use of money. Correspondingly, the mint takes on a new, more differentiated character, as we shall see below. In central Maharashtra, for example, not known as an important exporting region, wages, sales in the market, accounting systems, rents and taxation, and rural loans, possess a monetary character they either wholly or partly lacked in the seventeenth century. Even less in the eighteenth century than in the seventeenth, can economy, and thus money, be understood in merely regional or sectorial terms (a point to be further confirmed by the discussion of banking below).

In the late eighteenth century, mints increased in number in commercial and relatively remote regions alike. Malcolm counted nine mints in the small region of Malwa (zone 2), while in Mysore (zone 3) twelve were established in this period. In the Western Deccan (Maharashtra) many new mints were founded in these decades, although the full number remains unknown. Nor do we know how long each operated, nor the various periodicities of their production, but what is certain is that production is better calculated by region than by mint, in contrast to the earlier period in which particular mints frequently had a regional function (see Table 1.3). In addition, many new mints were established in small market towns as well as in the larger centres; this occurred in regions not necessarily involved in substantial cash cropping and manufacturing for distant markets. Many were founded to produce only copper coins of gimcrack quality while others continued to specialize in the factoring of high quality trading coinages. Using the craft intensive Mughal mint as a typological base, the mint not only becomes differentiated in terms of specialization and craft input, but also in those of the forces behind its day to day management and running. In several parts of the subcontinent, merchants and bankers are often found owning the mint or in managerial control, or else monopolizing access; this is true both of quality trading coinages and of gimcrack coppers.[10] The explanation lies in the adaption of mint production to a variety of different payment functions.

Two can be quickly identified: trading coinages need to be of established reliability over relatively large distances, variations thus confined within strictly narrow limits (and affecting form more than content). Indian Ocean larins and Spanish reals are early examples at the highest levels of international transaction, but the case can also be made for the subcontinent itself in the eighteenth century, when differentiation imposed a special need for reliable coinages. At these higher levels, the same is true of coinages used in the final stages of transmission of agricultural taxation, over which authorities often maintained an understandably tighter control. Below these levels, at that of actual payments of taxation by peasants, say, a host of less pure silver coinages (more variable in weight) were produced which tended to have a restricted local circulation. These probably circulated within the rural market towns and were used for payments and wages to the majority of ordinary people, the better coins reserved for long-distance transfers, for redemption of bills (hundis) and for payments and salaries to those higher on the social scale.

In addition, both agricultural production and manufacturing in India, were increasingly characterized by what is known as advance payments. Even in the seventeenth century advances played an important role in merchant-producer relationships. Merchants provided producers with the cash to purchase raw materials and foodstuffs (or to pay taxation at difficult times of the year), and received factored commodities, or marketable crops in return at preferential rates. For example, East India Company coinages were explicitly produced, in large part, as direct means of payment for raw cotton and textiles (cauris were imported for the same reason). Advances also need to be differentiated, however, in the late eighteenth century they take on a less voluntaristic, more coercive character in which low value coinages have a special function. It is very likely that several of the 22/3 mints so far identified in one political unit of central India, were established precisely for the purpose of producing monies for advance payments. This is especially likely to have been the case with gimcrack coppers, many being produced in small village mints, some of which remain to be identified. The need to pay advances to producers helps to explain why merchants became involved in gimcrack production, especially in regions like central India where commercial crops and textiles were of major importance.

An exception to this profusion of mints and coin types is Bengal, where, as we have seen, cauris continued to predominate below the rupee, being paid to labourers as wages and to manufacturers. Bengal thus seems to prove the rule; although prices tended to equalize towards the end of the century, we can suggest that here, where the East India Company began to achieve political and economic hegemony, it solved the headache of mint costs, production bottlenecks and competitive access to limited means of payment by continuing to import non-mintable media.

The reasons for gimcrack production lie in the need to cheapen costs of production and to increase flexibility. This was realized both inside the mint (by altering organization of the production line and the skills required) and also in terms of increasing numbers of mints in operation (which declining factoring standards permitted). Decline in quality of factoring of copper coin is readily observable in the crude, often rectangular cutting, the often very low quality of die design, poor striking and variable alloying.[11] In late eighteenth century England, we see tendencies of an exactly similar kind, again in response to local cash needs of a largely commercial character, private production (forgeries, clipping and tokens) filling the gaps left by state-run currency orders unresponsive to rapid change.

Some Data on the Transitions

Below, I shall briefly review the tables, which are intended to illustrate the changes discussed above. They present data that have not been collected together before, although a certain number of single cases have been cited in secondary works. The latter have sometimes led to false ideas, particularly in respect of supposed high costs of minting and the rigidity of hand production (contrast. for example, Table 1.4 with Habib 1982c, 361). This is why the figures collected in the tables are few in quantity and sometimes difficult to interpret.

Firstly, let us look at Table 1.1, showing the career of a single, but very important mint, Surat.[12] It is from the 1630s that imports of silver into the port become of special importance, output capacity growing rapidly, as shown in the career profile. Figures for the late seventeenth century are at present unavailable, apart from one doubtful case. Yet this is a period of expansion in silver supply so that one might expect even greater output of coin. In the early eighteenth century, the port of Surat and the manufacturing economy of its hinterland suffer decline (or a shift to a more peripheral role as producer of exportable crops, embracing some urban decline). But the longer term fortunes of output can perhaps be followed in Table 1.2 in which several mints in different parts of the subcontinent, and from the start of the seventeenth century to the early 19th century, are brought together. Such a small number of figures from such diverse types of location are difficult to compare and they require an essay in themselves. Here, we may contrast Surat in the early seventeenth century with Murshidabad in the early eighteenth, both mints of central importance in the leading commercial economies of their day (Gujarat and Bengal, respectively). Despite the use of hand technology in both cases, production appears to have increased considerably.

Unfortunately, all of these figures concern silver and gold. Lower standards of fabrication suggest higher production rates in the case of copper, certainly when calculated by region rather than by mint, and this would be expected given the large quantity of copper coin required in circulation. In this respect it is as well to remember that it is not the value of these different products which is of primary concern here but the quantity of items entering circulation.

Now let us look at a more remote rural region at the end of our period (Table 1.3). Production in Malwa (north-central section of zone 2) is relatively small if calculated by individual mint, but overall it is very large indeed, given that a seventeenth century mint such as Surat supplied a more than regional market (Surat's coins in particular are found widely dispersed in finds in the northern zone). Note that we are again dealing only with silver at a time when copper output in central India had become very substantial. What marks Malwa (and indeed much of central India) in the late eighteenth and early nineteenth centuries, are urban manufactures of quality textiles for inland markets and raw cotton production for Bengal spinners and weavers, apparently partly financed in the latter case by bankers based in distant cities.

This impression of change over the long-term may also be detected in Table 1.4. This appears to show a long decline in costs of seigneurage, at least in the north. Two reasons may be suggested: one, possible adaptation by the state authorities to the growing importance of commerce and commodity production;

two, the cut in production costs required to produce marketable coinages under changed conditions (argued above). Although actual costs of manufacture are less commonly recorded than seigneurage,[13] the latter includes certain salaries connected with mint production and could be reduced if output per unit of labour were generally increased. Both responses would have been necessitated by the need to produce viable coinages for mass consumption. Problems of cost must have been central in adapting mints and their pro-ducts to new usages for large numbers of ordinary, often relatively poor people (especially for the wide-scale return to copper in the north and its expanded use elsewhere – that is to say where costs squeezed against the value of the metal employed), as well as for manufacturing trades subject to increasing competition. In the latter case, prices were increasingly determined internationally and reduction of labour costs likely to have been decisive.[14] Certainly, in Bombay and Madras (as in London and Paris) in the seventeenth century, mint staff are observed protesting at changes attempted in production methods and salary levels.

The essentially provisional Tables 1.5a and 1.5b show differences in purity and weight per type of coin and per metal, illustrating our point concerning the variable standards of coins produced for different payment functions. This was intended to confirm my supposition that decline in purity affected certain types of coin rather than others. The silver content of commercial types, intended for interregional payments, varied between much stricter limits than others; by the same token, quality of factoring (cutting and striking) in these cases, settled at a fairly utilitarian level which if no longer 'artistic' was far from the crude productions of other coins.

In short, India's hand-produced coinages were adapted closely to the needs of a complexifying, increasingly differentiated economy, satisfying both local and long-distance needs for circulating coin as they developed in the course of the seventeenth and eighteenth centuries. In Europe, on the other hand, the 'alchemist' appeared in the guise of the mundane figure of the illegal coiner and clipper, and the producer of token coins, introducing a similar flexibility into systems otherwise characterized by too rigid and centralized management of production.[15]

Banking of the 'Old Type': The Means and Measure of a Larger Unity

A brief word must be given to banking, referred to as such by con temporary European merchants travelling in India, but generally characterized by specialized management of credit networks, money transfers and exchange dealings. The issue is of vital importance for understanding all aspects of the monetary economy, especially as concerns the measure of unity affecting the latter's highly fragmentary appearances and the nature of the changes affecting the eighteenth century. Unfortunately, it has been seriously neglected, with the result that we only have the barest impressions of its contemporary importance. For example, the widespread appearance and ubiquitous use of bills of payment (hundis) and credit certificates must have affected both circulation and prices, as well as stimulating trade and market-oriented production.

The overall position in the seventeenth century is unclear. Leonard and Richards have disputed both the scale of banking and its importance for state organization. However, both have important points to make, Leonard attacking the customary substantivist (even essentialist) treatment of bankers, and pointing to their central role in government, administration and economy, and Richards arguing that this is more true of the eighteenth century than of the seventeenth. What is well known is that the credit needs of foreign merchants in India, be they Persians, Armenians or European companies, were satisfied through indigenous credit facilities and instruments, centred both in the major ports and cities but also ordered in local agency networks at distant points of production. For example, in the early seventeenth century Dutch and English indigo traders obtained credit from the north Indian agents of Gujarat based bankers. The same[16] is true of purchases of cotton textiles over large areas of northern India, and in urban Gujarat. In addition, the largest financiers (at least) appear to have had agents and respondents m different centres of the international nexus of states in the subcontinent and also overseas, for example at Mocha and Bantam. Thus it is difficult to specify what changes in terms of scale had occurred by the late eighteenth century, when the monopolistic concerns of the Europeans were becoming an important factor in diverting Indian merchant bankers from direct participation in overseas trade in the Indian Ocean and Indies.

In the eighteenth century, however, it is abundantly clear that financial institutions and mechanisms were a fundamental aspect of the monetary economy, not only increasing the range and number of transactions, and closely linked to the production and use of coin, but providing a facilitative context decisively influencing a wide range of other spheres of late pre-colonial life (for example taxation systems, administration and systems of rights and properties). What needs especial emphasis is the increasing density of transactions involving banking and credit on the local level; this can be seen in commercial regions in the seventeenth century, but becomes characteristic of more remote and extensive areas, together with monetary transactions more generally, only in the course of the eighteenth century. Hundis were already important in central commercial regions in the seventeenth century, such as in Gujarat and the commercialized regions of the north, as well as in places of government, but it is in the eighteenth century that one reads that even in an economically backward area like Maharashtra, 'most' transfers, even of a highly local kind, were done by hundi. This coincided with the development of a much more monetized economy in the region, remarked upon above. Finally, transactions in coin need to be linked to the myriad small-scale credit letters in cash and kind which affected even the poorest social groups in at least some rural regions.

What I wish to point out, therefore, is that banking provides a different and illuminating perspective to the whole question of coin manufacture and money-use, one which we barely understand as yet, but which permitted a rare level of flexibility, allowed and articulated heterogeneous, but ultimately connected use – functions, and thereby, in turn, fostered the development of a varied coin typology. For the present, the best that we can do is to hold banking and finance in reserve as key factors in the understanding of the larger system.

A System of the European Type

The hypothesis worked out in the above sections is confirmed by the negative events following colonial occupation. However, the essential changes in the currency system occurred not in the late eighteenth century, when the East India Company began to build up large territorial bases of political control in the most important commercial regions, but in the early nineteenth century, when the process of political conquest was fairly complete. It is difficult to be certain about what is happening in the late eighteenth century: this is the period of great expansion and differentiation in coin production but also, in the last two or so decades, of the beginning of a fundamental change for the worse in India's international position with respect to supplies of monetary media and to commercial relationships with the old inter-Asian trading nexus. In addition, there is an increasing degree of monetary disorder caused by the military and political aspects of colonial conquest. The takeover in Bengal and parts of Coromandel in and after the middle of the eighteenth century, meant a progressive reduction of large-scale imports of bullion and copper in payment for exportable commodities, at the same time that Indian merchants were apparently being excluded from direct participation in overseas trading.[17] Control over a sizeable proportion of agricultural revenue provided the East India Company with an alternative means of payment, stimulating shortages of silver and copper in northern India.

In addition, the minting activity of the Company changes character, from participation in an indigenous system to increasingly interventionist and hegemonic activities. This reached a climax in the 1820s with the establishment of two huge coin mills at Bombay and Calcutta (imported factories, no less). These provided an order of output capacity quite different to the handicraft production of pre-colonial India and the early mechanized mints of pre-industrial Europe (Table 1.2). The establishment of this new level of capacity which reached 300,000 per day at Calcutta was matched by a rapid takeover of most indigenous mints in the early decades of the nineteenth century; these were gradually closed down in the next few years, the last important mints ceasing operations in the 1830s (see Table 1.6). Before the last phase of closure, the Company proceeded to concentrate production in a few of the old mills, especially those producing coinages used in collection of agricultural taxes. At the same time they took in large quantities of indigenous coin for reminting. Finally, the two new Company mints were left as the organs of a centralized currency order of the European type.

Siddiqi has described part of this process in a region of northern India, where the closure of the Banares and Farrukhabad mints, on which local transactions had come to depend, led to money famine and a decline in the number of local bankers (thus intensifying an earlier crisis). Such money famines also occurred in Maharashtra in these early decades, causing dire, if temporary local dislocation. It is not surprising that Siddiqi also describes the appearance of coin clippers and illegal minting to supply local needs in the former case, nor that a host of copper coins of diverse, often ancient origins appeared in the markets of the early nineteenth century. Finally, in these same decades, a few of the private mints left in the so-called 'princely states' (territories left under nominally autonomous governments, but in fact highly dependent on the colonial order) seem to have found a profitable business in supplying Company territories with hand-produced coins for popular use, exchanging below the rate of the official,[18] machine produced currencies. Once again, an analogy with late eighteenth century England is relevant, if this time with a different kind of emphasis.

In a broader view, the early colonial period sees the dismantlement of the currency systems of the old order, as well as much else of the infrastructure of the old economy. From both points of view we can speak of a process of relative demonetization, institutional as well as in terms of the factored materials of exchange.[19]

Conclusion

A final word needs to be said on the context of these changes. Monetization affected a broad spectrum of states in the rest of

Asia, as well as Europe itself. For example, the new or expanded use of copper coins was especially widespread. Such internal developments were linked to the great increase in trading activities during this same period. In the long run, an adequate appreciation of the meaning of monetization in any one of these different regions will need to take this broader framework into account.

III. Bibliographical Note

The following note replaces detailed footnotes and is directed to the needs of an audience for whom Indian economic history is essentially unknown. It does not pretend to be exhaustive.

The arguments in this essay are based on two more extensively documented essays (Perlin 1983b and 1987).

The formative work on the Mughal monetary system is that of Habib and his students, Hasan and Moosvi, published in a number of articles since the late 1950s. Habib gives a summary of their position: Habib 1982d, while S. Moosvi has begun a major revision (Moosvi 1987). Their findings tend to reflect the vicissitudes of the Hamilton debate in Europe.

The focus of this work is limited, however, being confined essentially to the Mughal monetary system, and neglecting monetary phenomena in the pre-Mughal Deccan of the seventeenth century and in Southern India. It also neglects developments in the eighteenth century, while attention tends to be dominated by silver. Habib has important points to make about the relative disappearance of copper, however, in the early seventeenth century (Habib 1987b). Except for the question of the impact of imports on prices, the international context and its ramifications tend to be neglected (both on the level of price formation and on the broader level discussed above).

With respect to these international questions, recent work on trade is very important for its emphasis on monetary media. Glamann 1953 and 1958 is especially useful on copper; Vilar 1976, is valuable on the international context, although in essence neglecting Asia; Chaudhuri 1978, and Prakash 1976 give information on the supply of silver and gold. There is little of value on cauris in pre-colonial India, and nothing on *badam*; here, we need to turn to the valuable work of Hogendorn and Johnson 1986 for serious study and information on the international aspects of this currency medium, especially its links with Europe and the Atlantic slave trade; Heimann 1980 is a pioneering essay on the Asian aspects of the trade. Finally Perlin 1987 brings together the scattered evidence for cauri – and badam – use in India, especially as relates to their function as a commercial payment medium in the seventeenth century. Speaking generally, however, the literature on Indian social and economic history has yet to be properly related to this new work on overseas commerce and supplies of monetary media, Om Prakash, being a rare exception. Of major importance, at least for its emphasis on international developments, is Richards 1983; Brennig 1983s contribution considers the relationship of imports to the 'march' southwards of silver in the seventeenth century, while Richards in his introductory essay (Richards 1983b) has important points to make about India and China as economic nodes of the early modem Asian world. Finally, I have drawn valuable information on the seventeenth century from H. van Santen's study of the activities of the Dutch East India Company in early seventeenth century India, especially with respect to credit and banking, and commercial cropping and manufactures in the hinterland van Santen 1982); this is another of the rare attempts to combine attention to overseas commerce with hinterland history.

Discussion of the broader context of growth in India, especially as concerns periods of apparent decline in post-Mughal northern India and post-Vijayanagara southern India, runs against the grain or generally accepted viewpoints. But see Hambly 1982 and Stein 1982 for belief but none the less valuable pointers. Stein's questions about monetization in southern India constitute an agenda for future research on this highly neglected region (they are but questions). Once more, Richards 1981 should be looked at for an unorthodox hypothesis, favouring increased monetization in the eighteenth century, broadly comparable to the arguments above. Despite what I have said concerning scarcity of data, it is abundant enough to reject Wallerstein's assertion (Wallerstein 1980,

108-9), based on an old article of Sperling and repeated recently by H.H. Nolte (1982, 58-9), that imported bullion and specie were absorbed not into circulation but hoarding and jewellery; this is one example among several of arguments which merely confirm the tendency to view India as not part of an international system of dependencies before colonialism.

Data on the eighteenth century is scattered and incomplete. Much derives from a long tradition of numismatic work, especially with respect to identification of mints and their products. As has been made clear above, this work is uneven, leaving serious gaps in our knowledge, even at this primary level of simple classification. However, Lingen and Wiggins 1978, is a valuable, but all too rare example of an attempt to treat these problems exhaustively on the level of the region. Reports, books and articles produced during the course of colonial rule, from the early nineteenth century on, provide much information on the early phase of colonial transition, but are also the source of a continuing tradition of misunderstanding about the nature of the monetary system. However, Bagchi 1982 and Siddiqi 1973 contradict orthodox opinion on this subject (Bagchi, indeed, complementing the view put forward in this article).

Otherwise, the study of the mint and coin production (both seventeenth and eighteenth centuries) has been seriously neglected, at least in so far as its internal organization, production character, and adaptation to changing demand is concerned.[20] Hand technology has seemed to stand for stagnation, single cases for the whole variety of mints and currency orders over the long period, while we lack even the identity and locations of many mints (as usual, our best information concerns the seventeenth century Mughal Empire).[21] In addition, if overall estimates of money supply (attempted by Habib and Moosvi, for example) have proved notoriously unsatisfactory for the seventeenth century Mughals, they have rightly not been attempted for the eighteenth. Rather, we are concerned with basic features such as the extent and character of monetization itself; thus my 'worm's eye' approach to the subject.

As for the broader economic context of the late eighteenth century, essential for understanding the observed changes in coin factoring, I use my own work on one pre-colonial backward region in the late eighteenth century, and draw inspiration from a small number of important articles on the transitional period in Bengal and Coromandel: Hossain 1979; Arasaratnam 1979; Mohsin 1973, and Prakash 1976.

The study of the crucial subject of banking and credit is relatively new, the consequent lack of sufficient data undermining our capacity to interpret pre-colonial economy; but pioneering work (almost entirely on the late eighteenth and early nineteenth centuries) is underway by G.T. Kulkarni, G.D. Sharma and C. Bayly, largely unpublished as yet (but see Kulkarni 1973, Sharma 1977, Robb 1993, and Bayly 1983). Habib 1972 has discussed hundis. The debate between K. Leonard and J.F. Richards over the role and development of banking is in *Comparative Studies in Society and History*, 21/1979 and 23/1981, but is concerned with the broadest generalities. Methodology in much of the new work is also a problem, being largely concerned with the careers and activities of individual bankers rather than a reconstruction of the network of relationships, contacts and facilities in which these individuals were involved.

Finally, comparison between India and Europe is rendered especially difficult due to disparities in research interest and a large complex of false assumptions fostered by compartmentalization of European and Indian historiographies. Steele 1982 on the role of expanding output and credit in the eighteenth century in increasing money supply, provides intriguing parallels, as does J. Styles remarkable essay on illegal clipping and coin production in the late eighteenth century England (Styles 1980). Production of large numbers of token coins in the early modem period (for example, see *The Times*, 2 March 1982, p. 12) is another indication of the parallel expansion of corn output and cash needs in early modern England and India, despite different organizational contexts. Spooner 1980 and Craig 1953 provide information on the difficulties of the transition to mechanized production in Europe; in contrast to Spooner I see hand technologies and mechanization as both having responded to increased demand, which leads me to the suggestion that the character of control over European currency systems had much to do with the introduction of machinery. Finally, Parker 1974 and Glamann 1974 (for example), provide information on the larger European and pan-Asian context of monetization discussed in this essay.

Together with the work on cauri in West Africa, comparison begins to give way to perception of a wider organization of economic development on an international scale.

Tables

The following tables are simplified versions of the originals, containing only selected information. The originals (for which see the bibliographical note) are accompanied by detailed notes on sources and on problems of interpreting them. Such sources are diverse, quotations differ in form (output, for example, may be expressed as capacity or actual production, or in terms of a quantity per hour, day, year or series of years – or even in terms of an income as a known percentage of actual output), and the contents of apparently identical types of quotation may be shown to differ more or less considerably (seigneurage, for example). The difficulty lies not simply in present scarcity of data but in the fact that its refinement has yet to be debated in the literature. In Tables 1.1-1.3, the essential concern has not been to calculate value of output but productivity in terms of numbers of items (thus metric weights are given only in the original versions); in relatively poor but highly monetized regions in which low value currency media are characteristic, the numbers of items entering circulation are more significant than their value, given the questions with which the present essay is concerned. Finally, the tables should be used in conjunction with the map.

TABLE 1.1: SURAT MINT OUTPUT

	Total output per day in no. silver coins (x thousand)	*Estimated output per 250 day year in no. of silver coins (x million)*
1634	5-9	1.25-2.25
1636	6-8	1.50-2,00
1645	22	5.5
1647	30	7.5

Source: Based upon Perlin 1987, Table 4.1.1.

TABLE 1.2: OUTPUT OF COIN IN DIFFERENT INDIAN MINTS (EXCEPTING SURAT)

Mint	*Years*	*No. coins per day (x thousand)*	*Estimated annual output (250 day) (million)*
Bagalkot	b. 1822	20	5
Benares	1762-64	12-20	3-5
Chandore	a. 1800	20	5
Indore	b. 1823	11	2.75
Murshidabad	1722	12.25	49
Rajmahal	1676	10	2.5
Sagur	b. 1823	7	1.75
Calcutta (factory with 5 steam engines)	1824	308	77

Note: a. = about; b. = before; calculations to nearest 1000 coins/day.
Source: Based upon F. Perlin, 'Money-Use', Table 4.1.2.

TABLE 1.3: A REGIONAL UNIT OF PRODUCTION (CENTRAL INDIA BEFORE 1820)

Mint	*No. coins per day (x thousand)*	*Estimated annual output (250 day) (million)*
Indore	11	2.75
7 other mints	8-10	2-2.5
Total capacity of 8 mints	67-81	16.75

Source: Based upon Perlin 1987, Table 4.1.3 (Malcolm, 1822, vol. 2, 85).

TABLE 1.4: SEIGNEURAGE COSTS IN DIFFERENT MINTS (IN CHRONOLOGICAL ORDER)

	The Northern Zone	
Imperial mint	a. 1595	5.0, 5.8 B/A
Rajmahal	1681	3.5 B
Rajmahal	1692	3.38 A
Rajmahal	1701	3.38 B
-place unknown-	1714-15	2.5
Murshidabad	1722-8	2.5 B
Murshidabad	1735	2.5
Ahmadabad	a. 1750	2.5 B
The Southern Zone		
Armagon	1626	(1.5) A
Nagapatnam	17th cent.	(0.75) A
Pulicat	1644-7	0.75 A
Fort St. George (Madras)	1666-78	0.5 A

Notes: a. = about; given that the transition to silver has been completed by the early eighteenth century. I include mints of zone 2 in the northern silver zone for purposes of this table.; A = gold, B = silver.
Editor's note: Perlin in Richards 1987,358-9 does not speak of seigneurage, but instead of 'duty %'.

TABLE 1.5a: RUPEE COMPARISONS

Type of rupee	*Value (Farrukhabad rupee = 100)*
Ujjain	98.78
Indore	98.6-98.8
Old Ankusi	97.08
Sri Sicca	96.5
Chandore	92.7-95.9
Malharshah	93.5
Bhopal	91.2-92.6
Bhilsa	86.9-88.9
Partabgarh	78.7-82.15

TABLE 1.5b: VARIATION BY WEIGHT OF SELECTED COIN TYPES (LATE EIGHTEENTH-EARLY NINETEENTH CENTURIES)

Type of coin	*Metal*	*No. of specimens*	*Variations as % mean weight*
Ankusi rupee	silver	18	1.98
Chandore rupee	silver	235	7.82
Shivarai paisa	copper	35	39.27

Source: Based upon Khatun, 1960, 224 'for Ankusi and Chandore rupees', and my own research in American Numismatic Society collection for Shivarai paisa.

TABLE 1.6: SAMPLE MINT CLOSURES IN THE EARLY NINETEENTH CENTURY

Mint	*Date*
Bagalkot	1823
Benares	1829
Broach	1806
Chandore	1830
Farrukhabad	1824
Kolhapur	1839
Nasik	1832
5 'Narbada' mints	1826
Pune	1834-5

Editor's Note: For further discussion of the issues raised in this chapter, see Perlin 1993.

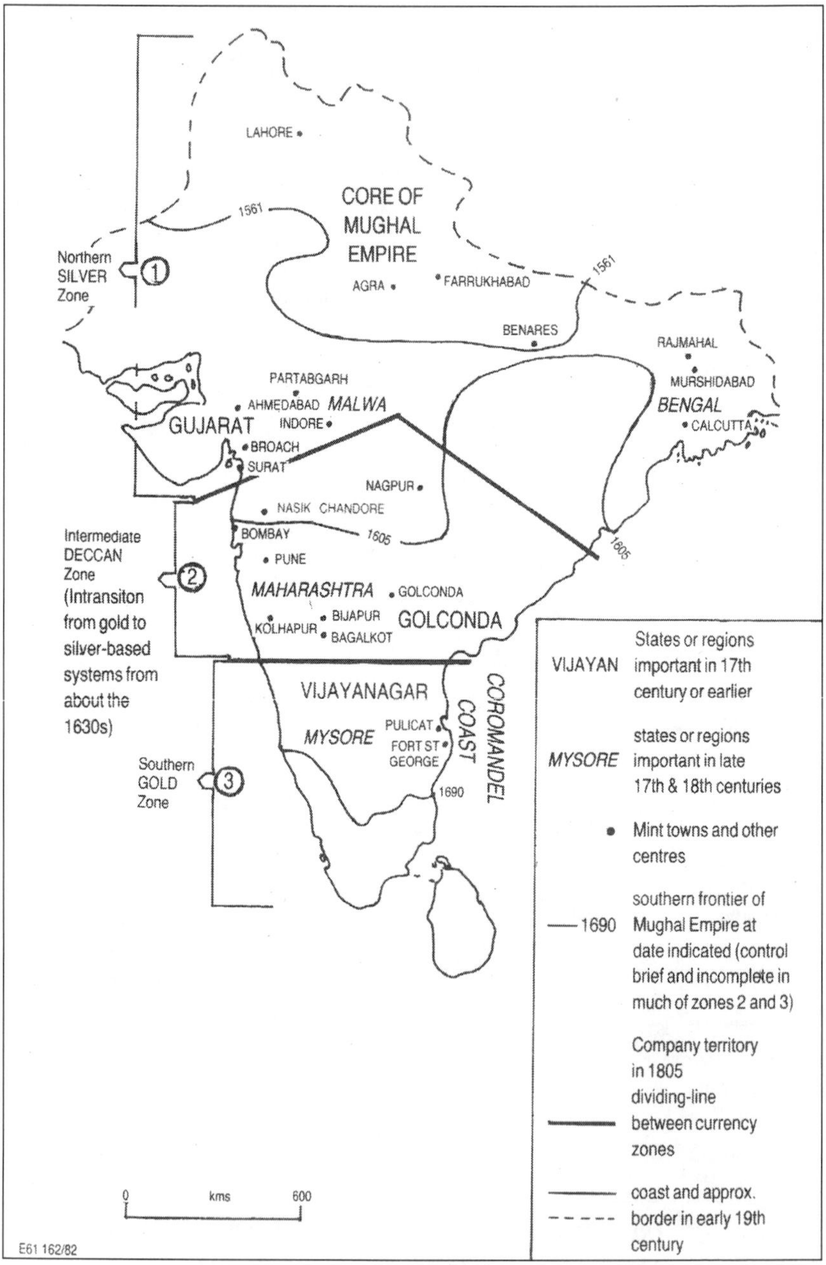

MAP 1.1: MONETARY ZONES, INDIA

NOTES

1. The map has been prepared by E. van Dijk, head cartographer of Erasmus University, whom I thank for expert advice. Full bibliographical references, and the location of my more detailed arguments and interpretations, are given in Part III (bibliographical note).
2. For example, Habib 1982b typically concentrates on Mughal monetary history in the late sixteenth and seventeenth centuries.
3. These remarks on decline of copper minting are based on Habib 1987b; however, the extent of this disappearance of copper from the early seventeenth century mint seems exaggerated to me, especially when seen from a more than Mughal perspective.
4. In fact, the question of access is much more complicated, as indicated by the contributions of Das Gupta 2000, Prakash 1987 and this author 1987. The remarkable purity and reliability of Mughal gold and silver coins was often remarked upon by European travellers.
5. Cf. Moosvi 1987, 9, 24.
6. Habib 1982d, 367-8; and also Kellenbenz 1981, 312-13.
7. In such cases, hoarding seems to serve simply as a demarcation procedure, negating the most interesting external evidence that events in India may be comparable in some way to those elsewhere, and sustaining the old compartmentalizations. [Perlin must be referring to the German historian Hans-Heinrich Nolte (see Nolte 1982; Wallerstein 1973-4. Ed]
8. Glamann 1953, 66, and 1981, 177.
9. Gimcrack production was not of course new, having characterized certain moments of Bahmani and Deccan Sultanate minting much earlier. In the same way, demand clearly outstripped the capacity of supply, quality thereby deteriorating. But these are the results of merely temporary pressures (production of a tribute coinage for example), our arguments concerning a general secular change in the character of demand itself. Temporary deteriorations, due for example to a recoinage, have frequently been observed in the case of Medieval England.
10. The general extent of such control over minting, and the variety of its forms, is unknown, but the cases available suggest that it might have been of strategic importance both in mint production and for the completely obscure problem of supply of raw materials to the mints.
11. In view of prevailing treatments, which assume hand-production to be relatively static, it is worth remarking that the career of the Indian mint between the seventeenth and eighteenth centuries displayed the flexibility characteristic of industries before industrialization. Premises were convertible to different uses. Production was easily adjusted upwards or downwards by increasing or reducing the number of the workforce or the number of hours worked.

12. The strategic location of the Surat mint is indicated by Martins contemporary view of Surat as one of the great silver entrepots of the world; whereas Cadiz transmitted its silver to other parts of Europe, that which came to Surat was mostly distributed within the subcontinent, Van Santen 1982, 83-4. Editor's note: Perlin must here be referring to François Marti, 1634-1706.
13. See note 20.
14. Cf. Arasaratnam 1980 for a discussion of the pressures of international competition on textile production and treatment of producers.
15. Cf. Styles, 1980, *Our Traitorous Money Makers*, for an excellent description of illegal activities and circulation of the products in eighteenth century England.
16. Van Santen 1982, 117-32, is especially useful on the transfer networks.
17. However, according to a private communication by Om Prakash (Editor's note: cf. Prakash 1994), this last point, well established in the literature, is in need of substantial revision.
18. One example among several consists of the 'shivarai paisa', crudely crafted coppers, pumped out in Satara state in the early nineteenth century (not the seventeenth century as commonly believed) and fed into the Pune market then under colonial rule.
19. See also the reference to A.K. Bagchi in the bibliography on demonetization.
20. The structure of mint organization remains obscure, varying in different parts of the subcontinent, over time, and per type of coins produced; the difficulty lies in evidence that mint master and merchant (the person requiring his 'raw material' to be coined) divided responsibilities over different parts of the production line, recorded costs thus not necessarily reflecting complete production costs, while 'seigneurage' is a category whose content varied from case to case.
21. Identification and classification must surely run hand in hand with adequate understanding of production and use of monies, yet much basic data is frankly unknown (for instance, the identity of numerous mints, their periods of working and types of productions, the range of circulation and type of use of the latter), especially as concerns low quality issues. This is both a consequence and a force behind the interpretations combatted in this essay, for example the 'essentialism' that permits, say, a figure for seigneurage or a description of the workings of a mint, to stand for seigneurage and mini working in the subcontinent at large and over two or more centuries.

2

Deep Monetization, Commercialization and Proletarization: Possible Links, India 1200-1900*

Jan Lucassen

Introduction

Economic and social historians traditionally attribute much value to monetization. They see this process – measured by the degree to which interpersonal exchange is expressed in money value or to which currency plays a role in this exchange – as a crucial step in economic development. And for that matter in social relations as well. May this be true in general, it certainly applies to India. Take, for instance, the famous Indian scholar and politician B.R. Ambedkar (1891-1956). From his time as a student at Columbia University when he showed interest in economic issues (his MA thesis in 1915 was on *Ancient Indian Commerce*), he held that the shift 'from kind economy to cash economy' was caused in the first place by 'the British system of revenue and finance.'[1] Without denying the impact of British colonial rule on Indian economic development, most professional historians interested in monetization have rather concentrated on earlier periods.

*An earlier version of this paper was presented on 15 February 2012 at the Workshop 'Money as Social Circuit: Anonymous Currency and Named Credit', organized by Akinobu Kuroda at the Institute of Advanced Studies on Asia, University of Tokyo. I thank the participants for their valuable comments.

Those of the so-called Aligarh school of history, in particular Irfan Habib (from the 1960s), Aziza Hasan (in the 1960/1970s), Shireen Moosvi (from the 1980s), and Najaf Haider (from the 1990s), have developed the theme of the monetization of the Mughal Empire by basing it mainly on sources written in Persian. Other Indian historians have studied the same topic primarily on the basis of Western sources, like Om Prakash, Sanjay Subrahmanyam and Sanjay Garg (who have looked at Dutch, Portuguese and English sources, respectively). Subramanyam's influential edited volume *Money and the Market in India 1100-1700* (1994) especially stands out. More recently, the economic historians Amiya Kumar Bagchi and Krishna Mohan Shrimali have made important contributions to this debate. In this respect the Canadian scholar John S. Deyell and his British colleague Frank Perlin certainly have to be also mentioned, among many others.[2] Deyell published a number of seminal studies since the 1970s in which he proposed and developed several methods to quantify Indian coin production. His data analysis focuses both on the period preceding the Delhi Sultanate and on the early Mughal period. Frank Perlin, a prolific British author, has been active in this field rather briefly, i.e. when teaching at the Erasmus University in Rotterdam between 1980 and 1995. Concentrating on eighteenth and nineteenth-century written sources on Maharashtra and northern India, he focused on coin circulation of small denominations issued by minor mints and their implications for economic and social history.

The work of these authors has found wide acceptance, but some of it has also triggered critical discussions, methodologically as well as historically. This has been the fate of, for example, Moosvi's attempt to establish the amount of stock of silver coins *c.* 1600,[3] and equally so Deyell's reconstruction of the period 750 to 1250, mainly on the analysis of coin hoards.[4] Perlin's conclusions about monetization and subsequently India's integration into a colonial empire which involved deindustrialization and relative demonetization (blatantly differing from Ambedkar in this respect!) have also been questioned severely. Shailendra Bhandare remarks that Perlin is not a numismatist, while Sanjay Garg comments that relative demonetization of India till the mid-nineteenth century 'can at best be a temporary and localized phenomenon'.[5]

The current historiography distinguishes five 'cycles of monetization' as Najaf Haider calls upswings in the use of coins[6]: the early Delhi Sultanate, the early Mughal Empire, the late Mughal Empire and especially its successor states, and, finally, the full-grown colonial state form, say, the second quarter of the nineteenth century onwards. Attempts to estimate absolute levels of monetization are extremely rare, and neither have the different sub-periods been linked directly. Nevertheless, most authors seem to think that each cycle represents a higher level than the previous one.[7]

Whether one agrees with specific scholars or not, basing themselves on the work of many numismatists not mentioned here, they have shown how important, feasible and promising the history of monetization of the Indian subcontinent can be. It goes 'beyond basic numismatic calendaring', although Sanjay Subrahmanyam (from whom I borrow this phrasing) in 1994 stated that the real monetary history of India before 1500 still remains to be written. He is convinced that for the time being there is a great need for precise regional studies, and I could not agree more.[8]

The direction of this essay is however different. Instead of restricting ourselves in time and space, I think we might already make some immediate progress by distinguishing clearly between different social functions of currencies.[9] After all, not all coins were used by all people. By concentrating on the functions of specific currencies (high, medium and small valued) we may not only advance in the field of monetary history, but also – more importantly – in understanding the implications of monetization for other historical developments, *including the history of work and of labour*. To begin with, we have to leave the general concept of monetization for the more specific concept of *deep monetization*. Most of the essay will be devoted to the application of this concept to India between 1200 and 1900, and methodological questions will have to dominate at this preliminary stage of the research. Finally, however, I will reach the ultimate goal of this whole exercise where I will reflect on the implications of deep monetization for long-term labour history.

Monetization, Deep Monetization, and Indian Historiography

Virtually all classical histories of monetization start by explaining the introduction of coins around the middle of the first millennium BCE, more or less simultaneously, in the Eastern Mediterranean, in India and China, by an increasing need for currencies in inter-regional and international trade.[10] In this narrative, coins and trade are inseparable. However, this may at best be only a partial explanation as well-developed international trade is much older and for millennia could do without currency. Besides, it was continued for another two millennia in other parts of the world (the Americas and sub-Saharan Africa). We therefore should be careful in exclusively linking trade with monetization. Instead, we should look for other exchange functions of currencies. Wage payments, for example, may be equally important or even more important for the explanation of the introduction of coins or of variations in their use over time. In contrast to most authors who restrict themselves to the role of money for a smooth exchange of goods (including trade), we have to include also the exchange of services (including work, both free and unfree).

Apart from the distinction between functions, we should try to link these with the outer appearances of currencies. Materials (mainly metals until one century ago, before the advent of small fractions of paper money), and weight should be considered most because they primarily determine the intrinsic value of means of exchange. In the case of fiduciary money, the outer appearance matters even more as the public can no longer derive value from weight and purity. In short, not all types of coins are equally useful for each type of exchange. Gold and heavy silver coins are mainly used for savings and trade settlements, medium-sized silver coins for the payment of taxes[11] and rent (and under certain circumstances also wages), whereas small silver but particularly copper coins (often erroneously called 'small change') are used in daily payments (including wages). Medium-sized coins fit best in systems of weekly or bi-weekly payments, smaller coins if wages are paid daily. Besides, small change is necessary in order to enable food and other market purchases by workers of all kinds. The production and circulation of small coins therefore may be related to the occurrence of wage payments.

Recently, some scholars have introduced the concept of 'deep monetization'. For Bhandare it 'involve[s] the use of coined money in the lowest stratum of a transaction system based on the introduction of cheap, low-denomination coinage', which he also calls 'microcosmic' money economies'. Koenraad Verboven does not give as much a formal definition, but makes two important additional remarks. First, that 'In deeply monetized societies social actors are tacitly and explicitly taught that specific social settings (for instance market exchanges) require money for exchanges and transactions to occur and that we can and should accept "money" in exchange for goods and services.' Second, 'that "deep monetization" does not imply full monetization. […] No pre-industrial economy ever came near to being fully monetized. Gift exchange, command economics and redistribution remained important structural principles that governed the flow of resources.' Without using the term, much earlier, Robert Wicks combined some of these elements by quoting Robert Renfrew – 'the existence of any low-denomination coinage, used within the jurisdiction of the issuing authority, is an indication of market exchange' – and by adding this comment: 'The presence of multiple denominations, especially in base-metal coin series, opens the door to wider usage, allowing for the possibility that the coinage was utilized in marketed transactions.' To summarize, this image of 'deep' denotes *the permeation of the usage of coins deep into society until reaching the large mass of the working population.*[12]

The proliferation of small-value coins points to increasing numbers of small-value transactions by an increasing part of the population, and might entail a shift from personal to impersonal obligations. Such shifts may be necessitated either by occupational specialization or by changing value systems in inter-personal relations. An example of the first is the shift at village or regional level from self-supporting households to occupationally specialized households where farmers, millers, bakers, shoemakers, soldiers, etc., have to exchange goods and services. The second may be exemplified by already specialized local or regional societies that no longer prefer to express their mutual dependency in terms of moral obligations, but rather in terms of credit and debt, expressed in money.

Processes of occupational specialization and monetization of this kind may occur simultaneously, but monetization may also develop long after occupational specialization takes off. Another variant – often simultaneous with occupational specialization – is the emergence of social inequality, where certain groups in society manage to impose tributary obligations on most others. Such tributary relations may or may not be monetized. The former is exemplified by monetary tax systems; the latter by the imposition of servitude, slavery, or other forms of unfree labour (for a summary see Figure 2.1).

It should be stressed here that we need a very broad approach to the way impersonal exchange of goods and services may be organized. Essential is the expression of mutual obligations in a standardized, impersonal way. There are three big variants. First, in goods (the concept of 'barter' covers this only partially where one good is exchanged against the other), like fixed grain payments for labour – documented already for Mesopotamia and Egypt before Alexander the Great.[13] Second, in metallic (or paper) currency – in the available literature best studied of all. Third, cur-

	Payments in kind	*Monetized payments*
Exchange of goods as a consequence of occupational specialization	Communal (jajmani-like) mutual obligations	Selling and buying own produce at commodity markets (and subsequent spending of earnings in markets)
Exchange of services	Communal and personal mutual obligations	Wage payments in coins (and subsequent spending of earnings in markets)
Imposition of obligations or duties	Tax payments in kind; Unfree labour	Tax payments in coins

FIG. 2.1: HUMAN EXCHANGE RELATIONS AND MONETIZATION

rency in non-metallic (and non-paper) forms, for which cowrie shells, bitter almonds and beads are well-known examples, but for which, in principle, any tangible and manually easily portable substance may serve. Many more distinctions of barter and currency are relevant and available, but they have to rest here.

It may be clear that monetization, and especially deep monetization, is directly linked to general historical debates, more particularly to those on economic development and economic growth, and on labour history. For those parts of the world where numismatic evidence is abundant, but written sources on monetization and occupational structures, for whatever reasons, are less abundant, there is already a certain tradition in numismatic and monetary history to use data on coin production as proxies for economic development at large. This also applies to India.

For many reasons, India seems to be also an extremely fine laboratory for the study of deep monetization. Frank Perlin already made a convincing plea for the importance of the production and circulation of the lower denominations. Many written sources corroborate the impact of small currency on the life of the population in general. Let me quote one about the scarcity of copper coins in Bihar in 1795:[14] '[…] this species of coin is the principal currency amongst the manufacturing and labouring class of people in this quarter, hence a deficiency of this currency in circulation, whether real or artificial, the evil will fall principally on the lower classes of people.'

This essay necessarily will have to develop first the necessary tools for the reconstruction of major trends in deep monetization. Although this concept as such is not restricted to specific parts of the world or specific periods, the focus in this paper is on India, 1200-1900. It also attempts to start a discussion on possible implications for the economic and social history of the subcontinent. The choice for this case is not only given by the rich historiography available on monetization and the recent publication of excellent catalogues which may serve as a solid basis of analysis. In the framework of global history in which increasingly continents and subcontinents are compared, India is always mentioned as an important case, but so far case studies lag far behind those on China and Europe.[15] As said, the relative lack of written sources for labour history before the colonial period might be an extra reason to look for alternatives as proposed here. The development of a long-term labour history of the Indian subcontinent may be enhanced by the study of long-term trends in deep monetization, more precisely of its relation with the processes of commercialization, commodification of labour, and proletarianization.

Available Data and Methodology: India 1200-1900

Whereas direct quantitative information on total circulation is lacking as a rule before the advance of modern economics in the second half of the nineteenth century, historians studying earlier periods have to rely on data about the composition of coin hoards or coin production. Frequency analysis of coin hoards is widely used in numismatics.[16] It tells us about historical preferences in hoarding coins (a proxy for but not identical to circulation patterns), and shifts in these patterns through time as the youngest coin in a hoard is mostly taken as a date *post quem* for the hiding. Apart from finding such shifts (a most important result as such!), hoard analysis is less suitable to reconstruct production figures over long periods of time. The most important reason for the limitations of this method is the lacking availability of information on most hoards that are turned to the surface, as most findings are not recorded as such and these coins reach the collector's market or disappear as scrap in the melting-pot. Therefore, those which come under the eye of specialists and receive able cataloguing can be seen only occasionally as representative of the content of all hoards. Besides, hoarding of small currencies is rather the exception because those who have to hide coins have an understandable predilection for gold or larger silver, which per weight represents more value. Thus, these minor denominations as a rule are found as stray finds, therefore escaping systematic numismatic analysis. Most importantly, the coin hoard method, because of differences in hiding practices (more or less, war and social turmoil in different periods) and in representativeness over time is less suitable for the goal set in this essay.

John Deyell's major contribution on Mughal coin circulation offers a quick introduction to the available reconstruction methods for long-term production trends, including the study of coin hoards.[17] This is also the basis of his later book on the period 750-1200.

One method he mentions there, but does not use himself, is the cataloguing of coin types per ruler, defining a coin type by ruler, mint and year.[18] Instead he adopts – in his own words - a less accurate approach, which is shown for copper coins in Table 2.1.[19] He

TABLE 2.1: DEYELL'S RECONSTRUCTION OF THE GENERAL AVAILABILITY OF COPPER COIN TYPES IN MUSEUMS AS 'A USEFUL INDEX OF THE RELATIVE ANNUAL COPPER COIN PRODUCTION DURING EACH REIGN' OF THE MOST IMPORTANT MUGHALS, 1556-1759

	Total number of specimens in 5 museums	*No. of mints*	*Average years per mint*	*Specimens in 5 museums per mint year*	
				D = A/BC	*D2 (excl. Elichpur)*
	A	B	C		
Akbar, 1556-1605	1304	59	40	0.552	0.552
Jahangir, 1605-27	85	12	23	0.308	0.308
Shahjahan, 1628-58	80	15	30	0.178	0.178
Aurangzeb, 1658-1707	145	26	40	0.139	0.130
Shah Alam I, 1707-12	35	12	5	0.583	0.218
Farrukhsiyar, 1713-19	6	12	6	0.083	0.091
Muhammad Shah, 1719-48	52	12	29	0.149	0.060
Ahmad Shah, 1748-54	18	3	6	1.000	0.500
Alamgir II, 1754-59	37	8	5	0.925	0.714

Source: Deyell 1987b, 161.

starts out by adding up 'the total specimens of copper coins for each reign preserved in five [most important British and Indian] museums' (column A in table). Next, he provides the number of mints in production per reign (B; according to Singhal 1953) and 'the average number of years the mints were in the possession of the Mughals for each reign' (C).[20] The relation between these three figures (D = A/BC) 'indicates a general decline in empire-wide annual copper production' from 1556 to 1748, which confirms broadly Irfan Habib's observations.[22] This trend shows even more clearly by leaving out one single mint (Elichpur in Berar) which in later reigns became the single most active copper mint. In a way Machhlipattan near Madras performed a similar local function (see Table 2.1).

A third method, used by Deyell, is the frequency analysis of coins from hoards. Two hoards, consisting of copper dams only (1,774 and 1,002 pieces respectively) turning out to be truly random samples, may therefore be taken as representative of the copper circulation in the Delhi *suba* in the years 1602-4. Such large hoards of copper coins are unfortunately rarely available for scholarly analysis in comparison with hoards of silver and even gold coins (see Tables 2.2 and 2.3).

In Tables 2.2 and 2.3 I have smuggled in a fourth method which Deyell mentions but applies only occasionally and unsystematically, which is the determination of the rarity of coins.[22] I have taken the opportunity to compare Deyell's results for frequency of circulation with actual collectors' market prices of old coins (as expressed in modern numismatic catalogue prices, and as available for CE 1600 onwards). This little experiment, covering only the last years of Akbar's reign, shows a high correlation between the relative frequency of *dams* in these two hoards and the frequency of similar pieces actually offered in the collectors' market, where prices between US $ 7-9 for (later) Akbar *dams* may be interpreted confidently as the indication 'very common (cc)' in other catalogues (see below). It may also serve as a preliminary introduction to the method applied in this essay that is explained below.

This in fact is a fifth method, the reconstruction of production figures and production capacity of mint houses in order to

TABLE 2.2: DEYELL'S RECONSTRUCTION OF THE AVAILABILITY OF COPPER *DAMS* FROM 10 MOST IMPORTANT MINTS IN TWO COIN HOARDS FOR THE PERIOD AH 963-92 (1554/5-1583/4) AS COMPARED WITH CATALOGUE PRICES

Rank	*Mint*	*Suba*	*Approximate tally of coins issued*	*Per cent of 445*	*Market price in quality Fine*	
					KM	*US$*
1	Narnol	Agra	445	100.0		
2	Ajmir	Ajmer	63	14.2		
3	Delhi	Delhi	47	10.6		
4	Fathpur	Agra	43	9.7		
5	Agra	Agra	42	9.4		
6	Urdu	none	37	8.3		
7	Dogaon	Awadh	35	7.9	28.19	7.00
8	Bairata	Agra	22	4.9	30.1	18.00
9	Alwar		18	4.0		
10	Lahore	Lahore	16	3.6		

Sources: Deyell 1987a, 56 (approximate tally of coins issued = the tally of type coins found for each mint, multiplied by the percentage of the number of minting years to the total number of minting years); Bruce 2008, 946-7 (only available for AH years 1010-13, instead of 963-92).

combine these with rarity indicators of coin types struck there. This is especially important because the same classical hammer- and anvil-method was used during the whole period studied here, with the exception of the big colonial mints of Calcutta, Bombay and Madras that came after 1835. This manual die-striking technique in India goes back to the fourth century BCE and was identical to the one practised in the Mediterranean.[23] The lower matrix was embedded in an anvil, the upper was in the form of a hand-held punch which was hit by a hammer man. Upper matrixes were worn much quicker than the lower ones. From a letter, written in 1804 by the British Collector of Allahabad, we know that for the

TABLE 2.3: DEYELL'S RECONSTRUCTION OF THE AVAILABILITY OF COPPER *DAMS* FROM 10 MOST IMPORTANT MINTS IN TWO COIN HOARDS FOR THE PERIOD ILAHI YEAR 30 (AH 993/994 = CE 1585/6) TO YEAR 50 (AH 1013/14 = CE 1605/6) AS COMPARED WITH CATALOGUE PRICES

Rank	*Mint*	*Suba*	*Approximate tally of coins issued*	*Per cent of 200*	*Market price in quality Fine*	
					KM	*US$*
1	Narnol	Agra	200	100.0	32.21	9.00
2	Urdu	none	172	86.0	32.29	7.00
3	Bairata	Agra	113	56.5	32.5	7.00
4	Chittor	Ajmer	71	35.5		
5	Gobindpur		69	34.5	35.12	7.00
6	Ajmer	Ajmer	58	29.0		
7	Delhi	Delhi	45	22.5	32.9	7.00
8	Dogaon	Awadh	45	22.5		
9	Ujjain	Malwa	36	18.0	32.28	9.00
10	Allahabad	Allahabad	33	16.5		

Sources: Deyell 1987a, 57; Bruce 2008, 946-7 (only Ilahi years 45-50, thus leaving out 30-44).

striking of silver coins, twenty-two upper and eight lower matrixes were needed, so nearly three times more upper than lower ones.

A sixth and last method, which so far is underdeveloped for copper coins but widely discussed for silver coins, traces the availability of metals for coinage. In this case copper mines and copper at imports into the subcontinent.[24]

On the basis of the foregoing historiographical and methodological overview, I will adopt the following approach to study deep monetization trends in the Indian subcontinent:

a. The unit of analysis is the entire subcontinent because in such a large geographical unit (like elsewhere in the pre-modern world), monetary circulation of coins was not confined precisely to the polities where they had been produced. This even goes for small coins, although less so than for higher-value coins.[25]

On the other hand, exchange of coins between the Indian subcontinent and surrounding territories (with a possible exception of Afghanistan) was limited until the nineteenth century, when colonial Indian coins started to circulate in e.g. East Africa, the Gulf and Malaya. In my database I distinguish between southern, north-western, north-central, and north-eastern India.

b. The time frame has been taken as long as feasible, which means the period 1200-1900. This is determined by the availability of good and coherent catalogues which is the case since a few years. An excellent starting point is the catalogue, published by Goron and Goenka in 2001, of all known coin types of the Delhi Sultanate and similar Muslim states. Before 1200, not only is cataloguing less well developed, but, more importantly, the dating of coins is much more uncertain. Mainly before the advent of the Muslim states, Indian coins rarely bear years in one of the prevailing eras and often even no reigns. Their dating is consequently too imprecise to allow for an attribution to quarter centuries in which they have been produced.[26] This after all is the shortest meaningful period possible, and therefore it constitutes my temporal unit of analysis (so, all in all, I distinguish twenty-eight quarter centuries). After 1900, another complication arises: the circulation of small-denominated paper money with a much shorter life time than coins.

c. Units of analysis are coin types, for which Deyell provides a useful definition: 'Essentially, numismatics is the science of classification of coins, and the unit of study is the coin-type, a differentiable category of coin possessing a unique appearance, metrology, metallic composition and message content.'[27] Numismatists, cataloguing coins of a certain period may sometimes differ about the value to be attributed to the variable 'message content' but all seem to agree that different texts are decisive. Although some would classify a different date or even a month (as practised in the Mughal's Ilahi-chronology) as a type, others do not consider differences in years as sufficient for typology purposes.[28] The latter method has been applied for this essay.

d. In order to catch deep monetization, I will restrict myself to small coins, here defined as all copper and billon coins, as well as silver coins weighing less than 5 grams. This excludes half rupee pieces and higher values from the sixteenth century, as well as similar coins in a more remote past. Heavier silver coins represented too much value for the common man and, as a consequence, were never received by the majority of the population or only a few times in their life.[29]
e. A listing of the small value coin types of India 1200-1900 provides only a first glimpse of deep monetization patterns. The next step, a reconstruction of their numbers in circulation, obviously provides much more insights. Only from 1835 is this possible for all issues of the British colonial mints (and even much later for the still surviving 'native' mints). Previously, such figures are available only for a handful of coin types. These will be used of course (see Table 2.6 below), but for the great majority an indirect method has to be found. In order to estimate coin production (and thus coin circulation) before 1835, we have to extrapolate from the data of the few types for which we have data, to the rest. The key proposal on how to do this, which is not used on a grand scale so far as I know, is to determine the rarity of coin types in the collectors' market as reflected in coin catalogues and to use it as a proxy for coin production.[30] For the catalogues to be used, this presupposes of course a certain uniformity in typology and indications of rarity, either expressed in symbols or in market prices. This is true for the six most important catalogues used for this paper. If we accept that there is overall a more or less fixed relation between actual rarity in the collectors' market and numbers struck in the past (as suggested in Tables 2.2 and 2.3 above), these catalogues provide us with a relative yardstick for measuring coin production intensity. Two sorts of information are available for different coin types (or even for separate years) in the major catalogues. First, qualitative indications of rarity, which are widely accepted among numismatists and coin collectors. These run from '*cc*' for *very common*, '*c*' for *common*, '*s*' for *scarce*, to '*r*' for *rare* and '*rr*', '*rrr*' and '*rrrr*' for higher degrees of rarity. Second, indications

of market prices, differentiated by degree of preservation. In this essay I will use only indications for the preservation quality 'fine' (i.e. showing 'fairly heavy wear over all of the coin', but still showing all important details), valuated in US $ at the time of publication of the catalogue (in this case editions varying between 2002 and 2008).

f. The penultimate step is the reduction of these two systems of rarity indication to one for the entire period. This has been possible because for some hundred coins, mainly dating from the seventeenth century, both indicators are available.[31] Fortunately, they show a high degree of consistency, which makes it possible to convert price classes into the symbolic rarity indicators, and consequently to apply one set of rarity indicators to the entire data base (see Table 2.4).[32]

g. The last step is the application of weights to the rarity indicators cc, c and s in order to present the results in one graph (see section under 'Relative Overall Trends: Acceleration and Stabilization Periods 1200-1900' and Figure 2.2, p. 349.).[33]

A database containing all types answering the specifications just discussed, and containing thousands of different types for the periods *c.* 1200-1750 and 1850-1900, is the basis for the preliminary conclusions in this essay. A few more words on the catalogues

TABLE 2.4: CONGRUENCY BETWEEN TWO SYSTEMS TO INDICATE THE RARITY OF INDIAN COINS IN DIFFERENT CATALOGUES

Indicated by symbols		*Indicated by market prices (in US $) for the grading 'fine'*
Very common	cc	0-10
Common	c	11-15
Scarce	s	16-25
Rare	r	26-35
Very rare	rr	36 and more
Extremely rare	rrr	
Only one or a few specimens documented	rrrr	

used may be useful.[34] For the greater part of India between 1200 and 1550/1700, an excellent catalogue by Stan Goron and J.P. Goenka is available for the sultanate of Delhi, its successors the Suris and its Muslim competitors and successors like the sultans of Bengal, Madura, Gujarat, Malwa and Kashmir. From 1600, world catalogues, although by far not as reliable as Goron/Goenka, may serve our purpose for the moment. The period in between the reigns of the three first Mughals is covered by an excellent catalogue for Babur and one for Akbar, but the intermediate reign of Humayun has not yet received equal numismatic attention and is certainly underrepresented in my database so far.[35] Also the coinage in the south deserves more attention than I could devote to it now.[36] Apart from these weaknesses to which a few dozen more missing types could be added,[37] my main problem lies in the century between 1750 and 1850, which for that reason is still missing in my database. As a consequence of the weakening of the Mughal Empire and the success of the colonial powers, first and foremost the British who prevailed in the second half of the eighteenth century, minting activities proliferated all over the country. On the one hand, this shows how important the demand for metal means of exchange was, irrespective of whether centralised polities could meet it or not. On the other hand, numismatic evidence of exactly which types have been made where and when is still very weak. Although the big world catalogues pretend that all information is available, detailed studies of the coppers in the early-nineteenth century demonstrate how wide the gap is between the prevailing catalogues and what we should wish to know.[38] I hope to contribute to narrowing this gap a little bit in the near future.

Another gap, which will never be filled by any cataloguing, however perfect, is quantifiable information on the circulation of non-metallic currency, especially cowries in north-eastern India about which a lot has been written already, and bitter almonds,[39] as well as on remuneration in kind (mostly grain) of labour and other services (see below). Consequently, the data presented restrict themselves to metallic small currency, but of course the circulation of non-metallic currencies and practices of payments in kind have to be weighed in any final discussion about proportions between payments and non-paid services (whether forced or not) on the other.

Historical Framing of the Numismatic Listings

Before jumping to the analysis of the database, we are reminded by Wicks that 'While the physical characteristics of a coin series, as well as its geographical distribution, can provide valuable clues to its function, the precise role of that coinage must be confirmed by a study of literary sources'.[40] Over the last years, I have had the opportunity to do exactly this by combining historical sources on wage payments, and the production and circulation of a number of copper coins in early nineteenth-century northern India, on the one hand, with numismatic evidence on the other. Occasionally, it is also possible to find more production figures of certain hand-struck coin types. Combined with information on their geographical distribution (from hoards and stray finds) this is a starting point for understanding their function. This basis is still too narrow to convert directly rarity indicators for all other types into production figures, but it is not to be excluded that a larger set of data will make such a procedure possible in the near future. This will also open the way to construct one common picture for pre- and post-1835 patterns. In the following subsections, two different types of evidence will be produced. To begin with, some state-wide cross-sections between 1300 and 1600, followed by production figures of a few dozen manually produced coin types as far as known to me, for the seventeenth, eighteenth and nineteenth centuries. Only at the end of the nineteenth century we touch firmer ground with the first national estimates of coin circulation, based on actual production figures.

'National' Cross Sections, 1300-1600

At the beginning of the fourteenth, the sixteenth and the seventeenth century, four widely diverging reports on state expenditure, state treasury at moments of 'regime change', and on taxation provide a first proxy for circulation patterns and maybe even figures.

Although full of uncertainties and providing coverage at the expense of depth, they are all we have for the earliest centuries covered in this essay. Enough reasons to present them here briefly.

State Expenditure and Coin Circulation: The Delhi Sultanate c. 1300

The earliest period for which at least some indications for coin circulation are available is the reign of Alauddin Muhammad, Delhi sultan 1296-1316. He is known for spending 10 million *tankas* cash per year on his 20,000 Turkish Mamluks (500 *tankas* per person) and 210 million *tankas* on his 900,000 cavalrymen (234 *tankas* per person).[41] Even if we do not accept fully the probably excessively high numbers of cavalrymen under arms as such, these are impressive sums of money. Most likely the coins needed had been produced recently by this same sultan.[42] Billon '6 *gani*' coins (25 per cent silver) weighing 3.5 grams were stamped during eleven years (AH 701-5 and 711-16). Besides, there were the equally heavy '2 *gani*' coins (containing *c.* 15 per cent silver), coined during seventeen years (AH 696-711 and 716). The mint house is not given, but supposedly it was Delhi where most gold and silver coins of this sultan were also struck under the famous mint master Thakkura Pheru. Both billon coin types are classified as 'very common' and therefore must have been produced in large numbers. Supposing that the Delhi mint mainly worked for the needs of the treasury, which in its turn had the army as its main expenditure, this mint house must have been able to coin per annum at least one million billon coins at the start of the fourteenth century.

State Treasury and Coin Circulation in the Mughal Empire c. 1526

After the battle of Panipat (1526) where Babur and his son Humayun defeated the Delhi sultan Ibrahim Lodhi, the acquired accumulated treasures of the Lodhis amounted to 70 lakh (7 million) pieces, donated by the father to his son. This treasure must have been Lodhi currency, more particularly *Sikandaris* or black *tankas.*[44] As the billon *tanka* of 80 *ratis*, weighed about 9 grams, the gift was bulky, weighing 63,000 kg of specie.

We may compare these figures to the taxes Babur could levy from the newly conquered territories, amounting to 520 million *tankas*. Only in Tirhut (northern Bengal, famous for its silver issues), the sum consisted of 255,000 silver *tankas* and 2,750,000 black *tankas*, but in all other provinces of the erstwhile Delhi, sultanate revenues were expressed in *tankas* without qualification.

If this information is correct and if we may suppose that, (a) this sum corresponds with the total circulation, and, (b) that this equals the total production of black *tankas* since Sikandar Shah Lodi (1488-1517), we are dealing here with an average annual production of at least 10 million pieces per year. Even if we extend the period back to the middle of the century, when Bahlul Shah Lodi (1451-1489) started his extensive coinage of *80 rati tankas* – extensive because these billon (16 per cent silver) *Bahlulis* now are classified by collectors as very common, the Delhi minting capacity is impressive. Covering in total three-quarters of a century, we reach an annual production of nearly 7 million pieces on average (see Table 2.5). Besides, billon and copper fractions were struck as well, all of which are still common or very common.

TABLE 2.5: PRODUCTION OF BILLON 80 *RATI TANKAS*, DELHI 1451-1526

Type (Goron and Goenka 2001)	*Rarity*	*Years struck (AH)*	*Number of years struck*	*Coin name*
D 690	cc	856-66, 872-92	33	*Bahluli*
D 705	cc	894-909	16	*Sikandari*
D 706	cc	900-22	23	*Sikandari*
Total			72	

In sum, we may conclude that the mint house of Delhi in the period 1451-1517 (when, apart from some tankas and their fractions, hardly other types were coined) had the enormous capacity of maybe 7-10 million pieces per year.

Taxation and Coin Circulation in the Bengal Sultanate c. 1550

According to the *Ain-i-Akbari*, the revenue of all Bengal (excluding Orissa) in the late sixteenth century was 472,726,681 copper *dams* (or 11,818,167 silver rupees or 12,831,152 silver *tankas*). Deyell compares this with his estimates of the great re-coinage in Bengal of 1493 (3.15 million *tankas*) and 1538 (2.68 million rupees), as well as with his estimates of average annual *tanka* production based on die-count analysis for the period 1493-1576.[44] Combining his annual production estimates with an average loss in circulation of 2.5 per cent he suggests a stable coin circulation of 30 million *tankas* between 1494 and 1519, a rise to about 37 million by 1538 and 30 million rupees in 1575. If the order of magnitude of all these estimates is acceptable, the two great recoinages mentioned must have affected 10 per cent of the circulating coins. It would follow also that *c.* 1550, annual coin production might have been one-thirteenth of annual revenue receipts, and that total circulation was sufficient to meet about three years of revenue demand (if fully realized) in the same coins.

Tax Sum and Coin Circulation in the Mughal Empire c. 1600

Having tried to establish a relation between Babur's tax sum and coin circulation/coin production, we may do the same for the Mughal Empire in *c.* 1600, when the total tax sum in the vastly expanded empire had risen to 3,630,000,000 *dams*.[45] In making the same assumptions *ut supra* – that this sum corresponds with the total circulation, and this equals the total production of *dams* so far (i.e. since the production of the *Suri paisas* from 1543 onwards), we are dealing here with an average annual production of at least 60 million pieces per year, or – taking the 10 most important mint houses – 6 million pieces on average per mint. Remarkably, this achievement is nearly the same as that of Babur's time, albeit that *dams* were much bigger than erstwhile *tankas* and therefore less easily produced, and, most importantly, that at the same time an impressive silver production had taken place.

Production Figures and Production Capacity of Traditional Mints, c. 1500-1870

Let us now move to more solid grounds where fewer assumptions have to be made and investigate production and production capacities of traditional mints, relying on manual striking. For two dozen of them sufficient numbers have been published, unfortunately some only for silver. Most and best figures are available for the early colonial period of the British occupation, when working mint houses in newly conquered territories fell into their lap, and which as a rule they tended to continue, at least for a number of years. Thanks to Paul Stevens' still ongoing work, ample information on these 'transitory mints' has become available recently, and can be added now to data provided mainly two decades ago by Frank Perlin (see Table 2.6).[46]

We may conclude that the main mint houses of north and central India, employing hundreds of workers, were well capable of striking up to 5 million coppers a year. If manufactured for years in a row, this implies dozens of millions of one and the same type, like it happened in the times of the Suris and Akbar. Smaller mints, as the examples of Broach, Surat, Saugor (until 1823), Bankot, Chhachrauli, Jagadhri, Chandore, Indore and Alwar show, may have produced under similar circumstances several hundred thousand or even several million pieces of one type. After partial mechanization, outputs of five million and more coppers per year became within reach.

Output figures for silver coins are overall slightly higher. Although struck by the same hammer-and-anvil technique their fabrication on the one hand took more time because less weight tolerance was accepted for the more expensive silver (roughly 20 times more than copper); on the other hand, minters earned higher piece wages by coining silver than copper coins, and had good reasons to speed up its production as far as possible.

All coins in this table have been compared to the available cata-

TABLE 2.6: MAXIMUM OR AVERAGE CAPACITY REALISED (MILLIONS OF PIECES PER YEAR) IN MANUAL COIN PRODUCTION

Mint	*Period (maximum production year in brackets)*	*Number of silver pieces*		*Number of copper pieces*	
		Annual average	*Annual maximum*	*Annual average*	*Annual maximum*
Surat	1634-72 (1647)	4.125	7.5 (10)	3.75	
Rajmahal	1676	2.5		-	-
Murshidabad	1722		12.16	-	-
Benares	1748-76			3	5
Ahmedabad	1750		(3.09-) 6.17	-	-
Calcutta	1758-75	(6.2)	*c.* 10	-	-
Pune and Chakand (Chakan?)	1793-1805	0.1-1.75			
Srinagar (Bundelkhand)	1794-1819	0.4-1.8			
Chandore	*c.* 1800		5		
Delhi	*c.* 1800-30		1-1.25		4
Amber / Jaipur	1802-03	(1.25)-5			
Farrukhabad	1802-05	3 – 3.4			
Surat	1802-13	0.07		1.15-1.28	
Broach	1803-29	0.9	1.84	0.75	0.96
Saugor	1806-23	0.4-1.08	1.7		
	1827-35*	2.15		5	
Bombay	1808-18			2.5-3	
Benares	1815-20*			7	
Ahmedabad	1817-18		2.62		
Bankot	1820-21			3-4.8	
Indore	1823		2-2.75		
Chhachrauli/ Jagadhri	1830			0.1-0.15	
Chandore	1832	0.18		1.7	
Alwar	1856-68			0.19	0.29
Indore	1875		3.0		

Note: * = with improved machinery (but not yet steam).[47]

logues – in line with earlier conclusions of this paper – turn out to be still very common in the collectors' market and valued accordingly.

Relative Overall Trends: Acceleration and Stabilization Periods 1200-1900

It is time now to come up with the results of the exercise so far: the weighted number of types struck 1200-1750, and up to now available in my database. As Figure 2.2 shows a clear pattern of ups and downs arises.

To begin with, the periods showing clearly an increase of production:

- A first acceleration took place in the period 1275-1325/75, followed by a low;
- A second acceleration in the period 1425/50-1525, followed by an even more impressive acceleration period;[48]
- A subsequent third and major acceleration from 1525 until at least 1600.[49]

It is too early to reflect extensively on these results, but a few

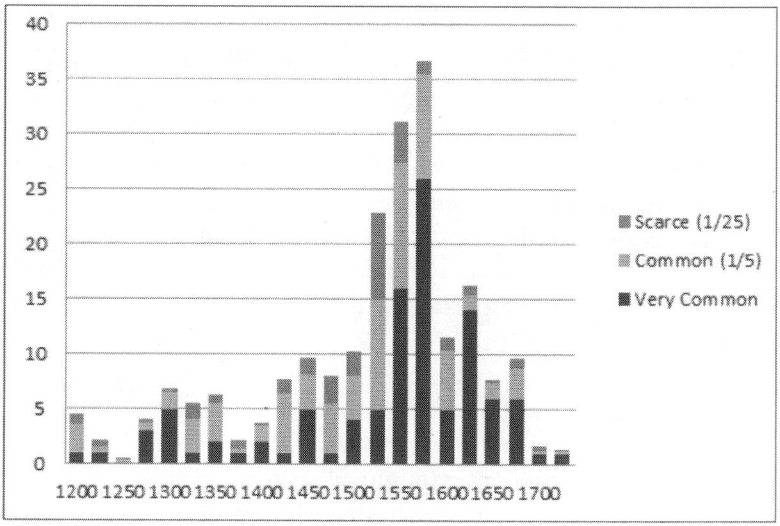

FIG. 2.2: WEIGHTED NUMBER OF TYPES 1200-1750

historiographical observations on the three acceleration periods may be in place.

The first acceleration period started with Balban on the Delhi throne (1266-87) and was continued under the Khaljis (1290-1320) and the first Tughluqs. In these years production per mint may not have changed substantially, but rather the number of mints was expanded from five mint towns under Iltutmish (1210-35) to twenty-one different ones under the late Khaljis and the first Tughluqs.[50]

The second acceleration period did not so much start in the Delhi sultanate (where only during the Lodhis from 1451 onwards did coin production pick up), but in other sultanates, like those of the Bahmani sultans of the Deccan, the sultans of Jaunpur, of Gujarat, of Malwa, and of Kashmir.

The third and most impressive production growth started under the short-lived Suri-dynasty in Delhi (1538-54) and the first Mughals, to find its apogee during the long reign of Akbar (1556-1605). At the same time, some of the sultanates (like Gujarat, for example) maintained a rather impressive production. Among the princes who had a lasting impact on coin production in India, Sher Shah Suri (1538-45) was maybe the most important one. His innovations in this field were the abolishment of the coinage of billon, which he replaced by an extensive series of copper coins (mainly *dams* of c. 20 grams, initially called *paisas*) and silver ones (rupees of c. 11 grams, originally called *tankas*), and the establishment of nearly forty provincial mints. Twenty of these also struck copper coins.[51] One can easily see that Akbar continued and extended the system, introduced by his Suri predecessor.

When we look at the regional patterns in the period of top production, 1525-1600, we see a remarkable shift from the north-west (meaning in this case especially Gujarat and Kashmir) to the central regions of the north.

The regional division also betrays the insignificant small-coin production of the north-east (predominantly Bihar and Bengal). This is probably due to the large share of the non-metallic *cowries* in that part of the subcontinent, documented extensively from the sixth up until the nineteenth century.[52] The relatively small share of the south may partially be due to under-registration because – as said before – some catalogues for southern issues still have to be processed. However, this certainly will not change the overall picture substantially.

What the figures collected so far do not yet show are two more upswing periods.[53] A fourth period is very likely to be situated in the second half of the eighteenth century when the failing production of the shrinking Mughal state and the demise of the vestiges of the last sultanates was more than supplemented by the proliferation of medium and small mints all over India. Perlin has very suggestively proposed this development without, however, strong quantitative arguments. According to him, this was the local and regional answer to a growing demand, related to the spread of new sectors depending on wage labour (e.g. poppy and indigo production).[54] A fifth phase started, as has been already demonstrated, with the advent of mechanized production in the 1830s.

The results presented here for *deep monetization* to a considerable extent fall in sync with partial conclusions available in the literature for *monetization at large*.[55] In particular, Akbar's prolific coin production has been emphasized already for a long time.[56] The data presented here are especially more precise on the surge in the heydays of the Delhi sultanate and especially on the sometimes neglected importance of the Suri prelude to Akbar.

Both the overall dating and the dating of the lows, however, deserve much more attention. In order to describe these less spectacular periods, we first have to pay attention to the technical problem of keeping a certain circulation at the same level. Due to wear and loss in circulation, numismatists apply 'as a rule of the thumb [that] a particular coinage issue would diminish to half its original issue in twenty years, to one quarter in forty years, and to one eighth in sixty years [or] the stock of coinage in circulation suffered a diminution of two and a half per cent annually unless replenished'.[57] As my analysis rests on twenty-five-year periods, this rule implies that in order to maintain the same level of circulation, production in a particular twenty-five-year period should stay at least at 62.5 per cent of the level of the previous period (and this last level should be maintained forever, so to say).

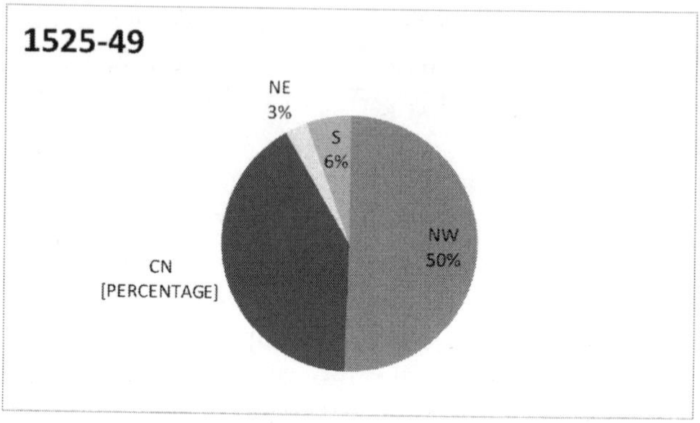

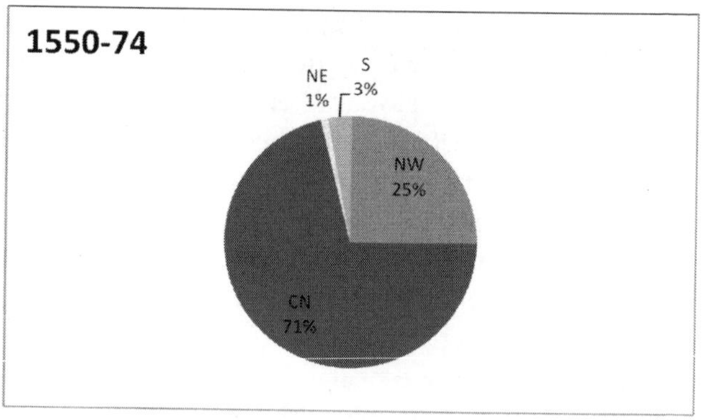

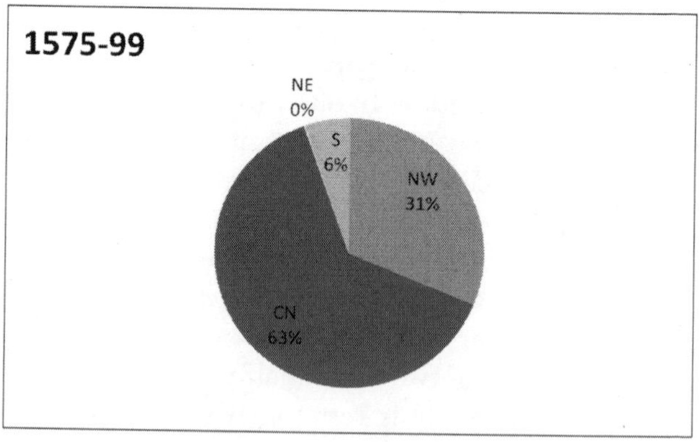

FIGS. 2.3-2.5: WEIGHTED COIN PRODUCTION NUMBERS PER REGION, 1525-49, 1550-74 AND 1575-99

Key: S = southern India; NW = north-western India; CN = central northern India; NE = north-eastern India

Taking this rule into account it is now possible to distinguish three periods of diminished coin circulation:

- The relatively short period from 1225/50 until 1275;
- The less clearly distinguishable period from 1325/75 until 1400/50 (the possible lull, 1475/1500, is not convincing enough to be discussed here);
- The long period from 1600 until at least 1750 (the preliminary end of my data base), only interrupted by a short recovery 1625-50.

Like before in the presentation of the upswing periods, some brief historiographical comments may already be made.

The decrease around the middle of the thirteenth century has not extensively been reviewed so far in the literature, in which all attention has been drawn by the discussion on the nature of 'Indian feudalism'. The ideas of R.S. Sharma on this phenomenon have been challenged eloquently by John Deyell in his classic *Living without Silver* (1990), but far from convincingly according to Subrahmanyam and later Shrimali.[58]

The low-swing period of the late fourteenth and part of the fifteenth century has drawn the attention of several scholars, but firm conclusions are still wanting. Haider suggests a silver famine as its cause and possibly something like 'second serfdom' as its outcome.[59]

Also, the low coin circulation figures for the seventeenth and especially for the early eighteenth century have been remarked by a number of historians and numismatists, but both causes and consequences stay in the dark.[60] One of the reasons may be the attention drawn by the massive inflows of the American silver since 1590, mainly via Europe, which immediately were converted into silver rupees with a high and stable purity. So in this case, monetization and deep monetization trends clearly do diverge. This growing gap between rupee circulation and small, mainly copper coin circulation was accompanied in the second half of the seventeenth century by a weight reduction of the copper *dam* by one-third. Concomitantly prices rose and possibly, therefore, money wages as well.[61]

From Relative Overall Trends to Absolute Production Figures and Circulation Per Capita

As the title of this essay shows, I am not so much interested in monetization for its own sake – however exiting a topic which combines material and archival sources – but in its effects on society, or, vice versa, as a reflection of societal change (particularly in terms of change in labour relations). Unavoidably, we then have to envisage a most difficult question: to what extent do the changing trends in deep monetization and demonetization affect the lives of 'ordinary people'? A most difficult question, because it asks for a conversion of overall national trends into trends per capita. This means that population data are needed, but precisely here lies a major problem as historians tend to disagree substantially. Besides, until the reign of Akbar no reliable demographic estimates whatsoever are available as far as I know, certainly not independently from numismatic evidence which itself often is taken as one of the indicators of economic development.

The first available written source for demographic history, the *Ain-i Akbari*, contains many statistical or semi-statistical clues for the late sixteenth century. Interpretations of these data however, have so far not led to unanimity among historians. Moosvi's estimate of roughly 150 million inhabitants of India certainly is the most influential, but there are serious challengers who argue for a mere 90 million.[62] As compared to the 197 million around 1800 on which there is widespread consensus, this means anyhow an increase between 1600 and 1800. If we are allowed to attribute a wider validity to population developments in Bengal (the best studied part of India in this respect), an important part of this growth must have taken place in the eighteenth century.[63] In the nineteenth century India's population increased from 197 million in 1800 via 237 million in 1850 to 285 million in 1900.[64]

What do these most wanting demographic basics tell us about deep monetization per capita? Unfortunately, nothing before the beginning of the sixteenth century because of lack of any data. However, even without population figures for 1500, we may safely conclude that the steep rise of deep monetization between 1500 and 1600 (some 200 per cent) cannot be explained by demographic growth alone, although it most likely will have taken place.[65] I suggest therefore that deep monetization per capita in the sixteenth century must have increased as well. By the same line of argument, the ensuing strong decrease of deep monetization 1600-1750 also must have meant a decrease per capita, taking into account the net population growth between 1600 and 1800, even if we would locate it mostly in the latter part of the eighteenth century. As I have not been able to establish deep monetization levels for the period 1750-1850 (although assuming growth as argued above), it is impossible to state whether this also means increased circulation per capita, given simultaneous population growth as demonstrated for Bengal.

In August 1829 the construction of the new mint in Calcutta was completed and its capacity enough 'to supply two-thirds of the coin required for the circulation of India'.[66] The rest had to come from the mints of Bombay and Madras. Between 1831 and 1835 the Calcutta mint, although not yet powered by steam (that only happened late 1835) threw no less than 87 million new coppers into circulation (both *pies* and half-*annas*).[67] This means more than 15 million pieces per annum on average.[68] Once fully mechanized and empowered by steam, these figures rose in the last decades of the nineteenth century, in certain years, from 100 to 200 million. Given a population rise between 1825 and 1900 of some 30 per cent this is an impressive (ten times) increase of production, even if we allow for the fact that the Calcutta mint in the 1830s only had to cater for the Presidency with at most 15 per cent of India's population[69] against – as we just saw – 66 per cent afterwards. According to this very rough yardstick deep monetization may have doubled or more[70] in the second half of the nineteenth century, which is in accordance with Ambedkar's notion as given in the introduction to this essay.

These coin production figures for India (mainly from the mints of Calcutta, Bombay and Madras, but occasionally also from private mint houses in Birmingham) can now be linked to authoritative circulation estimates and, thanks to official censuses taken, to estimates per capita (see Table 2.7).

TABLE 2.7: CIRCULATION OF SMALL COINS PER CAPITA, INDIA *c.* 1880

	Total circulation expressed in rupees	*Circulation per capita*	
		Expressed in rupees	*Expressed in most common denominations (either silver 2 anna pieces, or copper quarter-anna pieces)*
Small silver	92,600,000	0.366	3 (or one 2-anna and one quarter-rupee)
Copper	48,100,000	0.190	12
Total	140,700,000	0.556	

Source: Lucassen 2007, 367.

Now it is also possible to present this in concrete terms of the demand for coins to pay out wages by way of a hypothetical model (see Table 2.8). Nothing more, nothing less; but important, I think, to visualize possible links between labour relations and coin circulation.

This hypothetical model is based on the following assumptions: (a) that about the same time 10 per cent of the total population was remunerated in wages;[71] (b) this percentage of people were paid on an average one rupee per week; (c) these wages were paid out weekly; (d) in small coins (an equal mix of silver 2 anna pieces and copper quarter-anna pieces); and (e) that all these coins made the full circle within one month and without taking into account losses (*ut supra*). If these assumptions are acceptable and if this tenth part of the population needed half of the circulating small coins, whereas the other part of the working population which had to sell its produce in the market (much less frequently, so more likely in one, half and quarter-rupee coins) would need the other half as change and in order to pay their creditors, the results of this model would be consistent with the circulation figures given by contemporaneous financial experts.

The first virtue of the model is that the change of one parameter necessitates that of another one. For example, suppose that only three-quarters of the wages at the time were paid out in coins and

TABLE 2.8: HYPOTHETICAL MODEL OF THE DEMAND OF SMALL COINS FOR PAYING WAGES, INDIA *c.* 1880

Labour relations		*Weekly payments of one rupee per person*			*Monthly circulation per capita*
	Per cent		*Pieces*	*Rs.*	*Rs.*
Adults, working mainly for wages	10	Half in silver 2 annas	8	0.5	0.125
Adults remunerated otherwise (mainly peasants and craftsmen)	40	Half in copper ¼ annas	32	0.5	0.125
Not able to work (mainly children	50	Demand for small change to pay creditors weekly[72]			
Total population	100	Copper ⅛ and 1/12 annas	4	0.07	0.016
			44	1.07	
		Total demand for wage workers			0.266

the other quarter in kind (grain or rice), it might necessitate to increase the demand of the non-waged part of the population, the frequency of wage payments,[73] or the velocity for these small coins (more than one month), etc.

It also offers a first opportunity for historical comparisons with Akbar's time.[74] Najaf Haider, basing himself on Irfan Habib, estimates the share of the primary sector in the national income (Rs. 542 million at 11.42 grams of fine silver) at 66 per cent, comprising 85 per cent of the population. One-quarter of these depended on wage labour. Besides, the secondary sector (11 per cent of gross national product) and the tertiary sector (23 per cent of gross national product), comprising together 15 per cent of the population, mostly consisted of independent craftsmen, but also on wage dependents (he mentions building construction, mining, the *karkhanas*, the military and the civil service).[75] Together, no less than one-quarter of the households may have depended for their income on wages, which – like three centuries later – represented about 10 per cent of the total population.

It is tempting, but still too early I think, to make direct comparisons between the importance of wage payments at the end of the sixteenth and the end of the nineteenth centuries on the basis of the circulation figures of Figure 2.2 and Table 2.7 (of course taking into account different wage levels expressed in coins and different coins produced), before more is known on remuneration modalities in India during the last centuries. To this theme, the final section of this essay is devoted.

Intensity shifts of deep monetization in India 1200-1900 and labour history: suggestions for a discussion

In the earliest Indian texts, contemporaneous to the spread of coins in the subcontinent, wage as a means of earning one's living is mentioned. According to Manu seven acquisitions of wealth are consistent with *dharma*, including employment in labour. Gautama specifies for which societal classes this applies. Whereas the Brahman receives gifts and the Kshatriya lives from conquest, the Vaishya's modes of income are primarily agriculture, trading, tending cattle, and moneylending, but also wages. For the existence of a Shudra, only wages in exchange for the performance of service are available.[76]

If these are the basic rules of the game, with the advent of Islam, a new element was introduced as suggested by Hussain in his exemplary book on politico-economic development and monetization in mediaeval Bengal.[77] He points to a strong relation between increased coin circulation on the one hand and the spread of Islam, urbanization and state formation on the other. As urbanization implies increasing specialization into non-agricultural occupations, deep monetization patterns may in the first place be influenced by occupational shifts. The second factor has to be found in changing interdependency patterns and remuneration systems, in particular in the countryside, where in the period envisaged the far majority of the population lived. As Husain pointed out rightly, urbanization went hand in hand with Muslim state formation, both in the Sultanates and during the Suris and under Akbar. Wicks dubs this process 'monetary imposition'.[78] From the late eighteenth century colonialism provided the impetus for a new round of urbanization.[79]

Urbanization, state formation and the concomitant occupational specialization (including the military) certainly may explain the surge in per capita monetization during the sixteenth century, but for the demonetization trends in the period *c.* 1600 to 1750 and the recovery afterwards, important explanations certainly also have to be sought for in the countryside. Mostly in the agricultural sector, but we should not forget rural industries. The blossoming textile industries in South India, but also in Bengal and other regions implied a – sometimes partial – shift away from agriculture.[80] In the south this went hand in glove with the rather sudden increase of the production of small *kasu* (cash) coins in the second half of the eighteenth century.[81] The enlargement of my database with a great number of very common small south Indian cash coins, produced mainly after 1750 (although often not dated and even anonymous) by mints like Gingee, Thanjavur, Pudokkotai, Madurai, Sivaganga, Tirunveli, Trichy and Arcot will make this clear.

Two shifts in agriculture and their social implications have to be discussed here: shifts in entitlements from reciprocity to remuneration, and, where remuneration occurs, shifts from payments in kind to payments in coins. The simplest, but also persistent model of the Indian countryside is an endless landscape of fields and villages – leaving aside the so-called 'tribal areas'. In these villages, families of craftsmen and specialists in different occupations, confined in castes, were entitled to part of the local harvest as were, conversely, peasants to the products of the village specialists. This reciprocal type of labour relations, avoiding remuneration and payments, and in no need of markets, supposedly was the basic Indian social formation, and its entitlement system is commonly known as *jajmani*.[82]

A few years ago, the Japanese anthropologist Akio Tanabe has come up with a more developed model, encompassing many more families within one entitlement unit, and thus opening a window to monetization questions. He bases himself on the eighteenth-century of Khurda in Orissa, but suggests that it has a wider validity for the principalities and kingdoms 'in the hilly tracts in east and central India' and compares it with similar formations (the *nadu*) in south India.[83] In pre-colonial Khurda (1776/7), the basic and highly integrated social unit of entitlements no longer was the village, but rather a fortress and (ideally) twelve surrounding villages. This inter-village 'micro-regional' unit was linked to other similar units, forming together a kingdom in which also the king and the units mutually were entitled to goods and services (one of the main functions of the king was ritual sacrifice, which made it a 'sacrificial community').

Interestingly for us, the 1776/7 documents analysed at length by Tanabe, demonstrate 'the introduction of new administrative technologies such as accounting in *cowrie* currency, which reinforced the trend to monetization already under way as a result of the growth of a market economy that connected the locality to wider networks of economic exchanges.'[84] Remarkably, the same documents containing a complete monetized account or value assessment of all entitlements (the value of land, goods and services), contain only very few entries of actual payments in *cowries.* The actual payment of the shares to the entitlement holders was given mostly in the form of land (86.47 per cent of the total distributed resources), or of goods and services (12.17 per cent), whereas the actual usage of *cowries* as medium of transaction accounts for only 1.35 per cent of the total distribution of the resource in the system of entitlements.[85] That is only one part of the story, however, as *cowries* were used extensively in local weekly markets – but so far there is not enough data to ascertain to what extent market exchanges were important for the overall economic activities of the villagers.[86]

The study of the extent of markets certainly may provide an indirect clue for changing labour relations if only for the simple reason that where people buy and pay with coins, they must have earned the coins somewhere else. The emergence and demise of markets, their nature, and of the availability of shroffs (or *sarafs*) at markets[87] for exchanging silver and copper coins and *cowries*, should all be on the agenda of labour historians. More direct information on the occurrence of wage labour in agriculture and elsewhere and the extent to which wages were paid in cash or kind may be found in the works of early-colonial observers, like Francis Buchanan for Mysore and Bengal and William Henry Sykes for the Deccan, but for the problems posed here for a much longer period, they only can be a starting point, although a very valuable one.[88]

By way of conclusion, I want to go back to what is possibly the most fundamental discussion, that of the *implications of shifts between systems of reciprocal labour and labour markets and relations.* Robert Wicks makes the following statement:

> Although the main purpose of a monetary system is to facilitate the exchange of goods and services and the discharge of fiscal and other obligations, *the presence of money does more than simply reduce transaction costs.* With the advent of money, economic relationships become abstracted and less personal, motivated by values independent of such factors as kinship ties, the status of individuals involved in the transactions, and personal obligation. With the advent of money also cash payments tend to replace seasonal labour obligations, further weakening traditional means of maintaining power and influence. While it could be argued that these tendencies are the cause rather than the result of the adoption of money, they nonetheless signal that critical changes are taking place within the society.[89]

On several occasions, Wicks quotes Polanyi. Without doing injustice to earlier authors like Georg Simmel, it is no exaggeration to state that most other scholars in the field refer to the basic remarks on money use made by Karl Polanyi in the 1940s-60s.[90] In a strong statement which, if true, would refute the whole issue of this essay beforehand, he writes:

> Let us make our meaning more precise, No society could, naturally, live for any length of time unless it possessed an economy of some sort; but previously to our time [the mid-twentieth century] no economy has ever existed that, even in principle, was controlled by markets [...] Though the institution of the market was fairly common since the later Stone Age, its role was no more than incidental to economic life. [...] Division of labour, a phenomenon as old as society, springs from differences

inherent in the facts of sex, geography and individual endowment; and the alleged propensity of man to barter, truck, and exchange is almost entirely apocryphal.[91]

In a more nuanced way, he explains:

Indeed, all archaic kingdoms made use of metal currencies for the payment of taxes and salaries, but relied for the rest on payments in kind from granaries and warehouses of every description, from which they distributed the most varied goods for goods and consumption mainly to the nonproducing part of the population, that is, to the officials, the military, and the leisure class. This was the system practiced in ancient China, the empire of the Incas, in the kingdoms of India, and also in Babylonia.

In these, supposedly more homogenous societies, but also in more stratified societies, which he calls 'feudal' redistribution is the key next to production for one's own use, called 'householding'. 'We find, as a rule, the processes of redistribution forming part of the prevailing political regime, whether it be that of tribe, city state, despotism or feudalism of cattle or land. The production and distribution of goods is organizsed in the main through collection, storage and redistribution, the pattern being focused on the chief, the temple, the despot or the lord. Since the relations of the leading group to the led are different according to the foundation on which political power rests, the principle of redistribution will involve individual motives as different as the voluntary sharing of the game by hunters and the dread of punishment which urges the fellaheen to deliver his taxes in kind.'[92]

I have quoted Polanyi here at length, not only because he is such an influential inspiration for scholars still today, nor to ridicule his statements made nearly seventy years ago, but to show – notwithstanding his exceptional conceptual clarity – how imprecise his historical representation is, or, more generally, how he scarcely allowed for historical developments between the Neolithic and the Industrial Revolution. For him, even the Greco-Roman world, in spite of its highly developed trade, formed no watershed. No wonder that for Polanyi markets before the Industrial Revolution were primarily 'meeting places for long-distance trade'.[93] Even the advent of Mercantilism and of the putting out system did not change human relations:

> Whether the cheap machinery was owned by the worker or by the merchant made some difference in the social position of the parties and almost certainly made a difference in the earnings of the worker, who was better off as long as he owned his tools; but it did not force the merchant to become an industrial capitalist, or to restrict himself to lending his money to such persons as were.[94]

But the study of reciprocal relations need not be ahistorical, as the Khurda case has demonstrated already. This historicising tendency can also be found in what might be called a subsection of reciprocity studies, those dealing with gift giving in the tradition of the French scholar Marcel Mauss, and like Polanyi's theories leaning heavily on ethnographic evidence.[95] Just to give one example, Gadi Algazi has analysed feudal relations in rural southern Germany at the end of the Middle Ages and indicated that what looks like reciprocal obligations of lord (protection) and serfs (maintenance of the lord) was in fact the outcome of conflict: 'Reciprocity would turn from a fundamental norm to a disputable construct located within shifting fields of power'.[96] If this is true for historians of pre-modern gift in Europe, it equally might apply to historians of work and labour in India.

Reciprocity is certainly a constituting part of the history of the Indian subcontinent in the period under scrutiny (1200-1900), but that does not imply that we are faced here with immutable structures, making any attempt to write the labour history of India before colonialism uninteresting and therefore a waste of time.[97] Deep monetization patterns and especially shifts in these patterns cry for answers which take labour relations seriously into account. Apart from urbanization, state formation, militarization and the emergence of rural industries (all fascinating topics for labour historians in their own right), I suppose that changing labour relations in the countryside have to be considered seriously as well.

Appendix: The Structure of the Database

As an example of how the database is built (so far for the period 1200-1750 and 1830-1900; with some gaps for the south), I present here in tabulated form the results for the first quarter century 1200-24 (all-India)

TABLE 2.9: RARITY OF SMALL COIN TYPES, DELHI SULTANS, 1200-24

	Copper						*Billon*	*Silver < 5 grams*	*T*
	Adli L	*Adli H*	*½ Paika L*	*½ Paika H*	*Paika L*	*Paika H*	*Jital*		
Average weight in grams	0.6-0.8	0.9-1.6	1.3-1.7	1.8-2.5	2.7-3.6	3.8-4.5	3.0-3.6		
Types cc							1		1 (1*)
Types c						1	12		13 (3*)
Types s			3	1	2		16		22 (1*)
Types r	1	2	4	2	7	1	4		21 (0*)
Types rr							2	1	3 (0*)
Types rrr	1						1	1	2 (0*)
Types rrrr									0
Total number of types	2	2	7	3	9	2	36	2	63 (5*)

Notes: H = heavy; L =light; * = weighted numbers (without decimals), see Figure 2.2 above.

Source: Goron and Goenka 2001 (sv Delhi Sultans).

NOTES

1. Ambedkar 1947, 27, as quoted by Garg 2008, 203-4; cf. Subrahmanyam 1994, 2, 8 for a different view.
2. For important works of these historians see the Bibliography. I refrain here from mentioning specialized numismatic publications
3. Perlin 1987, 343-4; Perlin 1993, 238-9; cf. Moosvi 2002, 88 (where, not without humour, she characterizes her own attempt as one 'that I once bravely undertook'); for a critique of Moosvi see Subrahmanyam 1994, 213, 218.
4. Shrimali 2002.
5. Bhandare 2008, 37; Garg 2008, 206-8, reacting to Perlin's 'Growth of Money Economy' (1983), 27, 31.
6. Haider, see Part I: Studies, No. 6 in this volume, [300-02].
7. It may be superfluous to say that this has no implications as such for the development of national income or of real wages, cf. Scheidel 2010.
8. Subrahmanyam 1994b, 41, 43 (quotation), and 56. This is not to deny at all the importance of numismatics, as is shown, e.g. by the widespread use made by historians of Singhal 1953.
9. Cf. Wicks 1992, 6 borrowing from Joe Cribb: 'money is a convention established in relation to payments which dictates that particular objects with agreed measures of value are recognised as the regular means of discharging the obligation to pay', which implies pre-existing socially determined 'forms of transactions'.
10. The following after Lucassen 2007a.
11. Recently a nice example has been provided for Bengal, see Deyell 2010, 83-6.
12. Bhandare 2008, 37 (without reference); Verboven 2009, 91-3, 105, 119; Wicks 1992, 16. From private correspondence I learnt that Verboven 'invented' the term for a paper delivered in June 2008, independently from Bhandare. Bhandare was inspired by Perlin's work more in general, not by a specific passage. When using the term for the first time in 2008, both authors were not aware of each other. So far, I do not know of its usage before 2008.
13. Lucassen 2007a; cf. Wicks 1992, Verboven 2009, Scheidel 2011.
14. Garg 2008, 106, quoting the Assay Master of Patna Mint, 17 February 1795.
15. Parthasarati 2008 and 2010; see also Ellis 2005.
16. Deyell 1987b, 1990, 2011; Perlin 1993, 240-1 for critical remarks; Wicks 1992, 15-16.
17. Deyell 1987b. For coin types for which enough specimens are available for research die count analysis is also an option, see e.g. Deyell 2010.
18. Hasan 1967. For a critique see Subrahmanyam 1994b, 204 and Deyell 1976.
19. Deyell 1987b, 162: 'Alternatively the mint years figure may be calculated by adding together the mints issuing copper coins in each year of the reign,

as listed in the seven museum catalogues above, discarding duplication between catalogues. The former [the method he actually applies, discussed in my text] is a good approximation of the latter, and less tedious to perform, so I use it here. The results from both methods should be similar, certainly as to the trend; but the latter method will give more accuracy.'

20. Deyell 1987b, 162: 'which figure is not necessarily congruent with the number of regnal years in a reign: for example, during periods of expansion of the Mughal frontier during the reigns of Akbar and Aurangzeb, the southern mint towns were often occupied for only a fraction of the whole reign, and they reduce the total years of mint possession for those reigns, commensurately'.
21. Habib 1987.
22. Deyell 1994, 113, 135; Deyell 2010, 67.
23. The following after Garg 2007, 354-6. See also Deyell 2011. Already before the introduction of steam engines, several mechanical improvements had been introduced, which cannot be discussed here in detail, see e.g. Stevens 2008a for Bombay 1818-22.
24. Haider 2002, 60; Prakash, see Part I: Studies, No. 7 in this volume; Lingen and Lucassen, see Part I: Studies, No. 12 in this volume; Shimada 2006.
25. See Lingen and Lucassen, see Part I: Studies, No. 12 in this volume.
26. Consequently, a successful extension of this approach to earlier centuries would rather have to use hundred-year periods.
27. Deyell 1990, 13.
28. Deyell 1976 himself has shown what the impact can be of neglecting different typology systems for historical analysis, in discussing Hasan 1969.
29. Lucassen, see Part I: Studies, No. 13 in this volume; It also has the additional advantage that problems of re-striking of coins related to spatial differential price levels of precious metals, as sometimes occurred with silver rupees (and so not primarily emerging from demand for circulation purposes), practically can be ruled out – as can Gresham's law.
30. For earlier attempts to apply this method to specific coin types, see Lingen and Lucassen, see Part I: Studies, Nos. 10 and 12 in this volume.
31. Goron and Goenka 2001; Rahman 2005 (he does not distinguish between cc and c); Liddle 2005 (he does not distinguish between c and cc; in this case I have attributed cc to all types with four or more different issuing years; Valentine 1914 (only 6 falus of Humayun, all valuated by me as cc). These are compared to prices in Bruce 2008 and Krause and Mishler 2002: For the period 1600-24 this is possible for 72 rarity valuations out of 125 types in total; for 1625-49 for 32 out of 103 types in total; for 1650-74 for only 4 out of 45; and for 1675-99 for only 5 out of 78 in total.
32. Differentiation according to 14 weight-classes and even to metals (copper and silver) has yielded no significant results. That is why one conversion table suffices. For the analysis I will concentrate on the coins within the cc/c/s brackets.

33. This has been done rather arbitrarily on the basis of impressions from section 3 of this essay, 'Historical Framing of the Numismatic Listings'. As an experiment different weights have been tried out, but they do not influence the overall trends.
34. Goron and Goenka 2001, Bruce 2008 for the seventeenth century, Krause/Mishler 2002 for the eighteenth century, and Bruce 2004 for the nineteenth century.
35. Rahman 2005 for Babur and Liddle 2005 for Akbar, partially overlapping with Bruce 2008; for now I have only been able to use Valentine 1914 for Humayun (1530-40).
36. The two excellent catalogues for South India by Michael Mitchiner, published in 1998, use a different typology system from the others consulted by me and therefore I still have to adapt Mitchiner's system to make it compatible with the rest of my database. I expect that especially the coppers of the later Pallavas (thirteenth century), the later Pandyas (fourteenth century) and of late Vijayanagar may have an impact on my data for the south, but not overall.
37. For example, the (very ill dated) medieval Kangra jitals.
38. For example, Lingen and Lucassen, see Part I: Studies, Nos. 10 and 12 in this volume.
39. For example, Perlin 1993, 270-2; Deyell 2010; Jan Hogendorn and Johnson 1986.
40. Wicks 1992, 16; see also Lingen and Lucassen, see Part I: Studies, Nos. 10 and 12 in this volume; Lucassen, See Part I: Studies, No. 13 in this volume; see also the admirable series of articles by Paul Stevens (Stevens 2004a-d, 2005, 2006a-c).
41. Deyell 1990, 221, 225, 253-63. Deyell writes on p. 221: 'sums in the tens of millions and hundreds of millions silver tankas', thereby suggesting that the foot soldiers received other types of coins than the cavalrymen. Also, the remarkable difference in remuneration of horse- and foot-soldiers (500 vs. 234, where exactly the opposite relation might be expected) suggests that different coin types were involved. On the basis of Goron and Goenka 2001, 38-9 I think that the foot soldiers were paid out in billon 'six gani' coins against the horse soldiers in silver tankas. The latter coins of this reign, struck by the mint of Delhi during all years AH 695-715 are classified as 'very common' and as 'common' for the mints of Dar-al-Islam and Deogir. As the 1 silver tanka equalled the value of 60 billon coins of 6 gani, the salary of a horseman would be twenty-eight times as high as that of a foot-soldier. This seems a big difference, but given the maintenance of the horse and grooms this is not impossible.
42. Deyell 1990, 262 (fn. 11): In 1389/AH 718: 'at the present time the current coins are those of King Alauddin'.
43. Rahman 2005, 29-33, quoting H.N. Wright, *The Sultans of Delhi, their Coinage and Metallurgy* (Delhi, 1936), pp. 257-62 and Edward Thomas,

The Chronicles of the Pathan Kings of Delhi (Delhi, 1871), who states 20 Sikandaris per rupee and 8 Sikandaris per Shahruki.

44. Deyell 2010, 97-8.
45. Blake 1987, 133. For a discussion see Datta 2000 and Ellis 2005, 19 (net tax receipts or *jama* reached at best two-thirds of the sums imposed).
46. In a more elaborate working paper in progress, I have given more details. The references are included in the Bibliography of this essay.
47. For mechanization in Benares see Garg 2008, 127.
48. This conclusion will be reinforced probably by including Vijayanagar in the database in the future.
49. This conclusion will be certainly reinforced by including Humayun more completely in the database in the future.
50. Goron and Goenka 2001, 12-13.
51. Goron and Goenka 2001, 89-92; Deyell 1987a; Singhal 1953.
52. Deyell 2010, 73-5.
53. But which are confirmed by my preliminary results for his period; preliminary because the very proliferation of often smaller mints 1750-1850 provides some data collection problems for this period which I have not yet fully overcome. I hope to finish this final stage in the near future.
54. Perlin 1987; Perlin, see Part I: Studies, No. 1 in this volume; for an overview of the discussion regarding the 'revisionists' see Subramaniam 1994a; for later arguments see Datta 2000, Robb 2007, 124-50; and Mukherjee 2011.
55. Haider, see Part I: Studies, No. 6 in this volume, [300-02].
56. See e.g. Richards 1987, Subrahmanyam 1994a, 52; Subrahmanyam 1994B; Haider 2002, 60; Idem 2007, esp. 200 and 302ff.
57. Deyell 2010, 97.
58. Deyell 1990; Subrahmanyam 1994a, 11-19; Shrimali 2002; Haider, see Part I: Studies, No. 6 in this volume.
59. Haider 2002; Haider, see Part I: Studies, No. 6 in this volume.
60. See Subramanyam 1994A, 55-6.
61. Haider, see Part I: Studies, No. 6 and Prakash No. 7 in this volume.
62. Moosvi 1987, 399-405; Thapar 2002, 54; for much lower estimates see Ellis 2005, 19-20 basing himself on Ashok V. Desai and Sanjay Subrahmanyam.
63. Among others Datta 2000; this is a well-documented revision of Dyson 1989, 9 (based on Visaria and Visaria 1984) who states that between 1760 and 1820 growth was zero, possibly negative.
64. Morris 1974; Dyson 1989.
65. Remember that population growth in the nineteenth century was about 40 per cent and that only in the twentieth century it surpassed the 200 per cent threshold
66. Garg 2008, 262.
67. Garg 2008, 196; cf. Perlin 1993, 253-4 (after Pinsep, *Useful Tables* 38: 308,000 coins per 7-hour day); Bruce 2004, 723; as the total value 1831-5 was Rs. 1,238,508, we may suppose that the far majority of this production

must have consisted of half-annas. Catalogue prices show how extremely common these coins are – as we might have expected.

68. Cf. Garg 2008, 197: In 1835 the Calcutta mint master tried to assess the implications of plans to replace all circulating copper coins, in particular *trisul paisas;* by completely new and now fully mechanically manufactured new coin types. This operation would entail a loss of Rs. 571,340. Because the loss for defacing Rs. 10,000 worth of old and depreciated coins received at the rate of 64 pice per rupee was estimated at over Rs. 6,277 we may estimate the total circulation at that moment at 58 million pieces. For silver I have not found circulation data for the first quarter of the century, but for gold it is estimated at Rs. 24.5 million in 1796 (Garg 2008, 208), or over one rupee per inhabitant of Bengal – a figure which is not too meaningful as the big majority of the Bengalis would never touch a gold coin in their whole lifetime. For coin circulation in Bengal *c.* 1800 also see Gupta 1984, 240-5; Robb 2007, 129.
69. Mukherjee 2011, 165.
70. Velocity not only increased by more coins available, but from the late nineteenth century also with the advent of the railways, see Gupta 1984, 244-5. I suppose that the impact on the 1880 reconstruction (Table 2.7) still was limited enough not to disturb directly comparisons with previous periods.
71. Roy in IISH – Global Collaboratory on the History of Labour Relations.
72. In the period 1880-4 29.8 million copper 1⁄12 anna pieces were coined and 205 million ¼ annas, or about seven times more (no ⅛ anna pieces were coined in those years).
73. Cf. Prakash, see Part I: Studies, No. 7 in this volume, [325]: the frequency of wage payments (daily, weekly, monthly) co-determines the size/value of the smaller coins in demand for this purpose (only). As wage workers enjoyed not much credit, most of them needed to be paid weekly or even daily (see Lingen and Lucassen, Part I: Studies, Nos. 10 and 12 in this volume).
74. In this essay I will abstain from a comparison with the situation in 1918, as offered by Prakash, See Part I: Studies, No. 7 in this volume. For an interesting reconstruction of labour relations in Mysore *c.* 1800 see Sivramkrishna 2009, 721.
75. Haider, see Part I: Studies, No. 6 in this volume; cf. Ellis 2005. Haider does not take into account slaves separately. On the other hand, they too could be remunerated in cash, see Fukuzawa 1991, 116-30.
76. Derrett 1957, esp. 69-70, 76, 87, 90-2. cf. Lucassen 2007a.
77. Hussain 2003; cf. Deyell 2010.
78. Wicks 1992, 10 (and Chapter 3).
79. There is much need of a good and encompassing overview of urbanization figures for India before 1850/1900. Those in world overviews (like Chandler and Fox, *Urbanization, 800-1800*) and even those in overviews of India (Habib 1982, 166 and Visaria and Visaria 1984, 466) certainly are not

sufficient and should be supplemented with more recent ones (see e.g. Mukherjee 2011, 166 for Bengal).

80. Parthasarathi 2001 and 2011; Riello and Roy 2009.
81. Primarily based on the listings in Mitchiner 1998, 196-245, combined with Krause and Mishler 2002 (as far as these coins can be dated earlier, they might raise my results for the pre-1750 years). Textile workers in Bengal will have been paid mostly in cowries until late in the eighteenth century.
82. The literature on this topic is endless (for a classic presentation see Neale 1957, referring to Henry Sumner Maine's *Ancient Law*, 1906), but for a comprehensive discussion see Tanabe 2005.
83. Tanabe 2005, esp. 250-1.
84. Tanabe 2005, 357.
85. Tanabe 2005, 366 (Table 1).
86. Personal communication from Akio Tanabe, whom I would like to thank here cordially.
87. I am actually collecting information on taxes, paid by the shroffs (*sarrafs*) in the major markets of Bengal for their exclusive right to exchange copper coins (the 'pyce mahal') which might provide some more information. See also Mukherjee 2011.
88. Sivramkrishna 2009; Sykes 1838 (original reports 1826 and 1829); also see Mayer 2006. For the interpretation of such sources fundamental considerations are to be found in Verboven 2009.
89. Wicks 1992, 7 [my emphasis]. These critical changes also may involve monetary debt and credit relations and consequently power relations. Debt bondage is a case in point in Indian labour history, cf. also Verboven 2009, 112, 116-18; Graeber 2011 provides a gloomy picture of debt relations.
90. Poggi 1993 (based on Simmel 1922); Polanyi 1944, esp. chapters 4 to 6; Polanyi, Arensberg and Pearson 1957; Neale 1957; Dalton 1971.
91. Polanyi 1944, 43-4. He blames the 'fallacy' of attributing too much value to markets first to Adam Smith, followed by many others. His main authorities are Richard Thurnwald and Bronislaw Malinowski (cf. Wagner-Hasel 2003, 148-9), but also Firth and Weber.
92. Polanyi 1944, 51-2 (mainly after Thurnwald).
93. Polanyi 1944, 59, after Max Weber.
94. Polanyi 1944, 74.
95. Algazi, Groebner and Jussen 2003 (Gifts have to be distinguished from other forms of interaction like market exchange, compulsory tribute and barter); also see Wicks 1992, 14.
96. Algazi in Algazi et al. 2003, 127.
97. See also Washbrook 2010.

3

Labour and Deep Monetization in Eurasia, 1000-1900*

Jan Lucassen

The efficiency of economic institutions has been an inspiring topic for many economic historians.[1] Labourers, among the most important actors in economic life, shape and are also shaped by several institutions. Most labour historians concentrate on institutions regarding basic freedoms, such as freedom of employment, freedom of organization, and freedom to organize collective action. In addition, protective legislation regarding working hours, age at work, dangerous circumstances, and the like, are part and parcel of labour history.[2]

To date, modalities of payment and means of exchange have attracted barely any interest from this field, nor monetary history or numismatics.[3] Nevertheless, the institutions involved in producing and circulating currencies suitable for use in wage pay-

* This chapter has grown out of one conference paper, written for two different conferences. First, the workshop on Economic Institutional Change and Global Labour Relations at the IISH in Amsterdam (26-7 September 2014), and second, the conference 'Coins, currency, and crisis from *c.* 2000 BC to *c.* AD 2000. On silver, paper and trust in historical perspective' at the Vrije Universiteit in Amsterdam (12-13 December 2014). I thank the participants of these conferences and of two meetings where I also could present these findings (Osaka 3–4 March 2015 and Utrecht 29 June 2015) for their input. In this new version, the labour aspects have been elaborated on more fully, in another chapter the monetary aspects are central: 'Deep monetization in Eurasia in the long run', Lucassen, Studies 4 in this volume. Both chapters refer to each other and some overlap is unavoidable.

ments and for the daily expenses of workers do matter. This applies to all societies where currencies are used as means of exchange to pay for labour and services performed, which implies major parts of Eurasia and Northern Africa for the last two and a half millennia, and for the rest of the world for the last five hundred years. In this contribution, a brief introduction is provided, detailing the usage of currencies for paying wages and of the concomitant small change. It also follows, turning the argument around, that changes in circulation patterns may point to changes in labour relations. A more extended overview is provided of the implications of currency circulation for labour conditions and the welfare of workers – both as objects and as subjects – as we will see from several examples of labour protest against failing small-denomination coin circulation. This overview can only be tentative, and more suggestive than conclusive, not only because it covers such a large field, but also because of a lack of data and secondary literature.

The structure might accordingly appear a little strange at first sight. After an introduction about the usage of currencies by workers, and more specifically about their need for small change ('deep monetization'), I will proceed in three steps. I start with a comparative overview of monetization in Western Europe and surrounding countries, as this is the first occasion when such an overview has been possible. These insights are then used in an inductive way to paint a diachronic picture, using data for Britain, the Low Countries, and France. These long-term insights into the European situation are necessary in order to be used as input for the examination of two case studies outside Europe: India and China, to draw an overall picture of Eurasia from 1000 to 1900.

Why Remunerate Work by Paying Wages?

Some types of labour relations do not involve remuneration at all (corvée labour), some do, but only implicitly (reciprocal labour), others do, but only in the form of maintenance (unfree labour), and still others do in the form of wages in kind or in cash.[4]

Corvée types of labour in their most extreme form are one-sided: the polity requires labour just as it may require taxes in kind or cash. Apart from the cost of maintenance, which is needed when the corvée has to be performed far away from home, remuneration is out of the question. In a more benign form, such labour is remunerated in public goods (material or immaterial) or at least by the suggestion that the polity cares for its subjects.[5]

Implicit remuneration is provided in reciprocal labour relations, such as within self-subsisting households or groups of households working intensively together; for example, among hunter-gatherers. All members contribute through their labour, and the results are divided more or less equally. Unpaid work is also and foremost found inside the household, in which the head of the household works for the market, while notably women and children share the income by performing all the household chores for free. The Indian *jajmani* system has to be mentioned as well. In this highly formalized system, craftsmen in the village community provide free services to the local farmers in exchange for a share in the total harvest.

Unfree labour – if established on a permanent basis such as in the case of slavery and serfdom or on a (in principle) temporary basis in the case of convicts – requires maintenance, either provided in the form of minimal food and shelter, or in the form of small plots on plantations where labourers can grow their own food. Serfs are also allowed to work their own family plot.

Formal remuneration of labour only occurs in market societies where either small producers receive it for their products or services, or where labourers receive a wage. These formal remunerations may be in kind, in cash, or mixed. For example, payment in kind occurs in the case of share croppers, who work in exchange for half the harvest while the other half goes to the owner of the soil, who often also procures the seed and makes other investments. Like small, independent producers, share croppers have to sell the products of their labour on the market. Partial wage payments in kind occur when workers benefit from board and lodging (apart from remuneration in money), such as soldiers, sailors, and living-in servants do. Where this is not the case, and wage labourers or small independent producers form their own households, wages may be paid in kind or – much more commonly – in currency. For an overview of all possibilities mentioned in commodified societies, see Fig. 3.1.

The link between work, remuneration, and currencies is not straightforward. It is, however, important in Eurasia, a part of the world that had seen markets develop long before CE 1000.[6] To formulate it differently, apart from the relations mentioned – which pertain more to unfree than to free labour, and more to women and youngsters than to adult men – work in Eurasia was performed to a substantial extent in exchange for currencies, directly in the case of independent producers (farmers and peasants, craftsmen, traders and peddlers, transporters, shopkeepers, and performers of services) or indirectly in the case of wage earners.

By implication, the history of currencies and their circulation – covering the academic fields of numismatics and monetary history – might become important for labour historians, particularly in cases where not enough other indicators for labour relations are available. This is very often the case in more distant periods in time or in societies for which no or insufficient written sources for labour history exist. To put it extremely simply: if in such cases currencies particularly appropriate for paying wages suddenly disappear, this might be an indicator of the emergence of unfree labour and vice versa.

Deep Monetization[7]

Circulating currencies can actually have several functions. If primarily intended for large-scale or costly trade, or when substantial amounts of savings are concerned, they originally consisted of large coins – mostly gold or heavy silver pieces – and later on paper money, bills of exchange, and the like. If intended for payments of rent, taxation, or wages, smaller denominations are often needed. Whereas the remuneration for work is one side of the circulation of currencies, the spending of income is the other. Sums used in spending are normally smaller than the sums received as remuneration for work. Even farmers selling their seasonal harvests, who receive relatively large sums, will divide their spending between the payment of rents and the purchase of

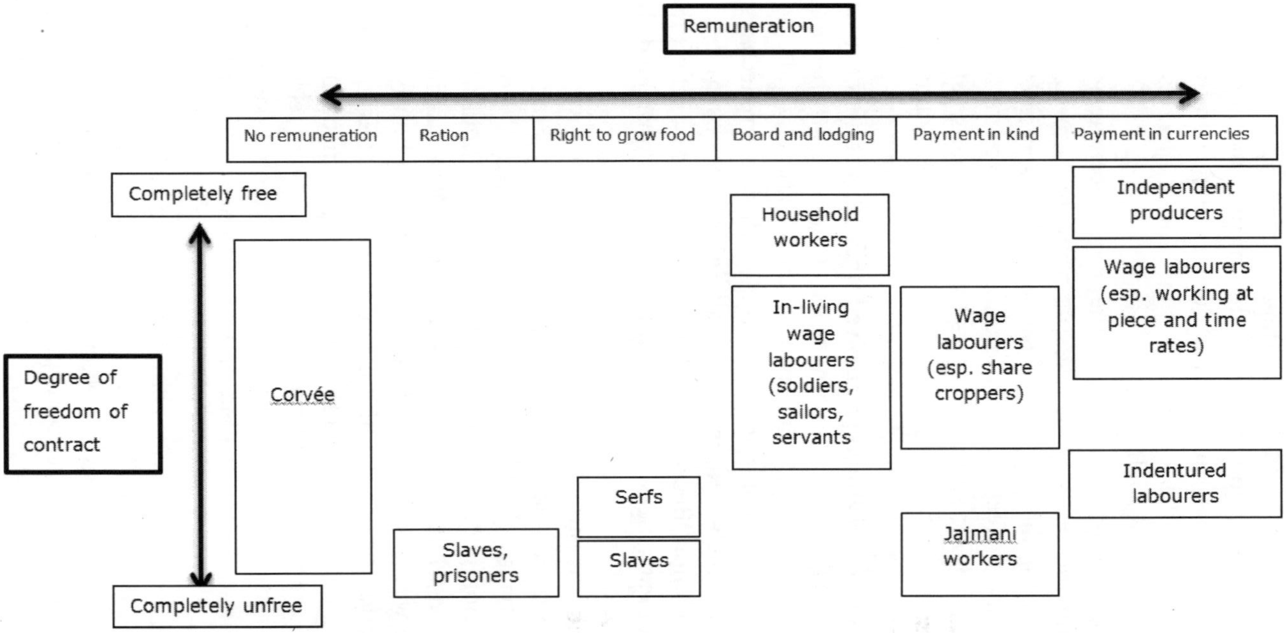

FIG. 3.1: THE RELATIONSHIPS BETWEEN TYPES OF COMMODIFIED LABOUR RELATIONS (VERTICAL FROM FREE TO UNFREE) AND OF REMUNERATION (HORIZONTAL FROM NONE TO MONETIZED)[8]

necessities for the continuation of their business, as well as food, clothing, and other goods that they do not produce themselves. All others – craftsmen and wage labourers – will spend most of their income on shelter, on food in shops and at markets, and if anything is left, on small luxuries.

The difference in size between the sums received as remuneration and the sums spent takes us from medium-size coins most suitable for the payment of moderate sums at intervals of one, two, or a few weeks (the predominant frequency for the payment of wages, but also for advances that many craftsmen could not do without), to the coins used for weekly or daily purchases. For these transactions, much smaller denominations are needed, both because of the amounts involved and because it is impossible for people to always pay with the exact money, thus creating a need for small change. The intensity of participation by individuals and households in a market economy is therefore reflected in the degree to which medium and small denominations are available for circulation. Because small denominations best reflect the frequency of exchanges in a society, they may be considered the ideal yardstick of commercialized human relations.

In order to measure this across space and time, I have recently proposed a formal definition of 'deep monetization'. I take this to be 'a substantial stock of currencies per capita in circulation, consisting of denominations equalling the value of one hour or less of wage work', in which 'substantial' is defined as 'a per capita stock equal to between five and ten times the prevailing hourly wage'.[9] The application of this definition to different societies may provide an indication not only of the levels of 'deep monetization', but also (and more importantly here) of shifts in labour relations at their root: shifts between remunerated and unremunerated work, between remuneration in kind and in currencies, and between frequencies of payment.

Clearly, for societies with abundant records concerning these shifts – such as Western Europe in recent history – a detour via deep monetization is less interesting, however, for most parts of the world before 1900, it could provide a useful approach. For many places and periods, written evidence of shifts in labour relations is not readily found or, even worse, virtually non-existent. Archaeological evidence concerning coin circulation, by contrast, is much more universally available, because of the metals used for most types of currency.[10] The academic discipline of numismatics is centuries old and has brought us not only catalogues of coins from all over the world, but also estimates or even precise numbers of the quantities produced and the circulation patterns, as mirrored in coin hoards and stray finds. Sometimes, deep monetization is almost the only possible approach to detecting shifts in labour relations. Most valuable, however, is its importance for enabling comparisons by providing a clear and objective measuring instrument through time and space.

Implications for Wage Payments and the Development of Wage Labour: Europe *c.* 1885

The first large-scale statistical overview of coin circulation in different countries that enables comparative research into deep monetization was made by the Austrian monetary statistician Ottomar Haupt (1839-98).[11] He produced a comparative table of coin circulation, including smaller denominations. With this detailed data, it is possible to reconstruct deep monetization levels (DML) for a number of countries (see Figure 3.2).

TABLE 3.1: DEEP MONETIZATION LEVELS FOR SEVERAL COUNTRIES, *c.* 1885[12]

	Country	*DML*
Deeply monetized	Belgium	10
	Denmark	9
	France	8
	Germany	10
	Netherlands	8
	Switzerland	8
Small credit	United Kingdom	4.9
Possibly deeply monetized	Austria-Hungary	12

(Contd.)

	Greece	6
	Italy	14
	Portugal	<17
	Spain	<15
Medium monetized	Egypt	2
	Norway	3.7
	Russia	1.5
	Sweden	2.2
	United States	2.7

The majority of the Western European countries show deep monetization levels (a per capita stock equal to between five and ten times the prevailing hourly wage), which vary between 8 and 10. For several technical reasons, it is very likely that the figures for Portugal, Spain (substantive exports of domestic small change to the colonies), Italy, and Austria-Hungary (a massive amount of small change minted, but not yet put into circulation) are too high, but nevertheless might belong to this group as well. The other countries deviate from this Western-European pattern. I will discuss them in four groups: first, Norway and Sweden; second, the Balkans (including Serbia and Greece, with far too high numbers for the same reasons as Italy and Austria-Hungary) and parts of the Middle East; third, the United Kingdom; and fourth, Russia and the USA.

First, Norway and Sweden contrast interestingly with the third Scandinavian country in this group, Denmark. Not only was Denmark much more prosperous than its northern neighbours, it showed much higher urbanization figures and concomitant occupational differentiation and agricultural specialization.[13] This situation apparently required a much greater number of transactions in Denmark than in Norway and Sweden. This is eloquently illustrated in the following description of the Norwegian countrymen (85 per cent of the total population) by the British Consul-General Crow, dated 9 November 1870, Christiania (Oslo).[14] He distinguishes three 'classes' among them: the seafaring peasantry along the coast, the 'Bonde', and the 'Field Bonde' or mountain peasant. The second group is the most important: 'The Bonde or real peasant is generally the owner of the land he farms. This class may be considered as the kernel of the nation. The property of the Bonde is not sufficiently large to exempt him from work, but large enough to afford him and his household establishment ample support. He farms in the majority of cases, *not so much to raise produce for sale* [emphasis added] as to grow provisions and everything necessary for spinning wearing-apparel.'

Second, the equally low figures for the Balkans (the DML of Serbia and Greece was temporarily so high because of oversupply), Turkey, and Egypt point to similarly low demand for small means of exchange as in Norway and Sweden, even if certain indicators of economic development (such as the high literacy rates in the north) differed substantially. It is, however, possible that this cross section shows a more primitive situation than in the preceding decades. According to Michael Palairet, political freedom in the Balkans went hand in hand with economic decline in the period from 1878 to 1914.[15]

Third, of course, the low DML of Britain – although with some imagination still within the minimum margins of my definition of deep – demands an explanation. This situation was an echo of previous ages characterized by the scarcity of small change. Muldrew and Selgin have indicated that it took the government 'well into the Victorian era' to supply the public with enough small change. Therefore, counterfeits and tokens found ready acceptance.[16]

Fourth, the low DMLs for the USA and especially for Russia also seem to be echoes from previous periods, in this case of the widespread use of unfree labour, maintained without paying wages. However, this point needs more research into the consequences of what Kolchin sketched as the commonalities of the post-emancipation USA and Russia: 'there was a common legacy of forced labour that Russia shared with the United States and with all other former slave societies as well. New forms of dependency that provided the ex-bondsman with at best semi-freedom became the rule.'[17]

Deep Monetization and Wage Labour in Europe in the Long Term, 1000 to 1950

For a few of the countries contained in the above list with deep monetization levels in the late nineteenth century, it is possible to go back in time, sometimes only a few centuries, as in France, sometimes back to the Late Middle Ages, as in the Low Countries, and sometimes even to the High Middle Ages, as in England. These three cases will help us to understand long-term trends in Western Europe. To start with, the country with the longest trend available: England.

England

After China, England has the longest series of coinage statistics and estimates in the world, starting from the late eleventh century.[18] The stage of deep monetization certainly had not yet been reached at the time of the Domesday Book (1086), let alone before.[19] Precisely when it started may not be known exactly, but there is no doubt that in the first half of the thirteenth century, pennies per capita increased fivefold, that in the second half of that century it doubled again, and that the same might have happened in the first half of the fourteenth century, just before the Black Death, after which levels fell back to those of fifty years before. If compared with the prevailing wage levels, the English DML already stood at 5 in 1282 – the first date for which enough quantitative evidence is available – to grow to 10 or more in the decades before 1351. These early and spectacular jumps run parallel to the equally early and rapid expansion of wage labour.[20]

More surprisingly, these levels could not be maintained from the second half of the fourteenth century onwards, and recovered only very slowly, never to reach those of the early fourteenth century. Calculations based on the output of the royal mint in London show DMLs of 3 in 1720, 4.7 in 1857, and the already mentioned 4.9 in 1885. The actual situation was slightly less worrying, as private tokens and counterfeits (officially condoned) filled the gap left by the authorities that were not willing or not able to provide their subjects with enough copper coins and small silver denominations. By including small change of all forms, DMLs in the seventeenth and eighteenth centuries may actually have oscillated around a meagre 5.

How did such an economically highly-developed society, where half of the population depended on wages, cope with this continuous shortage of small change?[21] Payments in kind of course were one alternative, but not greatly preferred by employers.[22] Group pay was another solution, although a very imperfect one. In 1794, a manufacturer explained:

> If the work of two men comes to near a guinea, or three men to near two guineas, we give them the gold and they must go together till they can get change by purchasing whatever they want. If they go to a grocer he will not give change unless the quantity of sugar, tea, etc. amounts to a certain sum, and then he stipulates for their taking a certain quantity of [bad] halfpence. […] It often happens that groceries are not wanted by poor men who come from villages around, who seldom care to take tea and sugar home; but they generally have a public house in the market town at which they call to refresh; And to it these two or three fellows (though not all countrymen) go, with a good excuse to get their gold changed: if they find, after drinking a pint or two, that they cannot succeed, what can they do but go to another house. […] But whether they get change at the first or second attempt, they are not served without taking several shillings in copper, and this of the worst quality that can be forced into circulation.[23]

More importantly, Craig Muldrew has pointed in particular to the extension of small-scale local credit reducing the frequency of cash payments in the seventeenth and eighteenth centuries. Payments to industrial workers could not easily be solved by using wages in kind. Here, wages were often in arrears, which implies that shopkeepers had to extend credit to wage labourers. Muldrew provides the following telling example from Birmingham: 'A shopkeeper who sued a brick maker in the Birmingham court of requests in the mid-eighteenth century claimed that the latter's master had told him that during the winter season the defendant 'can get only clay, consequently his wages are small; trust him what he wants, and I will see you paid in the summer'. Here, the brick maker's wages would have simply been turned into a debt owed by the master to the shopkeeper, eliminating the need for small change.'[24] At the same time, this implies that the brick maker was compelled to buy all his necessities from one and the same shopkeeper, with all the attached risks of abuse.

The Low Countries

After the demise of the highly monetized Roman Empire, a new round of monetization began with the emergence of towns in the southern Low Countries around 1100, followed by the north one century later. Similar to England, for several centuries only one single denomination was coined; the silver denarius or penny. Around 1300, a multi-fractional system came into being with the introduction of various silver denominations of two-and-a-half and eight *penningen*, greatly facilitating payments.[25]

For the Low Countries, data is not as abundant as for England, partially because of long periods of political decentralization.[26] The manorial system, in which people are bound to the land where they are forced to provide labour, had never been important in the northern maritime provinces, and in most others declined in the eleventh to the fourteenth century.[27] Instead, small-scale and independent labour on peasant holdings and in artisanal shops became dominant. Wage labour emerged afterwards in the form of mercenary armies, and in the building, public works, and transport sectors. Think of the construction of churches, town gates, and walls in this most urbanized part of the world. According to Van Bavel, in particular in the fifteenth and sixteenth centuries in coastal Flanders and later in the Guelders river area, Salland, and coastal Frisia, wealthy tenant farmers with 35 to 70 hectares emerged, needing much additional labour during harvest time and all year round. This happened at the expense of small tenancies, where families now had to supply their labour. The proliferation of numerous mini-tenants was also ideal for proto-industrialization.

Not by coincidence, from the mid-fourteenth century onwards – but not earlier – there appears to be a certain correlation between the denomination coined most frequently over a longer period, and the level of the daily wage. This correlation suggests that the demand side preferred a currency equivalent to four times a wage earner's full daily wage (*c.* 1350-1450). From the fifteenth century onwards, this reduced to one times for the worse-paid and two times for the better-paid wage earners.[28]

Does it also represent a situation of deep monetization? By 1550, the Low Countries as a whole were certainly deeply monetized, and this process must have already started earlier on in certain provinces, first in Flanders and later in Brabant, most likely in the fifteenth century.[29] The uncertainty about the exact timing is due to the lack of good population statistics combined with the validity of all Burgundian currencies in all provinces, irrespective of the province in which they had been struck.

Thus, the situation in the Low Countries in the mid-sixteenth century seems to have been in balance: a massive demand for small change and an equally abundant supply of it by the mint houses of Charles V and his son Philip II. The meagre success of the central authorities to limit maximum wages in 1560 points in the same direction. The Utrecht city government, for example, stated that 'wage setting is entirely God's work', which may be interpreted as a plea for the functioning of the forces of supply and demand.[30] However, the balance was not stable; not as unstable as in England, but in the Dutch Republic in particular, the circulation of small coins decreased in the second half of the seventeenth century. The country was prosperous, and overall coin production was impressive. The key merchants who commanded coins from the mint houses, however, were much more interested in the (comparatively cheap and thus more profitable) minting of large denominations than in the production of small silver and copper coins for the local market. Instead, the provincial governments in the seventeenth century tacitly condoned the circulation of (partially low-weight) copper coins, produced by small principalities and noblemen in border regions.

This example shows that supply and demand for specific denominations are not automatically in equilibrium. The more unified Burgundian Netherlands and the Kingdom of the Netherlands were apparently more willing to act than the decentralized Dutch

Republic, in spite of its very high *overall* level of monetization. An intermediate solution was the responsibility taken directly by the county of Holland in 1702, followed by other provinces (asking for orders from their towns), for minting small change: solid copper *duiten*, and in 1738, silver *pijlstuivers* (equal to eight *duiten*). How badly these *pijlstuivers* were needed became apparent in Amsterdam in August of that same year. Workers, aware of the new coin, no longer accepted the old inferior *wapenstuivers* and their protests culminated in the occupation of the town hall. They only could be persuaded to leave after a number of them had been offered sums of ten to twenty new *stuivers*. Occasionally the *stuivers* were not sufficient, such as when the Republic's richest banker, Henry Hope, ordered new *scheepjesschellingen* (six-*stuiver* pieces) in order to make weekly payments to the men who were building his mansion 'Welgelegen' near Haarlem.[31]

The Low Countries were already deeply monetized in the sixteenth century, and problems concerning the supply and demand of small change had been mastered well.[32] The occasional problems that arose in the Dutch Republic stemmed from its political structure and economic concepts, which determined who was responsible and which instruments were available. As a result, solutions were always inadequate, to the extent that in the second half of the seventeenth century, unofficial coins had to be allowed into circulation – just like in mid-seventeenth and again in late eighteenth-century England.[33]

France

Before we can speak of a (northern or north-western) European pattern, it should be supplemented by other case studies. This is not easy, because research on what might be termed the social history of coin circulation has only just begun.[34] Here, I can only briefly discuss the implications of some estimates for France, the largest country of Western Europe and as deeply monetized as the Netherlands around 1885, when the DMLs stood at 8 (see Table 3.1).

Between 1789 and 1810, a number of coin reforms took place,

mainly for ideological reasons. They combined a desire for science based politics with a demand for in-depth reports on the current circulation of the coins. These reports show DMLs of 11 up to 17 for the revolutionary years.[35]

In contrast to the situation in contemporary England, the French state took responsibility for the circulation of small change, but it should be noted that this was not a direct consequence of the French Revolution; it had much deeper roots. France's DML was already 12 in 1789. Although I do not know of earlier precise coin production figures, the introduction of the copper one and two *denier tournois* under Henri III (1551-89) was a particularly great success, apparently satisfying a huge demand, not only from townspeople but especially from small peasants and day labourers.[36] These denominations, coined in enormous quantities, were very small indeed, as hourly wage levels then stood at one *sou* or twelve *deniers*.[37] In addition – comparable with the Dutch Republic somewhat later – adjacent small principalities started massive production of similar coins, which were circulated widely.

Conclusions for Western Europe

First, deep monetization as a response to the commodification of labour – initially predominantly in the guise of independent producers, then gradually shifting to paramount wage labour – started in England around 1300,[38] spread to the Southern Netherlands in the late Middle Ages, to the rest of the Low Countries and possibly France in the sixteenth century, and to other parts of Western Europe at the same time or later on. Further to the east, variations in unfree labour had an effect on the circulation of small change, as recently demonstrated for eighteenth-century Russia. Serfdom was the norm, and only noblemen could own and employ serfs. Thus, non-noble industrialists there needed labour, but were not allowed to own serfs. Alternating legislation increased or diminished the possibilities for bourgeois entrepreneurs to hire serfs as paid labourers, and these fluctuations were large enough to directly influence the demand for copper coins. In addition, non-noble entrepreneurs are documented to have requested that the state authorities provided more copper coins in order to pay wages.[39]

Second, once achieved, deep monetization is not necessarily sustainable. Apart from shifts in labour relations leading to variations in demand for small change, the supply may vary along with the quality of state institutions responsible for the output of small change. When governments fail in this respect, like England between 1350 and 1800 and the Dutch Republic between 1625 and 1725, other suppliers may offer themselves from inside or outside the polity. Alternatively, credit relations may expand or contract accordingly.[40]

Deep Monetization and Wage Labour in Asia, 1000 to 1900

For two large areas in Asia, it is also possible to reconstruct the relationship between deep monetization and shifting labour relations over several centuries: India and China. For India, most evidence is available for the nineteenth century, but to a certain extent it is possible to go back to the Middle Ages. For China, circulation figures go back much longer in time, but information about labour relations still is very meagre for most periods. However, both cases enable us to put the results reached for Europe to the test in order to see whether we may speak of Eurasian instead of (West) European patterns.

India, 1200 to 1850

Coinage – and what is more, coinage of small denominations – in northern India, goes back 2500 years and its use is therefore as old as in the Eastern Mediterranean or China. Quantification is difficult and is, accepting many uncertainties, only possible from around 1200 onwards.[41] What is clear, is that there was a first acceleration of small-value coinage (copper, billon, and silver coins weighing less than 5 grams) in the period from 1275 to the mid-fourteenth century. Because these denominations hardly equal hourly, but instead daily wage levels, we have to speak of medium, rather than of deep monetization in northern India as a whole by 1300.

Firoz Shah, the Delhi Sultan from 1351 to 1388, made a serious attempt to strike more copper denominations, which is also confirmed by his court historian, Shams Siraj Afif:

> The thought crossed Firoz Shah's august mind that if poor people bought something from the market and a balance of half or a quarter *jital* was left of the amount paid, the shopkeeper would not have the quarter change. If the buyer let it go, he would lose money. If he demanded it from the shopkeeper how could he be paid when no such coin existed? In the end, the balance due to the buyer would be left with the shopkeeper. For these reasons, the transaction between the buyer and the seller would drag unnecessarily. Sultan Firoz Shah gave orders for the striking of a half *jital* coin called *adh* [literally 'half'] and a quarter *jital* coin called *paika*.[42]

A great leap forward towards deep monetization was seen in the short-lived Suri dynasty in Delhi (1538-54) and under Akbar, the first Mughal Emperor from 1556 to 1605. Billon (low-base silver) coins were replaced by copper 'dams' (initially called paisas), as well as fractions of a half down to a tenth of a paisa. Whole and half dams were struck in immense quantities in a great number of mints over many years consecutively. Especially the half dams and lower fractions may be considered as small change (smaller fractions were also made, but far less frequently). As craftsmen earned two dams per day or more, this suggests that a paisa equalled two to four hours work for craftsmen, and half a dam, one to two hours.[43] The number of copper coins in Akbar's probate inventory even suggests a DML of 12 for the Mughal Empire around 1600.[44] One of the reasons for this unexpectedly high figure may be the lack of small silver coins, which caused copper ones to be used instead.[45] Deep monetization must anyhow have made an impressive jump in the second half of the sixteenth century.

The picture in the seventeenth and eighteenth centuries becomes less clear. The production of copper coins in the seventeenth century definitely decreased, but the usage of cowries and to a certain extent bitter almonds became more widespread.[46] On the other hand, nominal wages rose, as a consequence of which, prevailing copper coins equalled hourly wages more than ever before. According to the VOC merchant Francisco Pelsaert, artisans in Surat and Agra in the years 1620-7 earned five to six *takkas* (or *paisa* to the value of a thirtieth of a rupee) per day.[47] As other wage data for the seventeenth century suggests, this entailed a substantial increase after Akbar, but it is very likely that prices rose as quickly, because Pelsaert comments:

> They know little of the taste of meat. For their monotonous daily food, they have nothing but a little *kitchery*, made of green pulse mixed with rice, which is cooked with water over a little fire until the moisture has evaporated, and eaten hot with butter in the evening; in the daytime they munch a little parched pulse or other grain, which they say suffices for their lean stomach.[48]

When the copper content of the *dam* was reduced by a third in 1663 we hear of the reaction of the workers in Ahmedabad:

> The administrator of buildings, gardens and other workshops of Ahmedabad City represented to the Celestial Court that [...] workers have declined to accept the new coins in place of the old, saying that the difference between them is in the order of 10:15. When the intelligence of this matter reached the August Presence [Emperor Aurangzeb], an order was issued to the Finance Minister of the province [of Gujarat] that, in the ratio 10:15, the daily wages should be paid at the rate of one and a half tanka instead of one tanka.[49]

Such reactions, demonstrating that labour was paid in cash as well as illustrating the agency of the receivers, may be shown with a few more examples. The first dates from 1797, when the spouses of Bengal artillery soldiers fighting overseas in the Mysore war against Tipu Sultan vehemently but successfully protested against the mode of payment of their husbands' salaries. Left behind with their children in the barracks of Dum-Dum, just south of Calcutta, they depended completely on these monthly allowances. One day, the officer in-charge was unable to find enough silver coins and tried to pay them in gold. As soon as the wives of the gunners and their assistants (*lascars*) found out that they would consequently receive less copper money from the money changers (shroffs), they turned to the poor officer who reported:

I could not even with some degree of force, prevail on the women (those of the Lascars in particular) to receive their allowances, as I received them from the Pay Office, as their tickets were made out of Sicca Rupees, and they insisted on receiving the pice according to the bazar currency [...] Every argument I used, could not prevail on the people to believe that I had not taken a Dustoor for my own trouble, in the case, my quarters were daily surrounded by the amounts of hundreds [...] who became clamorous and were so grose [*sic*] in their abuse, that I was often obliged to appease them by ordering the Sircar, and Shroff, to pay them the difference.[50]

The position of the shroffs was very strong indeed, and the British were unable to circumvent them. In 1810, for example, the Madras Government felt compelled to form an official 'Establishment of Shroffs' at the presidency. 'If you can't beat them, join them', must have been the consideration. However, this concession had its price. At an annual expense of the enormous sum of 240 pagodas, this institution voluntarily agreed to reduce exchange rates and standardize them.[51] This may have helped for a while in Madras, but not always and not everywhere. Twenty years later, an engineer in-charge of the building and maintenance of irrigation canals north of Delhi, having been sent there from Calcutta with boxes full of silver rupees, was confronted by workers who wanted to be paid only in exactly specified local copper coinage. Thus compelled to exchange his silver into copper, he complained about the shroffs that 'the price of pice is always raised when my works commence'. He even planned to go directly to the mint masters who he found out made the coins, but his masters in Calcutta frustrated this plan by ordering him to use instead the newly-minted official colonial coins. The creative engineer lost his case, notwithstanding his reply that:

The supply of *pice* ordered up will be utterly useless to me on the works without a special regulation of Government making the *pice* of the Calcutta mint the only legal copper coin throughout the Companies' territories. The *pice* in question cannot be introduced by an individual and will only subject me to infinite trouble and annoyance as no one will willingly take pay from me in a coin not in general currency.[52]

Another example of workers' protests against malpractices in wage payments dates from the navvies, maintaining and repairing the Sonipat division of the Western Jumna Canal north of Delhi in 1849. When they found out that their British overseer had systematically embezzled part of their earnings, they became so 'clamorous for their pay' that they lodged an official complaint with the executive superintendent, Lieutenant A.D. Turnbull. The lieutenant took action against his compatriot, stating 'It is impossible for work to be carried on while such irregularities exist. It is not to be expected that labourers will come to our works if they are not paid up regularly, but kept for long periods in arrears.' Thus the British felt compelled to investigate the case by an official Court of Enquiry at the barracks of the 42nd Regiment, Native Light Infantry, in Delhi, from 20 June until 12 July 1849.

Several foremen and workmen had to testify, which went reasonably well considering that they were illiterate. From the court case, for which 232 questions and answers were recorded, we not only learn precisely how the embezzlement had been organized, and that the accused were found guilty and therefore 'wholly untrustworthy and totally unfit to be retained', but also importantly that the wages were paid out exclusively in one particular coin, copper *takkas*, most probably imported from Alwar, 200 km south of the canal.[53]

Copper coin production in India was heavily dependent on Japanese and European imports. Production figures for Indian and Nepalese copper mines are very scarce, but overseas trade statistics show on average constant figures for Japanese copper imported by the VOC in Coromandel and Bengal, and rising figures for European copper imported by the EIC in Madras and Calcutta.[54] Combining all the data on nineteenth-century circulation levels, eighteenth-century copper imports, and fluctuations in intensity from the thirteenth century onwards, I am tempted to suggest that India underwent a first phase of deep monetization in the sixteenth century, which could barely be maintained in the seventeenth, returned to lower levels in the eighteenth, and surged to a second phase of deep monetization around 1800. This was then maintained throughout the nineteenth century.

Indian Deep Monetization Levels in the Nineteenth Century

For the beginning of the nineteenth century, more quantitative data at last becomes available, as the English had more grip on their dearly won new colony. We know that in the nineteenth century, proletarianization levels remained stable in the Deccan (about which there is more information below). If we assume that this trend is valid for India as a whole, we might expect that, all other things being equal, demand for small currency at the beginning of the century was the same as at the end of it. However, what about the supply side: the output of Indian mints around 1800? Most copper coins at the time were probably produced in mints under Indian control. The English wanted to replace these with their own coins, first completely in Indian (Persian) script, later with Latin script added on. In 1847, the collector of the Delhi district wrote that he needed 50,000 rupees 'for the use of his district to replace the native pyce', partly in order to pay the sepoys.[55] The efforts at replacement only became successful in the third quarter of the nineteenth century, and even then a number of 'native' mint houses remained active, some of them until India's Independence in 1947. This story demonstrates that the British institutions in India were less strong than the superpower of the time had wished for.

The colonial copper coin output for India in the first half of the nineteenth century already amounted to more than thirty-one million rupees, while a number of native mints were also still very active.[56] Given the lower population figures than half a century later (see below), this points to deep monetization already existing at the beginning of the nineteenth century. These impressions find some corroboration in the more precise figures for the district of Benares.[57] In 1808, the number of (copper) pice required for circulation in that district was estimated at 700,000 rupees, or roughly fifteen pice per capita. As the daily wage of a labourer was four pice, this would imply that the district as a whole was on the brink of deep monetization, especially if we include the number of cowries still circulating at the time in Bengal.[58]

There was certainly a demand for these copper coins, as demonstrated by a reconstruction of labour relations in the Deccan in the 1820s – the earliest data so far for India available in the Global Collaboratory on Labour Relations – which are not substantially different from the 1901 outcomes for about the same geographical area.[59]

TABLE 3.2: PRIMARY LABOUR RELATIONS (IN PERCENTAGES) IN THREE COLLECTORATES IN THE DECCAN IN THE 1820s[60]

Labour Relations Category	*Khandesh*			*Poonah*			*Dharwar*		
	male	*female*	*total*	*male*	*female*	*total*	*male*	*female*	*total*
1 not working	15	15	30	15	15	30	15	15	30
2 affluent	0	3	3	0	3	3	0	2	2
5 working in the household	0	16	16	0	23	23	0	18	18
7 slaves	7	0	7	8	0	8	6	0	6
12 a+b small producers	18	4	22	24	5	29	22	5	27
14 wage labourers	10	8	18	1	1	2	8	7	15
18 in state employ	4	0	4	5	0	5	2	0	2
Total	54	46	100	53	47	100	53	47	100

After all these estimates, we may end with the earliest reliable reconstruction of the total money supply of India, which dates from around 1880.[61] At that time, gold coins were used only for hoarding, for export, or in order to be melted down for ornaments. Silver coins were used for paying rents and taxes, and for petty trade transactions. The ordinary person, however, saw only the lowest possible denominations in copper.[62] Most surprisingly, these copper coins, with an estimated value of 48.1 million rupees – or a fifth of a rupee (three annas) per capita – expressed in hourly wages of a quarter of an anna, resulted in a DML of no less than 12.

This comparatively high level may need some qualification. Wages outside agriculture may have been slightly higher than a quarter of an anna, and working days may have been longer than eight hours, but even so the result would be a per capita copper circulation of more than five times the hourly wage. Further, the actual circulation of copper coinage is likely to have been higher, because the estimates may very well exclude both copper coins produced before 1862 – the first coinage under the British Crown – and the numerous humble 'native coins' that continued to circulate. Nevertheless, there are other reasons to suppose the conclusion that India was already deeply monetized by 1880 may be not too far off the mark. A recent reconstruction of labour relations for the subcontinent in 1900 shows levels of commodification (31.2 per cent self-employed and 12.1 per cent wage labourers) that are not very different from contemporaneous outcomes for European countries.[63]

Conclusion: India from 1200 to 1900

After a first attempt in the fourteenth century, northern India is very likely to have been deeply monetized in the sixteenth century. After possible dips in the seventeenth and eighteenth centuries, it was certainly back to similar levels in the early nineteenth century, which goes for the entire subcontinent in the later decades of the century. These are certainly unexpected results for a subcontinent that is hardly ever considered a candidate for serious economic growth. Although research in this field still is lacking, the ubiquity of paid labour (both independent and waged) and the insistence of wage workers for payment in specific types of small change may be termed remarkable. This not only points to much greater agency of Indian wage labourers than expected,[64] but also to small circulation circuits per type of coin before the middle of the nineteenth century. Political disunity may offer one explanation, but that is not very convincing if compared with Europe at the same time. Coin production might have been prolific, but state institutions in India hardly ever seem to have taken the responsibility for exchange ratios between silver and copper, leading to an enormous amount of power held by the intermediate layer of money changers. Consequently, workers tried to avoid exchange costs by insisting on the method of their wage payments. At the same time, this must have slowed down the velocity of money, which might point to an actual decline of deep monetization levels, especially during the period of decentralized coin production between around 1750 and 1850.

China

Like India, China has a tradition of small copper coin circulation going back well into the fourth century BCE. What is more, and unlike India, China's well developed central polities, characterized by much more continuity, were able to produce these small copper 'cash' coins centrally and – important for us – have kept production records since the Han (206 BCE to CE 220).[65] These show that average annual production of five to ten cash coins per capita was quite feasible, but also that in some periods many more were brought into circulation, leading to impressive stocks. Two periods stand out at once: The Northern Song (960 to 1126), with an annual production in the late eleventh century reaching over fifty cash coins per capita, and the Qing (1644 to 1912), with ten to twenty. The latter may seem much less impressive than the former, but the difference is smaller than one might think. On the one hand, the Song coins also circulated in Japan, which for centuries depended fully on imports of small change from China, and on the other, in the eighteenth and nineteenth centuries the stock of officially cast coins was supplemented substantially by illegally made specimens from all sorts of sources (including Vietnam), which demonstrates how great the demand was.

In the following paragraphs, I tackle two aspects: the methods of payments to workers, showing as far as possible the importance of cash coins for the functioning of the labour market, and the relationship between shifts in stock and shifts in labour relations. By way of conclusion, I discuss the comparability of the Chinese figures with those from other parts of the world.

The practice of daily payments in cash coins is abundantly testified to in official and unofficial written sources. Whether cash coins originated from castings in official mints did not matter, as long as they were accepted at the market and in shops. The government only intervened in grave cases of forgery, such as in 1794, when it closed down the Old Crow's Nest, a complete village of forgers in the mountainous border region of Sichuan and Guizhou. It had been active for eight years and in its heyday looked like a small town.[66]

Apart from the abundant availability of cash coins during most of the Qing period, what enhanced their use was also the accessibility of the courts for litigation cases regarding payments. Christine Moll-Murata found litigations in Baxian (Sichuan), over sums as low as 350 or 420 cash coins, at the time good for purchasing respectively 10 kg of rice or 2.5 kg of pork. Equally important was the likelihood for wage earners to win a case. It demonstrates, according to Moll-Murata, 'that to a certain extent, the "small people", who in their plaints and testimonies were required to refer to themselves vis-à-vis the authorities as "ants", harboured the hope that they would get their cash and acceptable working conditions by virtue of adjudication from the representatives of the state.'[67]

Hope could also spring from collective action, especially by craft guilds. In extreme cases, strikes would break out. The most famous one in this period is possibly the strike in one of the two large (more than 3,000 workers in total) metropolitan mint houses in Peking in 1741. Because of illegal wage deductions and bribery by their foremen, focusing on incorrect exchange rates between copper and silver money, a number of industrial actions took place. On one occasion, the workers in one of the factories climbed onto a mound within the mint, clamouring and shouting, and throwing bricks and tiles, even after troops had arrived. After several rounds of blanks were fired, the throwing stopped, but not the shouting. The prefect had the ringleaders punished, but at the same time requested that the emperor punished the foremen as well. It is also very probable that the workers received compensation for the illegal deductions and frauds committed by their foremen.[68] Methods of payment really mattered, and this was widely recognized.

The impressively deep monetization levels for the Song period are perhaps less surprising than those under the Ching. Kent Deng quotes the famous dictum by Eric Jones that Song China was just a 'hair's breadth' away from a genuine industrial revolution and adds: 'Counterfactually, if the stand-off between the nomads and the Songs had continued for another 200 to 300 years, China might indeed have become a capitalist economy.'[69] Another indicator for the growing importance of labour markets is the number of major cities, including the port Quanzhou, with a population of 100,000 households in 989, and Hangzhou – the capital of the Southern Song – with 550,000 inhabitants in 1165 and 1,240,000 in 1173.[70]

It also may be significant that around 1050, compulsory work for the Chinese state was converted into a tax, which had to be paid in cash. This suggests that self-employed peasants and craftsmen as well as wage earners became the new tax payers. From the twelfth century onwards, far fewer cash coins were produced, and Von Glahn emphatically states that bronze coin circulation virtually stopped for two centuries.[71] The partial replacement by paper money would not have been useful for regular wage payments or advances to craftsmen, and certainly not for their shopping. In the fifteenth century, the increase of private coinage brought some relief. The rise of 'bond servitude' in late Ming China implies a shift from free to unfree labour in those cash-ridden centuries.[72]

As they did during the Song population growth, the extension of labour markets and deep monetization went hand in hand under the Qing. This distinctive pattern of monetization intensity becomes understandable if we link it to shifting labour relations, in particular those described in detail by Christine Moll-Murata in the framework of the IISH-Collaboratory Global Labour Relations (CGLH).[73] Wage labour became increasingly important, especially from 1780 onwards, in various industrial sectors such as printing, porcelain making, and shipbuilding.[74]

China stands out for maintaining the circulation of one specific coin denomination, the 'cash' for more than 2,200 years. It is apparent that a large increase in monetization levels took place in the eleventh century, followed by a decrease between the twelfth and the sixteenth century, and again an increase in the eighteenth century. Although this periodization is important for the study of labour relations, it is not so easy to answer the question of what per capita stock would represent 'deep monetization' as defined in the introduction to this chapter. At first sight, the requirements of 'a per capita stock equal to between five and ten times the prevailing hourly wage' are more than fulfilled. However, we should not forget that a substantial proportion of the cash coins did not circulate as individual pieces, but as 'small' strings of (ideally) 100 pieces or 'big' strings of 1,000 pieces, which compares with medium and large silver coins in the southern and western parts of Eurasia.[75] With a few minor exceptions, multiple cash coins were cast and circulated by the state in large numbers only at the times of highest production in the Song and Qing periods. At these times it is apparent that there was a substantial demand for these larger denominations of five, and especially ten and higher cash coins.[76] In order to enhance comparability with other polities, it might be advisable to divide the Chinese DMLs by ten.

Conclusion

This chapter shows that for several parts of Eurasia, as a rule the degree to which people participate in a market economy is reflected by the intensity of which medium and small denomination coins are available for circulation. Small denominations best reflect the frequency of exchanges in society and so may be considered the best yardstick of commercialized human relations.

The concept of DMLs is used here as a yardstick for tracing shifts in labour relations. The chapter uses archaeological and other numismatic evidence as a supplement to and an alternative for written evidence of the history of work. It has proven useful for the multi-metal and multi-denominational currency systems that prevailed in the west and the south, but less so in the mono-fractional Chinese system (unless adjustments are made for the usage of cash coins strung together in units of 100 or 1,000 in order to pay larger sums because of the lack of intermediate denominations). Nevertheless, in all cases, shifts in the levels of monetization may indicate possible shifts in labour relations.

Available data for different parts of Eurasia (the Low Countries, France, India, and China) show unexpected results (see Figure 3.2): (1) similar levels of deep monetization in Western Europe and South Asia from around 1100 to 1900; (2) similar periods

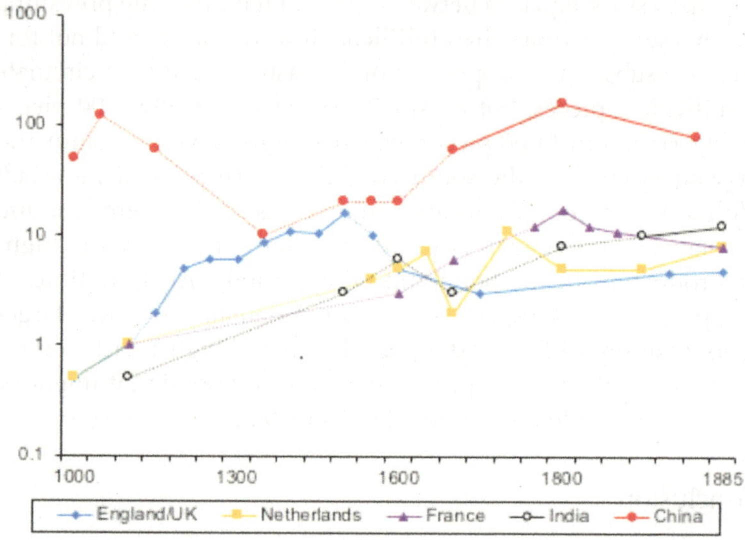

FIG. 3.2: DEEP MONETIZATION IN EUROPE AND ASIA, 1000 TO 1885

of increasing and decreasing levels overall, but diverging in the seventeenth and eighteenth centuries (an increase in Europe versus a decrease in India); (3) diverging developments between China and the rest; (4) the importance of institutions regulating coin circulation; and (5) the agency of workers if the circulation of the denominations they depend on is endangered.

To a certain extent, these results question accepted wisdom in debates on labour history, but also on the Great Divergence, urbanization, migration, and economic development. Although deep monetization did not automatically and directly follow the introduction of coins as currency, it took place everywhere much earlier than the advent of 'modernity' or the 'industrial revolution', and it is certainly not a prerogative of the West.

On the other hand, this institution is not a simple function of the demand for small change, as the supply side in particular is determined by a number of political factors, and therefore this institution can vary and appear somewhat unstable. One alternative for the demand for small change that is not met by sufficient supply is the extension of small credit (not shown in Figure 3.2). Variations in demand and supply explain why the lines in Figure 3.2 sometimes run parallel and sometimes do not.

In this chapter, two explanations have been proposed for the varying levels in deep monetization: first, actual shifts in labour relations, and second, shifts in the modes of payment, independent of such relations. As we have seen in the introduction, each form of labour relations (as defined in the GCLR) involves its own type of remuneration, which is linked to specific methods of payment. Actual shifts of many people engaged in free work to unfree work are likely to diminish the demand for small denominations, whereas shifts from reciprocal work to commodified work will have the opposite effect. Shifts in modes of payment may also occur when the supply of small change varies independently of developments in labour relations. In such cases, intervals of payment, and consequently credit relations, will have to change. Examples of both have been discussed: shifts in labour relations in all the countries analysed here, as well as changing credit relations in England between the fourteenth and the nineteenth century. Other shifts in DMLs still are not well understood (for example India in the seventeenth and eighteenth centuries).

Explanations for changing levels of deep monetization may be found on the demand side in shifting labour relations (free versus unfree; (de)commodification; independent versus wage labour), as well as in changing practices in frequencies of payment, and thus in the credit relations of workers that determine their power relations.

NOTES

1. E.g. Van Zanden 2008.
2. E.g. Steinfeld 1991; Biernacki 1995; Lucassen 2007; Van der Linden 2008.
3. Interesting for linking money (though not currencies) and labour is Reddy 1987; see also Biernacki 1995, Ch. 8.
4. Here, I refer to labour relations as defined in the Global Collaboratory on Labour Relations (GCLR), based at the IISH.
5. For an excellent overview of taxation systems worldwide, including corvée, see Monson & Scheidel 2016.

6. For practical reasons, tributary societies such as the Egyptian and pre-Columbian civilizations, let alone older societies, fall outside the scope of this chapter. See Lucassen 2013, and the site of the Collaboratory on the Global History of Labour Relations (CGLH) of the IISH, which provides a taxonomy of labour relations that are used in this chapter: see https://collab.iisg.nl/web/labourrelations.
7. More extensively in Lucassen, see Part I: No. 4 in this volume.
8. Cf. Simmel 1922, 284-91.
9. Lucassen 2014; Lucassen, see Part I: No. 4 in this volume.
10. A global introduction is provided in Cribb, Cook & Carradice 1990. Cf. Lucassen & Zuijderduijn, 2014.
11. Haupt 1886; 1894; see also *Report of the Committee* 1893, Appendix II, 213, 273-5.
12. Based on Lucassen, See part I: No. 4 in this volume, where it is also explained why the resulting circulation figures for some countries are far too high.
13. Cf. Grytten 2004 and Thue 2008.
14. *Further Reports* 1871, 362.
15. Palairet 1997.
16. Selgin 2008, 266, 295, 297; Muldrew 2007, 409.
17. Kolchin 1987, 375. For the circulation of tokens in the American South after the Civil War, see Lurvink 2014.
18. For an extensive discussion of English DMLs between 1300 and 1900 see Lucassen, see Part I: No. 4 in this volume.
19. Naismith 2012, especially 284-90 where he discusses the problems of small change in Anglo-Saxon England.
20. Cf. Bolton 2012, 27.
21. For estimates of the waged population, see Phelps Brown & Hopkins 1981, 70; Mayhew 2007, 213; Muldrew 2007, 395.
22. Muldrew 2007, 401.
23. Selgin 2008, 27-8, quoting Walter Merrey.
24. Muldrew 2007, 404.
25. For a general overview of circulation patterns in Europe, see Peter Spufford 1988; Spufford 2008. For the Low Countries, see Van Bavel 2010, 193-200.
26. What follows about the Low Countries and in particular its northern parts, is a summary of Lucassen 2014; most recent publications are Martiny 2014, and Vanhoudt 2015. See also Welten 2010.
27. Van Bavel 2006, 37-72; Van Bavel 2010, 200-4, 244-6.
28. Lucassen 2007C, 260-1.
29. Van Bavel 2010, 198-9.
30. Ibid., 208; at about the same time the English Statute of Artificers (1563) was prepared.
31. Lucassen 2014, 101-2.
32. Echoing Volckart 2008; in reaction to Sargent & Velde 2002.
33. Muldrew 2007; Selgin 2008.

34. Lucassen & Zuijderduijn 2014.
35. More extensively in Lucassen, see Part I: No. 4 in this volume (mainly after Desrousseaux 2012).
36. Cf. Béaur et al. 2010.
37. In the late sixteenth and seventeenth century, hourly wages were one rather than two sous, see e.g. Goubert 1968, 333-40, and Le Roy Ladurie 1969, 123. This coincides well with the end of the *denier tournois* after 1650 and of the *double tournois* after 1700.
38. Possibly also in Northern Italy (although not discussed here).
39. Bacherikov 2013. Information kindly provided by Bacherikov's academic supervisor Gijs Kessler. Cf. Florén 1994.
40. For an example from late medieval Normandy, see Cardon 2012.
41. Lucassen, see Part I: No. 3 in this volume.
42. Haider 2015. For the actual coins meant, see Goron & Goenka, 2001, 66. For frequency estimates see Lucassen, see Part I: No. 2 in this volume.
43. Lucassen, see Part I: No. 2 in this volume; Deyell 1987; Habib 1987 (see appendix by Deyell); Martin 2007; Wages in Habib 1987, 154; Prakash, see Part I: No. 7 and Haider, No. 6 in this volume; Haider 2015.
44. See Lucassen, see Part I: No. 4 in this volume.
45. See also hereafter the discussion of high deep monetization levels for China. For the low production of silver rupee fractions, see Prakash, see Part I: No. 8 in this volume, [337] and cf. Habib 1987, 145 ('It would therefore seem that everything that an ordinary person might buy in an ordinary North Indian city during Akbar's reign would have its price fixed in copper money. Only luxury and export items would need payment in rupees.'). See Haider 2015, 93-4 for a different view.
46. Habib 1987, 158-64; Haider 2015, 98-103.
47. Kolff & Van Santen 1979, 309 (wage; cf. 311 for servants 3-4 rupees per month, which at 30 paisa per rupee would mean 3-4 paisa per day) and 117 (exchange rate); cf. much less favourable exchange rates of 57-8 dam/paisa per rupee in these years: Prakash, see Part I: No. 7 in this volume.
48. Kolff & Van Santen 1979, 309; Haider 2015, 91 (quoting the English translation by Moreland and Geyl). See also De Zwart & Lucassen 2020.
49. Haider 2015, 311.
50. Lucassen, see Part I: No. 13 in this volume. For the payment logistics of Indian Maratha troops, see Lingen & Lucassen, Studies 9 in this volume.
51. Lucassen, See Part I: No. 13 in this volume.
52. Lingen & Lucassen, see Part I: No. 9 in this volume.
53. In addition, coin transport over large distances involved great risks of loss and robbery, see Lucassen, see Part I: No. 13 in this volume.
54. Shimada 2006. For details, see Lucassen, see Part I: No. 4 in this volume.
55. Jan Lucassen 2007c, 383.
56. More extensively in Lucassen, see Part I: No. 4 in this volume.

57. Stevens 2012, 264-5, 319-23, 336-42, 355-67, 378-9, 488. For information on the Benares Division, District, and City, see *Imperial Gazetteer of India*, Vol VII (Oxford, 1908).
58. Stevens 2012, passim; Lucassen 2007 (Introduction), 31-2; Hogendorn & Johnson 1986.
59. Lucassen & Stapel 2014. Following this, data for neighbouring Goa since the late 1830s (ongoing work in the framework of this collaboratory by Paulo Mattos, Lisbon) has confirmed this impression.
60. Lucassen & Stapel 2014, Tables 1-3.
61. More extensively in Lucassen, see Part I: No. 4 in this volume.
62. *Report of the Committee* 1893, Appendix I, 148-9.
63. Lucassen & Stapel 2014, Table 23. For Europe, see cross sections 1900 for Italy, Spain, and the Netherlands on. https://iisg.amsterdam/en/research/projects/global-collaboratory-on-the-history-of-labour-relations-1500-2000
64. For workers' agency in India in general from the late eighteenth to the nineteenth century, see Lucassen 2006; Lucassen 2012.
65. Lucassen, see Part I: No. 4 in this volume.
66. Cao & Vogel 2015.
67. Moll-Murata 2015 (276 quotation).
68. Vogel 2005. For mutinies caused by contentious modes of payment, see Kaske 2015, 378.
69. Deng 2015, 326.
70. Ibid., 325-6.
71. Von Glahn 2010, 39-56.
72. Chevaleyre 2013; Moll-Murata 2015.
73. Moll-Murata 2012. For the Middle Ages, see Von Glahn 2010, 50.
74. Moll-Murata 2008; 2015, 275-6.
75. As all Chinese cash coins were holed, they could be strung together.
76. For the 1854 issues, in use at least until 1879, see Kaske 2015, 371, 392.

4

Deep Monetization in Eurasia in the Long Run*

JAN LUCASSEN

Questions and Concepts

This chapter introduces a comparative method to measure deep monetization levels (DML) across time and space. Originally based on a case study for the Netherlands 1200-1940, its results are tested here for a number of countries in Eurasia in roughly the same time span. Why study monetization, and in particular deep monetization? Monetization, i.e. the increase in the use of currencies as a means of exchange in a society, may be regarded as the result of a demand for and supply of artefacts, such as coins and paper money. Monetary history is predominantly concerned with its supply side, and more especially with either the total sums

* This chapter has grown out of a paper written for two different conferences. First, the workshop on 'Economic institutional change and global labour relations', at the IISH in Amsterdam (26-7 September 2014), and, second, the conference 'Coins, currency, and crisis from *c.* 2000 BC to *c.* AD 2000. On silver, paper and trust in historical perspective', at the Vrije Universiteit in Amsterdam (12-13 December 2014). I thank the participants at these conferences and other meetings at which I gave a presentation (Osaka, 3-4 March 2015, Utrecht, 29 June 2015, Valencia, 1 April 2016) for their input. In this new version the monetary aspects have been elaborated upon more fully, while a chapter in a separate volume (here referred to as Lucassen 2017, and reproduced in this volume in Part I: Studies, No. 3) concentrates on labour aspects. Both chapters refer to each other, so overlap is unavoidable. I am grateful to Chris Gordon for his stylistic and linguistic revisions.

involved (e.g. mass inflation), or with the big denominations: paper money, gold coins (the gold standard being one example), and large-denomination silver coins (with the flow of Spanish silver from the Americas).

Here I concentrate on the demand side, and more especially on the small denominations – fabricated, as a rule, from base metal. That is precisely the type of currency used by the common man, i.e. many more social actors are directly involved in the use of small change than in that of higher denominations. Therefore, this aspect of monetary history is interesting for scholars wishing to understand the role of social relations in determining demand, but also in understanding reactions to an inadequate supply of small change. As will be demonstrated, these social aspects of monetary history are particularly promising for the study of long-term trends in social and economic history across Eurasia. Similarities and differences across time and space point to converging and diverging overall trends.

A key role of currencies is to serve as a means of exchange, i.e. in return for goods or for services.[1] Means of exchange for goods are needed in different forms of trade; means of exchange for services are especially needed to pay labour. In this way, labour remuneration may be seen as the demand side and the production and distribution of currencies as the supply side. This function has a very long history: for over 2,500 years the remuneration of work and currencies – the means of exchange in which remuneration is often expressed – are strongly interlinked in Eurasia. The relation between work and currencies therefore has a lot to tell us about both concepts.

The link between work, remuneration, and currencies is not straightforward. It was, however, important in a part of the world that had seen markets develop long before our period and in which tributary and self-sufficient reciprocal labour relations had already become insignificant early on.[2] In this world of 'commodified' labour, circulation of medium- and low-denomination currencies nearly always implies the remuneration of work, though remunerated work does not necessarily imply the circulation of currencies. The link between the two is weakest if currencies are primarily intended for large-scale or costly trade or for the hoarding of large savings. In those cases currencies consist of high-denomination coins – mostly gold or heavy silver pieces – and later on paper money, bills of exchange, and the like.[3]

There are three major situations in which work is not paid, or not paid in currencies.[4] First, we have the case of unfree and forced work. Of course here, too, minimal remuneration is necessary in order to keep the worker alive, but it is done in kind, either provided directly by slave owners or grown by the slaves themselves on plots and in time slots allowed to them. This form of labour without wage is also encountered on estates worked by serfs, who grew their own food on small plots on the estate unless ordered to work without pay for their lord. Secondly, remuneration may be paid in kind instead of in currency. Living-in servants, who work in exchange for board and lodging (plus a token remuneration in money), are a well-known example. Soldiers and sailors also receive a substantial part of their remuneration in kind.[5] The Indian *jajmani* system should be mentioned here too. Here, craftsmen in the village community provide free services to local farmers in exchange for a share in the total harvest for their consumption. Third, and most common, unpaid work is found inside the household, in which notably women and children share the income of its head, but perform all household chores for free.

To formulate it differently, apart from the relations mentioned – which pertain more to unfree than to free labour, and more to women and youngsters than to adult men – work in Eurasia was performed in exchange for currencies, directly in the case of independent producers (farmers and peasants, craftsmen, traders and peddlers, transporters, shopkeepers, performers of services) or indirectly in the case of wage earners employed by them.

The debate on the social implications, especially on the advantages and disadvantages of a monetary economy for the common man in early-modern Western Europe, has a long history. Some stress the negative effects of monetization for wage earners, others the more positive ones.[6] The optimists argue that increased 'dependency' on the market does not necessarily have only negative effects for the recipients of wages and other remuneration. As

Samuel Johnson wrote to Boswell in 1777, money earnings had a liberating capacity since those who lived off the land were also bound to it for lack of portable wealth. Wages paid in metal currencies, in contrast, supplied 'power of resistance and means of escape' from a feudal system.[7] This idea was fully developed by the German social scientist Georg Simmel (1858-1918) in his *Philosophie des Geldes*, originally published in 1900.[8] At the same time, he realized very well that this freedom is relative:

> It is not the bond as such, but being bound to a particular individual master that represents the real antipode of freedom. [...] Only in most recent times has the scarcity of domestic servants in large cities occasionally provided the possibility of turning down a position for imponderable reasons. Both sides consider this a major step towards the independence of servants, even though the actual demands of the job are no less heavy than they previously were. [...] A formally similar development emerges for wage labourers in a money economy. In view of the harshness and coerced nature of labour, it seems as if the wage labourer is nothing but a disguised slave. [...] From the subjective aspect, however, the relationship to the individual employer has become much more loose compared with earlier forms of labour.[9]

Before this debate can be settled we have to know more about actual monetization levels and the function of monetary exchange in daily life. If the remuneration of work is one side of the circulation of currencies, the spending of income is the other. Sums used in spending are smaller than sums received as remuneration for work. Farmers selling their seasonal harvests, who receive relatively large sums, will divide their spending over rent, the purchase of necessities to continue their business, as well as comestibles, clothing, and other goods that they do not produce themselves. All others – craftsmen and wage labourers – will spend most of their income on food and shelter and, if anything is left, on small luxuries.

We therefore should differentiate between sums received as remuneration for services (predominantly wages) and sums spent with these earnings. This brings us from medium-denomination coins most suitable for the payment of moderate sums at intervals of one, two, or a few weeks (the predominant frequency for the payment of wages, but also for advances that many craftsmen could not do without) to the coins used for weekly or daily purchases.[10] For these transactions, much smaller denominations are needed, both because of the amounts involved and because it is impossible for people always to pay with the exact money, thus creating a need for small change.

The degree of participation in a market economy is therefore reflected in the degree to which medium and small denominations are available for circulation. Because small denominations best reflect the frequency of exchanges in a society, they may be considered the most sensitive yardstick of commercialized human relations. To measure this across space and time, I recently proposed a formal definition of what scholars including Koen Verboven and Shailendra Bhandare have called 'deep monetization'. I take this to be 'a substantial stock of currencies per capita in circulation, consisting of denominations equalling the value of one hour or less of waged work'. The evidence presented in this and earlier articles suggests that 'substantial' may be roughly defined as 'a per capita stock equal to between five and ten times the prevailing hourly wage'.[11] In Figure 4.1 these definitions are recast in the style of a formula.

This approach provides a clear instrument to measure and compare monetization levels over time and space and to study the backgrounds to shifts. The application of this definition to different societies might provide an indication not only of levels of 'deep monetization', but also of shifts in labour relations at their root – shifts between remunerated and unremunerated work, between remuneration in kind and in currencies, and between frequencies of payment.[12]

The advantage of this approach is not only conceptual clarity as a precondition for historical comparisons, it also opens up methodological opportunities. Clearly, for societies with abundant records on mint output and circulation, links with social phenomena such as labour relations may be established immediately. For example, DMLs increase in tandem with proletarianization. However, for most parts of the world before, say, 1900, written data on output and circulation are lacking – even more so in the case of labour

$$\mu = \frac{M^{SC}}{P} \propto \frac{T^{SC}}{V^{SC}}$$

Where:
μ is the measure of monetization
M^{SC} is the total amount of available small change per capita
P is the price level of labour; we define this as the hourly wage
T^{SC} is a measure of the number of small-change transactions per capita
V^{SC} is a measure of the velocity of small change.

Monetization is inversely proportional to the velocity of small change. Here, small change is defined as all currency with a denomination equal to or less than an hourly wage.

Provisional definitions:

Low: $\mu < 1$
Medium: $1 \leq \mu < 5$
Deep: $5 \leq \mu < 10$
Extreme: $\mu \geq 10$ (indicating imbalances between small and insufficient medium-size denominations)

FIG. 4.1: DEEP MONETIZATION DEFINED[13]

relations. On the other hand, archaeological evidence on coin circulation is much more universally available, because of the easy preservation of metals used for most types of currency. The academic discipline of numismatics is centuries old and has brought us not only catalogues of coins from all over the world, but also estimates of quantities produced and circulation patterns as mirrored in coin hoards and stray finds.[14] This enables us to formulate more specific questions about the demand side behind increasing or decreasing levels of deep monetization. Often we have only the DM approach to detect shifts in labour relations.

This chapter offers a provisional overview of the available evidence on the emergence of and fluctuations in deep monetization in some important parts of Eurasia. For practical reasons the data presented here cover only the last millennium, even though the method could in principle be used from the very beginnings of coinage in Asia Minor, northern India, and China some 2,500 years ago. After a brief discussion of historical theories about the demand for small change, we will move from the known to the unknown. An initial overview of DMLs at the end of the nineteenth century is possible for several countries in the North Atlantic. From this empirical basis it is possible to reconstruct long-term developments for a few West-European countries and to find out when DM started there. The third step will be to apply these insights to long-term trends in India and China, which will enable us to conclude with some intra-Eurasian comparisons covering the last millennium.

Scholarly Attempts to Determine the Demand for Small Change

The problem of how to match the demand and supply of specific denominations is as old as the phenomenon of coins itself. Strangely enough, guiding principles for small coin production appeared only very late and date from the Enlightenment.[15] Possibly the earliest practical rule of thumb for the sufficient circulation of small change was formulated by Joseph von Sonnenfels (1732-1817), an Austrian member of the famous Illuminati. In the 1787 edition of his *Grundsätze der Polizey, Handlung und Finanzwissenschaft*, he remarked that mintmasters should not flood the market with small change, as this would drive up the price of large-denomination coins, thus endangering the collection of taxes. In a later edition[16] he defined what this implied in real terms: *Scheidemünze* (small change) should be produced 'so viel pro Kopf, wie die tägliche Consumtion der Arbeitenden Klasse beträgt' [in such quantities per capita as the amount of the daily consumption of the labouring class]. In a much-expanded edition in 1804 he formulated a fully-fledged theory, which is important enough to warrant being quoted at length from the original (Fig. 4.2).[17]

It is interesting to see that here Sonnenfels established the crucial link between monetization and wage payments that I derived from historical developments in the Low Countries (I was not aware of his study at that time). Since the mid-nineteenth century comparative statistics of coin circulation in different countries

'[…] die Münzkammern selbst müssen der Prägung der Scheidemünze Gränzen […] in einem Verhältnisse gegen die allgemeine kreislaufende Masse zu erhalten wissen. Es ist schwer dieses Verhältniss eigentlich anzugeben. Gemeiniglich wird von der Geldmasse eines States der zwanzigste Theil, oder 5% angenommen, welches zu unbestimmt scheint, da hier nicht vorzüglich das Verhältniss zu der allgemeinen Geldmasse, sondern das Bedürfniss der Ausgleichung, das ist, der kleinen Ausgaben in Anschlag kommen muss. Es ist wenigstens eine der Wahrscheinlichkeit am nächsten kommende Muthmassung, dass die Menge der Scheidemünze, auf das höchste angeschlagen, gleich seyn müsse, der Summe, wodurch die tägliche Verzehrung der arbeitenden Klasse bedeckt ist: da diese Klasse von dem täglichen Handlohne zu leben, mithin auch in Scheidemünze einzukaufen gewohnt ist. In den vorigen Auflagen war das Beyspiel dieser Berechnung auf folgende Art angegeben. Wenn bey einer Bevölkerung von 15 Millionen die Arbeitende Klasse 7 Millionen wären, und die tägliche Verzehrung eines Kopfes zu 4 Kreutzer, angeschlagen wird, sollte die umlaufende Scheidemünze 466,669 Gulden, ungefähr eine halbe Million betragen. Eine genauere Vervolgung der täglichen Auslage hat mich überführet, dass diese Summe viel zu klein seyn	The mint authorities must themselves decide upon the fractions of small change in a proper proportion to the general coin production. It is, however, difficult to determine this proportion. Usually, one twentieth part or 5 per cent of the total sum of coins in circulation is taken. But this seems to be too vague as in this case not the relation to the total sum in circulation matters, but rather the demand, and in particular the demand for means of exchange needed for small expenses. It is at least rather plausible that the amount of small change, estimated at most, must be equal to the sum that covers the daily expense of the labouring class. Because this class is used to living on daily wages, it is consequently used to paying with small change. In the previous edition I used the following example for this calculation. If in a total population of 15 million souls the labouring class amounts to 7 million, and if the daily spending per person is 4 *Kreuzer*, then the sum of all small change in circulation would have to be 466,669 *Gulden*. A more precise analysis of daily expenses has convinced me now that such a sum would be much too small. Therefore, the sum that remains for a few days with a family that receives its wages weekly should therefore also be taken into account, as well as the time this takes for the small change

würde. Es muss nämlich auf den Vorrath, den gleichwohl jede Familie, die wochenweise ihren Lohn erhält, durch einige Tagen liegen haben muss, auch auf die Zeit gedacht werden, durch welche die Scheidemünze umzulaufen hat, um wieder in die Hände der arbeitenden Klasse zu kehren: und nach diesem Anschlage scheint die Masse der Scheidemünze nicht zu stark angeschlagen: Dass sie seyn müsse gleich dem ganzen Wochenlohne der arbeitenden Volksklasse: das wäre bey 7 Millionen, die tägliche Erwerbung eines Kopfes in den andern zu 10 Kreuzer berechnet 7 Millionen.'	to circulate before it returns into the hands of the labouring class. And according to this consideration the amount of small change seems not to be assessed too high in the following way. It should be equal to the full weekly wages of the labouring class, which means for 7 million people with an average per capita daily income of 10 *Kreuzer* 7 million [*Gulden*].

FIG. 4.2: SONNENFELS'S RULE FOR ESTIMATING THE ACTUAL DEMAND FOR SMALL CHANGE (1804)

have become increasingly available, in particular within the framework of monetary unions such as the Vienna Monetary Treaty of 1857 and the Latin Monetary Union of 1865, as well as of the 1873 German Coinage Act and international monetary conferences, a direct successor to the Latin Monetary Union and first convened in Paris in 1867. Existing scholarly observations were now turned into official national legislation, stipulating how many coins of different metals and denominations were to be circulated.

An Overall Picture of Monetization at the End of the Nineteenth Century

Enough data on deep monetization for the different parts of Europe, some adjacent countries and the USA at about the same point in time are available only from the 1880s onwards. As a result of much trial and error by mint masters over the preceding centuries and much thinking since the Enlightenment, the working of supply and demand in the case of small currencies had resulted in scholarly works and concomitant statistics. These earliest large-scale statistical overviews of coin circulation in different countries enable us to conduct comparative research into deep monetization.

A pioneer in this field was the Austrian monetary statistician Ottomar Haupt (1839-98).[18] He produced a comparative table of coin circulation, differentiating between *Monnaie d'appoint* (small change, including small silver coins) and *Monnaie de billon* (base metal).[19] Unfortunately this distinction cannot be translated immediately into deep monetization, as in some countries hourly wages equal only base metal (copper, bronze, nickel, copper-nickel, billon) coins, whereas in other countries small silver coins also qualify. In the UK, for example, hourly wages of 7.2 pence in 1885 comprised the silver three pence and six pence coins. However, starting from Haupt's detailed data, it is possible to reconstruct DMLs for several dozen countries, including my original Dutch case (see Fig. 4.3).

This overview is of course very preliminary and needs a lot of fine-tuning (including better wage data for the same categories of workers), but some observations can be made. Most Western-European countries show DMLs varying between 8 and 10. Portugal, Spain, Italy, and Austria-Hungary probably also belong to this group. For the Iberian Peninsula figures have to be reassessed by deducting exports of coins to the colonies, for which I

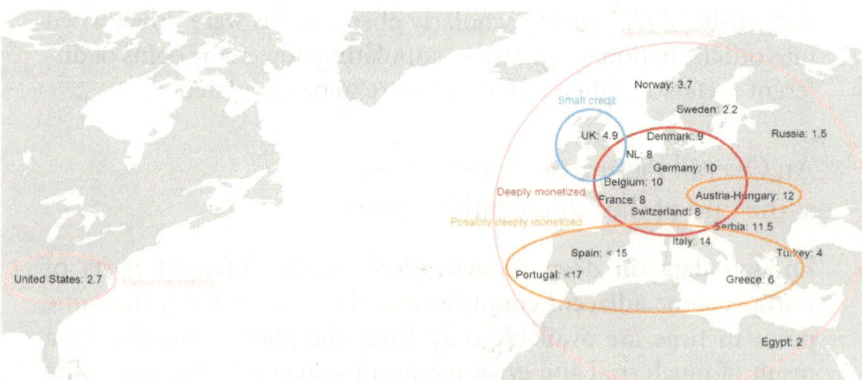

FIG. 4.3: DEEP MONETIZATION LEVELS (DMLS) FOR SEVERAL COUNTRIES *c.* 1885[20]

have been unable to find data. Austria-Hungary and Italy (as well as Serbia) are examples of countries in which recent coin reforms had temporarily caused the market (or at least the vaults of the mint houses) to be overstocked with small denominations. All other countries deviate from this 'main Western-European pattern'. They will be discussed in four clusters: Norway/Sweden, the Balkans with the Near East, the United Kingdom, and Russia with the USA.

Norway and Sweden contrast interestingly with the third Scandinavian country in this set, Denmark. Not only was Denmark much more prosperous than its northern neighbours, it had much higher rates of urbanization and concomitant occupational differentiation and agricultural specialization.[21] This situation apparently required many more transactions in Denmark than in Norway and Sweden. This is eloquently illustrated in the following description of Norway's rural population (85 per cent of the total population) by the British Consul-General Crow, written in Christiania (Oslo) and dated 9 November 1870.[22] He distinguishes three 'classes' among them: the seafaring peasantry along the coast, the 'Bonde', and the 'Field Bonde' or mountain peasant. The second group is the most important: 'The Bonde or real peasant is generally the owner of the land he farms. This class may be considered as the kernel of the nation. The property of the Bonde is not sufficiently large to exempt him from work, but large enough to afford him and his household establishment ample support. He farms in the majority of cases, *not so much to raise produce for sale* as to grow provisions and everything necessary for spinning wearing-apparel.'

The equally low figures for the Balkans (Serbia's DML was temporarily so high because of oversupply) and the Middle East point to similarly low demand for small change as that in Norway and Sweden, even if other indicators of economic development (such as the high literacy rates in Scandinavia) differed substantially. It is, however, possible that this cross section shows a more primitive situation than in the preceding decades. According to Michael Palairet, in the period 1878-1914 political freedom in the Balkans went hand in hand with economic decline.[23]

The comparatively low DML of Britain, midway between Greece and Turkey, cries out for an explanation (see the next section), one perhaps being the wide circulation of counterfeits and tokens.[24]

Finally, the low DMLs for the USA and especially for Russia seem to echo previous periods of widespread use of unfree labour, maintained without paying wages. These may be among the implications of what Kolchin has referred to as the commonalities of the post-emancipation USA and Russia: 'there was a common legacy of forced labor that Russia shared with the United States and with all other former slave societies as well. New forms of dependency that provided the ex-bondsman with at best semi-freedom became the rule.'[25]

As early as the eighteenth century variations in unfree labour had an effect on the circulation of small change in Russia. Productive work by serfs was the norm, and only noblemen could own and employ them. The emerging non-noble industrialists who needed labourers were not allowed to own serfs. Legislation was therefore introduced to permit, under certain conditions, bourgeois entrepreneurs to hire serfs as paid labourers. Because of resistance by the nobility, the scope to actually do so fluctuated heavily and laws were as easily promulgated as repealed. These fluctuations in legislation were significant enough to influence markedly the demand for copper coins: the higher the number of serfs entering the paid labour market, the higher the production of copper coin, and vice versa. Furthermore, non-noble entrepreneurs are known to have asked the state authorities to provide more copper coin so that they could pay out wages.[26]

DMLs in Western Europe in the Long Run: England, the Low Countries, and France

How old are the DMLs demonstrated at the end of the nineteenth century? Because of the ready availability of sources, Western Europe is a good starting point for the study of long-term shifts in DMLs, particularly in England, the Low Countries, and France.

England[27]

With the exception of China, England has the longest and most detailed series of coinage statistics and estimates in the world, starting in the late eleventh century. Production figures (Table 4.1) suggest that sometime in the course of the twelfth century the value of pennies per capita increased four to five times, that between 1250 and 1280 it doubled again, and that the same might have happened in the first half of the fourteenth century, just before the Black Death, after which levels returned to those of fifty years before.

The question is what these three spectacular jumps mean in terms of deep monetization. This stage had certainly not yet been reached by the time of the Domesday Book, let alone before.[28] But what about the situation in *c.* 1200, 1250, or 1300, when say 20, 40, and 80 pennies in silver coin were available per capita? Bolton is clear:

> By the mid-thirteenth century the concentrated money supply in England had probably reached the critical point that would allow coins to be used as the normal medium or agent of exchange. They could be used to buy and sell goods, to pay wages and other dues that peasants owed to lords. They could be collected as taxes and offered or demanded in lieu of feudal military service, and kings could now pay their much larger armies with coins.[29]

To understand how England had reached the situation described by Bolton, I will try to reconstruct medieval levels of deep monetization more precisely, based on the composition of the volume of specific fractions of silver currency in relation to wage levels. I use two methods: first denominations minted, and second archaeological evidence of coin usage. The story of silver coins is simple up to 1279, when only pennies were minted. In that year Edward I also started to strike farthings (quarter pennies), half pennies, and groats (four pence). The half-groat was added in 1351, the shilling around 1489, and larger denomination silver pieces from Henry VIII onwards. At the lower end of the scale, apart from debasements no innovations were made until

TABLE 4.1: MONETIZATION AND DEEP MONETIZATION LEVELS (DMLs) IN ENGLAND, THIRTEENTH TO NINETEENTH CENTURIES

Year	*Population (England and Wales unless otherwise stated), in millions*	*Coin: silver pennies per head*	*Volume of DM fractions in pounds sterling x 1000*	*Minted denominations below hourly wage*	*Money wage rate of building craftsman in Southern England, pence per hour*	*'Deep monetization' (DM)*		
						DM fractions		*DML*
						in pennies x million	*in pennies per head*	
1087	1.5-2.25	4-6						
1180	2.25-2.75	6.1-20.3						
1205	3-3.5	17.1-20						
1247	4-4.5	22.7-27.0						
1279	4.5-4.75	25.3-32.0			0.3			
1282	4.5-4.75	40.4-48.0	29	1/4d	0.3	7	1.5	5
1290	4.5-5.5	48	39	1/4d	0.3	9	1.8	6
1299	4.5-5.5	48.0-74.7	39	1/4d	0.3	9	1.8	6
1310	4.5-5.5	65.5-101.3	73	1/4d	0.4	17	3.4	8.5
			75	1/4d-1/2d		18	3.6	9
1319	4.5-5.5	82.9-122.6	93	1/4d	0.4	22	4.4	11
			95	1/4d-1/2d		23	4.6	11.5

1331	4.5-5.5	72.0-106.6	88	1/4d	0.4	21	4.2	10.5
			90	1/4d-1/2d		22	4.4	11
1351	3.5-4	56	40	1/4d	0.4	10	2.7	6.7
			100	1/4d-1/2d		24	6.4	16
1422		13	??	1/4d-1/2d	0.6	?	?	?
1470		29-33.6	??	1/4d-1/2d	0.6	?	?	?
1550-75	3.5		??	1/4d-1d	1	?	?	?
1650-1700	4.9		??	1/4d-1/2d	1.8	?	?	?
1720	6 GB		162	1/4d-1/2d	2.2	39	6.5	3.0
1857	28 UK		1264	1/4d-4d	5.4	303	10.8	2
			2961	1/4d-6d		711	25.4	4.7
1885	36 UK		5282	1/4d-6d	7.2	1268	35.2	4.9

Note: For population and coin production 1087-1470, see Bolton 2012, 25-7, 107, 224; for coin production 1279-1351, see Allen 2001, 603, 607 (see also his tables C and D). On later coin production, see Challis 1992, 689-92; on copper coin circulation in 1857 (Dyer and Gaspar 1992, 509; Selgin 2008, 299) and 1885 (Haupt 1894, 491), both supplemented by small silver, see Appendix 4.1. For wages see Phelps Brown and Hopkins 1981, 11-12. For some years I present two options, depending on the specific fractions to be included.

the introduction of the sixpence in 1550, and the three pence, three halfpence, and three farthing coin in 1561. From Charles I onwards, the smallest denominations were no longer made of silver. With a few minor exceptions, denominations smaller than farthings have never been minted in England.[30]

For a long time, the farthing was the only fraction meeting the DML criteria (i.e. coins equal to an hourly wage or less). From *c.* 1350 onwards half pennies have to be included for our purpose as the wage hike after the Black Death pushed carpenters' wages above four pence per day, nearly a half penny per hour. From the 1550s pennies, too, have to be taken into account, when daily wages for builders exceeded eight pence.[31] Although wage levels kept rising, for the period *c.* 1650-1800 we need only consider the circulation of farthings and halfpennies if we are interested in DMLs as, curiously enough, the coinage of all silver denominations less than the sixpence came to a complete halt under Charles II. It was not until 150 years later, under William IV, that three pences and groats (four pence) were once again minted.

With only very minor gaps, production figures for the half penny and farthing are available for the period 1279-1351. These enable us to follow in detail the deep monetization process in England. Actual circulation at certain dates has been reconstructed by Martin Allen. The two series differ because he takes into account both wastage and the production by mints for which no production figures are available and foreign coins circulating in England. His 'total currency' figures are therefore to be preferred, except for the last sub-period, for which his figures seem to be too low given previous output figures. For those years, total circulation of half pennies and farthings should be raised to *c.* 100,000 pounds.[32] By applying the proportionate output figures, we can roughly reconstruct separately the circulation of farthings and half pennies from the late thirteenth to the mid-fourteenth century (Table 4.2).

Now we see that the initiative to start coining farthings in 1279 not only raised the total output of silver coins substantially, but also enabled circulation levels to reach five small coins per capita, in this case farthings – a denomination lower than an hourly wage of 0.3d.

TABLE 4.2: MINT OUTPUT AND SMALL CURRENCY IN CIRCULATION, ENGLAND (IN POUNDS STERLING), 1279-1351[33]

	Pounds sterling x 1000						
	Known cumulative output by English mints			*Total currency in circulation*			
	½d.	*farthings*	*total*		*½d.*	*farthings*	*total*
1279-81	5.106	13.815	18.921	1282	11	29	40
1279-90	6.409	14.837	21.246	1290	16	39	55
1279-99	7.361	20.205	27.566	1299	1	39	40
1279-1310	8.071	32.237	40.308	1310	2	73	75
1279-1319	8.636	36.131	44.767	1319	2	93	95
1279-1331	8.698	39.146	47.844	1331	2	88	90
1279-1351	70.979	47.996	118.975	1351	60	40	100

English archaeology can help us to be more precise about the growing usage of small fractions than is possible on the basis of available production statistics. This is crucial because it turns out that there was a widespread custom of cutting pennies into halves and quarts before actual halfpennies and farthings were produced by the mints. This happened on a massive scale, as Richard Kelleher has demonstrated. Based on national data, he has been able to estimate the proportions of the three fractions in daily use (Table 4.3).

TABLE 4.3: FULL AND FRACTIONAL PENNIES, 1158-1279, AS FOUND IN ENGLAND[34]

	Proportions of number of coins found (percentage)		
	Pennies	*cut halves*	*cut quarters*
1158-80	60	30	10
1180-1247	50	40	10
1247-79	38	45	17

Applied to production figures (Table 4.1), this implies that, in the periods given, 4.2 per cent, 5.0 per cent, and 4.6 per cent respectively of all pennies had been cut into farthings. What this means is that in 1180 a maximum of one farthing per capita was circulating; in 1205 between 3.5 and 4 farthings; in 1247 between 4 and 5.4; and in 1279 slightly more, between 4.5 and 5.9 farthings. In relation to a supposed hourly wage of 0.3 pennies, this yields DMLs of less than 1 in 1180, about 3 in 1205, between 3.3 and 4.5 in 1247, and between 3.7 and 5.8 in 1279.

Combining output and archaeological evidence, we may conclude that – in accordance with Bolton – England and Wales may be said to have reached the stage of deep monetization already by the mid-thirteenth century. And this level was to rise until the days of the Black Death. For the cross section 1351, taking into account the circulation of halfpennies and farthings together, the DML was actually 16. This is *strictu sensu* too favourable, as the hourly wages (4d. per day for a building craftsman in Southern England) were less than a halfpenny, but substantially higher than a farthing.[35]

More astonishing, however, is the subsequent fall in this level. Although we have to wait for centuries before new solid DML data become available, it is very likely that DMLs must have fallen soon after the disastrous mid-fourteenth century, as by the early fifteenth century the total silver output of the mint was just 10 per cent of what it had been a hundred years before.[36] In the early eighteenth century, after the London Mint had been producing copper farthings and half pennies for decades, the DML was three, the same level as three centuries earlier, and no substantial change was to occur until the end of the nineteenth century,[37] assuming we consider only those coins officially minted. Because of the scarcity of small change, a number of private initiatives were taken, sometimes with official sanction, sometimes not – in practice nonetheless condoned by the authorities, which made no effort to prosecute illegal producers and distributors.

Occasionally the government allowed private individuals to provide small change, which helped cover the shortfall, at least between the early seventeenth and early nineteenth centuries. In 1613 James I authorized Lord Harrington to issue copper farthing tokens, and Harrington and his successors continued to do so until 1644, when issuance ceased by order of Parliament. As demand did not abate, in many towns this initiative was continued by private traders, who, between 1648 and 1672, produced enormous amounts of local farthings, halfpennies, and some pennies. In the mid-eighteenth century counterfeit halfpennies performed the same role, doubling circulation in the process.[38] And between 1787 and 1813 local tradesmen, alongside large firms like Boulton, resumed the practice of issuing private tokens, predominantly half pennies. To demonstrate the need for this private small change, it is enough to know that even these tokens were counterfeited, though less often so than the regal half pennies.[39] For the general public, this did not matter.

All in all, between 1613 and 1813 and sometime later England's DML may have been nearer five than three if we include small change of all sorts. When compared with the situation before the Black Death, that figure is still low for a well-developed country on the verge of becoming the 'First Industrial Nation', but it was less disastrous than official mint output figures suggest. During the nineteenth century this DML was maintained by the government at around five, apparently enough according to general opinion, as no major complaints of a structural lack of small change were heard.[40] When the Chancellor of the Exchequer, William Gladstone, reported in Parliament on 4 August 1859 about the actual number of copper coins circulating (see Table 4.1) and their poor condition, proposing to introduce new bronze coins instead, the debate was very brief. Nobody complained about the numbers circulating. Instead, the few members participating in the debate were concerned that the new bronzes might be the first step on the path to the much-feared decimal system in use on the continent.[41]

Since the late Middle Ages, England (and later the United Kingdom, including Ireland after 1820, when it ceased to mint its own coins), had for many centuries apparently gotten accustomed to much lower DMLs than the continent. We can question the wage levels used by most historians, consider the effects of clipping in the seventeenth and eighteenth centuries (reducing the value of small silver coins by cutting their edges), and more detailed mint statistics for specific denominations might be published. However, it seems unlikely our conclusion will be affected substantially.[42] How did the British cope with this situation? Let us turn to the demand side, in particular to the development of wage labour.

Before the Black Death, production figures for low-denomination coins seem to reflect demand among wage labourers for precisely these means of exchange. This is demonstrated by the introduction of farthings and half pennies in 1279, which obviated the need for the much-practised cutting of pennies, followed by half penny production outstripping that of the farthing in the 1330s. At that time, fields owned by the Westminster Abbey manor of Hardwicke in Gloucestershire could not be hoed because of a shortage of half pennies to pay the labourers.[43] Chris Dyer tells us that in the fourteenth century, 'The proportion of people who obtained most of their living from wage work must have exceeded one third over the whole country, rising to two-thirds in parts of the east. There were concentrations of wage-earners in large towns; in York, for example, 32 per cent of the contributors to the poll tax were called servants.'[44]

Pennies were needed to pay out the workers, who needed fractions to buy their necessaries at markets and shops. This social and geographical pattern is corroborated again by archaeology. Kelleher shows that the frequent use of cut farthings started at the London waterfront (the Vintry) as early as 1100, spreading first to other towns and especially to rural eastern England, then to the west-central region soon after 1200, and finally to the south-west and the north-west of the country.[45] The situation changed dramatically after 1350. By comparing the much larger small fraction output of Scotland in the late Middle Ages – which was more in step with general continental practice – with England, Nicholas Mayhew thinks England was exceptional:

> Mint tradition in England argued strongly against the production of copper, regardless of the needs of society, and the Scottish experience of black money was particularly negative. Mint contracts consistently failed to provide moneyers with an incentive to spend the extra time and effort necessary to produce adequate supplies of small change. Equally pressure on the mint to yield a royal profit may have pushed consideration of the needs of the economy into second place.[46]

This particular institutional set-up, leading to a serious undersupply of small change, was to last with minor ups and downs for more than four centuries. In 1696 the following complaint about the lack of coins was made from Ipswich:

> No trade is managed but by trust. Our tenants can pay no rent. Our corn factors can pay nothing for what they have had and will trade no more, so that all is at a stand. And the people are discontented to the utmost; many self-murders happen in small families for want, and all things look very bleak, and should the least accident put the mob in motion no man can tell where it would end.[47]

In 1672, copper halfpennies and farthings were introduced by the Royal Mint, and the great silver recoinage of 1696-7 remedied some of these complaints. However, this did not change the situation much. This replacement of the smallest silver coins by copper did not take place until some 150-200 years after most of the continent, although the proportion of wage labourers in England was already high and had not diminished; indeed, it had actually risen. In 1688 Gregory King estimated that 47 per cent of the population depended on wages. This figure had risen to 60 per cent by the beginning of the nineteenth century.[48]

Many solutions were found for this lack of official and less-official coins, in particular the lack of small change. Group pay was one of these, although a very imperfect one.[49] Payments in kind were another alternative of course, but – contrary to what is sometimes believed – certainly not one preferred by employers. As the accounts of Robert Loder, a large farmer, around 1600 demonstrate, he paid his servants about 10 pounds 5 shillings a year in food and drink and only 3 pounds 15 shillings and 6 pence in cash. But, Muldrew explains, he 'constantly complained that it would be cheaper to keep fewer "unruly" servants and instead rely on wage labourers, and as a result in 1612 he hired his servants at board wages.'[50]

Craig Muldrew's most important contribution to the debate is his emphasis on the most common solution, i.e. the extension of small-scale local credit instead of cash payments. That was Britain's basic answer to an endemic lack of small change. This credit could take different forms: wages paid in arrears for weeks, months, or more (i.e. credit provided by wage labourers to their employers), or the concomitant shopkeepers who got their bills paid too late (i.e. credit provided by shopkeepers to wage labourers). This might lead to direct contact between the employer and shopkeeper, circumventing the labourer and leaving him totally dependent on third parties.[51]

To sum up, as early as the mid-thirteenth century England was a deeply monetized country, possibly the first in Europe. However, after the Black Death its DML fell quickly, recovering only several centuries later to the same level, though not higher. That was exceptional in the European context for two reasons. On the supply side because of the failure of the state to produce enough small change, allowing private initiative to fill the gap in the period between the early seventeenth and the early nineteenth century; on the demand side because this situation, combined with the growing proportion of wage labourers, led to new practices of extending credit to poor people. This practice was apparently so successful that Britain's DML continued to oscillate at around five while other developed neighbouring countries showed levels twice as high. If this is a basic difference between Britain and the continent, its implications for labour relations and social relations in general deserve more scholarly attention.

The Low Countries[52]

As in England, after the demise of the highly monetized Roman Empire, the feudal society of the early Middle Ages was typically redistributive, at a rather low level of intensity. Markets were non-existent or unimportant for the great majority of the population, few cities were left, and wage labour was inconsequential. A new round of monetization began with the emergence of towns in the southern Low Countries around 1100, followed by the north a century later. One single denomination was coined, the silver *denarius* or penny. Somewhat later than in England, around 1300 a multi-fractional system matured with the introduction of various silver denominations of two-and-a-half and eight *penningen*, greatly facilitating payments.[53] From the mid-fourteenth century, but not earlier, there appears to be a certain correlation between, on the one hand, the denomination coined most frequently over a longer period and, on the other, the level of the daily wage. This correlation suggests that the demand side preferred a currency equivalent to four times (*c.* 1350-1450) and later once or twice a wage earner's full daily wage. From the fifteenth century on, this comes down to once for the worst-paid and twice for the better-paid wage earner.[54] Although it is still difficult to reconstruct per capita circulation for the Burgundian Netherlands – we have production figures for certain provinces only, and population figures are very uncertain – this type of situation, in which coin production patterns follow wage levels, strongly suggests that a situation of medium monetization began to emerge in the Low Countries from about 1350. It also indicates an important shift to wage labour, as demonstrated by Bas van Bavel,[55] and to a custom of independent producers receiving advances from merchants or customers at the same rate as labourers received their wages.

Does it also represent a situation of deep monetization? This is still open to debate, but by 1550 the Low Countries were surely deeply monetized, as Table 4.4 suggests.

This might have applied to the more advanced parts of the Low Countries already at the end of the fifteenth century, as evidenced by the massive imports of Scottish black money into the woollen industry in parts of Flanders and the Zeeland Delta between 1484 and 1505, where they met the need for small change,[56] and by the production of tiny (the lowest denomination was $\frac{1}{96}$th of an Utrecht *stuiver*) *holpenningen* by local authorities in Deventer, Nijmegen, Groningen, and some other parts of the east between 1460 and 1570.[57]

Yet the table demonstrates equally clearly that – as in England – once a high level of DM had been achieved, huge fluctuations could follow. Why did DMLs vary so much over time, and what kinds of solution were found for the regular lack of small change? Let us consider the fall in small-coin circulation in the second half of the seventeenth century. The country was prosperous, and overall coin production was impressive. However, the key merchants who

TABLE 4.4: PER CAPITA CIRCULATION OF SMALL-DENOMINATION COINS IN THE NETHERLANDS, 1550-1940, IN RELATION TO WAGE LEVELS (IN GUILDERS OF ACCOUNT)[58]

Cross section	*Circulation per capita*	*Hourly wage*			*Circulation expressed in terms of hourly wages*	
		Antwerp	*Amsterdam*	*The Netherlands*	*Antwerp*	*Amsterdam / The Netherlands*
1550 N&B	0.33	0.045	0.027		> 7	< 12
1600 N&B	0.42	0.100	0.077		4	5
1650 N	0.89		0.125			7
1700 N	0.30		0.125			2
1750 N	1.37		0.125			11
1800 N	0.68		0.125			5
1840 N&B	0.49		0.125	0.108		> 4-5
1890 N	1.68		0.208	0.203		8
1940 N	4.18			0.479		9

Note: N = the present-day Netherlands; B = present-day Belgium.

required coins from the mint houses were much more interested in the (comparatively cheap and thus more profitable) minting of large denominations than in the production of the small, silver *dubbeltjes* or *stuivers*. And insofar as they were interested in providing silver for coining small denominations, they sent most of the *stuivers* (0.05 guilders) and nearly all of the *dubbeltjes* (0.1 guilders) overseas.

After much hesitation, the response of the provincial governments to the high cost of small change was to increase the output of copper *duiten* ($^{1}/_{160}$ guilder) – and, for some decades, the tacit condoning of the circulation of (partially low-weight) *duiten* minted by small principalities and noblemen in border regions. When this proved insufficient after 1700, remedies were sought in improved machinery for striking *duiten* and government orders (instead of orders from merchants, which was the rule) for the minting of silver *pijlstuivers* after 1738. In the end, only the unitary state that emerged in the French period was capable of meeting public demand for small change.

This episode shows that supply and demand for specific fractions are not automatically in equilibrium. This is due not so much to technology as to which responsibilities governments are prepared to assume. Early on, the more unified Burgundian Netherlands and, later on, the kingdom of the Netherlands were apparently more willing to act than the intermediate Dutch Republic, in spite of its very high *overall* level of monetization.

Echoing Volckart (and *pace* Sargent and Velde), this case study for the Low Countries shows that the problems of supply and demand in relation to small change had been mastered as early as the sixteenth century.[59] The occasional problems that arose in the Dutch Republic stem from its political structure and economic concepts, which determined who was responsible and which instruments were available. As a result, solutions were always inadequate, to the extent that in the second half of the seventeenth century unofficial coins had to be allowed into circulation – just as in mid-seventeenth and again in late eighteenth-century England.[60] Craig Muldrew has pointed to the extension of small credit in similar situations in England; this might also have played an important role in the Netherlands after *c.* 1750. At the same time, these institutional shortages of small change – as a result of failing governments in certain periods in Dutch and English history – caution against any automatic link between supply and demand.

Yet before we can speak of a (northern, north-west) European pattern, the evidence for England and the Low Countries should be supplemented by other case studies. This is currently impossible because research on what might be termed the social history of coin circulation has only just begun.[61] Here, I can discuss only briefly the implications of some estimates for the largest country in Western Europe, France.

France

For France a good starting point is the revolutionary period, when a number of coin reforms took place, mainly for ideological reasons; they combined a desire for science-based politics with a demand for in-depth reports on the coins currently in circulation that had to be replaced. Contrary to the situation in contemporary England, the French state took full responsibility for the circulation of small change, resulting in high DMLs, varying between 11 and 17. For these years, deep monetization is reflected in coins equal to or lower than an hourly wage, which amounted to about two to three *sous*. Their circulation was particularly strong in the industrious northern departments. Also for France, output figures may be corroborated and detailed by archaeological evidence based on coin hoards and stray finds.[62]

How and when did these high levels come about? Was it not until 1789, when the Bastille fell, or earlier on? As the lowest silver fractions were six *sous*, the study of deep monetization of France between *c.* 1650 and 1810 may be restricted to billon and copper coins, all profusely brought into circulation, in particular since the end of the sixteenth century (see Table 4.6). The introduction of the copper one and two *denier tournois* under Henri III was a particularly great success, apparently gratifying a huge demand,[63] even to such an extent that – more or less as in the Dutch Republic somewhat later – adjacent petty principalities such as Bouillon and Sedan, Chateau Renaud, Dombes, Nevers and Rethel, and Orange started producing similar petty coins on a huge scale. I am not aware of there being reliable production data for small change in France before the end of the eighteenth century. The data available for the end of that century clearly show that by then France was deeply monetized (see Table 4.5). Awaiting more detailed information for the preceding centuries, I venture to suggest that this level had been reached already by around 1600.

Based on these three case studies, however incomplete, a provisional conclusion for Western Europe may be formulated. Deep monetization as a response to the commodification of labour – first predominantly in the guise of independent producers, grad-

TABLE 4.5: ESTIMATES OF COINS IN CIRCULATION IN FRANCE (IN *LIVRES*)[64]

	1789	*1801 (by Lambert)*	*1801 (by Desrousseaux)*	*c. 1806*	*1810*
Gold			986,000,000		746,231,976
Silver écu at 6 livres			1,700,000,000		1,863,014,796
Silver half écu			131,000,000		134,510,364
Silver 30 and 15 sol			23,000,000		25,278,019[65]
Silver 24, 12, and 6 sol			80,000,000		50,623,966[66]
Silver 5 franc			86,000,000		
Silver and gold (subtotal)	2,673,996,133	1,800,000,000	3,006,000,000		
Billon (1 and 2 sol)	12,398,786	12,000,000	12,000,000		9,601,414
Copper 'King's effigy'	22,758,547	20,000,000		5,000,000	
Copper sous 'de cloche'		20,000,000	18,000,000	15,000,000	31,302,897[67]
Copper 'Marianne'			20,000,000	15,000,000	
Subtotal billon and copper	35,157,333	52,000,000	50,000,000	35,000,000	40,904,3131
Grand Total	2,709,153,466	1,852,000,000	3,056,000,000		2,860,563,432
Billon/copper livres per capita[68]	1.26	1.73	1.67	1.17	1.08
Expressed in terms of hourly wage of 2 sous (DML)	12	17	17	12	11

TABLE 4.6: VALUE EQUIVALENTS OF SMALL CHANGE IN FRANCE, *c.* 1600-1810[69]

Denomination	*Deniers*	*Livre*	*Until 1793/4*	*1793/4-1815: decimal*
	30		Billon 1709-13	
				Bronze 2 *décime* An 4-5
2 sou	24	1/10	Billon 1738-64; bronze 1791-4	Bronze 1 *décime* An 2 [1793] 4-9 (1/10 franc); billon 10 *centime* 1807-10
	16		Billon 1696-1715	
	15		Billon 1641-1713	
Sou (sol) / douzain	12	1/20 (1/120 écu)	Billon *c.* 1450-1658; copper 1719-28; 1767-74; billon 1739-48; copper 1767-91; bronze 1791-3	Bronze 5 *centime* An 4-9; Copper 1808
½ sou / sizain	6		Billon 1628-58; copper 1710-12, 1719-24, 1767-91; bronze 1792-4	
	4		Copper 1696-1708	
Liard./ ¼ sou	3	1/80	Billon 1575-1655; copper 1649-1721, 1767-91; bronze 1792	
		1/100		Bronze 1 *centime* An 6-8
Double (denier) tournois (1/6 *sou*)	2	1/120	Billon *c.* 1300-*c.* 1580; copper 1577-1708	
Denier tournois	1		Originally silver; billon *c.* 1300-1586; copper 1575-1649	

ually shifting to paramount wage labour – may have started in England around 1250, in the most advanced parts of the Low Countries in the late Middle Ages, and spread to other maritime provinces in the sixteenth century and to France in the seventeenth century. Once achieved, deep monetization is not necessarily sustainable. Apart from shifts in labour relations leading to variations in demand for small change, the supply may vary along with the quality of state institutions. When governments fail, other suppliers from within or outside the polity might take over their role;[70] alternatively, credit relations may expand or contract accordingly.

4. India

Let us now turn to more easterly parts of Eurasia, and to relations between labour and coin circulation on the other side of the 'Great Divergence'. First India, which like Europe had been practising a multi-denominational and multi-metal currency system since the mid-first millennium BCE.[71] The earliest reconstruction of the total money supply in India dates from around 1880 (see Table 4.7). Following the same procedure as above, this will be our starting point, from which we shall go back in time to periods for which data are scarcer and more difficult to interpret.

India c. 1880

Gold coins were used only for hoarding, for export, or in order to be melted down for ornaments. Silver coins were used for paying rents and taxes, and for petty trade transactions.[72] At the end of the nineteenth century, silver coins played a much greater role in India than in Europe. In the words of an old India hand in 1892: 'the whole trade of India [...] is now conducted by the actual transfer of coin from hand to hand, except in the Presidency towns, and some of the large up-country towns, and even there you will see at the present day men paying their debts, by bringing in bags of rupees, rupees in thousands.'[73]

Throughout his entire life, however, the ordinary man would have seen only the lowest possible copper denominations.[74]

TABLE 4.7: COIN CIRCULATION IN INDIA, C. 1880[75]

	Total circulation (in millions of rupees)	*Circulation per capita*	
		(in annas)	*Expressed in terms of hourly wage of ¼ annas (DML)*
Gold coins	1,440.0		
Active silver rupee circulation	1,370.8		
Small silver coins	92.6		
Copper coins	48.1	3	12
Cowrie shells	insignificant		

At first glance, the conclusion that India was already deeply monetized in the last quarter of the nineteenth century – much more so than the European periphery at that time – may be surprising and in need of two qualifications. First, wages outside agriculture might have been slightly higher and working days might have been longer than eight hours, but even so the result would have been a per capita copper circulation exceeding five times the hourly wage. Second, the actual copper circulation was probably higher, because the estimates might very well exclude both copper coins produced before 1862 – the first coinage under the British Crown – and 'native coins' that continued to circulate. Further, a small proportion of the coppers consisted of half *anna* pieces, which have to be deducted. Yet there are other reasons to suppose that the conclusion that India was already deeply monetized by 1880 might not be too wide of the mark. A recent reconstruction of labour relations for the subcontinent in 1900 showed levels of commodification (31.2 per cent self-employed and 12.1 per cent wage labourers) that are not very different from contemporaneous outcomes for European countries.[76]

India 1800-80

The next question is when the threshold of deep monetization would have been reached in India: just before 1880 or much earlier? And did India experience the same sort of fluctuations we saw in Europe? These questions cannot be easily answered. Attempts have been made to reconstruct the silver and gold stock of India on the basis of import figures for bullion (India has no silver mines), but copper coins, the currency of the common man, are completely absent from these stories.[77]

What would the situation have been like at the beginning of the nineteenth century? To answer this question, it is important to know that, by that time, India was not a country dominated by self-sufficient peasants outside the market and therefore not in need of coins. On the contrary, preliminary reconstructions of labour relations suggest similar levels of commodification at the start and at the end of the century.[78]

At the beginning of the century, most copper coinage was probably produced in mints under Indian control, but their output is largely unknown.[79] We know more about the English production of copper coins for India in the first half of the nineteenth century (see Table 4.8). It shows that this initial attempt to dominate Indian copper production (before the mass production of reduced size coppers bearing Victoria's portrait, from 1862 onwards) already amounted to more than 31 million rupees, or more at a time when a number of native mints were still very active.[80] If we accept a total stock of coppers worth 40 million rupees and a population figure of roughly 200 million, the DML in the first half of the century would have been the same as around 1880.

These impressions find some corroboration in the more precise figures for the district of Benares.[81] In 1808, the amount of (copper) *pice* required for circulation in that district was estimated at 700,000 rupees.[82] Production figures for the preceding decades suggest that this was rather pessimistic.[83] The district, then still undivided, most likely coincided with the later Benares 'Division', with over five million inhabitants according to the census of 1901. Given an average population growth of 40 per cent in nineteenth-century India, the number of inhabitants may have been some 3.7 million in 1808, ten per cent of whom lived in Benares city. The per capita copper coin circulation thus amounted to 0.2 rupees or 3 *annas* or 15 *pice*. The daily wage of a labourer being 4 *pice*,[84]

TABLE 4.8: COPPER COIN PRODUCTION FOR INDIA BY THE ENGLISH (IN MILLIONS OF RUPEES), 1795/6-1858[85]

	English mints per Presidency				*Native mints*
	Bengal	*Bombay*	*Madras*	*Total*	
1795-6	0.03			?	?
1800-08	0.22	[1802-8 unknown but large-scale production]	[1803-8 unknown but large-scale production]	?	?
1809-12	1.29	0.28		1.57	?
1813-25	1.52[86]	[1820-9 unknown]	0.25	>1.77	?
1826-33	2.25			>2.25	?
1835-48	20.21			20.21	?
1853	0.46			0.46	?
1857	0.73			0.73	?
1858	3.68			3.68	?

this would imply that, with a DML of four, the district as a whole was on the verge of deep monetization. If we put aside questions of how representative Benares district was for India as a whole, the difference with 1880 is partly explained by the replacement of cowries by coppers, which took place on a massive scale in Bengal in the late eighteenth and early nineteenth centuries and causes figures for *c.* 1800 to be underestimated.[87]

India 1550-1800

Although we have almost no data on copper coin output before 1800, we are fortunate because the production of copper coin was largely dependent on Japanese and European imports, most of which went directly to the mint. Production figures for Indian and Nepalese copper mines are very scarce, but overseas trade statistics show on average constant figures for Japanese copper imported by the Dutch East India Company in Coromandel (200 tons per annum) and Bengal (100 tons) and rising figures for European (mainly Swedish) copper imported by the East India Company to Madras (from 100 tons in the 1750s to 200 tons in the 1760s) and Calcutta (from 100 tons in the 1730s to 300 tons in the 1770s).[88]

Before these growing copper imports in the later eighteenth century, confirmed by accepted impressionistic overviews of Indian numismatic history, output may have stagnated between say the first half of the seventeenth and the first half of the eighteenth centuries. This was in sharp contrast to the sixteenth century, when coinage activity increased threefold from 1525 to at least 1600.[89] Under the short-lived Suri Dynasty in Delhi (1538-54) and the first Mughal Emperor Akbar (1556-1605), mint output of gold, silver, and copper cannot be characterized other than as feverous. The previously common billon coins were replaced by copper *dams* of *c.* 20 grams (initially called *paisas*) and fractions down to one-tenth of a *dam/paisa*. This was an important step towards deep monetization as these coppers were struck during many consecutive years and in great quantities. Furthermore, they met the needs of wage labourers, as the wages for an hour of an artisan's work equalled between one-quarter and one *dam*.[90]

This impression of deep monetization being under way may be confirmed by Akbar's probate inventory. According to Francisco Pelsaert it recorded 230 million *Conincx peys* or *tacx*, making 766,666 *ropias* (30 *tacx* = 1 *ropia*). Supposing that this enormous quantity of *paisas* represents all the copper pieces minted during his lifetime, and that the massive Suri output still circulating more than balanced any wastage during Akbar's lifetime, this figure is equivalent to roughly 0.01 rupees or 3 *dams* per capita around 1600, when the population of the Mughal Empire is estimated at 100 million inhabitants. Divided by hourly wages of ½ to ¼ *dam*, this would yield a DML of between 6 and 12.[91] Too many uncertainties remain (for instance, the low output of small silver fractions might have been resolved by using more coppers), but it seems probable that deep monetization made much progress in the second half of the sixteenth century, although levels might have dropped subsequently before rising again after *c.* 1750.

India 1200-1550

As in Europe, however, the initial jump in Indian DMLs might well have occurred in the Middle Ages; quantifying this is very hard. Numismatic evidence for northern and central India from *c.* 1200 onwards[92] reveals an acceleration in the number of small-value coins (copper, billon, and silver of less than five grams) in India in the period 1275-1325/75, and a second acceleration between 1425-50 and 1525. Especially during the reign of Alauddin Muhammad Khalji, Delhi Sultan 1296-1316, in addition to gold and silver coins a huge number of two- and six-*gani* billon coins were put into circulation.[93]

Annual wages for unskilled workers (servants) were then 10 to 12 *tankas*, or $1\frac{1}{3}$ to $1\frac{3}{5}$ *jitals* per day, whereas for skilled workers like weavers and tailors they were 2-3 *jitals*. Given that, according to the famous mint-master Thakkura Pheru, the basis of the system was the one *gani-jital*, Alauddin's *dugani* (a 2-*gani* coin containing 8 per cent silver) and a 6-*gani* coin with 25 per cent silver equalled more or less the wages for between one and three days' work. For our DM criteria, copper *paikas* of ¼ *jitals* and its fractions, which gradually replaced one-*jital* pieces, are much more interesting therefore. Unfortunately, they do not occur in such large numbers as the billon pieces.

Firoz Shah, Delhi Sultan 1351-88, made a new attempt to ensure enough small change by increasing copper coin output, in particular the number of half and quarter *jital* coins, being aware of the fact that 'if poor people bought something from the market and a balance in half or quarter *jitals* was left of the amount paid, the shopkeeper would not have the quarter change'.[94]

In sum, precise data are lacking for India, but trends are certainly visible. Clear steps towards deep monetization were set in the late Middle Ages, but it was only in the second half of the sixteenth century that India might have had DMLs of between 6 and 12. It is likely that these could not be sustained in the centuries afterwards, but a new increase might have led to DMLs of ten in the nineteenth century. We may speculate why these levels are so surprisingly high, given our understanding of India's economic performance. One reason might be, as already suggested, that proletarianization and commodification had become more wide-spread than expected. Another might be the underdevelopment of credit for the poorly paid.

5. China and Japan

China 'invented' coins at roughly the same time as – though most likely independently of – northern India and the eastern basin of the Mediterranean. Nevertheless, it followed a different and very distinctive pattern.[95] The Qin state that eventually emerged victorious in 221 BCE adopted the so-called cash (*wén*) coins – cast round bronze, copper, or later brass coins with a square hole and a diameter of about two centimetres – as the only currency. This system was continued until 1900. It spread to Japan and South-East Asia, and was used in Vietnam until at least 1933. In China, with a few exceptions, no other copper, silver, or gold fractions were coined for two millennia. Alongside these cash coins, only silver ingots were used in wholesale trade and for hoarding. For convenience, cash coins could be stringed in units of (ideally) one hundred or one thousand pieces. This mono-denominational currency system offers far fewer research problems than the multi-denominational and multi-metal systems prevailing in the western and southern parts of Eurasia. Moreover, plenty of data are available on the Chinese production of cash coins from the very inception of the system.[96]

The production statistics show varying degrees of intensity. As a rule of thumb, replacements necessary due to wear and tear amounted to a minimum of one per cent of total stock annually. Given a total per capita stock of 400 cash coins (see Table 4.9), we arrive at about four cash coins per capita for replacement.[97] Greater production in this case means an increase in the stock, lower production a decrease.

Apparently, monetization levels rose sharply in the eleventh century, when an imperial official underlined its significance as follows:

TABLE 4.9: STOCK OF CASH COINS IN RELATION TO WAGE LEVELS IN CHINA, CE 9-1750[98]

Cross section in years CE	*Stock in billions*	*Population in millions*	*Stock per capita*	*Daily wage*	*Stock per wage sum*	
					daily	*hourly (=DML)*
9	20-30	60	300-500	<20	<15-25	<120-200
750	21.3-42.6		310-610			
1120	193.4-262	126	1530	145	11	88
1127	30 in private market and 98 in state treasuries	110	300 (1,200 if state treasuries included)			
1480				5-15 25-30		
1550	36-54	120-200	180-450	[25]	[7-18]	
1600	36-54	120-200	180-450	25-30		
1628-44				60		
1702			400		7-8	56-64
1750	122.8-146.8	300	400-480	50	8-9	64-72

The utility of money derives from circulation and loan-making. A village of ten households may have 100,000 coins. If the cash is stored in the household of one individual, even after a century, the sum remains 100,000. If the coins are circulated through business transactions so that every individual of the ten households can enjoy the utility of the 100,000 coins, then the utility will amount to that of 1,000,000 cash. If circulation continues without stop, the utility of the cash will be beyond enumeration.[99]

This was followed by a decrease between the twelfth and the sixteenth centuries, and an increase again in the eighteenth century. Although this periodization is important for the study of labour relations, it is not so easy to decide the question as to what per capita stock would represent 'deep monetization' as defined in the introduction to this chapter. At first sight, the requirements of 'a per capita stock equal to between five and ten times the prevailing hourly wage' are more than fulfilled (Table 4.9). However, we should not forget that a substantial proportion of the cash coins did not circulate as pieces, but as 'small' strings of (ideally) 100 pieces or 'large' strings of 1,000 pieces, which makes them comparable to medium and large silver coins in the southern and western parts of Eurasia.

The Japanese case can help us to distinguish between 'real small change' in the European and Indian sense and 'small change by default' in the Chinese sense. Until 1600 the Japanese imported Chinese cash coins and, with a few exceptions, did not produce their own coins. Tokugawa Japan, however, started to produce its own cast cash coins (called *mon*) alongside silver, gold, and paper currency.[100] That way it combined Chinese-like cash coins with a multi-metal and multi-denominational currency system. It is possible to reconstruct DMLs for *c.* 1640 and for the end of the nineteenth century. In 1640 only cash coins need to be counted according to our definition; in 1872 all copper coins qualify, including the highly devalued *tempo* pieces (cast 1835-68 and originally worth 96 *mon*); in 1879 we include all coppers plus the silver five-*sen* pieces and in 1883 again only the coppers[101] (Table 4.10).

TABLE 4.10: STOCK OF DML COINS IN RELATION TO WAGE LEVELS IN JAPAN, 1640-1886[102]

	Stock DM coins (millions)	*Inhabitants (millions)*	*Stock per capita*	*Average wage of carpenter*		*DML*
				Per day	*Per hour*	
1640	3,300 cash	25.000	132 cash	200 *mon*	25 *mon*	5.3
1872	5.6 yen	33.111	0.17 yen	0.50 yen	0.075 yen	2.7
1879	12.7 yen	35.769	0.36 yen	0.41 yen	0.05 yen	7.0
1886	15.1 yen	37.869	0.40 yen	0.23 yen	0.03 yen	13.3

As, after 1600, Japanese DMLs appear to have been in a range similar to those of other parts of Eurasia with multi-denominational and multi-metal currencies, we can now compare the Chinese DML *c.* 1700 (Table 4.9) with the corresponding Japanese figure somewhat earlier (Table 4.10). Given similarities between the economies of Japan and eastern China at this point in time, this suggests that only *c.* 10 per cent of the Chinese cash coins functioned as really small change and that *c.* 90 per cent circulated in strung forms as a medium-monetization means of exchange.

Finally, we can use the long Chinese coin production series to compare trends inside Eurasia. Interestingly, the chronology, which was rather similar between western and southern Eurasia, is different in China. There, monetization levels increased from the ninth century onwards, two or three centuries before India and Europe. The serious slump seen in China during the twelfth to the sixteenth centuries is not much visible in India and Europe, if we ignore the comparatively weak decrease seen during the Black Death. The increase in the eighteenth century can perhaps be seen in India as well, albeit slightly later. In the nineteenth century China clearly lagged behind.

This distinctive Chinese DML pattern becomes understandable if we link it to shifting labour relations, in particular those described in detail by Christine Moll-Murata in the framework of the IISH Global Collaboratory on the History of Labour Relations 1500-2000.[103] It is significant that, around 1050, compulsory work for the Chinese state was converted into a tax, to be paid in cash. This suggests that self-employed peasants and craftsmen, as well as wage earners, became the new taxpayers. Kent Deng quotes the famous dictum by Eric Jones that Song China was just a 'hair's breadth' away from a genuine industrial revolution.[104]

Labour relations changed dramatically from the twelfth and thirteenth centuries onwards and the rise of 'bond-servitude' in late Ming China implies a shift from free to unfree labour in these cash-ridden centuries.[105] This process is summarised by William Guanlin Liu as follows:

> While depopulation and deurbanization after the Mongol conquest significantly weakened the structure of domestic markets, the demonetization of the Chinese economy was directly caused by the rise of a command economy after the establishment of the Ming dynasty. The early Ming had little use for monetary exchange as it was operated on the basis of a barter economy and 'corvée services'. In essence, early Ming

farmers and artisans paid taxes in lieu of grains and other kinds of local products to the state and had little need for hard currencies.[106]

In the fifteenth century the rise of private coinage brought some relief.

In the eighteenth century a clear shift to working for the market is visible in the CGLH data collected by Moll-Murata. Whether this was due to an increase in wage labour or an increase in the number of small self-employed producers working for the market is not relevant. The former possibility is supported by the increase in wage labour in various industrial sectors such as printing, porcelain making, and shipbuilding.[107]

6. Conclusions

Building on earlier work on monetization intensities in India and on deep monetization levels (DML) in the Low Countries, this chapter demonstrates that the DML concept is appropriate for the analysis of long-term trends in major parts of Eurasia. A comparison of DMLs thus defined through space and time shows interesting constants, but also variations. Based mainly on traditional written sources, this chapter also draws on archaeological and other numismatic evidence. It has proven to be useful for the multi-metal and multi-fractional currency systems that prevailed in the west and the south, but also – with some caveats – for the mono-fractional Chinese system. In all cases, long-term shifts in levels of monetization are clearly visible.

The data available for different parts of Eurasia (the Low Countries, France, India and China) show the following results: (1) similar levels in Western Europe and South Asia from *c.* 1100 to 1900; (2) similar periods of increasing and decreasing levels overall, but diverging in the seventeenth and eighteenth centuries (increase in Europe, decrease in India); (3) diverging developments between China and the rest (see Figure 4.4). These results question to a certain extent accepted wisdom in historical debates on economic development. The similarity of the DMLs undermines the uniqueness of the processes of commodification and proletari-

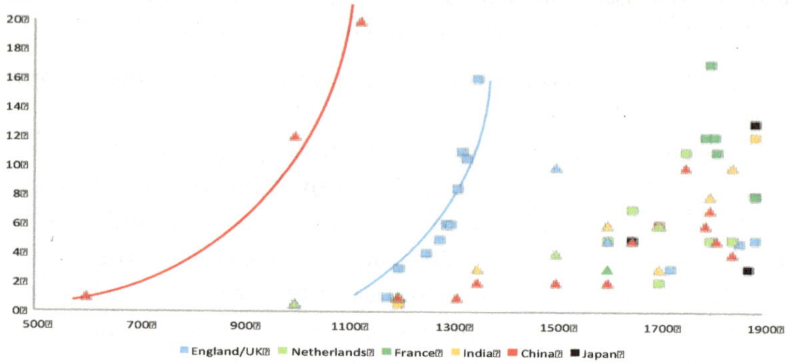

FIG. 4.4: DEEP MONETIZATION LEVELS (DMLs) IN EURASIA *c.* 600-1900[108]

anization in Western Europe. Here we see a strong link between monetary history and labour history. At the same time, similarities across Eurasia but also differences within Western Europe pose questions regarding the social function of credit. Why was Britain so different from the continent, while the continent showed more similarities with South Asia? Or, formulated differently, why the promulgation of deferred payments in Britain in contrast with more immediate payments elsewhere?

Are we justified in linking this to Margariti's observations regarding differing credit relations among medieval merchants in Egypt and the Indian Ocean? There, she observed long-lasting credit and debt relations among merchants within small communities sharing family ties and the same religion, in contrast to the quick disbursement of credit and debt between strangers: 'Perhaps nothing served better than minted coins – with their power to assign value to complex assets, their portability, and their eminent transferability – to facilitate risky transactions between members of different faiths.'[109] My hypothesis would be that this applies not only to payment for goods, but also to payment for services, including wage payments.[110]

Appendix 4.1: Deep Monetization Levels in Various Countries in the 1870s-80s

By combining the data on small-coin circulation in particular countries collected by Ottomar Haupt with evidence on wage levels and working conditions in those same countries as published in British parliamentary papers, it is possible to reconstruct deep monetization levels for the period around the 1870s to the 1880s.[111] For now, this reconstruction is possible for a handful of countries.

For each country, the following will be addressed:

- the hourly wage for ordinary workers;
- the fractions equal to that sum or less;
- the circulation figures of these particular fractions;
- these circulation figures per capita;
- these per capita circulation figures divided by the hourly wage, i.e. the *deep monetization level.*

TABLE 4.11 DEEP MONETIZATION LEVELS IN VARIOUS COUNTRIES IN THE 1870S-80S

Country	*Hourly wage for ordinary workers*	*Fractions equal to that sum or less*	*Circulation figures of these particular fractions*	*Circulation figures per capita*	*Per capita circulation figures divided by the hourly wage, i.e. the deep monetization level*
Austria-Hungary	10 *Kreuzer* = 1/10 *Florin* (assistant builder Vienna: *Further Reports* 1870: 554-9)	1858-91 all coppers (½, 1, and 4 *Kreuzer*) and billon coins of 5 and 10 *Kreuzer* qualify, from 1892 all coppers (1 and 2 *Heller*) and nickels (10 and 20 *Heller*) qualify, whereas 1 old *Kreuzer* = 2 new *Heller*	End June 1892, old billon coins 35.7 million *Florins*, old bronze 14.8 million, new bronze 0.2 million, new nickel 1.7 million, totalling 52.4 million *Florins* (Haupt 1894: 889-90)	1.22 *Florins* (Haupt 1894: 889-90)	12[112]
Belgium	0.25 Belgian francs or 25 *centimes* (a lot of data in *Further Reports* 1871: 21-66);	Bronze 1 and 2 *centime*, nickel 5, 10, and 20 *centime*	8.465 million francs in bronze and 6.6 million francs in nickel (Haupt 1894: 66, 227)	2.50 francs (Haupt 1894: 66,227)	10

Denmark	10 *skilling rigsmonts* (lower skilled workmen 6 *rigsdalers* per week = in 1854-74 96 *skilling rigsmonts* per day: *Further Reports* 1871: 141-3)	10 *skilling rigsmonts* (1854-74) ≈ 22 øre from 1874 onwards,[113] so that all bronze 1, 2, and 5 øre qualify as well as the (0.6) silver 10 and 25 øre pieces	700,000 kroner coppers in 1885 and 880,000 coppers in 1893 (Haupt 1894: 339-40); silver 10 øre production 1874-84 = 1,234,000 kroner, and silver 25 øre production 1874 = 2,035,000 kroner; resulting in a total of 3,969,000 kroner in small change in 1885[114]	1.99 kroner	9
Egypt	2 *piastres* (men in cotton factories 1 shilling a day, quarrying 1 shilling 8 pence, good excavators 2 shillings 6 pence, workmen 2 shillings = 20 *piastres*: *Further Reports* 1871: 148-58)	Until 1885 2 *piastres* (or *qirsh*) = 80 *paras* = $^1/_{100}$ pound; 1876-1909 2 *piastres* = 20 *ushr al qirsh* so that all coppers of 1 up to 40 *paras* struck in Cairo qualify; in addition, small silver pieces of 10 and 20 *paras* and 1 *qirsh*; from 1886-91 the Berlin mint provided nickels and bronzes	As production figures for small silver coinage are unknown before 1884, only coppers, valued at 152,734 Egyptian pounds, may be quantified (Haupt 1894: 71, 89-91)	Before 1884 0.022 Egyptian pounds in copper and an unknown but possibly equal sum in small silver, which would very roughly add up to 0.05 Egyptian pounds	2[115]

(Contd.)

TABLE 4.11 *(contd.)*

France	30 *centimes* (Charente: assistant artisans 3-5 francs per day, country labourer 2.50-3; Cherbourg town artisan 3, town labourer 2.25, country artisan 2.50, country labourer 2: *Further Reports* 1871, 171-85)	Bronze 1, 2, 5, 10 *centime*, silver 20 (hardly ever struck after 1869) and 25 *centime* (struck until 1848)	At the end of 1885 60 million francs in bronze coins (Haupt 1894: 674), plus silver 20 and 25 *centime*. Haupt does not distinguish between the different fractions of the silver *monnaie d'appoint* (all fractions between 20 *centimes* and 2 francs, totalling 250 million francs)	1.60 French francs in bronze and 6.50 francs in *monnaie d'appoint*, totalling for all denominations up to 25 *centimes c.* 2 French francs	8
Germany	1 *Silbergroschen* = 10 *Pfennigs* (Handarbeiter Silesia 1867-68 7 *Silbergroschen* in summer and 10 in winter: *Further Reports* 1871: 848-53)	As wages have risen since, all *Kaiserreich* copper fractions of 1 and 2 *Pfennig* and all nickels of 5, 10, and 20 *Pfennig* qualify	End 1885 45 million *Marks*; end 1892 61.5 million *Marks* (Haupt 1894: 66, 210-11)	100 *Pfennigs* or 1 *Reichsmark* (Haupt 1894: 66, 210-11)	10

Greece	40 *lepta* (*Further Reports* 1871: 194-201)	All coppers of 1, 2, 5, 10, 20 *lepta*, and silver 20 *lepta* (struck 1874-83) and 25 *lepta* (struck in very low numbers 1833-55)	October 1885 coppers circulating worth a total of 4.5 million drachmas (Haupt 1894: 135-7) plus silver *lepta* pieces, valued at *c*. 600,000 drachmas[116]	Copper 2.25 drachmas (Haupt 1894: 66), including small silver *c*. 2.50 drachmas	6
Italy	20 *centesimi* (*Further Reports* 1871: 210)	Copper 1, 2, 5, 10 *centesimi*, and silver *centesimi* (struck 1863-7)	Coppers struck 1862-86 at 76.2 million lire (Haupt 1894: 713-14[117]), plus 7 million lire in silver 20 *centesimi*[118]	2.75 lire	14
Norway	4 *skillings* (*Further Reports* 1871: 364-95)	4 *skillings* = 1/15 of the new 2 krone pieces and its fractions as struck from 1875 onwards = 0.13 ⅓ øre; therefore all bronze 1, 2, and 5 øre pieces qualify as well as the silver 10 øre pieces	In late 1885 400,000 kroner consisting of bronze pieces (Haupt 1894: 342-3), plus 681,000 kroner of silver 10 øre pieces struck 1875-83,[119] totalling 1,081,000 kroner	0.50 kroner	4

(*Contd.*)

TABLE 4.11 *(contd.)*

Portugal	30 *réis* (*Further Report* 1870: 152-7 rather vaguely suggests 300 *réis* per day)[120]	All copper and bronze fractions of 3, 5, 10, and 20 *réis* (silver only upwards of 50 *réis*)	1885 2 million *milréis* copper and bronze coins (Haupt 1894: 420-1)	0.50 *milréis* (Haupt: 1894: 421)	17[121]
Russia	10 kopeks (*Further Reports* 1871: 523-58)	Copper ¼, ½, 1, 2, 3, and 5 kopeks, silver 5 and 10 kopeks	10 million roubles in bronze coins (Haupt 1894: 766); plus[122] silver 5 kopeks 1867-85: 545,500 roubles and ditto silver 10 kopeks: 4,750,500 roubles, totalling 15,295,500 roubles	15.3 kopeks	1.5[123]
Serbia	20 *paras* (*Further Reports* 1871: 841)	All coppers of 1, 5, and 10 *paras*, all copper-nickel coins of 5, 10, and 20 *paras*	1,898,000 *dinars* in copper and 3,200,000 *dinars* in copper-nickel coins, totalling 5,098,000 *dinars* (Haupt 1894: 154)	Divided by 2.2 million inhabitants this yields 2.3 *dinars*	11.5[124]

Spain	0.8 *reales* (*Further Reports* 1871: 606-51)	0.8 *reales* = 8 *decimos* (1852-64) = 0.0304 oz. silver ≈ 23 *centimos*, according to the post-1869 system, which qualifies copper 1, 2, 5, and 10 *centimos* and silver 20 *centimos* (struck in insignificant numbers 1869-70) for inclusion	In 1892 57,199,652 pesetas in copper (Haupt 1894: 515-16)	3.50 pesetas (Haupt 1894: 515-16)	15[125]
Sweden	18 öre (*Further Reports* 1871: 656-7)	18 öre pre 1873 reform equals 20 öre afterwards. Therefore, the following fractions in 1885 qualify: bronze 1, 2, and 5 öre and silver 10 öre	At the end of 1885 900,000 kronor in bronze coins (Haupt 1894: 341), plus[126] 1,079,100 kronor in silver 10 öre coins, totalling 2 million kronor	44 öre	2.2

(Contd.)

TABLE 4.11 *(contd.)*

Switzerland	19 *centimes* (*Further Reports* 1871: 669-87)	All bronze (of 1 and 2 *centimes* or *Rappen*) and nickel coins (of 5, 10, and 20 *Rappen*)	At the end of 1885 4,500,000 Swiss francs (Haupt 1894: 147; cf. 139ff, 360ff, 840ff, and 893ff)	1.50 Swiss francs	8
Turkey	30 *paras* (300 *paras* per day for a married day labourer: *Further Reports* 1871: 713-47, esp. 720 for Anatolia; see also information for Izmir, Kurdistan, etc., elsewhere in this report)	Coppers of 1, 5, 10, and 20 *paras* (excluding 44,170,000 copper pieces of 40 *paras*, and equalling 1 *piastre*), plus silver 20 *para* pieces	At the end of 1885 in copper 73 million *piastres* (113 million *piastres* in total minus 40 million coppers of 40 *paras*, struck AH 1255/RY 17-23), plus 5 million silver 20 *para* pieces, struck from AH 1255/RY 9 [1847] to AH 1293/RY 8 [1883] (Haupt 1894: 828-9)[127] totalling 78 million *piastres*	3 *piastres* or 120 *paras* (25 million inhabitants: Haupt 1894: 829)	4

United Kingdom	7.2 pennies per hour (Phelps Brown and Hopkins 1981: 11-12)	All bronze coins (mainly farthing, halfpenny, and penny) as well as small silver coins (3, 4, and 6 pence)	At the end of 1885 1.6 million pounds sterling in coppers (Haupt 1894: 491),[128] plus 3.682 million pounds in threepences, fourpences, and sixpences,[129] totalling 5.282 million pounds = 1,267.68 million pennies	Divided by 36 million inhabitants (England, Wales, Scotland, and Ireland) gives 35.2 pennies	4.9[130]
USA	15 cents (*Further Reports* 1871: 853-937)	Bronze 1 and 2 cents, nickel 3 cents, copper-nickel 5 cents, silver 10 cents or dimes	At the end of 1885 15 million dollars in billon coins plus 13,085,546 million dollars in silver dimes 1853-85, totalling 28 million dollars	50 dollar cents (cf. Haupt 1894: 562)	2.7

NOTES

1. Useful definitions can be found in Haselgrove & Krmnicek 2012; Maurer 2006; Feinman & Garraty 2010. In this article money is generally taken as 'general purpose money' (Maurer 2006, 20).
2. See https://collab.iisg.nl/web/labourrelations.
3. Spufford 2002; Spufford 2008; Margariti 2014.
4. Figure 3.1 in Lucassen, see Part I: No. 3 in this volume; cf. Feinman & Garraty 2010, 171: 'in all economies, ancient or modern, market exchange, when present, coexists with other modes of transfer and exchange'.
5. See, for example, Cardon & Lemaire 2014.
6. A good overview for England can be found in Valenze 2006; Reddy 1987 offers eloquent, well-researched pessimism.
7. Selgin 2008, 6.
8. Simmel 1908, 746-7; Simmel 1922, 314-21; Simmel 2009, 297-303; cf. Valenze 2006, 21, 69, 184-8.
9. Simmel 2009, 299-300 (original: Simmel 1922, 316-17); cf. Peebles 2010, 230.
10. There is a great need for more studies in this field, but see Biernacki 1995, 352-62. For the visualization of circulation patterns of medium and small denominations, see Lucassen 2007c, 242 and Welten 2015, 173.
11. Lucassen 2014b. Consequently, there are two possible definitions of 'medium monetization'. First, in a system where multiple denominations coexist (as has been the case worldwide since *c*. 1900 and was the case in many parts of Eurasia long before then), by replacing hour/hourly by day/daily, as I have done (without using the term 'medium monetization') in Lucassen 2007a and Lucassen, see Part I: No. 13 in this volume; and, second, in a mono-denominational system (in East Asia, as will be explained below), by lowering the definition of the per capita stock to be equal to between one and five pieces. In this chapter I concentrate only on reconstructing 'deep monetization'.
12. Some colleagues have proposed using real instead of nominal wages. I consider this less appropriate and far less practical. In addition, an experiment by Pim de Zwart (IISH) regarding the Low Countries (see below) did not yield different trends, I am grateful to him for sharing these results.
13. I would like to thank Mathies Lucassen for his inspiration in designing this formula, which starts from Irving Fisher's well-known formula MV=PT. See, more extensively, Lucassen 2014b, 78.
14. Kelleher 2013.
15. Sargent & Velde 2002. My research in this respect is very preliminary.
16. Roscher 1881, 198-203, esp. 201, fn. 12 referring to Sonnenfels 1787, 287

(Part II, § 271) and Friedrich Jakob Schmitthenner (1796-1850). For the historiography, see also Rössner 2016.
17. Sonnenfels 1804, Part II, 393-5 (§ 237).
18. Haupt 1886; Haupt 1894; see also *Report of the Committee* 1893, Appendix II, 213, 273-5.
19. Haupt 1894, 66.
20. Based on Appendix 4.1 and Lucassen 2014b.
21. Cf. Grytten 2004.
22. *Further Report* 1871, 362; italics are mine.
23. Palairet 1997.
24. Selgin 2008, 266, 295, 297; Muldrew 2007, 409.
25. Kolchin 1987, 375. On the circulation of tokens in the American South after the Civil War, see Lurvink 2014.
26. Bacherikov 2013. Information kindly provided by Bacherikov's academic supervisor Gijs Kessler (IISH). See also Florén 1994 and Svirina 2014.
27. For this section I learned much from discussions with Peter Spufford, Richard Kelleher, and Craig Muldrew. Only after the completion of this manuscript I was able to consult Allen 2015, which broadly confirms my conclusions.
28. Naismith 2012, esp. 284-90, where he discusses the problems of small change in Anglo-Saxon England.
29. Bolton 2012, 27, 132-5.
30. Fractions of farthings (half, third, and quarter) were struck occasionally between 1827 and 1913, partially for use in Ceylon and Malta. Compared with the larger coppers, their total value was insignificant.
31. Hourly wages of building craftsmen in Southern England according to Phelps Brown and Hopkins 1981, 11-12 (daily wages divided by ten); cf. Bolton 2012, 267-8.
32. This may be explained by the fact that Allen – for reasons he does not mention – seems to exclude 1319-44 (Allen 2001, 602). However, in this intermediate period the output of halfpennies and farthings (more than 36,000 pounds worth) was even higher than in the last sub-period, 1344-51 (see Allen 2012, Table C2).
33. Output after Allen 2012, Table C2; total currency after Allen 2001, 603 (adjusted for 1351).
34. Kelleher 2013, 104-8, 324.
35. For new evidence on wages and mobility of labourers after the Black Death see Britnell 2015 and Dyer 2015.
36. See also Mayhew 2007, 217-18 and Allen 2012, 359-68.
37. Copper coinage in 1729-54, amounting to 818 tons or 175,000 pounds, will have improved the situation, but only slightly as it was also 'used as a means of filling the gap created by an attenuated silver circulation'. The next copper coinage, 1762-75, followed by a 24-year stop, amounted to only 234 tons (Dyer & Gaspar 1992, 434-8).

38. Dyer and Gaspar 1992: 436, 446-8: between 1797 and 1800 some 275,000 pounds in new copper coins had been brought into circulation 'best adapted to the payment of the Laborious poor' as requested by Parliament. According to Dyer & Gaspar, this was 'not far short of the genuine coin' circulating in 1797, not including the numerous private tokens and counterfeits still used everywhere; Valenze 2006, 34-43.
39. Muldrew 2007; Selgin 2008; Valenze 2006, 264-70.
40. Besides, token coppers circulated at least until the 1880s (Selgin 2008, 266).
41. Selgin 2008, 289; *The Parliamentary Debates (Hansard). Official Report*, 4 August 1859, *c.* 978-9.
42. James Campbell and Judy Z. Stephenson regard the figures published by Phelps Brown and Hopkins for *c.* 1700 as too high. Stephenson prefers 18 d. per day instead of the 22 d. of Phelps Brown and Hopkins (personal communication from Craig Muldrew). Following Stephenson, the DML around 1720 would be 3.6.
43. Mayhew 2007, 213.
44. Quoted by Mayhew 2007, 213-14.
45. Kelleher 2013, 48, 70-3, 102; Kelleher & Leins 2008.
46. Mayhew 2007, 219; cf. Gemmill & Mayhew 1995, Ch. 4; Spufford 2014.
47. Challis 1992, 387.
48. Muldrew 2007, 395; cf. Phelps Brown and Hopkins 1981: 70: 'If by a wage earner we mean one whose income in kind from any land he occupies is subsidiary, so that his material wellbeing depends mainly on his wages, then we believe it is generally reckoned that in the first half of the sixteenth century about a third of the occupied population in England were wage earners.'
49. Selgin 2008, 27-8; Lucassen 2017.
50. Muldrew 2007: 401, 404. On the relation between small credit and shortage of small change see recently also White 2016 for England and Smail 2016 for the Mediterranean. I would like to emphasize that this is not the same relation as between credit in general and the total money supply, which fluctuate much more in tandem, cf. Desan 2015, 191-230.
51. Cf. Selgin 2008: 208; Lucassen, see Part I: No. 3 in this volume.
52. More in detail see Lucassen 2007c; Welten 2010; van Laere 2013; Martiny 2014; Vanhoudt 2015; Welten 2015, ch. 8.
53. For a general overview of circulation patterns in Europe, see Spufford 1988, Spufford 2002, and Spufford 2008.
54. Lucassen 2007c, 260-1.
55. Van Bavel 2006.
56. Spufford 2014: most frequent were fractions of 3d. Scottish = 4 mite = ⅟₁₂th *stuiver* = 0.0042 guilders of account.
57. Pannekeet & Cruysheer 2013.
58. Lucassen 2014b, Table 3; for 1890 also Haupt 1894, 124-8 (per capita

circulation 1893 *monnaie de bronze* fl 0.40 and *monnaie d'appoint* – which includes the *kwartje* – fl 1.70).

59. Volckart 2008; Sargent & Velde 2002.
60. Muldrew 2007; Selgin 2008.
61. Lucassen & Zuijderduijn 2014.
62. See Desrousseaux 2012, 147 (Haute-Garonne / Toulouse 1811: 'les manouvriers, qui gagnent 15 à 20 sous par jour sont payés en cuivre et en billon'); cf. Prunaux 2013; Touitou-Michon & Michon 2013; Cardon & Lemaire 2014.
63. In the late sixteenth and seventeenth centuries hourly wages were more like one *sou* than two *sous*. See, for example, Goubert 1968, 333-40, and Le Roy-Ladurie 1969, 123. This coincides well with the end of the *denier tournois* after 1650 and of the *double tournois* after 1700; for wage labour in France see Béaur *et al.* 2010.
64. Desrousseaux 2012: 26-8, 88, 402-5: totals for 31 December 1813 (3,479,156,869 francs) and 1817, but without sufficient details for questions regarding deep monetization. See also Haupt 1894, 662-77.
65. I.e. 30 *sou* (17,811,193) and 15 *sou* (7,466,826).
66. I.e. 24 *sou* (19,894,514), 12 *sou* (27,287,641), and 6 *sou* (3,441,811).
67. I.e. 2 *sou* (12,118,818), 1 *sou* (16,920,391), 6 *denier* (2,190,035), and 3 *denier* (73,653).
68. Assuming a population of 28 million in 1789, 30 million in 1800, and 38 million in 1810.
69. Ciani 1926; Bruce 2004 and similar catalogues.
70. Cardon 2012; Cardon & Lemaire 2014.
71. Ray 2006.
72. *Report of the Committee* 1893, Appendix I, 148-9.
73. Ibid., Minutes, 81, question 1913. According to another interviewee it was only recently that paper money had begun to play a role. Ibid 118, question 2634.
74. Ibid 117, question 2629; Stevens 2012, 362.
75. Lucassen 2000c, 366-7, supposing a wage level for agricultural labourers of two *annas* per day of eight hours *Report of the Committee* 1893, Minutes, 57, question 1432. For similar estimates (unfortunately not including copper coins) see *Report of the Committee* 1893, Report, 21, and Appendix III, 307-8. See also de Zwart & Lucassen 2015.
76. Lucassen & Stapel 2014: Table 23.
77. The earliest attempt I know of is by Francis Capel Harrison (1863-1938), who estimated India's silver stock in 1493 at 290 million rupees, net imports 1493-1800 at 1,510.6 million rupees, 1800-35 at 611.9 million, and 1835-92 at 3,428.5 million. See *Report of the Committee* 1893, Appendix 3, 307-8. For modern estimates of imports since 1493, see Subrahmanyam 1994 and Prakash 2004.

78. Lucassen & Stapel 2014. Data for neighbouring Goa since the late 1830s (ongoing work within the framework of a collaborative project with Paulo Mattos, Lisbon) have since confirmed this impression.
79. Lucassen 2007c; Lingen & Lucassen; see Part I: Nos. 9, 10 and 12 in this volume.
80. Stevens 2012, 491-2; Lucassen, see Part I: No. 13 in this volume.
81. Stevens 2012, 264-5, 319-23, 336-42, 355-67, 378-9, 488; *Imperial Gazetteer of India* 1908 for information on Benares Division, District and City.
82. Stevens 2012, 264-5 in fact gives a figure of 700,000 lakhs or 70,000,000,000 units (1 lakh = 100,000). Supposing these units stand for coins, this would result in 20,000 *pice* coins per capita, which is impossible. The data for the districts of Burdwan, Jessore, and Purneah also clearly show that the units meant must be rupees.
83. Stevens 2012, 322 (annual *pice* production 1775-86 of about 6 million *pieces* as compared with a stock of 44.8 million *pieces* in 1808; 1782-1805 annual production in maunds, although incomplete, points in the same direction); ibid., 341 (*pice*, valued at 110,000 rupees or *c.* 7 million (*pice*) pieces, was supposed to be necessary for Benares in 1806-7, according to the Calcutta Mint Committee); ibid., 488.
84. Stevens 2012, 321 (in a report from 1786).
85. Stevens 2012, 168, 263, 266, 269, 488 (for the Bengal Presidency); Garg 2013, 164 (for Madras 1824-5), 172 (for Bombay 1809-19); Lucassen, see Part I: No. 13 in this volume, [383] (for 1835-48); Bruce 2004, 711 (for later years).
86. Stevens 2012, 488. However, Benares copper coin production 1826-7 (here Rs. 74,161 = 4,746,304 *pice*) is not consistent with ibid., 379: total 94,322 maunds = 9,432,200 lbs. troy (ibid.: 557) = 54,329,472,000 grains = 543,294,720 pice (ibid., 268) = 8,488,980 rupees (ibid., 269). I have borrowed here the lower figure of 74,161 rupees.
87. Stevens 2012, passim; Lucassen 2007a: 31-2; Hogendorn & Johnson 1986.
88. Shimada 2006, 107-28. For the ratio between Indian and foreign copper, see Prinsep, who in 1780 contrasted average annual copper imports (for four years) of 11,106.20 maunds with Rotas mines' production of only 2,000 maunds per annum (Stevens 2012, 112); for Indian copper mines see also Lingen & Lucassen, see Part I: No. 12 in this volume.
89. Lucassen, see Part I: No. 2 in this volume.
90. Lucassen, see Part I: No. 2 in this volume; cf. Deyell 1987, Habib 1987, Martin 1987; for wages Habib 1987, 154 and Prakash 1987; Prakash, see Part I: No. 7 and Haider, No. 6 in this volume; Haider 2015; De Zwart & Lucassen 2015.
91. Kolff & van Santen 1979, 117. Although Pelsaert here equates *paisa* and *taka*, for 1565 he equates one *taka* to 1/20th rupee (ibid., 84), suggesting 1 *tanka* = 2 *paisa*/*dams* which is correct (Haider, See Part I: No. 6 in this volume). On fluctuating *dam*: rupee rates: ibid.; Habib 1987, 145-50; Prakash, See Part I: No. 7 in this volume; inhabitants: Haider, see Part I: No. 6 in this volume.

92. Deyell 1990 has termed the preceding centuries as India 'living without silver'. For central and northern India see Lucassen 2014a, for southern India – still less researched – see Stein 1989, 41-2, and Palat 2015, 122-30, 161, 171-5.
93. Lucassen 2014a; Habib 1994; Haider 2011 and 2015.
94. Haider 2015: 90.
95. Lucassen 2005; Lucassen, see Part I: No. 3 in this volume (based on the work of Richard von Glahn, Hans Ulrich Vogel, and others); Wang 2004; Scheidel 2009.
96. Lucassen 2005, 431-2; Weirong 2005, 95-7; Burger 2008; Scheidel 2009, 154, 194, 199; Liu 2015; 68-76, 218-21.
97. Lucassen 2005, 432.
98. Lucassen 2005, 432, 439; Wang 2007, 67, 72 (wage of 600 coins per month for a captain, late Han); Von Glahn 1996, 85, 247; Scheidel 2009, 154; Moll-Murata 2005, 241; and Moll-Murata 2015: Appendix for wages. Stock, population and stock per capita *c.* 750, 1120, 1550, 1600 and 1750 after Liu 2015, 73 (123 for wages 1158 and 1480).
99. Shen Kua, quoted in Palat 2015, 145.
100. Shikano 2007; Kovalchuk & Depeyrot 2012. I would like to thank Christine Moll-Murata for her information.
101. Apart from the works quoted in the other footnotes, see also Gramlich-Oka 2008, Izawa 2013, and Noriko 2016.
102. For 1640: Izawa 2013, 15; Van de Polder 1891; production 1872-86: Matsukata 1899; wages: Hanley & Yamamura 1977, 192; Van Leeuwen 2007, 239.
103. Moll-Murata 2012; since elaborately confirmed by Liu 2015.
104. Deng 2015, 326.
105. Chevaleyre 2012.
106. Liu 2015, 74; cf. Von Glahn 2010, 83ff.
107. Moll-Murata 2008 and 2015, 275-6.
108. Squares indicate stock data and triangles estimates based on production trends.
109. Margariti 2014, 196; cf. Peebles 2010.
110. To push this speculative argument somewhat further: mixed religious populations as in parts of post-Reformation Europe and India after the introduction of Islam, but also in relation to caste distinctions, might have a bearing on conventions regarding small-scale credit and DMLs.
111. Haupt 1894 and *Further Reports* 1870 and 1871.
112. Haupt 1894, 890, commenting on the release of the new coins and notes, which appears to have been excessive given the existing stock.
113. Until 1874, 1 rigsdaler (0.4064 oz. silver) = 96 *skilling rigsmonts;* 1 krone (0.1929 oz. silver) = 100 øre from 1874 onwards. Therefore 1 skilling equals 0.0042 1/3 oz. silver, while 1 øre equals 0.001929 oz. silver, or 1 *skilling* ≈ 2.2

øre. Cf. Märcher 2013, who suggests that in Denmark deep monetization started in the late eighteenth century.

114. My calculation of total production for 1874-85 based on Bruce 2004.
115. Even after the new small coins had arrived from Berlin (126,217 Egyptian pounds in nickels and 5,317 Egyptian pounds in bronzes), Haupt 1894, 91 comments: 'On voit que l'émission de la petite monnaie se tient dans les limites très étroitement tracés.'
116. My calculation based on Bruce 2004.
117. There are reasons to believe that there was an extreme oversupply of coppers as none were struck in the twenty-eight years between 1867 and 1895; nickel 20 centesimi pieces did not appear until 1894. Compare this with neighbouring France.
118. My calculation based on Bruce 2004.
119. Ibid.
120. For similar wages on the Azores, see Further Reports 1871, 430-*7; f*or Madeira Further Reports 1871, 438-41.
121. Probably partially circulating in the colonies, such as Angola. See Haupt 1894, 423-4, and Crib, Cook & Carradice 1990, 238, 248, 253, 256-7, 262.
122. My calculation based on Bruce 2004.
123. A figure that subsequently rose. For instance, at the end of 1891 the small-change stock had risen to nearly 20 million roubles, giving a DML of nearly 2.
124. Note that all coppers were struck solely in 1868 and 1879 and all copper nickels only in 1883 and 1884, whereas coining these small denominations was resumed only from 1904 onwards. It is likely that at the end of 1885 smallest coins were still in stock in Belgrade, to be released into circulation only piecemeal in the years to come.
125. As in the Portuguese case, a substantial portion was sent to the colonies, especially Cuba, but also to Puerto Rico and the Philippines. See Haupt 1894, 314, 517, 691; Crib, Cook & Carradice 1990: 288, 290.
126. My calculation based on Bruce 2004.
127. Plus, my calculation based on Bruce 2004
128. Cf. 1.3 million pounds in bronze coins in circulation in 1877 and more than twice that sum around 1900. This increase was due also to automatic machines operated by pennies and to the fares of the new electric trams (Dyer & Gaspar 1992, 546).
129. Total production of threepence, fourpence, and sixpence coins 1817-85 was 5,231 million pounds (calculated based on Bruce 2004), less about 12 per cent for exports to colonies (Haupt 1894, 491) makes 4,603 million pounds, less 20 per cent withdrawn (the percentage estimated by Haupt 1894, 490 for all silver coins) gives a figure of 3,682 million pounds. The small amount of bronze exported to the colonies has been ignored here. For the circulation of English copper coins, valued at 35,000 pounds, in New South Wales (Australia), see Haupt 1894, 797. See also Dyer & Gaspar 1992, 546,

who report for 1877 that only 8.5 per cent of the bronzes had been shipped overseas.

130. On similar lines the DML for 1857 may be calculated as 2 by excluding the sixpence and as 4.7 by including it (copper coin circulation valued at 800 million pounds; see Dyer & Gaspar 1992, 509, and Selgin 2008, 299).

Sultanates and the Mughal Empire

5

The Price Regulations of 'Ala'uddin Khalji – A Defence of Zia' Barani

IRFAN HABIB

Zia' Barani's long account of the price-control measures of 'Ala'uddin Khalji (1296-1316), running to nearly seventeen pages of the printed edition, represents one of the most interesting portions of his work.[1] Some assessments of this account, it is true, have not been very complimentary to that historian. Moreland argued that Barani's facts may be accepted but for no better reason than that he 'did not possess the power of economic analysis' necessary for 'the invention' of such facts.[2] Yet it is precisely the unexpected 'economic analysis' that is rejected in a recent authoritative work; it is 'necessary,' it has been said, 'to distinguish Barani's facts from his conclusions'.[3] Now, Simon Digby, having the advantage of tracking down an earlier version of Barani's text would have us doubt the old writer's facts as well. 'Barani's inaccuracies,' says he, 'are even more extensive than has hitherto been supposed.'[4]

In what follows I propose to argue, first, that Barani's factual account is correct in all substantive matters; and, secondly, that, though the 'analysis' is his own, it is nevertheless sound and takes us much closer to the purpose, extent and consequences of 'Ala'uddin Khalji's measures than any other that has so far been offered.

I

A reader of Moreland's remarks might assume that if Barani's work were not there, we would not have known of 'Ala'uddin Khalji's price measures; and that his account, therefore, is uncorroborated. This is by no means so. The measures provided Amir Khuṣrau with yet another opportunity to insert panegyrics of his royal patron in the *Khaza'in-l Futuh*, a work written in 1311 or soon after.[5] There is the rather unjustly neglected account in the *Rihla* of Ibn Battuta, who was in Delhi from 1335 to 1342.[6] In 1350, 'Isami in his versified history, *Futuh-us Salatin*, devoted a section to the same subject;[7] and Nasiruddin Mahmud, the Chishti mystic, spoke on it twice at some length in his conversations recorded in 1354-55.[8]

Barani, who completed his *Ta'rikh-i Firuz-Shahi* in 1357, could not of course have had access to the narrative of Ibn Battuta; and it is most unlikely that he could even have heard of 'Isami's versified history, prepared for a hostile court. Barani does not give any indication of an acquaintance with Nasiruddin Mahmud's conversations, though he does mention the divine once.[9] It is, on the other hand, practically certain that as an educated man (and still more as a young friend of that poet) he must have read Amir Khusrau's *Khaza'in-l Futuh*; yet he does not seem to have used it directly in weaving his narrative of the military campaigns of 'Ala'uddin Khalji, for which chiefly the book should have served as a source. All in all, while we can confidently say that all the four accounts we have mentioned are independent of Barani, he, on his part, could not have seen two of these, and has probably not been influenced by either of the other two sources. Such independence should enable us to apply a simple test to check Barani's veracity. If the facts that he offers us are largely manufactured out of his ḥead, his account should be different in substantial particulars from what we get from our other sources, much briefer as they are. But if the reverse is true, that is, if his version matches with what these four sources tell us, he would stand vindicated, and there would be no reason to doubt the general veracity of his account. I, therefore, offer the following detailed comparison:

(a) Barani gives the prices of a very large number of commodities current under 'Ala'uddin Khalji. Simon Digby has traced an earlier version of Barani's work containing the prices of a fewer number of commodities.[10] The prices of food grains in both versions are identical with the exception of gram; in some other cases, the earlier version gives variant (possibly corrupt) quotations.[11] The question arises whether, when Barani later altered and expanded these earlier quotations, he did so from his head or from documentary evidence. Fortunately, Nasiruddin Mahmud gives us prices fixed by 'Ala'uddin Khalji for wheat, and red and white sugar; and these can be compared with those which Barani has recorded.

Nasiruddin Mahmud's prices are: 'Seven and a half *jitals* (one man of) wheat; half *diram* (½ *jital*), (one *ser* of) sugar; one *jital*, somewhat less (than one *ser* of) white sugar (*shakar-tari*).[12] Barani gives the corresponding quotations in his final version as follows:

'Wheat, one man for seven and a half *jitals*'; 'red sugar, three sers for one-and-a-half *jitals*'.[13] Thus wheat has the same rate; red sugar too is exactly half a *jital* for one ser; and white sugar, at one *jital* for 3/4 ser, suits the mystic's loosely stated price for it. The price quoted in Barani's first version for wheat is the same, and that for white sugar (1 *jital*, 1 *dang*, i.e. 1¼ *jitals*, for one ser) is closer still to Nasiruddin Mahmud's price; the price for red sugar is not provided.[14] With such corroboration, it would be hard to say that Barani has invented these prices, or set them down in his final version on the basis of just his memory or conjecture.

(b) Barani stresses that 'Ala'uddin Khalji's ability to induct grain into the market from the Imperial store-houses was a major factor behind the prevention of a rise in grain prices when the rains failed.[15] This is in fact the sum and substance of Amir Khusrau's statements on how the cheapness of grain was secured.[16] Ibn Battuta offers a more circumstantial account of this, approaching Barani closely in that he also refers to the undoing of the engrossers (*muhtakirun*).[17] 'Isami has a simpler but fairly straightforward account of the same measures, crowned by an expression of satisfaction at the destruction of 'all the engrossers' (*har muhtakir*).[18]

(c) Barani describes in detail the steps taken to ensure that the grain-carriers (*karvanis*) maintained an unending supply of grain to the city and sell at prices fixed by the Sultan.[19] Though his account is given from a point of view opposite to that of Barani, Nasiruddin Mahmud too ascribes the cheapness of the grain to the Sultan's success in managing the grain-carriers, whom he styles *nayaks*.[20]

(d) According to Barani, the cheapness extended to all other products, cloth of high and low grades, slaves, horses, etc., whose prices too were fixed; and the market for cloth, sugar and salt was placed on a piece of open ground called *Sarai 'Adl*.[21] Amir Khusrau says that all kinds of cloth (and he too names various sorts) were put on sale at low prices in the *Daru-l' Adl* (the name *Sarai 'Adl* is also deducible from averse), as also 'fruits and all necessaries of the table.'[22] Ibn Battuta similarly speaks of the Sultan acting to lower prices of meat and Daulatabad cloth.[23] Very low prices for quilted coats made of different kinds of cloth prevailing in 'Ala'uddin Khalji's time were recollected by Nasiruddin Mahmud.[24]

(e) The Sultan advanced money (a total of 20 lakh *tankas*) to the merchants (Multanis) to bring cloth (*aqmasha*) from various regions (Barani).[25] Ibn Battuta says 'Ala'uddin Khalji advanced money to merchants to bring oxen and sheep, as well as 'the drapery imported from Daulatabad'.[26]

(f) Barani says that wages under 'Ala'uddin Khalji were also very low, a mere fourth of what they were under his successor.[27] Low wages under 'Ala'uddin Khalji were similarly recalled by Nasiruddin Mahmud,[28] and by 'Ainu-l Mulk Mahru in one of his letters early in the reign of Firuz Tughluq.[29]

(g) According to Barani,[30] the administration of price-enforcement in the markets at Delhi was placed under the *Ra'is* in-charge of the *Riyasat-i Nazarat-i Mamalik wa Ihtisab*. He had to be a stern officer in order to deal with the 'shameless', 'lying' market-people (*Qaum-i bazari*). Amir Khusrau tells us of an honest *Ra'is* appointed by 'Ala'uddin such as 'speaks to the tongue-loose market-people (*bazarian*) with the tongue of the whip of justice';[31] and Ibn Battuta recounts how 'the *muhtasib*, called *Ra'is*', used to report the prices to the Sultan.[32]

(h) Barani says that stern steps were taken to prevent under-weighing (*kamdihagi*) by the shopkeepers.[33] Amir Khusrau similarly tells us of stern punishments for this offence; he adds that iron weights were ordered to be substituted for the stone weights.[34]

(i) Barani says that prices in the grain market were daily reported to the Sultan,[35] and the Sultan was concerned 'day and night' with the fixation of the prices of almost everything.[36] Ibn Battuta tells us of the report on prices being daily laid before 'Ala'uddin Khalji;[37] and so too 'Isami:

> From the market every day at sunset,
> The reporters (barids) brought the rates of grain prices;
> All those rates were laid before the King,
> One by one, every evening.[38]

Given the brevity of the other sources from which we have sought to verify Barani, we could hardly have expected a more extensive corroboration. Indeed, if one were to set aside Barani and reconstruct a picture of 'Ala'uddin Khalji's price regulations by simply assembling the other four early accounts, we would still get a considerable part of the skeleton, and a few of the many details, of Barani's spirited description. The essential merit of our other sources would, indeed, seem to lie in the service they perform of confirming so much of Barani's factual narration that we can safely repose confidence in the general truth of his whole account, including the part that the other four sources have failed to shed light on.

II

Barani goes much further than merely giving us a detailed narrative whose general reliability we may accept: he has a critical acumen, which the other sources so woefully lack. All the four of them simply attribute the measure to the benevolence of the Sultan who wished to serve the common weal. Of this supposition Barani was quite sceptical; but this may be better discussed at a later stage in this article. As for the practical measures by which the control was achieved. Amir Khusrau, Ibn Battuta and 'Isami can only tell us of the opening up of Imperial store-houses,[39] while Nasiruddin Mahmud, with partial support from Ibn Battuta, focuses on the Sultan's policy of advancing loans to merchants so as to enable them to bring supplies to the market.[40]

In his first version, Barani remains, on the whole, among the uninquisitive, with none of the analytical powers and attendant details of the final text. In between the two versions, then, he must have reflected. Sure enough, he too describes, and in detail, the use of imperial stores [see (b) in Section I] and the management of grain-carriers to ensure steady supplies [see (c) in Section I]. But we can see him asking himself further questions, to wit: (i) How were the Sultan's grain store-houses so full that they had enough within them to replace normal supplies whenever these failed in bad seasons? And (ii) of what avail would it have been for merchants to be assisted or coerced to bring in supplies, if they had to buy dear in order to sell cheaply, and so to proceed all the time at a loss? Any aid or constraint to sustain so profitless an undertaking would have collapsed: it could only succeed if grain were also made cheaper where it was raised; but how?

Barani's answers to both these questions are rooted in his description of 'Ala'uddin Khalji's land-tax policy.[41] There he says that 'Ala'uddin Khalji exacted half the produce as tax (*kharaj*) from every cultivator, measuring the land (*masahat*) and imposing on it the officially estimated grain-rate (*wafa*). In addition, he imposed a tax called *charai* on milch cattle and *ghari* on every house or hut.[42] The tax demand was high, and harsh measures were undertaken to see that there was no holding back of grain (*ghaban*) or uneven spread of taxation (*shutrgurba*).[43] The result was that the rural intermediaries – the khuts and muqaddams – were greatly impoverished, a point which Barani underscores.[44] In other words, at the expense of the peasantry and the higher rural classes, 'Ala'uddin Khalji obtained half the agricultural produce for the state. The limits of the area where this was done Barani carefully defines by mentioning a number of places lying within it; the territory extended from Lahore to Kara and from Katehar to Nagaur with the environs of Delhi at its core (see Map 5.1).[45]

Barani then shows how the magnitude and mechanism of the agrarian taxation enabled 'Ala'uddin Khalji to achieve both his objectives, viz., filling the granaries and securing to grain-carriers supplies at low prices. His statements are worth reproducing, in as literal a translation as possible.

Passage 1

The third regulation for establishing the cheapness of grain consisted in the collection of large quantities of grain in the Sultan's store-houses. The Sultan ordered that in the districts (*qasbat*) of the *Khalisa* in the Doab,[46] grain alone should be taken in lieu of the land-tax (*kharaj*), and that it should be conveyed to the Sultan's store-houses; in the 'New City' (Chha'in)[47] and in the Country of the New City, half of the royal tax (lit., the Sultan's share) be collected in grain alone, and this too[48] be stored in Chha'in and the districts (*qasbat*) of Chha'in. The said grain should be delivered to the grain-carriers (*karvanis*); as a result so much of the Sultan's grain reached Delhi....[49]

Passage 2

The sixth regulation for establishing cheapness of grain consisted in extracting letters (of assurances) from the revenue collectors (*mutsarrifs*) and functionaries (*karkunan*) of the (assigned) territories (*walayat*)[50] to the effect that they would compel the peasants (*ri'aya*) to sell grain by the side of the fields to the grain-carriers (*karvanis*) at the (fixed) prices. The Sultan ordered that the Royal Finance Ministry (*Diwan-i A'la*) should take letters from the officials (*shahnas*) and collectors (*mutasarrifs*) of the walayat[51] of the Doab, which is near the City (of Delhi), to say that they would demand the land-tax (*kharaj*) from the peasants with such harshness (*shiddat*) that the latter would not be able to bring the grain from the fields into their houses and engross it, and would be forced to sell the grain at low rates by the side of the field to the grain-carriers. As a result of the establishment of this regulation, the grain-carriers had no obstacle to face in conveying grain to the market (*mandi*), and grain supplies constantly reached the market. For their own profit, villagers also brought whatever they could from the fields to the market and sold it at prices fixed by the Sultan.[52]

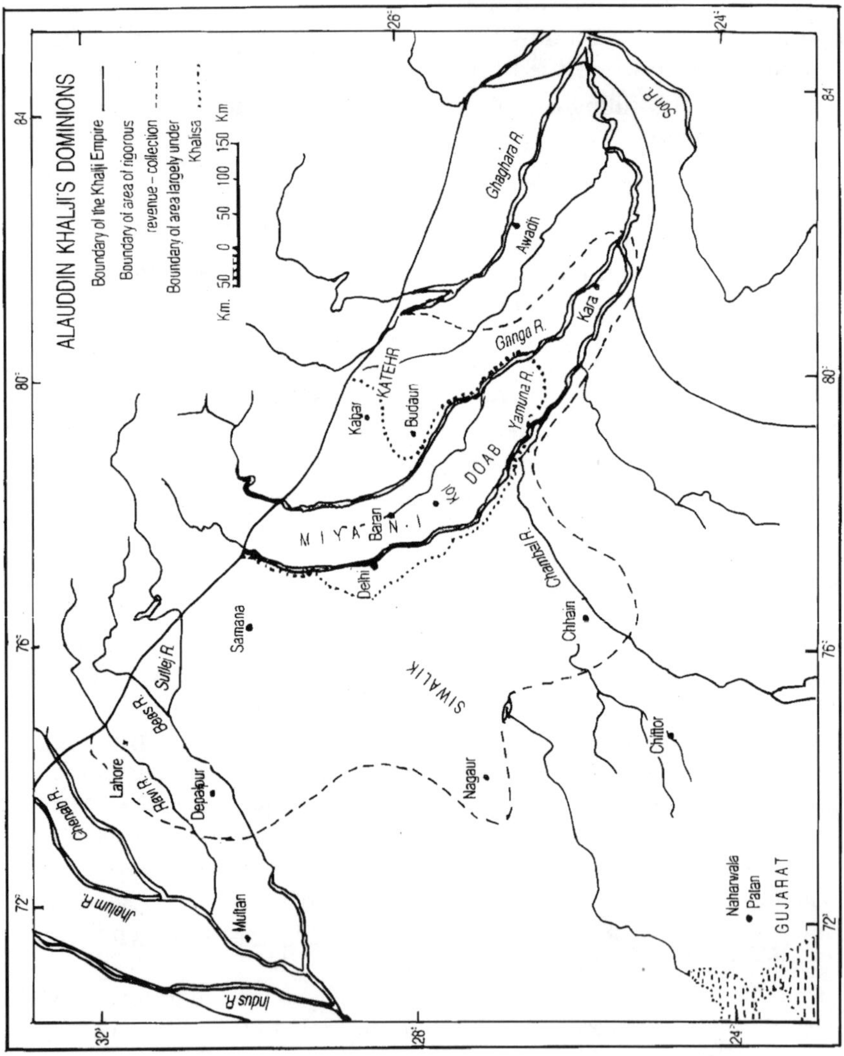

MAP 5.1. 'ALA'UDDIN KHALJI'S DOMINIONS

Barani sums up the device described in Passage 2, when he lists, as the second of the four causes for the success attained in reducing prices, 'the heavy magnitude of land-revenue (*kharaj-ha*), since the peasants, impoverished by the heavy tax-demand, had to sell grain and goods at prices fixed by the Sultan'.[53]

Each of the two devices described in the two passages thus led to a cheapening of the grain; the difference was that in one case the tax was collected in kind, in the other in cash.

Passage 1 describes what happened solely within the *khalisa* territories, that is, within tracts whose revenues were reserved for the Royal Treasury. In such territories lying within the Doab (including Delhi) the entire revenue was collected in grain; in those of eastern Rajasthan (the Chha'in tract) only half the revenue was collected in grain, the remainder presumably in cash.

Passage 2 relates essentially to the assigned territories, which seems to be the real sense of the word *walayat*. In contrast to the first passage there is no reference to the *khalisa*; and there would be no point in the Sultan's Finance Ministry taking letters of assurance from *karkuns*, *mutarrifs* and *shahnas*, if they were its own officials and not those of the *walis* or *muqtis*. In these territories grain was not taken in revenue, but the tax in money was to be so rigorously demanded as to force the peasant to sell part of his grain to pay the tax. Thus what the peasant was selling was not his own share, but really 'the Sultan's share' of the first passage, in lieu of which he had to pay the land-tax. There is no ground at all for supposing that Barani intended to imply that the very peasants who had parted with half the grain in tax, were now further 'compelled to part with the rest for a price, so that they had no grain left for their own families'.[54] Indeed, if the peasant had already paid the tax in the form of grain, there would be no scope for the recourse to the device of rigorously collecting the very same tax in order to make him sell. The fact that revenue under 'Ala'uddin Khalji was collected by the *walis*, or revenue-assignees, in money, and not in kind, is borne upon us by a rather late account of the proceedings of Ghazi Malik, the *wali* of Depalpur. In a particular locality within his charge he is said to have demanded 'the whole year's revenue in money (*naqd*)' in advance, instead of in instalments as hitherto.[55] This was, indeed, collection in money with a vengeance.

Barani's description of the two ways of getting grain supplies moving through taxation is, then, fairly clear. The only difficulty is posed by another passage, in which Barani tells us that 'the entire country of the Doab became in obedience (as) a single village and was brought into the *Khalisa*'.[56] Read with our Passage 1, this should imply that only grain was collected in the whole of the Doab; and there would be no room then for the measure described in Passage 2. But just after telling us that the entire Doab was made part of *Khalisa*, Barani goes on to say: 'The whole of its tax-revenue (*mahsul*) down to the penny (*dang o diram*) they brought into the Treasury, and it was out of it that they paid the salary (*wajh*) to the troopers and met the expenses of the Sultan's establishments.'[57] If so, the revenue must have been collected in cash, so that our Passage 2 would better describe the real conditions than Passage 1. The contradictions in these statements can, however, be reconciled by assuming that Barani has dispensed with certain necessary qualifications when making his statements in absolute terms. If we suppose (a) that the *Khalisa* was very extensive (though not all-inclusive) in the Doab, and within it in many villages the land-tax was levied in grain only; and (b) that cash was levied in many parts of the *Khalisa*, and in the territories of *walis*, who continued to hold *iqtas* in the same region, his various statements may become quite intelligible and mutually non-contradictory. The device of Passage 1 would be in force where conditions summed up in (a) prevailed, and a Passage 2 where those outlined in (b) held true.

To return to what I regard as Barani's main argument: grain supply at low prices depended upon the extraction of the agrarian surplus through the land-tax, brought directly into the Sultan's granaries or into the grain-carriers' hands by the rigour of the tax-demand. Insofar as the grain brought into the market was surplus produce, or grain above that needed for the producer's subsistence and for meeting the cost of other factors (seed, cattle, etc.), the 'costs of production' did not enter into the formation of the grain price. The floor for its sale price 'by the side of the field' was the size of the tax in money and the cost of its collection by the ruling class. This being so, grain prices could be arbitrarily set by the Sultan by linking them with the tax. What our Passage 2 tells us in effect is that instead of commuting *x* quantities of grain assessed as tax into *y* units of money at current market prices, the state now made this commutation at low prices arbitrarily fixed by it, and then enforced these low prices in the urban market, by assuring continuous supply of grain purchased by merchants in the villages at commutation prices set to match the fixed retail prices. There was an undoubted loss to the State in this, not commented upon by Barani, but obvious to us: if the commutation rates were lowered, the total revenue in money terms would be correspondingly diminished. Thus, one must assume that, unless wholly made up by an increase in the incidence of the land-tax, the total money revenue of the Khalji government should have fallen as a result of the price-control measures, though the real value in terms of grain tonnage might have been larger. We shall return to this question in the last portion of this article.

The reduction of food grain prices was central to a general reduction of prices, since it induced a lowering of the subsistence costs of labour. This Barani realizes very well, for he puts into the mouths of the Sultan's counsellors the argument that 'so long as strong regulations are not put into effect and firm balances not established for the cheapening of grain, the articles necessary for subsistence (*asbab-i ma'ash*) will also not become cheap'.[58] Barani's statement that wages were thereupon reduced to very low rates is corroborated by other sources [see (f) in Section I]. Barani says that the salary, obviously annual, of a servant or *chakar* under 'Ala'uddin Khalji was 10 or 12 *tankas*; this would be the equivalent of 1⅓ or 1 *jitals* a day.[59] 'Ainu-l Mulk remembered that the wages of artisans (*muhtarifa*) in the days of that Sultan were 2 or 3 *jitals* a day; and he clearly implies that the weavers' and tailors' wages were of this order.[60] The quotations in the two sources, one for unskilled, the other for skilled labour, match fairly well. It is not stated anywhere that 'Ala'uddin Khalji directly fixed servants' wages; but wages of manufacturing artisans might have been constricted by the prices fixed by the Sultan on 'the basis of the cost-prices (*barawurd*) of the articles and the profits of the seller'.[61] Amir Khusrau also writes as if the sale of their products by the artisans (*muhtarifa*) was closely supervised.[62] The reduction in wages would, in turn, mean that there would be less effective demand (in money terms) for goods, and this would, therefore, generate a strong deflationary pressure. Barani, indeed, remarks that one out of the four major causes of the prevalence of low prices was 'the lack of money (*bezari*) in the hands of the people', so that the saying went, 'One camel goes for a penny (*dang*), but who has one penny?'[63]

One can conjecture that if agricultural prices fell and wage-costs too were reduced, the prices of the goods manufactured within the price-control zone could be greatly reduced. Similar would be the case with those of the slaves: when wages of free labour fell, it would be unprofitable to use slaves bought at the old prices. Thus, prices of slaves, insofar as there was no alternative market to Delhi for them, could conceivably be brought down fairly sharply.

Yet, there would at the same time be a large number of commodities which came from areas outside the price-control zone. Their prime costs would not be affected by 'Ala'uddin Khalji's tax measures.

Such would be the fine cloth from Tebrez and Devagiri;[64] the cavalry horses, which except for the lowly *tattu*, must have been largely imported;[65] and also the imported slaves. If prime costs could not be changed, other steps could still be taken to reduce the margin between the cost in the place of origin and the retail price at Delhi. Barani describes how these steps were taken. Loans were advanced to merchants of high repute to bring in continuous supplies; engrossing was strongly suppressed; separate markets were established for particular goods to facilitate control and secure the buyers' direct access to caravan goods; the intrusion of brokers was dispensed with; and in the case of certain varieties of high-quality cloth, purchases were restricted to favoured classes (such as nobles and religious divines) so as to prevent the passing of the cloth into the hands of profiteers who might convey them to other more lucrative markets.[66] Clearly, the effort was to eliminate or reduce the component of speculative profits and intermediaries' share in the retail price. In the case of these particular commodities little more could perhaps have been done.

It would then seem that Barani's elaborations of his view that the price-reductions rested on a combination of heavy agrarian taxation and administrative measures of great rigour, are fairly adequately supported by the factual evidence he presents, and by the very logic of the situation whose details he supplies. This carries us to three more questions, which are closely interlinked: the area affected by the price reductions; the effects of the phenomena on the various sections of the population; and, finally, the motives of 'Ala'uddin Khalji in enforcing the regulations. On all these Barani has important information and observations to offer.

III

It is clear from Barani's language that the comprehensive measures for price-control that 'Ala'uddin Khalji sought to impose had the city of Delhi as their focus. Thus when he speaks of grain prices, he describes the control of the grain-market (*mandi*) at Delhi, placed under a *shahna* (Controller), Yaqut.[67] Grain supplies are said to have 'reached Delhi' continuously;[68] and, as a result, 'no famine occurred in Delhi'.[69] So, too, in relation to prices of non-agricultural commodities: A great cloth market was established at the *Sarai 'Adl*, 'an open ground inside Badaun Gate towards the Green Palace' at Delhi.[70] Merchants were advanced loans to bring 'high-quality cloth to 'the City' (Delhi).[71] When the brokers were eliminated in the horse-market, they were exiled 'from the City'.[72] On the other hand, there is no reference to similar measures taken in any other city.

The other fourteenth century sources are rather vague and self-contradictory about the extent of the price-control zone. Amir Khusrau says grandly that both 'the city-man and the villager' benefited from the Sultan's bounty; but his description of the *Daru-l 'Adl* (*Sarai 'Adl*) must solely refer to Delhi.[73] Ibn Battuta makes no definite statement,[74] but 'Isami says that 'Ala'udain Khalji entertained the ambition that 'Plenitude should be achieved, and scarcity banished; Thus may the City be protected'.[75]

Nasiruddin Mahmud specifically describes the absence of scarcity at Delhi under 'Ala'uddin Khalji and tells us how the Sultan arranged with the grain-carriers to bring grain to 'the City'. But he goes on to include 'the people of the world' among the beneficiaries of the measure.[76]

Similar vagueness about the locale of the price regulations is to be found in a letter which 'Ainu-l Mulk wrote (from Delhi or Multan) in the early years of Firuz Tughluq. In this, while dealing with a complaint over new taxes levied at Uchh, 'Ainu-l Mulk compares the prosperity of the artisans of his day (now being taxed) with the conditions prevailing under 'Ala'uddin Khalji when very low wages used to be paid. It may conceivably be argued that this means that Uchh was affected by 'Ala'uddin Khalji's price regulations; but for 'Ainu-l Mulk's argument it was not at all necessary that the artisans with whose conditions he was favourably comparing those of the artisans of his own day should also have belonged to Uchh.[77]

An explicit statement that the low prices had a more extensive domain than Delhi and its environs seems to have come, first of all, from Firishta, writing early in the seventeenth century. Before quoting the grain prices that he takes from Barani, he says: 'What (prices) were fixed at Delhi are as follows; from these one may imagine the rates (lit., conditions) in the other parts'.[78] This concern with an intriguing question does Firishta credit; but there is no proof that he had any authority to back his suggestion of similarly low prices prevailing elsewhere.

It has been contended that prices could not have been reduced just at Delhi, because, according to Barani himself. 'Ala'uddin Khalji wished to maintain a larger army at a smaller expense; and all expenditure on the army could hardly have been confined to Delhi.[79] But there is no doubt that much of it, at any rate, was so confined. The Sultan's troopers having been placed on cash-pay distributed from the Treasury,[80] would have been normally concentrated in Delhi. Here, too, was the large Army Camp – the *Lashkar*, of which we hear in Nizamuddin's conversations.[81]

There was, therefore, nothing unreasonable in the Sultan's

attempt to keep prices low at Delhi, the capital, the principal city and military camp of the Empire. But this attempt in itself necessitated control of prices at a number of other points. First of all, Barani himself tells us of the sale-prices of grain being set low throughout the Doab, 'being near the City,' so that the grain purchased at the price might be brought to Delhi for sale at profit (see Passage 2 in Section II). Thus, in the region around Delhi, a general fall in agricultural prices had to be enforced to enable supplies to reach Delhi. It is perhaps this lowering of the rural prices – attained through the tax-mechanism, as we have seen – which induced Amir Khusrau to speak rhetorically of 'the villager' deriving benefit from the cheapness of grain.[82] The fall in rural prices in the Doab would have affected prices in the towns within it as well. Similar conditions might be expected in the Trans-Yamuna tract comprising the environs of Delhi and the territory of Chha'in, where large granaries were established (see Passage 1 in Section II).

Beyond these extensions of the price-control area, it is difficult to see how prices could have been reduced where the kind of agrarian tax-measures taken in the Doab were not resorted to. In any case, if high agrarian-taxation was at the root of the success of the price regulations, it is not to be expected that its range went beyond the limits that Barani himself defines for the zone where 'Ala'uddin Khalji's heavy-tax system operated (see Map 5.1).[83] Multan, for example, would then be definitely excluded from the price-control zone. This is more positively established from Barani's own text, when he speaks of a Muslim theologian (Shamsuddin Turk), who, coming to India, decided to return to his homeland from Multan, where he 'heard' of 'Ala'uddin Khalji's indifference to religion. And there too he 'heard' of the Sultan's price-control measures.[84] We must assume from this that at Multan one could not directly experience this wonderful phenomenon. The existence of accessible markets not far from Delhi where higher prices prevailed, is shown by the anxiety displayed by the Sultan for preventing high-quality goods being cheaply bought by profiteers at Delhi and then conveyed to those markets.[85]

IV

Even if, as it seems to have been almost certainly the case, the price-regulations affected Delhi and its surrounding region only, these were a unique set of measures; and Barani unhesitatingly gives expression to a sense of awe at this notable administrative achievement. In fact, he put it, as 'a wonder of the age,' at the top of 'Ala'uddin Khalji's successes – even above his conquests and the repeated repulse of the Mongols.[86] Yet, here too, Barani's inherently critical bent of mind does not permit him to see the achievement in the same light as his contemporaries did.

To Amir Khusrau, the measure was an act of immense generosity on the part of the Sultan, undertaken for the sake of 'general comfort, the welfare of the elect and the public at large,' and of 'the general benefit of the city-man and the villager.[87] Ibn Battuta noted how 'the people of Hind' greatly praised 'Ala'uddin Khalji on this account.[88] 'Isami lauded the measures for the relief they gave to 'the people' (*khalq*), and classed their author among those sovereigns who 'grieve for the down-trodden (*zerdastan*) of the world', and 'always are benevolent towards their subjects (*ra'iyat*)'.[89] Nasiruddin Mahmud, the Chishti divine, recounted how Sultan 'Ala'uddin was anxious to do something from which 'gain would accrue to all people (*huma-khalq*); and this was secured through his price-control measures.[90] Barani himself puts into the mouth of Shamsuddin Turk a commendation of 'Ala'uddin Khalji's price-control measures which were 'of benefit to the entire humanity'.[91] Indeed, in his first version Barani wrote that in spite of his cruelties, 'Ala'uddin came to be regarded, owing to his price-control measures, as 'more benevolent and kind than one's own father and mother' by all people except the market-men (*bazaris*).[92]

Barani's own assessment of the benefits flowing from price-control was far more discriminating. The restraint may be seen when, putting the measures at the top among 'Ala'uddin Khalji's achievements, he refrains from expressly styling them a work of general public welfare.[93] This must be surely because his own analysis of their mechanics showed that the low prices did not mean an enhancement of the real income of all; on the contrary, they meant an increase in the real income of some and the diminution of that of many.

First of all, the entire fabric rested on a very heavy agrarian taxation. The peasants, 'from the headman (*khut*) to the menial (*balahar*),' had to part with half the produce;[94] not only that, the tax was to be realized with 'such harshness' (*shiddat*) that the peasants (*ri'aya*) would be forced to sell all the grain and hold back no surplus for stocking, or 'engrossing'[95] This reminds us of a later historian's remarks about the total helplessness of the peasants in the reign of 'Ala'uddin Khalji: Even when the *wali*, Ghilzi Malik, demanded a year's revenue in advance, they could do nothing; for no one could make any 'babble or noise' in the time of that stern Sultan.[96] One day, in 1315, conversation took a turn in the circle of Nizamuddln, the Chishti saint, to the subject of 'those who oppress the people and impose the land-tax (*kharaj* and *jiziya*) and the cess on cultivated fields,[97] – the present tense of the verb 'oppress' may be noted.

Large segments of the upper rural population were also greatly impoverished as they themselves became subject to tax-demand and were forbidden to levy their cesses (*huquq*). No longer could 'the *chaudhuris*, *khuts*, and *muqaddams* ride horses, wield arms, wear good clothes, and chew betel leaf'; even the women of the *khuts* and *muqaddams* had to take service in Muslims' houses.[98] Part of the grain and other rural products, which these classes consumed, must now have gone to Delhi and the other towns in tax payment, and so augmented supplies there.

In so far as the enlarged and continuous stream of supplies to Delhi and the neighbouring towns rested on the enormous deprivation of the countryside, these favoured the city against the village; and so the gain from the fall in prices accrued to the 'city-man' in general, and not to 'the city-man and villager,' as Amir Khusrau claims. The maintenance of low prices, even if under a rough rationing system during bad seasons,[99] made a deep impression on all our authorities. The prevention of the recurring famine conditions in Delhi – a great famine had ravaged it under Jalaluddin Khalji[100] – was certainly a good enough reason for the gratitude felt by the citizens of Delhi towards 'Ala'uddin

Khalji. But within the city, the gain from the low prices was by no means universal. We may leave aside for the moment the 'market-men' viz., the engrossers, the brokers and the like, whose profits were forcibly curtailed by the price regulations.[101] A major section of the population who seems to have had its real income reduced was that of the artisans and the unskilled labourers and servants. This arose partly because, as we have seen, the prices of manufactures came to be fixed as well, so that the income which the artisans obtained by selling then products was sharply reduced. 'Ainu-l Mulk contended that, though grain prices in 'Ala'uddin Khalji's time had not fallen to such low levels as prevailed at the time he was writing (Firuz Shah's reign), the artisans in the earlier reign used to earn far less (2 or 3 *jitals* a day) – indeed, almost one-tenth of what they earned in his own day.[102] Nasiruddin Mahmud recalled that under 'Ala'uddin Khalji, a tailor would charge 4 or 6 *jitals* for preparing a robe, whereas at the time he was speaking – *c.* 1354 – no less than one tanka (48 *jitals*) would be charged.[103] In his first version, Barani says that a tailor was paid 2 *jitals* only under 'Ala'uddin Khalji, as against half a *tanka* that he could get for the same work early in Firuz Shah's reign.[104] Else, here, he says that the 'wages of labourers' in 'Ala'uddin Khalji' time were a fourth of what they came to be under Qutbuddin Mubarak Khalji, and of the servants, one-sixth or one-tenth.[105] Under 'Ala'uddin, there had thus been 'a general lack of money (*bezari*) in the hands of the people'.[106] It is possible that the soldiers fared a little better. Their salaries too were fixed, and Barani's contention, as we shall see, is that the prices were lowered to enable the Sultan to pay lower salaries to soldiers. Barani's statement of the rates of the soldiers' pay in the final version is difficult to understand, and the text may be corrupt.[107] In the first version he says that 'Ala'uddin Khalji gave a cavalryman in salary 200 *tankas* for the *murattab* to provide him 'with weapons, equipage, tent, (draught) animals, a slave, a slave-girl, and one-poled (tent)', and another 78 *tankas* for the *do-aspa* to provide 'equipage, weapons and horse'.[108] This denoted a fair amount of prosperity for the cavalry trooper; and one recalls 'Ala'uddin Khalji's special concern for reducing the prices of horses and slaves.[109]

The greatest advantage from price-control would naturally have come to people who did not suffer from *bezari*, or lack of command over money. At another place Barani tells us that under Sultan 'Ala'uddin, 'things came to such a pass that except for the houses of the nobles (*maliks*) and commanders (*umara*), officials (*kardaran*) and Multanis (merchants) and *sahs* (bankers), little money (*zar*) was to be found anywhere'.[110] It was these classes, then, that stood to gain most from lower prices.

Though the 'market-men' suffered, as Barani tells us repeatedly, the merchant proper had a fairly respectable position in 'Ala'uddin Khalji's system; the Multanis indeed received large treasury loans to encourage them to bring supplies of luxury goods from distant places.[111]

The principal gainers of all must have been the nobles. Their revenues in money should, it is true, have contracted in the Doab and the Trans-Yamuna tract, as the commutation prices were so radically lowered. In terms of purchasing power, of course, this would not have been a contraction. At the same time the treasure already in their possession would have had its purchasing power greatly enhanced. Moreover, the revenues collected outside the limits of the zone where commutation prices had been reduced would be on the old scale, and yet be worth far more in Delhi in terms of goods. The special provision for supply of high-quality cloth at *Sarai 'Adl*, restricted to the nobility and theologians, illustrates the royal concern for the 'welfare' of the nobility.[112] Otherwise, too, the cheap supply of good horses and good slaves, from good-looking boys to ordinary workers,[113] must have been a matter of much satisfaction to this class.

The wealth of the nobility found one of its outlets in generous channels, the establishment of numerous free kitchens (*langars*) in Delhi and its environs, the distribution of free mantles to mendicants (*faqirs*), and the proliferation, as a result, of dervishes.[114] Those were therefore good days for religious men, as the Chishti saint, Nasiruddin would recall tearfully some forty years later.[115] Not surprisingly, under these conditions, there was a notable growth of religious devotion among Muslims that Barani observed as a special feature of the last ten years of 'Ala'uddin Khalji's reign.[116]

V

If we have now gone in our inferences and conclusions a little beyond Barani, the bedrock for them is still his analysis. He was aware that the price-control measures were not a universal boon' more he doubted if the motives in introducing these were purely philanthropic to the way every other contemporary commentator, without exception, has supposed.

Besides the courtier's claim by Amir Khusrau that the entire measure was an exercise in royal generosity,[117] we have the rather circumstantial story told by Nasiruddin in his conversations. Qazi Hamiduddin 'Malikut Tajjar', the Qazi of the Empire under 'Ala'uddin Khalji, once came to Awadh (Ayodhya), and there he invited Nasiruddin along with other guests to dinner. The Qazi recounted how once finding the Sultan deep in thought, he had respectfully sought the reason. The Sultan had replied that he was greatly conscious of God's bounty to him, and wished 'to do something whose benefit may reach all people. This was not easy to do, for even if he distributed his treasure, it would reach few people. So, the Sultan said, he had now hit on the design of cheapening the grain so that all might benefit.[118]

How Barani would have reacted to this obvious piece of public relations on behalf of 'Ala'uddin Khalji by a minister, one can easily conjecture. Qazi Hamiduddin Multani was by no means a favourite of Barani, who in fact regarded the appointment of that Prince of Merchants (*Malikut Tajjar*) to high theological office as a great scandal.[119] That there were many ordinary people who prayed for the Sultan and visited his grave as if he was a saint,[120] was simply proof that there was no end to credulity. How could a bloodthirsty tyrant like 'Ala'uddin Khalji have been a saint, and 'have received revelations and worked miracles'?[121] Barani quite firmly fails to see any sudden conversion of Sultan 'Ala'uddin to the creed of benevolence and social welfare.

At present it is next to impossible to credit or discredit the 'official' thesis of the Sultan's benevolent intentions which has reached us through Amir Khusrau and the *Khairu-l Majalis*.[122] Barani's view was different, and since this too involves a question of intentions as against hard visible facts, it is also difficult to accept or reject it. Nevertheless, as I hope to show presently, it is a very plausible explanation of 'Ala'uddin Khalji's real motives.

As is well known, Barani thought that the price-regulations came as a solution to a critical financial problem. This was caused by the continuous stream of invasions from the Chaghatai Horde in Transoxania. To protect the very heart of his dominions it became necessary for 'Ala'uddin to undertake a vast amount of expenditure. A fortified wall had to be thrown around Delhi; the ruined forts along the routes of the invasions had to be entirely rebuilt; and at several places new forts had to be erected. All forts had to be held by able castellans and provided with *ballistas* and military stores, and stocked with grain. Large armies had to be stationed at Samana and Depalpur. Above all, there had to be kept in readiness a very numerous army of trained cavalry with good horses and remounts (*nek-aspa*). These troopers needed to be paid such large amounts every year as 'to denude the treasury within five or six years'.[123] If the troops were to be employed within the existing resources, without completely draining the treasury, no more than 234 *tankas* could be paid in annual salary (*mawajib*) to the *murattab* or fully equipped soldier, who brought two horses along with all that he needed in the shape of tents, draught animals, slaves, etc., and 78 *tankas* to the *do-aspa*, or horseman with a remount, who was provided with all the equipment and a good horse by the State.[124] But such low payments could be put into effect only if the troops were still able to get all the articles and animals they were required to maintain and also such goods and services as were necessary for the maintenance or subsistence of their families, servants and slaves. The only way to achieve this was to reduce prices.[125]

The first portion of Barani's interpretation may be accepted. The recurring Mongol invasions were a fact, for which Barani may be supplemented by 'Isami. That 'Ala'uddin Khalji was obliged to put a very large amount of money into circulation is indicated by the spurt in the surviving coinage from his reign, which numismatists attribute to 'the enormous quantity of gold and silver' brought from the Deccan. From 1302-3 he issued gold and silver coins from two Delhi mints.[126] Clearly, the numismatic evidence would tend to confirm Barani's statement that 'Ala'uddin Khalji's treasury came under great strain owing to the Mongol invasions. This should make one still more repetitive to Barani's argument that it was mainly in order to check this expenditure without hurting his military resources that 'Ala'uddin Khalji attempted the novel device of forcing down prices.

This reading of 'Ala'uddin Khalji's motives has been censured on the ground, among others, that "Ala'uddin regulated the price of commodities that had no importance for the military".[127] However, as stated by Barani, the chief object was not the cheapening merely of the military stores and horses, but also the reduction of the salaries of cavalrymen and other troopers. This could not be done without reducing the costs of subsistence of the troops and their families, which, in turn, could only be achieved by reducing prices of food grains and manufactured goods needed by them. For the latter purpose, the general wage costs had to be reduced as well; and thus, to be successful in its object, the design required the reduction of prices of all goods whether directly required by the troopers or not.

A more serious objection arises out of a point I have already touched upon in Section II. The sale prices could only be reduced if the commutation prices for revenue purposes were also correspondingly reduced. In that case, the revenue collections would also be smaller. Where was, then, the gain for the Treasury if its income was also reduced along with the fall in prices?

At first sight this might more or less dispose of Barani's theory. But closer scrutiny suggests that the objection ignores the fact that all revenues of the Empire were not reduced by price-control, for, as we have seen, the price-control zone was limited to the region around the capital. Both the revenues and the expenditure were therefore divisible into two portions, (i) R and E being respectively the annual revenue collected and the annual expenditure incurred in the price-control zone, and (ii) Ŕ and É, the annual revenues and expenditure outside the zone. Now, suppose that early in 'Ala'uddin Khalji's reign, excessive expenditure had to be incurred in the area around Delhi, the future price-control zone. Then the revenues from outside of this central zone must flow in to meet the excess expenditure undertaken here. We may hypothetically represent the position as follows:

R	E	Ŕ	É	New Income [(R + Ŕ) - (E + É)]
50	90	50	25	-15

In other words, there would be a contraction of treasure by 15 units of money. Now, if prices were reduced by half in the central zone, R and E would also be reduced by half, while Ŕ and É would remain constant. So we may have:

R	E	Ŕ	É	Net Income
25	45	50	25	+5

The price-control measures could accordingly convert a net drain of 15 units of money per annum into a net gain of 5 units. It follows that price-control in the central zone would help to enlarge treasure, so long as the larger expenditure of the State took place in that zone, while a large part of the revenues was collected outside of it. We can see, then, that Barani's basic argument is theoretically very plausible.

Indeed, it can be conversely demonstrated that, if with changing circumstances, the points where the bulk of the expenditure was incurred began to move away from the central zone, price-control would no longer serve the purpose of maximizing the annual augmentation of the Sultan's treasure. Suppose that, while price-controls continued in the central zone, a large part of funds previously spent there is now spent outside that zone. The figures in our second illustration may, then, alter to:

R	E	Ŕ	É	Net Income
25	20	50	50	+5

R + Ŕ and E + É still equal the respective totals in our second illustration; the annual net inflow into the treasury stays at 5 units. But if the price-controls were now to be abolished, and the prices allowed to double in the central zone, R and E would increase correspondingly. As a result both R Ŕ and E + Ě would increase, but R + Ŕ more than E + É:

R	E	Ŕ	É	Net Income
50	40	50	50	+ 10

The net income would rise to 10 units, i.e. double itself. In other words, it would now be more profitable for the treasury to give up the attempt at price-control, and let R rise at the same pace as the 'free' market prices.[128]

It may, therefore, be that the abandonment of price-controls under 'Ala'uddin Khalji's successors partly derived from the shift in the main theatres of military and other expenditure. With the Mongols no longer a threat, beginning with the reign of Qutbuddin Mubarak Shah (1316-20),[129] the price-control policy could be scrapped – as, in fact, happened during that reign.[130] This is not to say that other factors, such as lack of administrative cohesion and the personal qualities of the succeeding Sultans, did not play a part in making the history of price-controls a short one. But the interest in treasure acquisition (which had also motivated 'Ala'uddin Khalji) should certainly have dictated, in the changed circumstances, a dismantling of the price-controls.

NOTES

1. *Ta'rikh-i Firuz-Shahi*, Saiyid Ahmad Khan, ed. W.N. Lees and Kabiruddin, (Calcutta: Bib. Ind., 1860-2). All my references under 'Barani' are to this edition. The portion dealing with prices appears on pp. 303-19. In S.A. Rashid's edition, vol. 11 (not formally published), the portion runs from p. 134 to p. 150. I have compared the two printed texts at important points with India Office MS 1.0.177177 (Ethe 211), transcribed in AH 1007/AD 1599 (microfilm in the Department of History, Aligarh).
2. Moreland 1929, 16.
3. Habib and Nizami 1940, 377. The chapter, 'Economic Regulations of 'Ala'uddin Khalji' (pp. 372-91), is credited to the late Professor B.P. Saxena, but has marks of considerable editorial revision by Professor Habib.
4. Digby 1971, 36n..
5. Khusrau 1853, text, 16-17, 20-3, for price-control measures; see 166 for the last date, Jumada II, 711 (=18 October 1311) in the text.
6. Ibn Battuta 1964, 429-30 and 1976, 41-2. Ibn Battuta dictated the account of his travels in 1355 (text, 701).
7. Isami 1948, 313-15; see also verses on 301, 605. This work is henceforth cited by the author's name, 'Isami.

8. *Khairu-l Majalis*, 1959, 185, 240-2.
9. Barani, 535.
10. Digby possesses in his collection (MS 57) a copy of the earlier version, and I am indebted to him for supplying me much information on this version. The version is also contained in the Bodleian Library, Elliot 353 (microfilm in the Department of History, Aligarh). I have used the latter MS, in which the portion relating to 'Ala'uddin Khalji's price-control measures occupies ff. 143a-44b. Since Digby 1982, 26n has promised to offer a detailed study comparing the two versions, I have refrained from entering into a detailed discussion of the significance of the first version.
11. Compare grain prices in Barani, 305, with those in Elliot 353, f. 144a. In Elliot 353, rice is omitted, and gram is rated at 4 *jitals* per *man* instead of 5. Prices of sugar, ghee and sesame oil in Barani, 310, may be compared with those in Elliot 353, f. 144a; the divergence is more marked here.
12. *Khairu-l Majalis*, 185. On 241, however, the divine says the price of 'grain' had come down to '7 *jitals* per *man*'. For *shakar-tari*, as meaning white sugar, see Tek Chand 1866, s.v. I take *diram* to be a synonym for *jital*.
13. Barani, 305, 310. MS 1.0.177/Ethe 211, however, reads one *jital* instead of 1½ *jital* for the price of 3 *sers* of red sugar; so also S.A. Rashid's text, 140.
14. Elliot 353, f. 144a.
15. Barani, 305-6, 308.
16. Khusrau 1853, 21.
17. Ibn Battuta 1964, 430; idem 1976, 42.
18. Isami 1948, 314.
19. Barani, 306-7.
20. *Khairu-l Majalis*, 241.
21. Barani, 309-16; the account of *Sarai 'Adl* is on 309-12.
22. Khusrau 1853, 21, 23.
23. Ibn Battuta 1964, 340; idem 1976, 41.
24. *Khairu-l Majalis*, 240.
25. Barani, 311.
26. Ibn Battuta 1964, 430; idem 1976, 41.
27. Barani, 385. Similar statements occur in the first version, Elliot 353, f. 144h, but the comparison is made with conditions at the time of writing (i.e. the early years of Firuz Shah's reign).
28. *Khairu-l Majalis*, 240.
29. Mahru 1965, 48.
30. Barani, 316-17.
31. Khusrau 1853, 16.
32. Ibn Battuta 1964, 429-30, idem 1976, 41.
33. Barani, 318-19.
34. Khusrau 1853, 16-17.
35. Barani, 308.
36. Barani, 316.

37. Ibn Battuta 1964, 429-30, idem 1976, 41.
38. Isami 1948, 315.
39. Khusrau 1853, 21.; Ibn Battuta 1964, 430, idem 1976, 42; 'Isami 1948, 314.
40. *Khairu-l Majalis* 1959, 241, Ibn Battuta 1964, 430, Idem 1976, 41.
41. Of the four causes of the success of 'Ala'uddin Khalji's price-control measures, Barani puts, as the second, 'the heavy magnitude of the land-tax (*kharaj-ha*)' (Barani, 321).
42. Barani, 288. The term *wafa* is explained by its use in 'Afif 1891, 180, as pointed out by Moreland 1929, 226. See Raychaudhuri andHabib 1982, 61-2, for 'Ala'uddin Khalji's taxation measures.
43. Barani, 288.
44. Barani, 287, 288, 291.
45. Barani, 288.
46. In the text '*Miyan-i Doab*,' 'Between the Two Rivers'. Wherever the name Doab appears in the passages translated by me, it should be assumed that the name in the original is *Miyan-i Doab*, meaning the land between the Ganga and the Yamuna.
47. *Shahr-i Nau*. According to 'Isami 1948, 271 (also 273), this was the name given to Chha'in, the famous town near Ranthambhor. Barani tends to confirm this when he says that after Ulugh Khan (who held Chha'in and Ranthambhor) died, he was succeeded in *Shahr-i Nau* by Malik 'Izzuddin Buraja (299). He adds that 'the land-tax in the New City (*Shahr-i Nau*) was exacted in the same manner as in the Environs of the City (Delhi) by measurement and (application of) crop rate per *biswa*'. This statement has obvious relevance here. For the identification of Chha'in, see Gupta 1975.
48. I follow 1.O. MS Ethe 211, ff. 198b-199a, and S.A. Rashid, text, 136, in reading *wa ham* instead of *wa huma* ('and all') as in the *Bib. Ind.* text.
49. Barani, 305-6.
50. I follow Ethe 211, f. 199a. The *Bib. Ind.* text (as well as Rashid) reads *wilayat*, country. Since the *wali* was another name for *muqti*, the word *walayat* (as distinct from wilayat in the singular) could well mean the *walis* or revenue assignees' territorial jurisdictions.
51. Ethe 211, f. 199b (supported by Rashid) reads *walayat* while *Bib. Ind.* text again has wilayat. See preceding note.
52. Barani, 307 (Rashid, 138).
53. Barani, 312.
54. Habib and Nizami 1940, 389.
55. Afif 1891, 37-8.
56. Barani, 323-4.
57. Barani, 324.
58. Barani, 304.
59. Barani, 395. The first version (Elliot 353, f. 144b) records still lower pay for the *chakar*, 'eight *tankas*, at most ten or twelve *tankas*'.
60. Mahru 1965, 48.

61. Barani, 316.
62. Khusrau 1853, 16.
63. Barani, 312: The comment on this argument in Habib and Nizami 1940, 391n, is perhaps unjustifiably harsh on Barani.
64. Barani, 311.
65. Barani 313. His earlier version contains references to the *daryai* (imported, sea-borne) and *baladasti* (Central Asian) horses sold at the controlled horse-market established by 'Ala'uddin Khalji (Digby 1971, 38-9).
66. For these various measures the entire account in Barani on 309-19 needs to be read. The harshness employed in putting them into effect is so firmly a part of current text-book history that one need not use up space in reproducing the details here.
67. Barani, 305 ff
68. Barani, 306.
69. Barani, 308.
70. Barani, 309.
71. Barani, 310-11.
72. Barani, 311.
73. Khusrau 1853, 20-2.
74. Ibn Battuta 1964, 429-30, idem 1976, 41-2.
75. Isami 1948, 315.
76. *Khairu-l Majalis* 1959, 185, 241.
77. Mahru 1965, 48.
78. Firishta 1874, 112.
79. Habib and Nizami 1940, 388.
80. Barani, 323-4.
81. *Fawa'idu-l Fu'ad* 1966,195 (meeting, 8 April 1314). Amir Hasan, who was a military officer, said that he now lived in the *Lashkar*, where he had obtained a house, and went to the City only once in 10 or 12 days. For the *Lashkargah* at Siri, see ibid., 311 (8 February 1318). See Athar Ali 1981, 11-12.
82. Khusrau 1853, 21.
83. Barani, 288.
84. Barani, 298.
85. See, especially, Barani, 311-12. The goods in *Sarai 'Adl* were not to be sold to merchants (*saudagar*) (p. 311). Further: The *Ra'is* gave permits (*parwanas*) for (purchase of) fine cloth to the commanders, nobles, great men and divines according to his knowledge of their circumstances of life; and if he knew that the person was not a merchant and (yet) wished to purchase cloth at the *Sarai 'Adl* at cheap rates and then sell to others taking it to other parts at a price four or five times the price at *Sarai 'Adl*, he would not give him the permit.
86. Barani, 339.
87. Khusrau 1853, 21.
88. Ibn Battuta 1964, 429, 1976, 41.

89. 'Isami 1948, 314-15.
90. *Khairu-l Majalis*, 1959, 241.
91. Barani, 298.
92. Elliot 353, f. 144b.
93. Barani, 339 ('cheapness of grain, goods and means of subsistence').
94. Barani, 287.
95. Barani, 307.
96. Afif 1891, 57-8.
97. *Fawaidu-l Fu'ad* 1966, 232. For the *jiziya* coupled with *kharaj* as signifying the single land-tax, see Raychaudhuri and Habib 1982, 61.
98. Barani, 287-8.
99. Barani, 308-9.
100. 'Isami 1948, 217-21; Barani, 212. Barani says grain then sold for 1 *jital* per *ser* or 40 *jitals* to the *man*.
101. Cf. Barani, 298, 312 ff., 340-1, 343. For the jubilation of the *bazaris* after the death of 'Ala'uddin Khalji, see Barani, 385.
102. Mahru 1965, 48.
103. *Khairu-l Majalis*, 1959, 42.
104. Elliot 353, f. 144b.
105. Barani, 385-6.
106. Barani, 312.
107. Barani, 303 (Rashid, 134). The text reads differently in Ethe 211, f. 194a; it omits all reference to *yak-aspa*, and is conformable in sense to the corresponding passage in the first version, but is much briefer.
108. Elliot 353, f. 143a. *Yak-chobi*, 'one-poled (tent)' may signify an umbrella as well.
109. Barani, 313-15.
110. Barani, 283-4.
111. Barani, 311.
112. Barani, 311-12.
113. Barani, 313-15.
114. *Khairu-l Majalis* 1959, 185, 240-2.
115. *Khairu-l Majalis* 1959, 185.
116. Barani, 341, ff.
117. Khusrau 1853, 20-1.
118. *Khairu-l Majalis* 1959, 241.
119. Barani, 298-9, 352.
120. *Khairu-l Majalis* 1959, 241-2; Barani's own first version, Elliot 353, f. 144b.
121. Barani, 265.
122. For an almost total acceptance of this version, see Habib and Nizami 1940, 373-9.
123. Barani, 303-4.
124. I give this interpretation of the text on the basis of Barani's first version (Elliot 353, f. 143a) read alongside his final version as in Ethe 211, f. 194a.

As noted earlier, the printed text (Barani, 303; Rashid, 134) is corrupt and the basis it offers for fixation of salary is difficult to understand. However, it should be noted that Elliot 353 reads 200 for 234, and Ethe 211 has 88 for 78 *tankas*.

125. Barani, 304. Barani offers the same motive for reduction of prices in the first version (Elliot 353, f. 143a), but much more briefly.
126. Wright 1936, 107-8.
127. Habib and Nizami 1940, 272.
128. One other possible argument may be that a low-price zone should have attracted bullion inflow from other areas so that in course of time the maintenance of low prices would become increasingly difficult. But this could only happen if (a) the price-differences between the zones were larger than transport costs for basic wage-goods like food grains; and (b) there was free trade. Neither conditions would seem to have existed. That large inter-regional price differences existed before the railways may be seen from the maps of average wheat and gram prices, 1861-70, in Khan 1978, 343, 348. Bullion movements did not bring about any price-equalization here.
129. Barani, 387. An alarm over a possible Mongol raid is, however, referred to in *Fawa'idu-l Fu'ad* 1966, 373 (conversation of 24 October 1319); it had led to a rise in prices, but this had by then abated. (Read *girani* for *nigrani* in the printed text.)
130. Barani, 384-5.

6

Structure and Movement of Wages in the Mughal Empire, 1500-1700

NAJAF HAIDER

This chapter explores four institutional factors which went into the making of the wage structure in the Mughal Empire. Focusing on the relationship between monetization, patterns of currency circulation and wage payments, it also raises historiographical issues crucial to the understanding of the over-time movement of money wages in the sixteenth and seventeenth centuries. It must be admitted that quantitative data on wages, prices, money supply and income are extremely limited and fragmentary for the whole of medieval India (1200-1800). It is only from the middle of the nineteenth century (1861) that one begins to get an unbroken statistical series on prices and wages. This explains the short treatment the subject has received in current historiography. However, there is sufficient evidence – some of it fresh – to commence an investigation into the process of wage determination and payment and to offer new interpretations for existing material.

The Mughal Empire was carved out of a number of regional states of India through the conquests and political alliances of the Timurid prince, Babur (1526-30), and his successors, notably his grandson, Akbar (1556-1605). Akbar was responsible also for giving shape to the administrative, fiscal and monetary institutions of the Empire. As a result of these efforts, the Mughal Empire expanded to include 100 million out of 145 million people estimated to have lived in India at the turn of the seventeenth century.[1] At that point in time, the estimated Gross National Product of the Empire stood at 542 million rupees (1 rupee = 11.42 grams of fine silver), of which the shares of the primary (agriculture and ancillary sectors), secondary (value added by manufactures) and tertiary (service) sectors were 66, 11 and 23 per cent respectively.[2] Agriculture was generally practised by individual peasants, some of whom possessed large fields, raised crops for the market and employed wage labourers. A large portion of the agricultural produce (often amounting to half its value) was claimed by the state in land revenue (*mal*) and commuted into cash to support the military and civil apparatuses of the Empire. Food grains and raw materials sold by the village to meet its tax obligations fulfilled the requirements of the urban society and economy. The urban economy was sustained by a large craft and service sector which generated a good deal of employment owing to low productivity and the luxurious lifestyle of the ruling classes.[3] The towns also became major centres for the supply of export goods by sea and land to the markets of the Middle East, Africa and Europe in the West and South-East Asia, China, Japan and the Philippines in the East. Returning ships and caravans usually brought foreign currencies or un-coined metal to reinforce the circulating medium and commence fresh cycles of exchange.[4]

No estimates are available for the size and composition of the workforce employed in the agricultural, industrial and service sectors, but there is sufficient evidence to suggest that wage labour existed in all three. Almost a quarter of the rural population (which made up an estimated 85 per cent of the total) was prevented from taking up cultivation as peasants by their caste status as menials and untouchables in order that they could be hired as wage labourers.[5] In the industrial sector, wage labourers were particularly concentrated in building construction and mining.[6] Although Mughal artisans were essentially independent producers, owning their equipment and raw materials, those who produced expensive craft products often worked as wage earners in the manufactories (*karkhanas*) established by kings, nobles and big merchants.[7] The same employers also hired a whole range of ordinary and skilled labourers in military and civil establishments in different capacities.

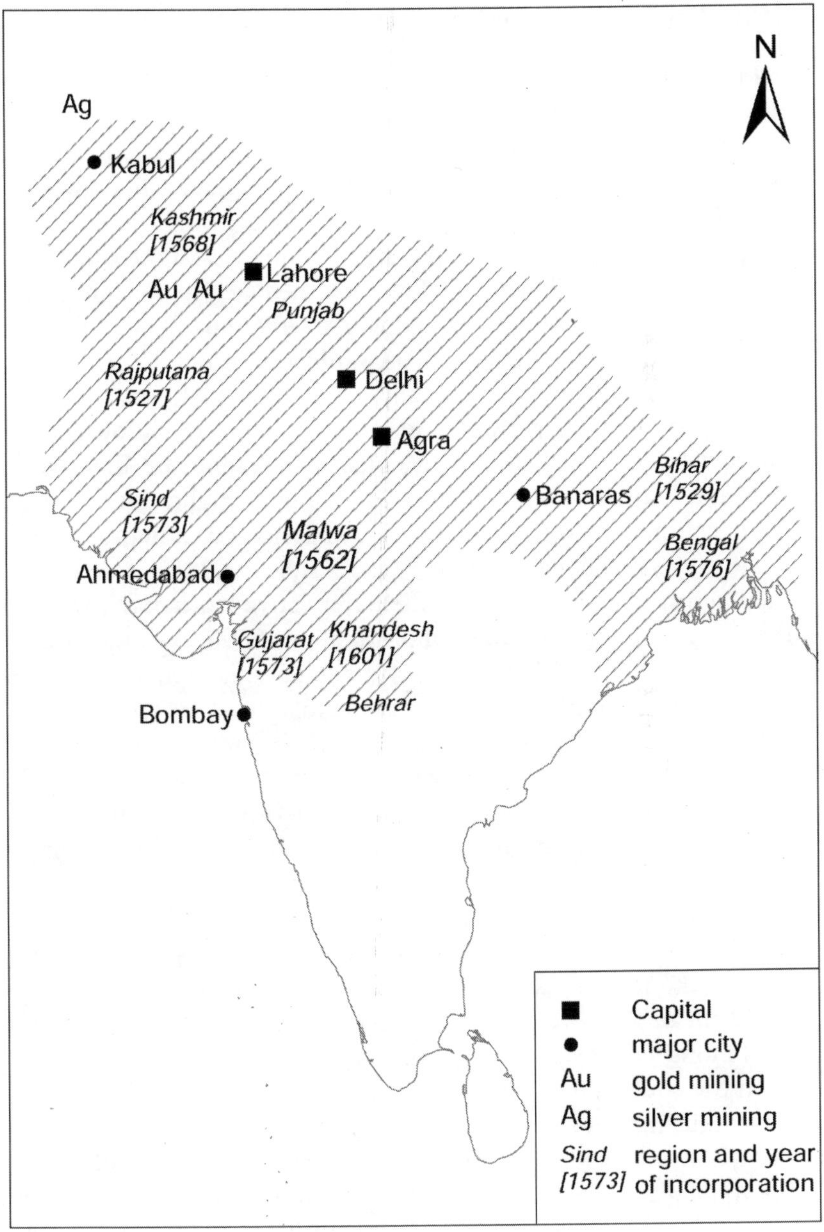

MAP 6.1. THE MUGHAL EMPIRE, 1526-1605

Time, Skill and Wage Formation

Paid in any form – benefits, commodity or money – wages represent the price of labour transacted at a given level of the market. The first and foremost components of the wage structure are time and skill. In any society free from servitude, a participant in a process (productive or otherwise) where labour is expended is entitled to receive something in return. The return may assume different forms but is generally reckoned by the time taken to conclude the labour process. In Mughal India, wages were mostly determined by taking the day, month or season as units of time.

In diurnal chronology, the day was reckoned from dawn to dusk. Francisco Pelsaert, a Dutch factor, who closely observed production and exchange in Mughal India, reported that artisans and craftsmen worked from 'morning to night'.[8] Describing the duration of time for which skilled artisans stayed in organized workshops (*karkhanas*), a Frenchman residing in India noted that they 'repair every morning to their respective kar-kanays, where they remained employed the whole day; and in the evening return to their homes. In their quiet and regular manner, their time glides away'.[9] No information has come to light so far on quantifiable working hours or the length of day in different seasons which formed the basis for fixing wages.

The month was either the Indian or Islamic lunar month of 29 days or the Persian solar month of 30 and 31 days.[10] According to one report, monthly wages of the servants in the Dutch factory at Agra were paid on the day of the 'new moon'.[11] Pelsaert is once again our authority for his statement that 'most of the great lords reckoned 40 days to the month' for paying wages.[12] This could mean that even though wages fell due on the first day of each month, they were paid on the tenth.

In the countryside, village officials and servants received their wages during harvest cycles of varying length (with their peak and slack seasons).[13] Although the salaries of Mughal officials (*mansabdars*) were fixed monthly, the bulk was paid during harvest seasons. This was because the majority of *mansabdars* were paid, except during 1575-81, with revenue assignments (*jagirs*), which required them to collect all the taxes stipulated by the state (mainly land revenue), keep the amount equivalent to their salaries and remit the balance to the exchequer. A small number of the *mansabdars*, especially those who received lower salaries, was paid in cash (*naqd*) directly by the exchequer every month of the year.[14]

There was no practice of paying weekly or fortnightly wages in medieval India. Piece wages were paid, as in the mint (Table 6.1) or in building construction by the amount of work done within an agreed period of time.[15] In the countryside, potters, tanners, and carpenters received piece wages for making cooking utensils, shoes and dishes of leaves used for dining. Potters were paid by the size of the dish, tanner by the quality of the shoes and the carpenter by tale where all items were of uniform quality.[16]

The reckoning of time for wage payments became complex when a particular skill was required to perform a piece of work. This was reflected in the wage differentials within the same sector as well as between different sectors at any one time (Tables 6.1 and 6.2).

TABLE 6.1: PIECE WAGES PAID IN THE MINT (*c.* 1595)

Category of Wage Earners	*Wages paid in dams for crafting 1000 coins of:*		
	Gold	*Silver*	*Copper*
	(169 grains/ 10.95 grams)	*(178 grains/ 11.54 grams)*	*(323 grains/ 20.93 grams)*
Blank-cutter (*zarrab*)	210.05	53.44	20.00
Silver smelter-assayer (*sabbak*)		54.00	
Weigher (*waznkash*)	17.50	6.76	0.44
Coiner and hammerer (*sikkachi* and *patakchi*)	14.00	5.38	3.00

Note: The hammerer received 1/6 of the total paid to the coiner.
Source: Abul Fazl 1872, *Ain i Akbari*, I, 16-18.

It is difficult to compare the figures in Tables 6.1 and 7.1 for the reason that we do not know the daily workload of a mint artisan. Unless we know the daily output of the mint, the size of the workforce in each department as well as the number of shifts, piece wages paid in this sector cannot be compared with time wages paid in another. Something, however, can be said about how skills were taken into account by employers when formulating payments. The higher wages paid to the blank-cutter were due to the delicate nature of his job which demanded exactitude, as all blanks had to be cut with shears to an equal size and weight (*kamil ul wazn*). Coin specimens preserved in museum and private collections betray advancing a margin for wear and tear, and tolerance (sanctioned deviation from the mint standard) a high degree of uniformity in weight, size and shape within a single series. In the case of precious metals, greater precision and time were also required to weigh the blanks on a fine balance. Compared to the silver weigher, the workload of the gold weigher for one thousand coins was higher because gold was weighed in smaller batches. Similarly, the job of the coiner was to fix and align the dies (Mughal dies were not pegged), place the blanks between them, examine the impressions formed on the obverse and the reverse, and prevent slipping, over-striking and cracking of the edges of the coin. In addition, he was required to provide the hammer and supervise the repair of the upper and lower dies. The operation demanded more skill and responsibility than the hammerer whose job was to strike the blow with measured strength at the instruction of the coiner. Thus, no separate allowance was made for the hammerer at the mint and he received a share of the wages paid to his superior partner.[17]

Wage Payment in Subsistence and Monetized Economies

Just as the circulation of commodities is facilitated by the availability of an efficient medium of exchange, wage payments too become increasingly frequent with the widening use of money. Once the wage sector is monetized, changes in currency circulation and prices begin to impinge on wage movements and income distribution.

Medieval Indian society is often characterized by the co-existence of two domains of economic activities: one of subsistence production in the village where the role of money is generally understood to be marginal and exchange was based on a socially established network of reciprocal obligations, and the other of a monetized economy where market relations of exchange prevailed. In the subsistence-oriented economy, payments were made to village workers and artisans from a common pool or on an individual household basis, though the forms they took are difficult to identify, as there was never any formal conceptualization of such payments as wages. Many artisans held revenue-free lands granted to them by the village community in lieu of the services they performed.[18] It is likely that the revenue due to the state on artisanal holdings constituted their wages. If this were the case, the state might have subsidized the costs of wage labour in the countryside by granting revenue concessions on land held by the village community for such purposes. Micro-level research on the identification and computation of rural wages will not only establish the incomes of the rural classes with greater certainty but improve our understanding of village economic organization (hitherto ascribed to the realm of autarchy and self-sufficiency) and the triangular relationship between the state, village community and rural labour market.

It is quite difficult to date the introduction of cash payments in village societies. At some point, services were indeed bartered and obligations were fixed and settled in kind or via the distribution of rights for the use of village resources, creating the impression of a 'natural economy'. Such practices continued in varying degrees even after the partial monetization of the village economy. In the absence of detailed micro studies of the different regions of the Mughal Empire, one cannot possibly fix a chronology for the transition from barter to monetized exchange and its impact on wage payments. We have, however, clear evidence that in the sixteenth and seventeenth centuries, the monetized sector of the Mughal Empire expanded at the expense of the non-monetized sector.

In those regions of the Mughal Empire which fell within the monetized sector and where there was greater contact between the market and the countryside, payments made to agricultural labourers and village officials were expressed and disbursed in cash. Village-level documents of the seventeenth century show entries in account books relating to cash payments made to officials and a money changer (*sarraf*). The peripatetic French jeweller, Jean Baptiste Tavernier, says that a village in India may indeed be very small if it had no money changer (*c.* 1666).[19] The presence of the *sarraf* suggests that the village community was drawn into the vortex of monetary economy by the seventeenth century and was familiar with the conception of exchange rates.

The Monetization of the Indian Economy

If we take a long-term view of the history of pre-modern India, three broad cycles of monetary movements can be discerned. The Indus civilization (2500-1500 BC) had no regular coinage and measures of grain or units of precious objects (gold, silver, cornelian, agate, etc.) were used as money to conduct local and long-distance exchange.[20] The Vedic Aryans (1500-700 BC) generally counted their wealth in cows, camels, horses and slaves, although there is evidence of the use of unstamped gold and silver pieces of different units (*pada*) and ornaments (*nishka*) for exchange.[21] The first cycle began with the circulation of silver 'punch-marked' coins (sixth century BC) on the eve of the rise of Buddhism and a 'second urban revolution', and reached its high point with the extensive use of gold and copper currencies in the Kushana and Gupta periods (first century to sixth century).[22] The cycle came to an end following a decline in the exchange network and commerce under the phase of 'Indian feudalism' (500-1000), in which gold coinage practically disappeared, silver money became rare and copper currency circulated on a moderate scale.[23]

The second cycle started with a gradual reorganization and expansion of the monetary economy in early medieval India (eleventh century), with the revival of urbanization and foreign trade, and subsequently the introduction of monetary and fiscal institutions from Central Asia.[24] The establishment of the Delhi Sultanate in the thirteenth century brought about a perceptible change in the production and circulation of money through a standardized multi-metallic currency system of gold and silver *tankas*, billon *jital* (base metal mixed with silver) and copper *paika*. The silver *tanka* (169.8 grains), and its fraction (half a *tanka*), was employed in higher value transactions, such as the purchase of horses, slaves, concubines and textiles, payment of servants' wages (fixed annually), payment of piece wages of a skilled craftsman, or money given out in charity. The gold *tankas* were minted in limited quantities to be used for high-value exchanges, gifts and imperial and elite hoardings.[25]

Most cash transactions below the value of a half *tanka* were conducted in a series of billon coins minted by the Delhi Sultans which were known by the generic name of *jital* (gross weight 56.61 grains). The prices of essential commodities, such as grain or garments and the daily wages of labourers and artisans were quoted and paid in *jitals*. From the mid-thirteenth century, the silver content of each *jital* was expressed in a unit called *gani* (2.83 grains), sixty of which could be exchanged for 1 *tanka*.[26]

In the copper currency sector, the heaviest coin of the early Sultans weighed 72 grains and was known by the popular designation of *paika* with its half called *adhva*.[27] The weight of the *paika* was meant to be equivalent to a quarter of the billon *jital* of 1 *gani*. Although the rate was susceptible to changes in the bi-metallic ratio, it was maintained for a considerable period of time. References to this coin in Persian literature are so few that it appears that either the *jitals* of lower values completely dominated the domain of petty transactions or the authors of historical works were far removed from the milieu in which copper coins were used on a regular basis.

A prolonged international crisis of silver from about the middle of the fourteenth century and the inability of the hinterland economies of the Sultanate to draw precious metals from the relatively rich currency regimes of the coasts brought the second cycle to an end.[28] Silver and gold were replaced by billon and copper coins, which became the principal media of exchange till the middle of the sixteenth century. The most remarkable sign of the downturn was the progressive debasement of the silver *tanka* to a point where it practically became a copper coin with a streak of silver and earned the designation *tanka i siyah* (black *tanka*).[29]

In the early stages of the final cycle, the currency system of the Mughal Empire represented the continuation of the billon-copper regime of the late Delhi Sultans. A new tri-metallic currency of pure metals was established in the wake of a series of developments within and outside India. The most important external development was the eastward transmission of European silver obtained from the mines of Peru and Mexico (Spanish colonies in America) to finance the Indian Ocean trade. With an annual supply ranging between 85 and 131 metric tons of silver, the Mughal Empire became the biggest importer of foreign bullion outside Europe in the late sixteenth as well as seventeenth century.[30] Estimates available for Ming China, a major recipient of foreign bullion in Asia, suggest an annual import of 43 to 46 metric tons of silver in the second half of the sixteenth century almost one third of the estimated figures we have for the Mughal Empire.[31]

At the same time that Spanish-American silver was on its outward journey to India, the Mughal Empire expanded westwards to embrace the coastal regions of Gujarat and Sind, which were direct recipients of foreign bullion not only from Europe but also Japan. In the second half of the seventeenth century, Bengal emerged as a major destination for the transmission of precious metals by the Dutch (VOC) and English East India Companies. The territorial expansion of the Mughal Empire created conditions for the integration of coastal hinterlands into a single network of commodity exchange, fiscal remittances and currency circulation.

The absorption of external and internal stocks of monetary metals was facilitated by the state and the market. The Mughal state adopted fiscal and monetary policies which streamlined and expanded currency circulation in the Empire. A policy of collecting taxes and disbursing salaries in cash was pursued to trigger a cycle of monetary circulation. In addition, a series of measures was taken from 1582 to create a standardized currency system through the replacement of regional as well as old and sub-standard coins with freshly minted Mughal currency.[32]

The Mughal mints were an important instrument of currency supply and control and operated in the major commercial and administrative centres of the Empire. The mints worked on the principle of open coinage which entitled the supplier of monetary metal and demonetized specie to receive freshly minted coins (in the same metal) on payment of brassage and seigniorage (mint charges). The mint price of the monetary metal (number of coins delivered by the mint) was always higher than its market price since the *sarrafs* (buyers for the mint cum money changers) charged commission on the sale of currencies. In the latter half of the sixteenth century, mint charges for coining rupees out of fine silver were a little over 5 per cent of the total output. The same coins were sold in the market at 6.5 per cent over and above their weight in fine silver. The cost of striking copper into *dams* was a little over 9 per cent of the total output, whereas its market price was 15 per cent. Since both rupees and *dams* circulated at a premium which was made up entirely of their costs (mint charges and commissions), their exchange rates were determined by the market. Whenever the demand for a currency outstripped its supply, the state took steps to expand mint production by cutting down or abolishing seigniorage and directing sales of monetary metals exclusively to the mint.[33]

Money changers and merchants offered a certain uniformity and cohesion to the areas covered by the network of monetized exchange by negotiating the movement of cash, goods and services across customs barriers and between different sectors of the economy through *commenda*, money changing (*sayrafi*), deposit banking, respondentia (*avak*), bills of exchange (*hundi*), commercial usury, and inland and marine insurance (*bima*).[34] The uniform and standardized currency system which emerged after three decades of intensive administrative and market changes was sustained by a constant flow of silver through foreign trade and its absorption into the circuit of exchange.

What impact did monetization, mint production and currency circulation have on the form of wage payments? With an increase in monetary circulation, it is logical to assume that wages took on money form on a bigger scale than before. This phenomenon is borne out by scattered references to money wages in Persian and European sources (Tables 6.1-6.4, 6.6-6.7). More specifically,

TABLE 6.2: MONTHLY WAGES PAID TO THE SERVANTS OF THE DUTCH FACTORY AT AGRA, 1637

Category of Employees	*Wages in Rupees*
Washerman	5.0
Groom	4.5
Servant of chief factor, Geleynssen de Jongh	4.5
Torchbearer	4.0
Servant of factor, Barents	3.5
Chariot driver	3.5
Gatekeeper	3.5
Peons (each)	3.5
Luggage boy of Geleynssen de Jongh	2.5
Keeper of the graveyard	2.0
Writer of letters in Persian	0.5
Barber	0.5

Source: Geleynssen de Jongh, NA 123.

the expansion of the monetized wage sector was precipitated by certain changes which took place in the pattern of currency circulation in the sixteenth century.

An important aspect of the monetization of the Mughal economy was the substitution of copper by silver from the second half of the sixteenth century in revenue and salary payments and in market transactions.[35] This was largely due to the heavy imports of silver, policies of the state, and the higher cost of production of copper which restricted currency circulation to areas lying closer to mines.[36] In such circumstances, it is likely that employers were encouraged to pay monthly wages in silver (Tables 6.2 and 6.3). Numismatic evidence suggests that there was a fall in the number of copper mints as well as the output of each individual mint in the seventeenth century.[37] However, copper currency did not disappear completely from the monetary scene even though an unknown portion of it was demonetized and fractional silver money (the *anna* or $\frac{1}{16}$ of a rupee) made inroads into the domain

TABLE 6.3 MONTHLY WAGES OF PEONS AND DOMESTIC SERVANTS, 1613-89, EXPRESSED IN SILVER

Year	*Place*	*Category of Wage Earners*	*Wages in Rupees*
1613	Agra	Lowest wage (Imperial Establishment)	3.00
1616	Surat	Domestic Servant	2.66
1622	Agra	Peon	4.00 *
1623	Surat	Domestic Servant	3.00 **
1623	Agra	Porter	4.00
1626	Agra	Domestic Servant	3.00-4.00
1634	Surat	Peon	2.22-3.11
1636	Surat	Peon	3.55-4.44 +
1636	Ahmedabad	Peon	3.55-4.44 +
1637	Agra	Peon	3.00-3.50
1659	Ahmedabad	Peon	4.00
1689	Surat	Peon	4.00

Note: * Rate quoted as 'high'; ** with food and clothing; + years of famine;
For rates quoted in mahmudis, the exchange rate was 1 rupee = 2.25 mahmudis.
Sources: Hawkins 1921, 99; Foster 1928, 66; Foster 1908, Vol. 2, 94, 222; Foster 1911, Vol. 5, 151; Grey 1882, I, 42; Pelsaert 1925, 62; Geleynssen de Jongh, NA 123; *Factory Records, Miscellaneous, Oriental and India Office Collection (OIOC)*, series G/36, Vol. 3, folio 133; Ovington 1929, 229.

of petty transactions. Usage of the principal copper coin of the Mughal Empire (*dam*) was retained and even expanded in areas where wages and salaries had to be paid in small amounts (Table 6.4). In 1611, an Englishman travelling from Surat to Agra met with a 'caravan of pisas [*dams*], bound for Baremporte [Burhanpur] to paye the soldiers, with a guard of 100 horses for feare of robbinge'.[38] A few years later, the state imposed a ban on the demonetization of copper coins to discourage the export of the raw metal to Iran where it fetched higher prices.[39] In the 1660s, a drop in the supply of copper created a crisis of small change in different parts of the Mughal Empire (see below).

The reasons for the survival of copper can only be speculated. Before the influx of international silver altered the monetary land-

TABLE 6.4: DAILY WAGES PAID IN COPPER

Year	*Place*	*Category of Wage Earners*	*Wages*
1572	Jaunpur	Labourers and Masons	Paid in *dams*
1626	Agra	Skilled Labourers	10-12 *dams*
1661	Surat	Ship Carpenters and Labourers	Paid in *dams*
1663	Surat	'Stewards'	Paid in *dams*
1666	Ahmedabad	Labourers	Paid in *dams*

Sources: Ilahabadi 1878, 108; Pelsaert 1925, 60; 'The parwana (order) of Raja Ragunath' [1661] *Biblioteca Apostolica Vaticana, Vatican, MS. Persiano* 33 (Unfoliated); Khan 1927, I, 267, 277-8; Foster 1922, Vol. 11, 121.

scape of the late Sultanate and early Mughal India, the dominant exchange media consisted of billon and copper coins at the higher echelons and fractional pieces and non-metallic currencies (cowrie shells and bitter almonds) at the lowest levels of the market.[40] With the coming first of gold (1500-50) and then silver (1550-1700), the top and middle layers of exchange came to be occupied by the two precious metals.[41] When the billon coin was withdrawn from circulation (the Mughal monetary authorities instituted a strict regime of purity), a greater demand for copper money was created at a time when the size of the wage-earning population was growing and a shift was taking place from kind to cash payments.

Money of Account, Currency Exchange and Wage Payment

Within the general framework of monetization, it is important to identify the relationship between the currency in which wages were fixed and the one in which payments were made. It is quite possible that wages calculated on a daily basis were either paid at the end of the day's work in one currency or were accumulated and paid after a month in another. Conversely, monthly wages stated in silver could be disbursed on a daily basis in copper money at the current rate of exchange if such money was plentiful. Disaggregating currency denominations would offer us an entry point into an interesting area of monetary history yet to receive scholarly attention, viz., the triangular relationship between currency denominations, rates of exchange and wage payments.

In mono-metallic currency systems, payments were made and accounts were kept in multiple units of a single coin which have constant values. In a multi-metallic currency economy, such as that of Mughal India, currencies of differing values co-existed and competed with one another to carve discrete spheres of usage in a complex network of exchange. Such a system had to cope inevitably with the problem of value relation and exchange in a market where the prices of currency metals were determined by supply and demand. One possible way was to adopt a stable currency as the standard of valuation in a given region, sector or time period and make necessary adjustments in accordance with fluctuations in the market.

In order to facilitate the transition from a billon and copper regime of the late Delhi Sultans to a tri-metallic system, with silver as the predominant metal, the Mughal chancery created a money of account called *tanka i muradi* (or simply *tanka*) which had a fixed value in copper.[42] Each *tanka* was equal to two standard copper coins of the Mughal Empire, known as the *dam* (also called *paisa*) weighing 323 grains. The *tanka* also appears to have had a fixed value in billon coins of previous mintages which circulated concurrently before getting demonetized. While the relationship between the *tanka* and the *dam* remained fixed throughout the sixteenth and seventeenth centuries, even when the introduction of a lighter *dam* of 216 grains (2/3 of the standard coin) in the 1660s threatened to disturb the ratio (see below), its silver or gold rate continued to fluctuate with changes in the market rates of exchange.

Most wage rates and salaries in sixteenth-century documentation were quoted in the *tanka*. This is quite understandable since the same money was used by the Mughal state to prepare its revenue statistics and balance sheets of income and expenditure. But this does not mean that salaries and wages were paid only in copper. Money was disbursed in different legal tenders depending on the magnitude of payment. This can be best illustrated by looking at the largest sector to which the state made payments. The salaries of *mansabdars*, out of which wages to servants in the military establishment were paid (see below), were originally (1574) fixed in a single currency but paid in silver, gold, and copper:

When someone by good fortune enters the fold of the army and the branding is conducted, the pay orders are issued without delay or costs. The salaries are fixed in *dams* while at the time of payment half is made out in rupees at the rate of 48 *dams*. The rest is paid in two equal halves: one in *muhrs* at the value of 9 rupees, and the other in *dams*. When the price of the rupee reached 40 *dams*, by the emperor's benevolence the same rate was reckoned in payment.[43]

Before we raise issues relevant to the working of a payment system such as this, one thing should be made clear about the copper denomination used in the above passage. All references to the *dam* here originally appear as the *tanka* in an early recension of the manuscript by the same author, Abul Fazl.[44]

In the final draft which Abul Fazl prepared for presentation to the emperor, all figures given in *tankas* were converted into *dams*, a task made easier by the fixed ratio which existed between the money of account and the copper coin. Thus, it is important to remember that wherever salaries and wages were quoted in the *dam* in the final draft (published text), the medium of exchange might not necessarily have been the copper coin.

Although the above structure of payment designed by the fiscal authorities broadly reflected the pattern of currency circulation in the various sectors of the economy in the third quarter of the sixteenth century, it was unlikely to have survived fluctuations in the exchange rates of monetary metals in the market. While the copper component of the salary structure remained unaffected, the silver and gold portions began to depreciate. When the system was barely a decade old, 10 per cent of the total salary of the bureaucrats and their soldiers was wiped out due to a 20 per cent fall in the copper value of silver in the market (from 48 to 40 *dams*). At an unspecified date during this phase (1574-82), the market value of the silver rupee slipped to 35 *dams*, leading to a further depreciation of salaries and wages paid out in precious metals (Table 6.5).

TABLE 6.5: PRICE OF SILVER RUPEE IN COPPER DAMS IN NORTHERN INDIA

Year	*Official Rate (tankas/dams)*	*Market Rate (dams)*
1574	24/48	48
1574-82	24/48	35
1582	20/40	40
1595	20/40	45
1606	20/40	102

Source: Data derived from Haider 1999, 338-45.

Two steps were taken to redress this situation. The first was to bring down the rate of conversion – from copper to silver (and also gold via silver) – to align it with the market. For the same amount of *tankas*, the recipients could now have more gold and silver coins (rupees and *muhrs*). The second measure was to treat the new rate of exchange as permanent. Thus, in 1582, an elaborate schedule of exchange rates was prepared by the finance minister, Todarmal, in which gold and silver coins of all types (such as those which lost weight and were passed at a discount) were expressed in the copper money of account (*tanka*) at a fixed rate. A silver rupee of full weight was exchanged for 20 *tankas* (or 40 *dams*) and a gold *muhr* for 360 *tankas* (or 180 *dams*).[45] The silver rate of the gold coin was fixed at the same level as in 1574. As a result of this measure – at least in Mughal revenue collections and salary payments – the real copper coin (*dam*) also became a money of account, since its value was fixed *ad infinitum* against silver and gold.[46] This could explain why Abul Fazl translated all figures from one money of account into another.

In order to keep the official exchange rates constant, the Mughal state offered additional payments to its officials and their soldiers whenever the market rate rose beyond the official rate.[47] As this was a cumbersome exercise which kept the fiscal balance sheet floating with every new development in the money market, it might well have been the reason behind the decision to frame new salary figures in rupees towards the end of the sixteenth century.[48] By now, the silver rupee had become the principal medium of exchange. At the same time, it was appreciating in value against copper (Table 6.5), and salaries and wages fixed in copper but paid in silver at the official rate of exchange meant loss for the exchequer. In certain departments of the fiscal sector, it was rational for the state to snap the link which it had maintained with the copper money of account owing to the multiplicity of issues during the period of transition.[49]

Outside the state sector, wages expressed in one currency and paid out in another gave rise to similar problems. We have a report from Surat (Gujarat), of 1663, in which the English factors highlighted the problem of accounting wages in silver and paying in copper: 'The mamody, that useth always in former time to bee at 20 and more pice, is now, by the dearness of copper, fallen to 13½ and 14 pice, whilst provisions noe whitt the cheaper; and the stewards disbursements are for the most part in pice, afterwards reduced into mamodies.'[50]

Here, the monthly wages of the stewards were fixed in silver *mahmudis* (a regional coin which remained in circulation against all odds) but paid out in copper pices (*dams*).[51] When the exchange rate of the *mahmudi* fell against the *dam* (from 20 to 14) due to the scarcity (dearness) of copper, money wages paid to the stewards dropped in value, while on paper they remained the same. Since the prices of provisions purchased by the stewards remained unaffected, their real wages fell. If the employers paid the servants at the old rate, the entry in their ledger against wages would have shown a higher outlay of *mahmudis* (hence the explanation in the annual letter to London).

The crisis of copper money created problems for wage earners in the state sector too. In Gujarat, when the shortage became acute, the *sarrafs* of Ahmedabad circulated a fiduciary (iron) coin, forcing the governor to organize supplies of copper to the mint and seek permission for the free coinage of imperial issues (abolition of seigniorage for one year).[52] The central administration acceded to the request only after reducing the weight of the *dam* by a third (215 grains). The reduction in coin weight interfered with the traditional *tanka-dam* (1:2) exchange ratio insofar as all payments stipulated in the *tanka* ought to have been made at the rate of three instead of two *dams*.[53] This, however, was not the case until the wage earners petitioned the government regarding the loss in their income. A chronicler of the city of Ahmedabad summarized these developments in the following passage which he reconstructed from the administrative documents at his disposal:

> The administrator of buildings, gardens and other workshops of Ahmadabad City represented to the Celestial Court that formerly the wages of the labourers had been paid in copper coins (*fulus*)[54] weighing 21 *mashas* [323 grains]. Since the said *fulus* have been withdrawn from circulation…, and *fulus* of auspicious Alamgiri stamp, the weight of which is fixed at 14 *mashas* [215 grains], have become current, workers have declined to accept the new coins in place of the old, saying that the difference between them is of the order of 10:15.When the intelligence of this matter reached the August Presence [Emperor Aurangzeb], an order was issued to the finance minister of the province that, in the ratio of 10:15, the daily wages should be paid at the rate of one and a half *tanka* instead of one *tanka*. From that date the *tanka* in Gujarat is rated at 3 *fulus*.[55]

Much like the English Company, the Mughal state had to resort to an upward revision of money wages (in terms of the units of currency) in its accounts. It went a step further to embrace the implications of this decision by crying down the money of account and assigning to the *tanka* a lower value in terms of the minted copper weight (2 lighter *dams* instead of 2 heavy issues).[56]

In the first two cases discussed above, the metal content of the unit of account remained stable while its value expressed in precious or base metal coinage altered as a result of a change in the bimetallic ratio. In the third case, the metal content of the unit of account was altered as the result of a change in the weight of the coin to which it was pegged. In all three cases, 'money wages' remained constant while 'real wages' declined until the anomaly was addressed either by making 'extra' payments or changing the system of accounting or adding 'money' to the book rates.

The Mughal State and the Wage Labour Market

The role of the Mughal state in institutionalizing a monetary economy has already been pointed out. The relevance of its military apparatus and the consumption pattern of its ruling elites for the wage sector is also worthy of attention. In the Mughal military establishment, the responsibility for maintaining soldiers, war-animals and servants was delegated to the rank-holding officials of the state (*mansabdars*) on the basis of guidelines issued by the imperial administration. The officials held a dual rank (*mansab*). Their personal rank (*zat*) denoted their position in the administrative hierarchy by a number (5,000 *zat*, for instance), and their obligation to maintain soldiers and war animals in their personal contingent (*khasa*). Their military rank (*sawar*) determined the number of cavalry troopers (*tabinan*) they were expected to bring to muster (5,000 *sawars*, for instance). The *mansabdars* received separate salaries and allowances for *zat* and *sawar* in accordance with their personal ranks, ethnic groupings, the number of cavalry troopers they theoretically maintained or brought to muster and the number and quality of horses (both *khasa* and *tabinan*). For instance, soldiers serving under Mughal and Iranian *mansabdars* were paid, in the last quarter of the sixteenth century, at the pre-muster (*barawardi*) rate of 25 rupees per month. Soldiers of the Indian *mansabdars* were allowed 20 rupees per month.[57] It was out of these salaries and personal allowances that the wages of the labour force employed in the military sector were paid. Abul Fazl has provided figures for the wages paid to the servants tending personal horses and elephants of the *mansabdars* as well as the horses of their cavalry troopers (the soldiers were not permitted to keep elephants).

TABLE 6.6: MONTHLY WAGES OF THE GROOM (*TIMARDAR*), 1574-5

Breeds of Horses	*Wages in Dams*
Iranian and Turkish	
Arab	63
Iraqi	63
Mujannas	60
Turki	60
Indian	
Yabu	45
Tazi	45
Jangla	45

Source: Abul Fazl 1872, *Ain-i-Akbari*, I, 176-8.

PLATE 6.1: CONSTRUCTION OF THE FORT AT AGRA FOR THE MUGHAL EMPEROR AKBAR

This is the second part (left hand side) of a double-page illustration to the *Akbarnama*, the history of Akbar and his empire authored by Abul Fazl. Among the various building activities depicted in the painting are loading and carrying of stones and mortars on heads by men and women as well as a beam fastened to bamboo sticks; mixing of mortars by masons (*raj*); and stone getting transported to the site in boats from the quarries of Fatehpur Sikri. The construction of the red sand stone structure commenced in 1565 CE (10th regnal year of Akbar) and took 8 years to complete. We know from another contemporary work (*Tarikh-i Akbari*) that 2,000 stonecutters (*sangtarash*) and 2,000 mortar and-lime makers (*gilkar o chunakar*) worked daily to build the fort (*qila*), along with 8,000 labourers (*mazdur*) who supplied stone and lime (*sang o chuna*). The painting was sketched (*tarh*) by Miskina and coloured (*amal*) by Tulsi Junior (*khurd*), both artists of Akbar's atelier. Source: © Victoria and Albert Museum, London. Used by permission.

TABLE 6.7: MONTHLY WAGES OF THE ATTENDANTS OF THE ELEPHANTS OF THE MANSABDARS, 1574-5

Category of Servants	*Types of Elephants and Wages in Dams*			
	Mast	*Shergir*	*Sada*	*Manjhola*
Driver (*mahawat*)	120	105	90	75
Assistant I (*bhoi*)	90	75	60	45
Assistant II (*meth*)	90	90	60	30

Source: Abul Fazl 1872, *Ain-i-Akbari*, I, 176-8.

The *mansabdars* were concentrated in cities which attracted an overwhelming proportion of cash revenue siphoned from the countryside, out of which a big urban craft and service sector was maintained. The king and the nobility owned and supervised *karkhanas* in which the ornaments of their luxurious life were fashioned. In the last quarter of the sixteenth century, there were 1,000 *karkhanas* in the city of Lahore alone which produced shawls, an item in which Akbar showed special interest.[58] Similarly, the construction of palaces, inns, monuments, etc., absorbed a huge labour force consisting of bricklayers, stone carriers, stone masons and others. Information on the size of the workforce employed in the building industry is quite desultory but the scattered figures recorded in chronicles and travelogues suggest that it was by no means small. The Mughal Emperors considerably enlarged the scale of building construction, which, under the Delhi Sultans, was already quite significant. According to one report, Alauddin Khalji (1296-1316) employed as many as 70,000 workers and craftsmen for the construction of his various buildings.[59] The first Mughal Emperor, Babur, made the following observation in his memoirs on the labour force engaged in building construction during his time (1526-30):

> Another nice thing is the unlimited numbers of craftsmen and practitioners of every trade. For every labour and every product there is an established group who have been practicing that craft or professing that trade for generations. For instance, in the *Zafarnama*, Mulla Sharaf writes eloquently that during Timur Beg's building of the stone mosque two hundred stonemasons from Azerbaijan, Fars, Hindustan, and other

places were employed on it daily. In Agra alone there were 680 Agra stonemasons at work on my building every day. Aside from that, in Agra, Sikri, Bayan, Dholpur, Gwalior, and Koil, 1,491 stonemasons were labouring on my buildings. There are similar vast numbers of every type of craftsman and laborers of every description in Hindustan.[60]

The numbers went up under his successors. The workforce engaged by Akbar for the construction of the Agra Fort comprised 2,000 stone cutters, 2,000 mortar and lime-makers, and 8,000 labourers (*mazdur*) supplying stone and lime. It was reported that 5,000 men worked daily to build the Jami Masjid of Delhi and 20,000 to construct the Taj Mahal during Shah Jahan's reign (1628-58).[61]

The service sector maintained by the elites of the Empire was equally large. By one estimate, there were 36,000 'officers and men' in the royal establishment, including 'porters, gunners, watermen, lakeyes, horse keepers, elephant keepers, small shot, frasses [*farrash*] or tent men, cookes, light bearers, gardeners, keepers of all kinds of beast. All these be payed monethly out of the king's treasurie; whose wages be from ten to three rupias.'[62] According to Pelsaert, every wife in a noble's harem had 10 to 100 maids in attendance, who were paid on a monthly basis. The figure for the imperial harem was 4,700 maids for 300 ladies.[63]

The state also contributed to the creation of a viable environment for offering employment. Although political interference was present (such as the exaction of forced labour), it did not materially affect the free-trade character of the Mughal state. There were no legal restrictions on accumulation (the law of escheat or confiscation of property of the deceased applied only to indebted nobles), business methods (including usury), and the movement of artisans and professionals. Indeed, the state attempted to break the monopolies of skill-based professions ensured by the caste system to boost the supply of labour in individual sectors (see below). The Mughal Emperor Aurangzeb's (1659-1707) declaration that the monopoly held by gold-wire drawers of the Srimal caste was illegal is a case in point.[64] We have the testimony of the Dutch factor, Geleynssen, that the Mughals followed their predecessors in allowing and encouraging artisans and workers to settle in newly founded cities.[65] The territorial unification and political stability offered by Mughal rule also appeared to have facilitated the short and long-distance migration of wage earners to areas of employment.

The Caste System and Wage Labour

It remains for us to assess the relevance of one of the most outstanding social institutions of India – the caste system – for the wage market. Sustained by kinship, endogamy, commensality and rituals of purity, the caste system created hierarchies which were difficult to breach. Caste seems to have had a dual impact on the determination of wages. In the agricultural sector, it helped to create landless labourers, mostly menial and ready to be hired, by excluding them from landownership.[66] Without the presence of this pool of resources, it would have been impossible for the upper caste peasantry (rich peasants, village headmen, *zamindars*, etc.) to cultivate their large estates at minimum cost. It is important to remember that the land-man ratio was favourable and cultivable waste could be occupied at no cost since the state promoted its ploughing for revenue. The caste system not only ensured the abundance of labour but kept agricultural wages to the level of subsistence. For the landholding village aristocracy specializing in the production of cash crops, this was an important source of wealth accumulation.

Since members of a caste could only practise their ancestral profession and could not switch to another easily,[67] rural manufacturing also received a plentiful supply of artisans such as cotton carders (*naddaf*) and oil pressers (*teli*), who might not have been able to find employment in their own villages. Gradually, the system gave birth to a class of itinerant artisans and labourers who hawked their skills from village to village. A contemporary European observer (1666-7) left a graphic description of one such social group servicing the cotton textile industry, arguably the most important in our period of study:

We went next to Gitbagh, five leagues from Mader, we met great many colies [koli], which are people of a caste or tribe of gentiles who have no fixed habitation, but wander from village to village, and carry all they have about with them. Their chief business is to pick and clean cotton, and when they have no more to do in one village they go to another.[68]

The description highlights another interesting phenomenon: the employment of family, women and child labour. Such labour was particularly visible in the building and mining industries where wage labour was harnessed *en masse*.[69] Here again, the employer not only had a much wider pool of resources (women working with members of their family or caste felt secure to venture out) but also at lower costs. Wages paid to women were less than those paid to their male counterparts for the same type and amount of work.

One way in which artisans and workers could have negotiated for a bigger role in wage determination was through the guild. But the emergence of a guild system in India was thwarted by caste formation. The caste system, although acting as a substitute, lacked the organization and apparatus necessary to boost the bargaining power of the group and safeguard the interest of the wage earners. Professional castes did have their headmen (*chaudharis*) but they were concerned more with caste matters, such as restricting the entry of outsiders to their profession. Although they mediated between the employer and the wage-earners, it appears that (except in the case of the corporate bodies of merchants and money changers called *mahajan*) they did not play any effective role in regulating wages in the way that guild masters did in medieval Europe.[70]

The caste system also encouraged a reverse trend in the wage sector. In certain professions, skills and trade secrets were jealously guarded and transmitted from one generation to another within the caste, a process which resulted in the preservation and intensification of skills.[71] An exquisitely calligraphed and illustrated manuscript was hailed at the Mughal court over a printed book, presented by the Jesuits, on account of its beauty, elegance and lower costs of production. Whenever demand for such exclusive craftsmanship exceeded its limited supply, which was usually the case, wages were set at a very high level. This explains the extraordinarily high wages paid to the blank cutter and assayer in the mint (Table 6.1), since both came from the highly skill-intensive sub-castes of goldsmiths and silversmiths. This also explains the restrictions placed on their migration out of the Mughal Empire but not between two imperial mints. When a monetary crisis occurred at Delhi in 1684, mint workmen were dispatched from Gujarat. The English, on the other hand, met with stiff resistance from local officials in their efforts to hire blank cutters and assayers for their newly established mint at Bombay.[72]

The 'Price Revolution' and Wage Movements

Just as wages are an expression of the value of labour and skill, prices are an expression of the money value of goods. The market value (purchasing power) of wages received in money could rise and fall with fluctuations in the level of prices. Ever since Earl J. Hamilton co-related money wages with prices in his treatment of 'profit inflation' and capital accumulation during the Industrial Revolution, the study of wage movements has assumed added significance. For the first time, at least in modern historiography, the power of money to bring about major changes in economic and social structure was persuasively espoused. However, W.H. Moreland, in his classic study of the Mughal economic organization, found no noticeable change in wage levels and took this to be a sign of stagnation.[73] Irfan Habib considered the possibility of money wages lagging behind prices, but for him the magnitude of profit inflation was too modest to hold wide-ranging implications for the economy.[74]

There are two points which need to be raised before we accept the views of the two most distinguished historians of the Mughal economy. First, Moreland's argument on the absence of wage movements was based on a misinterpretation of currency denominations in which wages were quoted in the sources. Moreland began his investigation of money, prices and wages with the assumption that copper appreciated in its value against silver at the turn of the seventeenth century due to its rising demand in the industrial sector and declining supplies from internal sources. Habib arrived at the same conclusion but from a different premise. Guided principally by the quantity theory of money, which states that the value of money depends on its quantity.[75] Habib argued that an influx of silver into the Mughal Empire in the sixteenth century depressed the rupee purchasing power of copper. Habib was writing at a time when, following Hamilton's stimulating study of Spanish imports and their effects, the European Price Revolution was increasingly understood to be a function of the rising quantity of silver.

This view of the value of silver, common to both Moreland and Habib, shaped their analyses of the movement of money wages in two respects. The first relates to the exchange rates of silver and copper coins, i.e. the ratio between the rupee and the *dam*. The second relates to their interpretation of currency denominations in which wages were fixed.

In the seventeenth century, most exchange rate figures for the copper currency, provided by European merchants, are quoted not in *dams* but in *paisas* (pice), the earliest quotation referring to the current rupee to 'be worth in Agra 102 pices 100, 98 and 96 for the money many times rise and fall'.[76] The document suggests a remarkable rise in the value of silver against copper, a phenomenon which defies the logic of the quantity theory of money. Moreland, who worked on these figures with the conviction that the value of silver fell against copper in the seventeenth century, found them inconsistent with the official rates supplied by Abul Fazl (Table 6.5) and forced upon the data new definitions of copper denominations. He assumed that the *paisa* (another term used for the *dam*) here denoted the half *dam* (*adhela* of the traditional Indian copper scale) and the *tanka* a *dam*.[77] For easy comprehension, the problem can be re-expressed as follows:

Seventeenth-century scale of copper currencies:

1 *tanka* = 2 *dams* or *paisas* = 4 *adhelas*
1 *dam* or *paisa* = 2 *adhelas*

Moreland's reading:

1 *tanka* = 1 *dam* = 2 *paisas*

Subsequent historians, sharing Moreland's conviction as well as his interpretation of Mughal copper currencies, read the data in a manner in which all references to the *tanka* and *paisa* in Persian and European sources stood respectively for the *dam* and the *adhela*.[78] There is no significant evidence, textual or numismatic, to make it necessary to suppose that a new scale of copper currency came into use by transferring the designation of one coin to another. We have already seen that the *tanka* was a double *dam*, and a copper coin weighing 646 grains (double the weight of the *dam*) was indeed minted for a brief period at the turn of the seventeenth century.[79] The doubling of the absolute value of the *dam* not only inflated the copper price of silver by 100 per cent but depressed all wages stated in copper currency.

Thus, while the daily wages of an unskilled labourer doubled between *c.* 1595 and 1637 (from 2 *dams* to 4 *paisas*), Moreland saw no change because he considered the latter figure to be equivalent to 2 *dams* (see the reading of the copper scale by Moreland). Such a misinterpretation of numismatic evidence marred the validity of all his calculations of wages and prices which he used for macroeconomic analyses.[80]

The data used by Moreland, and additional evidence, suggest that money wages did increase in the Mughal Empire in the seventeenth century. Monthly wages paid to an ordinary labourer rose from 1.5 rupees in 1595 to 3 rupees in 1613 and 3.5 rupees in 1637. The wages of a skilled groom also registered an upward trend between the two terminal dates (Tables 6.2-6.3). Further, we have figures of wages paid to mint workmen for comparison and corroboration.

The wages of the mint workmen were usually stated in proportion to the amount minted since they were not actively employed round the year and were called upon to work only when the mint functioned regularly. At all other times, it was customary for them to receive a subsistence allowance, apparently designed to keep skilled workers under contractual obligation, since such workers were not easily available everywhere and at all times.[81] There is evidence of local administrators controlling the movement of mint workers and often employing coercion to keep them tied to a particular mint.[82]

TABLE 6.8: WAGES OF BLANK CUTTERS FOR 1,000 SILVER COINS

Year	*Wages (rupees)*	*Mint*
1595	1.34	Agra or Lahore
[1676]	4.00	Surat
1694	4.50	Cambay
1694	5.00	Surat

Sources: References in notes 82 and 84.

From evidence available to us for the late sixteenth century, the *zarrabs* (blank cutters) were paid for the period when they were at work. These were given as 53.44 *dams* (1.34 rupees at the official rate of exchange) for minting a thousand silver coins.[83] By 1694, when the English needed workmen for their Bombay mint who could only be recruited from Gujarat, the *zarrabs* at Cambay asked for 6 rupees per month as 'diet' money and 4.5 rupees per thousand silver coins they crafted.[84] The *zarrabs* at Surat demanded a higher rate of 8 rupees for subsistence and 6 rupees per thousand of coining though they were reported to have been paid 5 rupees for the latter at the Surat mint.[85] The wages seemed to have more than doubled in the intervening period.

So far, we have been talking about the movement of money wages. However, it is real wages, money wages adjusted for price changes, which hold greater significance for an understanding of income distribution, accumulation and economic and social change. In the absence of an unbroken price series for a basket of commodities for any region of the Mughal Empire, one straightforward method adopted by modern historians had involved measuring the value of silver against a stable standard. Since the belief was widely held that silver depreciated in value (*a la* quantity theory), copper (as well as gold) was considered to be that stable standard against which silver prices can be judged. Consequently, changes in bi-metallic ratios became effective indicators of the general movement of commodity prices. However, we have seen how problematic any price history can be which is premised on the notions of quantity and value, particularly when the demand side of equation is ignored and comprehension of currency denominations is subordinated to monetary theory. Future researches in this field would require the compilation of fresh data to arrive at a better understanding of the factors working behind movements of prices and wages and their implications for different sections of the population.

NOTES

1. Broad estimates of the Indian population at the turn of the seventeenth century were offered on the basis of a comparison (and backward extrapolation) of the land-man ratio as it stood in the early twentieth century, and estimates of the ratio between per capita and total revenue. The results suggest a compound annual growth of 0.21 per cent between 1601 and 1871 in the population: Moosvi 1987, 399-405.
2. Moosvi 2000, 330.
3. Habib 1999a, 280
4. Haider 1996, 298-364.
5. Habib 1999b, 280.
6. For mining, see Moreland 1920, 141-2.
7. Raychaudhuri 1982, 279-81. For a detailed description of manufactories, see Verma 1994.
8. Pelsaert 1925, 60.
9. Bernier 1916, 259.
10. Nandram 1879, 4.
11. Geleynssen de Jongh Collection, National Archives, The Hague (NA) [hereafter Geleynssen de Jongh, NA],123.
12. Pelsaert 1925, 62.
13. Tennant 1803, I, 191-9.
14. Habib 1999a, 299-300.
15. Abul Fazl 1872, *Ain i Akbari*, I, 170.
16. Tennant 1803, I, 191-9.
17. Abul Fazl 1872, *Ain i Akbari*, I 18; Van Dam 1929, II, iii, 108-9; *Kaghzat i-Mutafarriqa* (Anonymous collection of administrative documents from eighteenth century Bengal), Oriental and India Office Collection, British Library, London, MS Add. 6586, folios, 57r, 58v-r; Bihari, *Hidayat ul Qawaid*, p. 150).
18. Habib 1999a, 156-8.
19. Tavernier 1925, I, 10.
20. Habib 2002, 46-7.
21. Habib & Thakur 2003, 10, 51; Gupta 1996, 2-3.
22. Kosambi 1981; Chattopadhyaya 1979; Gupta 1996, 8-52, 69-81.

23. Sharma 1987, 123-4; Shrimali 2002.
24. Deyell 1990; Gopal 1965; Chattopadhyaya 1994, 130-54.
25. Barani 1862, 280, 310-14; Sijzi 1966, 83; Khurd 1885, 516; Habib 1982b, 87-8.
26. Pheru 1961, 1-38; Afif 1891, 344; Barani 1862, 318. The best work on numismatic evidence remains Wright 1936. For a recent treatment of the billon *jital*, see Tye 1995, 57-61.
27. Pheru 1961, 37 (Table 29), 38 (verse 148); Afif 1891, 344.
28. Monetary historians of medieval Europe largely agree to a scarcity of silver in the late Middle Ages, prolonged and intense enough to designate it a period of 'bullion famine'. The case is most persuasively argued in Day 1987, 4-7. Also see Spufford 1988, 339-62; Munro 1983, 101. For a mid-fourteenth century crisis of silver specie in Egypt, see Lopez, Miskimin & Udovitch 1987, 124.
29. Haider 1998, 237-54.
30. Haider 1996, 298-364.
31. Von Glahn 1996, 133-40.
32. Haider 2005, 131-7.
33. Abul Fazl 1872, *Ain i Akbari*, I, 32-3; Khan 1927, I, 265; Haider 1996, 332-3, 354.
34. Haider 2002, 58-79.
35. Habib 1987B, 137-70.
36. For copper mines and mint production, see Deyell 1987.
37. Deyell 1987, 160-4.
38. Jourdain 1905, 150.
39. Foster 1906, Vol. 1, 142, 144. For more examples of wage payments in copper, see the next section.
40. Afif 1891, 344; Abdullah 1954, 83; Ilahabadi 1878, 108.
41. The first half of the sixteenth century was a period of the dominance of gold in the Indian Ocean trade, and the 'river of gold' which flowed through the Red Sea brought to the Indian Ocean markets a multitude of gold coins (*ashrafis*, *sultanis* and Yemeni *dinars*), all modelled on the Venetian ducat which itself came in large quantities. Barbosa 1989, I, 100-1; Pires 1967, I, 13, 17, 21, 43-4; Magalhaes Godinho 1969, 293-4.
42. Of the three essential functions of money – measure of value, means of exchange and mode of accumulation – the money of account performs only the first.
43. Abul Fazl 1872, *Ain i Akbari*, I, 196.
44. Abul Fazl, *Akbarnama*, Oriental and India Office Collection (OIOC), MS Add. 27247, folio 332r and passim.
45. Ibid.
46. 'Though the rate of 40 *dams* to a rupee could be higher or lower than the market price, in the payment of salaries this rate is recognized'. Abul Fazl 1872, *Ain i Akbari*, I, 26.

47. Ibid., pp. 176, 178
48. Ibid., pp. 180-5.
49. Silver depreciated owing to its huge influx between 1574 and 1582 when the process of its absorption into the exchange network had barely begun. The situation, however, changed after 1582, when steps were taken to monetize silver on a larger scale by centralizing the administration of silver mints and integrating them with the fiscal structure. It is also possible that silver monetization created huge reserves of replaced copper money that outstripped its demand (which too increased in absolute terms). This curious phenomenon - higher supply leading to higher exchange value escaped notice in all modern accounts for reasons which are explained below (The 'Price Revolution' and Wage Movements).
50. Foster 1922, Vol. 11, 121.
51. Foster 1911, Vol. 5, 151; Haider 2003, 134-52.
52. Khan 1927, I, 265.
53. Khan 1927, I, 265, 267, 277.
54. A generic Perso-Arabic term for copper coins.
55. Khan 1927, I, 267.
56. Khan 1927, I, 277.
57. Abul Fazl 1872, *Ain i Akbari*, 175; Habib 1967, 234.
58. Abul Fazl 1872, *Ain i Akbari*, I, 104.
59. Barani 1862, 341.
60. Babur 1996, 351-2.
61. Qaisar 1988, 13. For the wages paid to those employed in the building industry, see Table 6.1.
62. Hawkins 1921, 99.
63. Pelsaert 1925, 64.
64. Khan 1927, I, 292-3.
65. Moreland 1925, 75.
66. Habib 1995a, 106-7; Habib 1995b, 120-5, 130-6, 142-4; Habib 1995c, 169-75.
67. Pelsaert 1925, 60; Bernier 1916, 259.
68. Thevenot 1949, 10.
69. Habib 2000, 2-3.
70. Gupta 1970, 49-51. For suggestions that 'guild-type organisations of artisans and labourers' had control over labour supplies in colonial times, see Bayly 1983, 313-14.
71. Khan 1927, I, 292-3.
72. *Akhbarat i Darbar i Mualla* [Newsletter from the Mughal Court], Royal Asiatic Society, London, MS 2361, (folios arranged reign wise), 37th regnal year of Aurangzeb [1684]; *Factory Records, Surat*, Oriental and India Office Collection (OIOC), British Library, London, series G/36, Vol. 94, folios 28v, 93r.
73. Moreland 1923b, 173, 178, 194-5.
74. Habib 1982d, 378-9.

75. The modern version of the quantity theory, popular with the monetarists, stipulates that, *ceteris paribus*, an increase in the quantity of money causes a proportional increase in the level of commodity prices. For the latest statement of the modern version, see Lucas 1996, 661-82. The pre-history of the quantity theory is traced in Hegeland 1951, 1-25. Also see Vilar 1991, 163-5.
76. *Factory Records, Miscellaneous*, vol. 25, folio 96; Foster 1928, 48.
77. Moreland 1923b, 183, 330-1; Moreland 1923, 151-2; Pelsaert 1925, 29 (Moreland's note). Hodivala, the doyen of Indian numismatists, writing about the same time as Moreland, concurred with this interpretation. See Hodivala 1923, 140, fn. 2.
78. Habib 1961, 12, 18 fn. 2, 19 fn. 8; Habib 1982D, 370 (Table 10); Habib 1987B, 149 (Table 3), 156.
79. Specimens of minted *tankas* are described in the catalogues of museum collections.
80. A detailed critique is presented in Haider 1999, 338-44.
81. *Factory Records, Surat*, 94, folios 39v, 58v.
82. Ibid., folios 28v, 93r.
83. Abul Fazl 1872, *Ain i Akbari*, I, 17, 32-3.
84. *Factory Records, Surat*, 94, folio 58v. In an inventory of the costs incurred by the Dutch merchants for coining silver at Surat (*c.* 1676), the wages paid to the *zarrabs* ('seraeb, die de ropyen haar teecken en ronte geeft') were listed as 4 rupees per thousand coins. Van Dam 1939, III, ii, 109 (Appendix VIIIc). The date is inferred from the absence of seigniorage, abolished in 1676, in the total cost.
85. 'The jurobs demands [*sic*] 8 Rs. each the moneth when there is no business and 6 p. mille on al they coin: in the tanksal they have 5 p. mille'. *Factory Records, Surat*, 94, folio 39v.

7

Long Distance Trade, Coinage and Wages in India, 1600-1960

Om Prakash

A growing degree of monetization and an increasing use of wage labour have historically been among the more important ingredients of the process of transformation that the present-day developed economies experienced in the course of their economic development. Growing monetization signified an ever-larger proportion of the total transactions being conducted in the monetized sector involving, in turn, a continuously rising supply of money in the economy. Since money consisted overwhelmingly, if not exclusively, of metals – both precious and non-precious – the supply of money, in turn, came to be linked in a critical manner with the supply of the relevant metals. In the case of many countries, the supply of metals, particularly precious metals, was significantly dependent on imports.

Growing monetization was usually accompanied by a rising proportion of the total workforce in the economy being employed on a money-wage basis. While the wage rate itself would be a function of the demand and supply of the particular category of labour in question at any given point in time, the logistics of wage payments could be an important factor in determining the mix of coins of different denominations manufactured in the economy. If the norm of payment to wage labour was weekly rather than monthly, for example, a much larger component of the total coin output would probably be in smaller denomination coins. The norm of wage payment would, of course, itself be a function of both economic and non-economic factors. Consumption patterns in any society would also be subject to influence by the norm for wage payment.

Against the background of these very general observations, what was the situation like in India over the last half a millennium or so? At the very outset, it would be useful to distinguish between the pre-colonial and the early-colonial period (1600-1800) on the one hand and the colonial period (1800-1947) on the other. This is partly because there are major differences between these two periods in the matter of the availability of data on various economic indices, both quantitative as well as qualitative. Also, the considerations governing the output of coins and the supply of money in the economy in general were very different in the two periods. For the period between 1500 and 1800, I will argue that there was indeed a very strong causal link between long distance trade and the supply of money in the economy. This link worked through the overwhelming, indeed almost total, dependence of India during this period on imports for the supply of precious metals and to a smaller extent for that of non-precious metals including copper. As a consequence of the growing involvement of India in the early modern world economy during these centuries, there was a very large inflow of precious metals into the country with important consequences for the supply of money and the degree of monetization. One of the consequences of the accelerated pace of monetization would have been the use of wage labour on an increased scale. While the available qualitative evidence would strongly support these hypotheses, there is a great paucity of data for the period until 1800 relating to both the supply of money as well as the scale of wage employment, the usual wage rate and the frequency with which money wage payments were actually made.

The situation was completely different in the nineteenth and the first half of the twentieth century when India was under British colonial rule. As the export of Indian textiles to the West collapsed under the impact of the Industrial Revolution, India ceased to be a net recipient of precious metals from abroad. Indeed, in the 1930s, large amounts of gold were exported from India to Britain on commodity account. Also, from 1893 onwards, Indian coinage ceased to be 'free' coinage and the rupee became a token coin. But while the link between long distance trade and coinage got increasingly snapped, the information base regarding the supply of money and its breakdown into currency and coins denomination improves considerably during this period. On the question of wage employment and wage rate also, the data availability during the nineteenth and the twentieth centuries is much better. But there is very little information on the logistics of the wage payments, particularly on the link between frequency of wage payment and the denomination mix of the coin/currency output. An important reason for this would seem to be that the principal unit of account in the Indian coinage, namely the rupee, was a relatively small value coin in the context of the nineteenth century levels of prices and wages. The need for smaller denomination coins was correspondingly much smaller than in the earlier period when a large part of the total coin output would seem to have consisted of copper *dams* or *paisas*. Indeed, in addition to standardized money consisting of gold, silver and copper coins, Mughal India witnessed an extensive use of the so-called 'humble' money such as *cauris* (sea-shells), bitter almonds and so on to settle small value transactions including wage payments.

Long Distance Trade, Precious Metals and Coinage

In a well-known passage in his magnum opus, *An Enquiry into the Nature and Causes of the Wealth of Nations*, Adam Smith, the father of modern economic science, argued that 'the discovery of America and that of a passage to the East Indies by the Cape of Good Hope are the two greatest and most important events recorded in the history of mankind'.[1] While there clearly is an element of exaggeration in this statement, it nevertheless underscores the critical role of the two events in the emergence of an early modern world economy. The three principal segments of this economy, namely Europe, the New World, and Asia came together for the first time directly as a result of the great discoveries of the last decade of the fifteenth century. Unlike in the case of the New World, there had been a certain amount of interaction between

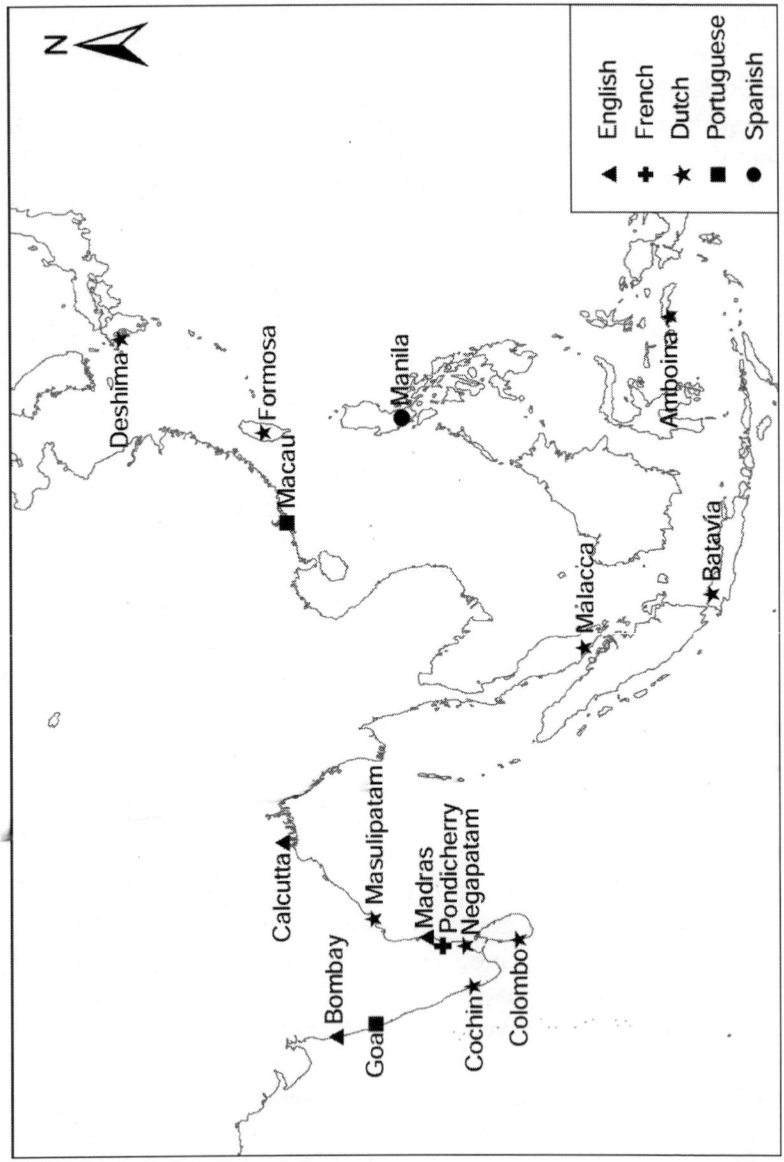

MAP 7.1: IMPORTANT EUROPEAN SETTLEMENTS IN ASIA, 1650-1780

Europe and Asia since antiquity and there is evidence to suggest that regular trade relations between the two continents went back at least to the early years of the Christian era.

What the discovery of the all-water route via the Cape of Good Hope achieved was the overcoming of the transport-technology barrier to the growth of the Euro-Asian trade. The volume of this trade was no longer subject to the capacity constraint imposed by the availability of pack animals and river boats in the Middle East. It was indeed a critically important coincidence that the discovery of the Cape route and of the New World took place almost simultaneously. For without the enormous quantities of American silver reaching Europe through the sixteenth century, the enhanced trading opportunities between Europe and Asia opened up by the Cape route would essentially have been frustrated. Euro-Asian trade had traditionally been one involving the exchange of Asian luxury and other goods basically against European silver and, to a smaller extent, gold. This 'bullion for goods' pattern of trade was an outcome of the inability of Europe to supply goods that could be sold in Asia in reasonably large quantities at competitive terms. Europe at this time had an undoubted overall superiority over Asia in the field of scientific and technological knowledge, but not as yet the distinct cost advantage that came with the Industrial Revolution in the late eighteenth and nineteenth centuries. This put the Asian, and particularly the Indian producers, with their considerably lower labour costs and a much longer history of sophisticated skills in handicrafts of various kinds, in a position of advantage over their European counterparts in the production of a variety of manufactured goods. As a result, Europe really had no option but to pay for the Asian goods overwhelmingly in terms of precious metals. Ever since the fourteenth century or so, the output of precious metals in Europe had by and large been stagnant, raising fears of deflationary tendencies cropping up. This, coupled with the bullionist inhibitions regarding the export of precious metals, would almost certainly have created a situation where the non-availability of significant additional quantities of precious metals for export to the East would by and large have rendered the opportunities opened up by the availability of the Cape route quite redundant. It is in this context that one must appreciate the critical significance of the two great discoveries that of the New World and of the Cape route to the East Indies having taken place almost simultaneously. It is from this time onward that one can legitimately speak of the emergence of an early modern world economy embracing in an organic and interactive manner all three of its principal components, namely the New World, Europe, and Asia.

In so far as the trade along the all-water route in the course of the sixteenth century was by and large not at the expense of the trade along the older water-cum-land route except perhaps in the early years of the century, the Cape route did lead to a fairly substantial expansion in the overall volume and value of the Euro-Asian trade. However, it was only after the English and the Dutch were able to remove the Portuguese stranglehold over the Cape route at the beginning of the seventeenth century that the really substantive expansion in the value of Euro-Asian trade began. The English East India Company, established in the year 1600, and even more so the Dutch East India Company chartered two years later, acted as the principal agents of this expansion, assisted later in the century by the French East India Company founded in 1664. Other European enterprises such as the Danish East India Company, the Ostend Company and so forth remained essentially on the fringes.

I would like to emphasize that my formulation of the early modern world economy is very different from Immanuel Wallerstein's construct of 'world economies' based on a 'world-systems' perspective. The space available to me does not permit a proper evaluation of Wallerstein's theory but it might nevertheless be useful to recall some of the key features of his analysis. The world systems perspective embraces the notion of both 'world-empires' as well as of 'world-economies'. A world-system, whether it is a world-economy or a world-empire, however, does not have to include the whole world so that there can simultaneously exist several world-empires as well as world-economies. A given world-economy can thus have areas external to it. There have existed in the past many world-economies, most of which became world empires and then failed: sooner or later an imperium expanded to fill the geographical space of this economy.[2]

The capitalist European world-economy, the focus of Wallerstein's analysis, arose during the period between 1450 and 1600. By the latter date, the core of this world-economy was located in North-Western Europe. Spanish America and Eastern Europe (Poland and Hungary) were peripheries, but Persia, the Ottoman and Russian world-empires, the Indian Ocean area and the Far East were external to it. This world-economy had trade relations with its external areas to be sure, but since these relations were based only on precocities, these areas were not yet incorporated into it. Some of these external areas were themselves world-economies or proto-world-economies. South Asia (also referred to as the Indian Ocean area) was one such world-economy which got incorporated into the capitalist European world-economy only after the middle of the eighteenth century.

According to Wallerstein then, in the early modern period while South America was peripheral to the capitalist European world-economy, the Indian Ocean area was external to it. This was notwithstanding the fact that precious metals (mainly silver extracted from the mines of Potosí and Mexico) were at the heart of the commercial relations between both Europe and the New World as well as those between Europe and Asia. The rationale of this evidently consisted in the fact that while in one case Europe received the critically indispensable precious metals, in the other it lost them to its trading partner. Without bullion

> Europe would have lacked the collective confidence to develop a capitalist system, wherein profit is based on various deferrals of realized value. This is *a fortiori* true given the system of a non-imperial world-economy which, for other reasons, was essential. Given this phenomenon of collective psychology, an integral element of the social structure of the time, bullion must be seen as an essential crop for a prospering world-economy.[3]

This is what made South America so valuable. In Wallerstein's words,

The production of gold and silver as a commodity made the Americas a peripheral area of the European world-economy insofar as this commodity was essential to the operation of this world-economy, and it was essential to the extent that it was used as money. Had the bullion of the Americas all flowed out to Asia, the Americas would have been just another external arena and Europe would have been merely an axis of three arenas – America, Europe, and Asia – obtaining its Asian luxuries at the price of the goods sent to the Americas. But the Americas were not interested in exchanging their bullion, and surely not in mining it. Therefore, the Europeans first seized Inca gold, then mined Potosi and Mexican silver, seeking ever-new mining areas (of which Brazilian gold would soon be the most important). They sent settlers to control the area of the Americas politically and to supervise the economic operations, and they imported labour as well. In short, they incorporated the Americas into their world-economy, primarily because they needed a solid currency base for an expanding capitalist system and secondarily to use the surplus in trade with Asia.[4]

Asia, on the other hand, remained external to the European world-economy because all that was received from that continent were non-essential luxury goods first spices and then the 'calicoes of the East Indies'. To quote Wallerstein yet once again,

At this epoch, the relationship of Europe and Asia might be summed up as the exchange of precocities. The bullion flowed east to decorate the temples, palaces, and clothing of Asian aristocratic classes and the jewels and spices flowed west. The accidents of cultural history (perhaps nothing more than physical scarcity) determined these complementary preferences.[5]

The reason I have quoted Wallerstein at such great length is not really because I am particularly concerned one way or the other about his classification of the New World as a periphery and of Asia as external to his capitalist European world-economy in the early modern period. What I indeed am concerned with is the widely presumed otherness of Asia as clearly brought out in the quotations from Wallerstein above. When imported into North-Western Europe, gold and silver was a commodity 'essential to the operation of this world-economy'. But when imported into Asia, the same commodity becomes an item of luxury consumption used 'to decorate the temples, palaces, and clothing of Asian aristocratic classes'. In the case of Europe, the essential character of the import derived from its use as money: in Asia, this valuable asset was frittered away by being used 'for hoarding or jewelry'.[6] Wallerstein is in very respectable company here. This is what the American scholar, Rudolph Blitz, has to say, 'In the Orient much of the specie went promptly into hoards or was demonetized and became a commodity satisfying the oriental penchant for ornaments'.[7] I believe that such a clear-cut dichotomy is indeed quite untenable and does not conform to a wide body of evidence available to us. Asia certainly was different from Europe but not necessarily in the matter of the role of imported precious metals in the long-term functioning of her constituent economies. And indeed whatever differences might have existed in this regard might not all have simply been a reflection of some mystic and implicitly irrational 'Oriental penchant for ornaments'.

Before I come to the case of India, let me briefly quote William Atwell on late Ming China. According to Atwell,

> Japanese and Spanish-American silver may well have been the most significant factor in the vigorous economic expansion which occurred in China during the period in question. This is true not only because of its direct impact on the silk and porcelain industries, although this clearly was of great importance, but also because an increase in the country's stock of precious metals upon which economic growth and business confidence seem to have depended would have been determined almost entirely by how much silver entered the country through foreign trade.[8]

There can be very little doubt that imported precious metals had traditionally played a similarly central role in the functioning of the Indian economy. The domestic production of these metals had always been marginal in India and the internal needs of the economy for coinage, consumption, and other purposes had overwhelmingly been met through imports. Until the sixteenth century, the Middle East, which itself obtained the bulk of its supplies from Europe via the Levant, was the principal source of these imports. It was indeed not without reason that the port of Mocha on the Red Sea was often described as the 'treasure-chest' of the Mughal empire. Following the discovery of the all-water route via the Cape of Good Hope and the arrival of the Portuguese in India, the Spanish-American silver also began arriving into India directly. Another important development characterizing the sixteenth and the first half of the seventeenth century was the emergence of Japan as by far the largest Asian source of both gold and silver. Through the agency of the Portuguese private traders operating under the so-called concession system, India was among the first major recipients of the Japanese precious metals. With the large scale participation of the Dutch East India Company in the seventeenth century in intra-Asian trade as an integral part of its overall trading strategy, the volume of Japanese silver and gold reaching India through the agency of the Company became extremely large, sometimes even exceeding the quantities imported from Holland. A good amount of the Japanese silver also reached China through the agency of the Chinese merchants, who apart from the Dutch, constituted the only group of foreign merchants allowed to come to Japan during the latter's 'closed-country' era. The growing integration of Asia into the world economy was clearly being accompanied by a growing integration of constituent economies within Asia.[9]

What impact did the growing import of precious metals into India as a result of her increasing involvement in the early modern world economy have on her economy and society? We have seen above that scholars such as Wallerstein and Blitz would have us believe that unlike in the case of early modern Europe, the growing availability of these metals in an Asian society would simply have involved either an increased conspicuous consumption of these metals on the part of the aristocracy and other rich sections of the society besides their growing use in the temples, or their simply being hoarded in response to an 'Oriental penchant'. The kind of effect associated with the import of these metals into Europe would therefore not have materialized in an Asian society. By far the most concrete of these effects in the case of Europe was the so-called 'price revolution' of the sixteenth century. A similar response is ruled out in the case of Asia for the simple reason that the first link in the chain, namely an increase in the supply of money, would not have come about in the Asian economies.

In my opinion such a view is quite unjustified and needs to be revised drastically. It would seem to me that in its essentials, the situation in Asia was not very different from that in Europe. There is first of all the question of the supply of money responding to a rise in the stock of precious metals in the system. I would like to suggest that the money supply in an Asian economy such as Mughal India was fully reflective of changes in her stock of gold and silver. The treasure imported by Indian merchants into the country was against goods they had sent out the previous season, and which they ostensibly would need to invest in the procurement of goods to be sent out in the next round. Similarly, the treasure brought in by foreign merchants, including the European trading companies, was intended for investment in Indian silks, textiles and other goods. In so far as foreign coins were not allowed to circulate in India, the very first step that would need to be taken by these merchants in the matter of raising the necessary purchasing power would be the conversion of the imported bullion and coins into Mughal Indian rupees. This could be done either through professional dealers in money known as *sarrafs* or by recourse to one of the imperial mints in the empire. In either event, there would be an automatic and corresponding increase in the supply of money in the economy. It is, of course, perfectly possible that a part of the increased money supply might eventually have been hoarded or withdrawn from active circulation. But in the present state of our knowledge, it would probably be futile to surmise on how significant or marginal this phenomenon might have been. Some observations could nevertheless be made in this behalf. In any society, hoarding of precious metals in the form of bullion or coins would be a function of the structure of asset preferences. Given the virtual absence of deposit banking facilities in Mughal India, hoarding on a reasonable scale can very well be interpreted as a perfectly legitimate and rational form of holding liquidity. The point is that the implied irrationality in the 'Oriental penchant' kind of story might in fact never have been there except perhaps at the margin.

A growing supply of money in response to a continuing import of precious metals would presumably have had implications for the functioning of an Asian economy along lines not necessarily very different from those in Europe. I have already referred to William Atwell describing Japanese and Spanish-American silver pouring into late Ming China as possibly 'the most significant factor in the vigorous economic expansion' which occurred in that country. The economic growth and business confidence associated with a rising stock of precious metals that Atwell talks of in relation to China would certainly not seem to have been confined to that country. In the case of Mughal India, for example, it would seem that the rising supply of money was leading to a significant acceleration in the process of monetization in the economy so characteristic of the period. The well-known growing monetization of the land-revenue demand during the period was clearly a part of this larger process. Another significant feature of the Mughal Indian economy was the rise of banking firms all over the empire dealing in extremely sophisticated instruments of credit. Many of these firms had enormous resources at their command. Probably the best known of these was the house of the Jagat Seths, operating from its headquarters at Murshidabad in Bengal.[10] Along with its other activities, the firm organized the transfer of Delhi's share in the land revenues collected in the province. I need hardly stress that there was an important organic link between the rise in the money supply and the growth of the banking firms in the Mughal Indian economy.

In the domain of employment, growing monetization facilitated the payment of wages in money to a growing proportion of the total work force. Logistics of wage payments would seem to be an important consideration in determining the mix of the coin output. Since paying the wages of an average workman on a daily, weekly or even monthly basis in terms of the principal coin of the Mughals, namely the silver rupee, would have been an impractical proposition, copper coins constituted a substantial proportion of the total Mughal Indian coin output. This output consisted of coins of three metals the gold *muhr*, the silver rupee and the copper *dam* or *paisa*. The basic coin constituting the principal unit of account was the silver rupee .The gold *muhr* was used mainly either for ceremonial purposes or for hoarding. The copper *dam* or *paisa* constituted a major medium of handling small-value transactions and was used extensively. A distinguishing feature of Mughal coinage was the extraordinarily high content of the relevant metal of a very high degree of purity in the coin. Thus the gold *muhr*, which weighted 169 grains troy, was practically of unalloyed metal of high purity. The alloy content in the silver rupee, which weighted 178 grains until Aurangzeb raised the weight to 180 grains, was also never more than about 4 per cent. The copper *dam* weighed 323 grains till 1663-4 when its weight was reduced to about two thirds of this figure. The coins were manufactured in imperial mints spread all over the empire. The procedure followed was that of 'free' mintage under which anyone could bring bullion, old coins or foreign coins to a mint and obtain after a lapse of time new coins in exchange. The number of coins delivered against a given quantity of metal depended upon the purity level of the metal surrendered. This was determined at the mint. A charge was made at the mint to cover the seigniorage, the loss of metal in the process of coining, and the cost of coining, which consisted partly of the cost of the necessary ingredients and partly that of the labour involved. As far as the question of the relative valuation of the coin of one metal in terms of each of the other two was concerned, this was left entirely to the market, and depended upon the relative market supply and demand of each of the three metals.[11]

In the case of the silver rupee, the new coin delivered by the mint was known as the *sicca* rupee. The value of this coin corresponded broadly to the value of the metal contained in it, plus the minting charges including seigniorage. The problem of wear and tear of a coin through use was tackled ingeniously by a complex system of equivalence based on a varying degree of premium being enjoyed by a new coin over older issues. The *sicca* rupee, defined as a coin minted during the current or the previous year, enjoyed such a premium over all older issues which routinely carried the year of issue on them. The rate of this premium was controlled for all practical purposes by a class of highly experienced and influential money dealers known as *sarrafs*. Once the premium enjoyed by a new over an earlier issue exceeded a threshold level, the old coin would simply be brought to the mint for recoinage. This would be encouraged by the government in so far as its income from seigniorage would go up. Since the coins were intrinsic and not token coins, the problem of debasement of coins did not plague Mughal coinage. It also seems that forgery of coins was generally not a major problem.

The Mughal coinage system involved monetary management by the state only in a limited way. The accretions to the supply of money were determined by the public itself subject to the availability of metals in the system and the capacity of the imperial mints. In this regard, the government was formally no different from any other member of the public except that its resource base was naturally larger than that of any private individual and the minting of its bullion would get priority. Further, the government could, and did, occasionally exercise its authority in directing the use of a particular metal for coinage. Thus in 1657 when an increase in the demand for copper coins in Surat took the rupee: *paisa* ratio to 1:40, while in 1642 it had stood at only 1:56, the *mutasaddi* (local governor) of Surat ruled that all copper imported into the city should be taken directly to the mint. In order to facilitate this, he banned the movement of the metal bought by the indigenous merchants from the Dutch East India Company (which was by far the single largest importer of this metal into the Mughal Empire, mainly from Japan) to places outside the city. This ban remained in force over the two succeeding years.[12] Mughal imperial mints were scattered all over the empire, though clearly some were more important than others, in terms of both the number of coins manufactured as well as the geographical area within the empire over which the issues of a mint ordinarily circulated. It is also important to realize that while the business of all the imperial mints was the crafting of refined metal into coins, this could be done under different entrepreneurial and technical arrangements. The available information suggests the existence of at least two distinct models along which the structure of a Mughal imperial mint was organized. The dominant model would seem to have been the one where Mughal state officials organized the work of production themselves. The alternative organizational arrangement involved the entrepreneurial function being delegated to the *sarrafs*. What was common to the two patterns was the strict control exercised by the government on the quality of the coins manufactured.[13]

The coinage system in south India was quite different.[14] Until the Mughal conquest of Golconda in 1687, the monetary system of the region remained firmly based on gold. The standard coin was the pagoda or *hun* (53 grains) stamped with the image of Vishnu. The pagoda's subsidiary coins, the half-pagoda and the *fanam* (5 grains) were also gold. The latter, heavily alloyed, was one of the smallest gold coins known and was extensively used for ordinary commercial transactions including wage payments. A copper coin weighing between 25 and 30 grains was called 'cash'. Since 1636, the Qutb Shahs had also been minting a limited number of Mughal silver rupees to symbolize their status as tributary chiefs. After 1687, of course, the Mughals issued gold *muhrs*, silver rupees and copper coins of the usual Mughal types from the Hyderabad mint. But the production of the older indigenous gold and copper coins as well as their extensive use in the region continued for quite some time. This flexibility was possible because a centrally controlled minting structure of the north Indian variety was conspicuous by its absence in the south. In the latter region, including Golconda and the Hindu territories further south, minting was decentralized subject to licence and a fairly large number of mints operated in the area, bringing out coins which were not always comparable in weight and fineness across mints. This applied with particular force to *fanams*, where the alloy content of the coins brought out by different mints could be very different.

Coinage and Wage Payment

Coming next to the relationship between coin output on the one hand and wages and the logistics of wage payments on the other, it should be obvious that the mix of coin output in any society would be determined by the proportion of small sized transactions to total transactions including wage payments. Thus if wages are paid overwhelmingly on a weekly rather than a monthly basis, the proportion of coins of relatively smaller value in total coin output would be considerably greater than if this were not the case. This proportion would be still higher if the norm of wage payments involved daily payment. In societies with a single-metal coinage, the smaller coins would obviously be fractions of the principal coin and would bear a fixed relationship to it. This would be the case under multi-metal coinage as well provided there was a fixed relationship across coins of different metals. In such societies the production of coins of different metals and denominations would largely be a matter of metal availability and convenience. Of course, if the relative market value of different metals in terms of each other were to undergo a significant deviation from the fixed norm, coins of the metal whose relative value was on the increase would tend to be melted down.

The situation in Mughal India was more complicated than this. Not only was coinage multi-metal-gold *muhrs*, silver rupees and copper *dams* – but also 'free' with the public having the right to take bullion, old coins or foreign coins to an imperial mint for conversion after a time lag into newly minted coins. Most importantly, there was no fixed relationship across coins of different metals. As pointed out earlier, the gold *muhr* was largely a ceremonial coin also used extensively as a store of value. But it did not figure with any prominence in the settlement of ordinary transactions which were taken care of either by the silver rupee or the copper *dam*. Unless otherwise specified, a claim or an obligation stated in terms of rupees implied settlement in terms of the *sicca* rupee, namely a rupee coin manufactured during the current or the previous year. Payments made in rupee coins manufactured prior to the previous year, namely the *chalani* or the *khazana* rupees, would need to be enhanced by a market-determined premium that the *sicca* rupee carried over these coins. In practice, however, this premium was fairly defined and subject only to marginal fluctuations. The situation, however, was quite different with respect to the relationship between the *sicca* rupee and copper *dam*. According to Abul Fazl, the author of the *Ain-i-Akbari*,[15] an administered *dam* : rupee rate of 48:1 was devised around 1575 for purposes of government transactions. But the actual market rate of exchange deviated quite considerably from this ratio. The *dam* was reported to have gone up as high as 35:1 sometime before 1583 when another administered rate of 40:1 was prescribed. This is also the rate quoted for 1595-6, the year in which the *Ain-i-Akbari* was written. This often created situations of great anomaly and hardship for parti-cular sections of the society. To take a specific case, in 1575 while the rates of salary payment that Akbar's *mansabdars*[16] were obliged to make to the troopers engaged by them were specified in *dams*, 50 per cent of the actual payment was to be made in rupees, 25 per cent in gold coins and only the remaining 25 per cent in copper *dams*. To help the cause of the troopers to the extent possible, the emperor laid down a rule that in the event the market rate of exchange between the *dam* and the rupee turned more than 40 *dams* to a rupee (the administered rate at the time being 48:1), the conversion rate actually enforced would be 40:1.[17]

The ideal way to avoid these kinds of situations would have been to enforce a fairly strict parity between the coin in which the claim/obligation was specified and the coin in which the settlement was actually made. In other words, the only way to insure a worker against the risk of fluctuations in the *dam*: rupee ratio would have been to both specify the wage in terms of *dams* as well as to make the actual payment exclusively in that coin. This was usually but perhaps not always the case. By the same token, a large payment eventually to be collected in silver rupees must also be denominated in the same coin. It is indeed the case that whatever information on wage rates is available in sources such as the *Ain-i-Akbari* is almost exclusively in terms of *dams*, irrespective of whether the basis of payment was daily or monthly (there does not seem to have been a tradition of weekly payment at all) or whether it was a time rate payment or a piece rate payment. The situation changed somewhat in the seventeenth century from about 1620 onward when one-*anna*, two-*anna*, four-*anna*, and eight-*anna* coins (all fractions of the silver rupee coin – one-*anna* coin being one-sixteenth of a rupee) were also coined, though the scale on which these small silver coins were manufactured does not seem to have been very large. The result nevertheless was that while during the sixteenth century, copper coinage was probably the dominant coinage in Mughal India, this was no longer the case in the seventeenth century. John Deyell, for example, has demonstrated an immense contraction of copper minting after the close of Akbar's reign.[18] Wage data for this period are, therefore, also found stated in rupee terms, though the overwhelming medium in which they continued to be specified was the copper *dam*.

The only important exception to this pattern would seem to be the specification and the payment of wages as indeed other small-value transactions in terms of units of different kinds of uncoined non-standardized money alternatively referred to as 'humble' money. In Gujarat, the preferred uncoined medium of exchange was the *badam* (inedible bitter almond imported from Persia), 36 of which reportedly went for a copper *paisa* in 1646.[19] Other such mediums were pieces of lead and tin, etc. But by far the most extensively used such medium at least in Bengal and other parts of eastern India was the *cauri* or a sea-shell. In 1646, a copper *paisa* (which carried the same value as the *dam*) was reported to be commanding approximately 80 *cauris*.[20] More than a century later, a *paisa* was stated to be equal to a *ponny* of *cauris* which might well have consisted of 80 pieces.[21] The Maldive islands, south-west of Sri Lanka in the Indian Ocean, were the largest world producers of these shells at this time. In the fifteenth century, Venetian merchants conducted a re-export trade of Maldives *cauris* in the Mediterranean, from which they were transshipped across the Sahara to the gold and textile centres of West Africa. Later, in the sixteenth century, the Portuguese transferred apparently huge quantities of *cauris* from the Maldives to Portugal for re-export to Guinea, Benin and the Congo. In the Indian Ocean, the *cauris* were the principal medium through which the Maldives obtained goods such as coarse textiles and provisions like rice, oil, and sugar from major trading partners such as Bengal. Indeed, the trade with Maldives was one of the principal branches of trade carried on by the Bengal merchants from the port of Balasore in the seventeenth and the early eighteenth century. It is remarkable that at a time when trade carried on from Bengal ports such as Hugli and Balasore was undergoing an overall decline in the early years of the eighteenth century, the trade between Balasore and the Maldives was on the rise.[22] Enormous quantities of these shells thus found their way into Eastern India. While there obviously were alternative uses for these *cauris* such as for ornamentation, probably the largest single use to which they were put were as a medium of exchange. Wages are, therefore, often found recorded as both specified and paid in *cauris.* Even land revenue was often collected in this medium. C.R. Wilson refers to the English East India Company receiving its land revenue from *zamindars* in Calcutta in *cauris* and then converting it into rupees.[23]

The amount of information available on wage rates in different occupations in early modern India is distressingly small. It is also incapable of generating any meaningful long-term trends. But before we come to a discussion of this information, it might be useful to draw attention to some data that are available on the share of labour cost in the total cost of production of certain varieties of textiles manufactured in Bengal. The first set of data pertain to the 1680s and relate to three grades of *khasas*, a staple variety of muslins. About two-thirds of the price obtained by the weaver under the Indian variant of the putting-out system covered the costs of the raw material while the remainder was the reward for his labour. The mark-up by the intermediary merchant (calculated on the basis of the price agreed upon at the time of the contract between the Dutch East India Company and the intermediary merchant) was 35 per cent in the case of grade I, 55 per cent in grade II, and as much as 142 per cent in grade III.[24] It is remarkable that a century later, in the case of textile after textile, the relative share of the weaver's reward in the value obtained from the European buyer had come down to a quarter.[25] The explanation almost certainly was the changed status of the labour market. The 1680's were characterized by a growing gap in the rate of growth of the demand for Bengal textiles by the Dutch and the English East India Companies and that of their supply leading to a marked increase in the bargaining strength of the weavers vis-à-vis the intermediary merchants and that of the latter vis-à-vis the Companies. The 1770s, on the other hand, were characterized by a ruthless domination of the market by the English East India Company in consequence of its newly found political leverage in the province. The poor weaver was at the complete mercy of the Company and could expect hardly anything over and above the barest minimum subsistence.

As noted earlier, the data on wage rates themselves are rather scanty and do not admit of the construction of a proper time-series. During the sixteenth century, the wage data are almost exclusively expressed in terms of copper *dams* on a daily basis. Table 7.1 lists the information available on daily wage rates in respect of two time periods. The first of these is the mid-1590s and the source of the information is the *Ain-i-Akbari* which has a brief chapter titled 'On the wages of labourers' sanctioned for the imperial establishment. The second time period relates to the years 1637 and 1638, though some observations pertain to the years 1627 and 1630. The source of this set of observations is the documentation of the Dutch East India Company and these relate mainly to employees hired by the Company. The 'soldiers' in this list were hired to accompany the Company's caravans carrying goods and at times specie from Agra to Surat, etc. The workmen were hired in 1638 for the construction of the Company's factory at Agra. While the two sets of observations are obviously not fully comparable with

TABLE 7.1: DAILY WAGE RATE IN MUGHAL INDIA

Category of workers	*Ain-i-Akbari (1595) (in dams)*	*Dutch East India Company sources (1637-8) (in paisas)*
Carpenter	2-7 (for grades 5 to 1)	10-13
Bricklayer	3-3½ (for grades 2 and 1)	15
Lime worker	5-7 (for grades 3 to 1)	7
Wood-sawyer	2	12½
Bamboo-cutter	2	
Thatcher	2	
Water-carrier	2-3 (for grades 2 and 1)	
Labourer (*majur*)		4-7
Labourer in warehouse		9
Attendant		5-7
Soldier		7
Weaver		8-9
Artisan		10-12

Source: Abul Fazl 1977, *Ain-i-Akbari*, I, 235-6; Van Santen 1982, 102.

each other, they nevertheless can be used to indicate the broad orders of magnitude. What such a comparison in respect of categories where information is available in both the sets reveals quite unambiguously is the distinct and substantial rise in the daily wage rate over the period. The only exception to this pattern were the lime workers.

How does one explain this? At least two variables need to be taken into account in this connection. One is the average price level of food items which would perhaps be the most important single constituent of the wage goods basket. The year 1638 witnessed an unusual rise in wheat prices in Agra from 91 *paise* per maund of 69 Dutch ponds at the beginning of the year to Rs.1.74 on 24 April, to Rs.2.67 on 3 May to return to Rs.2.11 per maund on 12 July 1638.[26] It is not clear how representative or long lasting this kind of rise was but it seems to have had a hand in the rise in the wage rate. Thus Wollebrant Geleynssen de Jongh, the head of the Dutch East India Company's factory in Agra wrote that 'one has now to pay the labourers and the attendants much more than before'.[27]

The other variable that one needs to take into account is the changing value of the copper *dam* or *paisa* which was the medium in which the wage rate was usually expressed in relation to the silver rupee which in the course of the seventeenth century increasingly became the standard Mughal Indian coin. A quick look at Table 7.2 which gives this ratio for the years between 1583 and 1702 mainly for the cities of Surat and Agra points to distinct phases in this ratio. We have already noticed earlier the difference between the administered rate of 48 *dams* and then 40 *dams* to a rupee on the one hand and the market rate of exchange on the other. In 1583 a rupee commanded only 35 *dams* in the market against the administered rate of 40 *dams* thus favouring the wage earner who was paid in *dams*. The situation, however, changed drastically in the second quarter of the seventeenth century with the rupee generally commanding 50 and more *paisas*. The high wages expressed in *paisas* that we noted earlier in respect of the 1630s perhaps need to be interpreted in this context. The picture changed drastically yet once again in the 1660s and the 1670s with the rupee commanding no more than 30 to 34 *paisas*. Unfortunately, we do not have wage rate figures for this period but the growing burden on the employers was becoming quite evident. In 1661, for example, the Director of the Dutch East India Company establishment in Surat wrote, 'Considering that all wages have to be calculated and paid in *paisas*, those who are obliged to make daily wage and other small payments have to carry a distinctly larger burden.'[28] Emperor Aurangzeb, who was having repairs done to his pilgrim vessel, the *Ganj-i-Sawai* the same year at Surat and was obliged to have payments made to the carpenters and other workmen reckoned in *paisas*, was similarly reported to be suffering a loss because of the 'dearness of the *paisas* at Surat'.[29]

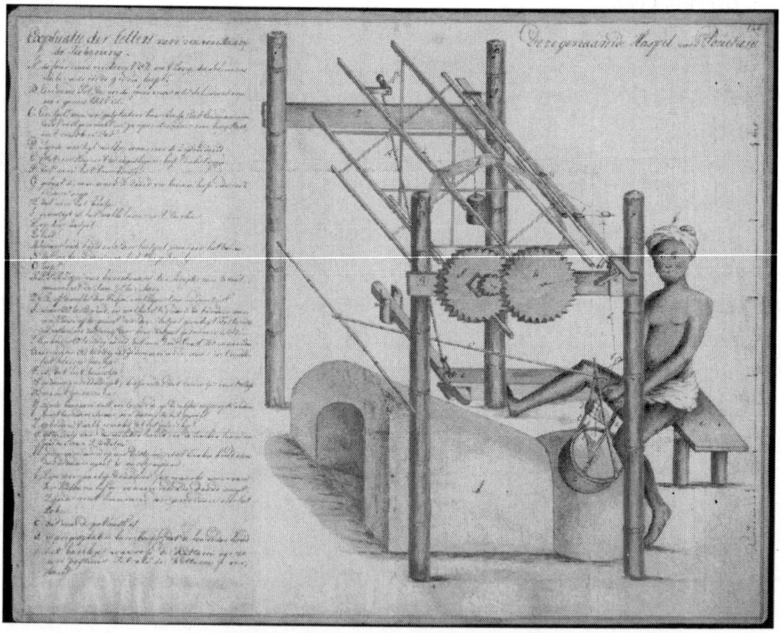

PLATE 7.1: DEPICTION OF THE SO-CALLED *HASPEL VAN POUCHON*: A MACHINE THAT INTEGRATES THE UNWINDING AND REELING OF SILK IN ONE PROCESS.

Source: ARA, Verzameling Buitenlandse Kaarten, Leupe (VEL) 1107, originally attached to a letter of J.M. Ross, opperkoopman at Cossimbazar, dated 27 December 1774 (VOC 3395, ff. 142-50). Used by permission.

From the point of view of the logistics of wage payments, it is interesting to note that according to Pelsaert, the month on occasions was regarded as consisting of forty days.[30] It is impossible to say how marginal or widespread this practice was. Also, itemized detailed information available in the papers of the Dutch East India Company on the costs incurred at the Rajmahal mint in Bengal in 1692 in coining gold bullion into *muhrs* includes items such as 'sweets for the beaters' and the 'cost of provisions for washermen and water carriers' employed at the mint in addition to the usual money wages paid to these categories of employees. Interestingly also, of the nine washermen employed at the mint, the seven employed on a permanent basis were paid Rs.2.75 per month while the two temporary ones received Rs.3 each.[31]

TABLE 7.2: RUPEE: *DAM* (PAISA) RATIO IN MUGHAL INDIA

Year	*City/Region*	*Dam (Paisas) per rupee*
1583	Agra	35
1623	Surat	57
1627	Agra	58
1630	Broach	41-3
1633	Gujarat	53-4
1636	Surat	56
1637	Agra	50-5*
1638	Agra	55-8*
1639	Agra	58
1642	Surat	56
1650	Surat	50
1657	Surat	40
1661	Surat	32
1662	Surat	30-1
1666	Surat	32-4
1681	Surat	30-4
1702	Surat	60-4

Note: *Monthly observations are available for Agra for 1637 and 1638. This figure represents the range for the entire year.
Source: Van Santen 1982, Tables 11 and 12, p. 114.

A Long-term Perspective

With respect to the questions of coinage and wages, there were both continuities as well as discontinuities between the pre-colonial and the colonial periods. While the degree of monetization in the economy would generally seem to have gone up in the nineteenth century, it was by no means the case that all or even the bulk of the wage payments were made in terms of money. Dharma Kumar's work on agricultural wages in the Madras Presidency, for example, establishes that in the early nineteenth century, the wages of both attached and casual workers were generally paid in grain, apart from perquisites of cloth and money.[32] A plausible explanation of the survival of a substantial non-monetized sector in India in the nineteenth and the twentieth centuries is that given the extremely high level of risk and uncertainty of Indian agriculture in conditions of erratic weather and price fluctuations, the typical farming household has always sought to protect itself by preserving an adequate minimum level of subsistence activity.

As for the system of coinage, the Mughal Indian norm of 'free' minting was discontinued as of 1893 with the closure of the Indian mints for the free coinage of gold and silver, with the government retaining the power to coin silver rupees on its own account. This was essentially an outcome of the rise in the international output of silver in the 1870s resulting in its substantive depreciation in relation to gold. As a result of this depreciation, the gold value of the rupee had fallen from about 2 shillings in 1871 to 1s.2d in 1892. This had aggravated the budgetary problem for the Government of India in so far as it had increased the burden of the home charges, namely its sterling obligations such as interest on public debt, pensions, payments to the War Office and the cost of government stores bought in England.

Between 1898-9 and 1915-16, a gold exchange standard operated in India. As from September 1931, following the British government's decision to abandon the gold standard, the rupee was officially linked to sterling. As for wage payments in money terms, they were now almost universally made in rupees (both notes and coins) making the production of smaller coins representing fractions of the rupee that much less necessary for the purpose. In 1918, for example, against a total of 1,354 million rupees worth of notes in circulation, the number of rupee coins was 279 million and of smaller coins only 1.62 million rupees worth.[33]

A study done in the 1970s comparing the purchasing power of the wages mentioned in the *Ain-i-Akbari* for Agra with those in the Government of India's *Labour Bureau's Family Living Survey of Industrial Workers* in 1958-9 for five major cities Delhi, Kanpur, Bombay, Calcutta and Madras produced the following results. For Akbar's time, the monthly average wage rate assumed was Rs.2.75. For 1958-9, the monthly wage assumed was Rs.90 for Delhi, Rs.77 for Kanpur, Rs.104 for Bombay, Rs.79 for Calcutta and Rs.66 for Madras. It was found that in terms of food grains, the purchasing power of wages in Akbar's time was consistently higher than that in 1958-9 in all the five cities except for one city and one commodity *moong* (a variety of lentils) in Kanpur. The purchasing power was also considerably higher in terms of milk, curd and clarified butter, and higher by smaller margins in terms of meat. However, both Bombay and Madras had a substitute in 1958-9 in the form of fish which was much cheaper relatively than goat meat in sixteenth century Agra. On the other hand, the twentieth century worker could buy more of vegetable oils, sugar and jaggery, more salt and spices and more of most vegetables.[34]

A more recent study attempts a comparison of real wages of weavers in south India with those in Britain during the latter half of the eighteenth century. The price of grain in each region is used to measure real purchasing power. For south India, grain wages have been calculated in terms of rice while for Britain the grain equivalence has been expressed in terms of bread. Since bread contains only 1,000 calories per pound and rice 1,500, the bread figures have been converted to their grain equivalents for comparison. In the mid-eighteenth century, the wages of rural and small-town weavers in Britain are stated to have ranged from 7s to 9s a week. This could purchase 65 to 75 pounds of bread, which is calorically equivalent to 40 to 50 pounds of grain. A London weaver is believed to have made 10s 6d per week, which translated to 60 pounds of grain. The highest earnings allegedly went to the silk weavers of Spitalfields, who in 1747 earned 18s to 21s a week, the equivalent of 120 to 140 pounds of grain. In mid-eighteenth century south India, the earnings of calico weavers in Cuddalore could purchase 65 pounds of rice per week. In 1800, a more highly skilled weaver in Tanjore made the equivalent of 85 pounds of rice a week. According to data from the 1790s, the manufacturers of finest calicoes in south India earned two and a half times more per week than a Cuddalore weaver, an amount which in the 1760s could have purchased 160 pounds of rice. It is then concluded that an average south Indian weaver's wages were higher than those of a weaver in rural and small-town Britain, and comparable to those of a London weaver.[35]

It should, however, be obvious that the conclusions of such studies are subject to strong reservations. In the latter study, the principal methodological problem would seem to consist in relying exclusively on grain consumption as an index of total consumption, both food and non-food, and deriving conclusions regarding real wages entirely on that basis. Data-wise, it is not at all clear how selective or representative the observations with regard to the money wage rate particularly with regard to south India are. Also, there is no indication at all regarding the relative weights in the total weaver population of the categories producing different varieties of textiles. A range of real wages from 65 to 160 pounds of rice without any idea of the relative weights of the different components in the weaver work force in south India indeed does not tell one very much.

From about the 1880s onward there is a considerable body of information on money and real wage rates prevailing in different sectors of the Indian economy. An important source is the official annual publication *Prices and Wages in India* started in 1861. But there are severe problems in the use of this information arising principally from lack of comparability across time and across industries in a given sector. In brief, however, the following picture emerges. The annual average of the agricultural real wage index calculated by K. Mukherji (1890 = 100) stood at 93 during 1871-3, 99 during 1878-82 and 96 during 1896-1900. This is the overall picture. The regional picture shows greater variation. Labourers may in fact have experienced an improvement in living standards in the major cash crop growing regions. Cash crop production meant increased demand for labour with increases in cropped area and/or labour intensity. Signs of material prosperity for the rural population can in general be seen in Punjab and Bengal. For the period 1900-20, the picture is quite positive for south India. In coastal Andhra, there is evidence suggesting that real wages in the 1920s were higher than in the 1900s. In districts (especially in Madras) where commercialization combined with large net emigration, there were signs of a rise in wages. After 1920, however, most studies find the onset of a declining tendency. Money wages fell sharply during the Great Depression. In some cases, real wages also fell. Dharma Kumar's conclusion that 'the agricultural labourers probably felt the effect of the pressure of population after 1921 more keenly than any other group' seems valid.[36]

In the modern industrial sector, the first major industry to come up was that of producing cotton textiles. The first mill was set up in Bombay in the 1850s by a Parsi entrepreneur, C.N. Davar. In the succeeding decades, both entrepreneurship and capital in the industry continued to be wholly Indian as did the market for its output. A total absence of tariff protection or any other form of assistance by the colonial regime notwithstanding, the industry registered a rapid rate of growth. By 1914, it had become the world's fourth – or fifth – largest cotton textile industry. Information regarding movements in the wage rate in the industry begins to be available only around 1875: until 1905 the wages were quite stable. This, however, should not be construed as evidence of unresponsiveness of wages to the pressures of labour shortage. In 1897, when plague caused thousands of workers to flee Bombay and when mills were desperately short of hands, wages rose more than 68 per cent in a few short months.[37] In the twentieth century, the wage rate level rose sharply between 1914 and 1923 mainly in consequence of a sharp rise in prices.

The interwar years required a contraction of the labour force as the industry struggled to resolve its economic difficulties. The years between 1926 and 1937 witnessed a steady fall in the level of wages. After 1937 the trend reversed and wages rose swiftly during World War II to the 1947 peak. But as in World War I, it seems clear that wages lagged behind wartime price rises and were pulled upward only by the cost of living.[38]

With respect to the modern industrial sector as a whole, the picture was somewhat more positive. As far as real wage movements in large scale factory industry are concerned, the best series both in terms of care of construction and explicitness of assumptions is the one by K. Mukherji. This series suggests relative stability (or slight declines) until just before World War I. From 1907-11 until immediately after World War I there was an obvious fall while the inter-war period saw fairly significant rises in real wages. Mukherji's data deviate from conventional wisdom in their suggestion that real wages did not decline during World War II.[39]

Summary and Conclusions

This chapter has examined the relationship between long distance trade, coinage, and wages in India over the past half a millennium or so. Over this period, the relationship across these variables was different in crucial respects as between the pre-colonial period stretching from the sixteenth to the eighteenth centuries on the one hand and the period of British colonial rule in the country on the other. In the pre-colonial period, the amount of money supply in the economy was critically dependent upon the amount of treasure imported from the rest of Asia as well as from Europe through the agency of both the Indian and other Asian traders on the one hand and the European corporate enterprises and private traders on the other. The Mughal Indian coinage system consisted of three metals gold, silver and copper but was not truly trimetallic in content because of the absence of a fixed relationship across the coins of the three metals. In order to avoid inconvenience and even more so the risk arising out of the uncertainty of the changing relative value of coins of one metal in terms of those of the other two, the practice followed was to generally specify obligations/claims in terms of the coins of a particular metal as also to collect/make payment by and large in coins of the same metal. The use of gold *muhrs* was largely confined to ceremonial occasions.

Large transactions were specified and effected in silver *sicca* rupees while small transactions, including wage payments, were made in terms of copper *dams*. This called for a certain mix in coin output and, if necessary, the state was willing to step in to help achieve such a mix. This picture was modified to a certain extent in the seventeenth century when silver coinage became relatively more important and coins representing fractions of the silver rupee were manufactured. Monthly wages are then found stated more and more in terms of silver rupees, though daily wages continued to be expressed in copper *dams*. Non-standardized 'humble' money, particularly *cauris* in the case of eastern India, was also an important medium of wage payments during this period. The actual amount of wage data available for the pre-colonial period, however, is rather scanty not admitting of the construction of time series or an analysis of long-term trends. But a careful analysis of the available data reveals a number of interesting outcomes. The daily wage data are overwhelmingly found expressed in copper *dams* or *paisas*. The rupee value of the wages obviously fluctuated in accordance with changes in the ratio between the silver rupee and the copper *dam* or *paisa*. It is useful to remember that between the late sixteenth and the late seventeenth century, the available evidence points to the existence of several distinct phases in this ratio. Whenever the value of copper coinage rose in relation to that of the silver rupee, the employers saw this as evidence of rising wage burden. The device of providing a part of the wages in kind was evidently intended as a partial protection against falling value of the copper coin and ensuring a certain minimum real wage rather than depending entirely on a purely nominal wage. One might also note that a comparison of real wages in Mughal India with the 1950s as also a comparison of real wages in south India with those in Britain in the eighteenth century was found to be exercises fraught with many problems.

The pattern of relationship between long distance trade, coinage, and wages was qualitatively of a very different kind in the nineteenth and the first half of the twentieth century. Following the stoppage of the import of treasure, there no longer was any relationship of consequence between the first two of the three variables. Free minting of the Mughal Indian vintage was abandoned towards the end of the nineteenth century and the money supply henceforth consisted overwhelmingly of notes though rupee coins and coins representing fractions of the rupee continued to be manufactured. The information on wage rates begins to be substantial from about the 1880s onward but problems of coverage and comparability abound making it possible to make only general statements regarding long-term trends.

NOTES

1. Smith 1976, II, 139.
2. Wallerstein 1974, I, Ch. 7.
3. Ibid., I, 46.
4. Ibid., 1980, II, 109.
5. Ibid., 1974, I, 41.
6. Sperling 1962, 450. Quoted in Wallerstein 1980, II, 109.
7. Blitz 1967, 40.
8. Atwell 1977, 5.
9. Von Glahn 1996; Richards 1983.
10. Little 1967.
11. Prakash 1988, 475-91.
12. Van Santen 1982, 109-10.
13. Prakash 1988.
14. Ibid., 1987.
15. The *Ain-i-Akbari* is part of a larger work that Abul Fazl Allami undertook on the orders of Emperor Akbar (reigned 1556-1605). The two volumes of his *Akbarnama* record the events of Akbar's reign, preceded by an account of the reigns of Babur and Humayun, Akbar's grandfather and father respectively. The third volume was devoted to recording the *Ainha-i-Muqaddas-i-Shahi* (the Sacred Imperial Regulations). It is this volume which is ordinarily referred to as the *Ain-i-Akbari.* I have used the third and enlarged edition translated from Persian by Blochmann 1977.
16. Under this system, all the senior military and civil administrative positions throughout the Mughal empire were held by officials known as *mansabdars.* From the time of Akbar onwards, each official held a dual numerical rank *zat* (personal) and *sawar* (cavalry).The *zat* rank determined the official's status in the hierarchy besides his personal salary per annum, while the other rank specified the extent of the military obligations of the holder in terms of maintaining a certain number of horses, troopers and military equipment to be made available for imperial service, whenever required. The *sawar* rank also determined the annual sum of money to be reimbursed to the

official against this obligation. The pay-claim of each official was met either in cash or through the grant of revenue collection rights over a specified area of land whose annual assessed revenue equalled the amount of the claim. Such areas were then known as *jagirs*. In the initial years of his reign, Akbar insisted upon meeting the pay-claims of the *mansabdars* exclusively in terms of cash, but the exigencies of administrative convenience later necessitated the increasing use of the *jagir* method. By the time we reach the period of Aurangzeb (1659-1707), revenue collection rights over nearly four-fifths of the total land in the empire had been alienated to the *mansabdars*.

17. Abul Fazl 1977, I 275; Habib 1987B, 137-70.
18. Deyell 1987.
19. Van Twist 1648, 58. The chapter containing this reference is reprinted, without its source being indicated, as Appendix Vc in Vol. II, Part III of Van Dam 1939, 100-1.
20. Van Twist 1648, 58.
21. *Nationaal Archief* [hereafter NA], *Voormalige Nederlandse Bezittingen in Voor-Indie* [hereafter NBV-I], No. 66, 'Bericht van den Koopman Johannes Mattheus Ross wegens de commissie in de arrengs (met bylagen)', 1767. Submitted to Director George Lodewijk Vernet on 26 December 1767. Appendix N, note 1. The volume is not foliated.
22. Prakash 1979, 43-70.
23. Wilson 1895-1917, I, 219-22; II, 254.
24. The precise figures were 65 per cent for grade I, 66 per cent for grade II and 68 per cent for grade III (Instructions by Commissioner van Reede tot Drakenstein to Bengal factors of the Dutch East India Company, 21 February 1687, NA, *Verenigde Oost-Indische Compagnie* (VOC), 1435. The volume is not foliated).
25. NA, NBV-I, 66, note 3. The volume is not foliated.
26. Van Santen 1982, 102.
27. Ibid., 93.
28. NA, L. Winnincx at Surat to Directors dated 17 December 1661, VOC 1234, f.115; Van Santen 1982, 115.
29. NA, L. Winnincx at Surat to Directors dated 17 December 1661, VOC 1234, ff.115v -116: Van Santen 1982, 115.
30. Kolff and Van Santen 1979.
31. NA,VOC 1502, ff. 1387-90.
32. Kumar 1965.
33. Chandavarkar 1983, 762-803.
34. Desai 1978, 53-79.
35. Parthasarathi 1998, 79-109.
36. Roy 2000, 80-1.
37. Morris 1965, 49.
38. Ibid., 51.
39. Ibid., 1983, 553-676.

8

Coin Circulation in the Bihar Fortress of Barharia, 1771

Jan Lingen and Jan Lucassen

In an earlier article, we had discussed the booty and, in particular, the coins found by the troops of the British East India Company (EIC) after the capture of the fortress of Deeg (or Dig), the second capital of the Princely State of Bharatpur in Rajasthan.[1] This siege, by a contingent under General Gerard Lake, with 5,000 infantry, lasted two weeks, from 11 until 24 December 1804.

Because such booties reflect the internal economy of a fortress and, more specifically, of the men defending it, this kind of information tells us about daily coin circulation patterns at the time. It is therefore interesting to analyze a second booty, found nearly twenty-five years earlier, after the capture of 'Burraria Fort' in north-western Bihar, located by road 850 km east of Deeg.

It shows, once more, how important it is to also take 'paper hoards' into consideration for our reconstruction of the coin usage of the common man and we hope that more such hoards may be dug up from military and other archival records. This is not entirely impossible because the booty in warfare had to be divided among the troops according to strict rules, which means precise recording in the first place as we explained in our previous article on this topic.

Burraria Fort and its Conquest

'Burraria' as it appears in the records in 1771 (see Appendix 8.1) may be identified with Barharia (बड़हरिया), presently a Block in the

Siwan district, situated in the north-western part of Bihar. Siwan was originally a subdivision of Saran sircar (district). This low-lying part of Bihar was mainly agricultural and its small peasant farms yielded three harvests per year, of which rice was the most important crop. Consequently, it was densely populated.[2]

Barharia Fortress, or remnants of it, still exists (see Map 8.1).[3] In 1771, it measured nearly one hectare and was described as follows:

> The Fortress itself is in the Usual Form of other Mud Forts, but the walls are rather loftier, from ninety to hundred yards square, with a high Bastion at each Corner; but the Ditch which constitutes the Difficulty of this Place, is not less than forty yards broad, quite full of Water the whole year round, & to appearance, as well as by Report, of a great Depth, nor is there any way of entering the Fort, but by a Boat.

Later, it was discovered that there was even an extra ditch within it.[4]

On modern maps, it can be found under the name 'Yamuna Garh,' situated southwest of Barharia on the road to Siwan. The ruins are still surrounded by a wide rectangular moat (see Figs. 8.1a and b).[5]

To understand the wider context of the capture of Barharia Fortress we must first turn our attention to the fiscal history of Bihar.[6] After the Battle of Buxar in 1764 and following the Treaty of Allahabad in 1765, the British acquired the rights to collect revenue (called *diwani*) in the name of the Mughal emperor.[7] This provided them with great economic power, but at a cost, as not all landowners were prepared to yield willingly to the new regime. Apart from a readjustment of the sums to be raised by the former Mughal subah (province) Bihar, they initially copied the existing system completely. In 1769, however, the Indian officials (*nazims*) were replaced by European supervisors, responsible for the collection per district, to be coordinated from 1770 by the Revenue Council, based at Patna.[8] The new system proved unsuccessful, and the system of European supervisors was abolished already in 1784. No doubt these British supervisors, functioning between 1769 and 1784, were not much beloved among the taxpayers. This was certainly true in 1770 because of the terrible and widespread

FIGS. 8.1a & b: BARHARIA FORTRESS, ACTUAL SITUATION FROM TWO DIFFERENT ANGLES. PIC. COURTESY: SANJAY GARG

famine in Saran, which forced the British to concede tax reductions.[9]

The direct collection of land taxes in Mughal India, as well as under the British, was left to the *zamindars*, the big landowners who, with the help of their right hands, called *patwaris*, were responsible for collecting taxes – of course, with a sizeable margin at the cost of the peasants, the actual producers. Unsurprisingly, in these early years of British tax collection in Bihar, we hear of difficulties with several of these *zamindars*, not only from the one for Barharia, the central figure in this article (see below). First and foremost, was Maharaja Fateh Sahi of Hussepur, who, from the inception of the new regime, refused to pay the revenue and, despite numerous military expeditions against him, was able to persist in his resistance from 1765 until he died in 1791.[10] Furthermore, Raja Jugal Kishor, *zamindar* of Bettiah (north of Barharia), and the

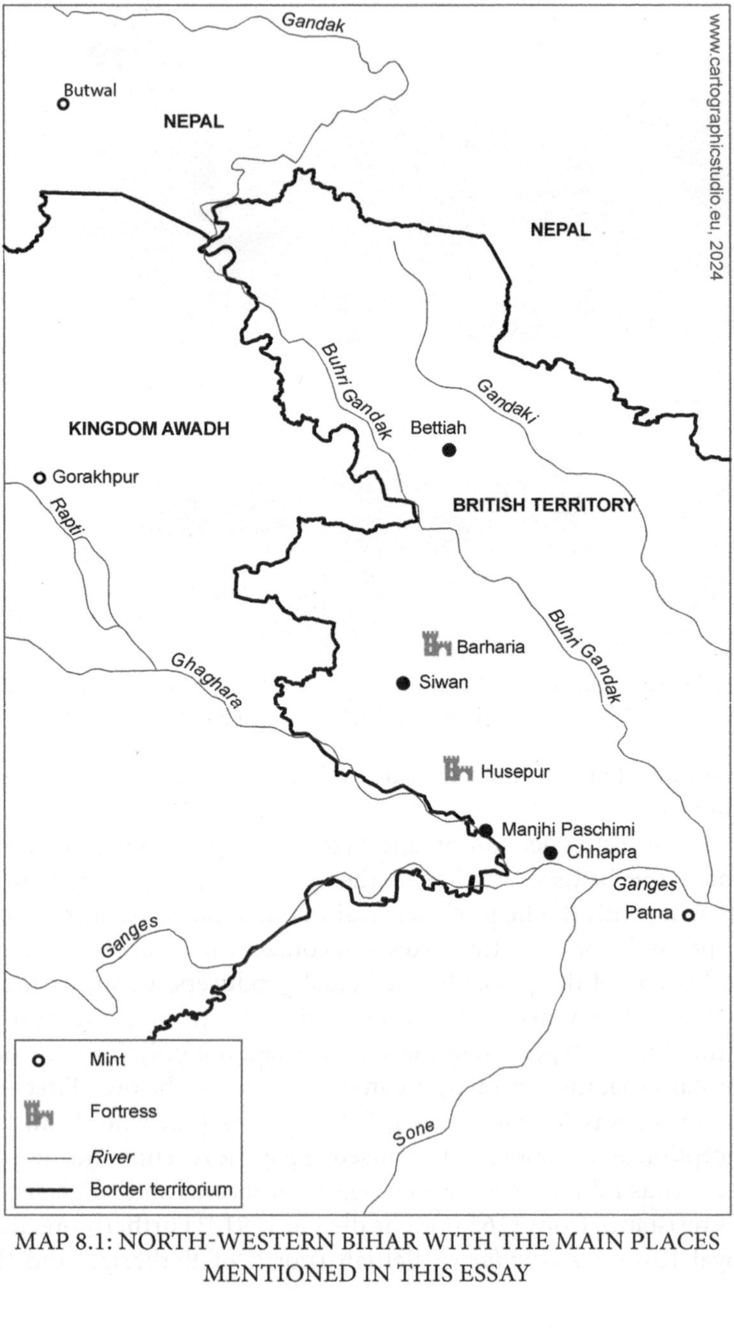

MAP 8.1: NORTH-WESTERN BIHAR WITH THE MAIN PLACES MENTIONED IN THIS ESSAY

zamindars Kripanarayan in 1770,[11] Raja Azamgarh in 1771,[12] and Maharaja Shitab Ray in 1773.[13]

Some of the *zamindars* also had a military significance, like Shaikh Fakr Ullah of Barharia. He even owned a fortress, which was strategically interesting for the British, most likely in their attempts to defeat Maharaja Fateh Sahi of Hussepur.[14] The oldest information we have about this fort dates from two centuries earlier, when a certain 'Kabul Mohammad of Barharia,' an Afghan Chief and supporter of Daud Khan (this is likely a reference to the last sultan of Bengal 1572-6), was among the opponents of Akbar.[15] In Bihar, the emperor had found a strong supporter in Raja Jubraj Sahi of Hathwa, who had fortresses at Kalyanpur and Hussepur, both in Siwan. In one of these battles between the Mughal emperor and his Bengali-Bihari adversaries, Kabul Mohammad of Barharia was killed by Jubraj Sahi. Although the Mughals prevailed, the fortress of Barharia seems to have remained in such a state that it could be used two hundred years later to resist the new masters of India, the British.

One of the new supervisors was Edward Golding (1746-1818), appointed to collect the land revenue in the sircar of Saran, which, since the readjustment of 1765, had the highest rate of assessment in north Bihar.[16] Such a job could be highly profitable because this young man, having arrived in India in 1763 at age 17, is said to have made himself a 'considerable' fortune on his return to England in January 1780 at age 35, having served the East India Company with 'unsullied honour and integrity.' This cannot have been possible with the as such fairly high salary of Rs. 1,000 for his monthly allowance, which he had decided to pay himself.[17] It was this Edward Golding who was confronted with the resistance of Raja Shaikh Fakr Ullah, the *zamindar* of Barharia.

When exactly Golding got the idea to take the Barharia Fortress by force is not known, but it is likely that he had already decided in January 1771 to force Shaikh Fakr Ullah to give up his fortress, the possession of which Golding considered essential for his wider attempts to bring Maharaja Fateh Sahi, the *zamindar* of Hussepur, to his knees. Golding suspected that the evil forces of the Marathas, and possibly of Awadh too, were behind the Maharajah. A second motive for taking the fortress will have been making Shaikh Fakr Ullah pay the revenue due for the Barharia *zamindari* in the famine year 1770, fully and in the required currency, i.e. 'sanwat' or 'sonaut' rupees, and not in 'inferior sorts of rupees'.[18] But how to proceed? Shaikh Fakr Ullah was an absentee landlord, who resided in Awadh, and therefore outside the EIC territory, and was not willing to go there. Nor could he be accused of an outright refusal to pay the taxes at that time. In the absence of this pretext, the preparations had to be made secretly, according to Golding.[19]

On 13 February, Golding had finalized his plans together with Captain Benjamin Ashe (1741-1808).[20] The attack should not be postponed as

> the present season is the best calculated for such an undertaking; The Harvest not being yet reaped, their stock of Provisions within the Fort, can be but small, And as the Zemindar will I hope have completed his first half years Rent, in about 15 Days more the remainder will be better secured, by making this Attack before the Grain is carried off, & it will likewise be an inducement to the Ryots to continue in their respective Habitations.[21]

Captain Ashe was convinced that it was not possible to take the fort by surprise because of the width and depth of the ditch and the height of the walls, which would require the construction of rafts and high ladders – preparations that would inevitably be seen by the defenders. He therefore proposed requesting a large gun, larger than the two three-pounders, now available at Siwan. In addition, three companies of sepoys were deemed necessary to occupy the place after making the breach. Two could march directly from Chhapra, the capital of the sircar situated on the northern shore of the Ganga. Together with Ashe's own company, marching via a different route from Siwan, they would surprise the occupants of Barharia Fort.

Golding proposed the following pretext to start the action against Shaikh Fakr Ullah:

> In order to be acquainted with the Man's Determination & to give him an Opportunity of delivering up the Fort, without being considered as a rebellious, & disaffected Zemindar, I would propose to inform him that

I had received an order from Patna, to remove the stores now at Sewan, to Barrareea as a Place of greater safety for a Magazine, & it is, therefore, necessary for him to withdraw his Family, & Dependants from thence, should he refuse, there would be a sufficient Reason for immediately attacking him, or his Compliance would answer the same End.

At the same time, a tahsildar could be ordered to collect his *zamindari's* revenue. Three days later, the Board of Revenue had already agreed, stressing the need for 'the utmost secrecy'. However, they did not want to act immediately.[22]

Nearly two months later, on 6 April, the time had come, and the Board of Revenue sent a letter to Golding that the two companies at Chhapra were ready to march via Manjee (Manjhi Paschimi), to be followed by the Artillery with two eighteen-pounders and a mortar. They were now in a hurry because the expected onset of the rains would make the passage through marshy land impossible.[23] In a last attempt to resolve matters peacefully, the Revenue Council at Patna suggested offering Shaikh Fakr Ullah, in exchange for his fortress, the revolting *zamindari* of Hussepur.[24]

On 15 April, Captain Ashe arrived on the outskirts of Barharia, which, with an estimated 1,000 troops and five pieces of cannon, was under command of Shaikh Abdoor Raheem, the *naib* (deputy) of Shaikh Fakr Ullah. Awaiting reinforcements with heavy guns from Chhapra, Ashe sent a messenger to the commander with a *parwanna*, an official ultimatum in Persian from Edward Golding, dated 25 *Zilhidge* (11 April), saying:

As the Fort of Burraria is now required for the Service of the Government and you are the Person in Charge of that Place, Captain Ashe is now going to lay up some stores there, and you are on his Arrival to deliver it up to him. Accordingly, your Compliance in this case will be for the advantage both of your master and yourself.[25]

The defenders answered immediately and unequivocally by shooting a sepoy of Ashe's company. At the same time, they sent a letter (unfortunately intercepted by the British) asking for assistance from a neighbouring *zamindar*.[26] Captain Ashe now seemed to panic and requested more troops and artillery, including two twenty-four-pounders. Fresh troops arrived on the last day of April under the command of Lieutenant-Colonel Thomas Goddard (*c.* 1740-83), answerable to Colonel Alexander Champion (+1793), commanding the First Brigade at Danapur Cantonment. This military reaction led to confusion on the British side about who was in the lead: the revenue authorities or the army. One of the issues was what to do after the expected and hoped-for capture of the fort 'as we [the Patna Council of Revenue] are told there is some money & Effects as well as stores in the Fort & the Zemindar is in arrears to the Government. We purpose desiring Col Goddard to secure them & send us a list of them.'[27] The conflict had now escalated to such an extent that the authorities at Fort William in Calcutta had to be informed.[28]

Finally, after three and a half weeks of siege, on 10 May, the defenders of the fort surrendered to Colonel Thomas Goddard. How that happened has not been reported, only that 'the Family of Shaik Facquir Ullaw are retired to the House of Mahomed Ally, a Neighbouring Zemindar.' Golding opined that the retention of one company under the command of Captain Ashe would be sufficient to stay at the fort but that all other troops should return as soon as possible to their quarters 'as the Deserted Inhabitants will be fearful of returning to the Districts till our troops are removed from them.' His concern was clearly the continuation of agriculture and, thus, of tax payments. The Council of Revenue opted for two companies.[29]

According to his instructions, Goddard took possession of all the movables in the fort, although he feared that 'the lenient terms' prescribed by the Council of Revenue meant that the defenders had been able to remove part of the valuables. Nevertheless, he had managed to safeguard a sum of about Rs. 15,000, albeit he considered it 'so trifling a sum' that he sought permission to distribute it among his troops, as had been done on an earlier, similar occasion.[30] This was not at all evident for the authorities at Patna and Fort William. The latter ordered that all effects found in the fort should be returned to their respective owners. A long conflict between Goddard (and his sepoys, to whom he must undoubtedly have promised the booty), on the one hand, and the civil authorities was to follow, the outcome of which is unclear. In any case, as late as 7 September 1772 Goddard had not yet returned the Rs. 12,000, said to have been taken from Fort Barharia.[31]

Edward Golding had other concerns, as we have seen already. Already within a week, he proposed to the Council of Revenue to release nearly all prisoners 'with all proper encouragement to Continue in the Country,' an important indication that the peasants belonging to the zemindari had been defending the fort, not professional soldiers. The exception were Emum Bucsh, the nephew, and Shaikh Abdoolah, the son of Shaikh Fakr Ullah. Golding had been assured by Abdoor Sittar Cawn, 'a Person nearly connected with & Belonging to Shaik Fuckeer Ullaw,' that these two important prisoners were willing and able to settle the revenue dispute of the *zamindari* and to convince the *zemindar* himself to meet Golding to resolve all issues. Golding was in favour of this idea because: 'The Prosperity and Cultivation of that District does certainly greatly depend on his Speedy Return and the Management of it being placed without the loss of Time under such part of his family as are already here.' As an extra argument he added piously that the inhabitants 'are really Attached to their Old Zemindar.'[32] We do not know the precise outcome of these negotiations and, admittedly, they are not important for our main argument, but we may suppose that, finally, matters were arranged more or less accordingly.[33]

The Booty

What the victors discovered in 1771, and apparently found worthwhile enough to register, can be divided into coins and precious metals, goods for use by the soldiers, as well as various other materials, which were worth putting up for sale. This latter category consisted of precious textiles (85 pieces of silk, 29 pieces of chintz, and nine pieces of gingham), two elephant teeth, and two small remnants of woolen cloth. This, as well as the big tent (*marquee*), must have been the property of the household of the raja himself, which was completely forfeited.[34]

The goods, meant for direct use by the defenders of the fort – as we have seen, some 1,000 tenant farmers, share croppers, and maybe even agricultural labourers belonging to the *zamindari* and mobilized by the raja – consisted of indispensable daily food (still unweighted grains of all sorts and part of the cooking pots and vessels used to prepare it) and, possibly, also the 225 pieces of white cloth. Central to our discussion are the coins and precious metals (gold and silver, as well as copper).

Gold Coins

The report distinguishes between old and, apparently, new gold *mohurs*, most probably the raja's savings. The 211 new *mohurs* are valued at 15 rupees each (derived from the total sum of 3,165 rupees).

As the regnal year 13 of Shah Alam II started in April 1771, the new golden mohurs must bear previous dates, most likely regnal year (RY) 10 and 11, struck by the EIC from 1769 with the name Murshidabad (also struck at Calcutta; Fig. 8.2).[35]

FIG. 8.2: GOLD *MOHUR* OF THE EIC, MURSHIDABAD, AH 1183/ RY. 11, WEIGHT 12.28 G., DIAMETER 24.3 MM. REF.: STEVENS 2.11; PR. 18; *KM*. 94.1 (PRIVATE COLLECTION)

The 54 old *mohurs* are more difficult to identify with certainty. The divergence between the book value of 15 rupees and the actual value of slightly less than 9 rupees (the total sum of Rs. 817:5 divided by 54 old pieces) is hard to explain. The 1766 issue of the Murshidabad *mohur* was put into circulation for 14 rupees.[36] However, in May 1768, the new mint master James Alexander (1730-1802) wrote that, despite the positive order of the government, this *mohur* 'now sells publickly in the bazar for 13 rupees 12 annas,' which was mainly due to the rise in the value of silver. The issue of 1766 proved to be a failure and the *mohurs* were then recalled by the Company at a considerable loss, at the original rate of 14 rupees. It is, therefore, unlikely that the Murshidabad *mohurs* of the 1766 issue were part of the 54 old *mohurs* with a book value of 15 rupees. What else they could be is pure guesswork (Figs. 8.3–8.4). *Mohurs* struck at nearby Patna (Azimabad) since Akbar's time may qualify most. Also, nearby Mu'azamabad (Gorakhpur) qualifies, but none of these possible identifications would explain the difference in book value and the actual value as mentioned in our source.

FIG. 8.3: GOLD MOHUR OF THE NAWABS OF BENGAL, BIHAR, AND ORISSA (10.4 G.), AZIMABAD (PATNA) I.N.O. ALAMGIR II, AH - /RY. 3 (1756/57) (ZENO 322809)

FIG. 8.4: GOLD *MOHUR* OF AWADH (10.91 G.) I.N.O. MUHAMMAD SHAH, MU'AZZAMABAD (GORAKHPUR), AH 1148/RY. 18 (ZENO 438.16)

Silver

The silver appears in three different forms: as 7,906 rupees without specifications, as 'old silver,' valued at Rs. 844 and as 'silver plates,' valued at Rs. 815:12. The first question is what is meant by old silver? Parallel to the distinction made between two sorts of *mohurs*, we may suppose that, also in this case, the silver old rupees are meant, to be distinguished from new ones, bearing RY 10 or 11. Alternatively, silver jewellery, belonging to the raja's family (or that of his commander) might be meant, and the silver plates may also have been actually used by them. Of course, old silver coins, old silver jewellery, and silver plates may eventually be brought to a mint for conversion into rupees, but jewellery and plates of course cannot be used to pay somebody directly, let alone the peasants defending the fort.

This considerable sum of good silver rupees may have had a savings function, like the gold *mohurs*. More likely, however, it represents the land revenue collected by the raja and claimed by his new British masters. At the same time, by refusing to hand it over to them, the raja could use it for the defence of his fortress, first by buying gunpowder or the raw materials to make it.

Like with the *mohurs*, and given the place and time, we must try to understand which rupees are being referred to here. There are several possibilities, among which the rupees struck at nearby Patna (Azimabad) are the most likely ones, followed by Murshidabad and, much less likely, Akbarnagar and Muhammadabad Benares, and, finally, Gorakhpur (Mu'azzamabad), see Figs. 8.5 to 8.9. Our argument for the Patna rupees follows from a report, written seventeen years after the events, here described by A. Montgomerie, the Collector of Chhapra.[37] According to him, the roughly 1.5 silver rupees in circulation in the sircars of Saran and Chhapra, were mainly those minted at Patna by 'the nawob of the Subah Behar' until 1768/9 (Fig. 8.5).

FIG. 8.5: SILVER RUPEE OF THE EIC (11.29 G.) I.N.O. SHAH ALAM II, AZIMABAD (PATNA), AH - /RY. 10 (1768/69). REF.: STEVENS 5.21; PR. 108; *KM*.; ZENO 169892

FIG. 8.6: SILVER RUPEE OF THE EIC (11.67 G.) I.N.O. SHAH ALAM II, CALCUTTA/MURSHIDABAD, AH 1181/RY. 8 (1766/67). REF.: STEVENS 2.75; PR. 90; *KM*.; ZENO 274453

FIG. 8.7: SILVER RUPEE OF THE NAWABS OF BENGAL, BIHAR, AND ORISSA (11.60 G.) I.N.O. MUHAMMAD SHAH, AKBARNAGAR, AH - /RY. 25 (1742/43). REF.: *KM*.436.4; ZENO 106559

FIG. 8.8: SILVER RUPEE OF AWADH (11.33 G.) I.N.O. SHAH ALAM II, MUHAMMADABAD BENARES, AH 1183/RY.11 (1769/70). REF.: *KM*.36.5; ZENO 261285

FIG. 8.9: SILVER RUPEE OF THE MUGHAL EMPIRE (11.37 G.) I.N.O. MUHAMMAD SHAH, MU'AZZAMABAD (GORAKHPUR), AH 1131/ RY. AHD (1719). REF.: *KM*.436.43; ZENO 236638

Copper Pice

The 54,875 pice, a considerable sum, was meant to pay the defence force. Counted meticulously, they unfortunately have not been valued in rupees and thus it is difficult to determine precisely which copper coins are meant. However, here, too, given the time and place, we may present some reasonable suggestions. In his 1788, report, A. Montgomerie also mentioned the most common copper coins in circulation in the sircars of Saran and Chhapra, both answering the demand sufficiently.[38] First, he mentions 2 million 'Goruckpoory pice', weighing 10¾ *masha* and 'equal to the best sort of copper,' and coined by the nabob of Oude (the king of Awadh); second 1.2 million 'Nepauly,' weighing 10 *masha*, and coined by the raja of Nepaul. Taking the situation in 1788 as a guideline, we come to the following interpretation for Barharia in 1771.

Gorakhpur Pice from Mu'azzamabad, Muhammadabad, and Gursaul imitations

One of the strongest candidates is the nearby Gorakhpur mint, coining under the name of Mu'azzamabad.[39] Originally, this town had a Mughal mint, producing copper *damris*, *nisfis*, and *dams* under Akbar between 1566/7 and 1579/80 (see Figs. 8.10-8.11), and again, between 1603/4 and 1605/6, and equally copper falus under Aurangzeb in 1669/70 and under Jahandar in 1712/13.

FIG. 8.10: COPPER DAM OF AKBAR, AH 963-1014/AD 1556-1605 (20.40 G.), GORAKHPUR, DAR AL-KHILAFAT, WITH 'NASIR AL-DIN' LEGEND

FIG. 8.11: COPPER *NISFI* OF AKBAR (9.68 G.), GORAKHPUR, ND, MONTH AMARDAD (LEO). COINS OF GORAKHPUR OFTEN SHOW A FIVE-POINTED STAR SYMBOL, AS SEEN ON BOTH THESE COINS OF AKBAR

Subsequently, this mint was exploited by the newly emerging Awadh state. While formally maintaining the name of Shah Alam II, this Awadh mint initially coined only silver and gold, but between 1763/4 and 1790/1, only copper *paisas*. They are documented for four different regnal years between 1763/4 and 1777/8, and thus, the mint was active in the period under scrutiny (Figs. 8.12 to 8.15). We even have production figures for the copper *paisas* for one year (AH 1190 or 1776/7), when an impressive number of 2,920,000 were struck (for the Benares imitations, see below).[40] This mint was closed in 1801 according to Francis Buchanan-Hamilton who wrote in 1813/14:

The coinage of copper, since the English Government [=1801], has been stopt, and a great deal of the money has been exported, so that in the town of Gorakhpur it was with much trouble that I could procure 200

FIG. 8.12: AWADH, MU'AZZAMABAD (GORAKHPUR), COPPER FALUS I.N.O. SHAH ALAM II, AH 1177/RY. 5 (1763/64) (ZENO 216752)

FIG. 8.13: AWADH, MU'AZZAMABAD (GORAKHPUR), COPPER FALUS (11.60 G.) I.N.O. SHAH ALAM II, AH 1181/RY. 8 (1767) (ZENO 334663)

FIG. 8.14: AWADH, MU'AZZAMABAD (GORAKHPUR), COPPER FALUS (12.9 G.) I.N.O. SHAH ALAM II, AH 1182/RY. 10 (1768/69) (ZENO 205309)

FIG. 8.15: AWADH, SUBAH MU'AZZAMABAD (GORAKHPUR), COPPER FALUS I.N.O. SHAH ALAM II, AH -/RY. 19 (1777/78)

Paysahs in order to estimate the average weight. In its place has been introduced a coinage equally rude, made in Nepal, but called Butauli, because it comes through that town. It is a trifle lighter than the old Gorakhpuri coinage, and 64 may be considered the average number given for a Banaras Rupee, but the exchange varies daily. In remote parts of the district, more of the original coinage remains. Cowries are on the same footing as in Shahabad.[41]

But that is not all. A series of copper *pice*, with the mint name Dar al-Fulus Muhammadabad, has been attributed, on account of this mint name, to Benares (Muhammadabad-Benares). However, the name of Benares has not been observed on any of these coins (Fig. 8.16).

Most of the coins in this series show a five-pointed star symbol typical for Gorakhpur (see Fig. 8.10-8.11 above) and it is tempting

FIG. 8.16: COPPER PICE (*c.* 1764), STRUCK WITH THE NAME OF DAR AL-FALUS MUHAMMADABAD

to assume that these coins are the ones referred to by Barlow when he writes that in the 5th year of Shah Alam II (1760-1806), so around 1764, the Benares mint struck 340,000 imitations, weighing 10 *mashas* (9,07 g.) 'with the die of Gorruckpore'.[42] The average weight of ten specimens of these coins is 10.65 gram, reasonably close to the reported weight of 10 *mashas*, thus confirming that, at Benares, 3,250 were struck out of one maund of copper, which would result in a pice of 10.7 gram.

Our argument for the Gorakhpur candidacy is not only the short distance between the two places (say 100 km as the crow flies) but also comes from archival sources. We have already seen the description of 1788, but next to this, we have several other reports from these years that corroborate the importance of the Gorakhpur *paisa*.

First, we have the detailed description of the Benares mint by G.H. Barlow in August 1787,[43] in which he states that: 'The pice current in the city and district of Benares previous to the establishment of the mint were coined mostly at Goruckpore in the

Soubah of Oude from a species of copper called Lungeree,'[44] which is brought from the Northern Hills. Besides, the circulation of Gorakhpur *pice* is also mentioned in several other reports from Bihar and Bengal. In 1787, they were said to be popular in Boglepore (Bhagalpur) and Rajemahl (Rajmahal), and in 1792 in the southern half of Tirhut (with the remark that under Mansur Ali Khan Safdar Jung (better known as Nawab-Wazir Safdar Jang, 1739-54) they were not only coined in Gorakhpur, but also in 'Abeed').[45]

At about the same time, there were complaints about Gorakhpur and Gursaul pice amassing with the postmasters and excise officers in places as far away as Berhampur and Murshidabad.[46] These Gursaul pice deserve an explanation because 'gursaul' is not at all a common historical or numismatic term. More importantly, it offers an explanation for the widespread circulation of Gorakhpur pice as attested in the records of the time. According to a circular of the Revenue Department of 4 December 1772, 'Gursaul' is a specification for rupees coined by private persons not in the established mints. Being a very base coin, they undergo another deduction besides that for deficiency of weight. This deduction or *batta* was 12.5 per cent in 1773.[47] In 1795, we encounter the same term for *pice*, so a *gursaul pice* must be a privately coined low-quality copper *pice*.[48] In this context, we believe that we dealing specifically with bad imitations of Gorakhpur *pice*. Such items are occasionally offered in the coin market, listed as being of Mu'azzamabad. The coins, however, are of crude and incorrect calligraphy and are missing a mint name, and presumably country imitations (so-called *kachcha* coins) and may be the enigmatic '*Gursaul pice*.' (Fig. 8.17). In Auction #21 of Virasat Auctions, Lucknow, three copper coins (lot 419, 420 & 422) are listed as being of Mu'azzamabad. The coins, however, are of crude and incorrect calligraphy and are missing a mint name, and presumably country imitations (*kachcha* coins) and may be the enigmatic *Gursaul pice* (Fig. 8.17).

In 1807, the role of the Gorakhpur *paisa* had become much less important in Bihar as it was stated that 'formerly' there were two types of copper *pice*: the single (*adhelee*) from Gorakhpur and the double (*tacka*) Muddoo Sahee.[49] Nevertheless, these pieces had a

FIG. 8.17: THREE COPPER COINS, PRESUMABLY PRIVATELY MINTED IMITATIONS OF GORAKHPUR *PICE* (VIRATSAT AUCTION 21, LUCKNOW, 16 JUNE 2024, # 419, 421, 422 RESPECTIVELY)

long life in certain pockets because we read that 'large quantities' of Gorakhpur pice were still circulating in Jaunpur district in 1835.[50]

If the Gorakhpur *pice* of various sorts, as described in this section, are meant in the Barharia case, then the proper ones weighing 10 *mashas* and 3 *ruttees*, and varying between 44 and 52 to the rupee, the 54,875 *pice* captured at Burharia Fort would have represented a value of roughly 1,150 rupees.

Nepali *Pice*

The second candidate is Nepalese coppers. Their circulation in the neighbouring parts of India is sometimes mentioned but seems to have been restricted to a few regions. In the same, just-mentioned report about Tirhut in 1792, Nepalese *pice* struck by the raja of

Nepal, inscribed 'Sittaram' and weighing 9 to 9.5 *mashas* dominate the northern half of the district. An Italian missionary, travelling in 1756 from Patna to the kingdom Tanahu in Central Nepal gave the following description: 'coins of Nepal (i.e. of the Kathmandu Valley) circulate more than those of India. The king has only copper money. No gold or silver money is issued by him.' None of the copper coins referred to can be positively identified as being struck by the raja of Tanahu, but it is not unlikely that he issued unstamped, or roughly stamped, lumps of copper of the type that circulated widely in Nepal and northern India throughout the nineteenth century. In an earlier account of 1707, another Italian missionary travelling the same route describes how, seventeen days after having left Patna, he reached Benjory in the territory of Raja Badal Singh, where 'Mogol copper pieces are not circulating, but other pieces are circulating, which are called Torrà.' The next day, he proceeded to Sankry where, 'in spite of the distance of only three kos [seven miles] from Benjory, and in spite of the fact that the locality is subject to the same Raja, the Torrà are not current, but only the pieces of the Mogol.' Five days after he left Benjory, the Father reached Nepalese territory at Sindhuli Gadhi and records that the money in circulation, both large and small, was all of silver.[51] Nicholas Rhodes describes such 'Anonymous Issues, *c.* 18th century–1880' and mentions three groups, viz.: Die-struck copper coins, '*ganda*' or four *paisa* (39-42 g) without a legible description (group a, see Figs. 8.18-8.19); Bhutwaliya or Gorakhpuri *Paisa* (group b, see Fig. 8.20); and Lohiya *Paisa* or Black *Paisa* (group c, see Fig. 8.21). According to Francis Buchanan-Hamilton (see above), the coppers called 'Butauli' (from what is now Butwal in Nepal) became in demand after the closure of the Gorakhpur mint in 1801.

Group A

FIG. 8.18: COPPER *GANDA* OR 4 *PAISA* (39–42 G.), CLEARLY DIE-STRUCK WITH AN ILLEGIBLE ARABIC INSCRIPTION. THE COIN IS SLIGHTLY MAGNETIC, AND HENCE MAY HAVE BEEN STRUCK IN EASTERN NEPAL. REF.: RGV 1349; ZENO 326334

FIG. 8.19: COPPER *DHYAK* OF 2 *PAISA* (20.43 G.), SIMILAR TO ABOVE. REF.: RGV -; ZENO 326335

Group B

FIG. 8.20: COPPER BHUTWALIYA OR GORAKHPUR *PAISA*: FINE COPPER, NON-MAGNETIC PIECES, USUALLY ROUGHLY RECTANGULAR IN SHAPE, THE HEAVIER PIECES *c.* 30 × 25 MM, THE LIGHTER c. 20 × 15 MM, WITH THE NARROW ENDS SLIGHTLY ROUNDED. THE SURFACE CAN BE EITHER SMOOTH OR ROUGH.

MAINLY EXPORTED TO INDIA VIA BUTWAL. THESE PIECES CIRCULATED EXTENSIVELY IN THE AREA AROUND GORAKHPUR (HENCE IT IS PROBABLE THAT THEY WERE ALSO NAMED 'GORAKHPUR *PAISA*'; MOREOVER, THEY HAVE ROUGHLY THE SAME WEIGHT). THEY WERE MANUFACTURED IN THE PALPA DISTRICT, BAGLUNG, AND BENI AREA, AND PERHAPS ALSO IN OTHER PLACES. THEY APPEAR IN THREE DENOMINATIONS, VIZ: RGV 1350 *GANDA* (4 *PAISA*) 40-4 GRAM; RGV 1351 *DHYAK* (2 *PAISA*) 18-22 GRAM; RGV 1352 DHEBUA (1 *PAISA*) 8-12 GRAM (ILLUSTRATED ABOVE; WITH WEIGHTS, RESPECTIVELY, OF 10.88, 10.15, 10.11, 9.57 GRAM; SIZE 18×18, 17×16, 18×18, 16×19 MM); ZENO 161218.

Group C

FIG. 8.21: LOHIYA *PAISA* OR BLACK *PAISA*, COPPER/IRON ALLOY,[52] USUALLY STRONG MAGNETIC AND MANUFACTURED IN MANY PLACES, MAINLY IN EASTERN NEPAL. SIMILAR IN SHAPE TO THE BHUTWALIYA *PAISA*. THESE PIECES CAN ONLY BE DISTINGUISHED FROM THE GORAKHPURI *PAISA* WITH THE AID OF A MAGNET. DUE TO THEIR IRON CONTENT, THEY HAD A SLIGHTLY LOWER VALUE THAN THE PURE COPPER *PIECES*. THIS TYPE OF *PAISA* CIRCULATED IN KATHMANDU AND THE EAST OF

NEPAL AND WAS FREQUENTLY EXPORTED TO THE CHAMPARAN DISTRICT. THEY APPEAR IN THREE DENOMINATIONS, VIZ., RGV 1350 *GANDA* (4 *PAISA*) 40-4 GRAM; RGV 1351 *DHYAK* (2 *PAISA*) 18-22 GRAM (ILLUSTRATED ABOVE); ZENO 326337; RGV 1352 *DHEBUA* (1 *PAISA*) 8-12 GRAM.

Taken together, the officially coined Gorakhpur *pice*, their imitations, called *gursaul*, and very crude Nepali coppers of roughly the same weight, called equally Gorakhpur pice or *bhutwaliya*, offer an explanation for why we encounter so often the denomination 'Gorakhpur *pice*' in the written sources of the late eighteenth century.

Benares *Pice*

The third, but somewhat less likely candidate is the Benares mint (called Muhammadabad Benares). Not less likely because of the distance but because it minted very irregularly copper coins before the seventeenth year of Shah Alam II (1775). According to the detailed and previously mentioned Barlow report, there have been only two, distinctive issues. Barlow mentions that the first coinage of *pice* at Benares took place in RY.23 of Muhammad Shah (1740/1) when Gowaul Doss Saho struck 100 maunds (3,483.6 kg) weight of *pice* with the die of the *sicca* rupee. The weight of each pice was 10 *mashas* – 3 *rattis* (*c.* 9.4122 g.). The total number of *pice* would be about 370,115 pieces, which would be equal to about 7,115 to 8,410 rupees at a rate of 44 to 52 a rupee (Fig. 8.22).

FIG. 8.22: SILVER *SICCA* RUPEE I.N.O. MUHAMMAD SHAH, MINT: MUHAMMADABAD-BENARES, DATED RY 22. AS THE *PICE* WAS REPORTEDLY STRUCK WITH THE DIES OF THE *SICCA* RUPEE OF THIS YEAR, THEY MAY HAVE THE SAME DESIGN.

Although this was a substantial number, for the next twenty years (until the imitation Gorakhpur *pice*, see above) there was no follow-up. Serious and annual production of copper coins at Benares mint was only resumed from the seventeenth year of the reign of Shah Alam II, so from around 1776 onwards – too late for the problem we have to solve now.

Najibabad *Pice*

The fourth candidate (but least likely candidate given the distance of some 800 km as the crow flies, and the weight of 18 *mashas*) is the important mint of Najibabad. We want to mention this possibility nevertheless in view of the following passage in a letter, written by Archibald Seton (1758-1818), member of the Bareilly Mint Committee on 26 January 1804:

> From the best information I have been able to obtain, it would appear that in former times, that is prior to the time of the powerful Rohilla Chief Nudjeeb ul Dowlah, there were no coined pice in any part of Rohilcund. The then copper currency consisted of oval pieces of that metal called Muddha Sahees which had neither letter nor figure of any kind stamped upon them but were supposed to weigh 18 *maushees* or 290 grains avoirdupois. About forty-five years ago Nudjeeb ud Dowlah coined pice for the first time at Nudjeebabad out of copper brought from the hills of Surreenagar. These pice which weighed 18 *maushes* were termed *nujeeb khannees*. Their circulation was not confined to the territories of the chief in question, which comprehended only the northwestern portion of Rohilcund but extended generally over the whole of that province *and even far beyond its precincts* [our italics].

How far is far remains unclear, but all this means that the successful production of the Najibabad *pice* started around 1760 at Najibabad, founded in the 1740s by Najib ud-Dawlah (who died in 1770).[53]

Comparisons

At Dig, in 1804, the booty listed silver and copper cash plus substantial materials for producing gunpowder, whereas at Barharia besides gold, silver, and copper cash uncoined precious metals, food for the defenders, and some other goods were also captured (for a full list see Appendix 8.1). A comparison between the two cases demonstrates interesting similarities and differences between the two cases (see Table 8.1).

TABLE 8.1: COMPARISON BETWEEN THE BOOTIES OF BARHARIA 1771 AND DIG 1804 (IN WHOLE Rs.)

		Barharia 1771	*Dig 1804*
New coins	Gold	3,165	None
	Silver	7,906	209,403
	Copper	Estimated 1,150	min 315 max 1,260
Old coins	Gold	817	Not mentioned
	Silver	844	
Uncoined precious metals	Silver	825	
Raw materials for making gun powder		Not mentioned	min 188,820 max 189,765
Grain		Not valued	Not mentioned
225 pieces of white cloth		Not valued	
Cooking vessels		Not valued	
Other articles		Not valued	
Total value			399,483

What immediately comes to mind is the poverty of Barharia in 1771 as compared to Dig in 1804. Apart from all other possible considerations, this has to do with the size of the two fortresses and the nature of their defenders. The size of the fortress of Dig may also be derived from the fact that it had facilities for making its own gunpowder within its walls. Concentrating on the total value of the coins (and for now leaving out the uncoined precious metals but including the 'old silver'[54]), the difference is also obvious: roughly Rs. 15,000 at Barharia against Rs. 210,000 at Dig, or fourteen times more. But as to the proportions of the value of gold, silver, and copper something interesting happens: at Barharia Rs. 3,982 or 29 per cent in gold, Rs. 8,750 (or 9,575 if the uncoined silver is included) or 63 per cent in silver and an estimated Rs. 1,150 or 8 per cent in copper coins against at Dig a quarter century later no gold at all, less than 1 per cent copper and over 99 per cent silver.

From the size of Barharia's defence force, we might conclude that about 1 rupee in copper money was available per head and a few (at a maximum 8) rupees in silver, apart from the fact that payment in cash took place next to payment in kind in the form of food and clothing (call it board and lodging). This combination of payment of wages in the form of cash and kind was very common in India.[55] These differences reflect most of all the difference between professional soldiers, Maratha mercenaries, who defended Dig, and peasants who had been drafted by their *zamindar* for the occasional defence of Barharia.

Appendix 8.1: NAI, Home Department Public Original Consultation 10 June 1771, No. 9 (a); and I. Cons., 1771, pp. 91-2

TABLE 8.2: COPY OF THE INVENTORY OF GOLD, SILVER, BRASS, AND COPPER &CA FOUND IN BURRARIA FORT 19 MAY 1771, ENCLOSED IN PATNA REVENUE COUNCIL

211	gold *mohurs*	3,165:00
	rupees	7,906:00
	silver plates weighing	825:12
	old silver weighing	844:00
	old gold weighing (54 *mohurs* 8:15 rupees each)	817:08
54,875	pice	
34	copper pots of different sizes	
17	brass pots of different sizes	
27	toothenague pots of different sizes	
1	country marqeece	
2	elephant teeth	
225	pieces of white cloth	
85	pieces of silk	
29	pieces of chintz	
9	pieces of gingham	
2	small remnants of woollen cloth	
	grain of different sorts, left in charge of captain Ashe the quantity not ascertained	

Appendix 8.2: Circulation of silver and copper coins in the Districts of Sircar Sarun & Sircar Champaran in 1788, including their estimated quantity and the degree to which this was considered sufficient.

FIG. 8.23: THE CIRCULATION OF SONAUT RUPEES AND COPPER PICE, IN THE DISTRICTS OF SIRCAR SARUN & SIRCAR CHAMPARAN

Denominations	*Where*	*By whom*	*Quantity in circulation*	*Extent to which the general demand is met*
Mohomed Shahy sonaut from 1 to 31 sun & Allum Giery sonaut 4 sun 	Patna Azimabad	The nawob of the Subah Behar	2½ lakh	The proper quantity to respond to the market ought to be five lakh

(Contd.)

Allum Shahy sonaut 1, 2, 3, 4, 6 & 10 sun	Yr. 10 EIC	Do	2 lakh	The same as above

Do do 5 sun	Nawab issue	Do	1½ lakh	This kind of rupee is not in demand
Do do 7 & 8 sun	EIC	Do	3½ lakh	This amount is almost adequate for the demands – only deficient about ⅙

Do do 9 sun	EIC	Do	2 lakh	This amount is not nearly enough to respond to the market. Six lack is estimated to be the amount necessary to meet the general demand
Allum Gury sonaut 1, 2, 3, 5 & 6 sun	EIC	Do	3 lakh	No great deficiency is observed for this sort of rupee

(Contd.)

Goruckpoory pice; 10¾ *masha* equal to the best sort of copper; real value at present 4: 1½; nominal value 5	Gorakhpur	The nabob of Oude	About 20 lakh	This quantity sufficiently responds to the demand
Nepauly; 10 *mashas*; real value at present 4¼; nominal value 4¾	Nepal	The Rajah of Nepaul	About 12 lakh	Ditto

Note: in the column 'by whom' we have made several corrections where the original states 'The nawob of the Subah Behar', whereas the emissions after 1765 were minted under the authority of the British East India Company (EIC).[56]

Source: NAI, Finance, Mint Committee Proceedings 18 August 1792, 482-8 (A. Montgomerie, Collector to John Shore, President & members of the Board of Revenue, Chuprah, 28 February and 16 May 1788).

NOTES

1. Lingen & Lucassen, see Part I: Studies, No. 9 in this volume. We thank Dr. Sanjay Garg for his generous assistance.
2. O'Malley 1908, 33 for the situation *c.* 1900, suggesting, however, that this was already the case in the centuries before.
3. Information from Dr. Garg who received confirmation of the fort's existence in 2023 from a former Block Development Officer in Barharia.
4. WBSA, LC, Golding to Patna Council of Revenue, 23 January 1771; Ashe to Golding 16 April 1771.
5. For a map, see https://tinyurl.com/33v684xr. The source for the photos is Google: Yamuna Garh.
6. All the information that follows was found in *Press List of Ancient Documents* Vol. 1. Series II: Comptrolling Council of Revenue Patna (Calcutta: Bengal Secretary Book Depot, 1917), pp. 30-48, 73-5, 81-9, 93-4, 101, 111-14, 157, 169, 181, 187, 211, 234, 373. The Press List only provides a detailed summary of the documents; the originals of this series are deposited in the West Bengal State Archives (WBSA). The references are to Copy Book of the Letters issued (indicated as 'LC'), by the Comptrolling Council of Revenue, and by Chief of Factory at Patna. The documents (in the form of typed out transcripts of the originals) used here have been kindly made available to us by Dr. Simonti Sen (WBSA) by mediation of Dr. Garg.
7. O'Malley 1908, 115-26; for a recent assessment, see Datta 2024, 238-56.
8. The members of this Revenue Council at the time of the Barharia troubles were George Vansittart (1754-90), James Alexander (1730-1802), and Robert Palk. For Vansittart, see https://www.historyofparliamentonline.org/volume/1790-1820/member/vansittart-george-1745-1825; for Alexander, see https://en.wikipedia.org/wiki/James_Alexander,_1st_Earl_of_Caledon. Both made a big fortune in India and returned to England to become members of parliament. We have no further information for Palk (related to, but not to be confused with his namesake 1717-98).
9. O'Malley 1908, 72-3.
10. O'Malley 1908, 26-8, 117-18; WBSA, LC, Golding to Council of Revenue 23 January 1771; Golding to the Council of Revenue undated (7 or 11 April 1771).
11. *Press List* 1917, 31, 94 about Jugalkishor (whether to restore him in his old dignity, Kripanarayan, and about Juggul Kissore, who had left the EIC territory; see also WBSA, LC, Patna Council of Revenue to Golding, 16 February 1771; Golding to the Council of Revenue undated (7 or 11 April 1771).
12. *Press List* 1917, 83 (warned not to support the *zamindar* of Barharia).
13. *Press List* 1917, 421-2 (no. 7). For Maharaja Sitabroy, see also WBSA, LC, Golding to the Council of Revenue undated (7 or 11 April 1771).
14. WBSA, LC, Council of Revenue to Golding, 5 February 1771.

15. Ansari 2019, 160-1, citing O'Malley 1908, 21. Similar information (without due referencing) at https://oroyalarchives.com/hatwa/.
16. O'Malley 1908, 115-26. After Golding's return from India, he became a member of parliament (like Vansittart and Alexander, see note 8 above), see https://www.historyofparliamentonline.org/volume/1790-1820/member/golding-edward-1746-1818.
17. *Press List* 1917, 31. For the approval: WBSA, LC, Council of Revenue to Golding, 16 February 1771.
18. For the great famine of 1769/70 in Bengal, see Datta 2000, 73, 91-9, 118-19, 238-74, 285-315; Datta 2024, Ch. 4.
19. WBSA, LC, Golding to Council of Revenue 23 January 1771; Council of Revenue to Golding, 5 February 1771; *Press List* 1917, 31.
20. We have not been able to find much information about him. His first name is given in *Press-List* 1918, 51 cited above. See https://www.geni.com/people/Benjamin-Ashe/6000000018736916824.
21. WBSA, LC, Golding to Council of Revenue, 13 February 1771.
22. WBSA, LC, Council of Revenue to Golding, 16 February 1771.
23. WBSA, LC, Council of Revenue to Golding, 6 April 1771; Golding to the Council of Revenue undated (7 or 11 April 1771).
24. WBSA, LC, Council of Revenue to Golding, 13 April 1771.
25. WBSA, LC, Ashe to Golding, 16 April 1771. The month *Dhul-Hijah* is the twelfth month of the Islamic calendar.
26. WBSA, LC, Golding to the Council of Revenue, 19 and 22 April 1771; this neighbouring zemindar may have been Mahomed Ally, who hosted the family of Shaikh Fakr Ullah after the reduction of the fort (WBSA, LC, Golding to the Council of Revenue, 11 May 1771). It is also possible that Shaikh Fakr Ullah himself came to the rescue (WBSA, LC, the Council of Revenue to Golding, 20 April 1771).
27. WBSA, LC, Golding to the Council of Revenue, 22 April 1771 (2 letters), A. Champion to the Council of Revenue, 29 April and 11 May 1771; Council of Revenue to Alexander Champion, 30 April, 4, 5, 6 and 11 May 1771; Golding to the Council of Revenue, 1 May 1771; Council of Revenue to Golding, 7 May 1771; Council of Revenue to Goddard, 7 May 1771. For Colonel Thomas Goddard (?1740-83), see https://discovery.nationalarchives.gov.uk/details/c/F69689. For Colonel Alexander Champion (+ 1793) who, a few years later, defeated the Mahrattas and became commander-in-chief, see https://en.wikipedia.org/wiki/Alexander_Champion_(East_India_Company_officer).
28. WBSA, LC, Patna Council of Revenue to John Cartier, President & Governor &ca Council of Fort William, 4 May 1771.
29. WBSA, LC, Golding to the Council of Revenue, 11 May 1771; Council of Revenue to Champion, 13 May 1771; Champion to the Council of Revenue, 13 May 1771.

30. WBSA, LC, Goddard to the Council of Revenue, ND (probably 13 May 1771); Council of Revenue to Fort William, 14 May 1771.
31. WBSA, LC, Council of Revenue to Champion, 18 May 1771; Champion to Council of Revenue 24 May 1771; Council of Revenue to Fort William, 25 May 1771; *Press List* 1917, 101, 111, 113, 157, 169, 181, 187, 211, 234, 373.
32. WBSA, LC, Golding to the Council of Revenue, 15 May 1771.
33. *Press List* 1917, 111-12, 114.
34. Maybe there were no fixed buildings in this mud fort, and the commander Shaikh Abdoor Raheem used this marquee as his dwelling during the defence.
35. Stevens 2012, 43, 89-91.
36. Stevens 2012, 33-6.
37. See Appendix 2. Alexander Montgomerie (1744-1802) mentions a circulation of 1.35 million rupees, distinguishing between six kinds of rupees, struck at Patna (Azimabad) from 1719 to 1768/9. Because he thinks that 1 million more are needed to meet the demand, there was room for other types.
38. See Appendix 2. He adds, for the Gorakhpur paisa: 'real value at present 4: 1.4; nominal value 5,' which seems to mean that 100 pieces equalled nominally Rs. 5. Likewise, for the slightly lighter Nepali paisa: 'real value at present 4¼; nominal value 4¾.' Taking the *masha* at 0.972 grams, these weights fit with our interpretations below.
39. For the following, see Kapoor & Master 2018, xxxiv, 8, 33, 70; *South Asian Coins and Paper Money* 2013, 21, 23, 25, 27, 72, 102, 139, 238; Gorakhpur is also mentioned regularly in the correspondence of Edward Golding from Saran in these years.
40. *South Asian Coins and Paper Money* 2013, s.v. Gorakhpur #A106.
41. Royal Asiatic Society London, Papers of Francis Bucanan-Hamilton, GB 891 FBH /7, Statistical Survey of the District Gorakhpur, Vol. 2, Book 5, pp. 128-9.
42. NAI, Finance, Mint Committee, Proceedings 26 June 1792, pp. 136-58 on copper coins, where all following information may be found, see Part II: Records, No. 3 in this volume.
43. NAI, Finance, Mint Committee proceedings 26 June 1792, 76-180. See Part II: Records, No. 3 in this volume, printed in a slightly different version in *Minutes of the Evidence* 1788, vol. 11, Appendix 432, 1987-90.
44. Presumably the Bhutwaliya or Gorackhpuri paisa, see Rhodes 1989 (RGV 1352).
45. NAI, Finance, Mint Committee, Proceedings 26 June 1792, pp. 136-58. 'Abeed' most likely is a misspelling for Awadh (Faizabad).
46. NAI, Home Department, Public original consultations, 2 January 1795, No. 7
47. Price 1876, 200-1. We encounter also the spelling 'gyasaul' and 'gyasaal.'

48. About Gursaul Pice, see an entry of 18 Jan 1795, in the Alphabetical Index to the Proceedings of the Board of Revenue, January to June 1796, p. ix, https://sadte.wb.gov.in/uploads/pdf/D12/D12776.pdf.
49. NAI, Finance, Mint Committee, Proceedings, 2 July 1807, pp. 7-9.
50. NAI, Finance, Mint Committee, Proceedings, 8 July 1835 pp. 97-8.
51. Rhodes 1989, Ch. V, pp. 170–203 on the coinage in the Nepalese Hills (catalogue numbers hereafter referred to as 'RGV').
52. Some examples were analysed in the Calcutta Mint in 1866 at the request of the British Resident in Nepal, Col. G. Ramsay, and were found to be 41.6 per cent copper and 57.6 per cent iron.
53. NAI, Finance, Mint Committee, Proceedings 1804-5, p. 25; cf. Stevens 2012, 472. See *South Asian Coins and Paper Money* 2013, 204 sub Rohilkhand: Najibabad paisa with known dates between AH 1176 (1762/3) and 1188 (1774/5), which coincides nicely with the archival data. For later copper coins from this mint, see our earlier article 'Copper circulation in Northern India in 1830' (see Part I: Studies, No. 10 in this volume).
54. If we exclude this, which is well defensible, proportions will shift only slightly.
55. Carvalhal, Lucassen & De Zwart 2023.
56. Stevens 2012, 184 ('Although the British had acquired control of all mints in the Presidency in 1765, Murshidabad, Patna and Dacca continued to be controlled by the Nawab and his officials until the end of 1769').

Successors: Princely and Colonial States

9

Warfare and Coin Circulation: Two Lakhs of Bharatpur and Bindrabund Rupees and 15 Bags of Copper Pyce, Captured at Dig on Christmas Eve 1804

JAN LINGEN AND JAN LUCASSEN

Dig (also spelled Deeg; alternatively known as Mahe Indrapur/ Mahendrapur) was the summer residence and, therefore, the second capital of the Princely State of Bharatpur in Rajasthan.[1] It came into possession of the Jats about the beginning of the eighteenth century, and, in 1751, its ruler acquired the title of 'raja'. His grandson, Raja Ranjit Singh, who ruled from AH 1190-1220 (1776-1805) decided to support the Maratha chief, Jaswant Rao Holkar, with money, provisions and men in the Second Anglo-Maratha War (1803-5).[2] During this war, Bengal forces of the British East India Company, called the 'Grand Army' and commanded by General Gerard Lake, marched from Kanpur on 3 September 1804. At that time, the strength of the Maratha army was estimated at 14,000 infantry and 160 guns, besides strong cavalry. A British Contingent under General Fraser with 5,000 infantry laid siege to Dig on 11 December 1804 (AH 1219, RY 47 of Shah Alam II), which surrendered on 24 December. Thereafter, Lake and his troops besieged the capital, Bharatpur, but without success. After four failed attacks, which cost the Company 3,292 killed and wounded (including 103 Europeans) the British had to give up on 22 February 1805. Peace was arranged, and Dig was restored to Ranjit Singh.[3]

A detailed report of the siege of Dig is available in the diary kept by James Young, one of the British artillery officers who took part in it.[4] Born in Glasgow on 2 October 1782, he matriculated from Glasgow University to join the East India Company in 1801. In 1818 he resigned from the Company, became the director of a business firm and was twice, in 1838 and 1839, sheriff of Calcutta. His diary describes how, in December 1804, the town and its fortress were defended by the majority of the Maratha infantry from inside, while their cavalry, under the command of Holkar himself, was freely moving around and attacking the British. The latter concentrated on the fortress which they bombarded for nearly two weeks until a breach was forced. On the early morning of 24 December when it was still dark, the fortress was stormed and taken by the British. During that day the population of Dig, including Holkar's infantry fled the town and took the road in the direction of Bharatpur, without the British being able to prevent this exodus as it was protected by Holkar's 10,000 to 12,000 strong cavalry.

James Young feared that they were also carrying with them 'the treasures of the Fort and Town',[5] but later on, he changed his mind and deemed this to be very unlikely as 'the fugitive would never have tempted the cupidity of their protectors, Holkar's ill-paid cavalry, by carrying with them any cash'. At that moment, the citadel was still held by 600 Jats, but these also retired on Christmas Eve and Christmas Day 'after breakfast, almost the whole camp went down to visit the fort and town'. Young was among them and called the town 'populous and flourishing' while admiring at length the new palace of the Raja, which he considered 'with its beautiful gardens, by far, superior, in every respect, to any building I have seen in India'.[6] The next day (26 December) at noon precisely, however, the tourist party was over, and the British army resumed its routine, including the taking of prize, in particular a search for the treasury of the Raja. Six officers were officially appointed as prize agents (entitling them to 5 per cent on all sales and 3 per cent on cash), under the leadership of Lt. Hay for the artillery. In the words of Young:

> The Prize Agents of the army have been very busy in the fort looking out, and digging for treasure and selling all property. Informers of treasure or property of any kind concealed get half of it if it is their own secured to them and one quarter if it is public or another's effects. 2 Lacks and 9,000 rupees have been dug up in the Fort and more is expected as by all the native accounts 50 Lacks of Rupees were always kept in Deeg. [...] several lacks of maunds (a maund is 80 lb.) of grain had been found which will be purchased by the Company and effects of greater quantity than value are selling by the auction daily for the benefit of the Prize Fund. A Lieut's share of what we have *already* realized will amount to about 400 rupees.

Young underlines *already* because 'Strong suspicions are entertained, that much money is concealed in the beautiful carved and fretted walls and pillars of the palace and our prize agents, of whom two are left for the purpose of searching in Deeg, I will dare say not stand upon much ceremony about pulling it to pieces [...]'.

Whatever efforts the British may have put in finding the rest of the supposed 500,000 rupees, they were in vain, as proven by the final overview of the Deeg booty (see Appendix), less than half of which consisted of cattle, ingredients for making gunpowder (saltpetre, sulphur and charcoal[7]) with cash making up the rest. Most goods like cattle and grain, including bags of copper pice, were immediately put into auction, the ingredients for making gunpowder were reserved for their own military use, and the silver rupee coins were handed over to Captain Staunton Deputy Field Paymaster.

The total sum of nearly 400,000 rupees of prize money was going to be divided among the troops, as James Young had expected already. This was a long-established custom, one of the extra stimuli for the troops. On an earlier occasion, the European and Indian troops present at the final victory over the Rohillas on 23 April 1774 were entitled to a sum of one million rupees according to the rules set out by a committee at Berhampur in 1787 – at least those still alive at the moment the money was disbursed some fifteen years after the battle.[8]

The capture of such big sums is not just a lucky coincidence for the victors but is very significant for the role coins played in these societies, and more particularly in the armies involved. In a careful analysis of what he considers as the decisive British successes in 1803, Randolf Cooper attributes these not to superior training, discipline and drill, nor to superior British artillery, but to British credit, i.e. the ability 'to buy out military forces or hire them on credit underwritten by the EIC. The promises of pay were enough to lure away entire battalions who had seen Maratha leaders stripped of their capital and credibility.'[9] Without capital, there was no victory, and this went for both armies, which consisted exclusively of paid mercenaries. It does not seem farfetched to link the presence of 200,000 rupees at Dig directly with the exigencies of war, in particular with the payment of the Maratha troops. This sum approximates to the annual pay of some 3,000 privates, or even 7,000 – if we attach credence to believing the rumour that 500,000 rupees were always kept available in Dig.[10]

The most important sum of what we might call the Dig booty was represented by 208,900 Bharatpur rupees. Comparatively insignificant were 50 'Bindrabund rupees', 453 'rupees of different kinds' and 15 bags of copper pice – unfortunately without details about the number of pice coins contained in one bag. The main question we would like to answer here is which coins are meant, but also what their role may have been in the coin circulation in Bharatpur around the turn of the century.

The Bharatpur Rupees

The Bharatpur state produced good silver rupees on a very regular basis in a number of mints, as well as a few half and quarter rupee pieces. Remarkably, production was not constant, neither for the state as a whole nor for its different mint houses (see Table 9.1). The small price variations between the different years and mints as reflected in actual market prices for collectors suggest a rather regular annual output, which might be put easily at a few hundred thousand per year and if need be even at a few million.[11]

In the beginning of Shah Alam's reign, basically two mints

were actively striking coins, followed by a break between his regnal years 17 and 23, after which it was resumed, initially on an irregular basis but from regnal year 29 onwards annually in Bharatpur, supported by the mints of Dig, Kumher and Wer (or Weir). In 1751, the Mughal emperor Ahmad Shah Bahadur bestowed Badan Singh (1722/3-1756), a Raja, with the title of Mahendra, and Suraj Mal (1756-63), a Kumar Bahadur, with the title of Rajendra and also made him *faujdar* of Mathura for a modest annual tribute. Badan Singh's title of Mahendra created the name Mahendrapur for Dig. Bharatpur became known as Brajendrapur on the coins.

The earliest coins for the State of Bharatpur are rupees in the name of Ahmad Shah Bahadur dated AH 1166/RY 6 (1752) with the mint name Mahendrapur. The first coins observed with the mint name Bharatpur, but subsequently Brajendrapur, are in the name of Shah Alam II, dated AH 1185 [*sic*] / RY 14 (1772/3). In Table 9.1 we summarize the available data on the production of rupees in Bharatpur state between 1759 and 1806. For purposes of reference, we have included Agra, although not part of Bharatpur, because it was the nearest important mint and, during the years AH 1175-88 under the control of the Jats of Bharatpur. This is not the place to discuss possible economic and political backgrounds of the discernible sub-periods of enlarged or diminished coin production of the princely state of Bharatpur, as becomes clear from Table 9.1. An exception may be made for the end of the period.

In AH 1201 (1786/7) four mints within Bharatpur State simultaneous started minting rupees. This increase in minting activities can probably be explained by the exigencies of war (in which the Marathas conquered Mathura and drove the Jats from Vindravan), including the payment of troops. It is, therefore, probably also no coincidence that in RY 46, during the war with the English, these four mints were active again producing rupees (see Table 9.1). It is not unlikely that these are the very coins which in such great numbers – over 200,000 (possibly out of a total of 500,000) – fell in the hands of the East India Company at the fall of Dig.

TABLE 9.1: RUPEES WITH THE TITLE OF SHAH ALAM II (1759-1806), PRODUCED IN BHARATPUR MINTS UP TILL THE END OF HIS REIGN (AH 1221/RY. 49, 1806)

RY	AH	*Akbarabad = Agra*	*Brajendrapur = Bharatpur*	*Mahendrapur = Dig*	*Kumher*	*Wer*	*Jawahargarh = Kumher?*[12]
Ahd	1174	X Moghul		X			
2	1174			X			
2	1175	X Jats		X			
3	1175	X Jats		X			
3	1176	X Jats		X			
4	1176	X Jats		X			
4	1177	X Jats		X			
5	1177	X Jats		X			X
5	1178	X Jats		X			
6	1178			X			
6	1179	X Jats		X			
7	1180	X Jats		X			
8	1180	X Jats					
8	1181	X Jats		X (118x/8)			
9	1180!			X			
9	1181			X			

9	1182	X Jats		X
10	1182	X Jats		X ¹3
10	1183			X
11	1184	X Jats		X (- /11)
12	1184	X Jats		
12	1185			
13	1184!			X
13	1186			
14	1185!	X Jats	X	X
14	1186	X Jats	X	X
14	1187		X (118x/14)	
15	1187	X Jats	X	X
15	1188	X Jats	X	X
16	1189	Najaf Khan		X
17	1189			X
17	1190			Najaf Khan
18	1191		X	
19	1192			
20	1193			X (119x/20)

(Contd.)

TABLE 9.1 *(contd.)*

RY	*AH*	*Akbarabad = Agra*	*Brajendrapur = Bharatpur*	*Mahendrapur = Dig*	*Kumher*	*Wer*	*Jawahargarh = Kumher?*[12]
21	1193		X	X (-/21)			
21	1194						
22	1195						
23	1195	X Muh. Beg		X			
24	1196			Mirza Shafi			
24	1197	X Muh. Beg					
25	1197	X Muh. Beg					
25	1198	X Muh. Beg					
26	1198	X Muh. Beg					
26	1199	X Muh. Beg	Sindia			X	
27	1199	Sindhia					
27	1200					X	
28	1200						
28	1201	X Ghulam Qadir					
29	1201	X Sindhia	X (12xx/29)	X (12xx/29)	X (120x/29)	X (12xx/29)	
30	1202		X				
30	1203	X Sindhia					

31	1203		X (12xx/31)	X		
32	1204		X (12xx/32)			X
33	1205		X	X		X (120x/33
34	1206	X Sindhia	X	X	X	
34	1207	X Sindhia	X			
35	1207		X (12xx/35)			
36	1208					
37	1209		X			
38	1210	X Sindhia	X (12xx/38)			
39	1211		X (121x/39)	X		
40	1212	X (121x/40)	X (12xx/40)	X (12xx/40)		
41	1214			X (12xx/41)		
42	1212!		X			
42	1214		X	X		
42	1215	X Sindhia		X		
43	1215	X Sindhia	X			
43	1216					
44	1216	X Sindhia	X			
44	1217	X Sindhia				

(Contd.)

TABLE 9.1 *(contd.)*

RY	AH	*Akbarabad = Agra*	*Brajendrapur = Bharatpur*	*Mahendrapur = Dig*	*Kumher*	*Wer*	*Jawahargarh = Kumher?*[12]
45	1217		X				
45	1218	X Sindhia	X (12xx/45)				
46	1218	X Sindhia	X	X	X	X	
46	1219	X Sindhia					
47	1219	X BEIC	X Siege of Bharatpur	Dig besieged by BEIC	X (121x/47)		
47	1220	X BEIC		Treaty concluded April 17th, 1805			
48	1220/ 1221						
49	1221/ 1222		X (12xx/49)				

Source: This table is based on data collected during the last four decennia by the first author on the coinage of the former princely states of Rajasthan. We present a simplified relationship between regnal years and AH years as other combinations (including blatantly erroneous ones) also occur.

FIG. 9.1: AR RUPEE MAHENDRAPUR (DIG) AH 121x/RY. 42

FIG. 9.2: AR RUPEE BRAJENDRAPUR (BHARATPUR) AH 1216/RY. 44

FIG. 9.3: AR RUPEE 'MAHENDRAPUR' (KUMHER) AH 121x/RY. 47

FIG. 9.4: AR RUPEE 'MAHENDRAPUR' (WER) AH 1218/RY. 46

The Bindraban Rupees

We now look at the 50 'Bindrabund rupees' which were part of the booty, and ask why such an infinitely small sum was emphatically distinguished from the Bharatpur and other rupees. To understand this, we have to go into some detail about the often misunderstood monetary history of Bindraban, the famous pilgrimage place on the right bank of the Yamuna.[14] During the reign of Aurangzeb Alamgir (AH 1068-1118/AD 1658-1707) the name was changed to Muminabad (= city of the faithful).[15] Contrary to what is suggested in the main catalogue[16], there never was a local or city mint in Bindraban. All coins bearing the name Bindraban or Muminabad were issued by larger territorial states, some at Bindraban proper, but most outside.

The Jats were the first to strike rupees in the town for a few years from about 1778 (AH 1192/RY 20 until RY 23), see Fig. 9.5.[17] In about 1786 (AH 1200/RY 28) Vrindavan came under the control of the Marathas and, according to F.S. Growse, Daulat Rao Sindhia established a mint there in 1786 from which a street called the 'Taksál-wali-Gali' derived its name – *taksaal* meaning mint.[18] Under Maratha rule, rupees in the name of Shah Alam II with regnal years running from 26 to 45 bearing the mintmark of a sword were produced (see Figs. 9.6 and 9.9), as well as copper paisas from regnal years 26 to 41, possibly also a ½ paisa with regnal year 37.

Apart from these two series, there is a very peculiar third series, to which the booty document almost certainly refers. After the Jats had been ousted from Vindravan they must have taken the rupee dies with them, and from AH 120x/RY 37 (AH 1209 or 1795) they continued striking Muminabad Bindraban rupees with the mint marks of a sword and *katar* (dagger), but – and this is most important – with a lower silver content (see Fig. 9.7).[19] Moreover, they seem to refer typologically to Bharatpur coins, the sword being the mint-mark for Mahendrapur and the *katar* for Brajendrapur. Whereas the British after they occupied Vrindavan discontinued the coin production there, the Bharatpur (Jat) rulers continued theirs until 1867. Most of these rupees and their occasional fractions of ½ and ¼ bear the frozen regnal year 44 (see Fig.

9.8). In the years 1859-67, these debased Bindraban rupees struck at Bharatpur – like the full-weight Bharatpur rupees proper – also showed the effigy of Victoria (see Fig. 9.10).

FIG. 9.5: AR RUPEE MUMINABAD BINDRABAN AH 1193/RY 21 (JAT ISSUE FROM VINDRAVAN)

FIG. 9.6: AR RUPEE MUNINABAD BINDRABAN AH 1207/RY 37 (MARATHA ISSUE FROM VINDRAVAN)

FIG. 9.7: AR RUPEE OF DEBASED SILVER MUMINABAD BINDRABAN AH 120x/RY 37 (JAT ISSUE FROM BHARATPUR)

FIG. 9.8: AR RUPEE OF DEBASED SILVER MUMINABAD BINDRABAN AH 121X/RY 44 (JAT ISSUE WITH FROZEN REGNAL YEAR FROM BHARATPUR)

FIG. 9.9: AR RUPEE MUMINABAD BINDRABAN AH 1218/RY 45 (LAST MARATHA ISSUE FROM VINDRAVAN)

FIG. 9.10: AR RUPEE WITH PORTRAIT OF QUEEN VICTORIA, 'BINDRABAN' 1859, STRUCK AT BHARATPUR.

Some of the existing confusion regarding these debased rupees may have been caused by Growse himself. Normally considered a very reliable author, he erroneously writes in the *Mathurá District*

Memoir: 'When the Jats were in possession of the country, they transferred it to Bharatpur, where what are called Brindábani rupees, are still coined.' This apparently is a slip of the pen for 'When the Jats had to leave the country [of Vindravan in 1784/ 5 ...]'.

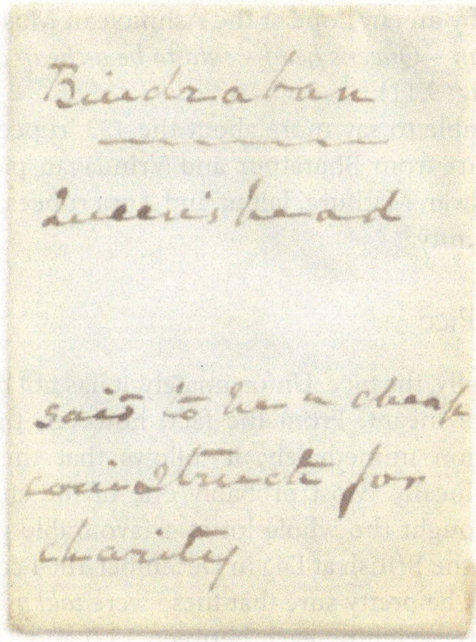

FIG. 9.11: ENVELOPE IN WHICH SUCH A RUPEE WAS PRESENTED TO THE ASHMOLEAN MUSEUM, OXFORD

Luckily he does not only add that the Bharatpur rulers continued this production until very late in the 1860s, but also why exactly these debased rupees were so popular: ' They are especially used at weddings, and when there are many such festivities going on, the coin is sometimes valued at as much as 13 annas, but ordinarily sells for 12.'[20] This points to a particular use of these debased coins, distinct from general circulation. Recently Hans Herrli mentioned the custom in Rajputana where 'marriage guests, who were expected to bring an auspicious number of coins, – e.g. 101, 108 or 1011 – as presents, often chose the rupees struck by the Marwar Thakur of Kuchaman that contained less silver than others and, therefore, allowed them to save some money.'[21] Similarly, the production of debased 'Brindaban' silver coins, might be connected to a special purpose, in this case collecting coins for charity disbursements at the famous temples of Vindraban where rich devotees spent enormous amounts of money, whereas poor ones depended on alms.[22] The interpretations by Growse and Herrli are corroborated by an envelope at the Ashmolean Museum with the text: '*Bindraban – Queens head – said to be a cheap coin struck for charity*' (see Fig. 9.11)[23].

It is impossible to say more about the 453 'rupees of different kinds', but apart from Bharatpur and Vrindavan pieces, we may think of i.a. Alwar, Mathura, Jaipur and Agra rupees, struck in the immediate vicinity.[24]

The Copper Pice

Third, and finally, the pice. Unfortunately, it has not been recorded which pice are meant. From the fact, however, that they were put into auction immediately, it follows that they must have been current locally. Most probably one of the shroffs (money exchangers) bought the whole lot at a favourable price. If these bags, taken by the British at Dig in December 1804 contained local pyce, we might be pretty sure that these were *takkas* struck by the Bharatpur rajas, weighing each between 17.0 and 18.5 g. On the one side, they show the name of the Mughal emperor Shah Alam II (AH 1174-1221 or AD 1759-1806) and, on the other, the mint name, regnal year and the respective mintmarks.

The mintmarks used at the period concerned are:

a. Brajendrapur (Bharatpur): a bold katar between *julūs* and the regnal year. Within the Persian character *sīn* of *julūs* a star, 4 dots or cross-mark with leaves attached above.
b. Mahendrapur (Dig): sword + *katar* (a push dagger with an H-shaped horizontal hand grip), the *katar* is located within the loop of the *sīn* of *julūs*.
c. Pseudo mint-name 'Mahendrapur'(struck at Kumher): a bold *katar* between *julūs* and the regnal year. Within the *sīn* of *julūs* a vertical bar between dots.

As they are poorly catalogued we provide a preliminary overview in Table 9.2 of the examples known to us.

TABLE 9.2: COPPER COINS WITH THE TITLE OF SHAH ALAM II (1759-1806) ON THE OBVERSE, PRODUCED IN BHARATPUR MINTS FROM RY 27 UP TO THE END OF HIS REIGN (AH 1221/RY 49, 1806)

AH	*Regnal year*	AD	*Brajindrapur = Bharatpur*	*Mahendrapur = Dig*	*Mahendrapur = Kumher*
			Mintmark a	*Mintmark b*	*Mintmark c*
1201	27	1785/6			
120x [1200 or 1201]	x8 [28]	1786		P	
	33	1790/1	T		
	38	1795/6			T
	40	1797/8	T		
1213	41	1798/9	T		
	42	1799/1800	T		T
1215		1800/1		P or T (Stephen Album, list 18-895)	
	44	1801/2	T		
1216	44		T		
1216	45	1802/3	T		
	45		T		T
1217	45		T	T	
	x6 [46?]	1803/4	T		
	47	1804/5	T		
1221	49 (Became also a frozen year on later issues)	1806	T		T

Source: Data as in Table 9.1, which means that dates only known from the literature (especially *SACPM* 2013, 260-1) have not been included although they do not contradict our observations; P= *paisa*, T = *takka*

On the paisas of Dig, the Hijri-date can usually be observed above the *shā* of *bādshāh*. On the Bharatpur issues the Hijri-date is located above *sikkah mubārak* and often off the flan. On the few specimens where Hijri dates are shown, they often do not coincide with the regnal year on the reverse. This would indicate that the dies were used until they were completely worn out or broken before they got replaced. Therefore, certain date combinations or regnal years may have been produced over a longer period of time or even became frozen, as happened with the last regnal year of Shah Alam II, viz., RY 49. The latest date combination so far observed is AH 1279/RY 49 (=1862). Bharatpur mint (Brajendrapur) seems, unlike the mint of Mahendrapur (Dig), not to have coined any other copper coins than *takkas*. Dig seems, particularly during the early period in the reign of Shah Alam II, to have minted paisas profusely instead of *takkas*.

Bharatpur continuously minted *takkas* from about the regnal years 40 to 49 of Shah Alam (1798-1806). They were produced very regularly with possibly a peak output for all three mints in RY 45, which fits well with the data on which the booty was seized. We, therefore, suggest this reflects an increase in the production of Bharatpur rupees and takkas during the second Anglo-Maratha War (1803-5). As large regiments were kept to defend the fortresses, they not only had to be paid out in silver rupees, but they also had to purchase goods at the local markets, which necessitated the availability of copper change.

As to the content of a 'bag' not much can be said for sure, but a bag of 10 *seers* = 9.331 kg would contain only 525 *takka* pieces. A bag of 1 maund = 40 *seers* = 37.324 kg would contain 2,100 pieces, which makes the total number of coppers seized not very impressive, say between 7,885 and 31,500 Bharatput *takkas* - at best 10 per cent of the annual output of one of its mints.[25]

FIG. 9.12: AE *TAKKA*, MAHENDRAPUR (DIG)
AH 1217/RY 45 (WEIGHT 17.00 G)

FIG. 9.13: AE *TAKKA*, BRAJENDRAPUR (BHARATPUR) AH 12xx/RY 45 (WEIGHT 18.22 G)

Conclusion and Epilogue

To conclude: the booty inventory made up after the capture of Dig on Christmas Eve 1804 does not contain numismatic surprises and seems to confirm the impressive output of the Bharatpur mints at that period. At the same time, it is significant for the history of coin circulation as it may explain why there was such a heightened minting activity in those years. It also shows the crucial role of the availability of coins for paying the troops as underlined by Randolf Cooper for the Anglo-Maratha wars. On top of this, it illustrates the extra incentive for soldiers provided by booty which trickled down to the lowest ranks.

This document does not tell us what Captain Staunton Deputy Field Paymaster did with the silver rupees. If he subsequently used them for local payments by the occupying troops, then the effect on the circulation will have been nil. But even if he sent the complete treasure to one of the EIC mints of Bengal for smelting and re-coining, the effect on coin circulation in Bharatpur state would not have been felt very much. Nor do the rarity indications in the modern coin catalogues provide a clue in that direction – unless of course in this way the total annual production of one of the mints – and especially that of Dig – vanished, which is not the case as it was still quite active up till well after 1857.

The sack of Dig on Christmas Eve 1804, may still have left another numismatic imprint. In 1803 during the 2nd Anglo-Maratha war, Lord Lake entered Delhi and on 16 September 1803 visited Shah Alam, who reportedly called him his 'friend and deliverer'.[26] From that date the British controlled affairs in Delhi, including the mint.

A particularly nice coin with floral borders was struck for the first time in AH 1219/RY 47 (18 July 1804 to 1 April 1805; see Figs. 9.14 and 9.17). These rupees and *mohurs* of the so-called 'wreath type' are described in the British Museum Catalogue as well as by Paul Stevens as: 'Obv. and Rev. Enclosed in wreath of roses, thistles, and shamrocks'.[27] However close observation shows no thistles nor any shamrocks. The wreath with the berries look more like holly that is used for decoration at Christmas with its red berries (see Fig. 9.15). The flowers look like roses, but could well be Christmas roses (hellebores; see Fig. 9.16).[28]

It was Shailendra Bhandare, on a discussion group on the Internet, who pointed to this connection with Christmas decorations. There must have been a particularly important event related to Christmas, for such rupees and *mohurs* to have been produced. It is tempting to assume that the success of the 'Grand Army' with the surrender of the Jat fort of Deeg on Christmas Eve 1804 may have instigated the design of these outstanding coins.

FIG. 9.14: WREATH TYPE AR RUPEE, SHAHJAHANABAD, AH 1219/ RY 47

FIG. 9.15: CHRISTMAS HOLLY

FIG. 9.16: CHRISTMAS ROSE OR HELLEBORE

FIG. 9.17: WREATH TYPE AV *MOHUR*, SHAHJAHANABAD, AH 1220/ RY 48

Appendix 9.1: Statements of prize property, captured from the enemy from 13-10-1803 to 10-04-1805 by the Grand Army under the command of the Right Honourable Lord Lake Commander in Chief &ca &ca &ca

S.P. Hay Lieutt & Arty Prize Agent, Agra 28-08-1805[29]

TABLE 9.3: STATEMENTS OF PRIZE PROPERTY, CAPTURED FROM THE ENEMY FROM 13 OCTOBER 1803 TO 10 APRIL 1805 BY THE GRAND ARMY

Where and when captured	*Names of articles*	*Remarks*
At the action of Deeg 13-11-1804	453 rupees of different kinds	Taken charge of by the prize agents
During the siege and at the capture of Deeg	208,900 Burtpore rupees	Taken charge of by the prize agents and delivered by them by order of the commander in chief to Captain Staunton Depy Field Paymaster
	50 Bindrabund rupees	Taken charge of by the prize agents
	15 bags of copper pice	Taken charge of by the prize agents and sold by public auction [together with other goods]
	552 maunds of salt and saltpetre	For the use of the garrison

	8000 maunds of firewood	
	57 maunds 20 seers of sulphur	
During the siege of Burtpore	[No cash or materials for manufacturing gunpowder]	
Total prize money from auctions, cash and goods kept, probl amount of the Fund	Rs. 399,483:6:8	
Minus rupees	Rs. 209,403	52.4%
Value of auctioned goods (including the copper pyce) and the materials for making gun powder	Rs. 190,080	47.6%

NOTES

1. About the middle of the nineteenth century, Bharatpur was a territory of 1,974 square miles with 650,000 inhabitants, see Growse 1978, 46 (the first edition dates from 1874, the second and enlarged edition from 1880); Herrli 2013, 22, fn. 38.
2. There is much confusion about the numbering of the Anglo-Maratha Wars, as explained in: Cooper 2003, 313-14, 343-4. Here we stick to the conventional but problematic indication, although the 1804-5 British campaign against Jaswant Rao Holkar may well be seen as separate from the preceding one in 1803; Khanna & Tandon 1985, 40.
3. Naravane 2006, 91-6.
4. Khanna & Tandon 1985. The original is to be found in the British Library (Add Mss 30516).
5. Khanna & Tandon 1985, 47.
6. These and the following quotes from Khanna & Tandon 1985, 50-2.
7. Lucassen 2012.
8. See *Fort William – India House Correspondence*, 94-5 (Letter from Court 8 April 1789), 238-41 (Letter to Court 16 August 1787), 251 (15 December 1787), 253-4 (12 January 1788); for the lists of thousands of names of those entitled to a share see *NAI, Military Board Proceedings* 21-10-1786).
9. Cooper 2003, 299, 327-34; cf. Kolff 1990 and Herrli 2013.

10. Cooper 2003, 227.
11. Lucassen, see Part I: Studies, No. 2 in this volume.
12. Kulkarni 2003, 17.
13. Also attested in a contemporaneous document, see Herrli 2013, 22, fn. 38.
14. Growse 1978, 189-93, 259-66.
15. *Mu'min* is a term, frequently referenced in the Quran, meaning 'believer', and more in particular 'a faithful Muslim'. *Mu'minabad* would thus lit. mean a 'a place of faithful Muslims' – a rather derogatory name for one of the most venerated centres of Hindu pilgrimage in India.
16. E.g. Bruce 2004, 621 ('Bindraban. This city, the modern Vrindavan, was not a princely state [...] The coins [...] display symbols of Awadh, Mughals, Delhi and Bartpur [*sic* Bharatpur], although it is clear that they were not mints of any of those authorities, especially in the British period'; The catalogue itself then distinguishes confusingly between 'city' and 'local' coinage). The same text in Bruce 2013, 270-2.
17. Unless otherwise stated, all data are from the same source as Table 9.1.
18. Growse 1978, 266.
19. Therefore, contrary to the opinion of Maheshwari & Wiggins 1989, 147-54 it is not difficult at all to distinguish the Maratha issues of RY 26-45 from the Bharatpur issues of RY 37 and later.
20. Growse 1978, 266.
21. Herrli 2013, 21, fn. 31, however without reference.
22. For the annual income of the temples, see Growse 1978, 266.
23. Image kindly provided by Shailendra Bhandare.
24. For Alwar and the other states mentioned, see Bruce 2013.
25. For some data on the transport of copper coins and the contents of chests (containing several gunny bags) see Lingen & Lucassen, see Part I: Studies, Nos. 10 and 12 and Lucassen, No. 13 in this volume.
26. Cooper 2003, 171-89, quote on 188.
27. Stevens 2012, 428-9, 433-4.
28. *Helleborus niger* is commonly called the Christmas rose, due to an old legend that it sprouted in the snow from the tears of a young girl who had no gift to give the Christ child in Bethlehem.
29. NAI, Military Board Proceedings, Friday 14-03-1806, 3774-81 (our selection from these long lists, whereby we concentrate mainly on the cash; the last two rows are ours, to simplify matters here taking all rupees at the same rate).

10

Copper Circulation in Northern India in 1830

JAN LINGEN AND JAN LUCASSEN

Production and Circulation of Copper Coins: No Simple Relation[1]

It is convenient to assume that states or other polities, like, e.g. towns, produce coins for internal usage, and that coin circulation is totally or at least predominantly national. This national perspective pervades most handbooks and catalogues,[2] although monetary historians and numismatists know many exceptions to this 'rule' – in particular gold and big silver coins, often used as export products. Famous examples are the Athenian tetradrachms, the Spanish pillar dollar and the Dutch golden ducat. In all these cases, coins could actually circulate far from the places of production and outside the polity which had authorized its legal production.[3]

In particular copper coins (and, for that matter, all coins of a low intrinsic value) are believed to have circulated primarily within the polity where they were produced for two obvious reasons. First, because of the fact that copper coins basically are fiduciary, which means that their production costs are below their nominal value and that consequently their acceptance depends on trust in the issuing authorities. Secondly, because of the relatively high transportation costs of these low-value goods.[4]

Nevertheless, copper coins can and do circulate outside the territory where they are produced legally or where their production at least is condoned by the authorities under two conditions: the one demand and the other supply-driven. Societies which have a high demand for coppers have a fine network of markets as well as a substantive number of inhabitants that are paid in coin, either as small producers (peasants or artisans) or as wage earners.[5] Demand for small currency in such highly monetized societies can draw in foreign or privately fabricated copper coins if the authorities for whatever political or commercial reason fail to supply enough themselves. Famous examples are the circulation of private tokens in mid-seventeenth and late eighteenth-century England,[6] but also the spread of Chinese 'cash'- coins in South-East Asia.[7] A variant is the importation in colonies of coppers produced in the homeland of which the exportation of Dutch-made copper *duiten* or *doits* in eighteenth- and early-nineteenth century Indonesia and Ceylon offers a good example.[8] On the supply side profit-driven foreign governments or private entrepreneurs, both national and foreign, must be available.

In principle two kinds of sources may provide the evidence necessary to reconstruct patterns of copper coin production for exportation and circulation in other polities: archeological, especially the analysis of coin hoards and stray finds, and archival. Understandably but unfortunately the archeological field is dominated by the analysis of silver and gold coin hoards, in particular those of more recent centuries.[9] Therefore, we very much depend on archival sources. However, these are rare because the producers of coins rarely supplied evidence about the fate of the coins after they had left the mint house.

One of the parts of the world where copper coin circulation seems to have been completely erratic and the result of haphazard circumstances is India in the eighteenth and nineteenth centuries. There a proliferation of mints can be observed, often in polities too small to warrant the existence of an own state mint. Consequently, exportation of copper must have been an option but the destination nearly always is unknown.[10] Gradually, more and more studies have been published on coin production there, but the study of copper coin circulation has yet to begin, and precise case studies are awaited.

In a recent article, we have shown how a concentration of

wage earners in a certain area may produce a substantive demand for coppers, which may be provided for by suppliers from outside. The case in point is the workers involved in the repairs and maintenance of the Western Jumna Canals, immediately north of New Delhi in the late 1840s.[11] This was before the colonial small change, produced at the Calcutta and Bombay mints, had reached this part of the colony. In exchange for their labour for the canal company the workers received wages, paid out in one specific copper coin, called in the sources the 'mansuri paisa'. According to us the mansuri paisa in this particular case has to be identified as paisas, produced in Alwar, a native state with coin factories at a distance of some 150 km away from the canal area in another polity (directly ruled British India) where they were used.

Several aspects of this case are interesting: the importance of wage labour for the circulation of copper coins, the importation of coppers over substantive distances, and the limitation of specific coppers to specific labour markets. In order to know whether the two latter features are exceptional or more general and to reconstruct circulation patterns of coppers the mansuri case now may be extended by new evidence. Fortunately, we came across a document which discusses the copper circulation around 1830 in a wider area, viz., the part of northern India between Delhi and the Himalayas, and thus including the region of our first case study.

Copper Circulation between Delhi and the Himalayas in 1830

In 1812 the British East India Company (BEIC) started the building of the Jumna Canals and many irrigation canals were to follow, the most famous of which was the Ganges Canal. After the completion of a canal the work was not finished because maintenance and repairs asked for continuous supplementary labour.[12] In 1823 Captain John Colvin[13] had been appointed by the Military Board (one of the most important departments of the BEIC in India, and *inter alia* responsible for the canals) to superintend Feroze's Canal, and from 1827 onwards he became superintendent of all irrigation canals in the Delhi territory. On an annual basis he spent about Rs. 6,000, which at a monthly wage of Rs. 2 to 3 for diggers or excavation workers equalled 2,000 to 3,000 working months. This made him an important employer in the region. On 15 June 1830 he had run into trouble when he had to pay his workforce, engaged in the maintenance of the Western Jumna Canals.[14] Not that he received insufficient money from his bosses in Calcutta. No, enough silver rupees had arrived which, however, he was compelled to change into coppers because the workers did not wish to receive their earnings in silver. The silver rupee roughly equaled more than a week's salary and was therefore too inconvenient to be used for small payments in the markets, or to creditors. Consequently, before pay day Captain Colvin always had to exchange his silver rupees into coppers. In the end therefore, the BEIC as an employer was dependent for its wage payments in copper coin on the local shroffs. The price they charged for copper coins expressed in silver rupees mattered therefore greatly.

It turns out that the shroffs, aware of this circumstance, combined and tried to draw extra profits as soon as new works started. As Colvin remarks: 'the price of pice is always raised when my works commence'. After a couple of years, he decided to investigate the possibility of circumventing the shroffs and striking a deal directly with two local mint masters. According to his information from the mint master of Chhachrauli this could be rather advantageous to the Company (as summarized by us in Table 10.1).

The mint master at Jagadhri explained to Colvin that he could strike a profitable deal only if he could provide raw copper at Rs. 50 per maund or less, because at a higher price it would be cheaper to buy existing copper coins from the shroffs. Colvin's dilemmas at Chhachrauli and Jagadhri are summarized in Fig. 10.1, from which it is clear that at a copper price of Rs. 50 per maund it was always more profitable in both places to produce coins rather than to exchange them, whereas at Chhachrauli this was even the case at a copper price as high as Rs. 60 per maund. As copper was available at Rs. 44, 42 or less this was a realistic alternative.

Despite this creative and profitable proposal, Colvin received a negative answer from the Military Board in Calcutta.[15] The

TABLE 10.1: COST OF PICE AT CHHACHRAULI

	Rate of pice per rupee*	*Total sum in Sonat rupees***	*Difference between highest and lowest price in rupees*	*Effected savings if purchased at lowest price (per centage)*	*Total production costs per maund of copper*** in Sonat rupees*
At highest exchange rate from shroffs	29.3	3,071	556	18	
At high exchange rate from shroffs	29.8	3,020	483	16	
At normal exchange rate from shroffs	30	3,000	465	15.5	
If bought directly from the Mint at Rs. 60/maund of copper	30	3,000	465	15.5	64:1:5.5
If bought directly from the Mint at Rs. 50/maund of copper	35.5	2,535	0	0	54:1:5.5

Notes: * 1 pice = 19,44 gram (see appendix: 1920 pice = 1 maund = 37.3242 kg.)
** 1 sonat rupee = 11.66 grams (see appendix: 3,200 rupees = 1 maund)[16]
*** manufacturing costs of 1920 pice = Rs. 4:1:5.5 (4 rupees, 1 anna, 5½ pice)

Governor-General in Council ordered the Military Board to inform Colvin that he had to use exclusively the copper pice coined at the Calcutta mint, 'the circulation of which it is supposed there can be no difficulty in introducing it into Delhi territory'. Colvin protested against this easy assumption:

the supply of pice ordered up will be utterly useless to me on the works without a special regulation of Government making the pice of the Calcutta mint the only legal copper coin current throughout the Companies' territories. The pice in question cannot be introduced by an

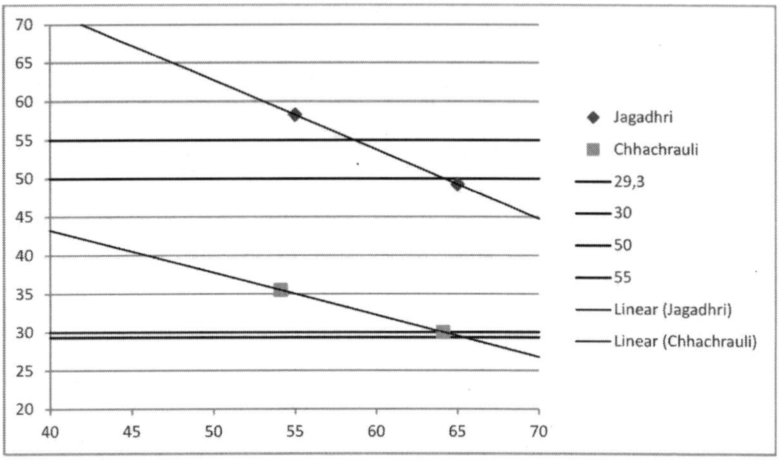

FIG. 10.1: COMPARATIVE COSTS OF COPPER COIN PRODUCTION AND COPPER EXCHANGE RATES AT JAGADHRI AND CHHACHRAULI 1830

Key:
x-axis: production costs (in silver sonat rupees) per maund of copper.
y-axis: number of copper pieces, received per 1 silver sonat rupee.

individual and will only subject me to infinite trouble & annoyance as no one will willingly take pay from me in a coin not in general currency; and in the Seik [Sikh] states, where the chief part of my work lies they will absolutely not pass and will only be received as copper at its value as such, and to their Independent States no regulation of the British Government will apply without special treaty on the subject. I conceive it would be most desirable object if our copper currency could be introduced throughout the British Dominions, but the [Military] Board will easily perceive it cannot be done by any individual.

However sound this argumentation might have been, Calcutta stuck to its decision to send up Rs. 5,000 in copper pice to Delhi, together with ordnance stores. The coins were ordered to be packed in twenty-five boxes each containing 12,800 pieces and to be loaded on board of one of the Ordnance Store Boats, guarded by two 'Podras/ Padars' 'for whom it will be necessary to make some arrangements for their accommodation on board the boat'. We do not know whether this shipment actually took place, but we

Fig. 10.2a

Fig. 10.2b

Fig. 10.2c

Fig. 10.2d

FIG. 10.2: TRILINGUAL (BENGALI, PERSIAN, HINDI) COPPER PICE WEIGHING 6.48 GRAM, COINED BY THE BRITISH AT CALCUTTA (FIG. 10.a; 1829, 6.43 G.), BANARAS (FIG. 10.b; 1827-9, 6.46 G), SAUGOR (FIG. 10.c; 1827-33, 6.21 G) AND FARRUKHABAD (FIG. 10.d; 1820-4, 6.50 G)

do know that eighteen to nineteen years later Calcutta coppers still were not readily available in the countryside north of Delhi and that only then the British started to distribute their own copper coins in sufficient numbers.[17]

From these loading specifications it follows that 64 pice were supposed to equal 1 rupee, which was indeed the official exchange rate. Although in reality this rate could fluctuate[18] it is unequivocally clear which specimen is meant: the copper trilingual pice weighing 6.48 grams as produced by the British mints with the fixed regnal year 37 of Shah Alam II (1795-1832/33) at Calcutta (1813-32/3 in Rs. 2,001,685 value or 128 million pieces) and Banares (1815-29/30 in Rs. 1.388.140 value or 89 million pieces), or with the fixed regnal year 45 at Saugor (1827-32/3 in Rs. 283.388 value or 18 million pieces) and Farrukhabad.[19]

More important for the question under discussion than the actual result of Captain Colvin's request are his efforts to find out which particular coins were accepted by the wage earners. He observed that there were strong regional preferences and that on average per region only one type of copper coin was used for wage payments. From Delhi northwards to the Himalayas this resulted in three distinct zones. The first consisted of Delhi and surroundings, the second of the canal area between Delhi/Karnal and Dadupur, say some 10 km south of the line Ambala-Dehra Dun, and the third from Dadupur northwards (see Map 10.1 and Table 10.2).

Although the area of circulation is clear, it turns out to be much more complicated to determine exactly which types of coin are meant. Although we are in a slightly more advantageous situation than when we started our hunt for the 'mansuri paisa' (after all, now we know the names of coins, their exchange rate, and their weight, we know where they circulated, and in two out of three cases we know where they were produced) it is not easy to identify the actual coins.

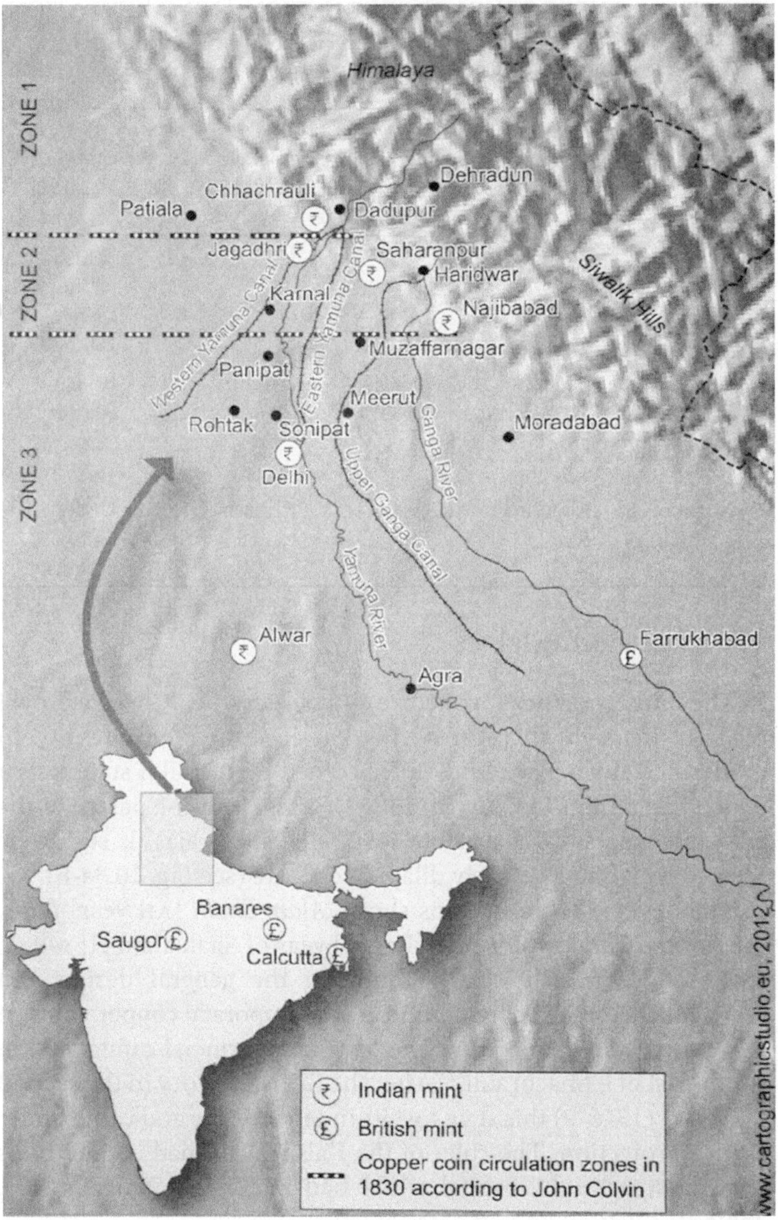

MAP 10.1: COPPER COINAGE CIRCULATION ZONES NORTH OF DELHI, 1830-48

Sources: Baker 1849, Plate 1; Cautley 1860, Part III, map between pp. 23 and 24.

TABLE 10.2: THREE ZONES OF PRODUCTION AND CIRCULATION OF COPPER COINS BETWEEN DELHI AND THE HIMALAYAS, ACCORDING TO COLVIN IN 1830

Zone		*Name of prevailing copper coin*	*Weight in grams*	*Where produced*	*Bazar rate*	*Political authority over the mint*
1	Delhi and surroundings	?	?	?	44	British territory since 1803-20
2	Between Delhi/Karnal and Dadupur	[small] Mensoorkhane pice	[*c.* 11.66/ 12.83]21	Jagadhri	50-5	British territory since 1829[22]
3	North of Dadupur	Cheecheerowli pice	19.44	Chhach-rauli	33	Under Sikh authority

The 'Cheecheerowli Pice'

In the most northern zone we encounter the 'Cheecheerowli pice'. At first sight this seems to be the easiest coin to identify. In modern catalogues we find a pice coined by the Sikh state Kalsia which had a mint in Chhachrauli.[23] In this town the palace of the erstwhile rulers of Kalsia state (1902-48 called rajas) is still to be seen – though in a severely dilapidated state (see Fig. 10.3a-b).

The obverse of these coins shows *Alam Shahi* [AH year] *fulus*, the reverse *Chhachrauli zarb* [Regnal year of Shah'Alam II] *sanah*, according to Herrli 'clearly imitating the general design and marks of the much more common contemporary copper coins of Saharanpur (see Table 10.3), the Mughal provincial capital 40 km south-east of Chhachrauli'.[24] After the British victory in the second Sikh War (1846-9) this state lost its independence and came under British protection. The ruler of the Kalsia states had copper fulus or dams struck at his capital, which had 5.520 inhabitants in 1901. Table 10.3 lists all known dates of issue.

FIG. 10.3a: THE OLD PALACE AT CHHACHRAULI FALLEN TO RUINS

FIG. 10.3b: REMAINS OF A WALL PAINTING, SHOWING THE UPCOMING INDUSTRIALIZATION, WITH RAILWAY LINES, FACTORY BUILDINGS, HIGH SMOKING CHIMNEYS, CANALS AND LABOUR WORKING ALONG IT. [Figs. 10.a and 10.b: Photos taken by Jan Lingen March, 2011]

FIG. 10.4: THE CHHACHRAULI PICE, DATED AH 1215/RY 41 (1800/1801)

The years reported (1799-1804) however predate by at least twenty-five years the situation encountered by Captain Colvin. This is strange: in 1830 these pieces still dominated a fairly large territory and the minting workshop was still fully operational. We must conclude that either the pieces mentioned in the literature have been continued with a so-called 'frozen year' or that pieces

TABLE 10.3: KNOWN DATES OF ISSUE OF THE CHHACHRAULI PICE

AH *date and regnal year (*CE *date)*	*Valentine 1914, page, number (and weight in grams)*	*Bruce 2004, page, KM number (and weight in grams)*	*Other references (and weight in grams)*
1214//41 (1799/1800)		p. 668, *KM* 32 (wrong transcription of year; no weight given; = Herrli 2004, 264)	
1215//41 (1800/1801)			Collection Jan Lingen (11.90 g) Fig. 10.4
1215//42 (1800/1)	138-9, no. 96 (= Wright 1907, 299, no. 2490 (17.36 g) and 2491 (14.64 g); = Herrli 2004, 246)		
1216//41 (1801/2)	138-9, no. 97 (2 retrograde, resulting in AH 1616; = Whitehead 1914, 418, no. 3202) (14.90 g); = Herrli 2004, 246		
1218//44 (1803/4)		p.668, no. 32 (no illustration; no weight given)	
(*c.* 1830)			Letter Colvin

with later dates have been melted down or have vanished otherwise, or, finally, that another, still unidentified, type was produced. As mentioned before the Chhachrauli pice shows much similarity to the Saharanpur copper coins, it is therefore most likely that at a later stage of their mint activities copies of the Saharanpur pice were struck at Chhachrauli. For an example of such an imitation see Fig. 10.12 below. The weight is still lower than the 19.44 g as concluded from Colvin's report but compares favourably with the earlier issues of Chhachrauli and Saharanpur. As the reported weight of 19.44 g was the theoretical weight and taking in account an usual allowance for wear and tear of 1 per cent and perhaps some other hidden fees, we come reasonably close to the issues of Saharanpur and its contemporary imitations.

TABLE 10.4: SOME CONTEMPORARY COPPER COINS OF SAHARANPUR MINT AND CONTEMPORARY IMITATIONS

AH date and regnal year	*Takka (weight)*	*Remarks*	*Inventory numbers Fitzwilliam Museum*
1214//41	16.71, Fig. 10.5		
1215//42	16.79, Fig. 10.6		
1215//42	16.32, Fig. 10.7		
1215//42	16.46, Fig. 10.8		
1217//44	16.29, Fig. 10.9		
121x//44	16.20, Fig. 10.10		
1218//45	16.45, Fig. 10.11	Fitzwilliam Museum	CM.IN.4208-R
1215//4 (5 or 9)	15.75, Fig. 10.12	Contemporary imitation	
1215//xx	14.44, Fig. 10.13	The obv. shows much similarity with the above coin	The reverse has no resemblance with any other coin in this series
Yr.45	14.16, Fig. 10.14, flag		
Yr.45	12.23, Fig. 10.15, as above	Fitzwilliam Museum	CM.IN.1278-R
Yr.45	12.71, Fig. 10.16, as above	Fitzwilliam Museum	CM.IN.1276-R
Yr.45	12.60, Fig. 10.17, as above	Fitzwilliam Museum	CM.IN.1280-R

Fig. 10.5

Fig. 10.6

Fig. 10.7

Fig. 10.8

Fig. 10.9

Fig. 10.10

Fig. 10.11

Fig. 10.12

Fig. 10.13

Fig. 10.14

Fig. 10.15

Fig. 10.16

Fig. 10.17

FIGS. 10.5-10.17: COPPER COINS OF SAHARANPUR MINT AND CONTEMPORARY IMITATIONS, AH 1214/RY. 41-5 (1799-1804).

The 'Mensoorkhane Pice' from Jagadhri

The 'Mensoorkhane pice', produced in Juguree / Jugadree (modern Jagadhri in Haryana) without any doubt under British authority in 1830, poses even more problems., Coinage of silver rupees has been reported so far only for 1789 and possibly 1800-5. A paisa (Fig. 10.9) with the (pseudo) mint name Najibabad has on account of similar silver coins been attributed to Jagadhri too. The only silver coin observed with the mint name Jagadhri, is in the name of Shah Alam II, dated AH 1205/RY. 31 (1789/90).[25]

FIG. 10.18: THE JAGADHRI RUPEE WITH MINT NAME JAGADHRI, AH 1205/RY. 31

FIG. 10.19: 'JAGADHRI' PAISA WITH MINT NAME NAJIBABAD, AH- /RY. 30

FIG. 10.20: 'JAGADHRI' RUPEE WITH MINT NAME NAJIBABAD, AH '112'/RY. 29

FIG. 10.21: 'JAGADHRI' RUPEE WITH MINT NAME NAJIBABAD, AH 1205/RY. 33

The British Museum holds a series of rupees struck with the name of Shah Alam in the regnal years 42-7 with a ticket saying 'Old Jagadhree rupee, struck by Rani Sookum'. Unfortunately, this Rani Sookum never has been identified.[26] Some examples of the so-called 'Old Jagadhree rupee, struck by Rani Sookum' are illustrated here:

Fig. 10.22, RY. 43

Fig. 10.23, RY. 46

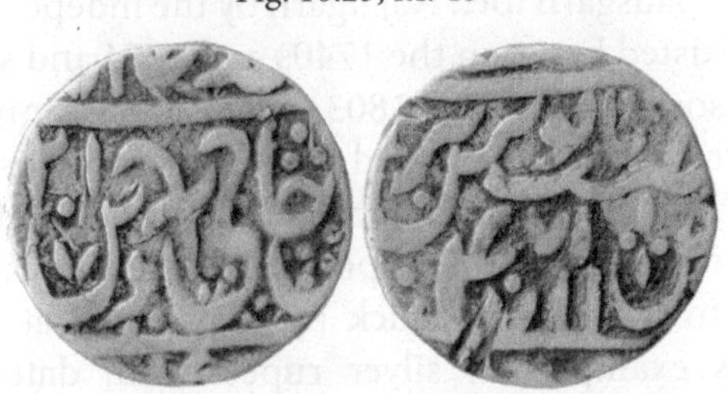

Fig. 10.24, RY. 47 (c. 1806)

FIG. 10.22-10.24: 'OLD JAGADHREE RUPEES, STRUCK BY RANI SOOKUM', *c.* 1800-6.

So far there is little evidence at hand to help identify the pice reported by Captain Colvin. As long as no specimens of a copper pice bearing the name Jagadhri become available we have to look out for a coin bearing another inscription, weighing *c.* 11.66/12.83 grams, leading to its acceptance at the rate of 50-5 per rupee (see Table 10.2), and – as Colvin calls these coins 'small' – suggesting a smaller diameter than the 24 mm of the Chhachrauli pice). Unfortunately, its name (*Mensoorkhane pice*) is not very helpful.

Like its successor in about the same region eighteen years later (the Alwar *takka*) it seems to have a rather generic significance. 'Mensoor' is rather similar to the 'mansuri paisa', according to our interpretation referring to the Persian noun 'manzuri' and meaning 'legal tender'.[27] 'Khane' might be the same as 'gani', originally a billon coin.[28] 'Mensoorkhane pice' might thus simply mean 'low value legal tender'.

We have made it likely that the Chhachrauli mint master thought it best to imitate an existing copper coin produced not far away at Saharanpur. If his colleague in nearby Jaghadri did the same – also in this case a full-fledged imitation, without changing the name[29] – we would like to suggest one possibility which meets at least all our specifications of metal, approximate weight and approximate size.

The Najibabad and especially the 'pseudo-Najibabad' pice meets indeed all these requirements. This copper coin was struck in Najibabad, Gausgarh fort, Najafgarh by the independent Rohilla state which existed between the 1740s and 1774 and subsequently by its successor Awadh until 1803, when it was annexed by the British.[30] Barry Tabor has noticed that there are coins bearing the mint name 'Najibabad' or 'Najibabad Dar ul-Khilafa' and later dates than AH 1218 (1803). This poses a problem because no coins are thought to have been struck by the British at Najibabad.[31] He mentions examples of silver rupees with dates as late as AH 1221//46 and with only regnal year 47 (these are the so-called 'Old Jagadhree rupee' as discussed above), as well as Najibabad copper pice as late as AH 1221//48. In table 10.5 we have summarized the evidence in as much detail as possible, available from one collection[32]

A series of small copper coins which show some affinity with the coins above (Fig. 10.38 a-j) should also be mentioned here. The coins show the mint name Najibabad and the figure of a vertical fish. All pieces show the regnal year 41, which would coincide with 1798/99, provided it is not a frozen year.

TABLE 10.5: COPPER NAJIBABAD AND PSEUDO NAJIBABAD COINS STRUCK UNDER AWADH AND POSSIBLY ALSO BRITISH RULE FROM AH 1205/RY 32 ONWARDS, *c.* 1790-1804

AH date and regnal year	*Takka (weight; symbols; mint name)*	*Paisa (weight; symbols; mint name)*	*Half paisa (weight; symbols; mint name)*
1205//32	17.59 (crescent, dagger) Fig. 10.25		
1208//34	17.76 (symbols unclear) Fig. 10.26		
1210//36	15.06 (crescent, dagger) Fig. 10.27		
12xx//37		9.72 (cross) Fig. 10.28	
1211//38	18.41 (crescent, dagger, sun) Fig. 10.29	6.17 (dagger) Fig. 10.30	
1210//40		7.23 (fish horizontal) Fig. 10.31	
12xx//41			5.91 (fish vertical) (as Fig. 10.34)
1215//42			4.44 (dagger) Fig. 10.32
1215//43			3.63 (fish horizontal) Fig. 10.33
1216//43	18.41 (fish vertical) Fig. 10.34		
1217//44		7.01 (star, sword, dagger) Fig. 10.35	
1218//4x		6.47 (fish horizontal) Fig. 10.36	
1218//47	18.41 (Kabirganj or Akbarganj) Fig. 10. 37		

Fig. 10.25

Fig. 10.26

Fig. 10.27

Fig. 10.28

Fig. 10.29

Fig. 10.30

Fig. 10.31

Fig. 10.32

Fig. 10.33

Fig. 10.34

Fig. 10.35

Fig. 10.36

Fig. 10.37

FIGS. 10.25-10.37: COPPER NAJIBABAD AND PSEUDO NAJIBABAD COINS STRUCK UNDER AWADH AND POSSIBLY ALSO BRITISH RULE FROM AH 1205/RY. 32 ONWARDS, *c.* 1790-1804

Fig. 10.38a

Fig. 10.38b

Fig. 10.38c

Fig. 10.38d

Fig. 10.38e

Fig. 10.38f

Fig. 10.38g

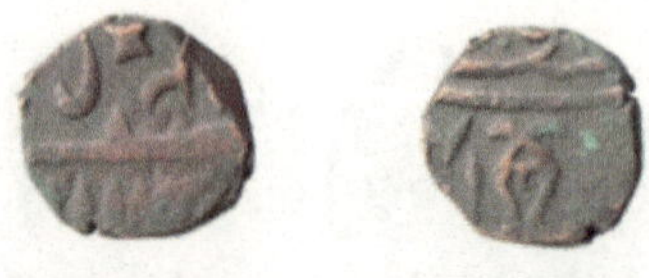

Fig. 10.38h

Fig. 10.38i

Fig. 10.38j

FIG. 10.38 a-j: HALF -WEIGHT PSEUDO-NAJIBABAD PICE WITH VERTICAL FISH, RY. 41 (1798/99, BUT PROBABLY A FROZEN YEAR)

The average weight of these pieces is about 4.95 g and therefore about half the weight of the coins of show with Fig. 10.44 to 10.47. For these reasons they may not be the enigmatic Mensoorkhane pice (Fig. 10.38 a-j), but pseudo-Najibabad pice.

An issue very similar to the coins of Fig. 10.38 a-j, but of better workmanship is illustrated in Fig. 10.39. A similar coin is illustrated in Valentine, p. 114, #177.

Fig. 10.39: 5.91 g.

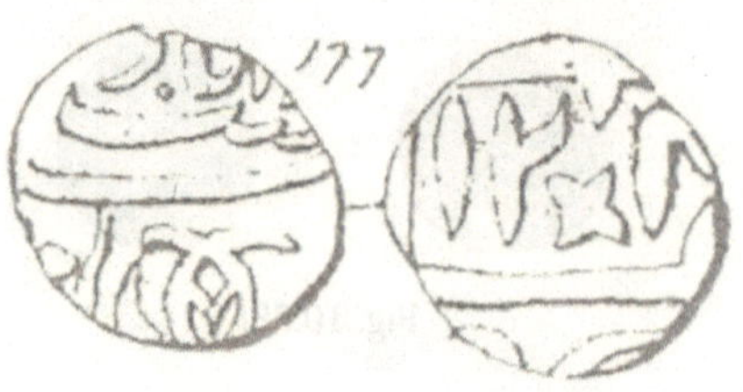

Fig. 10.40: Valentine #177

FIGS. 10.39-10.40: PSEUDO-NAJIBABAD PICE OF GOOD WORKMANSHIP FROM UNKNOWN PLACE, EARLY NINETEENTH CENTURY.

Valentine suggests that it was struck under Sikh rule. Particularly as two other coins (Valentine 178 and 179; Herrli 17.01.11) show a Sikh-legend. In that case Chhachrauli would be a more serious candidate for production of such pieces. As it is more likely, however, that Chhachrauli imitated the Saharanpur copper coinage, these coins must have been struck at some other nearby locality. Herrli (p.232) mentions that in 1785 'a Sikh army under command of Jassa Singh swept through Rohilkand and plundered the country as far as Chandausi, a town between Delhi and Bareilly. The Raja of Garhwal was made a Sikh tributary, and Najibabad was occupied for a short time by Sikh troops which on this occasion may have struck some paisas.' However, as the coins under discussion (Figs. 10.41-10.42) are dated later they cannot be attributed the Sikh activity in 1785.

Fig. 10.41: Valentine #178

Fig. 10.42: Valentine #179

Fig. 10.43: 5.79 g.

FIG 10.41-10.43: PSEUDO-NAJIBABAD PICE WITH THE LEGEND OF MAHARAJA SHRI PARDUMAN SHAH (1785-1803) OF GARHWAL.

The obverse is of typical Najibabad style and similar to the coins above (Figs. 10.39 and 10.40), while the reverse shows the legend of Maharaja Shri Parduman Shah (1785-1803) of Garhwal. On account of the date, year 41 on all the above coins (Figs. 10.38 to 10.43) they must be struck in 1798 or, more likely, in the early nineteenth century.

Finally, yet another enigmatic copper coin, reportedly frequently found in the area of Najibabad, might also have been known as the *Mensoorkhana* pice. The average weight (10.42 grams), however, doesn't exactly match with the calculated weight taken from Colvin (Table 10.2), but taking in account the allowance for wear and tear the coin compares favourable to the calculated weight by Colvin. It provides a comparable deviation in weight as the pseudo-Saharanpur *takka* which, we presume, was probably struck in Chhachrauli. Some examples of this enigmatic issue are illustrated below.

Fig. 10.44: 9.20 g.

Fig. 10.45: 10.96 g.

Fig. 10.46: 10.72 g.

Fig. 10.47: 10.57 g.

FIGS. 10.44-10.47: PSEUDO-NAJIBABAD PICE WITH AN AVERAGE WEIGHT OF 10.42 GRAM

All these examples show that in the political turmoil around 1800 not only Chhachrauli (as made evident by us above) but also Jagadhri and probably other mint houses in the region too, were still able to produce coins from dies which not necessary showed the name of the mint house and where obverse and reverse often got mixed. In this light we have a good candidate for the coins, offered to be produced for Colvin by the Jagadhri mint master. The slight deviation from the calculated weight can be easily accounted for, as discussed above.

The above illustrated (Figs. 10.44-10.47) coins, so far known as light weight 'pseudo-Najibabad *takkas*' with weights ranging from 9.20 to 10.96 grams perfectly meet the requirements of the 'Mensoorkhane pice'. At the same time we have found an answer to the riddle posed by Tabor. The latter coins are still quite common in the market, which is an extra argument for our interpretation.

The 'Dilhi Pice'

Finally, what is meant with the pice circulating at the rate of 44 per rupee in Delhi and surroundings around 1830? At first sight this might be related to the 'Dilhi', mentioned in John Prinsep's *Useful Tables* of 1834.[33] Prinsep writes that this coin circulated at a rate between 44 and 60 paisa per rupee. We suppose that he meant the paisa, struck in the name of the penultimate Mughal Muhammed Akbar II (1806-37) at the Delhi (named Shahjahanabad) mint from AH 1221//1 until AH 1233//12. During the first two years it shows exclusively text in Persian script, but from AH 1225//4 onwards an additional S in Latin script as an abbreviation for *Sanah* (year) has been added. The weight varies between 11.21 and 11.58 grams (average weight 11.41 grams), which differs considerably from the weight given in *KM* (12.9 to 13.8 grams).[34] The last known year, AH 1233 began on 11 November 1817 which perfectly fits Prinsep's information. Colvin was not acquainted with the weight or place of issue of this issue, but on account of the exchange rate of approximately 44 to a rupee the weight, by extrapolation, would be about 14.5 grams. As minting has been stopped twelve years earlier their number in circulation may have been decreased to such an extent that it boosted the exchange rate, compared with the copper coins of the more northern mints.

TABLE 10.6: THE 'DILHI' OR THE PAISA STRUCK IN DELHI BETWEEN 1806 AND 1818

AH date and regnal year	*Paisa (weight in gram)*	
1222//2 (1807/8)	11.58	Fig. 10.48
1225//4 (1810)	11.28	Fig. 10.49
1227//6 (1812)	11.21	Fig. 10.50
1231//10 (1815/16)	11.56	Fig. 10.51

Fig. 10.48

Fig. 10.49

Fig. 10.50

Fig. 10.51

FIGS. 10.48-10.51: DIHLI PICE AH 1222/ RY. 2 (1807/08) TO AH 1231/ RY. 10 (1815/16)

In 1826 serious consideration was given to resuming the coinage of coppers at the Delhi Mint. On that occasion we hear that the production of 120 pice out of one *seer* of copper cost between Rs. 1:7 and Rs. 1:14 at a maximum, of which one anna was for manufacturing costs and the rest for the copper.[35] This means copper costs of Rs. 55 to 72.5 per maund, or considerably more than estimated by Colvin four years later, and manufacturing cost of Rs. 2:8 per maund, consisting of 4,800 coins of 7.78 grams[36] each against Rs. 4:1:5.5 per maund, consisting of 1920 *takkas* of 19.44 grams each at Chhachrauli. The latter comparison suggests that the weight per coin determined manufacturing costs more than the number made.

However, the 'Dilhi pice' is not our only candidate. To complete the scene of copper coin circulation in northern India, a series of copper coins with the mint name Shahjahanabad should also be taken into consideration. This series of lighter 'fish paisas' seems not to be a product of the Imperial mint at Delhi, but were probably struck at a not identified mint place east of the Yamuna River and north of the capital Delhi. As Colvin mentioned that he was unacquainted with the weight and place of issue, these 'fish paisas' cannot, despite its low weight, be ruled out completely as the type of coin Colvin referred to.

TABLE 10.7: A SERIES OF LIGHTER FISH PAISAS WITH THE MINT NAME SHAHJAHANABAD

AH date and regnal year	*Paisa (weight in grams)*	*Legend*	*Reference Fitzwilliam Museum*
1205//32	8.43, Fig. 10.52	Falus Alam Shahi	
1208//35	7.29	Falus Alam Shahi	
1201//38, error for 1210//38	7.53	Falus Alam Shahi	
1212//38	7.54, Fig. 10.53	Falus Alam Shahi	CM.IN.4209-R
1212//39	7.22, Fig. 10.54	'Fazl-i-hami-din' couplet	CM.IN.4167-R
1412, error for 1214//41	7.21, Fig. 10.55	Falus Alam Shahi	
Yr. 48	7.97, Fig. 10.56	'Fazl-i-hami-din' couplet	

Fig. 10.52

Fig. 10.53

Fig. 10.54

Fig. 10.55

Fig. 10.56

FIGS. 10.52-10.56: LIGHT-WEIGHT FISH PAISAS WITH THE MINT NAME SHAHJAHANABAD, AH 1205/ RY. 32 TO RY. 48

Conclusion

For the second time we have been able to show in detail that coppers were needed to pay out wages in the second quarter of the nineteenth century in northern India. And, more importantly, that wage labourers clearly preferred certain copper coins over others, most likely because they knew what the purchasing power of these pieces was, whereas the value of alternative pieces varied too much or had to be negotiated constantly. However, for the second time we have run into considerable trouble in our attempts to identify exactly which concrete pieces changed hands. This trouble stems essentially from the circumstance that the coins reported in our main source, Colvin's letter of 1830, were not produced by the authorities in charge, in this case the British. It took them a long time, decades or more than half a century to strike coins for the newly conquered territories. This may be explained because many alternatives were at hand: the continued usage of old coinage (like the 'Dihlis' in and around Delhi, reported in 1830 when they were twelve years old at a minimum), the importation from neighbouring states like the 'Cheecheerowli pice' from Kalsia, reported in 1830 and the *takkas* from Alwar, reported in 1848, and, finally, the continuation of the old production of existing mints in the newly conquered territories, without however changing the outer appearance of the coins. Paul Stevens has provided many examples of this phenomenon and we may add to this list the 'Mensoorkhane pice', produced in Jagadhri according to our 1830 report, possibly to be interpreted as a light version of the pseudo-Najibabad *takka* (Figs. 10.44 to 10.47), but also as the reduced weight Shahjahanabad paisas, produced at an unknown mint (Figs. 10.52 to 10.56).

We may also observe the dynamism in what seems to be a fixed payment custom at a certain point in time. Whereas around 1830 between Delhi/Karnal and Dadupur the 'Mensoorkhane pice' and in and around Delhi the 'Dihli' were preferred by the workers, this had changed eighteen years later. Most likely because of the discontinuation of the production of these coins by the British, they had to import coins from elsewhere as long as their large coin factories in Bombay, Calcutta, Benares and Farrukhabad were yet unable to provision all of British India. This provided a chance for states like Alwar as we have shown. The new evidence also enables us to define more precisely the period in which the Alwar *takkas* must have been most in demand north of Delhi: roughly in the two decades between 1830 and 1850. We cannot be sure about the precise beginning, but it cannot have been long after 1830 as the exchange rates of the 'Mensoorkhane pice' and the 'Dihli' had already been rising substantially by that date, which must have made them less popular among the labour force. The massive transports of coppers from Calcutta to the north-western provinces in 1848 must have been felt in the circulation in the years afterwards and must have driven out the Alwar *takkas* sooner or later.[37] That also must have been the death-knell for the circulation of Chhachrauli pice in the north if they still were as popular there as they were twenty years before.

This new and more precise evidence for the emergence of demand for Alwar *takkas* coincides pretty well with our data on the production of this coin. After an interruption or at least a slow-down in the 1820s their production was resumed in the

1830s and continued at a larger scale from 1838/9 onwards.[38] This was Alwar's response to the demise of the Delhi and Jagadhri pice we would suggest. The extensive production of Alwar *takkas* in the 1850s and 1860s suggests either a slower introduction of the British-Indian coins in the north than supposed so far, or new outlets outside the parts of India, directly ruled by the British.

From our summary about the customs regulating the actual payment of wages in copper coins in Delhi and the regions north of it in the period 1830-48 (see Table 10.8) it follows that the coins that changed hands equalled 3.6 to 6 parts of a daily wage, or two to three hours of work.

TABLE 10.8: COPPER COINS USED FOR WAGE PAYMENTS BETWEEN DELHI AND THE HIMALAYAS, 1830-48

Zone	*Name of the coin in the sources*	*Identification*	*Exchange rate (number of coppers per rupee)*	*Number of coins per daily wage of 0.1 Rupee*[39]
North of Dadupur 1830	Cheeche-erowli pice	Pice produced by the Kalsia state in Chhachrauli (cf. *KM* 32, but later. It's also possible that an imitation of the Saharanpur pice, like Fig. 10.12, was struck there.)	44	4.4
Between Delhi/ Karnal and Dadupur 1830	Mensoor-khane pice	Pice produced in Jagadhri, as such so far unidentified in collections but possibly pseudo-Najibabad light *takkas* (Figs. 10.44 to 10.47)	50-5	5-5.5
Between Delhi and Panipat 1848	Mansuri paisa	Alwar *takka* (*KM* 15, 25, 35.1 and 35.2)	36	3.6

In and around Delhi 1830	Pice (Dihli)	Pice produced in Delhi until 1818 (*KM* 770 and 771; Figs. 48-51) Or the reduced weight Shajahababad paisa (Figs. 10.52 to 10.56)	44-60	4.4-6

This result compares rather well with more general observations about the number of coins received by a worker per payment elsewhere.[40] It also shows how worthwhile it is to add new pieces to the puzzle and in this way not only to contribute to Indian numismatic, economic and social history, but also to take part in debates which have an even wider importance.

Appendix 10.1: Letter of John Colvin, Captain, Superintendent of Canals, Office 25-05-1830, to Lieutenant Colonel Craigie, Secretary of the Military Board, Fort William

Sir,

I beg to submit for the consideration and orders of the Military Board the following connected with the extraordinary high prize of pice in these provinces which, having been now steadily so for several years past, may be expected to continue, entailing on Government a great extra expenditure, which the adoption of what I propose will enable me to counteract and effect a certain saving on my own line of works north of Kurnaul[41] and if I can get pice coined in sufficient quantity probably to a much greater distance along the canals under my charge.

The grounds on which I go are these, first in regard to the Cheecheerowlee[42] pice, the coin in which all payments to daily work people from Dadoopoor[43] upwards are made, including a large portion of the ordinary repairs of the Delhi Canal which I will suppose to account to sonat rupees 3,000 per annum of disbursement, in pice.

The general rate at which copper can be purchased in this neighbourhood is sonat rupees 60 per maund weighing sonat rupees 3,200, which are equal in weight to 1,920 Cheecheerowlee pice; the expence of coinage is rupees 4-1-5½ nearly per maund. The Cheecheerowlee Mint agrees to give me 1,920 pice of the above weight if I give in 1 maund of copper and st. rs. [Sonat Rupees] 4-1-5½ in cash. This at the above rate of copper would make 1,920 pice to cost sonat rupees 64-1-5½ or an average rate of about 30 pice per R. If I can [p. 1425] deliver copper to the Mint at sonat rupees fifty per maund, I should receive 1920 pice costing sonat rupees 54-1-5½, yielding an average rate of about 35½ pice per rupee. On the above sum of 3,000 rupees at these rates this would effect a saving of sonat rupees 465; Or, in other words, by supplying the Mint with copper at 50 sonat rupees per maund I should get the same number of pice for sonat rupees 2535 as at 30 per rupee I get for 3000 rupees. And as the price of pice is always raised when my works commence the saving effected would still be more, probably 16 to 18 per cent.

Secondly, in regard to the small Mensoorkhanee pice, the bazaar rate of which for several years past has raised from 50 to 55 per rupee, they could not be coined advantageously with copper at sonat rupee & therefore 3,200 would cost sonat rupees 65, yielding about 49¼ per rupee. With copper however at 50 rupees per maund the same number would cost sonat rupees 55 and give an average of about 58¼ per rupee; a difference of rate with the late and present nerrick sufficient to make it of consequence when the coinage would not counterbalance the saving. This latter pice is not at all current in the country above Dadoopoor but is the only one current from that down to Delhie where in the city and neighbourhood a third species of pice generally about 44 per rupee is the only currency, with the weight or place of coinage of which I am unacquainted.

In assuming my ability to supply copper to the mints of Cheecheerowlee and Jugudree (where the two first mentioned kinds of pice are coined) at sonat rupees 50 per maund, I go upon the bazaar rates of copper in Calcutta varying from sicca rupees 42 to 44 per maund which allowing for exchange and coinage and difference in weight might allow of my getting it up somewhere [p. 1426] about 50 sonat rupees per maund; and I conceive it probable the magazine rates of copper at Delhie may be still less.

If so, it would be advantageous my drawing my supply from thence. It is further proper to state I have applied to the British authorities at Jugadree and to the independent Sikh authority at Cheecheerowlee to know if they would coin copper for me at their Mints and have received their assents. If therefore the Military

Board approve of my making the trial I will do so either by indenting on the Delhi magazine for copper and receiving it at its value on the books of the Military Board as cash to account of the works, or I will have copper purchased in Calcutta and sent up to me whichever may be the most advantageous when I know the magazine rates. In the hope I may receive an early answer either approving or disapproving for my guidance.

RESOLUTION: Ordered that copy of the foregoing be submitted for the consideration and orders of Government.

Source: NAI/MB Proceedings, 15 June 1830, 1424-6.[44]

NOTES

1. We would like to thank Shailendra Bhandare, Paul Stevens and Barry Tabor for their suggestions and help.
2. Even the excellent *Coin Atlas* (Cribb, Cook & Carradice 1990) does not totally escape this orientation.
3. Spufford 2006; Welten 2010.
4. Sargent and Velde 2002.
5. Lucassen 2007a; Welten 2010.
6. Muldrew 2007; Selgin 2009.
7. Hall 1999; Van Aelst 2007.
8. Van Zanden 2007; Boncan 1986.
9. Welten 2010.
10. Perlin 1993 and 1994.
11. Lingen and Lucassen, see Part I: Studies, No. 12.
12. Baker 1849; Headrick 1988, 173-180; Lucassen 2006; Lucassen (see Part I: Studies, No. 13 and Lingen and Lucassen, No. 12 in this volume.
13. He may be identical to John Colvin (1794-1871) of Leintwardine, a Royal Engineer posted to India, where he collected fossils of strange animals that had been preserved in the rocks of the Siwalik area. He was also a key member of the Ludlow Natural History Society, and on his return to England he donated his collection to Ludlow Museum; he is not identical with John Russell Colvin (1807-57), the last Lieutenant-Governor of the North-Western Provinces under the BEIC (Colvin 1895).
14. See the full text in the Appendix. Later on, Colvin received the rank of colonel (Colvin 1833).
15. NAI/ MB Proceedings, 20-7-1830, 2394-5; idem 27-7-1830, 2641-2; idem 24-8-1830, 3383-4.

16. By Regulation XI of 1819 the Farrukhabad rupee became the standard coin of all the territories under the Government of Bengal, except in the Provinces of Bengal, Bihar and Orissa, which retained the Calcutta 19-*san* rupee standard. The weight 180.234 troy grains (= 11.6789 g.) and the edge provided with an upright milling. The Farrukhabad mint was closed 5 February 1824. To assist in the coinage required a new mint was opened at Sagar and commenced production in 1825. The weight of the Farrukhabad rupee struck at Sagar was 180 troy grains (=11.6638 g.). The minting at Sagar continued till 1835. The same Farrukhabad rupee with upright milled edge, was struck at Banares (1820-9) and Calcutta (1819-30). On February 1831, an order directed that the Calcutta 19-*san sicca* and Farrukhabad rupee struck at the Calcutta mint would have a 'plain flat milling only' and by regulation VII, 1833, the Farrukhabad rupee coined at the Calcutta mint was reduced in weight to 180 troy grains, the same standard then in force at the Sagar mint. The sonat rupee with which Colvin calculated must have been the Farrukhabad rupee of 180 troy grains or 11.6638 g., struck at Sagar between 1825 and 1835. The Indian maund is 37.3242 kg, divided by 3,200 rupees is exactly 11.6638 g. = 180 troy grains.
17. Lucassen, see Part I: Studies, No. 13 and Lingen and Lucassen, No. 12 in this volume.
18. Lucassen, see Part I: Studies, No.13 in this volume.
19. Stevens 2009, 33-5 (production statistics); Lingen and Lucassen, see Part I: Studies, No. 12 [210-11] in this volume; Bruce 2004, 722-3 (*KM* 56, 57, 64, A65); Pridmore 1957.
20. Stevens 2006, 20; for the data, missing in Colvin's report, see below.
21. Derived from weight and exchange rate of the Cheecheerowli pice.
22. *The Imperial Gazetteer of India* 1908, vol. 13, 75-376 (Jagadhri Town).
23. *The Imperial Gazetteer of India* 1908, vol. 10, 96 (Chhachrauli); idem 14, 320-1 (Kalsia); for images of a Sikh mint see Garg 2007, 362.
24. Herrli 2004, 264.
25. In a private collection in India and another one with a Mumbai coin dealer.
26. Also 'Jaghadri' rupees with regnal years 29 (Fig. 10.20) and 33 (Fig. 10.21) are known, bearing the mint symbol of Najibabad and a paisa, nearly identical to such a rupee has been recorded with a Mumbai coin dealer (Fig. 10.19).
27. Lingen and Lucassen, see Part I: Studies, No. 12 in this volume.
28. Goron and Goenka 2001, xvi.
29. For similar cases see Tabor 2010a and 2010b.
30. Tabor 2008; cf Bruce 2004, 590, catalogued as *KM* 132; Herrli 2004, 232; Stevens 2006, 19; Gommans 1993, 170-1, 193.
31. Stevens unpublished ms.
32. All collection Jan Lingen; because Valentine 1914, 112-14, nos. 167-76 (1183/11 until 1216//43 with title Shah Alam II) and 177-9 ('under Sikh rule') does not provide weights, we have left this information out here.

33. Prinsep 1858, 44-60 (originally published in 1834); Stevens 2006, 20-2.
34. Bruce 2004, 570-1, catalogued as *KM* 770 and 771. A lighter so-called *fish-paisa* is known from the Shahjahanabad mint, struck until AH 1214/41 (1799), average weight 7.615 grams (Figs. 10.52 to 10.56)
35. Stevens 2006, 21.
36. It has to be noted that the 1826 plan (the 'manufacture of one seer of copper into 120 pice') meant the coinage of pice which went more in the direction of the contemporaneous Calcutta pice of 5.8-6.5 grams than that of the heavier previously coined Dilhis of an average of 11.41 grams.
37. Lucassen, see Part I: Studies, No. 13 in this volume.
38. Lingen and Lucassen, see Part I: Studies, No. 12 in this volume; cf. Bruce 2004, 596.
39. Lucassen 2006, 57, 60 and Lucassen, see Part I: Studies, No. 13 in this volume suggests monthly wages of 3.5 to 4 rupees for natives at the north Indian canals around 1850, but data for Agra on 13 November 1830 (NAI, MBP, 4 January 1831, 6522) are much lower: Rs. 2 for water carriers (*bheesties*) and the lowest paid carpenters. Therefore, we to take here an average of Rs. 3 per month or Rs. 0.1 per day.
40. Lucassen 2007a.
41. Modern spelling Karnal.
42. Modern spelling Chhachrauli.
43. Modern spelling Dadupur, on the eastern bank of the Western Jumna Canal where a dam is situated, 14 miles south of the canal head at Tajewala and 38 miles north of its bifurcation near Indri (*Imperial Gazetteer* 1908, no. 14, 234-6; see Cautley 1860, map between 23 and 24: 'Sketch maps to accompany medical reports').
44. Literal transcription apart from the irregular punctuation and use of capitals by the scribe.

11

Pucka Pice in Fatehpur District 1839: The Wide and Long-lasting Circulation of Awadh's Coppers

JAN LINGEN AND JAN LUCASSEN

The transition from Indian to British colonial currency in India is a messy history. In theory, there is no problem: the all-powerful colonizers modernized and uniformed what they saw as an erratic and primitive currency circulation by hundreds of states and potentates in several steps, the last one being the introduction of the East India Company rupee and its fractions in 1835. In reality, the existing 'native' coinage served very well regionally and it took half a century before it could be said that the Imperial currency was the sole circulating medium of exchange.[1]

This long-stretched period of replacement of 'native' by British currencies and of their co-habitation is a major impediment to reconstruct levels of monetization and in particular of deep monetization. There is a great lack of knowledge about the circulation intensity of small change, because so far production and circulation figures of the 'native' mints in this period have hardly been studied.[2]

In fact, we are confronted with three different problems. First, the identification of the Indian mint houses and their production figures outside Calcutta, Bombay and Madras, the capitals of the three Presidencies.[3] Second, to what extent coins were circulating in the very same polity where they were produced. Those entities were not automatically synonymous, which may sound a bit odd for a modern reader until he or she realizes how many US dollars are actually circulating outside the United States. Third, the question at what pace particular 'British' denominations (especially of copper coins) have replaced 'native' ones.

It is difficult to come to grips with these problems unless we have more case studies on the basis of which we can make extrapolations for wider geographic entities. A number of examples of such studies on particular copper denominations from particular mints circulating in particular regions in this transitional period between say 1800 and 1850 is now available, and this article is meant to add to this.[4] Our starting point here is Fatehpur district, a part of northern India which already since 1801 had been under direct British rule, belonging administratively to the Allahabad Division of the North-Western Province since 1836 (see Map 11.1).

Working on the Grand Trunk Road: Fatehpur 1839

In the summer of 1839, Lieutenant Fraser, officiating superintendent of the Allahabad – Gursahaiganj Division of the Grand Trunk Road (GTR), had to solve the problem how to recruit a sufficiently large labour force for the improvement of the stretch between Allahabad and Kanpur.[5] This road – the main artery of the Mughal state inherited by the British – was particularly crucial when the alternative of river transport was halted during the dry season. The GTR-section between Kanpur in the west and Allahabad in the east is about 100 km long in Fatehpur district.

According to the estimates, approved by the Military Board in Calcutta, Fraser was supposed to replace the convicts used previously for this purpose, by free labourers. For 'ramming and tamping konkur' (modulated limestone – *kankar* – for road metal) he wished to form 13 gangs of 250 to 300 *bildars* each, for which he needed an advance of no less than 30,000 rupees. The problem was that the Military Board had expected that 3 rupees a month would be an acceptable wage, but on the spot, Fraser found out that this was unacceptably low. After all, in the British cantonments in that part of India for similar tasks, 3 rupees, 4 annas and 6 pice were paid per month of 30 days. As the task had to be completed in time and 'on principle of urgent measures requiring urgent treatment'

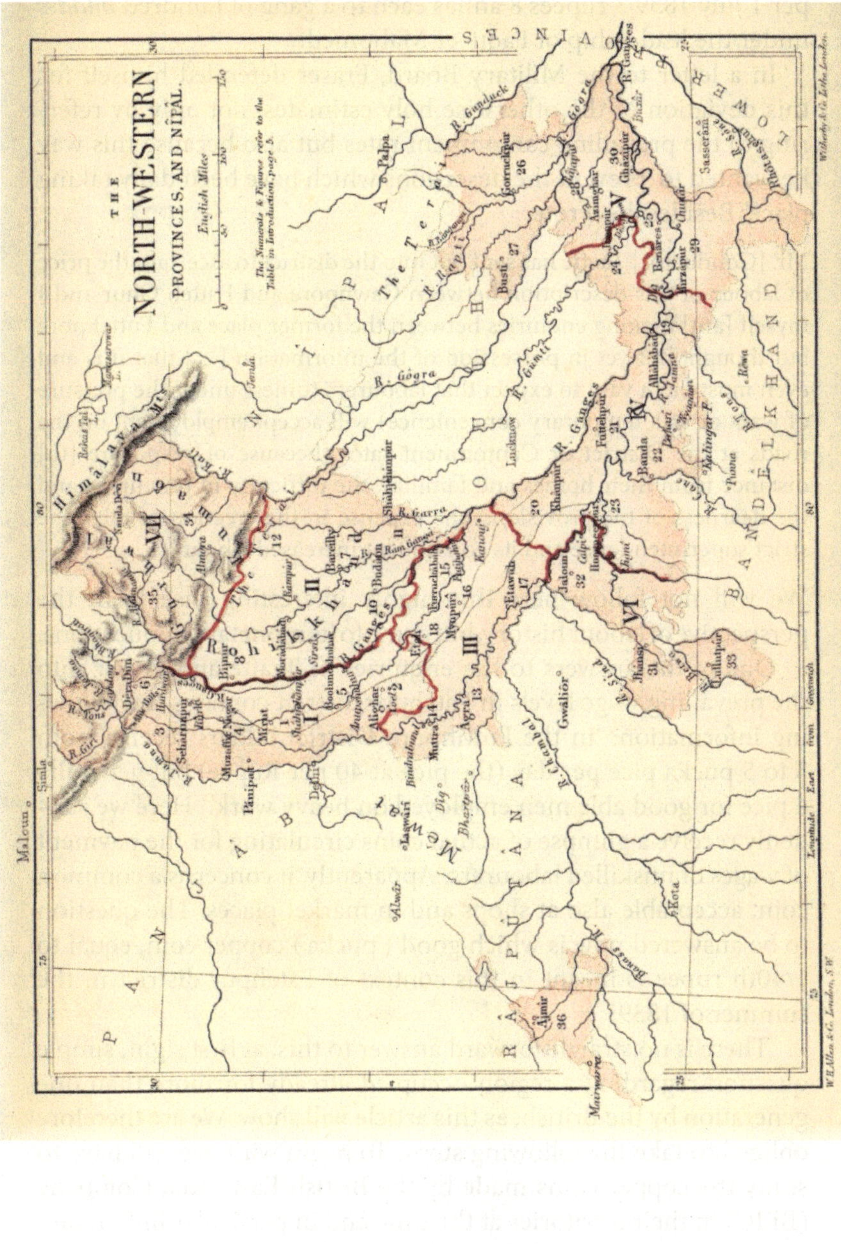

MAP 11.1: THE NORTH-WESTERN PROVINCES (FROM POPE 1880, 4/5).

he decided on his own to instruct his conductor Mr Taaffe to pay per 1 July 1839 3 rupees 8 annas each to a gang of hundred *bildars* under the leadership of Faqueer Mahomed.

In a letter to the Military Board, Fraser defended himself for this deviation of the otherwise holy estimates, not only by referring to the prevailing cantonment rates but also because this way he wanted to 'prevent the desertions which have been daily taking place'. Besides, he wrote,

> Mr. [Conductor] Taaffe has sent out into the district to ascertain the price of labour of this description between Cawnpore and Futteh Ghur and I myself [am] making enquiries between the former place and Futtehpore but thought not yet in possession of the information [...] that it is and even must be in vain to expect that labourers (unless under the pressure of want or as a temporary convenience) will accept employment on the roads at the District or Cantonment rates [because of] exposure [to] distance from their homes and families, the difficulty in procuring and the dearness of the provisions, the expense in the erection of huts, the strict superintendence and its consequent increased labour.[6]

We will not follow here this highly interesting case from the perspective of labour history, but come to its monetary implications.

One of the answers to the enquiries of Taaffe and Fraser into the prevailing wage levels in Fatehpur district contains the following information: 'in the Futtihpore District bildars receive from 3 to 5 pucka pice per day (the pice at 40 per Rupee) but generally 4 pice for good able men employed on heavy work'.[7] Here we suddenly receive a glimpse of actual coins circulating for the payment of wages of unskilled labourers. Apparently, it concerns a common coin, acceptable also at shops and in market places. The question to be answered now is which good ('pucka') copper coin, equal to 1/40th rupee is meant in this context of Fatehpur district in the summer of 1839?

There is no straightforward answer to this, at first sight, simple question regarding a region occupied already for more than one generation by the British, as this article will show. We are therefore obliged to take the following steps. To begin with, we will have to study the copper coins made by the British East India Company (BEIC) in their territories at the time and in particular in Benares.

Situated immediately east of Fatehpur district, Benares had been under Company rule already since 1775 and from there the British extended their influence in a north-western direction in the beginning of the nineteenth century. As we will demonstrate, the answer is not to be found there and we will have to look beyond the Company's territories. So, next we will turn to the copper coins circulating in the 'native states' south of Fatehpur in the nineteenth century, at the time nominally independent and at best only indirectly controlled by the British. Third, we will turn our eyes to the north for evidence of the existence of pucka, i.e. 'good, well made' copper coins equal to 1/40th part of a rupee, as mentioned explicitly by Lieutenant Fraser in Fatehpur district in 1839. Finally, we will draw a conclusion and sum up our arguments.

The Introduction of Copper Coins by the BEIC in the North-West Provinces

In the late eighteenth century, Benares district was the most western part of the Bengal Presidency. Beyond this, Indians ruled themselves. During the first thirty years of their reign in Benares, the British did not or hardly interfere with the production of coins in the very active local mint house.[8] Only in 1805 did they start to regulate mint production, including copper pice. Initially, until 1808, old coppers circulated at various rates. In December 1809, a regulation was published, authorizing copper pice for Benares. The copper coin struck at Calcutta for circulation in the province of Benares would be of pure copper and confined to the pice of one size only and with an exchange rate of 64 to the Benares *sicca* rupee. By 1810, the 1809 regulation meant that the old dump pice would no longer be acceptable as currency. However, as no new pice had got into circulation yet, and as after a period of six months 'dump' pice would no longer be accepted, great scarcity was created.

Requests for ample supply of the new pice didn't meet the approval of the Calcutta Mint Committee, who were not convinced that the coins were necessary. The Calcutta Council agreed that the minting of copper coins for Benares should cease for the time being and copper coins produced at Calcutta never got into circulation in Benares. This was the reason that the mint master at Benares asked for permission to mint copper pice at his own mint. A lengthy exchange of arguments followed in which the Mint Committee bluntly argued that the introduction of the new pice (minted at Calcutta) in Bihar had been successful.

The Collector of Benares, who was in favour of pice being produced at the Benares mint, added the following argument on 30 November 1811:

> It is universally acknowledged throughout the province of Benares that the copper currency of a fixed weight, standard and value is particularly wanted, and that at present all classes of the community are subject to great imposition and extortions from the shroffs and money changers in the exchange of silver for pice. Just at the present time the rates of exchange of pice in the bazar are from 23 to 23½ tacas per rupee (nearly 9 takas less in value than the double pice of Government coinage which would be sold at 32 per rupee).[9]

Finally, in 1815, machine-made copper pice were produced at the mint of Benares, and this continued till the mint was closed in 1830. Apart from the Calcutta mint, three mints in what later on was called the North-Western Provinces, still produced copper coins in the 1820s and 1830s, and so in principle, also for Fatehpur district: those of Benares, Farrukhabad and Saugor. When the British acquired the territories to which Fatehpur belonged in 1801, they at the same time became the masters of a number of working mint houses, of which those of Allahabad to its east and Farrukhabad to its west must have been the most important for Fatehpur. Together with most other mint houses, of what was to become known as the 'Ceded and Conquered Provinces', Allahabad was closed, but Farrukhabad (200 km from Fatehpur) was continued until 1824. Its copper coin production from 1820 to 1824 must have been substantive, although no production figures are known. Subsequently to its closure in 1824, the Saugor Mint, 300 km south-west of Fatehpur, turned out copper pice between 1827 and 1833 at the value of Rs. 283,388. The production of both mints was meant to be supplementary to that of the mint house of Benares, the capital of Benares district, part of the Benares Division of the same North-Western Provinces as Fatehpur. In total, easily

2 million pieces may have been minted in the three mint houses (Table 11.1).

TABLE 11.1: BRITISH-INDIAN MINTS PRODUCING COPPER COINS FOR THE NORTH-WESTERN PROVINCES, 1815-33

Mint house	*Production (in Rs.)*	*Official weight (g. copper)*	*Actual weight (g. copper)*	*Exchange rate in silver rupees*
Farrukhabad 1820-4	?	6.48	5.80-6.47	1/64
Saugor 1827-33*	283,388	6.48	6.11-6.50	1/64
Benares 1815-29	1,388,140	6.23	3.03**-6.76	1/64

Notes: * Saugor opened in 1825 (Stevens 287) and production of coppers commenced in 1826 (Stevens 288). The mint at Saugor closed in 1835, but mintage figures are only known from 1827-33.
** Many contemporary forgeries of these coins exist, most, if not all, light-weight coins (Stevens 404).
Source: Stevens 2012, 333, 379, 404-5, 455, 469, 488, 498

It may be clear by now that the British started to introduce their own copper coins rather late and hesitantly in this part of India, but most of all, that the copper coin of 1/40th rupee that Lieutenant Fraser was alluding to as the standard coin for wage payments in Fatehpur district in 1839 cannot be a pice officially coined by the British, because both before and after the introduction of the uniform coinage in 1835, they used coppers of 1/32nd rupee (the half anna pieces) and of 1/64th rupee (the quarter anna pieces). Consequently, we have to look for other mints.

Contemporary Copper Coinage in Neighbouring Native States, Especially in Bundelkhand

A quick look at the map shows that Fatehpur district at the time was situated in a rather narrow corridor of the British territory. North of it was the kingdom of Awadh and south the various principalities of Bundelkhand. For the first half of the nineteenth century there is only scant information regarding the circulation of native copper coins and their exchange rate against rupees, so we will start our investigation with a much later, but rather complete overview.

The Financial Department Proceedings, February, 1872 provide some inside information regarding the 'Manufacture of Copper Coins in Native States' in the North-Western Provinces around Mau Ranipur in the Jhansi district. Immediately striking is the mixture of official mint houses and production centres that imitate actual and antiquated coppers at a large scale. In a letter, dated 6 October 1870, the commissioner G.H.M Ricketts of Jhansi Division (some 200 km west of Fatehpur; see Map 11.2) wrote to the Secretary of Government, North-Western Provinces:

2. The Central Provinces have lately been inundated with a quantity of copper coin, made chiefly in imitation of an old Lucknow coin. Bearing a rude impression of the Lucknow fish; but several other native coins have also been imitated and their counterfeits circulated. 3. Police enquiry has shown that these coins are made in immense quantities in the Native States and Jagheers all around Mow Raneepore (Mau Ranipur). That town is a great mart for their purchase, and in and around Mow itself the manufacture of these coins has been constantly carried on. Every blacksmith and goldsmith in that neighbourhood is a proficient in the trade, and coins of any required kind can be purchased by the ton at any time in the Mow bazars.[10]

As far as British territory is concerned the Commissioner regards this practice as illegal and therefore it should be stopped. The major offender, according to him, is Tehree (Orchcha, near Jhansi). The Tehree chief is permitted to coin, but not to transfer the right. The Commissioner complains further:

It has been his practise to give (or probably to sell) licences to coin to numerous dealers in, and makers of coin in his territory, and our existing law cannot stop the practise. At present the coin is current for very nearly its value as common copper for manufacturing purposes. It has no standard value and rises or falls with the market rate of the metal.

According to another letter by J.V. Sturt, Officiating Assistant Commissioner, dated 16 February 1871,[11] the localities where coins were manufactured are said to be: Tori Futtehpore (or

MAP 11.2: ORCHHA PRINCELY STATE (1909, *IMPERIAL GAZETTEER OF INDIA*, CENTRAL INDIA MAP SECTION).

dependency of Orchha), Buncoree Orchha, Sursaie Allypore, and Kurrara Gurowlee, but, prior to British rule, they were all manufactured at Mow in the Jhansi district. Orchha or Tehree and Duttia are the only Native States west of the Dussan river having the authority to coin money. The pice of four descriptions, viz., Pootlee Shaie (Table 11.2, #7) and Nawabee of Lucknow (Table 11.2, #8), Tirsoolee of Nagpore (Table 11.2, #6) and Bala Shaie of Jalaun (Table 11.2, #5) had been extensively manufactured at the aforementioned places for at least twenty years or more, but in former times, before British rule, every kind given in the list is supposed to have been made at Mow itself.

According to Mr. Stratton, Political Agent, Bundelkhand, these coins have the impression of the Delhi coin on one side and they are evidently made after that pattern; the other side bears the mark adopted by the district or Government where, or by permission of which, they were manufactured.[12] Finally, Sturt in his letter dated 9 January 1871 provides an interesting observation that in the Bandah district, the manufacturers avoid the difficulty arising from stamping the pice with any particular mark by making it plain. These are called 'chikna pysa'.

We have tried to identify the original examples for the imitations made around 1870 in the various mints active in Bundelkhand as described by Sturt (Table 11.2 and Figure 11.1).

TABLE 11.2: COPPER COINS CURRENT IN THE DISTRICT OF JHANSI 1870

No.	*Name of the coin*	*District*	*Remarks*
1	Tope Shaie or Mogaolee	Scindia	Supposed to bear the impression of a gun or cannon.
2	Maharaj Shaie	Gwalior	Bearing the impression of a sword.
3	Lushkuree or Tirsolee or Guwaja Shaie	Ditto	With a trident.
4	Lushkuree	Ditto	Serpent's head (specimen not found).

5	Bala Shaie	Jaloun	The mark of a trident.
6	Tirsoolee	Nagpooree	As above, only of lighter weight.
7	Pootledar	Lucknow	Bearing the image of a man.
8	Nawabee or Muchlee Shaie	Ditto	Bearing the image of a fish.
9	Bhopal Shaie	Bhopal	Impressed with the word Bhopal, showing year and value.
10	Katar Shaie	Boondee Kota	Bearing the impression of a dagger.
11	Soobehdar Shaie	Jhansi	Bearing the impression of a horse.

Source: J.V. Sturt, Officiating Assistant Commissioner stationed at Mow. *Financial Department Proceedings*, February 1872, Mint and Currency, 22.

1. 'Tope Shaie or Mogaolee'
Gwalior, Daulat Rao Sindhia, 1794-1827, AE paisa (13.22 grams), i.n.o. Muhammad Akbar II, struck by Jean Baptiste Filose (1809-17) at Isagarh

2. 'Maharaj Shaie'
Gwalior, Baija Bai, 1827-33, regent for Jankoji Rao Sindhia, AE paisa (8.23 grams), i.n.o. Muhammad Akbar II, dated AH 1243 (1827/8)

3. 'Lushkuree or Tirsolee or Guwaja Shaie'
Gwalior, Jankoji Rao Sindhia, 1833-43, AE paisa (13.44 grams), with frozen RY 23.

4. 'Lushkuree' with serpent's head
AE paisa (6.29 grams). This issue was first struck in VS 1926 (1869) and therefore probably not found when the report was written in 1870.

5. 'Bala Shaie'
Jalaun, AE paisa (16.88 grams), i.n.o. Shah Alam II, dated RY. 31 (1788/9)

6. 'Tirsoolee'
Nagpur, AE paisa (9.34 grams), i.n.o. Ahmad Shah Bahadur. Reduced weight standard of 9 *mashas*, struck by Gordon during 1823-4.

7. 'Pootledar' or 'pootlee' shaie
Awadh, Muhammad 'Ali Shah, 1837-42, AE falus (11.95 grams)

8. 'Nawabee or Muchlee Shaie'
Awadh, Amjad 'Ali Shah, 1842-7, AE falus (11.76 grams)

9. 'Bhopal Shaie'
Bhopal, anonymous coinage of Sikandar Begum, 1844-65, AE 1 anna, AH 1276 (1859/60)

10. 'Katar Shaie'
Bundi/Kotah, AE *takka* (18.86 grams i.n.o. Shah Alam II, RY. 32 (1790)

11. 'Soobehdar Shaie'
Jhansi, AE paisa (16.1 grams). ND. Similar coins with a horse symbol were struck at Sironj, dated AH 1226 (1811)

FIG. 11.1: POSSIBLE ATTRIBUTIONS TO ACTUAL COINS OF THE ONES MENTIONED IN TABLE 11.2.

How to choose between this bewildering variety of coppers made by official and unofficial native mints? By 1839 most mints in the adjoining Bundelkhand district, which were formerly under Maratha administration, had become inactive. However, popular demand remained, which explains the large-scale imitating, or as the British would say: counterfeiting. These coins also known as *kachcha* coins will therefore not qualify for the coins Fraser used. The demand in 1839 for *pucka* pice indicates that these coins must have been produced at a legal mint house, controlled by a well-established administration. We therefore now have to turn our gaze to the north.

The So-called *Pucka* Pice Equal to 1/40th Rupee Found in Awadh

The third leg of our research trip leads to Awadh, opposite Fatehpur on the left or northern banks of the river Ganga. In order to prepare ourselves properly, let us first try to specify precisely what kind we are looking for when we speak of a copper *pucka* pice equal to 1/40th rupee in 1839 in this part of the country. Two clues will point most probably in the right direction: one from Bhopal and one from Bihar.

Traditionally, and as a rule, Indian coins did not bear an indication of their value (more specifically in relation to the silver rupee, the standard coin). Luckily in our period and region there is one exception. That is to be found in the Princely state of Bhopal, south-west of Bundelkhand. Beginning with the reign of Sikandar Begum (AH 1261-85/CE 1844-68) its mint house struck copper coins with a value impressed on it, viz., 1 anna (*ek anna*) with a weight of *c.* 30.08 g, as well as fractions of one half and one-quarter anna, weighing respectively 15 to 15.5 and 7 to 8 grams. The earliest dates on these coins with an explicit value indication were made in AH 1266 or 1849/1850, i.e. ten years after the year we are investigating. We therefore conclude that the copper *pucka* pice (= good coin, contra *kachcha* or bad coin), equal of 40 to a rupee, we are looking for, would accordingly be *c.* 12.25 g in weight. Which contemporary copper issue would meet this weight and may be the coin referred to?

For a slightly earlier period in this part of India, we know that copper coins, exchanged for 1/40th to 1/50th rupee have been circulating. That was in Bihar and more specifically in Patna, as testified by a paper, published by the Batavian Society of Art and Science (with its site at Batavia, now Djakarta in Indonesia) in its transactions of 1786 (Figure 11.2).

VI VERHANDELING DER MUNTEN, MAATEN EN GEWICHTEN VAN NEERLANDSCH INDIA	VI PAPER ON THE COINS, MEASUREMENTS AND WEIGHTS OF DUTCH INDIA
Cauris, zeker ſoort van Kinkhoorns, zynde in Bengalen gangbaar, na de quantiteit die 'er is; 4 Cauris doen een Gonda, 20 Gonda een Ponny, 16 Ponnys een Kaon; gemeenlyk doen 60 Ponnys of 4800 Cauris een Sicca Ropy, doch dit ryst ſomtyds tot 64, en daald ook weder tot 50 Ponnys.	Cowries, a kind of shells, are current in Bengal, according to the quantity; 4 are equal to a Gonda, 20 Gonda is a Ponny, 16 Ponnys a Kaon; usually 60 Ponnys or 4800 Cowries are equal to a Sicca Rupee, but this fluctuates sometimes from 50 to 64.
In Patna en Behaar doen 4 Cauris een Gonda, 3 Gonda een Damerie, 2 Damerie een Tjadauw, en 4 Tjadauws een Peza, waar van 40 à 50 op een Ropy gaan.	In Patna and Bihar 4 Cowries are equal to a Gonda, 3 Gonda a Damerie, 2 Damerie a Tjadauw and 4 Tjadauws a Peza, of which 40 to 50 are equal to a rupee.

FIG. 11.2 EXCHANGE RATES OF COWRIES, COPPER PICE AND SILVER RUPEES IN BIHAR, END EIGHTEENTH CENTURY (DUTCH ORIGINAL WITH ENGLISH TRANSLATION).

Source: Verhandelingen van het Bataviaasch Genootschap der Konsten en Weetenschappen, MDCCLXXXVI, VI, 451: Verhandeling der Munten, Maaten en Gewichten van Neerlandsch India.

Combining these two pieces of information we obtain the key for solving our question. In the neighbouring kingdom of Awadh, a prolific production of copper coins had been going on since the late eighteenth century. Under its ruler Wajid 'Ali Shah (AH 1263-72/CE 1847-56), an interesting innovation took place. In AH 1269 (1852/53) he introduced a series of copper coins of ⅛, ¼ and ½ paisa, bearing his coat of arms with the so far enigmatic numerals 3, 6 & 12 added to it. From the transactions of the Batavian Society it becomes obvious that these numerals must refer to a cowrie-related denomination system (see Table 11.3 and Figure 11.3a-d):

TABLE 11.3: RATIOS OF DAMRI, TJADAUW, PAISA AND RUPEE IN AWADH *c.* 1780-1860

Gonda	*Damerie/ Damri*	*Tjadauw*	*Paisa or Falus*	*Rupee*
3	1		⅛	
6	2	1	¼	
12	4	2	½	
		4	1	1/40-1/50

The cowries cowries-related exchange rates are also mentioned by Pridmore, who reports that the wages paid by the Company in 1757 ranged from 2 to 5 rupees per month for labourers and craftsmen. For daily or even weekly shopping, enormous amounts of very small value coin would have been required. In these circumstances, the cowrie shell served as an ideal medium for petty transactions and was widely used, well into the nineteenth century.[13] We suppose that because of referring to these ratios on copper coins, they must have been rather stable during the last decades of the kingdom of Awadh, abolished in the Indian rebellion against British rule in India in 1857-9 (called the Mutiny by the British).

11.3a: COPPER 3 GONDA (1 DAMRI OR ⅛ FALUS), AH 1270/RY. 8 (1.52 G)

11.3b: COPPER 6 GONDA (2 DAMRI OR ¼ FALUS), AH 1272/RY. 9 (3.04 G)

11.3c: COPPER 12 GONDA (4 DAMRI OR ½ FALUS), AH 1270/RY. 7 (6.04 G)

11.3d: COPPER FALUS, AH 1270/RY.8 (12.09 G)

FIGS. 11.3a-11.3d: COPPER ⅛, ¼, ½ AND 1 FALUS, STRUCK BY WAJID ʿALI SHAH, KING OF AWADH (AH 1263-72/CE 1847-56)

Verification of the weight of the copper paisa struck by the later rulers of Awadh shows that the weight of the paisa varies from 11.00 to 12.11 gram (Table 11.4).

TABLE 11.4: WEIGHTS OF AWADH PICE 1827-56

Rulers	*Weights of pice or falus (gram)*
Nasir al-Din Haidar Shah, 1827-37	11.80-12.11
Muhammad Ali Shah, 1837-42	11.53-11.93
Amjad Ali Shah, 1842-7	11.20-11.70
Wajid Ali Shah, 1847-56	11.00-12.00

Source: Kapoor & Master 2018.

Based on the calculations of the contemporary Bhopal coinage, the weight for a copper coin of 1⁄40 rupee, should be about 12.25 gram. Therefore, we cannot but conclude that the *pucka* pice referred to by Lieutenant Fraser in 1839 were the contemporary copper coins of Awadh State, more specifically those bearing the names of Muhammad Ali Shah (Table 11.2 #7) and his immediate predecessor Nasir al-Din Haidar Shah (Fig. 11.4). Besides, Wajid Ali Shah introduced a copper currency which shows the denomination on it, based on a prevailing accounting system and that the Fatehpur district was situated right across the river Ganga as seen from the kingdom of Awadh, and had belonged to that state before the British occupation, all point in that direction.

FIG. 11.4: NASIR AL-DIN HAIDAR SHAH (1827-37), AE FALUS, AH 1245/ RY. 3 (11.83 G)

We do not know their production figures, but the frequency of issues, their wear and tear due to heavy circulation, shows that these coins were widely used and accepted. Even today they are still relatively common in the collectors' market. We therefore may deduce that the Awadh pice (commonly called *falus*) may have been struck in pretty large numbers.

Summary and Conclusion

In Fatehpur district wages for common workers were paid out in 'pucka' pice, valuing 1/40th rupee. Searching for a concrete coin that qualifies for that description, we had to conclude, first, that this could not have been the official copper pice introduced two decades earlier by the EIC, to which this district had belonged since 1801. They went for 1/64th of a rupee and therefore were simply too light. Neither do the pice made in the various mints in Bundelkhand, south of Fatehpur, because at the time their circulation consisted mostly of irregularly made imitations, which were more heavy than the ones we were looking for.

The pice, produced in Awadh, north of Fatehpur do, however. This means that the British, still, in around 1840, were not able to cater for the demand of copper coins in the parts of India that they ruled directly. It also confirms the result of an earlier study on more westerly parts of the North-Western Provinces.[14] The British-controlled mints of Calcutta, Benares, Farrukhabad and Saugor had not been sufficient to meet the demands of the labour market. Instead, pice, made at official and unofficial 'native' mints circulated widely. Witness the use of these pieces in parts lost by that kingdom in 1801, like Fatehpur district (Figs. 11.3-11.4). Besides, this went on for the decades to come, as seen by the proliferation of imitations of Awadh pice long after the abolishment of that kingdom (Figs. 11.5a-b).[15]

Fig. 11.5a: Typical imitation of Awadh falus (11.65 g.)

11.5b: Imitation of AE falus of Wajid Ali Shah (11.20 g.)

FIG. 11.5a-b: IMITATIONS OF COPPER COINS OF AWADH, DATING FROM THE DECADES AFTER ITS DEMISE IN 1857

NOTES

1. Lucassen, Part I: Studies, No. 13 in this volume; Garg 2013; 2019.
2. Lucassen, Part I: Studies, No. 13; Lucassen, Part I: Studies, No. 4 in this volume.
3. Stevens 2011, 2019; for the Madras Presidency such an overview is still lacking. The Madras Mint itself closed down in 1869.
4. Lucassen, Part I: Studies, No. 13; and Lingen & Lucassen, Part I: Studies, Nos. 9 and 12 in this volume.
5. NAI, New Delhi, Military, Military Board Proceedings (MBP), 31 January 1840, 8915-25.
6. NAI, MBP 31 January 1840, 8919; Our interpolations between [ ]. For the history of wage labour see Lucassen 2021; for wage labour in India see Lucassen & Seshan 2022.
7. NAI, MBP 31 January 1840, 8921.
8. Stevens 2012, 304-411.
9. Stevens 2012, 359
10. *India Office Library & Records*, London, Financial Department Proceedings, February, 1872, Mint and Currency, 19, Letter No. 408.
11. Ibid., 20, Letter No. 74A.
12. By the 'impression of the Delhi coin' is referred to coins with the impression of the Mughal Emperor in Delhi or to those in Persian script in general.
13. Pridmore 1975, 197.
14. Lucassen, Part I: Studies, No. 13 in this volume.
15. Cf. Wiggins 1978.

12

The '*Mansúrí*' or '*Munsooree Paisa*' and its Use: Combining the Numismatic and Social History of India, *c.* 1830-1900

JAN LINGEN AND JAN LUCASSEN

The Problem: How to Identify a Mansuri?

Not seldom, an abyss yawns between the nomenclature of coins in historical sources (both in the form of actual coins and of money of account) and in coin collections. Many coins that are known from history do not seem to match actual pieces in coin collections. *Vice versa*, we hardly know the historical context, let alone the use of many coins that, as such, are very well known to coin collectors. The former problem can be due to the actual loss of coins, e.g. by remelting; the latter problem very often arises because of a lack of the right questions regarding the function of coins. Usage in 'trade and commerce' are the usual stopgaps in order to offer explanations. These may, in general, be of some value in the case of gold or silver coins, but as a rule, they do not apply to coppers. This mismatch between numismatics and history can be nicely illustrated in a not-so-remote past like India in the mid-nineteenth century.

In 1834, James Prinsep (1799-1840) published a list of the then-current copper coins in northern India.[1] In the case of the coins struck in Bombay, Calcutta, Farrukhabad or Madras, there is no doubt about which actual pieces are still now available in collections, he is speaking. In other cases, the coins he mentions are a puzzle. What does he mean, e.g. by a *Gokula* (*Gandasahi*), or a *mansúrí*? In such cases, only a combination of numismatic knowledge and more historical context about the usage of specific coins can bring about a satisfactory solution. In this article, we focus in particular on the *mansúrí* because our search for its meaning opens the possibility to combine historical sources and numismatic evidence; the sort of approach, we are pleading for in general.

For Prinsep, the *mansúrí* must have been such an obvious concept that he saw no need to explain which actual piece he was meaning. Otherwise, he certainly would have given more details, beyond the remark that this coin was current in 'Agra, etc.', that its weight in troy grains was 169 and its usual rate per rupee 58. But what was obvious for Prinsep no longer is for us. There are several reasons why in this case it is not easy to link the name of a coin in a historical source (e.g. the list by Prinsep) to an actual coin.

First, *mansúrí* does not seem to match a mint in the first half of the nineteenth century. Mussoorie, the place name that comes nearest in northern India, did not produce coins at all. Neither did Mansurpur near Saharanpur. Second, if the name of this coin refers not to a place of issue, it might do so to the name of the issuer. However, no prince with the name of Mansur was reigning, or for that matter striking coins in nineteenth-century India. Besides, Mansur is such a common man's name – meaning 'triumphant', 'victorious' or 'conquering' - that it does not ring a bell immediately. A third possibility seems at first attractive, but in the end, has to be rejected as well. The Jodhpur copper takkas produced from AH 1192 (CE 1778) until AH 1267 (CE 1850) bear on the reverse in Persian script not only the word Jodhpur in the upper half of the circle but on the lower half also Jodhpur's epithet 'Dar-ul-Mansur'.[2] And what is more, the consonant *sad* in the middle of *mansur* is placed in such a way that it is as it were the centre circle or navel of the coin. For anybody with a minimal knowledge of Persian the word *mansur* must have been seen as the most prominent word on the coin. However, we have to reject this attractive proposition because the Jodhpur *takkas* are simply far too heavy to meet our requirements as their weight is always over 20 grams. This would mean that the rate of the Jodhpur paisa to the rupee must have been in the range of 1:40, whereas Prinsep's *Mansúrí [paisa]* commands a rate of 1:58 as we saw.[3]

	Obv.: within decorated circle: جودپور دارالمنصور ١٢٠٥ Jodhpur Dar al-Mansur (Fictitious year) 1205
KM#13. Anonymous AE *takka*, fictitious date AH 1205/RY. 35, attributed to Jodhpur city Mint (eighteenth/nineteenth century). Weight 21.69 g, Ø 25 mm	Rev.: within dotted and decorated circle: ضرب مانوس میمنت جلوس سنه ٣٥ Zarb Manus Maimanet Jalus Sanah 35

FIG. 12.1: ANONYMOUS JODHPUR TAKKA AH 1205/RY 35, ATTRIBUTED TO JODHPUR CITY MINT (18TH-19TH CENTURY), 21.69 GRAM, SIZE 25 MM. OBV. WITHIN DECORATED CIRCLE *JODHPUR/ DAR AL-MANSUR* [FICTITIOUS YEAR] 1205; REV. WITHIN DOTTED AND DECORATED CIRCLE *ZARB/ MANUS/ MAIMANAT/ JULUS SAHAH* 35.

This forces us to go in a different direction. If we read *mansúrí* as *manzuri* (spelt with a *za* in the middle) instead of *mansur* (spelt with a *sad* in the middle), we have to translate it with 'sanction, permission, or approval'.[4] In this case, it is a rather neutral term, which indicates that a coin is legal tender, but as such, it tells us nothing about the actual coin meant.

Such a generic explanation is also suggested by the numismatist Charles J. Rodgers, who wrote at the end of the nineteenth century:

> In a heap of common bazaar coins in the northern towns of India at the present-day coins of Bhopal, Baroda, Gwalior, Indore, Amritsar, Lahore, Jummu and Srinagar (Kashmir) are the most common. But there is always a vast number of copper coins, the origin of which the coin dealers can tell us little about. The Mansuri pice are coins of this kind. They are, as a rule, oblong lumps of copper or brass. They are without inscriptions and generally have no devices on them. Of course, they are not of equal weight. In some bazaars remote from trade routes, I have seen shapeless lumps of iron or copper or mixed metal sold for coin. Strange though it may seem, these coins are in great demand. When a marriage takes place, it is the custom to distribute coins to faqirs and the poor. Over a hundred of the pice described above are obtainable for a rupee, whereas only 64 pice stamped in Government mints can be got for the same sum. Hence, it happens that the common bazaar money changer does a great trade in the old copper issues of the country. He buys up from villages and towns the money given away at marriages, etc., and in the marrying season drives a roaring trade in selling the same coins again.[5]

These seem to be the same pieces as those which used to circulate in Sirmaur district (Himachal Pradesh) as described by Lalman and Ritu: 'Numerous square rectangular and sometimes irregularly cut and defaced bits, popularly known as Mansuri paisas, have also been recovered from several sites from the area of our research'. They describe them as copper pieces of *c.* 20 × 20 × 6 mm. and *c.* 10.5 g. On the one hand, the two descriptions - one by Rodgers and one by Lalman and Ritu – point to the same objects, on the other hand, the weight of the *mansuri paisas* found in Himachal Pradesh is unexpectedly heavy for an exchange rate of over one hundred per rupee.[6]

Here we meet under the same name a *mansuri (pice)* of 1/100th rupee, whereas the *mansúrí* in the Useful Tables equaled 1/58th rupee. Of course, there is a time difference between the two data, but that cannot explain such a huge difference in monetary value. At the same time, it suggests that the *mansúrí* must have been extremely common before it was degraded to the state as described by Charles Rodgers, otherwise it would not have been able to lend its name to old and worn-out copper coinage.

Finally, only recently yet another reference to a *Munsooree* turned up in the archives. Paul Stevens found a reference to a coin of that name, which was produced at the Hathras mint some time before 1832, fluctuating in value from 64 to 66 per rupee. Besides, other Hathras pice (a 'Hathras pysa coined by [Rajah] Diaram 'which valued 45, and a *Nuwabee* which valued 53 to 54 per rupee) were produced by that copper mint and all were 'current only at Hathras [Surswe], Moorsawn and the villages around that, at Coel even they are at a discount'.[7]

In order to explain these divergent descriptions of the *mansuri* there is only one option. We have to look for a concrete historical context in which we can identify a specific coin as a *mansúrí* or *manzurí paisa*.

A Concrete Case: The *Mansúri Paisa* as Used in 1848-49

Fortunately, such a case is available for the payment of wages specified in *munsooree paisa* in 1849. Thanks to the extensive records of a 'Special European Court of Inquiry' that was set up in New Delhi in order to investigate charges of embezzlement against John Buttress, a British overseer of the Western Jumna Canal, we have enough detailed information to advance our argument.[8] During this court case that took place between 20th June and 12th July 1849 in the barracks of the 42nd Regiment Native Light Infantry it turned out that Buttress, in-charge of the canal section between Sonipat and Panipat, systematically had underpaid his workers who started to complain to the engineer. The questioning went into such a detail that we even hear about the actual coins in which the wages were paid to the workers.

For their maintenance activities like weeding and repairing the canal banks, the workers received in principle their wages fortnightly. According to the rules the superintending officer, based at Dadupur, monthly sent drafts on the nearest (English) Treasury to his seven (English) overseers, who in their turn had to cash them. In this case the draft had to be presented to F.W. Collins, Deputy Collector, Delhi Central Division, Treasury Office. From him, the overseer, or rather a *barkandaz* (who had to protect the treasury chest) sent by him, received the sum in new (*sicca*) silver rupees. These silver rupees were locally ('on the road' it is called on one occasion) exchanged against coppers. Thereupon, they were distributed over the main stations, about 10 miles or one march separated from each other along the canal. The treasury chest of each station or *chowki* of which the overseer kept the key, was guarded by a *barkandaz*. Of course, the coppers also could be paid out immediately to the workers.

On pay day the overseer or *mutsuddi* (his right-hand man) personally (only occasionally they enlisted somebody else like a *barkandaz*) called for the foremen, sometimes called *chaprassis*, mentioned in their particular abstract books of work people and daily cash account books (kept by the overseer in English, and by the *mutsuddi* in Persian), and paid them the money due for the past two weeks. Upon receiving the money the foremen immediately had to stamp the 'acquittance rolls' with their own seals. Together with the accounts, these stamped receipts had to be returned at the end of the month to the office of the superintending engineer. It seems that a dozen or so workers, e.g. groups of earth workers, grass cutters, or carpenters, had their own foreman. As a rule, the workers seem to have been paid by their foremen, and not individually. After receipt of the draft it took between six and ten days before the establishment actually was paid. This time was mostly spent in traveling with the draft, the silver and finally the copper pieces, while on average it took one day to travel 10 miles.

We will forgo here the way in which John Buttress, the overseer of the second section of the Western Jumna Canal, in cooperation with his *mutsuddi* Mahomed Zuma, managed to commit fraud despite such a transparent system of payments, but instead, concentrate on the actual coins used for these wage payments.[9] The workers on the Western Jumna Canal in 1848, 1849, and maybe also before that, invariably received their wages in copper coins called 'tukka', equaling two *Mansooree pice*. In all the accounts and calculations given before the court of enquiry, the exchange rate per Company rupee was 72 *munsooree pice*, or for that matter 36 *tukka*. This seems to have been no bone of contention between the canal establishment and the workers or their foremen. All the latter desired was a timely and correct payment of their wages, and the superintending engineer and his superiors could only agree. After all, that was the only way to find the work people and to secure the maintenance of this important irrigation canal.

So far, we have encountered four different rates for the *mansúrí paisa* (irrespective of its spelling): about 1/65th in or before 1832 in Hathras,1/58th in 1832-1834 in Agra, 1/72nd in 1849 in the Sonipat-Panipat region and 1/100th around 1890 in the northern towns of India, possibly in particularly in the Cis-Sutlej and in Hill states. We may, therefore, safely conclude that for each separate case we have to determine which actual copper coin was meant when we encounter *mansúrí* or 'legal tender' in the sources. We will try to do so for the 1849 case, as only there enough circumstantial evidence is available so far.

Where were the *Mansúrís* produced that Circulated in the Sonipat-Panipat Area in 1848-9?

So far we now know that the *munsoorie paisa* actually has been in circulation in the shape of a copper 'takka', equalling 1/36th rupee or two *munsoorree paisa* of 1/72nd rupee, and that it was a common coin north of Delhi in the Sonipat-Panipat area in the years 1848-9. On the basis of this knowledge, how can we come to the identification with an actual piece? Before we try to come up with the best possible suggestion, it is good to realize that it must have been a coin that was produced in great quantities. A closer look at the case of the Western Jumna Canal just mentioned, will show this easily because it may be safely assumed that fortnightly some 2,500 rupees had to be available to pay the workforce. This means no less than 90,000 copper *takkas* at the same time for this canal alone.

Of course, it is impossible to extrapolate from this single employer how many *takkas* must have been available in total for circulation in the Sonipat-Panipat area if only 1,400 canal labourers already needed such a large number of coins. The working population of this region may be estimated at least 200,000 individuals.[10] On the other hand, only about half of them will have worked for wages, and only a minority for money wages. Besides, not all the wages in this area had to be paid at exactly the same moment in time. Still, a circulation of millions of *takkas* is one of the conditions that has to be met by the specific coin we are looking for. It must have had a wide circulation, must have been widely accepted and consequently must have been produced in great quantities in the first half of the nineteenth century.

Which coin does meet all requirements mentioned above? From the list of mints in native states drawn up in 1869-70, we may conclude that only one particular mint at the time meets the requirements set forth by us for the *mansúrí paisa* on the Western Jumna Canals in 1849. If the time gap of twenty years between *c.* 1850 and *c.* 1870 does not spoil the game, we have to conclude that only the *takkas* of Alwar can be the coins we are looking for (see Table 12.1). Their exchange rate fits, and they have been struck in great quantities (see Table 12.2).

TABLE 12.1: EXCHANGE RATES OF COPPER COINS PRODUCED IN NATIVE MINTS, 1869-70[11]

Denomination	*Exchange rate (Government rupee)*	*Remarks*	*Reference (page in Proceedings Volume)*	*Our identification*
Calaba pice	1:80		16	Figure 12.2
Banswara (in Meywar) copper		1:80 Salum Sahee* or Odeypore Rupee	24	Figure 12.3
Rutlam, Jowrah, Syllana (all in Western Malwa) copper	1:64		19	Figure 12.4-12.6
Bikaner pice		1:53 Bikaner rupee	30	Figure 12.7
Marwar dhubboo circulating in Sirohie	1:40		28	Figure 12.8

Ulwur pice	1:36	27	Figure 12.9 -12.10

Note: * The source gives a weight of 7 *mashas*. If a *masha* of 17.6 grains (or 1.14 gram) is meant (as usual in Marwar) this would result in a coin of 7.98 gram. However, all Banswara paisa weigh between 10.3 and 11.6 gram. Therefore, we suppose that a half paisa is meant, although this piece weighs 5.5 gram (see Figure 12.3)

12.2 Colaba Pice (Janjira Island) Sidi Ibrahim Khan (AH 1265-97/ AD 1848-79) *KM*#26. AE paisa AH 1284 (AD 1867) Weight: 8.9 g, Ø 20 mm. Note: Obverse inscription retrograde	
12.3 Banswara *KM*#6. Anonymous AE ½ paisa (19th cent.) Weight: 5.50 g, Ø 17 mm.	
12.4 Ratlam Ranjit Singh (VS 1921-50/AD 1864-93) *KM*#22. AE paisa, VS 1927 (AD 1870) Weight: 8.92 g, Ø 19 mm.	
12.5 Jaora Muhammad Ismail (AH 1282-1313/ AD 1865-95) KM#5-6. AE paisa, AH 1284 (AD 1867) Weight : 7.74 g, Ø 24-27 mm.	

12.6 Sailana Dule Singh (VS 1907-52/AD 1850-95) KM#5. AE paisa, ND. Weight: 5.78 g, Ø 16-19 mm.	
12.7 Bikaner Sardar Singh (AH 1268-89/AD 1851-72) *KM*#41. AE paisa in the name of Queen Victoria / Sardar Singh. VS 1916 (AD 1859). The date VS 1916 became frozen. Weight: 7.70 g, Ø 18 mm.	
12.8 Marwar (Jodhpur) KM#14.2. Anonymous AE takka, fictitious RY 45, attributed to Pali Mint (18th/19th cent.). Weight 20.72 g., Ø 25 mm. (legend as on Jodhpur Takka above)	
12.9 Alwar KM#5 AE *takka* RY 30 (1788), in the name of Shah Alam II (AH 1173-1221/AD 1759-1806). Mint: Rajgarh Weight 18.63 g, Ø 21 mm.	
12.10 Alwar Sheodan Singh (AH 1274-91/AD 1857-74) KM#35.2. AE takka in the name of Queen Victoria / Sheodan Singh, AD 1870/ (13). Weight: 18.57g, Ø 20 mm.	

FIGS. 12.2-12.10: COPPER COINS OF NATIVE MINTS IN NORTH-WEST INDIA, 1869-70.

Captain J. Blair, Officiating Political Agent, Eastern States Rajpootana, wrote that 'about 100 years ago' a mint was formed at Rajghur by Maharao Raja Pertab Singh of Alwar. This prince reigned from 1772 until 1792, and he started the production of these *takkas* in 1774. His mint gave employment to fifteen artisans and workmen. In the nine years 1913-19 and 1921-2, Sumbut (1856-64) they produced on average 135.712 silver rupees per year and in the eleven years vs 1913-19, 1921-2, and 1924-5 (AD 1856-66) over 217,000 'pice [had been] coined'. From the context it is nearly certain that a production of copper coins at a total value of 217,000 rupees is meant. In the intermediate years vs 1920 and half vs 1923 the silver mint was leased out, hence there are no returns, but we may suppose that also in this period as many (or even more coins) have been made by the contractor than under direct state supervision. Crucial is Blair's wording: 'thirty-six pice go to the rupee'.[12] This is exactly the rate we are looking for!

Secondly, the production had been considerable over the years as can be concluded from two types of evidence (see Table 12.2): besides official production figures for the period 1865-8 we propose to use actual prices for these pieces in the coin collector's market as an indication for degrees of rarity.

TABLE 12.2: PRODUCTION OF COPPER *TAKKAS* FOR ALWAR, 1774/1775-1871

Identification (KM)	*Dates*			*Indications for production*		
	AD and regnal years	*AH and regnal years*	*VS*	*pieces*	*Rarety (1804-33 = 100)*	*Different years of issue as known from actual pieces*
5	1774/5-1798/9	(1173/) 16 = 1188-(1173/) 41=1213		?	60	18
15	1809/10-1833/4	(1221/) 4 = 1224-(1221/) 28 = 1248		?	100	15

(Contd.)

25	1838/9- 1855/6	(1253/) 2 = 1254- (1253/) 19 = 1271		?	50	9
*	1856	?	1913	179,136	?	1?
	1857	?	1914	165,528	?	1?
	1858	?	1915	142,416	?	1?
	1859/2	-	1916	245,088		
35.1	1860/3	-	1917	253,656	35	6
	1861/4	-	1918	275,760		
	1862/4 [*sic*]	-	1919	230,400		
	1864	-	1921	170,136		
	1865/9	-	1922	209,952		
*	1867	?	1924	227,548	?	2?
	1868	?	1925	290,844		
35.2	1870/13	-		?	35	2
	1871/15	-		?		

Sources and key: Identification and rarity after Krause & Mishler 2002, 702 and Bruce 2004, 596 (value for the quality fine for *KM* 15 is US$ 10;* Indicates that no actual pieces have been observed so far; Production figures after India Office Library and Records, Financial Department Proceedings, January 1876, Pros. No. 4: Mints in Native States and the desirability of having a uniform coinage throughout India, 27.

The combination of the two sets of data seems to suggest that in this case an actual market value of US $3.50 per piece in the preservation quality *fine* coincides with an annual production of about a quarter of a million pieces, whereas a market value of US $5.00 rather seems to point to a production figure of some 150,000 pieces. If it is acceptable to equal, accordingly, a market value of US $10.00 to a production figure of roughly 100,000 pieces, we would arrive at the following totals: 2.7 million pieces in the period 1774-1800, 1.5 million between 1800 and 1835, 1.5 million between 1835 and 1858, and 2.5 million between 1859 and 1871. In total this would result in more than 8 million *takkas* in the century between 1770 and 1870, or on average 80,000 pieces annually.

To put this in perspective it is important to know that the state of Alwar in this period on average will not have had many more than half a million inhabitants.[13] This is between two and three per thousand of the whole Indian subcontinent. However rough these population indications are, they are important in order to decide whether Alwar's *takka* production was high enough for successful exportation. We think it was. If e.g. we look at the demand of the Indian population at large for this denomination we have to look at the production of half-*anna* pieces in the great coin factories. In the nineteenth century the demand for this specific denomination was about one hundred million pieces. That at least is the output of the coin factories in 1835 (104 million pieces) and in 1862 (85 million pieces). Production in other years was insignificant. In other words, three Indians had to share one half-*anna* piece, whereas for every inhabitant of Alwar between ten and fifteen pieces had been produced between 1770 and 1870. To conclude, our candidate the Alwar *takka* may easily have been exported.

One of the reasons why Alwar was able to produce so many coppers was the local availability of copper ore. Blair's report also mentions the origins of the bullion needed for this large coin production: 'Copper is coined by the State. There are copper mints at Durelia and Jodawas, and an unworked copper mine at Debra. The miners pay a royalty of 10.5 *seers* per maund of copper dug out, and two *seers* go to the workmen and officials of the mint. The whole amount is coined into pice.' The average weight of the Alwar *takkas* was between 18 and 18.5 gram. Therefore, we may suppose that 50,000 pieces could be fabricated from one ton of copper. For the years 1856-68, for which we have actual production figures of Alwar's mint houses, this would boil down to a demand of between three and five thousand tons of copper. This seems to be consistent with what Ball tells us in his book of 1881 about the mines at Daribo (or Debra as he calls it): 'During the last 12 years the average annual outturn has been only 3 tons 8 cwts', or 3,454 kilos of copper.[14] It also seems to be consistent with what we know about copper prices in northern India.[15] In short, the local supply of copper must have been more than sufficient for the state's coin production. And *vice versa*, most or nearly all locally mined copper ore was smelted for the state's copper coin production. In view of the prohibitively high transportation costs of ores where no waterways were available, it is no coincidence that both the mines and the mints were all located in the southwest of the state.

All these computations, however rough they may be, lead us to the conclusion that Alwar must have been not only a successful producer but also an exporter of copper *takkas* to areas, which lacked copper mines. At least as long as they could not be supplied sufficiently by the new British mint factories in Calcutta and Bombay. One of such areas may have been the Sonepat-Panipat area, 200 km north.

Such an export is by no means unlikely, nor logistically impossible. A report from 1868 about counterfeit coins issued from mints in Jaipur depicts vividly how we have to envisage the long-distance distribution of coppers outside the realm of the issuer.[16] This is not to say that the Alwar production has to be defined as counterfeit. Rather to the contrary, but the distribution of its coins will have been organized along similar lines. The counterfeits, alluded to in the 1868 report, were made in 19 workshops in Khetri (less than 100 km north-west from Alwar) and in 13 workshops in Chirawa, north of Khetri.

Under the silent approval of the rajah of Khetri and his local representatives, who received their percentages, local wealthy *sahookars* had less fortunate members of their caste, as well as *lohars* produce great quantities of counterfeit short-weight copper *pice* (especially of the Gwalior type) out of locally mined copper. These coins were transported by camel loads to their agencies in towns like Agra, Mathura, Ajmer, and Gwalior, all at a distance of 200 to 300 km. It is supposed that monthly 20 camels laden with counterfeit *pice* made their way from Chirawa to Agra. As each camel carried some 300 rupees worth of *pice* this transport route alone must have represented an annual production worth 72,000 rupees! Apparently, the demand for such coppers must have been enormous, even in British territory, like Agra, which the great coin factories in Calcutta, Bombay and Madras for decades already had been providing with new standard copper coins.

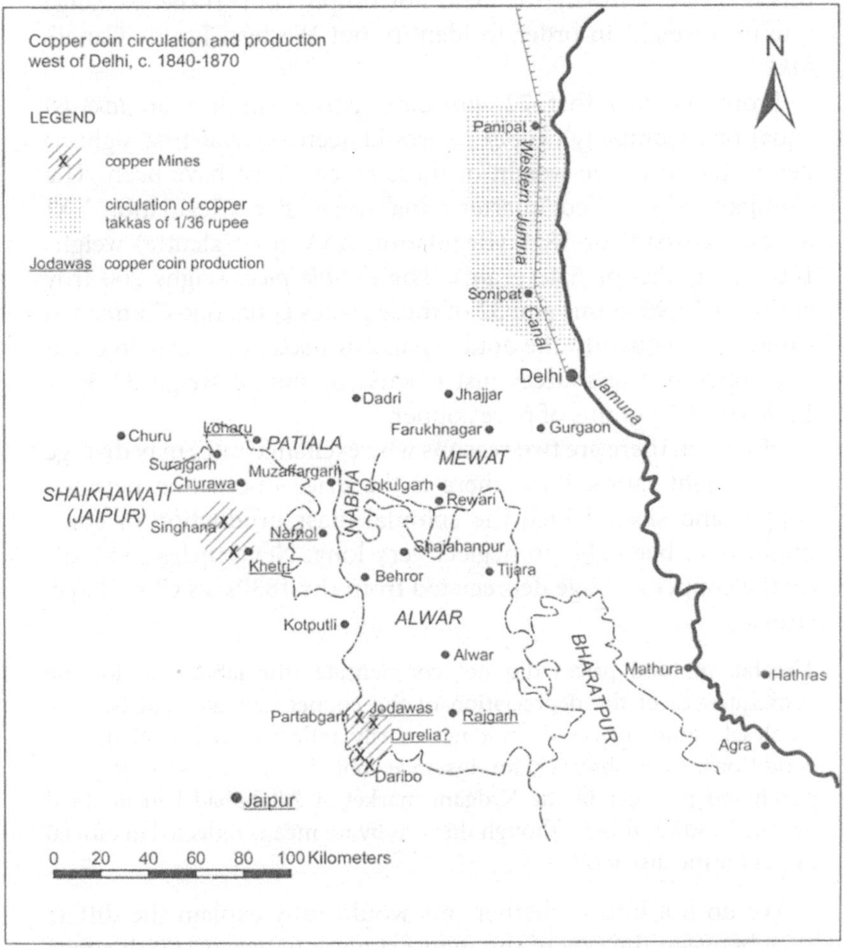

MAP 12.1: COPPER COIN PRODUCTION AND CIRCULATION IN THE WIDER DELHI AREA WEST OF THE JAMUNA RIVER, *c.* 1840-70

Exchange Rates of Coppers

If our attribution of the *takkas*, used for wage payments in the Sonepat-Panipat region in the late 1840s to Alwar makes sense, one problem still has to be solved: the relation between the bullion used to produce a certain piece and the exchange rate versus the silver rupee. This is by far not straightforward as we will show, and this is the reason why we could not simply convert the exchange rate into weight in order to identify out Western Jumna Canal's *takkas*.

From the fact that 72 *munsuree paisas* (in fact 36 *takkas*) equal one Company's rupee, it would seem easy at first sight to determine what the weight of these pieces must have been. The Company *pice*, called 'quarter anna' since 1816 (Regulation XXI for Farukhabad) or 1817 (Regulation XXV for Calcutta) weighs 100 troy grains or 6.48 grams. The *double pice* weighs 200 troy grains or 12.96 grams and 32 of these pieces equal one Company's rupee. Consequently, the double *paisa* or *takka*, of which 36 equal one rupee in the sources just discussed, should weigh 32/36 × 12.96 or 11.52 grams of pure copper.

However, there are two reasons why exchange rates may diverge from weight ratios. First, there is the price fluctuation between copper and silver which the colonial mass production of coins might have been able to neglect very long. Nevertheless, in reality the copper coinage depreciated from the 1830s, as Chris Bayly stresses:

> The fall in food prices did not compensate [the labourers] for the consequences of the depreciation of the copper coinage, and besides, wholesale grain prices do not necessarily reflect actual local market conditions. One observer, for instance, noted that the price of grain purchased per seer in the Kydganj market at Allahabad had doubled between 1802 and 1833, though this was by no means reflected in official prices for the district.[17]

We do not know whether this would fully explain the difference between the rate of the *mansúrí paisa* between 1/58th rupee in 1832-4 and 1/72 rupee in 1849 because this would imply a copper inflation of about 1 per cent per year. Nevertheless, it may have played a certain role.

The second, and probably more important reason is that not only the weight of coppers must have determined their market value, but – as Table 12.3 shows – apparently also other factors and considerations.

TABLE 12.3 COPPER COINS FROM THE LIST OF PRINSEP, ARRANGED FROM 1/46 DOWN TO 1/80 RUPEE AS COMPARED TO THE *MANSÚRÍ PAISA*

Name	*Identification*	*A: weight in troy grains (or grams) according to Prinsep*	*B: weight in grams according to numismatic evidence*	*C: usual rate per rupee (Prinsep)*	*D: ratio A:B (grams)*	*E: ratio A:C*
Rewasahi	*KM* 14 (Fig. 12.11)	220 (14.26)	14.77, 4.79, 14.94	46	0.96-0.95	4.78
Lucknow new	*KM* 140 (Fig. 12.12)	185 (11.99)	12.01, 2.14, 12.20	46	1.07-0.98	4.02
Mathura old	*KM* 37 (Fig. 12.13)	147 (9.53)	9.58, 9.75	46.5	0.99	3.16
Nawasahi	*KM* 98 (Fig. 12.14)	197 (12.77)	11.16, 1.41, 11.64	47	1.10-1.14	4.19
Bombay 1797 (4 VEIC)	Probably a mistake for Madras: *KM* 398, Pr 316 (Fig. 12.15)	212 (13.74)	13.76	48	100	4.42
Mansuri (Prinsep)	See Table 12.4 below	169 (10.95)	?	58	?	2.91
Agra paisa	*KM* 505 (Fig. 12.16)	148 (9.59)	9.41, 10.33	60	1.02-0.85	2.47
Gwalior old	Mohd. Akbar Shah: *KM* 59, 64, 75 (Fig. 12.17)	146 (9.46)	8.22, 8.44, 9.14, 9.29, 9.31, 9.32, 9.33, 9.38	62	1.12-1.01	2.35
Bahar (probably Bihar)	Probably Benares paisa 1815-21: Pr 309, *KM* 27 (Fig. 12.18)	101 (6.55)	6.35-6.42	64	1.03-1.02	1.58
Calcutta 1817	*KM* 55, PR 206 (Fig. 12.19)	100 (6.48)	6.46 [*KM*], 6.18, 6.39	64	1.00-1.05	1.56

(Contd.)

Farukhabad 1816	*KM* 64, PR 335A (Fig. 12.20)	100 (6.48)	6.20	64	1.04	1.56
Bombay 1832	*KM* 231.1/2, PR 207/208 (Fig. 12.21)	100 (6.48)	6.12, 6.38, 6.47 [*KM*]	64	1.06-1.00	1.56
Madras 1832	Probably *KM* 431 (1825)	100 (6.48)	?	64	?	1.56
Patna 1817	See Bihar above	101 (6.55)	6.35-6.42	64	1.03-1.02	1.58
Mathura new	Double of 270 grains not observed: M/W T2a-b?	135 (8.75)	8.30, 8.50?	68	?	1.98
Gokula (*Gandasahi*)	lit. A coin with a *ganda* (cf. Gandasa: a pole-axe or battle-axe; or *ganda*: an aggregate of 4 cowries or 4 pice) M/W MUC T30?	110 (7.13)	?	70	?	1.57
Nepal paisa	*KM* 490	164 (10.63)	10.62	80	1.00	2.05

Sources: Krause/Mishler 2002 and Bruce 2004 (for identification and weight in grams); Maheswari and Wiggins 1989; Pridmore 1975; Prinsep 1858 for other data; the ratios are ours.

The reason for the widely diverging relation between copper weight and exchange rate against the rupee in a situation where the 'native' coppers still had a high intrinsic value as compared with the highly fiduciary British coins may be differences in alloy, variations in alloy and weight of the pieces concerned (which made frequent counting or weighing necessary), transaction costs (especially transportation costs), but also and maybe most confidence and other non-technical reasons.[18]

12.11 Rewa

(Prinsep: Rewasahi)
Jai Singh Deo (VS 1866-92/ AD 1809-35)
KM#14. AE 2 paisa, ND
Weight: 14.94 g, Ø 20 mm.

12.12 Awadh

(Prinsep: Lucknow new)
Ghazi al-Din Haider (AH 1234-43/AD 1819-27)
KM#140. AE paisa, AH 1234/ RY. 26 (fictitious ry.)
Weight: 12.14 g, Ø 23-24 mm.

12.13 Bindraban

(Prinsep: Mathura old)
KM#37. AE paisa, date partly off flan.
Mint-name: Islamabad Mathura.
Weight: 9.58 g, Ø 19 mm.

12.14 Awadh

(Prinsep: Nawasahi, so called Lucknow old; also known as *Machhlisahi*)
KM#98. AE paisa, ND.
Weight: 11.41 g, Ø11 × 20 mm.

12.15 BEIC, Madras Presidency

(Prinsep: Bombay 1797, marked 48 to a rupee, VEIC and arms)
KM#398; Pr.#316. AE dub 1797
Weight: 13.76 g, Ø 31 mm.

12.16 Agra

(Prinsep: Agra paisa, current in Agra district)
KM#505. AE paisa AH 1196/ RY. 24 (1782). Mint-name: Akbarabad.
Weight: 9.41 g. Ø 18-19 mm.

12.17 Gwalior

(Prinsep: Gwaliar, old. Marked Muhammad Akbar Shah)
KM#59, 64, 75. AE paisa AH 1232/RY. 1x (1816/17), in the name of Muhammad Akbar Shah II (AH 1221-53/ AD 1806-37)
Weight: 8.22 g, Ø 18-19 mm.

12.18 BEIC, Bengal Presidency

(Prinsep: Bahar = Bihar = Patna 1817)
KM#27; Pr.#309. AE Benares 37 san or trisuli pice (period 1815-21)
Weight: 6.43 g, Ø 24 mm.

12.19 BEIC, Bengal Presidency

(Prinsep: Calcutta 1817)
KM#55; Pr.#206. AE one *pai sikka* (Calcutta, issue 1817)
Weight: 6.39 , Ø 26 mm.

12.20 BEIC, Bengal Presidency

(Prinsep: Farukhabad 1816)
KM#64; Pr. 335A. AE 45 san single pice (Farukhabad, issue 1816)
Weight: 6.20 g, Ø 25 mm.

12.21 BEIC, Bombay Presidency

(Prinsep: Bombay 1832)
KM#231.1/2; Pr. 207/8. AE quarter anna 1832/AH 1247 (Bombay, period 1832-3)
Weight: 6.38 g, Ø 25 mm.

FIGS. 12.11-12.21: COPPER COINS FROM THE LIST OF PRINSEP (1834), ARRANGED FROM 1/46 DOWN TO 1/80 RUPEE

Conclusions

The *mansúrí paisa* was a rather common name for copper coins in nineteenth century northern India, but it did not refer to one specific coin, it rather was a generic name for legal tender coppers in general (see Table 12.4).

Which type of coin Prinsep was alluding to when he mentioned the circulation of *mansúrís* in the Agra area in 1832-4 is not certain. However, the *munsooree paisa* in the Sonepat-Panipat area in 1849 or rather the *takkas* with the double value can most likely be identified as Alwar *takkas*. The *mansúrí pices* described by Rodgers may well be the same kind of pieces as found in the Sirmaur district in Himachal Pradesh one century later and described by Lalman and Ritu. So, after all, at least four different types of coins may have been called by more or less the same word.

About one of these we know more. The '*munsooree* paisa' we encounter in the Sonepat-Panipat area performed an important function in the payment of wages. The much cheaper *Mansúrí pice* at the end of the nineteenth century will have been used as small change in the market place and the shops.

To sum up: this survey provides not only numismatic evidence about the occurrence of a certain type of coin, at the same time it shows how and why this particular type of coin was used. Of course, many factual questions remain still unanswered. At the same time the results obtained so far seem to justify the mixed methodical approach followed here. The results arrived at so far are only

TABLE 12.4: THE *MANSÚRÍ PAISA* IN THE NINETEENTH CENTURY SUMMARIZED

Source and date of observation	*Name in source*	*How many in a rupee*	*Weight (grams)*	*Area of circulation*
Stevens (2006) after Bengal consultations (1833)	*munsooree*	64-66	?	Hathras, (Surswe), Moorsawn and surroundings, and at Coel at a discount
Prinsep (1834)	*Mansúrí*	58	1095	Agra, etc.
Eastern Jumna Canals (1848)	*munsooree* paisa (= 2 *takka*)	72	?	Sonepat-Panipat
Alwar (1869-70)	*takka*	36	18.11-18.76	Alwar plus export
Rodgers (1894)	*Mansúrí* pice	100 or more	?	the northern towns of India
Lalman & Ritu (period not given)	*Mansúrí paisas*	?	9.683-10.931	Sirmaur district

possible by combining numismatic and historical evidence, or – to be more precise – historical evidence about the functioning of the labour market. We would like to propagate this specific angle, in particular in the study of the use of Indian coppers. References to trade or retail trade are not sufficient to understand the usage of this type of coins. We have to know how the common man and woman acquired the coins before they could spend them. Working for wages certainly was one of these ways.

NOTES

1. Prinsep 1858, 62-3 (one of his *Useful Tables*, published originally in Calcutta, 1834).
2. Krause & Mishler 2002, 731 (*KM*#12.2-14.2); Bruce 2004, 664 (*KM*#14.2).

3. Cf. Also India Office Library and Records, Financial Department Proceedings, January 1876, Pros. No. 4: Mints in Native States and the desirability of having a uniform coinage throughout India, 28: 'the *dhubboo* or 1/40th rupee, in general circulation in Sirohie, comes from Marwar, in particular – it is believed – from Jodhpur and Pallee'; according to Upadhyaya 1973, 90 the Jodhpur coppers were either called *bhimshahi* (heavy ones of 2 *mashas*, produced in the period 1793-1803, and used as the standard in the weighing of opium) or *dhabushahi* (with a weight of 310-20 grains (cf. Prinsep with 169 grains for his *mansúrí*).
4. Platts 1988, 1078.
5. Rodgers 1894, 123-4.
6. Lalman and Ritu 1999, 83-4, plate XV, nos. 118-22. Unfortunately, they do not provide a reference for their statement 'popularly known'. Referring to this study, but without other independent reference, Herrli 2004, 238 tells that a.o. *mansuris* were produced in Loharu (not far from Chirawa and Khetri, see below) between 1845 and 1865 for the Cis-Sutlej Sikh and some Hill States. In Herrli 1993 and 1998, 228 this reference is still missing, so he must have had also other reasons to use the expression *mansuri* in this context. However, he does not give them. Do all these references in the end go back to Rodgers, without mentioning him?
7. Stevens 2006, 22 (after IOR, Bengal Consultations, P/162/48, 29 March 1833, No. 3).
8. NAI, Military Board Proceedings 16 October 1849, 8963-9052. For this canal see Baker 1849.
9. See Lucassen, see Part I: Studies, No. 13, cf. Lucassen 2006a and 2006b.
10. In 1891 the tahsil Sonepat counted 224 villages with a population of 189,490; in 1901 it had grown to 203,338 inhabitants, whereas the town Sonepat then counted 12,900 inhabitants. In 1891 the tahsil Panipat counted 172 villages with 184,856 inhabitants; in 1901 it had 196,284 inhabitants, whereas the town Panipat then counted 26,914 inhabitants (*Imperial Gazetteer of India* XXIII, 1908, 82 and XIX, 1908, 397). Taking into account that India's population growth was over 20 per cent in the period 1850-1900 (see footnote 12 hereafter), we may suppose that the combined tahsils with their capitals counted some 325,000 inhabitants around the middle of the century.
11. India Office Library and Records, Financial Department Proceedings, January 1876, Pros. No. 4: Mints in Native States and the desirability of having a uniform coinage throughout India', 27; cf. For the meaning of this report see Garg 1998 and 2001.
12. From the context we conclude that the government rupee is meant. It is nevertheless worth mentioning that the Alwar rupee must have had about the same value as the English rupee: 'the ulwur rupee contains 10 *mashas*: 5.5 *ruttees* of silver and 2.5 *ruttees* of copper - total 11 *mashas*', which means 3 *ruttees* more silver, but 4 *ruttees* less copper than the government rupee. In vs 1917 (1860), the metal content of the Alwar rupee was altered to

10 *mashas*: 3.5 *ruttees* of silver and 4.5 *ruttees* of copper. In vs 1921 (1864) again, now to 10 *mashas*: 2 ruttees of silver and 6 ruttees of copper. Finally, in vs 1923 (1866) Alwar returned to the old standard. This is confirmed by Prinsep 1858, 63: Rajgarh (the mint place shown on the Alwar coins, despite the fact that some issues were actually produced by other state mints) *pice* of 274 troy grains and a usual rate of 36 per rupee.

13. Alwar had 828,487 inhabitants in 1901 (*The Imperial Gazetteer of India* 1908). As the population of the Indian subcontinent grew with some 20 per cent between 1850 and 1900 (Visaria and Visaria 1983, 488): this would result for the period under scrutiny in a population figure for Alwar between 500,000 and 600,000.
14. Ball 1881, 259-60; Which period exactly is meant is unclear, but we suppose it will have been the 1870s.
15. These estimates are corroborated by the fact that at about the same time locally mined copper was selling in northern India at 224 pounds per ton (Ball 1881, 271). This would put the Daribo annual production on average at 761.6 pounds or 11,422.5 rupees, or – if totally coined – more than 400,000 *takka* pieces. We have to bear in mind that we only have data about the output of the Daribo mines. The production of the other mines of Partabgarh and Jodawas still have to be added.
16. Foreign Department Proceedings, Finance-A, July 1868, Proceedings Nos. 11-13, 16-20. Cf. for the background of this report Garg 2001.
17. Bayly 1983, 295. It is possible that Bayly neglects too much the local copper mining for coin production (cf. idem, 243 about copper imports from abroad; for these see Shimada 2006).
18. Cf. Garg 2001, Part II: 'the money changers [...] charged varying rates of discount (batta) on different species of coins in the market which resulted in continually fluctuating exchange-rate between British and the Native currencies'.

13

The Logistics of Wage Payments: Changing Patterns in Northern India in the 1840s*

Jan Lucassen

Introduction

In his overview of the history of money and credit in India between about 1850 and 1950, A.G. Chandavarkar puts forward two major points. First, extrapolating from the National Sample Survey in the 1950s, he stresses the importance of the non-monetized sector in India in the twentieth century, and for that matter, in earlier periods; then he emphasizes our lack of knowledge of the so-called non-institutional sector, consisting of indigenous bankers and moneylenders, a sector that 'remains the least researched and documented portion of Indian economic history, both past and contemporary'.[1] For at least three reasons, theoretical as well as empirical, both those statements are problematic.

First, it is questionable to what extent this sort of twentieth-century evidence, whatever virtues it may or may not have, can tell us anything about the situation a hundred and more years before without additional historical evidence. Furthermore, the modern distinction between institutional and non-institutional and the consignment of 'indigenous' financial intermediaries squarely to the latter category is debatable.[2]

*I would like to thank Om Prakash, Sanjay Garg and Dirk Kolff for their valuable comments on an earlier version of this text.

Second, there are good reasons to believe that for ages past monetization had played an important role in India. Two examples will illustrate that. Two and a half centuries before 1850 a famous text about the state of the economy shows the highly monetized character of Indian society. In the late-sixteenth century manuscript *Ain-i-Akbari* the Mughal Empire is described as follows: 'The inhabitants of the towns and the country perform their transactions by means of money. Every man uses it according to the extent of his necessities [...] It is absolutely necessary for the continuance of the human race, as men obtain by money their food and clothing.'[3] According to Frank Perlin, one of the first historians to draw our attention to the relationship between coin production and coin circulation in India, that applies even more strongly to the eighteenth century. He characterizes the period as follows:

> continued monetization was associated with an increased density of local economic activity and money-use, affecting regions well beyond the more commercialized areas of the subcontinent, such as Bengal and Gujarat. Put briefly, the strictly monetary changes of the 18th century were marked by increased use of money among broad sections of the population, for wages, loans and market exchanges.[4]

Perlin distinguishes between two levels: first, trading coinages of established reliability over relatively large distances which were also used in the final stages of transmission of agricultural taxation, and for payments and salaries to those higher up the social scale; and second, a host of less pure silver coinages, more variable in weight, which circulated within rural market towns and were used for actual payments of taxation by peasants as well as for payments and wages to the majority of ordinary people.[5]

Third, Chandavarkar's two assertions are not consistent with each other. As long as we have no good idea of the importance and extent of the 'non-institutional' part of the financial sector, how can we state with any degree of certainty that 'currency developments [...] possibly affected only one half of the economy'? Especially as Chandavarkar remarked that 'the non-institutional sector [...] even to this day accounts for the major portion of internal finance.'

In theory, there are several ways to tackle this unsatisfactory situation. For practical reasons we will here concentrate on the mid-nineteenth century – Chandavarkar's starting point. Two strategies seem to offer themselves for studying monetization in India of that time. We could begin by examining the reconstruction of the occupational structure of the population and look at the extent to which its income depended on remunerations in money, or we could consider money circulation.

Although the first strategy seems more obvious, it is actually very complicated. It is well known that at the end of the nineteenth century between a quarter and a third of the population derived its income from agricultural wage labour, and another quarter from paid work in industry or services. However, it is not easy to determine exactly what sort of sums were involved.[6] Besides, some part of agricultural wages was paid in kind, but how big a part? Looking through the nineteenth-century gazetteers, examples of payments in kind (mostly in grain) seem to appear as frequently as payments in money. In and around towns money seems to have been the rule. But how can we substantiate such an impression?[7]

In his very detailed reports on the economy of the Deccan in the first decades of the nineteenth century, Colonel William Henry Sykes (1790-1872) devoted much space to his estimates of the prevailing wage rates because 'The amount of wages of agricultural labourers is of so much importance to the class *constituting the major part of the community* and it assists the judgement so materially in estimating the condition of the people'. The maximum monthly wages of adult male labourers amounted to six rupees with board and lodging, and eight rupees without. Women earned five-eighths of what a man could make.[8] Wages were paid in grain when grain was cheap and in money when grain was dear.[9] Of course, we need many more reports like that in order to draw firm conclusions for India as a whole. Nevertheless, the fact that labour was so important in a rather backward part of the subcontinent (Sykes shows how unimportant trade with other regions was) is interesting enough at the start of this enquiry.

The second strategy – the reconstruction of money circulation – entails the study of the institutional infrastructure necessary to the functioning of a monetized economy, such as the production of coins and other currency, their distribution, and the practices of moneylenders and bankers. Money circulation or the transfer of sums of money takes place on several levels. Large sums change hands in international and wholesale trade and between countries, say Britain and India; payments of taxes and rents, and private hoarding, all require smaller sums; and still smaller sums are involved in the payment of wages. Finally, the smallest amounts are used in general purchases from retail traders. As most people transact at the lower levels, those taken together make the best indicator of the degree of monetization of a country so we shall concentrate here on that sort of money circulation, for which Frank Perlin has proposed the following model to describe and analyse.

He emphasizes the important role of advance payments in the relationship between merchant and producer: 'Merchants provided producers with the cash to purchase raw materials and foodstuffs (or to pay taxation at difficult times of the year), and received factored commodities, or marketable crops in return at preferential rates.' He continues:

> Advances also need to be differentiated; however, in the late eighteenth century, they took on a less voluntaristic, more coercive character in which low-value coinages have a special function. It is very likely that several of the 22/23 mints so far identified in one political unit of central India were established precisely to produce monies for advance payments. This is especially likely to have been the case with gimcrack coppers, many being produced in small village mints, some of which remain to be identified. The need to pay advances to producers helps to explain why merchants became involved in gimcrack production, especially in regions like central India where commercial crops and textiles were of major importance.[10]

What is missing from his very attractive model are wage payments. Taking into account the large part of the population who depended on that type of income, this is a serious problem, even if we do not yet know to what extent wages were paid in cash or kind. Perlin does not work out how coins struck by local mints came into the hands of wage earners. And he is not the only one, as general studies in this field are lacking in the nineteenth century. In this essay, an attempt will be made to discuss this particular level of money circulation.

More specifically two case studies of public works in northern India in the 1840s will be presented here along with detailed information about actual wage payments, the coins used, their origin, and the way they travelled from the mint to the purse of the wage labourer. In that very decade the British tried to introduce their own centrally produced coins in even the remotest parts of the country in order to replace what they called 'native' coins. Therefore, it is fortunate that the first case falls just before the success of their attempts, and the second just after such a fundamental change in what might be called the logistics of wage payments.

In order to understand the two cases properly we must first briefly describe the basics of coin production and coin circulation in India at that time as well as the considerations that guided colonial policy in the matter.

Coin Production and Coin Circulation in India in the First Half of the Nineteenth Century

Until the beginning of the nineteenth century colonial powers in India were unable to develop an independent monetary policy, for legal, military, and practical reasons. Legally because their doing so would have been a serious infringement of the sovereignty of the Indian princes, and above all of the Great Mughal in Delhi. Only a century and a half after the establishment of their first settlements, the British were militarily strong enough to have done it, but in practice existing Indian coin production was sufficient. The Indians therefore did not need the colonial power, neither to set it up nor to reorganize it, and by their appearance, weight, and fineness the British-produced coins, especially their silver ones, fitted into the current Indian systems.[11] Throughout northern India, and including the British strongholds of Bombay and Calcutta and their dependencies, coin circulation was dominated by the age-old silver rupee; and in the south, including Madras and its dependencies, by the gold pagoda and *fanam*.

Things did not change immediately after the British were able to demonstrate their superior military power in the second half of the eighteenth century and to start administrative centralization by appointing a Governor-General for all India in 1773. In 1793 the new masters tried to exclude anything other than their own coins from Bengal.[12] Only during discussion of Lord Liverpool's *A Treatise on the Coins of the Realm*, which was published in 1805 and arrived in Calcutta in 1806, were the first serious ideas formulated about a new monetary system for the whole of British India. The Governor-General selected silver as the standard for unlimited legal tender, but no action was taken until 1818, when the British felt strong enough to introduce a uniform bimetallic standard for all three presidencies (Bombay, Madras, and Bengal). For the time being, that meant the production of uniform silver rupees and gold *mohurs*, but still bearing traditional inscriptions in Persian. Each of the three presidencies continued to strike different copper coins.[13]

In 1835 the British East India Company unified its coin production; until then it had been separate for each of the three presidencies. But at the same time it did more, for symbolically the change could hardly have been more fundamental: to central and northern India it signalled a farewell to the age-old Indian, or in fact Persian style of coins, which were now replaced by European-style ones. Not only did the physical size change of the rupee and its fractions, but also the devices upon them. An Indian with one of the new copper coins in his hand could not avoid the sight of the Company's crest, and the more fortunate who received silver were confronted, instead of fine Persian calligraphy, with the portrait of King William IV, or in due course of Queen Victoria.[14]

Thanks to a number of recent studies by Paul Stevens[15] we are better able to understand the situation in this intermediate period between about 1800 and 1835 when the British prevailed militarily but had not yet centrally produced uniform coins for all their possessions in India. Stevens's detailed articles about the Bombay and Bengal presidencies reveal a variety of monetary policies which are confirmed by data from other parts of India. After the conquest or submission of new territories, the first concern of the British was to divert taxes to their coffers. The locally responsible British officers – called 'collectors' – started to make inventories of coins in circulation in their district and they sent specimens to the assay master at the Bombay mint. As a result, official lists were drawn up showing the rate at which specific coins were to be accepted for tax payments.

The coins circulating in British territories in this intermediate period had various origins. If they were neither old nor had originated in adjacent territories, it might have been that they were produced by existing mints, which of course now fell under British supervision; but they might just as well have been struck in the workshops of newly established mints. If the former was the case, as a rule the new masters had the quality checked, through their collectors, by the assay master in Bombay and as long as coin was proven to be good 'native' production it could continue without any alterations in design or appearance. Exceptionally, full-time British mint masters were appointed under the immediate control of the Mint Committee in Bombay, as happened in Surat from 1800 to 1815.[16] But even if that happened, local minters who had been in the trade for generations continued to be responsible for actual coin production.

Normally, the existing situation did not change with the new overlords. Instead of the Mughal or an Indian prince, now it was a British collector who decided when and how many coins of a certain denomination had to be minted, by the authority of his superiors in Bombay, Madras, or Calcutta.[17] European symbols were introduced on some coppers, including the abbreviation 'VEIC' (United East India Company), but that was far from being the rule, and silver coins went on showing traditional Persian script. Whenever they needed new coins, the British preferred to issue a public advertisement inviting tenders for a specific order, either for a stated period or by way of payment of a certain percentage to the minters. In the latter case production could be suspended at any time. By way of regular assays of specimens, checks were carried out to ensure that the contractor kept to the conditions of his contract. That all implies it was not only existing mints that were considered for new orders, and indeed a dearth of coin might even lead to the opening of new 'native' mint houses where none had been working before, as happened in Bankot in 1819.[18]

Coins received by such methods were put into circulation by the collector as payment to troops[19] or were exchanged in the collectorate for old coins received as tax payments, which could then be melted down. It proved to be a delicate process in the case of coppers, because in no way did either the soldiers or the local moneylenders, called *shroffs*, accept unquestioningly the exchange rate determined by their new colonial masters. In that period the *shroffs* still proved to be strong enough to dictate the market and to determine the 'bazaar rate'. As a consequence, the British were sometimes forced to place some of their new coins into circulation at a loss.[20]

It would be a mistake to suppose that only the government ordered coins from the mints. From Mughal times onward, individuals could offer bullion to have it recast as coin, according of course to government specifications. At the Benares mint between 1814/15 and 1826/7 a total of 68,995,110 rupees were coined of which roughly 65 per cent was for individuals and 35 per cent for the Company. For the much smaller production of 7,362,523 rupees between 1814/15 and 5 February 1824 at Farrukhabad the ratio was the inverse of that: 38 per cent was for individuals, with 62 per cent for the Company.[21]

The case of Saugor in 1828 illustrates that British officials appreciated the supply of private bullion for coinage as much as the local merchants relished the presence of a mint house so that they could have their bullion made into coins. Local merchants were prepared to pay two instead of the usual 1 per cent for the coinage of their bullion in order to keep the local mint open. Its withdrawal from Saugor, the British officials feared, 'will be detrimental to the realization of the Land Revenue, which is paid in the superior coin, and will render the payment of the troops more difficult and expensive'.[22]

In the sources, the wholly Indian mints under British supervision in the Bombay Presidency in the period from about 1800-35 are called 'provincial' mints, which seems to be a better description than the recently proposed term 'transitional' mints.[23] After all, they represented the continuation of an existing system of production and circulation with only one exceptional change, to the script on some of the coppers. The transition in those years was for entirely political or practical, numismatic purposes, rather than for economic and financial.

In Bombay coin production under direct British supervision went on in the traditional way until November 1830 when the Presidency mint started production of copper coins (quarter-*anna*) with machines driven by three steam engines.[24] Until then this mint had been unable to meet demand, and even afterwards it was difficult. That is why a number of 'provincial' mints continued to be active along traditional lines: the last ones were Poona until September 1834 and Ahmedabad until 1835.

Why did the British choose to replace a properly working system of coin production and coin circulation, a policy which meant an enormous investment in large new coin factories in the capitals of the presidencies? Superficially it seems a silly question. Why would a successful, modern colonizer *not* wish to introduce its own uniform system? If, however, we follow the arguments as laid out in the correspondence of those in charge in the early decades of the nineteenth century,[25] it will become clear that the alternatives to the existing system were not so easy, that British coin policy was not at all straightforward, and that considerations were much more practical than ideological, and more political than purely economic.

The British naturally disliked having to deal with a lot of different coins, or being dependent on the power of the Indian minters' families and of *shroffs*, and always feared that they – and their subjects – were being fooled.[26] Of course they despised 'the old Indian letter'd barbarous looking coins';[27] and the fact that the names of the Delhi Mughals continued to adorn British coins.[28] Besides which, they thought that European-style coins were much harder to copy: 'Of all devices, the native characters are perhaps the easiest to be copied by the native Indians; and apprehend the human head is the most difficult; animals and trees follow next; because they require animation and gracefulness in the delineation, which the native artists have never yet attained.'[29] But these considerations were not the main drive behind their attempts at uniform coin circulation and concomitant centralized production, which demanded huge investments.

For interregional and international merchants in India it was not uncommon to have to deal with different coins in one and the same place or in different towns and parts of the country – something that was still quite common in Europe too at the time. In theory there existed a bewildering variety of coins, but in practice the gold and large silver coins they encountered tended to be similar. If we confine ourselves for a moment to the silver rupee we find that, in fact, by the beginning of the nineteenth century only five different rupees really mattered in the whole subcontinent under British rule: the Benares rupee, the Calcutta *sicca* rupee, the Farrukhabad rupee, the Arcot rupee, and the Bombay rupee. In 1819 and 1821 the Benares rupee was discontinued and substituted by the Farrukhabad rupee. In 1824 it was decided to have the Bombay rupee struck to the same weight and fineness as the Arcot rupee of Madras, and in the same year the Farrukhabad rupee was conformed to the standard of the Arcot rupee. Consequently, from 1824 onward there were only two standard coins left in India: the heavier and purer silver Calcutta '*sicca* rupee' and the approximately 6.3 per cent lower-valued (because lighter and less pure) 'Arcot rupee'.[30] Given India's size and population, that was a very high degree of uniformity, one – it should be noted – not yet reached in Europe by a long way.

Some experts, such as William Bentinck in 1807 (later he became Governor-General), observed that there was no interchange of coins between the presidencies, and some, such as Mr Roebuck, later the mint master at Madras, saw that therefore a general currency would be of no advantage in the negotiation of exchanges.[31] Others, like the directors of the Company, were of a different opinion, and they would certainly have been right in that under particular circumstances, such as for speculative purposes, coins could be exported in great numbers from one part of India to another.[32] But lack of a general currency is no inherent impediment to trade.

The problem arising from the variety of coins therefore did not lie with the merchant classes in so far as they had to pay in silver or gold; rather it arose with the various groups, particularly soldiers, which depended on the government for their income. Answering complaints about the negative effects on the payment of troops caused by fluctuations in the exchange rate, debasement of coins, or fraudulent practices by the *shroffs*, as early as 1800 the directors of the British East India Company spoke out in favour of 'a thorough reform in the coinage and the establishing of one coin throughout the Company's possessions to which may be added one weight and one measure'.[33]

That was plain enough English emanating from a revolutionary Europe, but Indian reality proved to be a tough nut in the decades to come. Two aspects of wage payments in general, and specifically regarding troops, bothered the British most of all. There were the problems arising from the exchange of high-value silver money into coppers, and then those from the deployment of troops in regions with different and thoroughly unfamiliar circulation patterns. Both problems could lead to dissatisfied soldiers and other wage earners, situations that had to be avoided at all costs.

Soldiers in general were paid in silver and in the south occasionally even in small amounts of gold, but that was not money they could use in the marketplace, or in the shops. In a letter to Madras, the directors showed that they were well aware of it:[34] 'It is evident while the troops are paid in gold and silver, and are obliged to have recourse to the shroffs for the exchange of that money into copper, before they can purchase the common articles of subsistence, that the shroff will require some *batta*, or allowance for his trouble'. But if copper coin was scarce, the *batta* would rise, as had happened before during those years. This could lead to the situation in which soldiers who expected to receive 48 *dubs* for their Arcot rupee according to government regulations, in reality could get no more than 43 *dubs*. Consequently 'the troops and others who only require the value of a few dubs for their daily support, must be very considerable sufferers'.[35]

But the soldiers and their families were not meek sheep. Instead of suffering they were prepared to become troublesome over such issues, as the following example from Bengal in 1797 will show.[36] As

FIG. 13.1: 'SHROFF, MONEY DEALER, HINDOO, DELHI', SITTING ON HIS TABLE IN FRONT OF A MUSLIM CUSTOMER

'Their trade is the exchange of money, the giving change for rupees in pyce or copper coin, and for pyce in cowries. There is generally an established rate for change [...] Before him his day-book into which he enters the most minute transactions, and beside him his box and small bags of money. The stall of the shroff is not unfrequently one of the gossip places of the community.'
(Albumen print, 163×123 mm, published in 1869 in Volume IV of *The People of India. A series of photographic illustrations of the Races and Tribes of Hindustan. Courtesy:* Alkazi Collection, New Delhi).

the Indian and European soldiers of Lieutenant Colonel Hussey's detachment had been sent to the coast, their families were entitled to monthly allowances. H. Grace, the Brigade Major of Artillery at the camp at Dum-Dum just south of Calcutta was unable to get silver coins and tried to pay the families in gold. As soon as the wives of the soldiers found out that they would consequently receive less *copper* money in the end from the *shroffs*, they turned to poor Grace in considerable anger. He reported to the secretary of the Military Board:

> I could not even with some degree of force, prevail on the women (those of the Lascars in particular) to receive their allowances, as I received them from the Pay Office, as their tickets were made out of Sicca Rupees, and they insisted on receiving the pice according to the bazar currency, which varies from the value of those received from the Pay Officer it seems [...]. Every argument I used, could not prevail on the people to believe that I had not taken a Dustoor for my own trouble, in the case, my quarters were daily surrounded by the people to the amount of hundreds [...], who became clamorous and were so grose in their abuse, that I was often obliged to appease them by ordering the Sircar, and Shroff, to pay them the difference.

For their services the *sircar* received from Grace Rs. 20 monthly and the *shroff* Rs. 10. Besides these expenses – which Grace of course expected the Military Board to reimburse him for – his total loss of Rs. 83:06:04 consisted of the payment to the writer and a large book 'for the purpose of entering the names of the men, and their families and other particulars, to the amount of seven hundred lines'. He ends his complaint that not only he, but also two other officers had suffered similar losses.

What could the government do to remedy such a situation? In 1810 the directors in London were prepared to issue as much copper coin as possible, although the largest should not be too heavy for small silver coins were more useful. The production of the smallest copper coin (3/4 pice, or 1/16 anna) would no doubt cause a loss, but the directors were prepared to have its production started 'as in India articles of the first necessity are comparatively cheap, we would willingly bear this encreased charge, when it offers a well-founded expectation of greater convenience to the lower orders of society, and especially to the troops'.[37]

What the directors seem to have forgotten is that India, precisely because of its need for financially affordable small change, had for ages been accustomed to import cowrie shells from the Maldives, and they were a medium which even as late as around 1880 had a very large circulation. At that time, 5,309 equalled a rupee, which meant 332 to the *anna* and 28 to the *pie* (until 1848 the smallest copper coin produced by the British).[38] *Cowries* were especially popular in Bengal where right up to the end of the eighteenth century to a very large extent they replaced copper. In other parts of India bitter almonds served the same function as small change.[39]

Apart from providing enough small change the government attempted to regulate the money exchange too. For example, the Madras government formed an official 'Establishment of shroffs at the Presidency'. As *shroffs* by tradition were already organized into guilds of a sort, we can imagine that the governor convened the headmen of the different *shroff* guilds under his jurisdiction in order to make uniform agreements with them. The policy had its price, however, to be paid by the government. At an annual expense of 420 pagodas this organization voluntarily agreed to reduce exchange rates and standardize them.[40]

But these measures were not enough to prevent problems in cases when troops or civil servants had to be sent to areas of colonial India where different rupees were in use. An early example is known regarding troops sent from Madras to Ceylon in 1796-7.[41]

Somewhat later, all over India military pay was calculated on the same principle, on the basis of an imaginary currency called the 'Sonaut rupee'. In the provinces of Bengal, Bihar, and Orissa (the Lower Provinces of the Bengal Presidency) the official exchange rate of 100 Sonaut rupees equalled 95 *sicca* rupees and 11 *annas*, whereas in the Upper Provinces of the same Presidency and in the Bombay and Madras presidencies the same pay equalled 100 Farrukhabad, Arcot, or Bombay rupees. That caused difficulties when the government wanted to send troops from the Lower Provinces to other parts of its territory or vice versa. In the first case, a soldier received more rupee coins, but 2 per cent less silver; in the second case more silver, but 4.5 per cent fewer rupee coins.[42] Even the members of the Board of Directors in London 'can readily conceive the difficulty that must be found to satisfy a person under these circumstances' and stated: 'Under the present system many complaints have been made on the score of losses which the troops have suffered by the mode in which their pay has been calculated'.[43]

Notwithstanding the clear disadvantage of maintaining two different rupees, the directors in their apparently chaotic meeting of 11 March 1829 (against the prevailing bureaucratic custom many passages in the records were crossed out and reformulated) still shied away from introducing one uniform rupee for British India. The choice between one of the two would lead either to wage increases for soldiers and civil servants or to taxation problems. Ten years before, taxes had been fixed in the prevailing rupees, and these rupees could not now simply be changed. The tax-paying *zamindars* would undoubtedly pass on any real or perceived tax increase to cultivators, who in turn would certainly raise the prices of their products 'and thereby cause a nominal rise in the prices of articles of ordinary consumption in the various bazars'.[44]

It is impossible here to repeat all the pros and cons that were discussed in this long meeting, but the conclusion was that everything should remain the same:

> As great difficulties offer themselves to either of the views taken of the question under consideration and as the evils to be apprehended by a future alteration of the currency far outweigh, in our deliberate opinion, any advantages on convenience attendant upon such alteration, we have determined that the currency of British India shall remain on the footing on which it now rests, namely the Sicca rupee to continue as the currency and legal measure of value in the Lower Provinces of Bengal, and in other districts in which that coin now performs those functions; and that in the rest of the provinces and districts under British authority and dominion, the new rupee of the Madras standard be considered the only legal measure of values. We therefore positively direct that no measures be adopted in respect of the alteration proposed in any of its parts nor any other alteration of the currency without previous communication with us on the subject'.[45]

In those years the directors were also very concerned about the losses incurred by the brand new coin factory in Calcutta,[46] a gigantic operation driven by five steam engines with a total capacity of 138 horsepower built between 31 March 1824 and the end of 1829 and delivered by Boulton and Watt. Production started in the summer of 1830 with masses of copper pie pieces.[47]

Contrary to the clear decision taken by the directors in 1829, the Governor-General and his Council in Calcutta let themselves be convinced by James Prinsep who since 1832 had been assay master and secretary to the Mint Committee[48] and urged in favour of a uniform currency. Unilaterally in 1835 they decided to introduce a new and uniform coinage for the whole of British India, and when their bosses in London found out they were not amused, answering: 'We cannot but feel extreme surprise at a change so extensive and so important having been determined upon, not merely without our approval, but in direct opposition to our instructions.' But what could they do? Things had got out of hand already and India was far away, so they concluded they must acquiesce in the situation with the following words:

> It is scarcely necessary to add our most positive injunction that you will in future pay implicit attention to the instructions which we may see fit to issue for your guidance. We are aware of the inconvenience and confusion which would now result from the abandonment or suspension of the plan which you have thus prematurely and unadvisedly determined to adopt [...] though we cannot but entertain the apprehension that the course you have pursued, in violation of our express injunctions, may yet involve your Government in very serious embarrassment while the alteration of the currency in which your accounts are stated will unquestionably occasion great inconvenience and great confusion.[49]

Only when the British gained the capability to produce enough coins themselves could they try to suppress the existing Indian coin-production centres in the directly occupied territories. And at last they could try to convince the princes in adjacent territories to conform their coinage to the colonial standard. The process was complicated and took more than a century, to be finalized only in the first year of India's independence. One reason for its complicated nature was the proliferation of coin-production sites after the weakening of the Mughal state in the eighteenth century.[50] Even more serious was the central importance attached by the princely states themselves to their right to mint coins. In 1836 the directors of the British East India Company over-optimistically stated: 'No means however but those of friendly advice should be employed. When one or two of the principal States shall be induced to concur in our views, the others will probably follow the examples.'[51]

To conclude, the major reform of 1835 which might have appeared to be the unavoidable result of a process of centralization and imperial administration was in fact a case of bare-faced insubordination. But the centralization of production in three large factories was only the beginning, because the circulation of their products all over the country took many years. The replacement of the Bombay Presidency coinage by the uniform Indian copper coinage of 1835 took nine years. Bombay was in the heartland of British influence; for the rest of the country it would be 1880 before it could be said that the Imperial currency was the sole circulating monetary medium.[52]

The period was a time for which it is possible for us now to reconstruct the money circulation in India as a whole, by combining the general observations of Richard Temple who had been finance minister of India from 1868 to 1874[53] and the very detailed computations of the silver circulation by Atkinson[54] (see Table 13.1).

TABLE 13.1: HYPOTHETICAL REPRESENTATION OF THE TOTAL MONEY SUPPLY OF INDIA, *C.* 1880 (IN MILLION RUPEES)

	Amount	*Additional sources and comments*
Deposit money	600-1,000	Temple 1883, 301: 50-100 million in sterling worth of *hundis* (Atkinson 1903, 110; 1 rupee = 19.96 pence)
Paper money	59.9	Issue of paper money without coin reserve to date
Gold*	1,440	Temple 1883, 297-8: 122 million in sterling
Silver (rupees)**		

(Contd.)

active rupee circulation	1,370.8	
coin in treasuries	278.0	
coin melted***	487.7	47.7 in coin melted in native mints; 437.0 in coin melted into ornaments
small silver coins	92.6	1880-1: small coin and copper circulation 140,7000,777 minus copper (subtracted here, see below)
Copper coins****	48.1	Temple 1883, 296: four million in sterling
Cowrie shells	?	
Total approximately	4,500-4,900	
Per capita (Rs.)*****	18-19	Temple 1883, 296: population 253 million

Sources: Atkinson 1898, 144-5; idem, 'Rupee Prices', 110, idem, 'Silver Prices in India for 1897', but for the following qualifications:
* Anonymous, The Currency Question, 38-9: 'Until 1835 or thereabouts gold coins constituted a recognized part of the Indian currency and they were received by the Government in payment of its demands until 1852 [...] though [since then] gold coins have not been in use as legal tender [...] there is no part of India in which gold coins are not well known and procurable, and recognized as a form of money, the value of the chief gold coins being regularly entered in the 'Prices Current'.
** Temple 1883, arrives at considerably higher figures than Atkinson 1898, but his method is much less accurate. I have therefore opted to follow Atkinson.
*** Because of the easy and frequent conversion of coin into ornaments and vice versa this item has been included in this overview. Some of the gold too was kept in the form of ornaments.
**** Temple 1883 does not give a source. Most likely this figure is an underestimate because he seems to consider only the lighter coppers, coined in the Calcutta, Bombay, and Madras mints since 1862, while omitting the still widely circulating earlier British (see Tables 13.4 and 13.5 below) and 'native' pieces.
***** Cf. Ellstaetter 1894, 21, for the much smaller result (four rupees per capita) arrived at by Sir David M. Barbour, who one-sidedly attributes his low result in comparison with Europe to the greater extent of barter transactions in India.

Each sort of money showed a distinct circulation pattern. *Hundis* and paper money mainly served the traders. Gold was used primarily for savings,[55] as were silver rupees to a great extent for the less fortunate;[56] migratory traders preferred silver money too.[57] Copper, some small silver, and to an even lesser extent silver rupees dominated the daily circulation for the common man,[58] including his wage payments. Finally, in certain parts of the country cowries were still used as small change.

As will be shown, the smaller denominations – mainly coppers – that had to be brought into circulation by means of wage payments required very specific logistical considerations. How many coins of a certain denomination had to be available at what moments in which places, and how were they to be moved from the point of production to the point of distribution? Thanks to the administrators who had to deal with such questions we can learn much more about the use of money at the bottom of the scale, in the realm of the wage earners.

Traditional Logistics of Wage Payments: The Case of the Western Jumna Canal[59]

Between 1817 and 1825 the British restored a number of canals north of Delhi, canals which dated originally from the mid-fourteenth century and had fallen into disuse in the eighteenth century.[60] This irrigation system, taking water from the west bank of the Yamuna, and watering most parts of modern-day Haryana or the areas of Ambala, Karnal, Hisar, Rohtak, and Delhi, was called the Western Jumna Canal. However, it soon became clear that the irrigated lands did not receive enough water and that they became salty. Disease was common among the inhabitants of the area. Much repair work was needed; this began in earnest from 1846 onward, but only between 1870 and 1882 could the restoration effort be declared truly successful.

For the maintenance and repair works the canal was divided into seven sections, one of which – on the main branch, called the Delhi Canal – was the 'Soneput Division', west of Panipat and Sonipat [Soneput]. The European establishment of the Western Jumna Canal fell under Proby T. Cautley, the director of canals at the Military Board and at the time based in Roorkee. The Western Jumna consisted of the executive superintendent Lieutenant A.D.

Turnbull based at Dadupur, three assistant superintendents, and nine overseers. Sergeant John Buttress was the overseer of the Soneput Division, running 48 miles – equal to four days' march – southward from Kokrana west of Panipat to Chota Thanna, 20 miles north of the centre of Delhi (see Map 13.1).

To each overseer, as well as to Sergeant Buttress, was attached a native establishment consisting of one *mutasaddi* (an Indian accountant or clerk; in this case Mahomed Zuma), two *khalasis* (Indian servants), three *chaukidars* (watchmen), one bricklayer's mate, a carpenter's mate, a blacksmith's mate, and a guard of *barkandazis* (police constables) for the protection of his treasure chest and tools. Buttress had a *daffadar*, called Gulaum Hossain, based in Chota Thanna, who commanded eight *barkandas*.

Every month the overseer and his *mutasaddi* had to deliver, in English and Persian script respectively, their accounts and progress reports to the superintendent for inspection and insertion into the general books of the canal.[61] The *mutasaddi* had to keep a record of all workers, to muster them when visiting a work site, and to see them paid.[62] If the overseer was not present the *mutasaddi* was supposed to pay the workforce, normally through their foremen. As a rule, foremen were illiterate and so unable to keep formal written records of their own. Nevertheless, they must have had a means of knowing which worker had earned what sums. One of them who had stated clearly that he could neither read nor write had an excellent recollection after nearly four months. He then remembered the payment of even so small a sum as three pice.[63]

Such was the scene for a major case of embezzlement investigated by an official Court of Enquiry at the barracks of the 42nd Regiment, Native Light Infantry, in Delhi from 20 June until 12 July 1849, providing us with many details regarding wage payments. Sergeant Buttress had taken up his appointment on the canals in 1840.[64] His headquarters were at Chota Thanna, the southernmost point of his division and not too far from Delhi, where his wife and mother-in-law, a Mrs Foy, lived. Apart from his establishment, he commanded hundreds of workers engaged in the never-ending repairs to the canal embankments. The inspection report of

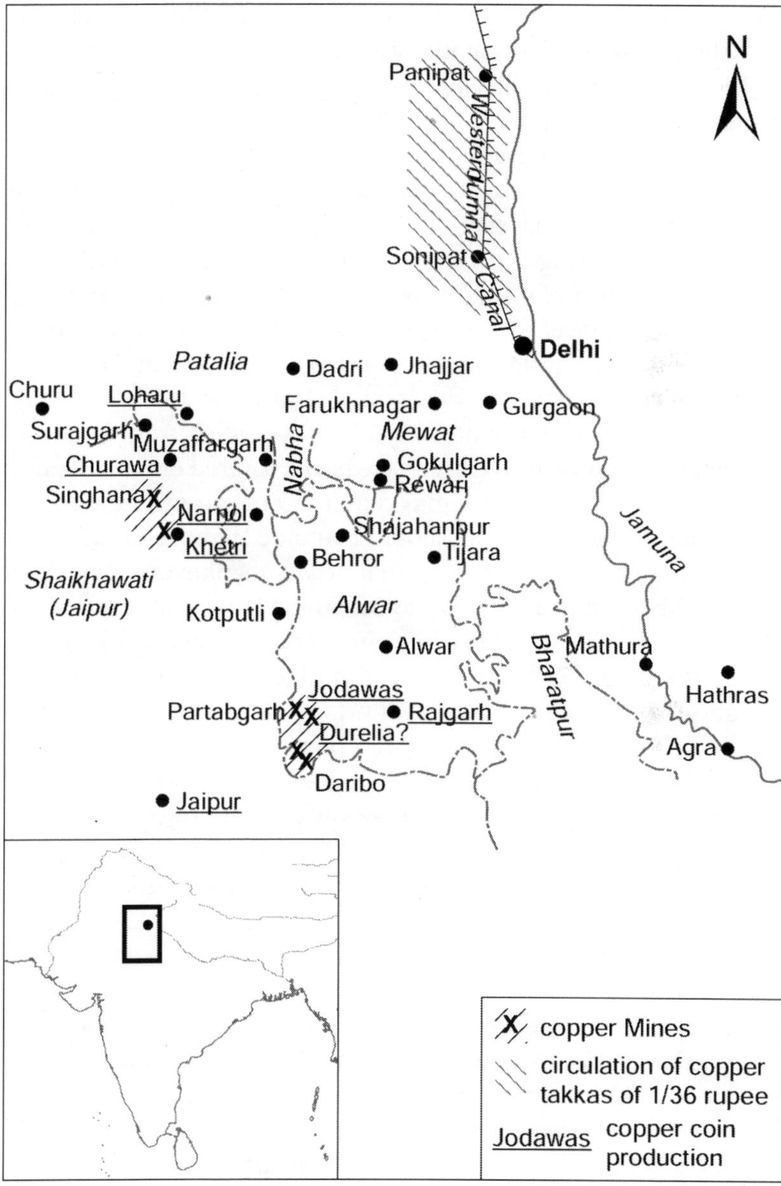

MAP 13.1: COPPER COIN PRODUCTION AND CIRCULATION WEST OF DELHI, c. 1840-70

Cautley, drawn up in January and sent to the Military Board on 12 February 1849, sums up many defects.[65]

Most of the more than twenty bridges of the division needed repairs and the ramps of some of them were totally missing. This section, of four first-class and five second-class *chowkis* (service buildings) as well as nearby mango graft plantations kept up by their own *malis* (gardeners), had very bad embankments; the western one bearing a road had been cleared but the berm only partially so, much of it still being covered with high grass and jungle. The clearance of the eastern bank had not taken place at all in many spots. A great danger to the canal banks were the manifold irrigation cuts through the roads, made by the local farmers to tap off canal water. What is more, in the central section from Koobroo via Jooah to Bhutgaon 'edgings have been required on both banks. In fact, the whole of these banks require to be raised', and Cautley continues: 'either that boats should be made to move in the canal so as to urge the silt forward, or that new embankments should be made'. The worst situation was found in the most southern part of this division: 'The canal has become a great straggling basin and extends now far beyond its original limits. The banks on the left are absorbed. There is in fact at Bhutgaon no passage along either bank. I would recommend a regular board of works at this place.' To sum up, it was not a normal canal as we are used to think of such waterways, but in fact a big, never-ending project, requiring many hands to keep it in shape. Even if we agree with Cautley that the section's bad condition in February 1849 'is not an evidence of Sergeant Buttress' interest in the charge over which he is placed'[66] it could not be denied that unusually high waters could severely threaten the canal.

How many workers were needed for the maintenance of this division? General overviews are not available, but occasionally some concrete information is provided for specific working parties, as the following three cases will show. The first pertains to the party of the *chaprasi* Elahi Bux and *khalasi* Ali Khan. Together they were the supervisors during the months of February and March 1849 of the 'clearing of the canal along the banks' between Noultah and Pulree, a stretch of less than five miles.[67] Occasionally the *mutasaddi*, who at that time lived about half a mile from the works, came to oversee things to gauge how the work was proceeding. We know how many days and men were involved in February 1849 (see Table 13.2).

TABLE 13.2: MAINTENANCE WORKERS BETWEEN NOULTAH AND PULREE (*c.* 5 MILES), FEBRUARY 1849

Dates	*Beldars*	*Coolies*	*Total*		
			men	*days*	*man-days*
1 February 1849	20	40	60	1	60
2-4 February 1849	30	50	80	3	240
5-13 February 1849	c. 55	c. 70	c. 125	9	c. 1125
	8	10	18	10	180
14-27 February 1849	12	13	25	2	50
	13	17	30	2	60
Monthly total				27	c.1715
Average					c. 63.5

Source: NAI/MB, Proceedings 16 October 1849, 8994-5, 89999, 9020 (detailed answer no. 145 by Elahi Bux, more or less corroborated by the less complete answer no. 171 by Ali Khan).

The large fluctuations in the number of workers suggest that Elahi Bux and Ali Khan acted as foremen for workers who contracted themselves casually by the day or week. Perhaps a nucleus of about ten *beldars* and ten coolies held a sort of permanent position, but the others seem to have been engaged as needed from the surrounding countryside. The hiring was one of the tasks of the foremen and the division of the work over the days of the month suggests a fortnightly pay day. The total wage sum for this month of February must have been over Rs. 200 as the normal minimum monthly wage for this kind of work was Rs. 3 and 8 *annas*, or Rs. 3.5. Although the *mutasaddi* and the sergeant had promised on several occasions to pay out the wages, the hapless pair had never received their pay for February, and Elahi Bux remarked that the workmen 'whenever they see me become very clamorous for pay'.

Even during the investigation on 4 July, the wages for February were still in arrears. The sum was higher than another sum mentioned for the same group in March. Then the two supervisors received somewhat over Rs. 54, probably for work done by their gang in January.

The second party was headed by Girdhairi, the carpenter who had to repair the railings of the bridge and the roof of the second class *chowki* at Jutowl in the same month, February 1849. He employed for this work other carpenters who spent in total 112 days on the job – some fifty days on the bridge and sixty on the *chowki*. If all of them worked full-time that month there must have been four men, which does not seem unreasonable for the type of work. The carpenter originally earned Rs. 8 per month, but later his salary seems to have been reduced to only Rs. 5. We may suppose that his mates earned Rs. 3.5 per month.[68]

The third party were under Oorie. He was a *beldar* and acted as the foreman of a gang of labourers cutting grass along the canal. For this group he received 1,100 *takkas* or about Rs. 30 for January. In February his men had worked ten days, for which Sergeant Buttress owed them total day wages for 117 coolies and 81 *beldars*, which means that Oorie's gang consisted on average of 12 coolies and 8 *beldars* every day. If we suppose that the monthly wages of these men were Rs. 3.5, or 146 *takkas*, and consequently some 3 *takkas* per day, then Oorie's gang worked in total 366 days in January as against 198 days in February. Or, based on an unchanged composition of the gang in those two months, eighteen calendar days in January as against ten in February. I suspect that on the other days those men were engaged in agriculture.

Normally, wages were brought to Oorie by a *barkandas*, but from the beginning of 1849 the flow of money dried up and although he complained to Buttress and to Mahomed Zuma his *mutasaddi* Oorie received the above sum only in March for work done in January. Even his complaint that the 'men were clamorous for their pay' did not help him for the time being, for Oorie did not receive all the arrears for February, March, April, and May until June from Sergeant Dixie, Buttress's colleague in the Hansi and Western Division of the Jumna Canal and who in the end had to repair all the mistakes made by Buttress.

Because of the contradictory evidence it is not possible to determine exactly how much money was spent on wages on the Western Jumna Canal. If my estimate is right that Buttress on average spent Rs. 750 monthly during the dry season and that most men were engaged on the basis of wage rates of Rs. 3.5 per month (see Table 13.3), at least 200 workers were engaged full-time on this section during the dry season. For the seven sections of the Western Jumna Canal, that would add up to 1,400 labourers in total. In reality more individuals would have found employment from the canal's supervisors as we have seen that even during the dry season most grass cutters must have worked part-time.

TABLE 13.3: WAGE RATES ON THE WESTERN JUMNA CANAL, 1848/9

Function	*Monthly wage in rupees*	*Names and other particulars*
Mutasaddi	10	Mahomed Zuma
Carpenter	8 (5)	Girdhairi (he also pays out wages, see above)
Bricklayer		Moolah (claims Rs. 54 for February)
Chaprasi (mustered)	5	Sheetal / Seetul (also responsible for the payment of Rs. 100 for workers at Jooah)
	?	Elahi Bux (he also pays out wages, see Table 13.2)
Khalasi	?	Ali Khan (he also pays out wages, see Table 13.2)
Gardener	5	Durmee; Narain
	4.5	Kurjee
	4	Bhawani; Matadeen
Driver of bullocks	4	Oodah, Jivan; Hussain
Beldar	4	Merai (he pays out wages totalling Rs. 71)

(Contd.)

	3.5	Hussun Khan (originally *barkandaz* at Rs. 4, paying out wages totalling Rs. 100, later on degraded to *beldar* at Rs. 3.5)
	?	Oorie (he pays out wages as head of the grass cutters, see above); Hursnoo
Pioneer or digger	3.5	Sheetal; Bowany Deen; Indul; Inggoo; Bakhtar; Gunnoor; Thuckrea; Gohan; Jorey
Personal servant of *mutasaddi*	2	?

Source: NAI/ MB, Proceedings 16 October 1849, 8983-9010.

In conclusion, the total sum for wages that had to be available per season for the whole canal must have been more than Rs. 30,000. If we know exactly how those wages were paid, we can determine how big a sum had to be available on payday. Thanks to the embezzlement of canal money by Sergeant John Buttress and the enquiries it triggered we are able to do so.

Why Buttress was no longer satisfied with his normal salary we do not know, neither can we tell when he started to take canal money for his private use, but it might have started as early as 1845 or 1846. From then on Buttress's *mutasaddi* Mahomed Zuma ostentatiously spent much more money than he could have earned officially, most likely because of his emulation of embezzlements perpetrated by his immediate boss. In November 1848 several foremen had a dispute with Zuma, whom they accused of 'theft and twenty other accusations [...] That I did not pay them the full sums'. Apparently, this was a concerted action by *chaprasi* (also called *khalasi*) Sheetal, *beldar* mate Merai, *beldar* Indul, *khalasi* Deenah, and others. The results of the dispute must have been very unsatisfactory for the men because Sheetal (who probably acted as their leader) and others lodged an official complaint with Lieutenant Turnbull against Buttress on 22 December 1848 'of not having received their pay for months in which their stamp has been affixed to the acquittance roll sent in'.[69]

Perhaps confirmed in his doubts about Buttress by the results of Cautley's inspection visit at the beginning of February, Turnbull – with the approval of the Military Board in Calcutta – decided to make a personal inspection visit, and eventuality not unexpected by the suspects. Early in March Buttress had been informed that Superintendent Turnbull wanted to examine his account books and in the same month the superintendent had all the cash money of Buttress's section secured by two *barkandas*, Shaik Amand and Hoossain Bux.

When Turnbull arrived on the scene in the first week of April 1849 complaints rained down about arrears, but Zuma also complained about Buttress and vice versa. Zuma remarked about his boss: 'I have asked the Sergeant a hundred times for money to pay them. He always made some excuse, that there was no money. But when it arrived, they should have it. Work for two months is still unpaid.'[70] All evidence pointed to the embezzlement by Buttress of at least hundreds and perhaps even thousands of rupees, but what he or his wife did with it remains unclear, though his *mutasaddi* had already drawn suspicion upon himself by his spending habits. Sergeant Dixie had heard that Zuma with his official salary of Rs. 10 'has been living for the past two or three years at full 25 rupees per month. I myself know him to have a wife, that he likewise keeps a fancy lady and also two horses, one of the horses is a much better one than I can afford to keep.' Zuma himself told the court that he paid a private servant Rs. 2 a month and that he also kept a 'tattoo' (pony). Sheetal was of the opinion that Zuma 'kept two servants, two horses and two women besides his wife'. Apart from all these shady circumstances the *mutasaddi* was accused from many sides of not paying out the salaries and not supervising properly. On one occasion he was absent for nine days because he was grazing his own cattle on the banks of the canal .[71]

All these accusations, and a few more, as well as the inspection of the account books and the counting of all the money left over in the treasury chests of this section led Turnbull to ask for an official Court of Enquiry to investigate all the irregularities and accusations. That was readily agreed to by the Military Board as the very principle was at stake of public works performed on the basis of a free labour market. In the words of Turnbull: 'It is impossible for work to be carried on while such irregularities exist. It is not to be expected that labourers will come to our works if they are not paid up regularly, but kept for long periods in arrears.'[72]

During nine sessions held between 20 June and 12 July 1849 with the help of an interpreter dozens of men were heard in person and some of them even cross-examined. All the account books of Buttress and Zuma were compared meticulously with each other and with Turnbull's. Having heard the answers to its 232 questions the court unanimously concluded that Buttress had embezzled 'considerable sums of money drawn from the government [...] and therefore they have the painful duty to perform of giving it as their opinion that sergeant Buttress is wholly untrustworthy and totally unfit to be retained in any responsible situation of trust under the Government'. Without any pain the court also stated 'that Mahomed Zuma or *munshee*, and Seetul [Sheetal] *chupprassee*, are neither of them trustworthy, and both wholly unfit to be retained in the service of Government'. The members of the Military Board, having read all the proceedings with appendices on 16 October 1849, confirmed the conclusions drawn in Delhi and left it to Cautley to decide the fate of John Buttress.[73]

Apart from the fact that the case reveals a lot about labour relations, it offers a detailed insight into the logistics of wage payments on the Western Jumna Canal. My reconstruction of the normal procedure is as follows. According to the rules the superintending officer, based at Dadupur, sent monthly drafts on the nearest British Treasury to his seven British overseers, one for each of the seven canal sections. The overseers had to cash the drafts, so Buttress, for example, had to present the draft to F.W. Collins, Deputy Collector, Delhi Central Division Treasury Office. From him the overseer, or rather one of the *barkandas* sent by him, received the sum in new silver *sicca* rupees. The silver rupees were exchanged locally ('on the road' it is said on one occasion) for coppers, whereupon they were distributed among the main stations, about 10 miles or one march away from each other along the canal. The money was locked up in treasury chests in the *chowkis* built there, and guarded by a *barkandas*, while the overseer kept the key.

On pay day – ideally each fortnight, but in the case studied here more irregularly, sometimes after three weeks or monthly – the overseer or his *mutasaddi* personally called for the foremen mentioned in their particular abstract books. These books were kept by the overseer in English and by the *mutasaddi* in Persian and the foremen were paid according to these books. Occasionally the overseer enlisted somebody else such as a *chaprasi* or *barkandas* to assist, and sometimes individual workers were paid by the canal officials, but as a rule they received their pay from their foremen. If nothing went wrong, it took from six to ten days from the receipt of the draft by Buttress to the payment of the actual wages to the foremen, that time being spent mostly in travelling with the draft, then carrying the silver and finally the copper pieces. On average ten miles of travelling took a day to cover.

As we have briefly seen already, crucial to the whole thing was a system of checks and balances whereby the foremen upon receiving the money had to stamp the acquittance rolls with seals issued to them. However, that was exactly where everything went wrong in the Sonipat-Panipat Division of the Western Jumna Canal in the late 1840s. During the inspection tour by Turnbull in the first week of April and during the sessions of the Court of Enquiry, it turned out that for some time past the foremen had not kept their personal seals with them but had given them to Mahomed Zuma, the *mutasaddi*. Consequently, Zuma could seal whatever pieces of paper he liked and the relationship had been broken between actual payments and the sums mentioned on the acquittance rolls. After the complaints to Turnbull by the foremen and their workers in November and December, Buttress had decided to take the seals from his *mutasaddi* in order – and here Turnbull quotes Buttress verbatim – 'to be certain that the *moonshi* played no tricks with them'. That was not at all logical, as Turnbull remarked about his overseer:

> He could give no reason for not allowing the seals to remain in the possession of their respective owners, but it appears that whenever pay was issued – if the *moonshi* did not happen to be with the sergeant – all the seals, kept by Sergeant Buttress were sent up by the *Burkundauze*, who took the money round the division, to the *moonshi* wherever he was. That he attached them one after the other (not in the presence of the

man to be paid) to the acquittance Roll and then returned them to the *Burkundauze* who gave them back to Sergeant Buttress.[74]

In order to come to a definitive reconstruction of what happened on pay day, we now have to discover what kind of currency and denominations were used. From all the available evidence it is clear that only one coin was used in all these wage payments: a coin called *taka* or *takka*, which equalled 'two *munsoorie pies*' (or *paisa*), while 72 *munsoorie pies* or 36 *takkas* equalled one of the Company's rupees. Clearly then, normal payments on the canal involved large numbers of coins, which would have weighed a lot. That circumstance becomes clear in a rather amusing account from Turnbull when he tried to find out from Buttress what exactly had happened to a certain sum of Rs. 51. That amount

> had by mistake not been placed under charge of the *burkundauze* [...] but that it was put in a small box (stated by him to be a brandy box) with a lock and key attached and brought down without his knowing it to Chota Thanna (his residence). On being asked how it was possible, to carry 51 Rupees, worth of pice (equal to, at the usual rate of exchange 3672 copper pices) in a small box, Sergeant Buttress then stated that they were not in Pice but in Rupees, but Sergeant Buttress had on the first day written down both these amounts as in pice with his own hand.[75]

There are good reasons to believe that the *takkas* referred to here had been made in Durelia and Jodawas, both places where a mint for the state of Alwar was established.[76] These *takkas* weighed about 18.5 grams, so were much heavier than what one would have expected on the basis of their official exchange rate, for two copper *paisa* pieces as made in Calcutta weighed only 13 grams. A sum of Rs. 100 in Alwar *takkas* – a quite common number in the texts about Buttress's embezzlement – would have weighed more than 66.6 kg, a weight which a pony at least, or a donkey or some other pack-animal would have been required to transport.

The next question is how often did wage payments on the Western Jumna Canal take place? We have seen that the ideal was fortnightly, but the reality might well have been monthly. Let us therefore work out the implications of those two possibilities for a total wage sum of over Rs. 30,000 per season. In the case of fortnightly payments 90,000 copper *takka* pieces would be needed, and for monthly payments twice that sum, 180,000 pieces. On condition that the pieces could be back with the *shroffs* before the next pay day, that was the number of pieces needed for one employer. Of course in the area, roughly 200 km further north, between Alwar and the canal there were many more groups of workers who needed their wages regularly, although normally in much smaller units than were needed by the Western Jumna Canal establishment. On the other hand, many more coppers originating from other mints might have circulated in that area, but the *mansúrí paisa* must have been quite common otherwise the workers would have complained about difficulties encountered in spending them in the marketplace or in shops. Anyway, it is certain that some multiple of the sums mentioned here must have circulated. As far as Alwar *takkas* are concerned it is indeed quite possible because the total production of the Alwar mints in the hundred years from 1770 and 1870 must have amounted to around eight million copper *takka* pieces, equal to about 160,000 kg of copper, or an average of 1,600 kg a year.

Outside Alwar there were conspicuously more mints concentrated in the same part of India, both legal and illegal ones.[77] The great number of different native states in that part of India, recognized by the British and because of it claiming the right to coinage, 'the most unmistakable insignia of sovereignty' as Garg calls it, goes some way to explain this extraordinary concentration of coin factories.[78] Most of their coinage was legal, but semi-legal production and outright falsification schemes could be found too. The main reason for this concentration of mints must have been that there existed a great demand for all these coins, including the counterfeit ones, in the more densely populated and urbanized river plains north of this production nucleus, and up to hundreds of kilometres away from it. The counterfeit coins were made in no fewer than nineteen workshops in Khetri, less than a hundred kilometres north-west of Alwar, and in a further thirteen workshops in Churawa, which was itself north of Khetri. With the unspoken approval of the Sultan of Khetri and his local representatives, who of course received their percentages, local wealthy *sahookars* forced less fortunate members of their own caste to produce great quantities of counterfeit short-weight copper pice, especially of the Gwalior type.

We can only guess at the total output of these legal, semi-legal, and illegal coin workshops. Apart from Alwar not much is known about production figures. At Alwar's mint in Rajgarh, fifteen artisans and workmen were employed, and at an estimated daily production of 240 pieces per person (which was the productivity of the Colaba mint per person) there would be 3,600 pieces per day made by the whole factory. As the annual production in the years in question reached nearly 300,000 pieces it follows that these workmen could have been employed only part-time.[79] As the actual collectors' value of the Alwar copper coins does not diverge substantially from that of most of the other mints in that part of India, we might conclude provisionally that the copper demand of all these mints was consistently similar.[80] With over thirty official mints in the area, that would amount to a total annual production of between 150,000 and 200,000 kg. Part of it would have been retrieved from melting down old coins which had become less useful because of wear and clipping. How much was made from re-melted coin is hard to say, but we may suppose that the central Indian mints needed at least 100,000 kg of raw copper per annum, either by way of imports or from local mining.

Let us now investigate to what extent the latter scenario was feasible. It is the more relevant because the question might be posed, 'What is the link between copper mining and copper-coin production in this area?' India used to have two major copper-producing areas: more important was Bengal with the Singhbhum district and Hazaribagh; but second came Rajputana, where copper was found in the northern parts of the Aravalli range on the Malwa Plateau situated between the rivers Yamuna in the north and Narmada in the south. All other production areas, one of which was the Nellore district in Madras Presidency, were insignificant in the second half of the nineteenth century. All mints under examination here were situated in this second mining district.[81] Around 1880, copper mines in that part of India were in the British district of Ajmer and the following princely states: Alwar,

Bharatpur, Jaipur, Udaipur, Bundi, and Bikaner. Although Indian copper was well suited to coin production[82] and some mines, as in Alwar, worked exclusively for the mint, competition from cheaper British copper was so strong that local copper mining at the time was diminishing quickly.[83] So the proximity of mine and mint was even more significant.

By 1880 Alwar had only one copper mine still in operation, in Daribo. The others, though previously extensive, had been deserted: the ones in Durelia and Jodawas (Indawas) only recently, and the one at Partabgarh after an accident in which a large number of miners had been buried alive.[84] Average annual production by the thirty-two families (totalling eighty-eight persons) amounted to about 3,500 kg of copper – six times more than that in weight of ore. Including the roasting over cow dung of the pounded ore, the refining process required 14,000 kg of charcoal. The entire copper thus processed was coined in the Alwar state mints situated, like the mines, in the south-west of the state. Locally gained copper was good then for more than half the total amount needed, while the rest would have consisted of worn coins re-melted.

In Jaipur State the mines of Singhana, Khetri, and Babai yielded most.[85] It is reported that all copper mined there was cast into small bars and ingots and sent to the mint where it was 'cut up and fashioned into coins'. Production figures for these mint houses are unavailable, but they must have been much higher than in Alwar State. In the Kulhari mine, one of several found in Khetri, no fewer than twenty-seven men were employed just in draining it. The owner of some of the Jaipur mines, the Raja of Khetri, is said to have received Rs. 14,000 for the lease of the Singhana mines, while claiming on top of that a sixth of the value of the copper. Nevertheless, work gangs, each of eight Muslims – 'said to be the poorest of the population' – tried to acquire concessions at the annual auctions.

For the other states in Rajputana no details are available, but what data we do have suggest that in certain places such as Khetri, ores found round about might have been sufficient for all local coin production, while in other parts such as Alwar they could have met somewhat more than half the demand, but elsewhere probably less. The many reports about deserted mines suggest moreover that in earlier times the link between mining and minting must have been even stronger. To sum up, we may suppose that the concentration of copper-coin production in this part of India can be explained at least partially by the local supply of copper ore, but fragmentation of political authority must have played a role too.There remains then a final problem: the method used to transport all these coppers to the places where wages were paid.[86] That job was done by camel loads to the agencies of the mint houses in towns like Agra, Muttra, Ajmer and Gwalior, all at a distance of 200 or 300 km. It is supposed that every month twenty camels laden with counterfeit pice made their way from Churawa to Agra, and as each camel carried some Rs. 300 worth of *pice* this transport route alone must have represented an annual production worth Rs. 72,000. Apparently, the demand for such coppers must have been enormous, even at places like Agra in British territory, where the great coin factories in Calcutta, Bombay, and Madras had for decades tried to provide the economy with new standard copper coins.

Colonial Logistics of Wage Payments: When the Calcutta Copper Coins Reached the Ganges Canal

As we saw earlier, by 1835 the British had successfully assimilated the several coinages of the East India Company's three presidencies into one uniform coinage. From that year onward large amounts of uniform copper coins of one-twelfth, one-eighth (struck only in modest numbers – 62 million pieces, or half a million rupees – with the year 1853 on it), one-quarter, and one-half *anna* as well as silver coins of two *annas* and higher silver and gold denominations left the modern mint factories in Calcutta, Bombay and Madras, although the later closed in September 1869 (see Table 13.4). As we have seen in the case of wage payments on the Western Jumna Canal, however, that does not mean that their production was enough to meet the immediate demand even of British India, let alone of all India. We may suppose that it took at least ten years to supply just Bengal and the directly ruled parts of the subcontinent around Bombay and Madras with the new coins.

TABLE 13.4: PRODUCTION OF COPPER COINS FOR BRITISH INDIA IN CALCUTTA, BOMBAY, AND MADRAS, 1835-48

Denomination	*Production years as they appear on the coins*	*Production*		*Production per capita (rupees)*
		In pieces (millions)	*In rupees (millions)*	
⅟₁₂ *anna* (1 pie)	1835-48	220	1.150	
¼ *anna (1 pice, pyce*, or *paisa)*	1835	978	15.280	
½ *anna*	1835	121	3.780	
Total copper coins	1835-48	1,319	20.210 (in *annas* 323.360)	0.09 (in *annas* 1.44)

Sources: Bruce 2004, 711-12 (for the quarter annas see also Stevens 2006c; according to Visaria and Visaria 1983, 466, 488 the population of the Indian subcontinent was 224 million.

Although a totally British-dominated institution like the Western Jumna Canal in 1848-9 seems still to have exclusively used locally produced coppers for its wage payments, and local coin production continued on a grand scale for decades, we can date the introduction of coppers into the North-Western Provinces of British India reasonably precisely to the years 1847-9.

In a letter of 17 April 1847, the Accountant C. Grant explained to A. Shakespeare, Assistant Secretary to the Government in the Financial Department of the North-Western Provinces at Agra, how the requirements for coins were made up. First came the military payments: 'The great bulk of disbursements is to the troops, who, it is well known, are exceedingly sensitive on any point connected with their pay.'[87] From another letter, written three months later from Delhi, we learn that the official collector there 'alone requires 50,000 rupees worth for the use of his district to displace the Native Pyce', to which Grant adds: 'The double pyce or half anna pieces are in no demand and are not taken willingly by the sepoys. I therefore beg that the future dispatches of copper coin may include only the single pyce of which 64 go to the Rupee'.[88]

For European troops higher denominations were needed. After the conquest of the Sikh state by the British in 1849 they discovered that very little of the Company's copper money was in circulation in Lahore or in the Punjab in general. But even more, small silver was needed, as becomes clear from the order sent to Calcutta 'for the special use of the annexed districts [...] The Punjab, Peshawar and Mooltan Districts [...] especially where European Troops are located'. For this purpose, Rs. 200,000 in half-rupee pieces, Rs. 100,000 in quarter-rupee pieces, and Rs. 200,000 in single-pice pieces were demanded.[89]

On top of these requirements came the wages needed for the execution of the Ganges Canal works. As J. Thornton, Secretary to the Government of the North-Western Provinces wrote on 10 May 1847: 'The total expenditure [on the canal] cannot be accurately stated but will probably be not less than 10,000,000 [or] One Crore of Rupees which will be spread over a period of 5 or 6 years according as agency to carry on the works can be procured [;] a possible expenditure of 20 or even 30 lacs in a single year is contemplated'.[90] The Ganges Canal, in modern Uttar Pradesh, was at 562 km, excluding branches, one of the longest canals in the world. When the bulk of its construction was taking place from 1848-54 tens of thousands of workers were employed at a time on earthworks, brickmaking, construction work, and related transport activities.

If we suppose that as a rule these activities were confined to the dry or cold period and therefore lasted only half the year, each worker, earning on average Rs. 4 per month, had to be paid Rs. 24. If we then suppose that at least Rs. 1.5 million per annum were spent on workers' wages, over 50,000 workmen were needed at a time. We know that in just the first district of this canal as many as 3,500 brickmakers were needed in the season 1846-7, which makes a figure of 50,000 workers for all activities in several districts not at all unlikely.[91]

These are not just academic calculations and deductions, for there is a very reliable yardstick for measuring demand for coins and for copper coins in particular: the exchange rate of *pice* per rupee. Officially set at sixty-four, the value of the copper could rise with increasing demand. In Benares, the bazaar exchange rate was sixty-three on 24 April but fifty-one or fifty-two on 10 May 1849,[92] meaning that government officials who had to pay wages in copper and so had to change silver rupees in the bazaars of Benares could receive fewer coppers than the official exchange rate, which it was apparently beyond them to enforce. For the government's paymasters it meant wage increases of 2 to 20 per cent for as long as they were dependent on the market.

We may conclude that in 1847 in towns like Delhi, Benares, Mirzapore and Allahabad the conversion from 'native' to 'government' copper was forced by a mismatch between the increased demand from the officials who had to pay the wages to the army and for the public works, and the laggard supply from the native mint houses. In the same letter from Delhi quoted above we read: 'as the Delhie Pyce which has become much worn is not esteemed as formerly, the Govt new single Pyce or quarter anna Pieces is now in great demand in the Bazar [...] I am of opinion that if a sufficient quantity of govt Pyce were supplied the native pyce would soon be put out of use.'

But that was precisely the problem. 'Sufficient' meant an enormous number of new coins. For the Delhi district alone Rs. 50,000 in copper money were deemed necessary,[93] and the mint houses could not meet the increased demand. In December 1847 it was clear that the current supply of copper at the Calcutta mint was insufficient for the heavy requisitions of the North-Western Provinces and a further supply of copper from Britain was necessary.[94] The production of enough copper coins in the mint was only one of the logistical problems that had to be faced. Transport was perhaps as difficult as production: the first part of the trip from Calcutta to the west could be made by boat to Benares, or, if the river Ganga was not too shallow during the dry season, to Allahabad, flats towed by steamers being used for the purpose. For the coin transports of 1846-8 the cargo boats *Luckia*, *Goomtee*, and *Kaleeganga*, the troop boats *Soane*, *Jellinghee*, *Soorma* and

Bhanguruttee, and the passenger boats *Sutledge* and *Matabanga* are frequently mentioned.

To spread the risk if something went wrong with one of the boats, not too many coins could be loaded onto each flat. For example, in 1848 the *Soane*, towed by the steamer *Lord William Bentinck*, 'was suddenly discovered to be making water fast and to have a good deal in her, though the hold had been carefully examined about half an hour before'. If the captain of the steamer had not instantly towed the flat onto a bank, she might have gone down in deep water. 'It was discovered on getting the water out of her that the leak was caused by a rivet having broken in the shank, leaving the head inside. The rivet-hole was stopped and the vessel proceeded.' The superintendent of marine who described this near-accident had consequently given instructions that as far as possible shipments must be divided between two vessels if the amount exceeded one lac or twenty boxes. If the amount were less the sum should be carried in the steamer as the safer vessel. Further, care should be taken not to load more than five or six lacs onto any one vessel, except in cases of emergency when one vessel could be loaded with coins up to the value of ten lacs.[95] From this correspondence we also learn some details of the way the treasure was packed on board. In the case of the near-sunken flat, one box contained Rs. 5,000, which is 58.3 kg of silver, and the same weight would have been the norm for copper coins. The boxes contained coin bags or 'gunnings', separated from each other by partitions or 'lashings'.[96]

On arrival in Benares or Allahabad the coins had to be transported over land further northwest, which was feasible only in the dry season, and called for heavy protection, which meant in practice that the army had to escort the money transports as part of annual manoeuvres. It was already common practice to take advantage of the movement of troops during the cold season to escort transports in the other direction of indigenous coins (Nanakshahi, Farrukhabad, or Salem Shahee rupees for example) worth millions of Company rupees destined for recoining in Calcutta, or of indemnity money. In 1846, Rs. 3 million were sent from Delhi to be joined in Mainpuri by 200,000 from Gwalior.[97]

Finally, even once the coins had arrived at the work site the dangers were not over, as Mr Volk, a German who was executive overseer of the Third Division of the Ganges Canal, found.[98] To pay the wages to the workforce, engineers like Volk repeatedly had to carry large amounts of money into the field, so they were accompanied by armed guards. Mr Volk then, arrived in Bulandshahr on 22 October 1847 with a thousand rupees locked up in the treasury chest. Because he did not need so much money Volk tried to leave Rs. 400 with the local collector, but for unknown reasons he failed to get rid of the surplus. On 5 November he reached his building site at the canal but was unable to muster the necessary number of men required for his safety. Normally, an executive overseer would have at his command a number of carefully selected guards (*barkandazis*). They would have been screened by a *daffadar* who received increased pay for ensuring the trustworthiness of his men. Furthermore, 'several respectable natives' had to give bonds of Rs. 500 each. Volk, who believed that even those measures together were insufficient and that 'only soldiers of the line ought to be entrusted with guarding government money', thus found himself in an awkward position and 'was obliged to select [his] Establishment from amongst those that offered their services without security.' One turned out to be a rotten apple. While Volk was asleep, early in the morning between 2 and 4 o' clock on 30 December 1847, Ahmed Khan, at the time acting as guard in charge of the chest, took it away never to return.

It is possible to reconstruct the pace at which the North-Western Provinces were supplied with new coins from Calcutta (see Table 13.5). In May and June 1846, the government of the NWP started to send requests to Calcutta for the new single *pice* coins, to be sent in sums of Rs. 5,000 per steamer, and the first of them left the capital on the last day of July.[99] From the table it is clear that silver rupee coins were the priority and that the biggest numbers of *pice* were shipped only in the first half of 1848. It is also clear that the *pice* was preferred over the two other copper denominations, the pie apparently being too small and the half-*anna* too big for wage payments. Among the silver coins the rupee dominated, apparently for paying the European soldiers. Although Table 13.5 does not specify which silver denomination among the rupee fractions was the most popular, it was undoubtedly the small silver two-*anna* piece.[100]

TABLE 13.5: VALUE OF COINS TRANSPORTED FROM CALCUTTA TO THE NORTH-WESTERN PROVINCES VIA GOVERNMENT BOATS TO BENARES AND ALLAHABAD, CUMULATIVE FOR VARIOUS DATES, 1846-8

Dispatched from Calcutta up to the following dates	*Copper coins*			*Silver coins*		*Total value (in rupees)*
	1/12 anna	*¼ anna*	*½ anna*	*2, 4, 8 annas*	*rupee*	
31 Dec. 1846	0	[23,000]	0	?	[750,000]	[773,000?]
28 May 1847	0	[75,000]	0	?	?	5,000,000
11 Nov. 1847	0	110,000	0	?	?	?
3 Dec. 1847	0	120,000	0	75,000	7,000,000	7,195,000
25 Dec. 1847	0	165,000	0	75,000	7,000,000	7,240,000
30 July 1848	0	355,000	0	115,000	7,000,000	7,470,000
7 Aug. 1848	0	355,000	5,000	115,000	7,000,000	7,475,000
12 Aug. 1848	0	425,000	5,000	115,000	7,000,000	7,545,000
19 Aug. 1848	0	445,000	6,000	115,000	7,000,000	7,566,000
8 Nov. 1848	5,000	485,000	5,000	115,000	8,500,000	9,110,000
Total in millions of pieces	0.96	31.04	0.16	If only 2-*anna* pieces 0.92	8.5	41.58
Total in kg	2,073.6	301,139.2	2,073.6		99.11	305,720.2

Source: NAI, Financial Department. For reconstruction on 31 December 1846: Index to Proceedings Financial Papers 31 July (no. 66), 28 August (no. 30), 4 September (no. 32), 11 September (no. 45), 18 September (no. 48), 16 October (no. 28); for 28 May 1847: total in Index 28 May (no. 32); reconstruction of *pice* dispatched by deducting Rs. 45,000 from 120,000 on next date, based on ibid. 24 December (no. 33) and 31 December (no. 51); for three other dates in 1847: Proceedings Financial Papers 3 December (nos. 29-30), 10 December (nos. 34-5), and 25 December (nos. 50-1); for 1848: Proceedings Financial Papers 15 July (nos. 50-4), 12 August (nos. 51-2), 19 August (nos. 57-8); 11 November (nos. 30a-b).

Figures are available for 1849 too but they would distort the picture as the British territories in that part of India had been widely expanded by that time after the conquest of the Punjab.

Conclusion

The way in which wages were paid in the North-Western Provinces in the late 1840s shows that analytical studies of Indian monetary history based on primary sources can, as A.G. Chandavarkar hoped more than twenty years ago, shed new light on the 'non-institutional sector' during the period of 'indigenous' coin production. The scale of the production of both legal and illegal copper coins and of the way they were used for the payment of wages suggests that the monetized sector was more important than has previously been thought. A similar conclusion can be drawn from the description of the introduction of the new colonial coins after 1835, showing the viability of pre-existing coin-circulation patterns and the initial inability of the colonial administration to meet the demand for copper coins by its own efforts.

Although it is too early to quantify the monetary sector and in particular the part played in it by wage payments, the events described here show that it is worthwhile to reconstruct the nature of 'indigenous' coin production and circulation both before and after the introduction of centrally managed colonial coin production, and to trace the gradual replacement of the former by the latter. The cases discussed in this essay enable us to make some important revisions to the Perlin model.

First, within the lower segment, coins were brought into circulation not only by payments made as advances to more or less independent producers in the manufacturing and cash crop sectors. Important too were wages paid directly to labourers such as those building and maintaining the irrigation canals, or serving the Army.

Second, not all the coins used for the payment of wages can be simply dismissed as gimcrack. The demand must have been substantial as alongside officially minted coins such as the *mansúrí takkas* used on the Western Jumna Canal or those of the Indian princes, there was substantial demand for illegally produced coins. Quantification of the different modes of production is still awaited, as is that of copper mining in India for monetary purposes.[101] In future research, it seems advisable not to state repeatedly that important sectors of the Indian economy were not monetized, but instead to concentrate on the monetized part of the transactions. Only through a detailed understanding of its workings and through it of its extent can we come to more solid conclusions about the nature of the Indian economy in the past, and place it in a comparative perspective internationally. This essay suggests too that monetary institutions have to be visualized much more broadly than simply organized or controlled directly by the nation state, a colonial state, or even by states as such. The characterization of 'indigenous' production and its circulation, whether legal, semi-legal, or wholly illegal, as informal is not terribly helpful. And the same goes for the *shroffs*. Most production of coins was by all means legal, and in so far as illegally produced coins were actually used it cannot be excluded that it was done by perfectly legal bodies, including British-owned or dominated firms. As long as the wage earners could use such coins at the expected rate in the market, as had been the custom in England half a century before, both private and illegal coinage served a purpose too.[102]

NOTES

1. Chandavarkar 1983, 765-6 (quotation 766).
2. This distinction is similar to the highly problematic one between the formal and informal sectors; see Bhattacharya and Lucassen 2005.
3. Subrahmanyam 1994b, 30; cf. Prakash 1988 and Haider, see Part I: Studies, No. 6 in this volume.
4. Perlin, see Part I: Studies, No. 1 in this volume.
5. Perlin, see Part I: Studies, No. 1 in this volume.
6. Krishnamurty 1983, 534; Fukazawa 1983, 178; Chaudhuri 1983, 163-71; Prakash 1992, passim.
7. For the Punjab see Bhattacharya 1992, 191-4.
8. Sykes 1838, 320 (identical to British Library, India Office Records, European Manuscripts, D 149, Report on the Deccan by W.H. Sykes, 1829, Tenures second report, 627) – my italics.
9. BL/IOR/Eur. Mss/D/144, Report on the Deccan by W.H. Sykes, 1829, vol. 13, 554; cf. (but less outspoken) Sykes 1838, 321-3.

10. Perlin, See Part I: Studies, No. 1 in this volume. Bengal with its predominance of *cowries* (imported by the Company) below the rupee 'being paid to labourers as wages and to manufacturers' is the exception that proves the rule. See also Garg 2007, and Gupta 1984, 240-5.
11. Thurston 1890, 16, 20-1, 24-5. In southern India the colonial powers enjoyed more political freedom, but there too they adapted to the existing systems. See Deyell and Frykenberg 1982, 13-14.
12. Thurston 1890, 38-43; Temple 1883, 292.
13. Thurston 1890, 51-67; MacLeod 1898, 11-17; Dadachanji 1948, 195-203; Liverpool 1805.
14. Deyell and Frykenberg 1982, 19.
15. Stevens 2004a, 2004b, 2004c, 2004d, 2005, 2006a, 2006b, 2006c. See also Wiggins 1996 (but much more superficial than Stevens), Doty 1998, 185-228, and Garg 1992.
16. Stevens 2004d, 29.
17. It is important to realize that an alternative payment system existed too. In Ahmedabad, 1780-1820, a *giro* system was used by the local merchants; see Stevens 2004d, 25.
18. So, in this period, the British were not yet simply aiming at the closure of as many 'native' mints as possible, as stated by Bayly 1983, 403.
19. See in addition to what follows Stevens 2005, 20.
20. Stevens 2004a, 30-1.
21. BL/IOR/EIC/E/4/733, 87-272, Bengal Despatches, letter 17 August 1831, especially 152.
22. Ibid., 180-90 (quotation on 189-90). Unfortunately, no further explanation is given for the eagerness of the Saugor merchants, except for the assertion of the local British agent that they had 'speculated largely in the purchase of bullion, with the view of having it coined at the Saugor Mint'; see 180-1.
23. Stevens 2004c, 24.
24. Doty 1998, 214-21.
25. For this chapter I have restricted myself to the outgoing letters ('despatches') of the Court of Directors in London for the period 1796-1842 (the period that is indexed by the British Library). I fully realize that this can only be a starting point and that further research is needed.
26. Extensively illustrated in Sykes's reports on the Deccan (BL/IOR/Eur. Mss/D/142, 541-4; D/149, 597-9; not in Sykes 1838). For modern views on Indian bankers and *shroffs* see Chatterjee 1993; Chakrabarti 1997.
27. Doty 1998, 203 (Forbes 5 May 1831), cf. also 190; BL/IOR/EIC/E/4/905, 42-66 (Madras Despatches, letter 6 March 1810), esp. 60 ('the superiority of British workmanship' in contrast to Indian in coin production).
28. Thurston 1890, 39; BL/IOR/EIC/E/4/899, 277-92, Madras Despatches, letter 10 February 1807, 291-2: 'We [the directors] are happy to find our Governor [in Madras] expressing an opinion so entirely in unison with our own, that the name of the Mogul need no longer be continued in the inscription of our

coins, as no national prejudices require our authority to bear the semblance of a delegated trust'. Notwithstanding this dislike, three years later the directors decided to postpone this part of the reform of the coinage of India because the Supreme Government in Calcutta had warned against this radical step. See BL/IOR/EIC/E/4/905, 157-192, Madras Despatches, letter 6 March 1810, esp. 187-8; Deyell and Frykenberg 1982, 15-19; Stevens 2006c, 22.

29. Doty 1998, 220 (Hawkins, 18-27 February 1827); cf. Thurston 1890, 56, 64.
30. BL/IOR/EIC/E/4/725, 5-92, Bengal Despatches, letter 11 March 1829, esp. 11-24; in 1829 the *sicca* rupee – the legal standard of 175.923 troy grains – was intrinsically 6.6 [the text on p. 20 states 6.5] per cent more valuable than the Arcot rupee of 165.000 troy grains.
31. BL/IOR/EIC/E/4/899, 277-92, Madras Despatches, letter Public 10 February 1807.
32. As happened in the 1820s when the Madras mint imported bullion from elsewhere for the coinage of silver rupees which to a great extent were immediately exported to Calcutta. See BL/IOR/EIC/E/4/944, 101-18, Madras Despatches, letter Public 29 January 1834, esp. 104-10.
33. BL/IOR/EIC/E/4/889, 353-6, Madras Despatches, letter 28 April 1800, quotation on 355-6.
34. BL/IOR/EIC/E/4/905, 42-66, Madras Despatches, letter 6 March 1810, 53-4.
35. Ibid., 55. It could also make a difference in which coin they were paid as becomes clear (65-6) from the weavers in 1804. If paid in gold pagodas they could obtain for that coin 197 copper *dubs* compared with only 185 copper *dubs* for the silver equivalent of that same pagoda. For major problems in paying Bengali weavers some years earlier see Chakrabarti 1997, 89-93.
36. NAI/MB, Proceedings 26 January 1795, 2211-12; cf. ibid., 2092-4.
37. BL/IOR/EIC/E/4/905, 182-3, Madras Despatches, letter 6 March 1810. In 1831 the Bombay Presidency required 164 million pieces of 100 grains each [i.e. quarter-annas pieces] to be fabricated from 1,100 tons of copper (BL/IOR/EIC/E/4/1056, 137-44, Bombay Despatches, letter 22 February 1833, esp. 140-1).
38. Temple 1883, 294: 266 *cowries* equalled one *penny* (in 1880-1 one rupee equalled 19.96 pence according to Atkinson 1903, 110-12); cf. BL/ IOR/ EIC/E/4/725, 353-6, Madras Despatches, letter 28 April 1800; Thurston 1890, 36.
39. Thurston 1890, 50; cf. Bertsch 2000. In 1757 the British produced their first coppers in Bengal, in order to pay the labourers employed in building Fort William in Calcutta. See Rhodes 1999 and Kathotia 2006. The copper *annas* of this series were equivalent to 270 *cowries*. For *cowries* see too the Introduction to the present volume.
40. BL/IOR/EIC/E/4/905, 173-4, Madras Despatches, letter 6 March 1810; Temple 1883, 300 (about the guilds).

41. BL/IOR/EIC/E/4/886, 688, Madras Despatches, Military Department, letter 7 May 1800; cf. idem E/4/889, 353-6, Madras Despatches, 28 April 1804; idem E/4/905, Madras Despatches, 6 March 1810, 42-66.
42. BL/IOR/EIC/E/4/725, 5-92, Bengal Despatches, 11 March 1829, 19-21. This text continues (24): 'he finds himself subjected to an apparent reduction of nearly 4.5 per cent from the sum he before received', which must pertain to the number of coins received. According to this same source (16) one Calcutta *sicca* rupee equalled 175.923 troy grains (which makes 16,833,563 troy grains for 100 Sonaut rupees or 95.11 rupees) against 165.000 troy grains for the other rupees (which makes 16,500,000 grains of fine silver for 100 Sonaut rupees). The difference in intrinsic value of 333,563 troy grains is a reduction of approximately 2 per cent (cf. calculations in the margin of 65).
43. Ibid., quotations on 25 and 29-30.
44. Ibid., 52.
45. Ibid., 72-5.
46. BL/IOR/EIC/E/4/738, 701-27, Bengal Despatches, letter 4 September 1833.
47. Doty 1998, 197-203; Tann and Aitken, 1992, 207-10. Cf. BL/IOR/EIC/E/4/738, 721, Bengal Despatches, letter 4 September 1833 (on average the Calcutta Mint produced 3,745,820 pieces per year in the years 1824/5 to 1828/9) with Perlin, See Part I: Studies, No. 1 in this volume (after the installation of five steam engines it produced 77 million pieces per year).
48. On James Prinsep (1799-1840), see for instance Shirras 1920, 94-5, 98-100.
49. BL/IOR/EIC/E/4/748, 149-59, India and Bengal Despatches, letter 27 July 1836, quotations on 150-1 and 157-8. There is nothing about this grave case of insubordination in either Thurston 1890, 63 ff., or Stevens 2006c. For a similar case of insubordination in coinage matters dating from 1781 see Shimada 2006, 127.
50. Perlin, see Part I: Studies, No. 1 in this volume, [307]; for an example see BL/IOR/EIC/E/4/740, India and Bengal Despatches, letter 3 January 1834, 1082-6.
51. Garg 2007; Deyell and Frykenberg 1982, 21-2; the quotation is from BL/IOR/EIC/E/4/747, India and Bengal Despatches, letter 9 March 1834, 469-70.
52. Stevens 2004a, 31 and 29.
53. Shirras 1920, 109-14, 477.
54. For a different model and for later figures see Shirras 1920, 167, 230-2, 460, 462, 478-82.
55. Temple 1883, 296; Ellstaetter 1894, 16 (in particular in the south and in the cities of the north), 117. Gold was used as savings irrespective of its age or demonetization; see Deyell and Frykenberg 1982, 5-6.
56. Temple 1883, 293, 296. Forty years later Shirras estimated that on average each man kept in his house two rupees per annum, or say ten rupees for a household of five: 'the agriculturalist always looks on the rupee as a store of

value, protected against climatic vicissitudes and the ravages of rats and ants' (Shirras 1920, 10, 16).

57. Ellstaetter 1894, 14 (after a report on the district of Shimla by E.J. Sinkinson, 1886).
58. Ibid., 114. By far the most important wage payments in silver (whole and half) rupee pieces were destined for the 200,000 strong army (*c.* 1890 with an annual budget of some 200 million rupees, mainly spent on salaries). See Ellstaetter 1894, 71.
59. NAI/MB, Proceedings 16 October 1849, 8963-9052.
60. Baker 1849; *Imperial Gazetteer*, 16, 1908, 234-6; on the history of canal building in India in general see Whitcombe, 'Irrigation'; for Cautley see also Lucassen 2006b.
61. Baker 1849, 61-8.
62. NAI/MB, Proceedings 16 October 1849, answers to questions 64, 98-110, 180.
63. NAI/MB, Proceedings 16 October 1849, answers to questions 100, 145.
64. NAI/MB, Proceedings 9 November 1849, 10655.
65. NAI/MB, Proceedings 26 June 1849, 3190-3208.
66. Ibid. Cautley's critique of Buttress on 3202 and 3207. In comparison to the overseers of the other divisions of the Western Jumna, Buttress's performance was by far the worst according to Cautley.
67. Cf. NAI/MB, Proceedings 26 June 1849, 3190-3208, where Cautley writes about his visit at the beginning of February 1849 to section 10 from Noultah to Sirdhana: 'The banks on this line are only cleared in part. All the road or right bank is cleared but the berm is not. The left bank is only partially cleared. None of these banks have been repaired.'
68. Cf. NAI/MB, Proceedings 26 June 1849, 3198, for the sort of work Cautley deemed necessary in this canal section. The head carpenter claimed (see idem, Proceedings 16 October 1849, answer to question 196) that Buttress owed him 'for work people Rs. 15:4 and Rs. 17:8 for 112 carpenters employed', which I think should be interpreted as a total sum of Rs. 32 and 12 *annas* for 112 workdays at Rs. 3.5 (or possibly Rs. 4) monthly.
69. NAI/MB, Proceedings 16 October 1849, answers to questions 45 (second quotation), 48, 91-6 (first quotation), and 105.
70. NAI/MB, Proceedings 16 October 1849, answer to question 187.
71. NAI/MB, Proceedings 16 October 1849, answers to questions 63, 94, and 105.
72. NAI/MB, Proceedings 16 October 1849, 9031 (Report by A.D. Turnbull of 11 May 1849)
73. Ibid., 9018-22, 9050-2. From the proceedings it is unclear why Sheetal, who seems to have started this whole case is ultimately considered to have been an accomplice of Buttress and Zuma.
74. For the usage of seals see NAI/MB, Proceedings 16 October 1849, answers to questions 46-52, 87-92, and 9026-7 for the quotations. Unfortunately,

no information is available about this type of usage of seals by foremen (or workers) from other sources. The lowest ranks in society for which the usage of personal silver or copper seals is documented so far are village heads (*watandar*) in the seventeenth and eighteenth centuries. See Bhandare and Godbole 2007, 34-5.

75. NAI/MB, Proceedings 16 October 1849, answers to questions 9, 112, 127, 139, 154, 166, 226, 229, and 9037-8 (quotation), 9042.
76. See Lingen and Lucassen, see Part I: Studies, No. 12 in this volume.
77. Lingen and Lucassen, see Part I: Studies, No. 12 in this volume. In the 1860s and 1870s there was a great demand for counterfeits of local coppers; see Kulkarni 1990, 68-72.
78. Garg 2007.
79. BL/IOR/Financial Department Proceedings January 1876, Proceedings no. 4; cf. Stevens 2006b, 21.
80. The actual collectors' value (according to Bruce 2004) of the coins mentioned here is of course a very crude yardstick, but overall the only one available until we have more production figures.
81. All information from Ball 1881, unless indicated otherwise. On Rajputana, see 259-64.
82. King and Pope 1891, 146, quoting the mint master at the Calcutta mint.
83. Ball 1881, 259, 268; cf. Hunter 1893, 728-9.
84. Compare Ball 1881, 259-60, with BL/IOR/Financial Department, Proceedings January 1876, no. 4, 27.
85. Ball 1881, 260-3 and plate IX between 264 and 265.
86. NAI/Foreign Department, Finance A, Proceedings July 1868, nos. 11-13, 16-20, esp. no. 12 (dated 25 March 1868), para. 10.
87. NAI/Financial Department, Proceedings Financial Papers 28 May 1847, no. 29.
88. NAI/FD, Proceedings Financial Papers 10 December 1847, no. 35, Grant to Thornton, Agra 11 November 1847, referring to an accompanying letter (no. 36) from the officiating collector of the treasury office in Delhi of 24 July 1847.
89. NAI/FD, Proceedings Financial Papers 2 June 1849, nos. 50-54; cf. idem, 28 May 1847 (letter Agra 17 April 1847: nulled 'Furrukhabad Rupees' that should be sent to the mint for recoinage 'are at a great discount and are strongly objected by the troops and others').
90. NAI/FD, Proceedings Financial Papers 28 May 1847, no. 31.
91. Lucassen 2006.
92. NAI/FD, Proceedings Financial Papers 31 May 1847, nos. 67 and 72; cf. idem, 28 May 1847, no. 29: 'I do not think it creditable to the Govt. to be run to the last farthing, particularly when the state of the Treasuries is known to every Banker in the Country, a class who are not slow to take advantage of such knowledge'.

93. NAI/FD, Proceedings 10 December 1847, no. 35 (letter from Agra, 11 November 1847).
94. NAI/FD, Proceedings Financial Papers 10 December 1847, no. 38 (letter from the Government of India to the Mint Committee of 10 December 1847). The situation could vary from one region to another. For a description of coin circulation in the district of Birbhum in Bengal during the first half of the nineteenth century see Gupta 1984, 240-5.
95. NAI/FD, Proceedings Financial Papers 13 July 1848, nos. 11-12 (in the cold season 1847-8 another flat had sunk near Calcutta and very little of the treasure had been recovered).
96. NAI/FD, Proceedings Financial Papers 2 June 1849, nos. 87-8.
97. Based on NAI/FD, Index to Proceedings Financial Papers 29 May 1846, nos. 43, 45; 26 June 1847, nos. 60, 63; idem, Proceedings 29 May 1846, nos. 43-5 (the Delhi and Gwalior transports); and 28 May 1847, no. 29.
98. NAI/MB, Proceedings 19 May 1848, 1670-81.
99. NAI/FD, Index to Proceedings Financial Papers 12 June 1846, nos 44, 46.
100. Precise figures are not available, but two-*anna* pieces are mentioned most, followed by half-rupees or eight-*anna* pieces, while quarter-rupees or four-*anna* pieces were least popular (Index to Proceedings Financial Papers 30 April 1847, nos. 75 and 76; 4 June 1847, nos. 71-3; 10 December 1847, nos. 34-6; NAI/FD, Proceedings 10 December 1847, nos. 35, 37, 39).
101. According to Prakash, 1998, 155, in the Mughal period copper coinage seems as a rule to have depended to a great extent on the import of raw copper.
102. See Bose 1996, for plantation money for instance.

PART II: RECORDS

This Part II offers a selection of *c.* 50 documents grouped into 33 closely related rubrics connected to the money of the masses, i.e. the circulation of copper (plus small silver) coins and sometimes *cowries*. It is mainly based on my research at the National Archives of India in New Delhi and, in one case at Goa. I have not attempted to make complete transcriptions of every document reproduced here. Instead, I have selected those passages which are directly informative about the questions treated in this volume. The references will enable readers to find the document interesting enough for further research.

Each rubric (record or group of records) will be preceded by a short introduction (in italics, in order to distinguish it from the archival source text) and therefore annotation will be sober.* I have mainly made cross references to the Introduction, the documents, other records in this list, and the appendices for more context. Also, the index of geographical names can be useful in this respect.

1. List of Bazarucos from Diu/Damão and Destined for Mozambique, January 1685.
2. Printed Advertisement for the Circulation of New Copper Coins at Calcutta, 24 September 1781.
3. Report on the Copper Coinage of the Benares Mint by George Hilaro Barlow, August 1787.
4. Letter from F. Mure, Sub Treasurer, Reporting an Undue Accumulation of Copper Coin in the Treasury, and Suggesting Measures for Preventing a Still Further Accumulation, Calcutta, 13 May 1788.
5. Correspondence of the Board of Trade on a Plan to Fix a Certain Number of Pons of Cowries per Rupee for Paying to the Weavers, 17 June, 24 July and 10 August 1792.
6. Replies to Questions from the Board of Revenue of 12 June 1787 Regarding the Circulation of Metal Currency in the Different Collectorates of Bengal and Bihar, 10 July 1787 to 24 July 1792.
7. The Reception of Copper Pice for Postage and Customs, Calcutta 31 August 1793, 18 April and 10 December 1794, Berhampore, October 1793, and Moorshedabad 21 October 1794.
8. Problems with the Acceptance of the Fiduciary Copper Coins Issued by the EIC, 23 April 1794.

*The main reference for all documents related to the minting activities of the East India Company in Bengal is Stevens 2012.

9. The Demand for Copper Pice at Patna, 30 April, 8 and 15 May 1794.
10. The Export of Turkish Copper via Persia to India, Basra, 31 July 1797.
11. The Staff and Workings of the Benares Mint 1802.
12. Copper Currency in the Province of Benares, 9 July and 26 October 1806.
13. The Shroffs at Bombay, 7 December 1806.
14. Extra *Pice* for Behar Province, Patna 8 July 1807, and Benares, 19 September 1808.
15. The Circulation of *Tirsuli Pice* at Benares, 21 May 1813.
16. The Circulation of *Cowries* and Copper *Pice* at Cuttack, 26 September 1817.
17. Manufacturers of Counterfeit Coin in the Kingdom of Awadh, 22 January 1827.
18. Copper Coin Minted at Saugor, 27 April 1831, and its Consequences as Still Felt in 1847.
19. Suggestions how to Introduce New Copper Currency from the Calcutta Mint in the Delhi Territory, 14 June 1831 to 13 September 1831.
20. Plans for the Issue of Newly Designed Copper Coins at the Calcutta Mint, 2 August 1831.
21. Circulation of New Copper Coin from the Calcutta Mint, 13 April to 8 May 1832.
22. Proposal from a Merchant to Purchase Large Numbers of *Pice* from the Calcutta Mint, 3 May 1832.
23. The Circulation of Pice from the Calcutta Mint, 4 June 1832.
24. The Consequences of the Closure of the Farruckabad Mint in the Upper or Western Provinces, 29 October to 26 November 1832.
25. Circulation of Old Copper *Pice* in Assam, 19 June to 14 August 1833.
26. The Circulation of Copper Coins in the Lower and Western Provinces, 19 July 1833.
27. Petition by the Petty Shopkeepers of Calcutta, 14 August 1833.
28. Bombay Government's Attempts to Suppress Mints, 17 September to 10 November 1834.
29. Remittance of Old Copper *Pice* from the Post Office to the Calcutta Mint, 10 September to 30 November 1841.
30. Report Called for Regarding Operations of Mints in Native States, 6 February 1847.
31. Gold, Silver and Copper Coins, now or Formerly Current in Central India States 1865-1866.

32. Coinage in Native Territory of Various Native Currencies in Bundelkhand, 26 September 1870 to 4 June 1872.
33. Closing of Bhopal State Mints, 7 July 1897 and 11 February 1898.

1

List of Bazarucos from Diu / Damão and Destined for Mozambique, January 1685

[*List of bazarucos, packed in 28 barrels, which will sail with two ships in this month of January 1684 [Easter Style, so 1685] to the factory of Mozambique, in total 9,962 xerafins. (60 reis = 1 tanga; 5 tangas = 300 reis = 1 xerafin (= 1678-1680 0.6800 gr. of gold or 1683-1700 10.57 gr. of silver); 750 bazarucos = 600 reis or 1 bazaruco = 0.8 reis or 375 bazarucos = 1 xerafin). These bazarucos can be identified as single tutenag bazaruços of c. 4.2 grams, made at Diu or Damão 1670-1680 (possibly also double bazarucos of c. 6.2 grams) was afterwards deemed 'unnecessary'. It predates the first coinage for Mozambique proper by 40 years.*

See the introduction of Ch. 4 of the Introduction; Gerson Da Cunha 1880, 78, 88; Ferraro Vaz & Correia de Sousa 1980, 190, 210; Gomes 2007, 623.]

Lista dos bazarucos que vão em cada hum dos vinte e oito barrils que, nesta monção de Janeiro de 1684, se remetem ao feitor de Mocambique com nove mil novecentos sesenta e dous xerafins.

TABLE R.1: LIST OF DIU OR DAMAO BAZARUCOS, PACKED IN 28 BARRELS, DESTINED FOR MOZAMBIQUE, JANUARY 1685

Barril no.	*Value*		
	xerafins	*tangas*	*reis*
1	339	2	36
2	373	2	24
3	380	3	12
4	372	1	48
5	341	3	36
6	402	1	24
Subtotal	2,210	0	00

Barril no.	*Value*		
	xerafins	*tangas*	*reis*
7	373	1	36
8	378	3	24
9	400	0	00
10	400	0	00
11	350	0	00
12	350	0	00
Subtotal	4,462	0	00

Barril no.	*value*		
	xerafins	*tangas*	*reis*
13	350	0	00
14	350	0	00
15	350	0	00
16	350	0	00
17	350	0	00
18	350	0	00
Cumulative subtotal	6,562	0	00

(Contd.)

Barril no.	*Value*		
	xerafins	*tangas*	*reis*
19	350	0	00
20	350	0	00
21	350	0	00
22	350	0	00
23	350	0	00
	350	0	00
Cumulative subtotal	8212	0	00

Barril no.	*Value*		
	xerafins	*tangas*	*reis*
24	350	0	00
25	350	0	00
26	350	0	00
27	350	0	00
28	350	0	00
	350	0	00
Grand total	9962	0	00

Source: NAI, Goa, Feitorias #2316, Livro de registo dos alvarás, cartas etc. de differentes feitorias, 1 vol., 1667-84, fol. 133vo.

2

Printed Advertisement for the Circulation of New Copper Coins at Calcutta, 24 September 1781

[*Advertisement for the circulation throughout the provinces under the East India Company of the series of copper coins, issued from the private mint of John Prinsep at Pultah, 1781-3; printed with corrections in ink.*

See ch. 3b and 3d of the Introduction and Pultah in Appendix 2, as well as Part II: Records, No. 8.]

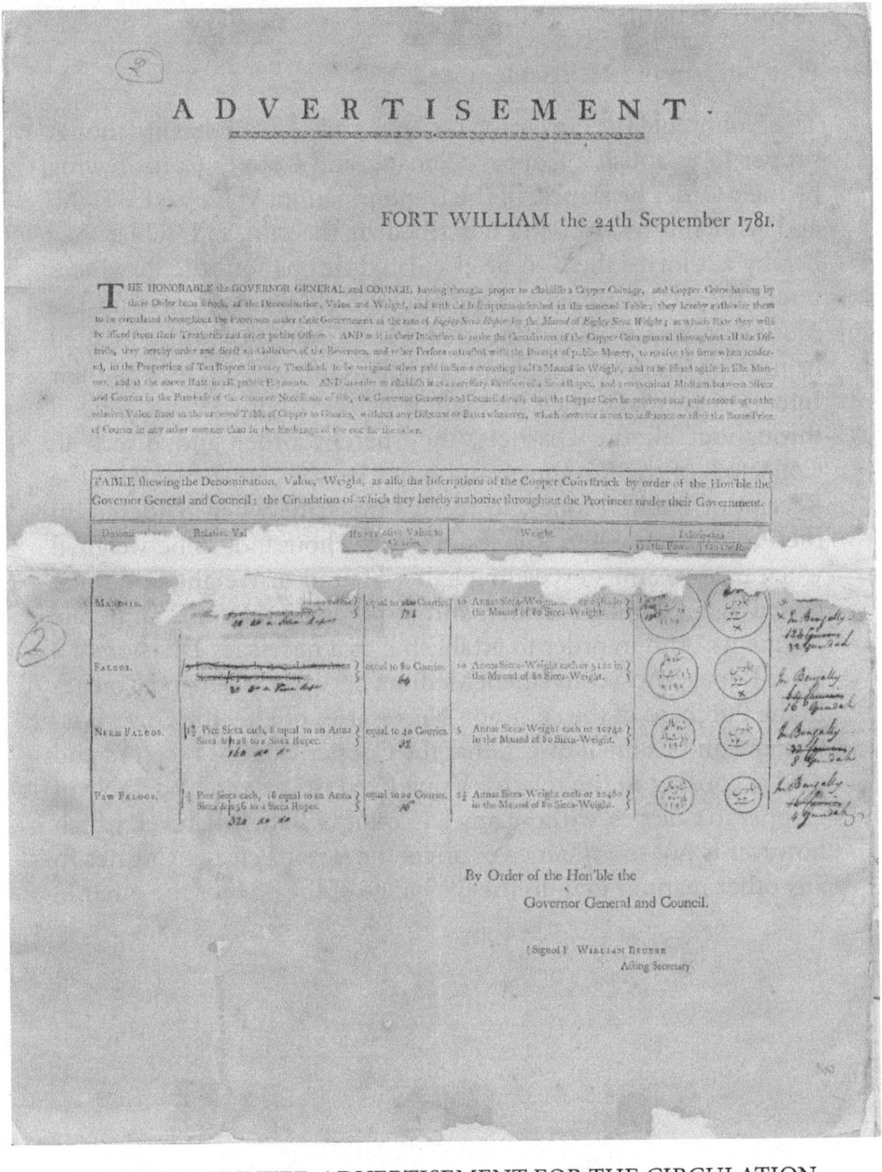

ADVERTISEMENT.

FORT WILLIAM the 24th September 1781.

THE HONORABLE the GOVERNOR GENERAL and COUNCIL having thought proper to establish a Copper Coinage, and Copper Coins having by their Order been struck, of the Denomination, Value and Weight, and with the Inscriptions described in the annexed Table; they hereby authorize them to be circulated throughout the Provinces under their Government at the rate of *Eighty Sicca Rupees* for the *Maund of Eighty Sicca Weight*; at which Rate they will be issued from their Treasuries and other public Offices. AND as it is their Intention to make the Circulation of the Copper Coin general throughout all the Districts, they hereby order and direct all Collectors of the Revenues, and other Persons entrusted with the Receipt of public Money, to receive the same when tendered, in the Proportion of Ten Rupees in every Thousand, to be weighed when paid in Sums exceeding half a Maund in Weight, and to be issued again in like Manner, and at the above Rate in all public Payments. AND in order to establish it as a necessary Division of a Sicca Rupee, and a convenient Medium between Silver and Couries in the Purchase of the common Necessaries of life, the Governor General and Council direct, that the Copper Coin be received and paid according to the relative Value fixed in the annexed Table of Copper to Couries, without any Discount or Batta whatever, which however is not to influence or affect the Bazar Price of Couries in any other manner than in the Exchange of the one for the other.

TABLE shewing the Denomination, Value, Weight, as also the Inscriptions of the Copper Coin struck by order of the Hon'ble the Governor General and Council; the Circulation of which they hereby authorise throughout the Provinces under their Government.

Denomination	Relative Value	Comparative Value to Couries	Weight	Inscription On the Face	Inscription On the Reverse
MADDEIS.	[illegible]	equal to [illegible] Couries. 128	10 Annas Sicca-Weight [illegible] in the Maund of 80 Sicca-Weight.		
FALOOS.	[illegible]	equal to 80 Couries. 64	10 Annas Sicca-Weight each or 5120 in the Maund of 80 Sicca-Weight.		
NEEM FALOOS.	1½ Pice Sicca each, 8 equal to an Anna Sicca & 128 to a Sicca Rupee.	equal to 40 Couries. 32	5 Annas Sicca-Weight each or 10240 in the Maund of 80 Sicca-Weight.		
PAW FALOOS.	¾ Pice Sicca each, 16 equal to an Anna Sicca & 256 to a Sicca Rupee.	equal to 20 Couries. 16	2½ Annas Sicca-Weight each or 20480 in the Maund of 80 Sicca-Weight.		

By Order of the Hon'ble the
Governor General and Council.

[Signed] WILLIAM BRUERE
Acting Secretary

PLATE R.1: PRINTED ADVERTISEMENT FOR THE CIRCULATION OF COPPER COINS, ISSUED FROM THE PRIVATE MINT OF JOHN PRINSEP AT PULTAH, 1781-3

Advertisement

Fort William the 24th September 1781

The Honorable the Governor-General and Council having thougt proper to establish a Copper Coinage, and Copper Coins having by their Order be struck, of the Denomination, Value and Weight, and with the Inscriptions described in the annexed Table; they hereby authorize them to be circulated throughout the Provinces under their Government at the rate of *Eighty Sicca Rupees* for the *Maund* of *Eighty Sicca Weight*; at which Rate they will be issued from their Treasuries and other public Offices. And as it is their Intention to make the Circulation of the Copper Coin general throughout all the Districts, they hereby order and direct all Collectors of the Revenues, and other Persons entrusted with the Receipt of Public Money, to receive the same when tendered, in the Proportion of Ten Rupees in every Thousand, to be weighed when paid in Sums exceeding half a Maund in Weight, and to be issued again in like Manner, and at the above Rate in all public Payments. And in order to establish it as a necessary Division of a Sicca Rupee, and a convenient Medium between Silver and Couries in the Purchase of the common Necessaries of Life, the Governor-General and Council direct, that the Copper Coin be received and paid according to the relative Value fixed in the annexed Table of Copper to Couries, without any Discount or Batta whatever, which however is not to influence or affect the Bazar Price of Couries in any other manner than in the Exchange of the one for the other.

TABLE R.2 COPPER COINS ISSUED FROM THE PRIVATE MINT OF JOHN PRINSEP AT PULTAH, 1781

Table shewing the Denomination, Value, Weight, as also the Inscriptions of the Copper Coin struck by order of the Hon'ble the Governor-General and Council; the Circulation of which they hereby authorize throughout the Provinces under their Government

Denomination	*Relative Value to the Rupee*	*Relative Value to Couries*	*Weight*	*Inscription*	
				On the Face	*On the Reverse*
Madosie	6 Pice Sicca each, 2 equal to an Anna Sicca & 32 to a Sicca Rupee	equal to 160 Couries	20 Annas Sicca-Weight each or 2560 in the Maund of 80 Sicca-Weight	*	**
[corrections in pencil]	40 to a Sicca Rupee	128		In Bengally 128 [corrected in 32] Gundah	
	3 Pice Sicca each, 4 equal to an Anna Sicca & 64 to a Sicca Rupee	equal to 80 Couries	10 Annas Sicca-Weight each or 5120 in the Maund of 80 Sicca-Weight	*	**
[corrections in pencil]	40 to a Sicca Rupee	64		In Bengally 64 [corrected in 16] Gundah***	
	1½ Pice Sicca each, 8 equal to an Anna Sicca & 128 to a Sicca Rupee	equal to 40 Couries	5 Annas Sicca-Weight each or 10240 in the Maund of 80 Sicca-Weight	*	**
[corrections in pencil]	160 do do	32		In Bengally 32 [corrected in 8] Gundah***	

(Contd.)

	¾ Pice Sicca each, 16 equal to an Anna Sicca & 256 to a Sicca Rupee	equal to 20 Couries	2 ½ Annas Sicca-Weight each or 20480 in the Maund of 80 Sicca-Weight	*	**
[corrections in pencil]	320 do do	16		In Bengally 16 [corrected in 4] Gundah	

By order of the Hon'ble the Governor-General and Council

(Signed) William Buere

Acting Secretary

Note: *Persian inscription: 'Shah Alam Badshah 1190'; **Idem: 'falus 22 zarb'; ***these corrections are meant to be added to the lowest part of the reverse.
Source: NAI, Home Department, Public Original Consultation, 24 September 1781, No. 28, pp. 1175-7.

3

Report on the Copper Coinage of the Benares Mint by George Hilaro Barlow, August 1787

[*Report on the Benares Mint by George Hilaro Barlow (1763-1846), one of the members of the committee, August 1787. The report contains a general introduction and sections on the silver, (pp. 76-136), the copper (pp. 136-58) and the gold coins (pp. 158-80). Barlow proposes branches of the Calcutta Mint at Patna, Murshidabad and Dacca, where the public can have their gold and silver coined (as Calcutta was too far away), instead of converting it into jewellery which was pawned with the Banians and thus not used for circulation. Here only the section on the copper coins will be reproduced.*

NB: Because the original pagination in ink, to which the indexes refer, has mostly been lost, there is a new pagination in pencil, which will be used here.

See also Part I: Studies, No. 8 and Benares and Gorakhpur in Appendix 2. The report has also partially been printed in Minutes of the Evidence 1788 (Vol. 11, 1787-1790 for copper coins); for Barlow see A Brief Sketch 1811.]

Copper Coin

The pice current in the city and district of Benares previous to the establishment of the mint were coined mostly at Gorruckpore in the Soubah of Oude from a species of copper called Lungeree which is brought from the Northern Hills. The first coinage of pice at Benares was in the 23rd year of the reign of Mahomed Shah when Gowaul Doss Saho struck over hundred maunds weight with the dies of the sicca rupee. The weight of each pice was 10 maashah 3 ruttees, the same as the pice of Gorruckpore and 44 to 52 exchanged for a Rupee.

From that period to the end of the 4th year of the present King's reign no pice were coined in the Benares Mint. In the 5th year Balgovind farmer of the mint, having purchased some European copper from a follower of Cossim Ally Khan's coined it into pieces of 10 maashas, and stamped them with the die of Gorruckpore. The number exchanged for a Rupee varied from 45 to 48.

The coinage of pice was again discontinued till the 17th year of Shah Aulum when Daoga Sund Metre obtained permission from Rajah Chyte Sing to reestablish it. The new pice were 10 mashas 3 ruttees in weight and pass current in the bazar at about 50 or 51 pr R.

In the 18th year Kashwan Malla brought a large quantity of copper from Calcutta and farmed the coinage of pice and the exclusive privilege of buying and selling copper in the city of Benares from the Raja for 5,000 rupees. The weight of the pice continued at 10 m 3 r and passed in the bazar or market at about 52 or 53 per rupee.

In the 19th and 20th year* the coinage was declared free and those who brought copper received pice in return after paying the customary duties. For one maund of Kodaleah copper Benares weight (84 Rs 6 As to the seer) the merchant received back from the mint 3,250 pice weighing 10 m 3 r after deducting all charges which amounted to about 7 r 12 a pr mnd.

In the 21st year a considerable revolution took place in the copper coinage. The Nabob Vizier issued orders to the officers of the Allahabad Mint to reduce the weight of the pice to 9 m 2 r. The merchants finding that their maund of copper yielded 3,650 pieces at Allahabad, whereas at Benares it produced only 3,250 carried all their copper to the former place. The coinage of pice at the Benares mint was in consequence at a stand, only 29 maund being coined during this year. Large quantities of the new Allahabad pice were brought down by the merchants to Benares. Raja Chyte Sing at first refused to authorize the currency but at length gave his con-

* In the margin in a later hand: AD 1779.

sent at the solicitation of some of his dependents, who were to share the profits with the merchants. The Allahabad pice of 9 m 3 r were accordingly declared current and ordered to be received in payment in common with the old pice of 10 mashas 3 ruttees. It is here necessary to mention that under the native government it is customary to proclaim the value of all new money issued from the mint, and it is deemed an high offence to demand a batta on a coin stamped with the name of the Emperor. Hence the facility with which the farmers of the mint circulated their debased coin, the merchants not daring to refuse the receipt of it during the year of its currency. When Raja Chyte Sing therefore declared the Allahabad pice current at Benares in common with the old pice, the bankers unable to make any distinction between them, contrived to lower the value of pice altogether, in which they were assisted by the large importations from Allahabad.

In the 22nd year Raja Chyte Sing at the representation of his mint master, whose profits were diminished by the descendance of the copper coinage ordered pice to be coined of the same size and weight as the Alllahabad pice, which contributed greatly to overstock the circulation.

In the 23rd and 24th year after the expulsion of Chyte Sing, the same weight of 9 m 2 r was continued and the price of pice continued to fall till the late famine in the 25th year when they sold at 13 [*sic*] for a rupee. At about this time Mr. Hastings arrived at Benares. The poor complained that the cheapness of pice added to the dearness of grain rendered them unable to subsist on the wages they received for their labour. The Collector of Customs at Benares represented that a considerable part of the duties were paid in pice and that he lost near 50 per cent in exchanging them for rupees. Mr. Fowke was in consequence directed to inquire into the state of the copper coinage, but it does not appear that either in this or the following year any measures were taken to complete the reform.

In the 27th year the late Resident Mr. Grant forbid the currency of the old pice of 9 m 2 r and ordered that no pice should be issued from the mint under 10 mashas 3 ruttees, and that Goruckpoor pice weighing from 10 mashas to 10 m 3 r and Benares pice of

10 mashas 3 ruttees should pass at the same value. The prices immediately rose to 58 per rupee.

In the 28th year when it was supposed that a sufficiency of the new pice had been coined for the circulation of the city, the Goorackpore pice were also forbidden, and only the new Benares pice stamped with a Tirshool or Trident and weighing from 10 mashas to 10 m 3 r and the Goruckpore pice restamped and not under 10 mashas were declared current. From the commencement of this year to the present time the price of the pice has fluctuated between 56 and 58 per rupee. These regulations however have not yet extended to the interior parts of the country where the old pice of different weight are still current.

Weight, Quantity, &ca Pice Coined in the Benares Mint

TABLE R.3.1: COPPER COINS, ISSUED FROM THE BENARES MINT, 1733-86

		Weights		*Quantities coined*	*Variation of the bazar price per rupee*	
		mashas	*ruttee*		*from*	*to*
Mahomud Shah	From 15th to 21st			[None]	44	52
	22nd	10	3	[over 100 maunds]	44	52
	23rd to 30th			[None]	44	52
Ahmud Shah	1st year			[None]		56
	2nd			[None]		52
	3rd			[None]	52	50
	4th			[None]	50	48
	5th			[None]	50	45
	6th			[None]	46	47
Aulum Gheer	1st year			[None]	47	48
	2nd			[None]	49	47

	3rd			[None]	47	46
	4th			[None]	48	46
	5th			[None]	47	44
	6th			[None]	44	43
Shah Aulum	1st year			[None]	42	43
	2nd			[None]	42	41
	3rd			[None]	44	42
	4th			[None]	46	44
	5th	10		340,000	45	48
	6th			[None]	48	46
	7th			[None]	46	47
	8th			[None]	48	47
	9th			[None]		48
	10th			[None]		48
	11th			[None]		52
	12th			[None]	53	52
	13th			[None]	52	51
	14th			[None]	50	47
	15th			[None]	40	47
	16th			[None]	48	46
	17th	10	3	2,307,500	50	51
	18th	10	3	11,421,250	52	53
	19th	10	3	4,858,000	54	55
	20th	10	3	3,139,500	57	58
	21st	9	2	[29 maund] 44,250	56	57
	22nd	9	2	2,854,300		61
	23rd	9	2	1,865,150	59	60
	24th			[None]	67	68
	25th	9	2	2,737,500	93	77
	26th	9	2	22,056,950	73	69
	27th	9	3	5,690,750	62	58
	28th	9	3	384,800	58	56

At present the coinage of pice is at a stand. The Kodaleah copper from which they are made now sells for about 56 rupees per maund and the market price of pice is 58 per rupee so that the dealers in copper would sustain considerable loss by sending it to the mint.

TABLE R.3.2: PRICE OF COPPER, BENARES 1787

Price of maund of copper Rs. 84:6 to the seer at Benares	56:00	
Duties to the coinage, loss in smelting, &ca	7:14	
		63:14:0
For one maund of copper the mint returns 3,250 pice of 10 m 3 ruttees each which at 58 pr rupee (the present current value) is		56:00:6
Loss		7:13:6

Should the price of copper fall, or the value of pice rise, the merchants will again bring their copper to the mint. This fluctuation however in the copper coin is a constant source of oppression to the poorer part of the community. In order to explain this it is necessary to mention that the rupee is considered as the measure of value of all other metals, and articles of merchandise. When grain therefore sells for 50 seers per rupee, and pice pass current in the market at 50 for a rupee, the labourer who receives four pice per day, can purchase two seer of grain with the produce of his day's works, but if pice should fall to 75 per rupee, he can only procure half that quantity. During the late famine in the year 1783 grain rose to 15 seer for a rupee and pice (owing to the deficiency in the weight and the circulation being overstocked) fell to 93, so that the calamities of the famine were much increased by the diminuation of the value of the copper coin.

From the above account your Lordship will perceive that the pice instead of being a medium of commerce are more variable in their value than the articles they are made use of to purchase. The shroffs who trade in the coin are the only gainers. Government itself often sustains a considerable loss on such part of its revenues as are collected in pice, but the poor on whose care and happiness the prosperity of the country must depend, are the great and constant sufferers.

In order to remedy these evils I beg leave to submit the following regulations to your Lordship's consideration:

1st That one species of copper coin be declared current throughout the Company's Dominions.

Remark: The regulations made in the pice by Mr. Grant have extended no further than the city of Benares, Gazipoor and Chunar where the new Tirsholee pice of 10 mashas to 10 mashas 3 ruttees have been introduced. In the interior parts of the country pice of every kind are current and vary in their value as much as any other article of trade.

2nd That the weight and impression be the same.

Remark: Any difference in the weight or impression affords the bankers the opportunity of making a distinction and charging batta the same as on rupees.

3rd That the pice be restored to their proper weight of 10 mashas

Remark: When the pice are restored to their proper weight, there will be no difficulty in establishing their currency. The reluctance with which the people have received the Calcutta pice, I should conceive has arisen from their great deficiency in weight. The Calcutta pice weigh about 6¼ mashas. Every person having a bill on government, payable within the provinces, is obliged to receive one rupee in pice at 64 per rupee, the rate at which they are ordered to be issued from the treasury and to pass current in the market. The Benares pice weigh from 10 mashas to 10 mashas 3 ruttees and at present pass current in the bazaar at 55 per rupee. The Benares rupee is also intrinsically 3-4 per cent less in value than that of Calcutta, and copper at Calcutta must always be much cheaper than at Benares. It would appear therefore that number of pice issued from the treasuries in the provinces for a rupee are not intrinsically worth above 9 annas. Should it therefore be determined to reform the copper coinage and make one species current throughout the Company's dominions, the district of Benares included, I should conceive it would be more expedient to raise the Calcutta pice to their proper standard instead of lowering those of Benares to the Calcutta weight. It also appears to me that the Company's imports of copper will be much affected by this diminuation of the weight of the coin. If Government order that a pice containing 6½ mashas of copper shall pass for the same value as those which formerly contained 10 mashas, the demand for copper to supply the annual circulation will diminish in proportion. The quantity of pice coined in the 26th year in the Benares mint alone will shew that this demand is by no means inconsiderable. In fixing therefore the weight and number of the reformed copper coin which should exchange for a rupee due regard should be had to the average price of copper in order that the intrinsic and nominal value of the quantity so exchanged may not exceed the amount of the duties on the coinage and the loss in melting. The division of tuckas, (two pice), single pice, half pice and quarter pice or chehdams (six dams) established at the late coinage in Calcutta appears to me well calculated for the purpose of commerce, the two latter tho' not at present current in the markets will be received without reluctance when containing the proper quantity of copper. The Calcutta die should be sent to the mint of Moorshedabad, Patna, and Benares and the whole stamp be contained upon the surfaces of the coin in order to prevent it to it's being clipped or defaced.

4th That persons bringing old copper coin to the mint shall receive back an equal weight of the new coin without any duty or fee whatever.

Remark: This appears to be the only method of calling in the old coin without subjecting the proprietors to a loss. The holders of the light Calcutta pice bearing the stamp of the 22nd year of the reign will indeed suffer considerably but as these pice were issued under the sanction of Government and the public have been made to receive them from the treasury at an over value, your Lordship will judge how far it is incumbent on Government to take the loss for itself. A banker who has any quantity of old coin in his possession will never bring it to the mint unless he can get as much as it will fetch on the market. Government therefore in order to get in the old pice must subject itself to the expense of the recoinage. This expense cannot be very considerable in the copper coin as the loss in melting and the wages of the workmen will be amply paid by the duties on the coinage of bar copper which I should recommend to be continued. In order to circulate the new coin with greater facility a quantity of pice should be sent to every collector equal to the demand of his district. These should be paid away or sold at the established number for the new rupee. Persons bringing old copper coins should receive back an equal weight of the new pice, and the holders of the old Calcutta pice should receive the difference between the weight of the 64 pice at present issued from the treasuries and the weight of the new pice which shall be declared current for a rupee or for every 64 pice one rupee should be delivered. The same precautions which I have recommended for enforcing the currency of the silver coin will be equally necessary for the new pice. All payment in the old pice should be declared illegal and the judges of the Adawluts and collectors should be instructed to punish such shroffs who should buy or sell pice at a different rate from that established by Government.

Source: NAI, Finance, Mint Committee Proceedings 1792, 26 June 1792, pp. 136-58.

4

Letter from F. Mure, Sub Treasurer, Reporting an Undue Accumulation of Copper Coin in the Treasury, and Suggesting Measures for Preventing a Still Further Accumulation, Calcutta, 13 May 1788

[*Proposal for a more restrictive cap on the proportion of copper coins allowed in the paying out of bills of exchange because of an undue accumulation of copper coin in the treasury.*

See also Part II: Records, Nos. 7 and 29.]

F. Mure, Sub Treasurer, to the Governor General in Council, Treasury Office, 13 May 1788.

My Lord,

Doubts having arisen respecting the interpretation of Your Lordship's orders, that all bills of exchange drawn in the remittance of the revenues should be paid one moiety in silver and the other half in the usual currency of Calcutta, and as the shroffs upon such occasions are ever quick sighted to their own interest and are glad to make any evasion, I request your Lordship's permission to make it publick in the *Calcutta Gazette* that no proportion of copper will in future be received in the moiety of silver. I beg leave to submit it to your Lordship's consideration whether such an advertisement is not the more necessary at this time, as there is between seven and eight thousand rupees of copper in the treasury.

Source: NAI, Home Department, Public Original Consultation, 16 May 1788, No. 8.

5

Correspondence of the Board of Trade on a Plan to Fix a Certain Number of Pons of Cowries per Rupee for Paying to the Weavers, 17 June, 24 July and 10 August 1792

[*For its exports of Indian textiles the EIC used a putting out system, providing the cotton cloth weavers with advances and collecting their products according to piece rates. In several parts of its Indian settlements it established factories or residences where the products were collected by the "commercial resident" to be sent to the shipping ports. Lakhipur in Bengal was one of those factories, subdivided into ten "aurungs", each organizing and overseeing the production process in a number of villages. The weaving wages in the contracts were expressed in rupees, but for payments in daily life the weavers needed cowries, of which the exchange rates to the rupee varied. Deteriorating exchange rates caused serious problems for them and consequently a demand for higher wages.*

See Ch. 3d and 4c of the Introduction, Part II: Records, No. 6 and Part I: Studies, No. 7.]

Proceedings 21 July 1792

S.L. Chauvet, Sub Secretary to the Government in the Public Department to the Committee for Superintending the Mints, 4 July 1792.

Gentlemen,

I am inclined to forward you my extracts of a letter from the Board of Trade and of that from the commercial resident at Luckipore to which the former relates and to refer the subject of them to your consideration

Extract of a letter from the Board of Trade, dated 29 June 1792.

1st We transmit for the information of your Lordship in Council extract of a letter dated the 17th inst from the Resident at Luckipore shewing losses and embarrassements which exist in the circles of his business from the sicca rupees appearing not to be current at its value proportioned to the Dus Massa.

2nd We do not take upon ourselves to recommend the Residents suggestion for a regulation fixing a certain number of pons of cowries for the actual exchange of sicca rupees into cowries. We do not conceive that such a measure could be enforced since cowries are in fact no other than merchandise and are constantly fluctuating in value here, and we believe in every part of the country where they are exchanged for silver.

3rd We have required the resident to state the amount of the loss incurred in May ere we form any opinion on the question in the 2nd paragraph of his letter.

Extract of a Letter from the Resident Luckipore to the Board of Trade, dated 17 June 1792.

Para 2

There has arisen a loss in issuing the sicca rupees to the weavers in advances in the month of May which I have not included in the Journal Parcel waiting your orders whether this loss is to be carried to the head of Revenue Department as heretofore, or of charges to be put on the cloths. This loss is less than was usually sustained in exchanging the siccas at Dacca for Duss Massa Rupees; and until a specific table of the value of the component parts of a rupee shall be established the fluctuation in the bazaar will generally create loss. I have been obliged to issue the Siccas at ½ an anna better than Duss Massa, which is less by 1½ pun than the former rate of batta between siccas and Duss Massa.

Para 3

At Luckipoor the weavers are able to dispose of the sicca rupees at the rate they were issued in May, but at Colinda the new Siccas you sent me are of no greater value in the bazaar than Duss Massa rupees; and those of 16 and 11 Sun are subject to a batta of 2½ pun. That is, the poora Duss Massa Rupee and new siccas are exchanged at 60 puns, the old siccas at 68. The weavers sustained last month this loss, and they object to receive advances at the rate issued in May of ½ an anna or 3½ per cent.*

Para 4

If the number of pons to be given for a sicca rupee was fixed and this regulation enforced, there would be some certainty, but at present the bazaar podars manage to depreciate the value of the sicca rupee, and it cannot be expected the weavers will receive their advances at a greater value than they pass for. The orders of Council of the 26th August 1791 do not apply to the payments in the *mofussil*. My business being confined to poor people and the rupees issued require being exchanged into pons couries &ca for purchasing rice, cotton &ca.

Para 5

These transactions of the weavers are carried on by the bazaar or cutcha amount, consisting of couries gundas, pons, and cawns. These have a definite and fixed value, but the number of pons composing a rupee altho' in the account valued at pons 64 per Duss Massa, yet it frequently indeed generally happens that the money changers only give 58, 60, 62 &ca. This fluctuation creates much trouble and loss to the weavers. And to fix for the intended currency (i.e. Sa Rs) a specific and unalterable quantity of each description, agreeable to their respective values would benefit the country and very materially care the inhabitants.

* Editor's Note. As ½ anna is 1/32nd part of a rupee this way of expressing ratios, common at the time in India, equals 3.5 per cent. For the same procedure see also Record 6.

Para 6

The cause of the sicca rupees having become so current in the Chittagong Province arises from their having been introduced at a period when the relative value of the Sicca and Duss Massa specie was established by Government, and the scarcity of the Duss Massa specie now in circulation is owing to the remittance made by the collector to the mint masters at Dacca, and there being no merchants that specifics [*sic*] has not been introduced. It is even difficult to obtain Duss Massa Rupees at present in Chittagong.

The very reverse is the situation of these Aurungs. There is no established batta, few paid into the collections and a large quantity imported by the private traders and if after the Poonea is held, the siccas do not rise in values, the cloths must necessarily be increased in price.

Proceedings 20 September 1792

*H.J. Scott, Resident Collinda Aurung to Board of Trade, Putta Haut Factory, 24 July 1792**

[...] I have inspected the books of the podars of the Luckipore market for several years past and do not find the entry of a sicca rupee until the month of Bysaa last. They have always been refused in the currency, and the few that made their way into these districts I am informed were issued either as Duss Massas and sometimes even at a lower rate.

The Board will observe that the present rate of exchange in the bazaar is equal to that at which the sicca have been issued by the factory, i.e. 2 pons better than Duss Massas. But the weavers are still discontented, and it is with great difficulty I can get them to receive them at this loss to the Company. I apprehend the subject of their complaint originates more properly elsewhere.

I have in a former letter mentioned that the sudder accounts are kept in sicca rupees. The engagements between the riots and

* Editor's Note. The beginning of the text is missing because pp. 549-51 of this volume have not been preserved.

their *talookdars* are made in Duss Massas. When this deficiency in the accounts was first introduced, a specific batta was established at the sudder for the receipt of the coins collected in the *mofussul*. At present this is done away, and the coin paid into the collector's treasury, if not siccas, is taken at the bazaar rate at Comilla. From the nature of the *kistbundee*, revenue is required when there is little or no produce in this country. Consequently the zemindars are obliged to borrow for the purpose of fulfilling their engagements, and become dependent on the many lenders. The different species of rupees collected in the *mofussul* pass of course to them and they are taken, perhaps to the orders of Government, at the bazaar rate. Duss Massas are, I understand, at from 6 to 7 per cent, and arcots from 8 to 9 worse than siccas in the Tipperah bazaar. Consequently, at present when the sum of sicca rupees introduced by this factory (for none of the gentlemen about Luckipore have imported them) not being sufficient to answer the call of the Revenue Department, the Duss Massa rupees of nearly equal value to the sicca rupees in the *mofussul*, are received at the sudder at a very material loss to the riots. The *zamindars* who subject themselves to the intervention of podars, and depend on them for regular supplies to discharge the demands of Government, must conform to their wishes, and what appears most advantageous to the podars is the rule to the *zamindars* whilst this influence exists, and it will until the arcots and Duss Massa have been all called in, the sicca rupee will not attain its true value in the *mofussul*. Duss Massas and arcots being received at the above rates by the podars are not, I believe, paid into the collector's treasury. That would defeat their end, but are returned to the country, and sold or exchanged to an advantage of 3, 4 & 5 per cent. But should the podars be even obliged to dispose of the arcots or Duss Massa, at Tipperah they are purchased for the purpose of commerce and returned to the market to the same advantage. [...]

At present there is no coin but rupees in these aurungs, and the number of cowries to be received in exchange depends on the money changers. It was owing to their opposition (which was very natural as they were so materially concerned in the event establishment) that I failed in making the sicca rupees current, and even reduced me to the necessity at issuing them at a loss on the former established relative value, or to give up the investment. I am convinced within myself that, if a copper coinage was to be established and the director directed to promote its circulation, the opposition it might at first meet with, would be very soon overcome.

The cause of the failure heretofore made for its establishment, did not arise from the objection of the inhabitants to the coin, but to its valuation. Government issued it at an advance I believe, upwards of 25 per cent on the selling price of copper in Calcutta. Even at its extention it passed in the Calcutta bazaar at a considerable excess on the price of copper.

Had the pice been issued at an advance of 10 per cent on the cost of the copper in England, the pice would I really believe not only have obtained a general currency but bore a premium. The ease and convenience to the country is not the only advantage. It would ensure a constant sale at a fixed price for a large quantity of the Company's imported copper. The copper, I imagine, does no[w] cost the Company 40 shs per maund in England or 32 per cent. […]

The constant complaints on the subject of loss, and the refusal of many weavers to labour for the Company whilst their advances are made in sicca rupees, give me very great disquietude, on account my inability to gratify your wishes to the extent of the order of investment. And I very much doubt whether I shall be able to do more than furnish the additional lac of rupees mentioned in my letter of the 17th as I apprehend a great deficiency of cloth this month from the foregoing causes.

The Board of Trade to Earl Cornwallis Governor-General in Council, Fort William, 10 August 1792

My Lord,

1st Having received a letter of the Resident at Luckeypore containing much information regarding the confused state of the coinage in the districts where his business lies, we think it proper to lay before your Lordship the enclosed copy thereof, and are sorry to observe that these circumstances in the coinage are likely to be attended with the effect of a defalcation in the investment to the amount of current rupees 202,091.

2nd The exchange of the sicca rupees for Arcots, which the Resident formerly suggested for removing his difficulties was (as we reported to your Lordship under date the 7th March) disallowed by us.

3rd His proposition respecting a copper currency we have not given any attention to, the subject not being under consideration.

4th The cloths of his aurungs being greatly in demand in Europe, we are exceedingly unwilling to relinquish any part of his allotment and have therefore again urged him to use his endeavours for investing the whole amount though at some loss upon the sicca rupee.

Source: NAI, Finance, Mint Committee Proceedings, 21 July 1792, pp. 245-51; idem 20 September 1792, pp. 552-63.

6

Replies to Questions from the Board of Revenue of 12 June 1787 Regarding the Circulation of Metal Currency in the Different Collectorates of Bengal and Bihar, 10 July 1787 to 24 July 1792

[*On the initiative of their superiors in London (General Letter Court of Directors 22 December 1786, para 22) the Board of Revenue at Fort William (Calcutta) started an enquiry in all collectorates about the actual circulation of currency and to what extent is was sufficient (12 June and 12 October 1787). The collectors very inventively tap into different sources of information, like of their own tax records, zamindars and bankers or shroffs. The Mint Committee, established in 1792, used this information to determine its course.*

As a rule, mainly extracts on the copper and cowrie circulation have been transcribed here. The replies by the collectors of Moradbaug, Kishenagur / Nuddea and Islamabad only pertain to silver coins; the same goes for Purnea 1787 (though adding: 'There are no copper coins current in this District'). For the reply of the Collector of Lakhipur / Luckeypore see the previous Part II: Records, No. 5.

See Ch. 3d and 4a of the Introduction, and Part II: Records, Nos. 5 and 8.]

J. Sherburne, Coll[ecto]r to John Shore, President & Members of the Board of Revenue, Beerbhoom, 11 February 1788

Gentlemen,

I have to reply to your letter of the 12th October, desiring me to inform you of the quantity of silver I estimate in circulation in the districts under my charge, the proportion of each specie whether I apprehend any inconveniency arises from the variety of coins or there is any want of specie.

Since the receipt of these your commands I have revolved the subject frequently in my mind without being able to find any date from which any conclusive deductions may be made or the points in question satisfactorily established.

The first idea I have of the subject is that the capital in specie must hold some certain proportion with the raw and manufactured produce to be circulated by means of it.

2nd That this capital must be greater or less in proportion to the number of times it can be issued and received in the course of a year. I estimate the raw and manufactured produce of Beerbhoom in the following manner:

TABLE R.6.1: CALCULATION OF THE DEMAND FOR SILVER COINS, BEERBHOOM, 1788

Present jumma	564,043	
Bazee Zemin and Chakran establishment 258,519 beega at 1 Rs	258,519	
		822,562
Deduct chakran included in the jumma		3,023
Gross revenue		819,539
Considering the province easy as [...] and the estimate of this revenue arising to the proprietors of bazee zeemin moderate, I suppose the sum of the public and private revenues to be ¼ of the gross produce. This will consequently amount to	3,278,156	
Allowing the inhabitants to consume 2/3 of this produce	2,185,437	

(*Contd.*)

There will remain for trade & exportation	1,092,719
Manufactured produce in white goods, raw silk, shell lack, cutch, iron &ca	700,000
	1,792,719
A trading capital as it is advanced [in the] months before any returns are made I imagine cannot in this country be issued and received more than twice a year. To circulate this raw and manufactured produce it will consequently require one half the amount in specie or	896,359
From this is to be deducted the imports in salt, species battle[mit?] and the internal consumption of the manufactured produce which I think cannot be estimated at less than the broken numbers	96,359
Estimated specie Rs. (about the amount of the gross revenue)	800,000

Judging from the coins I have received in the collections I estimate the proportions may be as follows:

TABLE R.6.2: PROPORTIONS OF DIFFERENT KINDS OF RUPEES, NEEDED FOR BEERBHOOM, 1788.

	annas
Siccas	7
Sonauts	7
Arcot & Dookey	2
	16

I understand the coins of this country are very little if any additional value on account of the st[ate]. If so, I apprehend no inconveniency can arise from a[bout a] quarter or less variety and as it seems to be admitted[ly] an inherent principle of commerce to find its own level, any arbitrary regulations in this point might possibly be attended with greater injury than benefit to it. certain it is that in this province the Sonaut Rupee is more in demand for the purposes of trade than any other specie, and therefore bears something more than its intrinsic value, but that may be attributed to the force of local prejudice and to the *mofussil* revenue amounts being kept in this specie.*

I am by no means satisfied with the result of this mode of estimate as I feel an involuntary conviction that the imports must amount to a larger sum, which would reduce the capital in specie to less than I imagine to be, and the only apology I can make for my temerity in writing on a subject I so little understand, and which seems to require the greater depth of mercantile experience in deference and obedience to your orders.

I have not observed any deficiency of specie in circulation but no criterion m[ay] be formed from the present year as the fai[lure] of the crops in other parts has drawn the Byparries and Merchants hither from every quarter.

Robert Adair, Coll[ecto]r to John Shore, President & Members of the Board of Revenue, Boglpore, 22 December 1787

Account of the several species of silver and copper coinage current in Zeelahs Boglepore and Rajemahl [...].

Copper coins current in Zeelahs Boglepore and Rajemahl

TABLE R.6.3: TYPES OF COPPER COINS, CURRENT IN BOGLEPORE AND RAJMAHL, 1787

		Weight in mashas
No. 1	Old pysa of Maddoo Sahy in Gurrauckpore	18
No. 2	New faloos coined in Calcutta, value ½ anna	13
No. 3	New faloos coined in Calcutta, value ¼ anna	6½
No. 4	New pysa struck in Gorruckpore	10½

[...] There does not appear to be any want of specie in circulation in these districts.

* A similar statistical exercise for Bissenpore, amounting to Rs 534,359 in specie circulating has not been transcribed here.

D.H. Mc Dowall, Collector to President & Members of the Board of Revenue, Rungpore, 25 September, 23 October and 2 December 1787

Gentlemen,

In consequence of your letter of the 12th June '87 enclosing extract of a letter from the honble the Court of Directors requiring specimens of all the silver coins of Bengal, I have now the honor to transmit to you an account of the Narranny and French Arcot Rupees, the only coins peculiar to this district together with 3 specimens of each which I hope will prove satisfactory. [...] There is no copper coin in circulation in these districts.

G. Hatch, Collector to President & Members of the Board of Revenue, Dinajpore, 10 July and 29 December 1787

Gentlemen,

I have received your letter of the 12th of June accompanying copy of the 22th paragraph from the Honble Court of Directors and desiring I will transmit the informations and samples therein required, what specimens of every specie of silver and copper coinage current in Bengal, with a concise history of each, particularly specifying where coined, by whom, weight, fineness, real and nominal values, quantity supposed to be coined annually, and as far as ascertainable, what quantity are supposed to be in circulation, and how far such quantities are proportioned to the general wants.

The rupees (of which samples now accompanying) are the currency of this district and are denominated Sonauts, Azeemabaddee or Patnye and French. The Sonaut Rupee falls in its value and looses its original name of Sicca after a certain number of years have elapsed and which the title of Sonaut implies. This rupee was the coinage of Moorshedabad.

The Azeemabadi or Patnye Rupee is of the same weight and fineness with the Sicca, but of less value. This rupee bears on the face of it the title under which it circulates, and is of the coinage of Azeemabad or Patna.

The French rupee is 2½ ruttee less in weight than the Sicca or Azeemabadi but as far as I can judge is somewhat superior to them in fineness and is of foreign import.

They all vary and lose alike in current value from deficiency in weight and defect in shape, appearance and alloy in proportion to the degree of the deficiency or the defects or of both. The first point is ascertainable upon a fixed principle. The latter is enveloped in mistery and only to be revealed by the interpunction of shroffs, all of whom differ in the rate to be paid for the loss upon the [...] according to the judgements they form upon it and their decision is arbitrary and final.

The annual received from the district is the only standard by which any conclusion with respect to the quantity of each specie in circulation can be drawn. The proportion paid to the remainder as revenue is nearly 2/3rd sonaut and of the remaining 1/3rd 3/4th French & 1/4th Azeemabaddee. In forming of a more accurate judgement of the actual quantity of the three species in circulation throughout the district allowance must be made for the exchange or shroffage carried on in the *mofussil*. The quantities of each specie are apparently proportioned to answer every emergency. The samples are packed in three parcels containing 10 rupees of each assortment.

A. Montgomerie, Collector to John Shore, President & Members of the Board of Revenue, Chuprah, 28 February and 16 May 1788.

Gentlemen,

[...]

An Account of the different Sonauts current in the districts of Sircar Sarun & Sircar [Chhaprah].

TABLE R.6.4: RUPEE CIRCULATION, SARUN AND CHHAPRAH, 1788

Denominations	*Where*	*By whom*	*Quantity in circulation*	*How far proportioned to the general wants*
Mohomed Shahy sonaut from 1 to 31 sun & Allum Giery sonaut 4 sun	Patna	The nawob of the Subah Behar	2½ lacks	The proper quantity to answer the market ought to be five lacks
Allum Shahy sonaut 1, 2, 3, 4, 6 & 10 sun	Do	Do	2 lacks	The same as above
Do do 5 sun	Do	Do	1½ lacks	This kind of rupees is not in demand
Do do 7 & 8 sun	Do	Do	3½ lacks	This amount is nearly adequate to the demands only deficient about 1/6th
Do do 9 sun	Do	Do	2 lacks	This amount does not near answer the market, six lack is estimated to be the amount necessary to supply the general wants
Allum Gury sonaut 1, 2, 3, 5 & 6 sun	Do	Do	3 lacks	No very great deficiency is observed in this sort of rupees
Goruckpoory pice; 10¾ masha equal to the best sort of copper; real value at present 4: 1½; nominal value 5	Goruck-pore	The nawob of Oude	About 20 lacks	This quantity sufficiently answers the demand
Nepauly; 10 masha; real value at present 4¼; nominal value 4¾	Nepaul	The Rajah of Nepaul	About 12 lacks	Ditto

M. Day, Coll[ecto]r to John Shore, President & Members of the Board of Revenue, Dacca, 22 November 1787

Gentlemen,

[…] There are no copper coins in circulation in this division. […] With respect to the amount specie in circulation with the quantity of each kind it is impossible for the reasons already assigned to mention with any degree of certainty. The trade of this district including every article of its commerce, I estimate and believe to be near one crore of rupees, allowing therefore that each article of its revenue will admit of two returns in the course of 12 months and the whole sum respectively engaged for to be advanced, a trade to that extent may be conducted by a currency of 50 lacks. But as the cloth trade which I estimate on an average to be from thirty to 40 lacks admit but of one return to the merchant in the above period and the whole amount engaged for being necessary towards the completion of investment I conclude the sum in general circulation through the year to be from 60 to 70 lacks of rupees. It has already been observed that the general currency of this province both in commercial and revenue matters is the Arcot specie. The currency of the Sicca specie is solely confined to the town, and in amount does not exceed 5 lacks. The balance whatever the circulation from the above remarks may be concluded to exist is entirely the Arcot currency.

Thomas Law Coll[ecto]r to John Shore, President & Members of the Board of Revenue, Gya, 6 August 1787 and 5 May 1788

Gentlemen,

[…] The following is a statement of the specie which accompany this in triplicate

TABLE R.6.5: COIN CIRCULATION, GYA, 1787-8

No.	*Coins*	*Value*	*Explanation*
1	Pice	70 per Sa Rupees	The pice fluctuate in value so much that they cannot scarce be termed a coin. Petty shroffs trade in them as any other article. The Company circulated a few from Mr. Prinseps Mint but they are now reduced to bullion. Since my arrival they have directed from 80 per Sa Rs to 60
2	Pice	Double the value of No. 1	
3	Sonats	105:4 per Sicca	These are so numerous and various that the bankers tired with repeated vexations and reciprocal extortions for batta &ca frequently interchange them in sealed bags without count or examination
4	11 Sun	Sicca	The stamp on some being abraded by friction or disfigured by 'assay marks' suffer an arbitrage batta by the bankers to equalize them with standard under the name of 'Chupote' effaced, 'Mullut' worn, 'Suranky' indented
5	12 Sun	Sicca	
			The Calcutta 19 Sun have been latterly introduced which I attribute to a balance of trade in favour of Behar, and it may be proper here to observe that as gold is not taken in payment at the Company's Provincial Treasuries, the Mohrs will never be thrown into extensive circulation

The old coins must gradually diminish by being fuzed into ornaments, paltes &ca and it were easy and beneficient to establish one currency, I will not however presume to intrude beyond my immediate Province. [...]

The quantity of species in Behar may amount to fifty lacks or about one year's revenue, for if twenty lack of rupees or indeed half that sum was required at once, not all the bankers could raise it. The revenue being receivable every month and immediately [reflux]ing for saltpeter, opium, cloth and the army prevents a stagnation. The balance of trade has lately introduced the Calcutta 19 Sun which supplies the place of the old coin gradually diminishing by fusion and abrasion.

If the distresses of Madras had not required exports of grain from Bahar, and foreign ships had not taken cloth during the war, Government must have received its revenue in kind for the remittances to Calcutta in specie by the Patna Council had exhausted the Province by that period.

T. Brooke, Acting Collector, Burdwan to John Shore, President & Members of the Board of Revenue, Burdwan, 31 May 1788

Sir and Gentlemen,

[...] Respecting the copper coin there is scarce. Any in circulation in this district, excepting a very few of the new Calcutta pice.

Robert Lindsay and J. Welles to John Shore, President & Members of the Board of Revenue, Sylhet, 30 October 1787

Gentlemen,

In reply to your letter of the 12th instant desiring the necessary information respecting the species of rupees in circulation permit me to inform me there are not 500 rupees of any kind in circulation throughout the district. The few that make their appearance are bad Arcot sold in the bazaar from 4 cawns 8 puns to 5 cawns according to the number in the market. Cowries are the only currency and from the extreme poverty of the district and inhabitants in general they are more useful for the purposes of traffick and to purchase the produce of the lands from the ryot than silver.

J. Welles to John Shore, President & Members of the Board of Revenue, Sylhet, 9 May 1788

Gentlemen,

[...] There is not above 6[00] or 700 rupees to be found in Sylhet and those bad Arcots and that no copper coinage of any species passes in the district. The revenues are paid in cowries and all mercantile transactions are carried on through the same currency.

Robert Bathurst, Coll[ecto]r to John Shore, President & Members of the Board of Revenue, Tirhoot, 5 and 12 May 1788

Gentlemen,

[...] The rupees circulating in this collectorship are sicca of the Moorshedabad and Calcutta mints and sonat of the Patna mint. Other species may occasionally be introduced into the country by traders in exchange for the productions of it, but not being admitted in revenue transactions they are passed away at a loss (proportionate to the necessities or to the ignorance of the possessor), which induces the mahajans and shroffs to take them up for the purpose of sending them to places where their currency is established.

The quantity of sonat rupees in circulation may be estimated at 450,000 to 500,000 while the siccas will not exceed 100,000. The sonat rupees have by far the most established currency in commercial and revenue transactions. Indeed in most districts under my charge the collections are made in sonat rupees, and in these districts it does not appear that any other specie circulates. In others when the collections are made in sicca rupees, the specie has some circulation, for altho the sonats are here in use for most purposes, yet the Cabooleats being for sicca, the Beopanies or Carreers find their account in bringing rupees of that denomination to purchase grain and other articles. But the coin so introduced does not remain in the country. It is appropriated to the payment of the revenues and is thus brought in and carried away every harvest, neither is the quantity so brought sufficient for the purpose, for the *malguzars* generally pay apart in sonaut rupees upon which the aumils are accustomed to take batta of 1 anna or more per rupee.

Enclosed are statements of the established rates of batta in Tirhoot &ca. These rates are not liable to vary unless when the merchant finds an opportunity to impose upon the inexperience of the party. Such variations cannot be ascertained & if they could it would be needless to specify them since they depend solely on the avidity and the ignorance of the party.

From what has been said it will sufficiently appear that no inconveniences are felt here from the variety of species now existing, except the profits which the shroff may have the opportunity of making, and which are neither frequent, nor considerable.

I have only to add that I have no reason to suspect any want of coin for the circulation of this district.

Statement of the rates of batta established by the merchants of Tirhoot &ca on the receipt of Moorshedabad sicca rupees

TABLE R.6.6: EXCHANGE RATES MOORSHEDABAD SICCA RUPEES, TIRHOOT, 1788

	As	*G*	*Cs*
11, 12 & 15 sun p rupee		10	
Phoolshikest (defaced)		1	½

Statement of the several rates of batta established by the merchants of Tirhoot &ca on the receipt of Azeemabad Hursunna rupees

TABLE R.6.7: EXCHANGE RATES AZEEMABAD HURSUNNA RUPEES, TIRHOOT, 1788

	As	*G*	*Cs*
Mullet a little defaced per rupee		5	
Chuppott more defaced		10	
Selputt quite defaced	1		
Sooraka a hole in the side		10	
Googedar a hole in the edge		10	
Toota cracked		10	
Ghyr Saul private coinage	2		
Furruckhseerees (Furrockseers per Govt Rs)		15	
Sunchar Furrakee not quite round		2	2

Rob[er]t Bathurst, Coll[ecto]r to John Shore, President & Members of the Board of Revenue, Tirhoot, 13 May 1792

Gentlemen,

I have the honor to receive your letter of the 12th June 1787 covering extract of the general letter from the Honble the Court of Directors dated 22nd December [17]86 and directing me to procure and transmit the information and samples therein required.

I have now the pleasure to transmit specimens of the different species of silver and copper coinage current in the districts under my charge, viz.

No. 1 Twelve sicca rupees
No. 2 Twelve Hursunna rupees
No. 3 Twelve Gorackpore pice
No. 4 Twelve Nypal pice.

The sicca rupees are of the mints of Moorshedabad and Calcutta of 19, 15, 12 & 11 suns. The circulation of which in this collectorship is estimated by intelligent persons at one hundred thousand.

This conjecture (as well as those I shall have occasion to offer concerning the other species in circulation) is undoubtedly vague, but no method has occurred of ascertaining the quantity with any degree of precision. Upon considering however a variety of facts relative to this subject, I have been led to concur in the estimates what have been furnished me. Such estimates are indeed always vague, but are particularly difficult in a district which has a constant and easy interchange on an extensive and open boundary. As the particulars relating to the sicca rupees will from other quarters be furnished more fully and more accurately than they possibly could be from hence, I have thought it superfluous to attempt to offer any information to the Board upon this head.

The Hursunna or sonaut rupees were coined at the mint of Patna under the authority of the then Nazims. None have been coined for many years and much of what is in circulation is of very distant dates. I have been unable to procure any correct information of the rules of the Patna mint, but I have understood that the Patna rupees ought to have been coined of the weight of 10 ½ mashas and of 49 parts in 50 fine, but it may be doubted whether they were ever coined of the value of which they purported to be, and are certainly now much worn by length of time, as well as debased by accidents or knavery. Conceiving that is the intention of the Board to cause an assay to be made to ascertain the weight, fineness and intrinsic value, concerning which it has not been in my power to obtain satisfactory information, I have only to add that the nominal value of sonat rupees is 5¼ per cent worse than sicca rupees, and that the quantity in circulation may be estimated at four hundred and fifty thousand.

The Gorackpore pice were coined at Gorackpore and Abeed by the authority of the Nabob Vizier Munsoor Aly Khawn Sufder Jung. None have been coined since his time. They weigh 10½ mashas and are current in the southern pergunnahs of the collectorship, where they pass at 63 to 66 per rupee at a medium (but the variations are occasionally considerable). The quantity in circulation in this district may amount to the value of 20[000] to 25,000 rupees.

The Nypal pice are coined by the Raja of Nypal and are inscribed Sittaram. They are current in the northern pergunnahs of this collectorship and weigh 9 to 9½ mashas, and pass at 72 to 76 per rupee. Their value varies at times beyond those limits. The amount in circulation may be taken at 25[000] to 30,000 rupees. I have in vain attempted to learn what amount is annually coined, neither have I been able to procure any particulars about the place and origin of the coinage, but however they have obtained a currency, it is certain that they are not now introduced into the country in any quantity worth noticing.

It is to be observed that the variations in the nominal value of pice (above stated) follow those in the price of copper at Patna, which is the great mart of these districts. From an average of the prices which copper has borne at Patna for a number of years can alone be deduced the real value of these pieces, but I have not the opportunity to prepare such an average, for which reason I have omitted to attempt to state the real value of the Gorackpore and Nypal pice.

With respect to the amount of specie in circulation and the

relative quantity of silver and copper coinage, I have no reason for supposing that they are otherwise than well proportioned to the wants of the people.

William A. Brooke, Coll[ecto]r to John Shore,
President & Members of the Board of Revenue,
Shahabad, 5 May and 4 June 1788

Gentlemen

[…]

The batta between siccas and sonauts is so very fluctuating depending on a greater or less demand of the one or the other that I can only observe that the variation is from three to 5 per cent The amount of rupees in circulation I conceive to be about seven lacks, and of the pice to the amount of five thousand rupees. This sum I consider as too inconsiderable for this Division.

The variety of species is certainly productive for inconveniences such as impositions of shroffs and bankers on farmers and ryotts, as well as confusion in the adjustment of litigated accounts. These can never be removed till one general coin be established throughout the country.

Account of different coins in circulation at Shahabad, Cheynpore, Sassaram & Havely Rhotas.

TABLE R.6.8: COIN CIRCULATION, SHAHABAD, CHEYNPORE, SASSARAM, AND HAVELY RHOTAS, 1788

No.		*Number*	*Suns*	*Weight (massa: ruttee)*	*Loss on weight (m : r)*	*Net weight (m : r)*
1	Patna sicca	3	12	10:4		10:4
2		3	11	10:4		10:4
3	Patna sonaut	3	10	10:4	0:1	10:3
4		3	5	10:4	0:1½	10:2½
5		3	5	10:4	1:0	9:4
6	Benares coins	3	17	10:2	0:2	10:0
	Mr Prinsep's new pice			6:4		

Gooruckpoory pice	6:4
NB some pice one ruttee less in weight	
At Arrah 64 pice p rupee	

W. Wroughton, Coll[ecto]r to John Shore, President & Members of the Board of Revenue, Momunsing, 7 May 1788

Gentlemen,

[...] In treating of this subject I must of necessity repeat much of what I said in my address of the 28th August [1787] accompanying the specimens I transmitted of each species as the different sorts therein mentioned are the rupees in circulation throughout the Dacca province. The Selberris Mehals alone is annexed to the collectorship receiving and paying in the Mofussul sicca rupees. Their names are Cogmirries, Burrabazzoo, Allyah and Saknee and the different talooks that have been separated from them, the aggregate jumma of which amounts to SaRupees 146,241:4:13:1. I am told a few sicca rupees have been occasionally been introduced into Momensing, Alephsing and one or two mehals contiguous, but in that case they are retained for the revenues and only go as good arcots in commercial transactions.

The quantity of different species supposed to be in this district is particularized in the account enclosed in my letter above alluded to and from subsequent enquiries I have no cause to alter what is therein specified.

I mean not however that the whole 6,135,000 is in constant circulation. Much is hoarded up by people who chuse not to speculate and who are disinclined to lend out their money. These are the whole body of zamindars, talookdars &ca who would rather involve themselves in debt than break in upon their hoards. All that specie is lost to the country and is only restored in small quantities at births, marriages, and religious ceremonies. The splendor with which they are sometimes celebrated even by those who are known to be involved is only to be accounted for by the above circumstance.

The real quantity of arcot rupees in constant circulation is – not from the best information I can gain – supposed to exceed 20 or 24 lacks. The sicca rupees are almost totally confined to the town in which there cannot be less than 12 lacks employed entirely for the payment of the revenues of government in which specie they have been received for the last 22 years. These are again issued from the treasury for the purpose of the Company's advances, and as arcots alone are the currency of the Mofussil that specie must be obtained. These periods being well known to the shroffs the exchange rises accordingly and when an extraordinary demand has been made, it is a known fact arcots have been estimated at an equal value with siccas, while at other times there has subjected a difference of 16 per cent. This is what has occasioned so constant a loss to Government, has been so severely been felt by individuals and is so detrimental to trade. [...]

Agreeable to the rate of batta here specified all rupees are shroffed. They are then when required exchanged into siccas at the bazaar prices which vary as follows:

TABLE R.6.9: SEASONAL EXCHANGE RATES FOR RUPEES, MOMUNSING, 1788

	Rs	*As*	*G*	*C*
In the month of June at the [per] anna per cent	6	4		
July, August and September from 6:4 to	7			
October, November, December and January with little variation	10	8		
February and March from 7 per cent to	6			
April and May	5	12		

Source: NAI, Finance, Mint Committee Proceedings, 18 August 1792, pp. 404-47, 482-548.

7

The Reception of Copper Pice for Postage and Customs, Calcutta 31 August 1793, 18 April and 10 December 1794, Berhampore, October 1793, and Moorshedabad 21 October 1794

[*Small denominations had to be accepted to a certain limit by public offices under the EIC according to the Regulations of 1 September 1785, partially repealed on 23 August 1793, and 6 September 1793. Consequently, copper coins tended to accumulate at post offices and with collectors of customs. The exchange of copper into silver at market rates by the shroffs posed problems to the functionaries who refused to be made responsible for the inevitable losses in the process.*

See Ch. 4c of the Introduction and Part II: Records, Nos. 4, 15 and 29.]

Home Department Public Original Consultation 16 September 1793, No. 12

Letter from Charles William Blunt, Postmaster-General to the Governor-General in Council, 31 August, 1793

My Lord,

I have been honored with the receipt of your commands thro' your Sub Secretary under date the 23rd current, acquainting me that the regulation of the 1st September 1785 has been repealed and that it has been notified to the public in the Gazette, that copper pice were to be received at the General Post Office.

From the time the receipt of pice beyond one anna in the rupee took place a very small excess of pice has been received at the post office, but according to the present regulation the receipts in copper will be always large, probably wholly in pice. For as the amount payable on each letter or package, the postage of which is less than one sicca rupee is made payable in copper, it will only happen to trible letters (of which few come to the post office compared to single and double) that any silver can be demanded. To illustrate the above it is only necessary to remind the Board that a single letter from Benares (the highest postage) is only seven annas and a double letter only 14. And I hope the Board will pardon the liberty I take in remarking that if a person sends a number of letters to the office, altho' the postage of the whole should exceed a rupee, still as the postage of each letter will not amount to that sum, it will be optional in the person to pay the amount in silver or in copper.

I have presumed to point out these circumstances to Governor-General in Council, not from any personal inconvenience that can arise to myself as Postmaster General, but from the confusion and delay which must happen in receiving and counting out a number of pice every night in postage on two or three hundred letters, in the short space of time it is necessary to receive them. It is also worthy of remark, that the Board not having specified what kind of pice are to be received in payment of postage the Post Office will be liable to continuous disputes and altercation from the sender of the smallest kind, vizt 128 to the rupee.

From the accompanying extract of a letter from the mint-master* it appears that four and eight anna pieces can be struck off, as they always have been, with great facility. May I therefore be permitted with due submission to suggest to the Board, that instead of pice being received where the postage on each letter and package does not exceed one rupee, the regulation be limited to four annas, which would very much facilitate the receipt of letters at the Office every night as the change would be counted and deliv-

* Editor's Note. Not copied in these consultations.

ered with little more delay than at present. But as the regulation is now formed, the dawks instead of going out at ten every night will seldom set off before eleven or twelve. And how far an alteration or uncertainty in the hour of the dawks setting out might affect a delay in their being forwarded at the several stations, I cannot say.

I take this opportunity to mention to the GGinC, that the daily attendance required from the clerks in Post Office is much more constant and late than at any other public office, Sunday and all holidays not excepted, the hour of dismission being generally from 10 to 11 o' clock at night, and I beg permission to observe the impossibility of procuring attendance so much later as the reception of the whole of postage in pice must occasion, at all events. I would therefore wish to recommend to the Board, that the Office be shut all the year round at gun fire as a period notorious to all and attending no dispute.

Home Department Public Original Consultation 18 November 1793, No. 23

Lieut. H. Read, Postmaster at Berhampore to Charles William Blunt, Postmaster-General, Berhampore, 5 October 1793

Sir,

I have the pleasure to transmit you the monthly Post Office accounts for September.

The difficulty of procuring Companys (Pultah) pice has been for this month past a cause of constant dispute and vexation. The gentlemen of these cantonments who in general wish to avail themselves of the permission of Government to pay their postage in copper, I think it a great hardship to have the current pice of this place refused, particularly as it is with great difficulty the Pultah are to be procured. In the other hand without special instructions from you I cannot receive any other as Mr. Oldfield, Collector of Moorshedabad refuses as I before wrote you to receive any other than the Pultah pice in the treasury. I request therefore to be favor'd with your instructions how I am to act in future.

Home Department, Public Original Consultation, 2 January 1795, No. 7.

Thomas Myers, Acctt to the B[oar]d [of] Revenue to William Cowper, President & Members of the Board of Revenue, Fort William, 10 December1794

Gentlemen,

1st. I have the honour to lay before you a copy of a letter from the Collector of Moorshedabad, in which he represents that the Goruckpoor & Gursaul pice received by him from the Deputy Postmaster at Berhampore at the value of SaRs 613 cannot be issued at the rate at which they were received.

2nd. As these pice were not I apprehend circulated under the sanction of Government, it appears to me that it may perhaps be advisable to authorize the Collector to issue them at their current value, and to charge such loss as may be sustained thereon to profit and loss.

3rd. I beg leave to enclose the specimens of the pice in question, which were transmitted to me by the Collector.

C. Oldfield, Collector of Moorshedabad to Thomas Myers, Accountant to the Board of Revenue Fort William, Zillah Moorshidabad, 21 October1794.

Sir,

I have been duly favored with your letter of 15th instant & in reply have to inform you that in compliance therewith I have granted a receipt to the Deputy Postmaster at Berhampore for the pice paid in by him on the 15th August 1793 at the rate they were received by him for postage, vizt.

TABLE R.7: COPPER COINS (THREE TYPES) RECEIVED BY THE POSTMASTER OF BERHAMPORE, 1793\

		at pice per SaRs	*SaRs*
Old Pultah pice	7,040	32	220
Goruckpoore	13,216	32	413
Gursaul	6,400	32	200
	26,656		833

2nd. As however it will be impossible for me ever to pay away the Gorruckpoorie & Gursaul pice at the same rate, they now selling in the bazaars at the rate of 9 gundahs or 36 pice per the rupee, I shall therefore be obliged to you, to inform me whether I may pay the away at the bazaar rate, or what I am to do with them.

3rd. For your satisfaction & information, I herewith beg leave to transmit to you a Goruckpoorie & Gursaul pice, both of which if weighed against a Pultah pice you will find are considerably deficient in weight.

Finance, Mint Committee Proceedings 2 October 1795, pp. 348-350

Members of the Board of Trade to John Shore, Governor-General in Council, Fort William, 21 April 1794

Honble Sir,

We beg leave to lay before you extract of a letter dated the 18th instant, which the Custom Master has addressed to us in consequence of the Regulation of the 6th September 1793 relative to the copper coin, and as there must be a great accumulation of this coin in offices where there are daily receipts of fractions of rupees we request your instructions respecting the disposal of it, as well in the present as in other instances.

Extract of a Letter from the Custom Master to the Board of Trade, dated 18 April 1794

I have the honor of laying before you an account of the copper coin now in my treasury, and beg to know in what manner I am to dispose of it. I must further observe that by adhering to the order of Government mentioned by the Sub Treasurer of receiving the copper coin in the fractional parts of one rupee, I shall at the end of every month have a large quantity of the copper coin in my hands. For instance, suppose I receive duties from fifteen different people in the course of the day, and that the fractional parts paid by each man may amount, on an average, to seven annas in this case, I shall have received in copper in the course of one day six rupees nine annas, without a possibility of paying away more than three or four rupees in the course of the month. If some remedie is not applied I shall in the course of a few years have all the copper coin of Calcutta in my office. I can see no remedy unless my office is made an exception at the General Treasury, or that I am prohibited from receiving copper coin in any part or parts.

Sources: NAI, Home Department, Public Original Consultation, 16 September 1793, No. 12; idem 18 November 1793, No. 23; idem 2 January 1795, No. 7; NAI, Finance, Mint Committee Proceedings, 2 October 1795, pp. 348-50.

8

Problems with the Acceptance of the Fiduciary Copper Coins Issued by the EIC, 23 April 1794

[*The Indian wage earners were very keen on receiving copper coins, valued according to the actual copper price and not according to fiduciary rates as the EIC preferred, like in its Regulation of 16 September 1792 (of which the Prinsep issues of 1781 were a first example). Therefore, the Calcutta laskars, serving under their serangs on the pilot schooners, preferred the coppers minted by Awadh State. The proposed new trilingual copper pice were introduced by the Calcutta Mint in 1800.*

See Ch. 4a and 4d of the Introduction and Part II: Records, Nos. 2 and 9.]

Cudbert Thornhill to John Shore, Marine Office, 23 April 1794

Sir,

With due deference and respect I beg leave to lay before you the very great difficulty we are under from the present disinclination the lascars have to serve on board the pilot schooners, by reason of a considerable portion of their pay coming to them in pice. The amount abstract for each vessel for a month's pay is received from the Pay Office in gold mohurs and pice, that is one per cent in pice besides the fractional part, after which they have to change the gold mohurs into rupees for the purpose of paying each individual, at the shroffs, who charge them 9½ annas on each gold mohur as a compensation for changing it, and the fractional part of the rupee is handed to them in pice. Their complaint is that the loss they sustain on the batta, together with the pice which the syrangs have brought and exhibited to me, declaring the people in the bazaar refuse to take them, is a greater diminution of their wages than any time heretofore.

I humbly request the Honble Board will be pleased to take the forgoing into consideration and afford such reliefs as shall appear to be most meet.

Governor-General's Minutes and Resolutions

The present very defective state of the copper currency has long been a subject of general complaint, but particularly amongst the lower orders of the people, on whom it occasionally operates as a heavy grievance.

2nd That the nature and extent of the evils experienced from the defective state of the copper currency may be clearly understood, it is necessary to premise that silver is the measure of value throughout the country, and that all goods and commodities are valued by the rupee.

3rd When pice therefore fall in value, or, in other words, when more than the usual or fixed number are exchangeable for a rupee, it follows that the day labourer who receives a given number of pice for his hire cannot procure the usual quantity of grain or other articles for his daily subsistence, and is consequently subjected to distress. Similar hardship is experienced by other descriptions of the lower orders of the people who receive payment in pice.

4th On the other hand, when the value of pice rises above the usual rate the loss falls upon those who pay in pice, as the labor or commodities which their rupee when exchanged into pice will then command, must be proportionately less.

5th The correspondence referred to in the margin* will show that both these effects have been felt at different periods as circum-

* Acting Colls of Boglepore with Lieutt Coll Pearrington's letter on the distress for pice recorded on the Mint Procs of the 31st May 1793 Board of Trade's letter & enclosure; also a letter from the master attendt on the same subject above recorded.

stances have contributed to increase or reduce the value of pice in different parts of the country.

6th This constant fluctuation in the value of the copper coin is a source of great profit to the shroffs who combine to raise and fall the value of it in the different parts of the country, buying it up when they have depreciated it, and selling it at an enhanced value when they have accumulated so large a quantity as to render the remainder in circulation at the places to which their influence may extend insufficient for the dealings of the inhabitants. Exclusive of this source of advantage they likewise desire a large profit from trafficking with the numerous sorts of old and counterfeit pice which have a local currency in the different parts of the coutry, in the same manner as by the exchange of the old rupees.

7th Previous to stating any propositions for a new copper coinage it may be necessary to notice the principles on which the copper currency was regulated under the native administration, and the rules that have been prescribed regarding it by the British government.

8th Under the Mogul administration the silver coin was the only measure of value and legal tender of payment. Gold mohurs and pice were struck at the mints for the convenience of individuals who carried gold or copper to be converted into those coins. But the Government never fixed the number of pice which should be considered as equivalent to a rupee, any more than the number of rupees that should pass in exchange for a gold mohur. Like other commodities, the gold and copper coin were left to find their value in the market, compared with the common standard of valuation the rupee.

9th As a necessary consequence of the above principle the quantity of copper contained in the number of pice exchangeable for a rupee was in general nearly proportionate to the average price of copper in the market, or, in other words, the nominal and current value of the coin was nearly the same as the intrinsic value.

10th From the year 1772 when the mints at Patna and Dacca and Moorshedabad were withdrawn, no pice were coined in the provinces until the year 1783, when a contract was concluded with Mr. Prinsep for coining pice on account of Government.

11th Under this contract 5,285 bazaar maunds of pice were delivered between the 29th November 1781 and the 31st of October 1783. These pice were of four descriptions, whole pice denominated pucka pice, and weighing twenty annas, and half pice, quarters and eighths of proportionate weight.

12th The pice were delivered to Government at the rate of sixty sicca rupees the bazaar maund of eighty sicca weight to the seer, and issued by them at the rate of eighty sicca rupees the maund or 32 pucka pice, 64 half pice, 128 quarter pice or 256 eights for the sicca rupees.

13th From the annexed statement furnished by the Import Warehouse keeper, it appears that at the above period the price of sheet or manufactured copper was about forty-eight current rupees the factory maund, so that the nominal value of the coin was about 74 per cent above its intrinsic worth. Government therefore in the first instance gained a profit of above 33 per cent on the amount coined; and the contractor the difference between the price at which he delivered the coin to Government and the value of the copper and the expence of converting it into coin.

14th When the principles by which the copper coin was circulated under the native administrations are adverted to, it will not be deemed extraordinary that the people should receive with reluctance a coin so much overvalued, or that much counterfeit and bad coin should have been introduced into circulation.

15th The rules which were adopted for introducing this new copper coin into circulation appear to have been subversive of their object. Persons who received payments from the public officers were obliged to take 1 per cent in pice at the fixed valuation above mentioned. The coin indeed was received at the Treasury, and made a legal tender of payment to individuals at the same rate, but as the persons who received these large sums in copper could not compel any manufacturer or trader to take them for advances or dispose of them in the purchase of goods it obliged them to sell the pice for silver or gold to the shroffs, who of course exacted a discount upon them proportionate to their current value in the markets, and when they had occasion to make any payment to the treasury, paid them at par, thereby deriving a profit on the exchange of the pice as often as they passed through their hands. This depreciation of the coin of course obstructed its currency.

16th In Calcutta and its vicinity, the whole pice have in general passed at the rates of thirty-four, thirty-five, and sometimes thirty-six for the rupee. In the interior parts of the country where they have been introduced, they have often circulated at thirty-eight and forty for the rupee, and the half pice in the same proportion. But the quarters and eights were invariably rejected by all classes of people in the markets, and it was long a trade to buy them up from persons who are obliged to receive them from the Public Treasuries, and to pay them to Government at par. The whole pice have lately risen in value in Calcutta, but this as ascribable to Government having withdrawn a great proportion of them from circulation, and to individuals being no longer obliged to receive them excepting in payment for the fraction of the rupee. But in the interior parts of the country the copper coin still consists of the above descriptions of Calcutta pice, the pice coined previous to and in the early part of the Company's administration, the pice from the Vizier's and other neighbouring countries and a much longer proportion of counterfeits of each, which are constantly fluctuating in value in different places from the causes above described.

17th The desideratum in the copper coinage of this country is that a given number of the coin should pass universally for the fractional parts of a rupee, or perhaps half a rupee or eight annas, and no more, in all purchases and payments whatever. To effect this desirable object the following appear to be the principles on which the copper coinage should be regulated.

18th The intrinsic value of the coin should be nearly equal to its nominal worth, estimating it according to the moderate average price, so as to preclude individuals from deriving any advantage from counterfeiting the coin. This is the great evil to be avoided, but which would be the necessary consequence of estimating the copper at too high a value, and prevent the coin being generally received at its fixed value. On the other hand, supposing the copper be rather undervalued, it can only produce the effect of occasioning some of it to be melted down when particular circumstances may cause an unusual rise in the price of copper. This however can rarely happen to any great extent. At all events it is an evil of comparatively little importance, being attended in its consequences only with the trouble of throwing a further quantity of the coin into circulation, the additional quantity of copper required for which can always be imported with advantage from Europe.

19th The sheet copper is the proper sort of copper for coining into pice. From the annexed statement [not transcribed here] it appears that the average price of this copper at the Company's sales for the last ten years is the current Rs. 46:1:1½ per factory maund of sicca weight 72:11:7 to the seer. The price however has risen at different times within the above period considerably higher and at the sales in January 1794 it was near forty-eight current rupees.

[...]

24th A half anna pice of thirty-two annas weight would be too heavy a coin for circulation and any smaller subdivisions of a rupee than a one hundred and twenty eighth part appear unnecessary, as in transactions in which a smaller sign of value are required, the couries are invariably used throughout the country. It appears expedient therefore that there should be only two descriptions of copper coin, a whole and a half pice, the former to pass at the value of a quarter of an anna, and the latter at half a quarter of an anna.

[...]

26th These regulations are in abstract as follows:

1st That people in all parts of the country may be apprized of the value at which the coin is issued by Government, and to be received and paid by the public and by individuals the value should be inscribed on one surface of it in the Persian, Bengal, and Nageree, the three characters used in business in the different parts of the provinces.

2nd Instead of obliging individuals to receive copper to the amount of one per cent as at the last coinage the coin should be declared a legal tender of payment for the fractional parts of half a rupee or eight annas and no more, and all the officers of Government should be prohibited receiving or issuing any larger amount in copper in receipts and disbursements made on the Public Account

3rd As the coin is to be made on account of Government, it should be struck at the Calcutta mint and not at the three city mints. The Calcutta mint will always be able to furnish a sufficient quantity of the coin for circulation, and by confining the coinage to this mint Government themselves will be able to regulate the issue of it in proportion to the demand for it in the country. [...]

Resolved accordingly as follows:

That a regulation for the establishment of a new copper coinage for the provinces of Bengal Behar and Orissa, in conformity to the principles stated in the above minute be framed and printed and published agreeably to the 41. Regulation of 1793.

That such part of the Calcutta or Prinsep's pice now collected in the General Treasury as may not be wanted for current purposes be transmitted to the mint master at Calcutta with directions to coin them into pice and half pice of the weight proposed, and that they be furnished with the proper inscriptions for the dies, and desired to submit samples of the coin to the Board for their approbation. That the Board of Trade be directed to furnish the mintmaster with three thousand maunds of the sheet copper proper for coining into pice from the copper of that description which may be now in the Company's warehouse or from the expected imports of the present season.

Source: NAI, Finance, Mint Committee Proceedings, 2 October 1795, pp. 351-65 and 369-83.

9

The Demand for Copper Pice at Patna, 30 April, 8 and 15 May 1794

[*The want of copper coins in Bengal and the failure to circulate the Prinsep pice, minted at Pultah in 1781, induce the mintmasters of Calcutta and Patna to consider the proper remedies. Calcutta clearly takes the lead, which resulted in the coinage of copper half and whole pice by the Calcutta Mint in 1795/96.*

See Part II: Records, No. 8.]

Public Original Consultation 12 May 1794, No. 14

Extract by Ja[me]s Miller, Mint Master at Calcutta of a letter dated the 30th April, received from the Assay Master at Patna the 7th May 1794

I beg leave to represent to you an evil that exists at this place that in my opinion ought to be laid before Government, this is the great scarcity of copper coin which is at all times in great demand in this quarter and the currency of it better established than in most other parts of the country. At present the dearth is such that only twelve annas or forty-eight pice can be procured for a rupee. Whether this dearth proceeds from a real scarcity or monopoly I cannot readily find out but in consequence of applications from all the principal merchants to the Mint for a supply of pice and at the request of the Magistrate I have coined a few sheets of copper into pice and have encouraged the propagation of a report that a large quantity of copper is coming from Calcutta for the coinage of pice here, with a view of opening the hoards if the scarcity proceeds from monopoly, but this has not had the desired effect.

Should you think proper to represent this business to the

Governor-General in Council I am of opinion that one fly press and two cutting machines to be employed at the leisure intervals of the other coinage would very soon furnish a sufficient quantity of pice to reduce the price to 16 annas per rupee that I will with much pleasure undertake the business on account of Government.

Public Original Consultation 12 May 1794, No. 14A

Extract of a letter, dated the 8th May, from the Mint Master to the Assay Master at Patna, requesting certain information, and stating that the question of copper coinage is under consideration

...

7. In regard to what you say of copper pice, I am most fully convinced of the entire rectitude of your intention on that subject, but I must strenuously dissuade you against the shortest prosecution or repetition of the trial you mention to have made in regard to pice, either at the instance of principal merchants or any other sanction whatsoever, that comes not duly from the hands of Government.

8. I beg you to do me the justice to consider this admonition as proceeding from the justest principles of propriety, and the sincerest desire to preserve you free from censure, for which reason I cannot entertain a doubt of your paying as much attention to it as if I had employed stronger terms in which to express myself on this occasion.

9. You may however rest assured that I shall make such use of the intimations you have given me on this article, as may appear to be most conducive to public utility; and in addition to the information with which you have favoured me, I would request you to loose no time in stating the weight, intrinsic and nominal value, and place of coinage of the copper pice current in your districts; of how many sorts they consist, and how many of each sort (if more than one) go current for the Sicca Rupee. I would also particularly desire you to apprise me what are the different prices of copper of each sort in the neighbourhood of your Mint, how much of each sort you may be of opinion could be bought up from the publickly understood state of the markets; and which kind of each you would recommend in preference to others for the coinage of

pice. Also of what weight each copper coin should be, which in circulation may represent the value of half an anna sicca, or six pice, according to the English mode of account, and whether you think 32 or 64 to the rupee would form the most convenient and suitable copper coin for circulation.

10. In so doing you will doubtless have regard to the difference you would recommend between the intrinsic value, agreeably to the market price and the nominal value in circulation with such reasons as in any way may influence your judgement on the subject.

11. As I have no desire to conceal any matter that can be in any wise be necessary to your information I am to apprize you that the Government have for some time past had in contemplation the subject of a copper coinage, but hitherto it has not been determined upon.

12. Your communications may therefore be highly useful, in answer to the queries above proposed, but I need scarcely after this intimation on my part, urge the necessity of confining it to yourself alone; as the promulgation of such intention would tend to influence the price of copper, and enable individuals to take advantage of the moment: hence I conceive it would be perhaps more politic, rather to discourage than encourage an expectation of the adoption of that matter.

Copy of a letter from Ja[me]s Miller, Mint Master, to Robert Blake, Assay Master at Patna, requesting him to furnish specimens of copper pice to enable the Board to form a proper judgement as to its coinage, Calcutta 9 May 1794

Sir,

Upon further consideration of the subject of that part of my letter of yesterday, which relates to copper pice, I conceive it would enable Government to form a more compleat judgement of the sort of copper coin that should be adopted, if you would immediately send down one piece of each sort that circulates in your neighbourhood; as also of those which you mention to have struck off at your Mint (and which to guard against the consequences of the possible miscarriage of my letter) I here repeat must be instantly discontinued. These coins I should suppose might be sent by one or two daks at most.

Public Original Consultation, 2 June 1794, No. 25

Copy of a letter from Robert Blake, Assay Master at Patna, to Ja[me]s Miller, Mint Master, forwarding some specimens of copper coin, and answering certain questions regarding them, Patna Mint 15 May 1794

Sir,

I was yesterday favoured with your letter of the 8th and this morning with another of the 9th instant. As I have it in my power to furnish you with all the information you required regarding the copper coin I shall reply to that part only in order that you will receive it by return of the dawke.

I am greatly obliged by your observations in the 7th & 8th parag of your letter of the 8th instant. I beg to assure you that I have been particularly cautious in this transaction not to expose myself to censure by extending it beyond the limits of an experiment and this not exceeding 10 maunds.

I find that the pice coined by Mr. Prinsep is held in most esteem here, musters of which I send you. There are half and quarter annas 32 & 64 per a rupee and the only copper coin in circulation in this quarter coined under the sanction of Government. Their intrinsic value as a coin is seldom lower than 70 small and 35 large for a rupee & I find that 32 half annas or 64 quarters weight 38 sicca weight or half a seer of the Patna weight, hence a maund of copper will coin into 80 SaRs.

The present price of copper at this place is 44 to 45 SaRs per Md of 76 SaWt per seer. The sort which I think the fittest for the copper coin is the sheets of the thickness of the half anna piece of this about 500 mds can be procured here together with 500 mds of the thickness of half an inch which would require some labour to laminate into strips before it is cut into blanks.

I am of opinion that the copper coin being cut into blanks with the cutting machines and struck in a fly press with a guide or register (in the manner the accompanying musters were struck) will be as great a check to the natives counterfeiting the copper coin as the milling is to the rupee.

The accompanying musters 1, 2, 3, 4 pass current as single pice with a batta of one anna on the rupee worse than these coined by Mr. Prinsep. The state of this coin is such as I doubt not will point out the necessity of its being reformed. From every information I can obtain I find that four parts out of five of the copper coin in circulation in this quarter is of the kind muster 1, 2, 3, 4 and at this time no more than from 54 to 56 per a rupee in the country, but at Patna where Mr. Prinsep's new pice only are current they are not to be procured at any rate.

Source: NAI, Home Department, Public Original Consultation, 12 May 1794, No. 14 and 14a, and 2 June 1794, No. 25.

10

The Export of Turkish Copper via Persia to India, Basra, 31 July 1797

[*The near-continuous warfare between France and its allies (including the Dutch) and England from 1792 to 1815 raised the price of copper at the world market. This, and the problems in the Dutch shipping of Japanese copper to India led to a search for alternative sources for copper, i. a. for minting coins. One venue was the procurement of Turkish copper via Persia for the Indian Mint houses.*

See Ch. 3c of the Introduction.]

S. Manesty, Resident at Bussora to Jonathan Duncan, President and Governor etc. in Council at Bombay in the Commercial Department, Bussora, 5 June 1797

Hon'ble Sir,

I have the honor to transmit a duplicate of my address of the 25th March and to acknowledge the receipt on the 4th May per *Viper* of your commands of the 30th January with their several enclosures and I shall herein communicate to your Honble Board such information on the subject of the exportation of copper from this country for sale in the markets in India as the wishes expressed by the Supreme Government and your commands above mentioned require.

After observing that the intelligence on the subject in question by William Page custom master at the Presidency and by him submitted to your consideration has, considering the deficiency of his sources of information, some merit as an outline, I will here more closely and particularly reply to the several queries contained in the address of the Board of Trade at Fort William to the Honble the Governor-General in Council dated the 13th December 1796.

To the first query 'From what places the copper lately brought from Bussora to India may have come, the distance of those places from Bussora and from water carriage, how many days it may take to convey the copper from the mines to water carriage, and how many days it may be coming by water to Bussora?' I respectfully reply:

That the mines from where the ore is extracted which produces the copper exported from Bussora are two in number, the one called the large and the other called the small mine, that they are situated in Anatolia a province of Turkey in Asia, and distant from Diarbeker a considerable town of that province, the large one about 150 miles and the small one about 90 miles. That Diarbekar lies within 4 miles of the river Tigris and about 500 miles from Bussora, that copper might be conveyed from Diarbakir to the Tigris in 2 hours, but that the navigation of that river between the vicinity of Diarbeker and Mosul, a city situated on the banks of it being insecure, is at present carried to Mosul by land, a distance of 150 miles.

To the second querie 'If possible the price at the mines and the expence of transportation of it to Bussora?' I respectfully reply:

That the price of cake copper at Diarbekar where the ore is brought from the mines is smelted and cast into cakes, at present averages thro' the year about 50 Bussora mamodies for 18 English pounds and that the expence of the transportation of copper from Diarbekir to Bussora including the duties payable on it at different places on the way is about 50 per cent.

To the third query 'Whether it be liable to any duties at the mines whether to any to the sovereigns of the countries through which it may pass, and to any when exported from Bussora and what in each instance?' I respectfully reply:

That the ore is not subject to any duty at the mines nor on its entry into Diarbekir, that cake copper is subject to an export duty at

Diarbekir of 2 per cent, to an import duty at Mosul of 2¼ per cent, to an import duty at Bagdad of 2 per cent, to an import duty at Bussora of 8⅓ per cent, and to an export duty at Bussora of 5½ per cent.

To the fourth querie 'under whose government the country in which the mines are situated may be?' I respectfully reply:

That it is under the government of the Ottoman emperor.

To the fifth query 'Whether the mines are worked under the direction of European miners or of natives?' I respectfully reply:

That the mines are worked under the direction of and by Greeks, having under them Muslim labourers.

To the sixth query 'The price at which it has sold at Bassora in the last and in preceding years, the answer to which is expected?' The answer to which is expected to express the comparative value of the Bussora money with the Bombay Rupee and the comparison of the Bussora weights with the English Avoirdupois Pound or the Calcutta Buzar Maund, I respectfully reply:

That the price of copper at Bussora has varied and gradually risen during the six last years from mamoodies 80 to 129. 9375 ds. For the attaree maund of Pounds English 30 and that ten Bussora mamoodies are equal in value to one Bombay rupee.

To the seventh query 'the quantity which has been exported from Bussora in the last and preceding years' I respectfully reply:

That the quantity of copper exported from Bussora for sale in the markets of India has from the year 1791 in which it amounted to about 16,000 attaree maunds gradually increased to about attaree maunds 70,000 the amount of the export of that article in 1796.

To the eighth and last query 'What quantity of copper the mines may annually yield whether it be probable they may admit of increase and to what extent?' I respectfully reply:

That the quantity of copper produced from the ore extracted from the mines has on an average during the six last years exceeded the weight of 250,000 attaree maunds and that the mines are so very rich and extensive as to render incalculable their possible capability of production.

In addition to the foregoing close and particular replies to the several queries of the Board of Trade, which I will flatter myself be considered as clear and satisfactory ones I beg leave respectfully to communicate the following general information, in further elucidation of the important commercial subject to which they relate.

The copper mines in the vicinity of Diarbekir are worked under the Superintendence of a Turkish Bacha of three tails who under the title of Vizir il Madaan or Bacha of the Mines has charge of them, of gold, silver, and lead mines, situated in the same neighbourhood. The present Bacha of the Mines by name Yusuf Bacha has the honour to be married to the sister of the present Ottoman Emperor Selim, and having been the companion of his youth and confinement of the Seraglio at Constantinople, enjoys the confidence of his Sovereign in a very high degree. The Bacha of the mines has great power, lives in great state, & has the command of a very considerable military force. He works the gold and the silver mines on account of the Ottoman Emperor from whom he farms those of copper and lead. The Bacha of the Mines will therefore for his own immediate benefit naturally endeavour to extract from the copper mines as great a quantity of copper ore as may be possibly vendible and he conveys the ore to Diarbekir on his own account where it is smelted and prepared for sale under the superintendence of his immediate agents. The copper produce from the ore extracted from the mines circulates in all directions from Diarbekir and whilst a considerable portion thereof finds its way through Bussora to India, other portions are conveyed to Persia, Armenia, Georgia, Constantinople, the Coast of Syria, Egypt and even to Europe. The mines are worked as before mentioned by and under the direction of Greeks having under them Muslim labourers. The ore is smelted at Biarbekir by Armenians. The ore is conveyed to Diarbekir on horses, camels, mules and asses. Merchants cannot purchase the ore at the mines. They buy copper at Diarbekir. The copper is conveyed from Diarbekir to Mosul on horses, camels, mules and asses. The copper is laden on rafts at

Mosul and conveyed on them to Bagdad. The copper is conveyed from Bagdad to Bussora in boats of different kinds and sizes varying in burthen from 5 to 35 tons. The copper is of superior quality.

I will here take the liberty respectfully to state to your Honble Board, that the fears entertained by the Board of Trade of the recent importations in India of cake copper from Bussora injuriously affecting the sales of the consignments of copper made by the Honble Company to the Presidencies in India are premature and that a reference to former commercial records might have justly removed them by proving that when the Honble Company made considerable consignments of copper to India, the consignments thither of that article were proportionally small. The copper exported from Bussora is only chosen by the merchants here as a vehicle for the conveyance of funds to India as returns for goods sold by them or to be employed there in the provision of the various manufactures of that country, and certain European articles suited to the Bussora market and to the consumption of the inhabitants of the surrounding territory, not as a commercial article promising an encouraging gain to a mercantile speculation, and I am convinced that if the future importations in India by the Honble Company of good battery copper gradually become adequate to the demand for that article, the exportations of it from Bussora will proportionally decrease and finally cease and the merchants engaged in the trade between Bussora and India will consequently be reduced to the necessity of selecting other commercial articles for remittances and abandoning adventures in copper.

Source: NAI, Home Department, Public Original Consultation, 31 July 1797, No. 2.

11

The Staff and Workings of the Benares Mint 1802

[*Manual manufacturing of coins, and in particular of coppers, has been documented best for the Benares Mint. In 1775 the EIC had taken over the Benares mint, and wished to have information about its functioning, also because of suspicions of fraud by Raja Amba Shunker the mint master or darogha (he died 5 May 1802 and was provisionally succeeded by Lolla Rampershand, and in June by Sheikh Ally Ahsun). No fraud was found and the manual production under Indian management compares favorably to the mechanized procedures of the Calcutta mint under British management.*

See, Part II: Records, Nos. 3 and 12, and Appendix 2 (s.v. Benares). More details are available in the same volume, proceedings of 1 and 6 April 1801, 27 May and 3 June 1802.]

J. Neave, J.S. Grant, J.D. Erskine [Members of the Benares Mint Committee] to the Calcutta Mint Committee at Fort William, Benares, 11 July 1801

Gentlemen,

On the 4th May we received your letter of the 25th April, and now do ourselves the pleasure to reply to your different questions.

1st The officers of the mint are only six in number, viz., darogha, assay master, mushrif, tehveeldar, rowenna and wozunkush. The darogha Raja Amba Shunker has a superintendence over all the concerns of the mint which seems to be loosely exerted and indefinitely applied, in his sunnud of appointment the rowenna is included as forming a part of his office. The assay master is Govind Dauss, grandson and adopted son of the late

Cawn Dauss, the duties of his office are explained by its title, his sunnud includes the appointment of wozunkush. The mushrif writes down the daily as well all other accounts and deposits them in the office. The tehveeldar receives all the government duties, and disburses the produce under verbal authority from the darogha. The rowenna is considered as nazir to the mint, and carries into effect the orders of the darogha. The wozunkush is immediately under the assay master and weighs gold and silver of every denomination. These officers receive no salary and their russoom will be explained when treating on the coinage and manufacturers, which will also bring to view all the other advantages they derive. No. 1 is a detail of the establishment fixed and contingent as authorized by the late Resident of Benares Mr. Jonathan Duncan, the amount is defrayed from the produce of the government duties.

2nd We cannot learn that any change has taken place in the mode of conducting the detail of the mint since Benares became subject to the British Government, but there are other changes we deem deserving of notice. When the profits of the mint were vested in the residents, its power extended to levying duties on very many articles, even carpet and leather sellers were not exempt. Mr. Duncan abolished all these miscellaneous duties on the 31st December 1790. The pensioners to the mint were transferred to the Adowlut.

3rd The form observed from the receipt of bullion to the issue thereof in coin is as follows. The mohagen carries his bullion to the mint master who transfers it to the *chandysaz* or sodha, whose business it is to melt the same and eject the dross. This done, the Chowdry of the derrabs cuts the mass into pieces (indefinite as to size and weight) and gives them to the mohagen, who causes them to be weighed in his presence at the cutcherry. The assay master then audits the proper alloy and delivers the silver to the *gudasgeer* who melts it into ingots and re-delivers it to the assay master who ascertains the standard, and gives them to the derrabs to be made into blanks, which blanks the *wozunkush* weighs, and admitting all those of proper weight they are transferred to the siege by whom they are stamped and counted. The remaining form is the delivery of the coin to the owner by permission from the darogha.

4th The accompanying number 2 will shew you the duties levied in behalf of Government, and fees received by the officers of the mint on the gold silver and copper coinage and the manner in which they are appropriated. Under the head of 'charges defrayed at the mint' we must introduce the workmen who are neither noticed in the establishment nor do they receive any part of the public duties. They are paid by the mohagens in the proportions laid down in No. 3, which concludes all the demands on them for coinage, with the exception of 70 rupees which they must pay to the mint as entrance money on first sending bullion for coinage or for Passa 56* of which are received by Government Rs. 15:13:6 are paid to the darogha and rowenna, the same amount to the assay master and wozunkush and the balance equally divided between the mushrif and tehveeldar. To bring all the duties levied on coinage in one point of view we have to observe that:

TABLE R.11.1: MINTING COSTS, BENARES 1801

	R: A: P
Gold bullion pays for every hundred gold mohurs	21:09:0
Gold mohurs coined from gold mohurs	13:08:6
Silver bullion for every hundred rupees	2:05:0
Kitteci rupees	1:15:0
Goorshahy	1:07:0
Mooteris	0:14:0
Sheet copper including loss by the coinage for every maund of pice	7:14:0
Bar ditto	6:04:0
And mooteris	0:04:0

We enclose No. 4 being an account of the entrance money paid by workmen taking up their professions.

No. 5 explains the amount of *nuzzerana* which the officers of

* Passa or ingot, see below.

the mint receive under that specific head. You will perceive by No. 6 that there is no check whatever over the mint, and we cannot much wonder at the want of regularity as the superintendence of that department we should suppose to have been taken up by the Collector, because he received officially the net monthly proceeds.

5th We enclose Nos. 7 and 8 being the account required from Raja Amba Shunker and Govind Dauss.

6th There are four classes of manufacturers connected with the mint:

1st Powteas gold and silver wire drawers. This class consists of nine persons only who claim an exclusive privilege of the trade on the grounds of ancient usage. On the death of any of these manufacturers the next lineal descendant succeeds to the trade. Their workshops are contiguous to the mint.

2nd Taneeces, manufacturers of gold and silver thread. This is a numerous class consisting of above 1,200 workmen.

3rd Chuppereeas, manufacturers of badileh (flattened gold and silver thread). Of this class there are about two hundred. An apprentice to this trade pays 5 rupees into the mint. Of this sum four-fifths are carried to the credit of Government and one fifth is distributed in the following proportions among the officers of the mint: to the darogha and assay master each one third, the remaining third is equally divided among the mushrif, wozunkush, tehveeldar and rowenna.

4th Batunharas, manufacturers of gold and silver lace. There are about twelve hundred workmen of this class. An apprentice pays into the mint Rs. 3:2 which is appropriated in the same manner and in the same proportions as above.

Over all these classes of manufacturers the darogha of the mint exercises the control of setting any matters of dispute but the assay master has no authority over them in any respect.

The silver from which these manufactures are prepared is in the first instance sent by the merchant to the mint where it is formed into passa or ingots for the purpose of being drawn into wire. The ingots being proved by the assay master to contain the established proportion of alloy (which is from 6 to 8 grains in the weight of a rupee) are then stampt with the seal of the darogha and delivered to the merchant upon his paying a duty to Government according to the following rates:

TABLE R.11.2: ASSAY COSTS OF INGOTS, BENARES, 1801

On passa or ingots	*Made from*	*Rs: as per 100 tollahs*
1	Chaudee bullion	2:08:00
2	Jennis: all silver coin except the current sicca rupees of Calcutta, Moorshedabad, Patna and Benares	2:00:00
3	Sun rupees of Calcutta, Moorshedabad, Patna and Benares	0:15:06
4	Gotee, silver obtained from burnt embroidery and cheda fragments of passa	1:05:06

On the two last descriptions of passa there is a drawback on the duty of 1 anna 6 pice allowed in favour of Gopal Dauss Sah, and Gooal Dauss Sah, and of 1 anna in favour of Ummuchund Cawn Jee and Ullum Chund in consequence of their ancestors having been heretofore concerned in the mint.

A merchant upon first engaging in the trade and before he becomes entitled to send silver to the mint to be made into passa pays 70 rupees entrance money one fifth of which is distributed among the officers of the mint in the manner before mentioned, and the balance is carried to the credit of Government. He also pays entrance money previous to his being entitled to have passa manufactured into wire. The following are the sums paid on this account by the different descriptions of merchants:

TABLE R.11.3: ADMISSION COSTS FOR MERCHANTS WANTING TO HAVE INGOTS ASSAYED, BENARES, 1801.

	Rs.
Brahmin, Butteree, Bad Furosh	250
Gujerattee, Uggerwallee	125
Soonnee, Zergur	45

Of this money one fourth is paid into the mint, of which sum a fifth is distributed among the officers of that department in the proportions before mentioned, and the balance is brought to credit of Government. The remaining three fourths are deposited with Suddanund Dauss, an agent on the part of the merchants and manufacturers, and when a considerable sum has thus been accumulated in his hands, it is appropriated to festivals and charitable purposes. Out of this money there is also an annual present of Rs. 100 made to the darogha of the mint in the cold season and of Rs. 4 to the assay master on account of preserving the weights correct.

Every dealer in passa pays annually into the mint at the time of the Dussara 1 rupee which is distributed among the officers as above. The Powtias are on all occasions required to submit the passa which they may receive from merchants to the inspection of the darogha of the mint and on no account whatever to manufacture it into wire until they shall receive his order to that effect. Previous to manufacturing gold wire they are also required to allow the gold into the mint to be weighed where a duty of 3 annas per tolah is levied on it on account of Government.

7th In reply to the 5th paragraph we beg leave to state that no one of the chowdries are officers of the mint. They appear to be merely agents for different manufacturers. They are appointed by them and their business is to send for the workmen and to give them information when their services are required, and to call the manufacturers together upon festivals &ca. The emoluments of the different chowdries have been stated to us as follows:

1st The Chowdry of the taneeces receives 8 annas and some sweetmeats from every apprentice on his first entrance, and one rupee from persons engaging in the gold and silver thread trade; one tanga also in the rupee on all sums paid to the manufacturers who are employed through is agency.

2nd the Chowdry of the choporeeas receives one rupee from apprentices and some sweetmeats, one rupee from persons engaging first in the Badla trade, and one tunga in the rupee as above.

3rd the Chowdry of the batunharos receives six annas from apprentices and two pice a month from the traders in lace.

8th The objection offered by the merchants and dealers to a separation from the mint is the apprehension they entertain of the passa being debased and the trade in consequence injured. We fully admit the strength of this objection and do not recommend any alteration in the present mode of conducting the manufactures so far as the powtias or wiredrawers are concerned, but we see no reason why the mint should exercise any control over the other classes of workmen or over the manufacturers, who appear to suffer from vexatious impositions equally oppressive to themselves as hostile to the interests of Government.

Were these evils removed we conceive the state would benefit by increased exports, and of the nature of these evils our various enclosures and details will afford ample information.

9th We are unable at present to state with any degree of precision how far the gold and silver stuffs can be considered as constituting the source of the wealth and commerce of this city. The dealers and manufacturers have afforded us no distinct information on the subject. We have however applied to the custom master and trust from his answers and other sources to form a tolerably exact estimation of the proportion which these manufactures bear to the other manufactures of this city.

No. 8: Enclosed in Letter from Mint Committee Dated 10th May

Establishment of the mint, the amount of which is paid from the Government duties levied on coinage.

TABLE R.11.4: ESTABLISHMENT OF THE BENARES MINT, 1801

Fixed monthly charges		*Per month*	*Per annum*
Naib darogha	15:0		
Mushriffs mohurrer	8:0		
Daroghas ditto	10:0		
Assay master's mohurrer	7:8		
Sehja Novees	7:8		
Wokeel	10:0		
House rent	25:0		
14 peadahs, two at Rs. 4 and twelve at 3	44:0		
		127	1,524
Contingent annual charges			
Paper, pens 7 ink		11	
Scales		5	
Books for the office		12	
Charity to the Brahmins at the Dussara		20	
Ditto at the Salonoo		20	
At the Dewaly the cutcherry is supplied with new shuteringees &ca		25	
			93
Total mint charges per annum			1,617

No. 9: Enclosed in Letter from Mint Committee Dated 10th May

Duties levied in behalf of Government on the coinage:

- On gold bullion sixteen rupees and one anna for every hundred gold mohurs.
- On gold mohurs, made from other gold mohurs, the impression only being defaced, 8 rupees and six pies, and the same amount when melted for recoinage.
- On silver bullion one rupee and six annas for every hundred rupees.
- On Kiticee rupees 1 per cent.
- On Goorshahy do. Eight annas per cent.
- On copper one rupee and eight annas on every maund of pice.

Fees levied by the officers of the mint exclusive of the Government duties.

TABLE R.11.5: BRASSAGE COSTS AND APPORTIONMENT TO CERTAIN MINT SERVANTS, BENARES, 1801

On gold bullion coined into gold mohurs; and the same amount is levied when gold mohurs are recoined or defaced	*Per cent (Rs : as : p)*
Darogha and rowenna	1:4
Assay master and wozunkush	1:4
Mushrif	0:4
Tehveeldar	0:4
On silver; the same amount is levied when gold mohurs are recoined or defaced	
Darogha and rowenna	1:3
Assay master and wozunkush	1:3
Mushrif	0:3
Tehveeldar	0:3
On copper	
Darogha and rowenna	0:5
Assay master and wozunkush	0:5
Mushrif	0:1
Tehveeldar	0:1
Naib darogha	0:2
Per maund of pice	0:14

Memorandum in Explanation

Gold mohurs made from gold, mohurs by defacing the old and substituting the Benares stamp are styled 'Mooteris' and none have been made during the superintendence of the present darogha of rupees, many come under this head as will be seen in the account of the coinage of the five last years.

The *rowenna* and *wozunkush* are servants to the darogha and assay master and in fact receive no part of the fees, but a salary from their respective masters, in whose sunuds they are mentioned.

Kiteice rupees are those which bear a royal stamp, and all are considered as such not coming under the head of Goorshahy. This denomination embraces agreeably to Mr. Duncan's orders – sanctioned by Government – dollars as also tuppery large and small coming from the eastward, which are in fact lumps of silver, and the following rupees:

Pondicherry
Lucknow
Allahabad
Furuckabad
Calcutta &ca from the eastward

No. 10: Enclosed in Letter from Mint Committee Dated 10th May

Fees paid by the mohagens to the workmen of the mint exclusive of Government duties and fees of the mint officers.

TABLE R.11.6: PIECE WAGES FOR COINING GOLD, BENARES MINT, 1801

On gold bullion	*Rs : as : p per cent*
Gudasgeer or sodha on every Rs. 100 mohurs	0:4:0
Siegee	0:4:0
Mohurkun	0:1:0
Balapaesaz	0:1:0
Annas	10

The derrab has for his labour one masha and two sooruks of gold for every 100 mohurs, which may amount to one rupee and fourteen annas. The same amount also when gold mohurs are melted for recoinage, but when the impression is only defaced he has five sooruks of fifteen annas per centum. The other workmen also receive as above with the exception of the gudasgeer who is not concerned in the transaction.

TABLE R.11.7: PIECE WAGES FOR COINING NEW SILVER, BENARES MINT, 1801

On silver bullion	*Rs : as : p per cent*
Chandysah or sodha	0:4:0
Derrab	0:4:0
Gudasgeer	0:1:6
Siegee	0:0:6
Balapaesaz	0:0:3
Mohurkun	0:0:3
Chashnygeer	0:0:3
Chowdry of the derrabs	0:0:3
Annas	11
Charity to the Bramen	1
Annas	12

TABLE R.11.8: PIECE WAGES FOR COINING OLD SILVER, BENARES MINT, 1801

On mooteris rupees	*Rs : as : p per cent*
Derrab	0:2:0
Mohurkun	0:0:3
Balapaesaz	0:0:3
Seigee	0:0:6
Annas per cent	3

TABLE R.11.9: PIECE WAGES FOR COINING NEW COPPER, BENARES MINT, 1801

On copper puttea or sheet copper	*Rs : as : p per cent*
Seigee	0:4:0
Mohurkun	0:1:0
Balapaesaz	0:2:0
Chowdry of the derrabs	0:1:0
Derrabs	2:12:0
Lohar	0:1:0
For every maund of pice	4:4:0
Besides the merchant suffers a loss of wear and tear of 1 seer of copper	1:4:0
Total rupees per maund	5:8:0

On bar copper is to be deducted from the above estimate one rupee for the lohar who is not employed and ten annas being only half a seer of copper lost in the coinage which make the rate on bar copper Rs. 3:14 for every maund of pice.

TABLE R.11.10: PIECE WAGES FOR COINING OLD COPPER, BENARES MINT, 1801.

On mooteris or old pice	*Rs : as : p per cent*
Seigee	0:4:0
Mohurkun	0:1:0
Balapaesaz	0:2:0
Chowdry of the derrabs	0:1:0
Derrab	1:2:0
For every maund of pice	1:10:0

No. 11: Enclosed in letter from Mint Committee Dated 10th May

Entrance money paid at the mint by various workmen, vizt:

TABLE R.11.11: ENTRANCE MONEY TO BE PAID BY SERVANTS OF THE BENARES MINT, 1801

Derrab dukandar		
Government		40:00:0
Darogha & rowenna		4:02:6
Assay master & wuzunkush		4:02:6
Tehveeldar		0:13:6
Mushriff		0:13:6
	BsSaRs	50:00:0
Derrab assamy [I]		
Government		15:00:0
Darogha & rowenna		1:04:0
Assay master & wuzunkush		1:04:0
Tehveeldar		0:04:0
Mushriff		0:04:4
	BsSaRs	18:00:0
Derrab assamy [II]		
Government		7:00:0
Darogha & rowenna		1:04:0
Assay master & wuzunkush		1:04:0
Tehveeldar		0:04:0
Mushriff		0:04:4
	BsSaRs	10:00:0
Gudasgeer		
Government		100:00:0
Darogha & rowenna		6:04:0
Assay master & wuzunkush		6:04:0
Tehveeldar		1:04:0
Mushriff		1:04:4
	SaRs	115:00:0
Punnasaz		
Government		20:00:0

Darogha & rowenna		2:01:3
Assay master & wuzunkush		3:01:3
Tehveeldar		0:06:9
Mushriff		0:06:9
	BsSaRs	25:00:0

Tickleesaz the whole to Government BsSaRs 12:08

No. 12: Enclosed in letter from Mint Committee Dated 10th May

Annual nuzzerana received by the officers of the mint

TABLE R.11.12: PIECE RATES, TO BE PAID BY SERVANTS OF THE MINT TO THEIR SUPERIORS, BENARES MINT, 1801

All mohagens or beoparies in coinage or passa pay at		*Which are divided*	
The Dussera	Rs. 4	Darogha & rowenna	Rs. 1:4
The Hooley	Rs. 4	Assay master & wozunkush	Rs. 1:4
		Mushriff	Rs. 0:4
		Tehveeldar	Rs. 0:4
		Naib darogha	Rs. 1:0
	Rs. 8		Rs. 4:0
The Chandysaz or Sodha and Siegee		*Which are divided*	
The Dussera	Rs. 6	Darogha & rowenna	Rs. 2:8
The Hooley	Rs. 6	Assay master & wozunkush	Rs. 2:8
		Mushriff	Rs. 0:8
		Tehveeldar	Rs. 0:8
	Rs. 12		Rs. 6:0
The other workmen of the mint pay at		*Which are divided*	
The Dussera	Rs. 3	Darogha & rowenna	Rs. 1:4
		Assay master & wozunkush	Rs. 1:4

		Mushriff	Rs. 0:4
		Tehveeldar	Rs. 0:4
	Rs. 3		Rs. 3:0
The Chandysaz or Sodha and Siegee			
The Dussera	Rs. 10		
The Hooley	Rs. 10		
	Rs. 20		

The chooly feroshes pay to the *darogha* every year three rupees supposed to be 40 in number.

No. 13: Enclosed in Letter from Mint Committee Dated 10th May

[the collector at Benares writes on 7 June 1801:]

I have no specific authority for my control over the mint, that I have no regulations as a guide for my conduct, that I have issued no orders or regulations for the better management of it and that I have never yet been able to investigate the accounts of receipts and disbursements delivered by the darogha of the mint who has always refused to attest them with his signature.

No. 14: Enclosed in Letter from Mint Committee Dated 10th May

[Assay report about the standard of the Benares rupees 1776 (AH 1190) - 1802 (AH 1215): outcome is 8 annas per cent worse than the sicca standard of Calcutta, but hardly any progressive diminution notable.]

No. 15: Enclosed in letter from Mint Committee Dated 10th May

A statement of the difference of expense between the native process of coining used at Benares and the improved process of coining which has been introduced at Calcutta.

TABLE R.11.13: SILVER COIN PRODUCTION, BENARES MINT, 1796/7-1799/1800

The coinage at Calcutta in four years or from 1796/7 to 1799/1800 inclusive has been

	[4 years]	*Average for one year*		*Total charge*	*Average charge*
gmn	324,544	81,136			
Rs.	5,552,817	1,388,204	1,409,340	542,582	135,645

TABLE R.11.14: SILVER COIN PRODUCTION, BENARES MINT, 1796/7-1800/1

The coinage at Calcutta in in five years or from 1796/7 to 1800/1801 inclusive has been

Rs.	*[5 years]*	*Average for one year*	*Total rate of mint duties Rs: As per cent*	*Charge of coinage*	*Average charge*
Goorshay	7,912,313	1,582,462	1:7	22,747	
Mooteria	703,177	140,635	0:14	1,229	
Kitie	53,280	10,656	1:15	534	
Satie	84,810	16,962			
		1,750,715		24,510	
Add establishment of the mint fixed & contingent				617	
				26,127	
Deduce the average of the mint duties received by Govt				10,299	*15,828
Difference					119,817

Note: *The whole of this charge is paid by the merchants exclusive of SaRs 10,299 paid to Government.

Hence it appears that the mint expenses of coining 1,469,340 pieces in Calcutta amounts to Sicca Rupees 135,645 whereas the mint expenses of coining a greater number of pieces (1,750,716) at Benares amounted to no more than SaRs 15,828 which exhibits an estimated saving of expence in the Benares process of coining compared with the improved process adopted in Calcutta of SaRs 119,817 per annum.

No. 16: Resolution

The Governor-General in Council on a consideration of the above letter and enclosures does not think it would be advisable either to abolish the mint at Benares or to alter at present the mode in which the coinage at that mint has hitherto been conducted.

With a view however to the introduction of such rules as may appear to be necessary – for guarding against the issue of any coin from the mint in future which may be either defective in workmanship or deficient in weight or standard, and for preventing any undue exaction from the merchants and other abuses by the native officers of the mint, His Excellency in Council orders that The Agent of the Governor-General, the Magistrate of the City, and the Collector of the Province of Benares be constituted a permanent Committee for the superintendence and control of the mint, with directions to submit to Government the draft of such rules as they would recommend to be adopted for their own guidance in the execution of the duty assigned to them, and for the general conduct of the business of the Benares mint.

Ordered likewise that the committee be directed to prosecute the enquiry into the charges preferred against the officers of the mint and to report to Government the result.

Ordered that the foregoing orders be communicated to the Committee at Benares and to the Committee at Calcutta.

Ordered likewise that the former be furnished with a copy of the report from the Calcutta Committee for their information and consideration in preparing the draft of the rules above required for the future management of the mint at Benares.

Ordered that the 2 Persian and 1 English enclosures accom-

panying the above letter be deposited among the records of the Secretary's Office.
Exd
H. Boileau

Source: NAI, Revenue, Mint Proceedings, 25 May 1802, pp. 149-67a.

12

Copper Currency in the Province of Benares, 9 July and 26 October 1806

[*The circulation of copper currency in the province of Benares in 1806 and its origins is the topic of two highly informative letters from Thomas Yeld, the newly appointed English mint and assay master of the Benares mint. He held this position of mint master at least until 1823.*

See Ch. 3c, 3d, 4a and 4c of the Introduction, Part II: Records, Nos. 11, 14 and 15, and Appendix 2 s.v. Benares.]

T. Yeld, Mint & Assay Master, Benares to
Mint Committee Benares, Mint Office 9 July 1806

Gentlemen,

My attention has for some time been engaged in an enquiry into the currency of this province with a view to a report on the subject in general, but my investigation having as yet been more immediately confined to the copper currency, the evident it admits of & which are in daily practice I deem it my duty to submit to Government without delay and have to request you will please to submit this address to the Honble the Governor-General in Council in such manner as you may deem most proper.

There is no regulation for the weight, size, or impression of pice that can be the least check on any person making them privately without fear of detection as the accompanying specimen will clearly evince. A great part of the pice now in circulation have been made in Oude, the Rewa Rajahs country and other places out of the district & smuggled into circulation imperceptibly.

The weight of pice when made being in a great measure regulated by the then current price of copper their relative value instead of being afterwards reckoned by weight, according to the present price of copper is determined by number & this is not only influenced by the price current of copper but by other circumstances that will be detailed hereafter.

The present copper currency is a source of the greatest hardships and loss to that class of people least able to bear it, the daily labourer & working artist. Their poverty obliges them to take their pay daily which is always reckoned to them in the common divisions of the rupee by annas & this is paid to them according to the current price of pice by number. When they carry these pice to the Bunyahs for the purchase of their daily food, they will not receive them according to the value of them in the anna, but at a rate by which the retail purchaser is imposed on never less than one anna in the rupee.

But it is seldom the poor coolie who gets his anna & half or two annas a day is able to afford of one article to the amount of one pice. He has therefore to undergo the further imposition of the Budleeahs or money changers by reducing his pice to gundahs of couries, whose established custom is to make two pice per rupee profit. The Bunyahs on this again lay a tax by receiving the couries at a less rate than they have brought at generally equaling the profit they make by receiving pice, so that the poorer class of the Honble Companys subjects in this district pay from near seven to upwards of 13 per cent dearer for the necessaries of life than those who are able to go into the market with silver.

The rich are also not exempt from the operation of the price of pice on their daily consumption since the rate of many things in the greatest demand, milk, eggs, some kinds of grain & many other articles are regulated by the current number of pice in the rupee, but the greatest injury the rich suffer is at the season of marriages in their families, when if they have not had the precaution of laying in a stock of pice necessary for the occasion the Budleeahs and richer Bunyahs make their harvest by previously hoarding up their pice & raising the price of them at this season of the year from four to ten in the rupee. Altho' the rich by neglect may suffer equally with the poor man yet the poor one is not less exempt if he has a marriage in his family, as on these occasions they always borrow to the utmost extent they can get credit for & the lender never fails to advance in silver & receive back in pice at the season of the year they are cheapest.

This latter being an imposition voluntarily entered into, may not present any very urgent claims for redress but the daily sustenance of so numerous a body of subjects as constitute the laboring class in this populous province demands every amelioration that can be suggested for their relief. Actuated by these considerations a zealous discharged of the duties of the office committed to my charge, and that the relief required may be made a source of profit to Government I venture to submit to the attention & consideration of the Honble the Governor-General in Council specimens of a new copper coinage, with such remarks as have occurred or been suggested to me on each kind.

TABLE 12.1: PROPOSAL TO COIN 4 DENOMINATIONS OF COPPER COINS, BENARES, 1806

		Number to the Rupee	*Weight (grains troy)*	*Diameter inches*
No. 1	a double pice	32	240	1¼
No. 2	a single pice	64	120	1
No. 3	a half pice	128	60	¾
No. 4	a quarter pice	256	30	6/101

In fixing on these divisions I have been led to enquire into the Bunyahs mode of keeping small accounts and have adopted their subdivisions of the anna as most likely to be convenient to them and relieve those dealing with them.

I at first made but three divisions from the fear of making the coin too small. The fourth was made at the suggestion of an intelligent native who stated that it would in a great measure obviate all application to the Budleeahs that recourse to them only on the lowest division of cauries would be required.

In fixing on the above rates of weight I am assumed that the

Honble Company are able to afford copper at forty rupees the factory maund and have doubled the expence of making the old pice. This, according to my calculation will give the expence of a factory maund of new copper pice fifty-five rupees and the number made equal to sixty-six rupees, having a profit of eleven rupees, about 17 per cent. But in the expence of making the old pice there being a Russoom to Government of one rupee eight annas a maund reckoned, which on being doubled will add to the profit above stated somewhat above four rupees eight annas per cent. Should this rate require any reduction I would recommend its being made by taking of forty, twenty, ten & five grains from each respective kind of pice.

If the machinery of the Calcutta Mint could be employed in laminating and cutting the Derabs, it would greatly reduce the expence of making the pice, but I would by no means advise the impression being stamped in Calcutta as the prejudices of the Natives in its being struck at Benares should in my opinion be conceded to & the expence would be so little more than it could be done for in Calcutta as not to be worthy consideration.

In issuing a new coinage it appears to me a serious object to Government to call in the old at the least expence possible. This has had its consideration to me in fixing the weight of the new, and on weighing a Rupees worth of new pice with a rupees worth of old at the [late / usual]* rate of forty-six to the rupee, the old exceeds [the late / new]** at an average of three pice, in taking the old pice therefore at the medium rate of the year of forty-eight to the rupee, a great inducement would be held out to the holders of the old pice to exchange them & the loss to Government would not be quite two thirds of the expence of recoinage.

I cannot acquire any authentic data for the quantity that would be required and on this head can only give the general result of various opinions of several intelligent Natives asked on it, which is that three lacks of rupees of the different kinds should be prepared to commence with.

* Paper damaged: my interpretation. Ed.

** Paper damaged: my interpretation. Ed.

It would be as contrary to the liberal sentiments of the British Government in India as to sound policy to attempt to force a new coinage. I would therefore recommend to its being left to find its own way into circulation with this only preference, that the old pice should not be taken or issued in any public payment, and that the prescribed number of either species of the new should be a legal payment either public or private for a rupee, or its division of annas and that no pice should be made but on account of Government.

T. Yeld, Mint & Assay Master, Benares to Mint Committee Benares, 26 October 1806

Gentlemen,

I have the honor to acknowledge your letter enclosing a requisition from the Calcutta Mint Committee of the price current of copper in the Benares bazar for one year distinguishing the variation in the price monthly and also the sicca weight of the seer and moond by which the copper is sold.

2. The price of copper and many other articles of general trade in the Benares bazar being regulated by the great mercantile mart of Mirzapore it appears to me more to coincide with the spirit of the Calcutta Mint Committee enquiry to furnish the price current of that mart than to adhere literally to their orders. The sale of the article in the Benares bazar is confined to the mere consumption of the makers of copper pots and other utensils for house use and being in the first instance furnished by the Mirzapore merchants varies from the Mirzapore price only in the expence of transportation from six to eight annas in the maund.

3. To save the Calcutta Mint Committee trouble I have inserted a corresponding column reducing the price to the rate per Calcutta factory maund taking the seer at seventy-five Benares Sicca Rupee weight.

TABLE R.12.2: MONTHLY COPPER PRICE AT MIRZAPORE AND CALCUTTA, 1805-6

Year and month	*Description of copper*	*Price per Mirzapore maund of 97½ Benares Sicca Rs. to the seer*	*Price per Calcutta factory maund of 75 Rs. to the seer**
1805			
January	Japan stick copper	64	49:3:8
	English stick copper	62	47:11
	English sheet copper	67:12	51:1:10
February	English sheet copper	67:12	51:1:10
March	English sheet copper	67:12	51:1:10
April	Japan stick copper	66	50:12
	English stick copper	64	50
	English sheet copper	69:12	54:6:2
May	English sheet copper	69:12	54:6:2
June	English sheet copper	69:12	54:6:2
July	English sheet copper	69:12	54:6:2
August	English sheet copper	69:12	54:6:2
September	Japan stick copper	67	51:8:6
	English stick copper	65	50
	English sheet copper	78:12	64:6:8
October	English sheet copper	78:12	64:6:8
November	English sheet copper	78:12	64:6:8
December	English sheet copper	78:12	64:6:8
1806			
January	Japan stick copper	68:8	52:11
	English stick copper	66:8	51:2:4
	English sheet copper	72:4	55:9:2
February	English sheet copper	72:4	55:9:2

(Contd.)

*Possibly also due to transcription problems there are inconsistencies in the conversion of the two last columns.

March	Japan stick copper	70:8	54:3:8
	English stick copper	68:8	52:11
	English sheet copper	74:4	57:1:10
April	English sheet copper	74:4	57:1:10
May	Japan stick copper	73:8	56:8:6
	English stick copper	71:8	55
	English sheet copper	74:4	59:6:8
June	English sheet copper	74:4	59:6:8
July	English sheet copper	74:4	59:6:8
August	Japan stick copper	79	60:12:2
	English stick copper	75	57:11
	English sheet copper	81	62:4:10
September	English sheet copper	81	62:4:10
October	English sheet copper	81	62:4:10

Source: NAI, Finance, Mint Committee, Letters received by Mint Committee, 1806-7, pp. 35-42, 55-7.

13

The Shroffs at Bombay, 7 December 1806

[*In his extensive comments on proposals from the Board of Directors of the EIC to introduce a uniform currency for all parts of India under its jurisdiction, Helenus Scott, the assay master of the Bombay mint makes many critical remarks, concluding that this is not a good idea for the time being. A small selection of his arguments related to the logistics of coin circulation (including costs of transport and insurance), but especially to the essential function of the shroffs for the exchange between gold, silver and copper, has been transcribed below.*

See Ch. 4c of the Introduction and Part II: Records, No. 18.]

H. Scott, Assay Master Bombay to Jonathan Duncan, the Governor of Bombay, 7 December 1806

Hon'ble Sir,

According to your desire I now lay before you such observations as have occurred to me on the Honble Company's Letter No. 2 with its appendix. I shall proceed according to the order of the paragraphs that appear to me the most important.

[…]

10. Paragraph 20 and 21. These are most important paragraphs. The adoption of this proposal requires in Bombay the utmost caution and consideration, for instead of the good that is intended, it may produce much inconvenience and very serious mischief. I am very far from meaning to call in question the principle that in every country there can be but one metal which is the measure of property, or as Ld Liverpool* calls it the principal measure of property.

* Charles Jenkinson, 1st Earl of Liverpool (1729-1808) authored *Treatise on the Coins of the Realm* (1805).

The question however, still remains to be decided, whether the value of other coins is not to be determined by the public authority, whether other coins, which are the representatives of the coins which are the principal measure are to be regulated by the value of bullion in the market, and the will and the speculation of individuals. In this part of India I have no hesitation in saying that it is absolutely necessary to fix the value of every denomination of coin by the public authority. Should it be otherwise ordered both the Government and the people would be a prey to the shroffs in a manner fortunately unknown to us in all time past.

11. No man without considerable experience in this country can form an opinion of the influence and the arts of shroffs. They hold in their hands almost the whole specie of the country. Their houses are connected in every part of India. Their whole life is spent in the trade of gaining money by exchange and by every other means connected with this art. They follow the same trade from generation to generation, they subtle and acute from long and early habit, and are divided from the rest of the people not more by their cast, than by their means of living, in which they allow none to participate. Their influence is great and extensive, nor is it even in the power of Government on many occasions to protect itself against their combinations. If any denomination of the coin were left here to find its value in the market instead of being fixed by Government, it is certain that this would be done by the shroffs as their own interest might dictate. No other part of this community would have influence in fixing the rates, for the shroffs hold in their hands almost all the specie and would be the entire masters of the exchange. In Europe the people have many resources, the money of the country is there in many hands, and if one class of men were disposed to be selfish and unreasonable, others would be found of a different disposition who would correct or lessen the evil. If it has been thought that the leaving the value of some coins unfixed by Government would expose in Europe the people to fraud and imposition from money jobbers and others, how much more dreadful must the evil be in this country, where the people are more ignorant, and where the money jobbers have an influence beyond all comparison more extensive.

The shroffs have the command of nearly all the specie or could very soon secure a command of it. They too would monopolize the bullion and it cannot be doubted, but that whenever it was much for their interest, they would alter the values that the metals bear to each other in the market, to the great loss of the Honble Company, and the ruin of individuals.

[...]

14. For many years past the amount of silver coin in the circulation of this place [Bombay] has from the causes already detailed become quite insignificant. The troops have been paid by means of gold and copper and most of the ordinary business of the place has been carried on without the assistance of silver. When purchases of silver or of gold are made in Europe the theatre is so extensive, that it may be impossible for any man to determine which of the two metals has altered in its value with regard to other goods. The matter is very different here. We see precisely the causes of the variation, it is a demand for silver for a particular purpose above what this place can for the time supply.

[...]

25. One of the most material objections to the plan of a General Mint is the inconveniency that will arise to many classes of men on this side of India, from the want of Mints in their neighbourhood. The natives from time immemorial have been accustomed, with their Princes of every cast, to the conveniency of mints, in which they could convert their silver or gold into the ordinary coin of the country. We have at this moment several mints to the northward, which were established in ancient times. Those are the mints of Surat, Cambay, Broach and Baroda. In all of these mints they coin rupees which differ somewhat in value. This in the rich and populous country of Guzerat, where money transactions are carried on daily to a vast amount, must produce much loss and inconvenience to individuals and much gain to the shroffs. This inequality of value in the rupees of neighbouring districts gives rise to a thousand speculations in exchange, in which neither individuals, nor the Government itself, can at all times be protected from fraud. If the money of all could be equalized, the Surat rupee should be adopted for the whole, or what is the same thing, the

general rupee as now proposed for India. The Province of Guzerat would certainly afford a proof of the advantage to be expected from a general and uniform currency. In order to accomplish it, it would be necessary to suppress some of the mints, perhaps all of them, but Surat. The distance between those parts is not very considerable, they are separated by civilized and highly cultivated countries, nor would the transport of money involve any very great risk or expence. The plan even to this extent could not be executed without opposition. The shroffs would instantly see the ill consequences of it to themselves, they would occasion difficulties and excite murmurings. They would mislead the opinion of the people, and altho' we should in the end carry the point, yet it would for a time raise some suspicion and ill will.

[...]

33. I shall mention but one bad effect more that would arise from the adoption of this measure. The natives would certainly as a last resource send their bullion to be coined in the Mahratta mints in their neighbourhood, and we should be overwhelmed by a base coinage. This constantly takes place to a certain degree even at present, when they have not the same motives for it.

[....]

35. It is needless for me to observe that conclusions drawn from Great Britain may in many cases but ill apply to this vast country. The transit of money from any part of Great Britain to another is safe, expeditious and cheap. The distances are insignificant, and it need neither pass by sea, nor thro' hostile nations. One of our settlements in India is not more accessible to another than America is to England, and after all the facilities of communication that we have created, or shall ever be able to create, they must have with regard to each other many of the inconveniences that attend the connection of distant, and even of foreign countries. [...]

Source: NAI, Finance, Mint Committee, Letters received by Mint Committee, 1806-7, pp. 173-216.

14

Extra Pice for Behar Province, Patna 8 July 1807, and Benares, 19 September 1808

[*Even after decades of British occupation of Bihar and the province of Benares, the English authorities are still very insecure about how to take care for a sufficient circulation of small fractions. They blame the shroffs because of their manipulation of the exchange rates, price fluctuations in the copper market and the copper smiths because of imitating official coins. A smooth functioning of the copper coin circulation of the province of Bihar is estimated to need between 500,000 and 700,000 pieces.*

See Ch. 4a and 4c of the Introduction, Part II: Records, Nos. 12 and 15.]

H. Douglas, Magistrate, Patna to
S[ecretar]y Mint Committee, Patna 8 July 1807

[...]

2nd Some time ago, being a good deal alarmed at the great reduction of the number of pice for a rupee, and supposing that it might in some degree proceed from a combination of the shroffs at Patna, I wrote to the magistrates of the different zillahs of Behar who informed me that the same thing had taken place in their district.

3rd Formerly there were only two kinds of pice, called single (adhelee) Goruckpore, and double (tucka) Muddoo Sahee. Afterwards Government coined single and double pice and the husseras (or copper smiths) made pice in imitation of them, which from that are called hausseras pice. The Muddoo Sahee pice are not current now in Patna.

4th Before the coinage by Government 52 single pice went for a rupee; after that the number rose to 64 which continued for a short time, and it then fluctuated for many years. But for five or six years prior to 1807 it varied from 56 to 58, and at the present time it is 60. It is to be observed, however, that during the hot months, when so many marriages take place, the number of pice invariably falls.

5th To the best of my information the reduction of the number of pice for a rupee is occasioned by the increased price of copper (that was many years ago 45 rupees, and is now from 68 to 70 rupees a maund) which certainly prevents the husseras from making pice. And by there not having been any coinage by Government for a very long time, during which great quantities must have been carried away.

6th Be the cause however what it may the effect of the reduction of the number of pice for a rupee is severely felt; and the evil calls loudly for a remedy which can only be afforded by a coinage of pice. But to what extent or what number of pice Government can now afford to coin for a rupee, I have not the means of ascertaining, nor is it perhaps expected that I should give my opinion on the subject.

7th I should think that the best way would be to reduce the weight of the pice so as to give 64 for the rupee, and to exact a Regulation prohibiting a less number than that being paid in exchange for a rupee.

8th The number of petty shroffs in Patna, whose sole business it is to deal in the exchange of pice was formerly very small, but it has now increased to perhaps 300 or 400 and their profit, in fact, operates in the nature of a tax on pice.

Mint Committee at Benares, to G. Dowdeswell,
S[ecretar]y to Govt in the Revenue Department,
Fort William, Benares, 19 September 1808

[...]

4th With respect to the immediate distribution or introduction into circulation of the very trifling sum of pice hitherto received and expected at the Collector's Treasury, it occurs to us that a serious objection arises in as much as the supply is so far less than the requisite quantum, and the profit which the exchangers or vendors of old pice do now make, is so large, that they may be induced to buy up or obtain the whole quantity of Government pice thrown into the market, in order to longer enjoy the great advantage of their trade, and this speculation they may the more surely engage in as they have already seen the length of interval which has occurred without the introduction of the new coinage so long rumoured.

5th The medium price at which the old pice have been sold in the bazar of this city for the last year is 24 tuckas or double pice for the rupee, which when compared with the established value of the Government coin makes a difference of 8 tuckas, the which difference would diminish the profit hitherto derived by the venders of the old pice nearly 25 per cent and we therefore conceive it would be worth the whole of the persons to buy up this small quantity of Government coin either to keep it by them till the circulation shall have been so extended as to be beyond their means to supplying it, or availing themselves of the great scarcity to compel the purchasers to take it at their own arbitrary value. It therefore in our opinion becomes indispensably necessary that a sufficiency for immediate circulation should at once be thrown into the market and not by small parcels, as the only measure of preventing abuses totally subversive of the intention of Government in introducing the new copper coinage.

6th The late Acting Collector of Benares formerly reported to the Board of Revenue that pice to the amount of seven lacks of rupees would at least be required for the whole of the province.

7th At the same time that we consider the quantity stated by that gentleman to exceed the absolute necessity, even if we suppose that five lacks of rupees of pice would suffice, and draw our inferences from the time that already has elapsed since the measure of coining pice at the Calcutta mint, and remitting to the Benares Treasury was first sanctioned by Government when now only 20,000 rupees worth are in store (and the collector informs us that he has advice of only 40,000 rupees more being on the way) we may reasonably fear that the necessary quantity for circulation cannot be received with a year or more. [...]

Source: NAI, Finance, Mint Committee Proceedings, 5 May 1807-1 February 1811; see No. 5, pp. 7-9, and No. 30, pp. 45-8.

15

The Circulation of Tirsuli Pice at Benares, 21 May 1813

[*The trident (tirsuli) was one of the traditional mint mark of Benares, used on its manually made copper pice until 1806. It was, however, not used on the machine-made light-weight pice of the Calcutta Mint, made for Benares from 1807 until 1809. The trisul reappeared on the Benares pice, manufactured from 1815 until 1829. The Benares Magistrate suggests another abuse of the shroffs, but is not very clear as to the issues meant.*

See Ch. 4c of the Introduction, and Part II: Records, Nos. 7, 12 and 14.]

W. W. Bird, Acting Magistrate to George Dowdeswell,
Chief Secretary to the Government Fort William,
Magistrate's Office City of Benares, 21 May 1813

Sir,

I am under the necessity of soliciting the Authority of the Right Honourable the Governor-General in Council to put a stop to an abuse which exposes the poorer classes of the inhabitants of this city to considerable inconvenience.

2. Since the coin denominated Tirsooli pisa was originally established as the copper currency of the city of Benares no measures have been ad[vanced/dressed] to renew it and the inscription on these pice has of course by process of time and circulation become more or less indistinct. In this inscription is a tirsool, from which the shroffs, availing themselves of the circumstance abovementioned have lately altered the current value of the pice in which the tirsool is defective by reducing it 11 per cent below the pice in which the tirsool is found to be entire.

This distinction, set up by the shroffs is merely fictitious, and does not arise of any depreciation in the intrinsic value of the coin. I send by way of illustration specimens of both descriptions, a pice in which there is a defect in the tirsool, tho' the rest of the inscription may happen to be perfect and the coin itself of equal weight and real value with a pice bearing the mark of the tirsool in which there may be no such defect loses 11 per cent in current value for no other reason than the defectiveness of the tirsool. With this distinction hardly perceptible in some instances to general observation, the shroffs alone are well acquainted, which enables them to impose upon the ignorance of the public, and derive an advantage by purchasing the pice in question at the nominal and selling them at their real value.

3. But the labouring class of people suffer most. They receive their daily wages in copper pice, and as the money price of labour is the same as it was before, the shroffs made to be paid in pice containing a defect in the tirsool, looses 11 per cent of his earnings. The retail shopkeepers, who deal chiefly with the labouring poor, are paid for their articles in pice, and are compelled to demand them their customers at the rate which is required by the shroffs to whom they exchange them for rupees. This innovation accordingly presses most heavily upon those who on account of their indigence are the least capable of supporting it.

4. It has also introduced an uncertainty into the current value of the copper coin which serves as a cover to exaction, for instance the Agents of the Collector for the retail sale of stamp paper are paid for this commodity in pice, but being required to remit the amount periodically to the Public Treasury in rupees, they must dispose of their copper to the shroffs, and consequently indemnify themselves for the loss of 11 per cent to which they are liable by raising the price of the paper to the purchasers. This, by leaving so much to the discretion of the agents, opens the way of course to unlimited abuse, for which there can be no effectual remedy without removing at once the evil in which it has originated.

5. Since this evil is found to originate in a distinction purely fictitious, and is in reality nothing else than a fraud concerted a month or two ago by a combination of interested persons to serve

their own purposes, it is very desirable to remove it, and for that purpose I recommend that Government authorize me to issue a proclamation declaring all tirsoolee pice, whether retaining the mark of the tirsool or not to be current as theretofore at the same value, and received at an equal rate in discharge of all public and private demands as the established copper currency of the place. This measure, I submit, is indispensable, not only to remove the abuses already introduced, but to prevent the introduction of new ones which the avarice of any combination may in future attempt to impose upon the public.

Source: NAI, Finance, Mint Committee Proceedings, 27 May 1813, pp. 4-7.

16

The Circulation of Cowries and Copper Pice at Cuttack, 26 September 1817

[The province of Cuttack became under British rule as a part of the Bengal Presidency in 1803. Still no copper coins were circulating there at that time until 1817 when this report was drawn up. What mattered for the working class was the exchange rate between cowries and the silver rupee, which allegedly was manipulated by the shroffs. Reference is made to earlier attempts to fix the rate between cowries and the copper pice of John Prinsep in Bengal in 1781.

See Ch. 3d and 4c of the Introduction, and Part II: Records, No. 2.]

J.W. Sherer, Accountant General to Holt Mackenzie,
Secretary to the Government, Territorial Department,
Fort William, 26 September 1817

Sir,

I have the honor to acknowledge the receipt of your letter of the 15th ultimo, communicating the sentiments of the Honorable the Vice-President in Council on the alleged depreciation of cowries in Cuttack after a consideration of my report on that subject submitted to Government under date the 28th of July last.

2ndI beg leave to state that in suggesting the measure of fixing the value of couries in Cuttack by enactment as the fraction of a rupee or rather of a pice vizt. 4 cowons of couries equal to 1 Calcutta Sicca Rupee, 1 pun of do. to one copper pice, I had simply in view the object of preventing the shroffs and mohajuns in that district from debiting and crediting this currency in their accounts at arbitrary and fluctuating rates, as it was alleged they did do, to the injury of many classes of the inhabitants, and I inclined to think that fixing the value of couries as a money of account might afford satisfaction, if not much actual relief to the complainants from the circumstance of such measure having been suggested by themselves both to Mr. Scott Waring, the Collector of Cuttack in 1811, and to the present Collector in the present year.

3rd With regard to the rate there appeared to me to be propriety in preserving the rate at which assessments of land in Cuttack had been and still are converted into rupees; and I did not apprehend that giving couries a somewhat enhanced value in account as the fraction of a rupee or of a pice would tend much to enhance them generally or much to impede the introduction of pice. Whereas if true as alleged, that silver was monopolized by the mohajuns for the sake of depreciating couries in account and running up heavy debts in this currency against the poorer classes who require accomodations in silver to pay their revenue, it might perhaps have put a stop to such exactions, to render a debt irrecoverable by law which exhibited couries at a lower rate than 4 cawons per rupee for such accomodations. When pice were first issued from the Calcutta mint for circulation in Bengal it was exacted under date 24th September 1781 that the copper coin should be received and paid according to the relative value fixed in a published table of copper to couries without any discount or batta whatever, which however is not to influence or effect the bazar price of couries in any other matter than in the exchange of the one for the another.

4th Having offered with deference this explanation I would beg however not to be understood as reurging the measure of fixing the value of couries in Cuttack as one of much importance.

5th On all accounts it seems desirable that a copper currency should be established in Cuttack as in the other districts of the Lower Provinces. The value of couries in account is not elsewhere regulated by authority and the measure suggested by me on the ground explained above would certainly, if adopted, would have formed an exception and might have tended to keep up an inconvenient distinction in respect of currency between Cuttack and the districts of the Lower Provinces.

6th With regard to the copper currency now circulating by authority of Government in the Lower Provinces* it appears to me desirable to extend it to Cuttack and to give it the sanction of the Law, which it still requires throughout those provinces. I beg leave therefore to suggest that the Mint Committee may be instructed to prepare a regulation for that purpose.

Source: NAI, Finance, Mint Committee Proceedings 10 May 1818, No. 45, pp. 96-8.

* In the margin: pice weighing 9 ans each and issued at 64 for a rupee.

17

Manufacturers of Counterfeit Coin in the Kingdom of Awadh, 22 January 1827

[*Until 1857 Oude or Awadh was an independent kingdom (capital Lucknow), although under considerable British influence. Allegedly tolerated by the local authorities counterfeiters of British Indian rupees were active in five villages in the pargana of Deryabad. In 1820 the Benares Mint ended the production of rupees with its own distinctive mark, but continued to produce the so-called Farrukhabad Rupees until 1830. This possibly opened possibilities for counterfeiters. Disguised as pilgrims to Benares, a holy city for Hindus on the boards of the river Ganga, they brought them in circulation in territory under direct British rule. A complaint was filed with the British Resident at Lucknow, requesting him to ask the Awadhi government to take action.*

See Ch. 4b of the Introduction, and Part II: Records, Nos. 14 and 15.]

Extract from the Proceedings of the Honble the Vice-President in Council in the Judicial Department, 1 February 1831

D.B. Morrieson, to Henry Shakespear, Secretary to Government Judicial Department at Fort William, Magistrate's Office City of Benares, 22 January 1831

Sir,

I consider it my duty to bring the following circumstances to the notice of the Vice-President in Council.

2. On the 27th April and 27th June 1827 Mr. Hamilton, the Magistrate of this city, reported to Government the substance of information he had received and the steps taken by him to cause the apprehension of a set of manufacturers of counterfeit coin in the dominions of His Majesty of Oude. In consequence of his exertions, I understand, several of the forgers were apprehended, and are at present in confinement at Lucknow, but I regret to state that a stop has not been put to similar nefarious transactions, and the quantity of bad coin now brought into our territories from a set of villages in Oude has become a serious evil. Since the abolition of the Benares Mint it has been notorious that counterfeit coin to a large amount has got into circulation in the city, and every exertion on my part was directed to discover the source; but, owing to the extreme difficulty of obtaining timely information, it was only within the last few days that I was enabled to get a satisfactory clue.

3. Several men, inhabitants of Oude, under the disguise of pilgrims were apprehended, and upwards of 2,000 of the counterfeit rupees found, partly upon them, and partly buried in the bed of a nullah not far from the city where it had been deposited by them till such time as a bargain with the Kulwars for its sale could be struck. The confessions of these men, added to information I have derived from other sources prove without a doubt the existence of a very extensive establishment of forgers at Deryabad, from whence a regular and copious supply of counterfeit rupees is sent for circulation into our territories. I beg to subject a short memorandum of the names, places of abode, and other particulars regarding these people, whose recognition I should have no difficulty in effecting. I likewise send three of the rupees as specimens of the manufacture.

4. I am fully convinced that these forgers are not only tolerated by the Oude zamindars, aumils and other local authorities, but are the sources of considerable profit to them and that rigorous as well as prompt measures must be adopted for their suppression. From the circumstance of their existence out of the Honble Company's Dominions, it is impossible for the magistrates of the neighbouring zillahs to extirpate them, and all measures for the prevention of the entrance of the forged coin into our district must from

their own nature be productive but of little good – the facilities of importation, as well as the profits of the illicit trade for counterbalancing the strictest precautions and the risks of detection. It is not to Benares alone that these supplies of coin are brought, but to all the neighbouring districts; tho' this city from its size, wealth, [and] importance forms, I doubt not, the chief mart thro' which it gets into circulation. And now that I have been able to get a good clue I have every hope of laying hold of many more of the utterers as well as of considerable sums of the false coin.

[…]

Memorandum reported to in Paragraph 3

TABLE R.17: NAMES OF RUPEE COIN FORGERS, BENARES, 1831.

Names of the forgers	*Names of the villages in which they reside*	*Names of the zamindars upon whose estates they reside*
Bullahee and Boree of the caste of Zirgurs or Jewellers	Dheema in the Pergunnah of Deryabad	Rakun Moosulman
Rambux Jeweller and his brother (name unknown)	Burayebad in Do Do	Sahibdeen Rajpoot
Bholaye and Bhikuna Jewellers	Nowhuryah in Do Do	Baboo Hurdut Singh
Hemaye Jeweller	Duroundah in Do Do	Rambux Bythe
Four other Jewellers (names unknown)	Bazpoor in Do Do	

Remarks

These forgers are all of the caste of jewellers and the proprietors, upon whose estates they reside levy a tax upon each shop, the rate of which is said to vary according to circumstances. They are all known to carry on their traffic thro' the connivance of their zamindars. It has been ascertained that the usual rate at which the coin sells is from 10 to 12 rupees per hundred. Three years ago the rate was as high as from 25 to 50 and the cause of this great alteration can only be attributed to the greater increase of the spurious money.

The specimens of the rupees herewith forwarded show that they have evidently been recently coined and to prevent friction on the road, which by rubbing off the coating of silver would at once expose their true nature, they were conveyed and found in bags filled with bran. The broken rupee exhibits a great admixture of copper, but as far as the external workmanship and appearance go, it must, I think, be generally allowed that the forgery has been very skillfully executed.

Source: NAI, Foreign Department 1830-9, Proceedings 11 February 1831, Nos. 72-3, P.C.

18

Copper Coin Minted at Saugor, 27 April 1831, and its Consequences as Still Felt in 1847

[*In 1818 the British took over the Maratha Mint of Saugor, which remained active until its closure in 1835 in favour of the fully mechanized Mint of Calcutta. For decades this caused a penury of especially copper trisul pice in central India. Still in 1847 the British Agent in Bundelkhand recommended the opening of three new cheap mints, at Saugor, Agra and Neemuch. Nevertheless, the authorities in Calcutta were not willing to reconsider their decision to centralize the mintage for British India as much as possible.*

See Ch. 4a of the Introduction and Part II: Records, Nos. 13, 19, 24 and 26.]

D. Presgrave, Mint Master at Saugor to J.C. Smith, Agent to the Gov[erno]r Gen[era]l Jubulpore, Saugor Mint Office, 27 April 1831[*]

[...]

With reference to the 4th paragraph I beg to state that copper has been always purchased at the lowest rate at which it was procurable here, but I have the pleasure to inform you that the maund weight at which it is bought at this mint is equal to one maund and a quarter of the weight by which it is sold in Calcutta, the Saugor weight being one hundred new Furruckabad rupees the seer.

The copper coined now yields to Government after paying all expenses about 25 rupees a maund or 35 rupees 12 Annas per cent according to the rates at which it is purchased.

* Pp 93-100 reaction Mint Committee: Saugor Mint to be continued provisionally.

When the new copper coinage was first established at Saugor it was deemed expedient on the issue of the new currency to prevent loss to the merchants and to the public to purchase the old pice at the rates at which such copper was selling in the bazar and this rate has been from 80 to 70 rupees for the Saugor mint maund above mentioned.

Since copper has been purchased from the merchants who have imported it from Mirzapore the constant endeavour has been to get it as cheap as possible which I have not I hope it will appear been altogether unsuccessful when the Mint Committee take in consideration the difference between Calcutta and Saugor weight. The distance from Calcutta to Mirzapore and from thence overland to Saugor on camels, buffaloes or bullocks being a distance of more than 300 miles.

The Saugor mint maund weighs 4,000 new Furruckabad rupees which is but 2⅙ drachms short of 103 lbs avoirdupois, and yields 7209 copper pice of 100 grains each.

7209 Copper pice at 65 to the Furruckabad rupees, the rate at which they are sold to shroffs and merchants are equal to SaRs 110: 14½ annas.

TABLE R.18: PRODUCTION COSTS OF COPPER COINS, SAUGOR MINT, 1831

The cost of making a maund containing 7209 copper pice is as under durabs labour		
	at 27 per hundred pice	11:12:0
Press men's labour for strucking 7,209 copper pice		0:08:0
Loss on melting of seraps or seysil Wasting on making planchets charcoal for firing seissible Ditto for annealing planchets Wood for blocks under the anvils, mootakas pootellies and hammer handles, iron, steel and kherie of making dies, chambes mootooka kuttenahs Guzzee cloth, cotton rope, oil for striking press		4:02:6

Gunney and twine for 2¼ bags for packing the pice Carpenter's labour for making hammer handles, blocks, mootakas, pootellees Blacksmith's labour for cutting copper, making dies chanblies &ca &ca &ca and engraving dies All of which is done by contract	15:14:6

Residencies, Central India Agency, Coins, Mints, No. 51 of 1847

*Agent Governor-General, Bandlecund to Secretary to Government of India with the Governor General Simla, Jhansie, 27 May 1847**

Sir,

I have the honour to acknowledge the receipt of your letter of the 8th January last, with enclosure from the Honourable the Court of Directors No. 28 dated the 21st of October 1846.

[…]

11. The work will, however, with the advantage of these cheap mints be one of time, for it has always been found a task of great difficulty to substitute a coin of higher for one of lower intrinsic value. For sufficient evidence of this we have only to go to the districts of Banda, Humeerpore, and Jaloun which border upon the Jumna, and all the Saugor territories. There the smaller rupee coined at the Native Mints still forms the great mass of the currency. The work of absorbing the Balasahee rupee coined at a mint that has ceased to work for thirty years, has been lately going on in the Jaloun district. The settlement was in some parts of this district made in this coin, and it has been received into the treasury, and sent for recoinage to the Calcutta Mint. These rupees have become so scarce that they commonly circulate in the market at par with the Company's rupee in that district, though they are twelve per cent

* See also NAI, Foreign Department 1847, Mints, No. 220.

less in intrinsic value. Indeed the landholders paid their revenue in Company' Rupees at par, being unable to get Balasahee rupees at a lower rate in the market. The Collector purchased Company's Rupees with some of them at par to pay the Government establishments, and credited the profits to Government, and it amounted from May 1844 to 30 April 1846 to 25,452. And at last Govt consented to receive from the Landholders Company's Rupees instead of Balasahees at a premium of 6:4 or 1/16th per cent insead of 12:8 or 1/8th, the rate which obtained when the settlement was made, and the process of absorbation began. And the landowners considered the indulgence as a very great boon.

12. Now the present mode of sending all the absorbed coins to the Calcutta Mint, even from part of Jaloun, which borders on the Jumna River is attended with great cost and still greater inconvenience and harassment to the troops. I had lately to send two companies of Infantry from Jhansi 70 miles to Orae, there to take charge of a batch of these coin and escort it to Allahabad, and thence to return to Jhansi. This trip took them the greater parts of the hot winds, and it has to be repeated more than once very year. What will the duty be if we attempt the same operation in all the districts of central India, so far removed as most of them are from navigable rivers. Our regiments would be inadequate to the duty in their present strength and numbers. Cheap mints at the points I have indicated would obviate all the difficulty, and be a source of profit instead of expense to Government.

13. As much loss and annoyance is felt by the mass of the people from the state of the copper as of the silver currency; and it was I believe from the copper coinage that the Saugor Mint received the chief part of its profits, at the same time that it prevented the very great inconvenience that is now felt at all times and in all the Saugor and Nerbudda District from the attempts to supply them with copper coins from the Calcutta Mint. They never reach the districts in the quantity and at the time they are required; and the complaints I receive of the fluctuations in value, and consequent loss and inconvenience are incessant.

The cheap mints I have suggested would remedy this evil everywhere, at the same time that they would pay a great part of their costs by an uniform copper coinage for all central India.

Source: NAI, NAI, Finance, Mint Committee Proceedings 1831, Pt. II, pp. 23-8; Residencies, Central India Agency, No. 22: 1726 / 1863: Currency question in C[entral]. I[ndia]: Reports on mints in the Native States of Bundelkhand (1846-7), No. 51 of 1847.

19

Suggestions how to Introduce New Copper Currency from the Calcutta Mint in the Delhi Territory, 14 June to 13 September 1831

[*The Public Works, and in particular the digging of irrigation canals north of Delhi from the 1820s to 1840s needed big amounts of copper coins for paying out wages. The British had closed the Delhi Mint in 1818, except for the occasional striking of presentation pieces for the last Moghul. The production of the Delhi pice was dearly missed although the need for small change was partially fulfilled by Mints in the still independent Sikh State. Nevertheless, all initiatives to reopen the Copper Mint of Delhi in 1826 and later failed. Besides, a smooth acceptance of the fiduciary British Indian copper coins was not at all self-evident.*

See Studies 10-13 and Part II: Records, Nos. 18 and 24.]

W.B. Martin, Acting Rest & Chief Commissioner of Dehlie to Mint Committee, Office of Rest & Chief Commissioner Dehlie, 16 March 1836

Sir,

I have the honor to submit for the consideration and orders of Government the accompanying copy of a letter addressed by me to the late Resident and Chief Commissioner and of its Enclosures.

W. Frazer, Commissioner to W.B. Martin, Resident and Commissioner Dehlee, Commes Office, Dehlee 13 September 1831

With reference to your letter of the 3d June last with its enclosure on the subject of a copper coinage I have the honor to forward copies of six letters from the Principal Assistants of the five divisions and the Superintendant of Canals, and to add that I see no objection whatever to introducing the standard copper currency as its use will depend entirely on the price of copper in the market. If laborers get more copper by taking standard pyce they will be glad to get them, if less they will raise their hire.

2. If it is desirable to introduce the currency the pice received may be paid away to artisans and laborers employed in the Public Works and from the Treasury.

3. The price of copper and value of pice may be compared by trying their sale in the bazar.

Copies

From Principal Assistant, Southern Division, 23 June 1831

I have the honor to acknowledge the receipt of your letter dated 14th June and its enclosures relative to the introduction of a standard coinage into this territory.

2. I imagine no difficulty will arise in affecting a speedy circulation of copper pice in this district. A proclamation by the Resident that the coin in question will be received and paid at a certain rate of exchange will at once give the coin a standard value in the money market.

From Officiating Prin[sipa]*l Asst, Rohtuk Division 23 June 1831*

I have the honor to acknowledge the receipt of your letter dated 14th June and its enclosures relative to the introduction of a standard coinage into this territory.

2. I see no difficulty to be apprehended in the circulation of the coin whatever either from its novelty or from ignorance of its value if the introduction of it is preceded by distinct proclamation.

3. The introduction of the copper pice might be immediately commenced in making trifling payment.

4. And if in the notices the relative value between the current metals be clearly stated it will destroy the power which monied men now have of over or under valuing copper to their own advantage and to the great inconvenience of the ignorant and the poor.

5. Nor would this manner of fixing the exchange at least rendering it more permanent than it is now is at all I should think injure any fair dealer. Commodities vary in the value they bear to metals much more often and suddenly than metals do in the value they bear to one another.

6. The continual exchanges exhibited in the market tables of copper coin assuming silver as the standard appear therefore fraudulent and the prevention of them would readily be understood by both parties affected, the agricultural dealer or anyone else and the banker.

7. I believe the novelty of the introduction would last only a day indeed. I have no doubt a Government paper currency might be brought into extensive circulation in this part of India.

The little risk in transporting it or of being robbed of it are great inducements to merchants whose agents or correspondents are distant and it would be convertible into money at every Government treasury. I have frequently enquired into this subject among trading men and always found nothing novel promising benefit an innovation even to a Hindoo.

From Superintendent of Canals, 14 June 1831

I have the honor to acknowledge to reply to your letter of the 14th instant and in reference to the conclusion of the 2nd paragraph of its enclosure I beg to state my opinion that until the currency of the coin in question is established supplying me with these pice with which to pay my people would only have the effect of drawing off the work people to where they could get pice which were in general currency and this possibility to the great detriment of the works, in the neighbourhood of Dehlee where these pice might attain a currency my works are not many. In the district where more extended these pice being utterly unknown would cause nothing but annoyance and delay in the works and in the Northern Division of the Canal in the Independent Sikh States where my greatest expenditure of pice lies they would not be received at all, the only current copper coin being that coined at Chuchuroulee.

In reference to the last paragraph of your enclosure if

Government be prepared to make the Calcutta pice the only legal copper money, I should suppose a plentiful supply under exactment of Government would answer the purpose, but so long as the other kinds of pice is now in circulation are permitted these new ones will only be received with reference to their value as copper. When the last of that ranges above their money valued they will be melted up and when the contrary they will be current at a deteriorated value unless this be specially guarded against and if they hang from their nominal value they will be equally inconvenient with those now in use. The experiment of introducing them has I believe been made in the military cantonment Meeruth where I understand no one is allowed to refuse receiving them at their nominal value. A similar measure enforced by penalty might in time bring them into general use and this would doubtless be a great inconvenience to all who had the charge of extensive works by simplifying accounts.

From Principal Assistant, Northern Division, 26 June 1831

I have the honor to acknowledge the receipt of your letter dated 14th June with its enclosure.

If the copper coinage alluded to is declared to be a legal tender and that it is not likely from its intrinsic value to be objected to by the community I cannot apprehend any difficulty in effecting its circulation. Perhaps pice to the extent of one or two hundred rupees in value would prove a sufficient supply for the demands of this district in the first instance and this amount would rapidly be put in circulation if a small percentage on all payments from the Government Treasury were ordered to be made in pice or even if the fractional parts of Rupees were to be paid in the new coinage.

From Collector, Central Division, 28 June 1831

I have the honor to acknowledge the receipt of a letter from your office of the 14th instant with enclosures relative to the introduction of a standard copper coinage into this territory and in reply to state that in my opinion the measure is exceedingly desirable and can be effected without any difficulty.

2. I would propose that the supply of new pice received from the Presidency Mint or such portion of it as may not be remitted to the other Divisions be deposited in this Treasury and be appropriated to payments in lieu of the copper currency now in use and that a proclamation be issued throughout the city directing all persons to receive them as the current coin and at their fixed value.

From Principal Assistant, Western Division, 16 August 1831

I have the honor to acknowledge the receipt of your letter dated 14th ultimo and in reply to state that I do not perceive any practical difficulty in introducing the new copper coinage into currency provided it be simultaneously introduced by proclamation through the other Divisions of the Dehlee territory.

The only parties who will suffer from the measure are the money changers who at present derive large profits from the trade in pice.

There is no distribution of pice to any extent on account of Government in the district excepting through the Superintendent of the Canal but as the supply of copper coinage is so inadequate that sometimes only 56 pice can be procured in exchange for the rupee and as on occasions of marriage or other ceremonies when money is usually distributed in small sums, the tax falls very heavily upon the parties, it will be a great source of advantage and convenience to the zamindars if they be allowed to exchange their money at the local treasury on paying a small fee to the treasurer for the additional labour it will involve in the same way as a small charge is sanctioned at the General Treasury on procuring small silver coin.

I am not at present prepared to state the amount of copper coinage which may be required to meet the wants of the district but the supply recently received from the Presidency will meet but for a very short time I imagine the demands of several divisions of the Territory.

The present currency is I believe superior in intrinsic value to the new coinage but its price will of course be considerably deteriorated by the proposed substitution and I shall feel obliged by your informing me upon what terms it is to be received in exchange.

Source: NAI, Finance, Mint Committee Proceedings, 3 April 1832, No. 6, pp. 53-9.

20

Plans for the Issue of Newly Designed Copper Coins at the Calcutta Mint, 2 August 1831

[*As part of the centralization policy of the Calcutta Mint from 1831 to 1835 copper pice, half anna and pie coins were coined, bearing texts with the value in three languages without any reference to the East India Company or the king of England. By taking such a step the directors in London feared the consequences of offending the Moghul at Delhi. The mint master at Calcutta did not feel such inhibitions as is clear from his proposal in 1831. The first portrait of an English king on EIC coins appeared on the silver rupee and its fractions, introduced in 1835 (William IV) and on British Indian copper coins only from 1862 onwards (Victoria).*

See Studies 13 and Part II: Records, No. 18.]

R. Saunders, Mint Master to H.H. Wilson, Secretary to the Mint Committee, Calcutta Mint, 2 August 1831

Sir,

With reference to the 4th paragraph of my letter of the 24th ultimo I have the honor to suggest that in the event of Government sanctioning the coinage of the double pice & single pice of account therein proposed to be struck in the mint, the pieces shall bear legends as follows:

On the double pice weighing 200 troy grains 2 of which go to the anna.

½ anna	
نیم انہ আধা আসা	HALF ANNA আধা আসা

ILLUS. R.20.1: PROPOSED DESIGN OF HALF ANNA COIN.

On the pie of account weighing 33, 333 troy grains 12 of which go to the anna.

1 pie	
یک پاي ऐक पाई	ONE PIE এক পাই

ILLUS. R.20.2: PROPOSED DESIGN OF ONE PIE COIN.

The legend on the present copper coin weighing 100 grains of which 4 go to the anna struck in conformity with Reg. XXV of 1817 is as follows.

1 pie	
شاه عالم باد سا جلوس مانوس سنه	এক পাঐ সিক্কা یک پاي سکہ ऐक पाई सिक्का

ILLUS. R.20.3: PROPOSED DESIGN OF ONE PIE SICCA COIN.

but as the diameter of the proposed pice of account will be seen to be much smaller, the inscription on the present coin cannot conveniently be adopted but it may be inserted on the double pice should government consider it to be preferable to the more simple and less expensive legend now preferred.

Source: NAI, Finance, Mint Committee Proceedings 1831, Pt II, pp. 216-17.

21

Circulation of New Copper Coin Issued from the Calcutta Mint 13 April to 8 May 1832

[*From 1831 to 1835 the fully mechanized Calcutta Mint produced millions of copper pice, half anna, and pie coins. Having the problems in mind of putting in circulation earlier issues in the Bengal Presidency, the Mint authorities discussed the logistical questions at stake. This way they wanted to make sure that the new copper coins were going to be used as effectively as possible, including attempts at diminishing the power of the shroffs by giving them an official role in the distribution. It is noticeable that together with copper coins also the smooth circulation of small silver fractions is deemed necessary.*

See Ch. 4b and 4c of the Introduction, and Part II: Records, Nos. 20, 22 and 23]

H.H. Wilson, S[ecretar]y Mint Committee of Calcutta to J. Prinsep, Secretary to Government, General Department, Calcutta Mint Committee, 3 May 1832

Sir,

1st I am directed by the Committee of Superintending the Affairs of the Mint at this Presidency to submit for the orders of the Honble the Vice-President in Council the accompanying copies of a letter of the mint master dated the 13th ultimo, and a minute by Mr. Barwell on the subject of facilitating and extending the circulation of the copper currency.

2nd At present the circulation of copper coin in Calcutta is impeded by the exclusive issue of them from the General Treasury, from which comparatively few persons, and those not of the poor classes who most require the accommodation, are likely to receive them. The value of the new coins, the double pice and 1/3 pice are also yet but little known, and advantage is taken of the ignorance of the people to exchange but two instead of three of the latter for a pice, to the consequent loss of the persons thus receiving them.

3rd In like manner the circulation of the copper currency in the Upper Provinces is obstructed by their being issued only through the Collectors' Treasuries and by their value imperfectly appreciated. They have, also in many places to contend with copper pice which, though of crude execution, are of greater weight and metallic value, and have accordingly a preference in the market.

4th To remove these impediments in Calcutta, the mint master proposes that the Sub Treasurer be authorized to employ podars in the principal public places in and about the town, who shall supply all applicants with copper coin in exchange at the Government rate, being remunerated either by a monthly salary or by a commission. The latter he considers preferable. He also recommends that copies of the Regulations regarding the new copper currency shall be printed and stuck up in the shops of these podars and in the principal bazars. Mr. Barwell concurs in these propositions, recommending also occasional proclamation by the beat of drum and specifying the places where the shops shall be established.

5th Mr. Barwell also states that the head podar of the treasury is willing to undertake the establishment of the shroff exchange shops for the distribution of pice and small silver coin upon a commission of one pice in the rupee. Another native has offered to purchase Rs. 1,000 worth of pice at the same rate, and Mr. Barwell is of opinion that sales of this kind might be made to petty exchangers. At the same time he is of opinion that the same control could not be maintained over the purchasers as over the shroffs established through the treasury podar, and consequently prefers that arrangement.

6th Similar measures are recommended by the mint master and Mr. Barwell for the mofussil, with the addition of declaring all other pice than those coined by this Government illegal. Mr. Barwell also recommends that the podars of the Collectors should be authorized to exchange the new pice for the old.

7th In these recommendations the other members of the Committee concur, except in the last, as the exchange of the old for the new pice might have the effect of encumbering the Treasuries with a quantity of copper coin not easily converted into the new currency, and might operate to keep up the fabrication of the old pice, as these, although of more metallic value than the new, exchange for more than the value of copper they contain, and would be profitably converted into an equal number of new pice at 64 to the rupee. It may be better therefore merely to declare them illegal & prohibit their receipt at any public office, and in time they may be melted and worked up in copper or brass utensils. With this modification the Committee beg to recommend the measures suggested for sanction of the Government.

8th In addition to these arrangements the Committee also think it advisable that due notice shall be given in the Government Gazettee that all persons applying direct to the General Treasury, or to any of the mofussil treasuries for a quantity of pice, not less than 10 rupees in value, shall be furnished with them at the established rate (64 to the rupee), free of all charge. Also with small silver coin for 10 rupees and upwards to the extent of 500 rupees, the last arrangement until further notice. In the mofussil also the issue of allowances to prisoners in jails, to indigent prosecutors and witnesses and to labourers in public works shall be made as extensively as possible in half anna pice and 1/3d pice at the rates fixed by Regulation, a notice may be stuck up in the places where the pay is issued.

9th The mint master has also submitted a statement of the cost at which a boat office in Calcutta is willing to undertake the conveyance of pice to different places inclusive or exclusive of insurance. In the former case no guard would be requisite. The Committee believe that this plan will be found more economical than the dispatch of pice through the Commissariat.

No. 2 Enclosure

R. Saunders, Mint Master to H.H. Wilson, Secretary to the Mint Committee, Calcutta Mint, 13 April 1832

Sir,

I have to request that you will bring to the notice to the Mint Committee that in consequence of the Sub Treasurer having an accumulation of new copper coin to the extent of nearly a lack of rupees at the General Treasury, none has been sent from the Mint for some time past whereby we have now in hand copper coin to the value noted in the margin, and more is in progress of coinage.

TABLE R.21.1: COPPER COINS (SINGLE PICE, ½ ANNA AND PIE) IN SUPPLY AT THE CALCUTTA MINT, 1832

	Rs. worth
Single pyce	13,000
Half anna pieces	30,000
Pie pieces	29,000

2. It is said that the new pie pieces are still being disposed of by the shroffs in the Calcutta Bazar at the rate of 2 instead of 3 to the old pice, owing to the public being ignoranted of the rate at which they should circulate, and that from the same cause the new half anna pieces are not in general circulation. Mr. Barwell states that copper coin cannot be distributed to the public directly from the General Treasury without great inconvenience to that establishment and on order from the Court of Directors directs that all coins should be sent from the Mint to the General Treasury.

3. Under these circumstances I would suggest that the Sub Treasurer be authorized to employ temporarily a few podars to be stationed in the principal bazars in Calcutta and its suburbs. These persons may daily take from the Treasury the quantity of copper they may be able to dispose of, giving of course adequate security from the same. They are to give copper coin in exchange for silver to any person who may apply to them at the Government

rate of exchange, and to engage under a heavy penalty to do this without any charge for shroffage during the time they may be so employed. They may be remunerated either by a monthly salary or by a commission on that value of copper coin they may thus put into circulation.

4. Extracts from the Regulations with translations relating to the rates at which copper coins are to circulate and to their being a legal tender for fractional portions of a rupee may be printed, and after having been proclaimed by beat of drum, copies may be stuck up in the principal bazars and at the Treasury podars shops.

5. A certain number of copies with specimens of the coinage be sent to the several collectors and paymasters; the regulations in like manner being proclaimed thru' the different districts. A quantity of the copper coin should be sent to those officers with instructions to use their endeavours to put them into circulation. Of all other copper coin than that struck at the Government mint should I think be prohibited within these provinces.

6. Accompanying a memorandum of the charge at which I have ascertained that a boat establishment in Calcutta is willing to convey copper coin to the principal stations on the river, inclusive of insurance for the delivery of the same. In the former case the necessity for sending a guard with the remittances will of course be dispensed with.

No. 3 Enclosure

Memorandum of charges of boat hire for the conveyance of copper pice from the new mint to the undermentioned stations, Calcutta, 14 April 1832.

TABLE R.21.2: CHARGES OF BOAT HIRE AND INSURANCE COSTS FOR THE CONVEYANCE OF COPPER PICE FROM THE CALCUTTA MINT ACROSS THE BENGAL PRESIDENCY, 1832

	Value in SaRs	*Boxes*	*Boats*	*Tonnage of books of each of these boats*	*Boat hire including accommodation for sepoys*[*]
Moorshedabad	15,000	87	2	400	45:8
Bhangulpore	10,000	40	2	400	76:8
Patna	10,000	40	2	400	102
Sarum	10,000	40	2	400	102
Ghazypore	10,000	40	2	400	136
Benares	10,000	40	2	400	136
Allahabad	10,000	40	2	40	170
Cawnpore	10,000	40	2	400	204
Furruckabad	45,000	180	4	500	560
Meerut	15,000	87	3	500	360
Dacca	15,000	87	3	400	102
Sylhet	10,000	40	2	400	102
Chittagong	15,000	87	3	400	153
Ghowhattee	15,000	87	2	500	240
	200,000	935	33		2,489

TABLE R.21.3: INSURANCE AND OTHER CHARGES FOR THE CONVEYANCE OF COPPER PICE FROM CALCUTTA MINT, 1832.

	Insurance		*Peon & Policy Fee*
	Rate per cent	*SaRs*	*SaRs*
Moorshedabad	1	150	10
Bhangulpore	2	200	15:10
Patna	2 ½	250	20
Sarum	2 ½	250	20
Ghazypore	2 ½	250	26
Benares	3	300	26

* Seven clays additional hire to the above rates for boats proceeding via the Soonderbunds.

Allahabad	3 ½	350	32
Cawnpore	3 ½	350	38
Furruckabad	4	1,800	36
Meerut	4½	675	74
Dacca	1½	225	20
Sylhet	4	400	20
Chittagong	4½	675	29
Ghowhattee	3	450	33
		6,325	454:10

No. 4 Enclosure

J. Barwell, General Treasury, 18 April 1832.

That the poorer classes of natives would be greatly benefited by a more extensive and general issue of copper money and particularly of the pie pieces will not, I imagine, be for a moment doubted by those who have considered the subject. The receivers of money at the General Treasury [that] have generally to receive in large sums are for the most part rich, do not require, and are consequently unwilling to receive copper money and cannot be forced to take more than the fractional part of a rupee. It is troublesome & tedious to count out any considerable sum of copper coin, and parties receiving money at the Treasury will not undertake it. It is evident therefore that copper money never can obtain general or extensive circulation even in Calcutta or the Lower Provinces by means of actual payments from the General Treasury. At the same time it is necessary under the existing orders of the Court that all money and of course this description should pass through the Treasury from the mint. The suggestions contained in the 3rd, 4th and 5th part of Mr. Saunders letter are in my opinion well calculated to get the copper money into circulation and defeat the tricks and trickery of the shroffs, in addition, however and with a view to further extend the circulation of the copper & the small silver coins, I would beg to suggest that in making remittances to the Salt and Commercial Agents, the Sub Treasurer be authorized to transmit a considerable portion in these coins to [be] distributed by them in making their advances. This will, no doubt, give the Agents or the native Amlah employed some additional trouble and will, in all probability, be objected to by them. As however the extension of the circulation of these coins must prove a public convenience, a boon to the poor and an object with the Government, such objectives will not, I imagine, be listened to. Mr. Saunders proposes that the podars to be employed in the exchange of copper money should be remunerated either by a monthly salary or a commission on the amount of coin exchanged. I am disposed to give the preference to the latter, considering it that mode of payment which combines private interest with the upright and active discharge of the Public Duty. The head podar of the General Treasury is willing to undertake the establishment of shroffs exchange shops at the undermentioned places, to give every security for the due and upright discharge of the business, and to conduct it at the rate of one pice in the rupee (i.e.) he is to be allowed one pice on each rupee's worth of copper and small silver coins exchanged, which is equal to one rupee and 9 anna per cent.

Public notice must of course be given of the intended measure, and every possible precaution taken to prevent fraud and extortion on the part of those employed. I beg also to bring to the notice of the Committee, that a native, who is aware of the proposed measure, has offered to purchase Rs. 1,000 worth of copper if allowed one pice in the rupee or one rupee and nine annas per cent, and is of opinion that he could dispose of ten thousand rupees worth of copper in the course of the month. He would no doubt sell to the smaller shroffs, and they would of course exact some profit from the party exchanging. Were we to adopt this mode, we would not have the same control over the parties as we shall over the exchange shroffs we may establish. The names of every individual so employed will of course be paid for in Bank Notes or Rupees, and a commission of one rupee & nine annas per cent allowed to the end of each month on the amount so taken. Not only should public notice be given by beat of drum &ca but as that may be forgotten in a short time, I would propose that a Board be fixed up at each exchange shop with the notice: 'Government Shroff Shop

64 pice for a rupee, 3 pie pieces for a pice and 12 pie for one anna. This should be written in Bengallee, Nagree and Persian.

It is very desirable in my opinion, to establish the same description of exchange shroffs shops all over the country and would suggest the expediency of doing so by means of the different Collectors. It is also in my opinion very desirable to call in the various copper coins now in circulation in the Upper Provinces and to substitute that lately issued from the Calcutta Mint. This might be done by means of these exchange shroff shops at little or no loss to Government. If it does not interfere with, and is not contrary to the existing regulations of Government I would beg to suggest to Government the expediency of declaring all copper coin, except that now issued from the Calcutta Mint, illegal, and authorize the Collectors (who should also be empowered to authorize the podars of the exchange shops established by them) to exchange them, pice for pice up to a certain period. To effect this it will be necessary to supply each Collector with a large quantity of the new pice, which can be done more conveniently at present than at any other time as the mint has little or nothing but copper to coin.

Government Exchange Shroff Shops proposed to be established in Calcutta:

1 shop to supply to [each of] these [5] places:

Collingah, Chandney Choke, Dhurrumtottah &ca
Bow-Bazar, Loll Bazar, Radah Bazar
Burra Bazar, Muchooa Bazar, China Bazar
Jora Sauko Nyah Bazar, Chitpore-Road, Simlah
Haut Kholah, Soba Bazar, Saum Bazar, Baug Bazar.

Source: NAI, Finance, Mint Committee Proceedings, 8 May 1832, No. 1, pp. 67-75.

22

Proposal from a Merchant to Purchase Large Numbers of Pice from the Calcutta Mint, 3 May 1832

[*Undoubtedly aware of the plans of the Calcutta Mint Committee to give the shroffs an official role in the distribution of the new copper coins, one of them already makes an offer for the distribution in Calcutta.*

See Chs. 4b and 4c of the Introduction, and Part II: Records, Nos. 21 and 23.]

[*Letter of a merchant, undersigned in Bengali script Shri Rambokondrao Sen, to the Mint Committee, Calcutta, 3 May 1832.*]

Understanding a quantity of pice being issued from the Mint I beg to offer tender to purchase one lack rupees worth under the following terms:

1. I take lack rupees pice which is 64 in a rupee,
2. I would take a quantity 5,000 rupees at a time,
3. The whole quantity to be cleared within 4 months,
4. I will pay down cash I receive the copper,
5. For the due performance of my contract I would deposit 500 rupees which is to be forfeited if I fail,
6. You are not to sell pice to any merchant until my contract is over,
7. For my profit I require 1/9 pr ct [per cent] or one pice from every Rs. or 65 pices a Sicca Rupee.

Source: NAI, Finance, Mint Committee Proceedings, 1832, Nos. 351-474 (see No. 442), p. 260.

23

The Circulation of Pice from the Calcutta Mint, 4 June 1832

[*The proposals for facilitating and extending the circulation of the new copper currency as discussed in April and May 1832 by the Calcutta Mint Committee, the Mint Master and Government were continued in June. The main issue still was how to prevent the shroffs to make excessive profits from distributing the coppers.*

See Chs. 4b and 4c of the Introduction, and Part II: Records, Nos. 21 and 22.]

The Mint Committee to the Secretary of Government, 4 June 1832

With reference to the orders of Government conveyed in Mr. Secretary Prinsep's letter of the 8th May, the Committee beg to record their entire concurrence in the opinion expressed by his Honor in Council that when the appearance of an attempt to force the copper coin into circulation beyond the natural demand, would not only be inexpedient but mischievous, and they cannot think that the measures recommended by them for the adoption of Government could have any such injurious tendency.

The object of the Committee was to facilitate, not to force the circulation of the copper money, and in this they were actuated by two motives, vizt the interests of Government and the convenience of the public, and particularly of the poorer classes.

The large profits derived by Government from the copper coinage renders it an object to afford every facility to its circulation. That the circulation falls short of the natural demand is shewn by the profits derived by the shroffs in the exchange, one of whom has established a shop near the Post Office and derives a considerable and permanent profit from it.

The only applications now made for copper money at the General Treasury are by the rich, to defray the expenses of religious ceremonies and to give to the poor, or by the shroffs for the purpose of exchange and profit.

With a view to encourage and facilitate the circulation of the copper coinage, the Sub Treasurer has, for some time past, been in the habit of accommodating parties with it in exchange for silver or bank notes, but the poorer classes who alone require a constant supply of copper money, are unable to come to the Treasury and exchange even to the extent of ten rupees, nor would it be expedient could they do so to make a retail exchange shop of the General Treasury. The poor man must still have recourse to the shroff to exchange his rupee, who no doubt will continue to exact from him the batta.

The establishment of exchange shops, as justly observed by Mr. Wilson, in answer to Mr. Prinsep's note, do not force the pice into circulation, it only affords facilities to the people to procure them, and it may be added, to the only class of people who require a constant supply of copper money, and who are unable to obtain it, except at a considerable loss, which they are least of all able to bear. The establishment of the exchange shops appear therefore to be the only effectual means of obviating this hardship, and of affording to the public the means of obtaining the requisite portion of copper circulation without being subjected to the extorsion and trickery of the shroffs.

This is evident then from the foregoing statement that the issue of copper coin at par from the Treasury, in the application of parties requiring it, has failed to stop the retail of pice at a higher rate than that fixed by Government, and it is as obvious that the failure is to be attributed to the circumstance of it's not affording to the poorer classes, who most require it the necessary facilities of obtaining it. The issue of the notices directed by the Government will certainly inform all who can read, of the relative value of the copper and other coin, but we apprehend will fail to remedy the evil; the shroff will not exchange without a profit, and cannot be forced to do so, and the poor man whose daily disbursements are made in copper money, must continue to pay the batta, not having the means of purchasing to the extent of 10 rupees at the Treasury. It might not perhaps be deemed becoming in the Committee to urge the subject further, till after the experimental measure of Government has been tried, and the principal object of this minute is to show that the measures recommended by the committee are well grounded.

Source: NAI, Finance, Mint Committee Proceedings, 1832, Nos. 351-474, pp. 309-12.

24

The Consequences of the Closure of the Farruckabad Mint in the Upper or Western Provinces, 29 October to 26 November 1832

[*Several reactions to a report by the Sudder Board of Revenue on the possibly inconvenient effects in the Western Provinces of the Bengal Presidency of the closure of the Farukhabad mint in 1824 and the Benares mint in 1830. Logistical improvements for conveying the coins from Calcutta to the western parts of the Presidency (in particular the regions of Agra, Aligarh, Bareilly, Delhi, Gorakhpur, Hathras and Meerut are mentioned) are awaited from the introduction of steamers on the rivers Ganga and Yamuna.*

See Part II: Records, Nos. 13, 18, 24, 26, and Part I: Studies Nos. 9 to 12.]

No. 1

W.H. Macnaghten, Secretary to the Governor-General, to G.M. Batten, Officiating Deputy Secretary to Government General Department Fort William, Camp Agra, 26 November 1832

Sir,

With reference to Mr. Secretary Prinseps letter dated the 9th ultimo submitting copy of a report from the Sudder Board of Revenue for the Western Provinces and the documents accompanying it. containing information as to the effect of the abolition of the Benares mint, I am directed to transmit for submission to the Honble the Vice-President in Council the enclosed copy of a minute recorded by the Right Honble the Governor-General on this date.

The original papers which accompanied your letter under acknowledgement are herewith returned together with the two original papers referred to in His Lordships minute.

No. 2 Enclosure (Minute)

William Cavendish Bentinck, Governor General,
Financial Department, Camp near Agra,
26 November 1832

The Sudder Board of Revenue for the Western Provinces in their report of Government under date the 3rd September upon the question of the inconvenience which the public has suffered by the abolition of the mints at Benares and Furruckabad describe upon the authority of several of the Collectors the following causes of it.

2. That besides the increased exchange value of silver generally the Government coinage has a premium varying in some districts as high as ten per cent in exchange against foreign coin or bullion.

3. That the pressure of the scarcity of the legal coinage falls with extremity upon the agricultural classes, who are obliged to procure it for the payment of their revenue, while the merchants and traders find a sufficient medium of exchange in the foreign and local currencies, which are not received at the Government Treasuries.

I took the opportunity in passing through Allyghur and Hatrass, where much business is transacted as well as at Agra to consult some of the principal European and Native Merchants upon the state of the exchange. Mr. Beckett, belonging to the former firm of Mercer and Company, resident for some years at Allyghur, a very intelligent person, furnished at my request a memorandum upon the subject. I also procured a similar communication from Mr. Wright, a very extensive land holder and indigo manufacturer in the neighbourhood of Agra whose opinions entitle much weight. These papers are annexed to the present minute. The native merchants gave information every much to the same effects.

The facts, bearing upon the present question, upon which they seem to be agreed, and may therefore be taken for granted and safely acted upon are:

1st That the Company's Rupees coined at the Benares and Furruckabad mints form the principal circulating medium, and that there is no scarcity of it as asserted in the Board's report to Government.

2nd But that great inconvenience is felt from the number of Company's Rupees of light weight in circulation, that the batta to be paid is a cause of embarrassment and delay in all pecuniary transactions but more especially in the payment of revenue to the public Treasuries.

3rd And that in consequence the reestablishment of a mint where these light coins and other bullion could be at once exchanged into others of good weight without delay and without imposition on the part of the Collectors Officers would be a great public convenience.

Upon tis last point I have no doubt whatever. The only consideration seems to be whether the means of such conversion can be more cheaply afforded by the mint at Calcutta or by a mint at Furruckabad. The superiority of the coinage at Calcutta would give a decided preference to the whole work being done at that mint, were it only for the facility that would be offered of distinguishing the false from the real coin. But a decision must depend on both the expense and dispatch with which the interchange can take place between Calcutta and the Provinces, and this will turn I think entirely upon the success of the new steamers about to be sent from England. If they can make the voyage in any reasonable time say a month or five weeks to Allahabad or Furruckabad, I should think, including all other advantages of this mode of communication, that a decided advantage would be in favour of the whole coinage being made at Calcutta. If the result should be different it will be greatly to be regretted that an establishment of such excessive cost and magnitude should have been so uselessly formed.

No. 3 Enclosure

Memorandum of J.O. Beckett, Agra, 19 November 1832

Regarding the inconvenience felt from the abolition of the Furruckabad Mint my knowledge does not extend beyond the limits of the Zillah Allyghur in which I have resided for nearly 8 years as a merchant and indigo manufacturer during which time I have had charge of several villages and I should say that little or no inconvenience has been felt from the abolition.

[…]

In the 18th paragraph of the Board's letter it is stated that all mercantile transactions are carried on through the medium of the foreign coinage. The Board seems to have misunderstood this. The foreign coinage, have alluded to, is a nominal coinage. The actual foreign coin is not used in these transactions, at Futtyghur for instance almost all the staple articles of commerce are priced in the old Furruckabad rupee of the Nawabs mint because it was the custom before the Company's Mint was established, but though the price is fixed in the foreign rupee, the render always expects to be paid in the Company's Rupee at the regular premium. The same takes place at Delhi, Barelly, and in Bundlecund. At Calcutta even many articles are priced in the current rupee, which does not exist as a coin. So difficult is it at any place or in any country to root out old customs, however in the Coel district all prices are quoted in Company's Furruckabad Rupees. […]

Regarding the copper coins current in these parts the following are some particulars:

The pice current at Hatras are:

> 1st the Hatras pysa coined by Diaram which fluctuates in value from 36 to 46 for the rupee, their general value is 45 per rupee.
> 2nd the Munsooree of 64 to 66 per rupee.
> 3rd the Nuwabee 53 to 54 per rupee.

The Hatras pice are current only at Hatras, Lursure, Moorsawn and the villages round about, at Coel even they are at a discount.

At Muttra are current:

> 1st the Nuwabee
> 2nd the Munsooree
> 3rd The Muttra pysa 46 to 50 per rupee
> 4th the Bhurtpoor pysa 42 to 45 per rupee

The Hatras, Bhurtpoor and Joypoor pice weigh 18 masha and

the Muttra pyce weigh only 9 masha, yet in Muttra there is but a small difference in the relative values of these pyce.

At Agra are current:

1st Gwalior pyce from 70 to 84 per rupee
2nd Agra pyce at 70 to 84 per rupee

These pyce also weigh near 9 masha yet their value is not much more than half of the Muttra pyce in Muttra.

At Coel are current:

1st the Nuwabee
2nd the Munsooree

But all the others are to be seen there and pass at a discount.

The relative value of pice with the rupee is not guided by the scarcity or plenty of either coin, but is regulated by the surrafs to suit their own purposes. During the months when Hindoos celebrated their marriages the surrafs raise the price of copper coin because there is a great demand for pyce made by the marrying parties to distribute during the Buiah. The moment the marrying time is over the price is lowered and the pice flow back into the surrafs hands, much to their profit. In fact the poor man is a loser in every transaction of money changing with a surraf. It would therefore be a great boon to the lower classes if there were only one good copper coinage of fixed interchangeable value with a rupee.

No. 4 Enclosure

Memorandum of N. Wright, n.d.

The number of various copper coins current throughout the Upper Provinces is a source of very great inconvenience to the lower classes, especially to those travelling through the country and were small silver coins to be had the inconvenience would not be so much felt.

No. 5

The Mint Committee of Calcutta to the Vice President in Council, Calcutta Mint Committee, 29 October 1832

Honorable Sir,

We have the honor to acknowledge the letter of the Secretary to the Government in the Financial Department of the 9th instant transmitting copy of a report from the Sudder Board of Revenue for the Western Provinces and copy of a letter addressed to the Secretary to the Governor-General and calling upon us to report on the subject of the alleged deficiency of Furruckabad coinage in the Western Provinces and in case of its existence what will be the most economical way of remedying it and provide the necessary supply.

2. With respect to the deficiency it is first to be remarked that considerable difference of opinion prevails as to the fact as by the subjoined list of authorities:

TABLE R.24: OPINIONS ABOUT THE ALLEGED DEFICIENCY OF FURRUCKABAD COINAGE IN THE DISTRICTS OF THE BENGAL PRESIDENCY, 1832

Those who state that great inconvenience is felt are	*Those who state that no inconvenience has been felt are*
Commissioners	*Collectors of the following districts*
Agra	Agra
Barellee	Belah
Benares	Calpee
Goruckpore	Goruckpoor
Meeruth	Meeruth
Moradabad	Mozuffernugur
Collectors	Mynpooree
Aligurh	Sirpoora
Azimghur	
Barelly	

(Contd.)

Boolundshuhur
Furruckabad
Ghazeepore
Moradabad
Muttra
Pilleebheet
Shahjahanpore
Saharunpoor
Suheswan

---

3. In some of the cases officers employed in the same district as at Agra, Goruckpore and Meerut give a different report, and although the weight of authority leaves no doubt that inconvenience is felt, yet it seems likely from this discrepancy of opinion that it is not of very general operation. It appears to be restricted very much to the upper parts of the Doab and the district of Barelly.

[....]

9. It can scarcely be necessary for us to call the attention of Government to the alteration that the last few years have been made in the commercial relations of British India. In place of a large surplus import of bullion of which a very large proportion went to the Upper Provinces, the import has scarcely, if at all, exceeded the export on public and private account. The balances of the Up Country treasuries have been drawn to Calcutta for the purpose of dispatch to Europe and the remittances formerly made to the Upper Provinces for purchase of cotton &ca have almost entirely ceased, as the supply from the only quarter from which it could come to any extent, importation by sea, has been thus cut off, it follows that a diminished circulation must ensue, and the prices of commodities decline. To what extent this has been actually the case the returns which we understand that the Accountant General has called for will shew, although the Board admit that there is an abundant supply of 'foreign' coinage for commercial purposes, we presume that the necessary consequence of diminished import and change of commercial relation is not yet very extensively felt. At any rate it is obvious that the re-establishment

of the Furruckabad Mint cannot contribute to remedy a real scarcity as it cannot convert into coin the bullion that does not exist.

10. The diminished supply of Government currency is a different question, but with all deference to the opinions expressed, we doubt if it has been created to any extent by the abolition of the Furruckabad Mint. One of the reasons for the abolition of the Mint was its inefficiency in the supply of the Upper Provinces with Government coin. In 1816 the officers of the Mint applied for leave to coin copper as they had no silver coinage. In 1818 it was stated in a letter from the Mint Committee to Government that the Mint did not seem to be well situated for the purpose of supplying the provinces in which the Furruckabad rupee was the legal tender, as the circulation of Goruckpore consisted chiefly of Lucknow rupees, and that of Bundelcund of Srinagur rupees. In the letter of the Mint Committee to Government of the 26th July 1819 it was also stated that the annual amount of individual coinage had averaged for 6 years about 18 lacs a year, but that for three years from 1814 to 1816 it averaged but 484,000 a year, and again in a letter from the Mint Committee dated the 8th November 1823 it was shewn that from 1820/1 to 1822/3 the average individual coinage was but 18 lacs a year, that in the third of these years it was but 8 lacs, and that it might be expected to fall off considerably 1823/24 as the first four months of the year had coined but 41,000 rupees.

[…]

14. As far therefore as the scarcity of coin and enhanced value of money are real, dependent upon diminished import of bullion upon its augmented export, upon the alteration of the course of trade and we may add upon the reduced expenditure of Government, we can offer no suggestions calculated to effect its removal. As far as the scarcity is artificial proceeding from the relative deficiency of Government currency, and the great abundance of local coin, not receivable in revenue payments, we trust it may easily be remedied by the temporary receipt at the Public Treasuries of local coin, and the gradual substitution of the Furruckabad Rupee.

Source: NAI, Finance, Mint Committee Proceedings, 29 March 1833, pp. 111-25, Nos. 1-5.

25

Circulation of Old Copper Pice in Assam, 19 June to 14 August 1833

[*The State of Assam, which lost its independence to Burma in 1824, only coined gold and silver, the small currency being cowries. After the British victory over Burma, Assam was gradually incorporated into the Bengal Presidency. In 1833 it appeared that old copper coins from the Presidency had found already currency among the peasants (ryots) from the sales of their harvest. They used it to pay their land tax individually, and therefore in small sums, directly to their new masters, who subsequently were loaded with huge sums in copper.*

See Ch. 3d of the Introduction and Part II: Records, No. 20.]

J.C. Robertson, Agent to the Gov[erno]r Gen[era]l to Pol[i]t[ical] Agent's Office N.E. Frontier, Cherrapoonjee, 9 July 1833

Sir,

I have to request that you will lay before the right Honorable the Governor-General in Council the enclosed copy of a letter to my address from Lieutt Rutherford and of my reply to the same on the subject of the receipt of Revenue.

2. I beg to add that in my opinion the exaction of silver in the payment of revenue in Assam will for the reasons stated by Lieutenant Rutherford greatly obstruct the introduction of that system of village settlement upon which its future condition in great measure depends.

H. Rutherford Lt in Civil Charge to J.C. Robertson Commissioner of Revenue 7th Division Cherrapoonjee, Central Assame Collectorship 23 June 1833

Sir,

I have the honor to forward the copies of letters that I have addressed to captain Davidson an Accountant General on the subject of the receipt of the old copper pice into the treasury.

2. I was obliged to forbid the receipt of the same from a current report that the coin was procurable in the Lower districts of Bengal at a very reduced rate. From which it was natural to suppose that it would immediately if received at its former value into this treasury become an article of import. I deemed it my duty pending your sanction and more accurate information to prohibit the receipt of the same in order to save myself from responsibility and the ryots from being deluded into the sale of their produce for a coin which has now become a mere article of trade at its intrinsic value as a metal.

3. I was hastened to this by measure by some large tenders in copper, and the ryots stating that they had received the same for the sale of produce from which source they alone were capable of paying their revenue.

4. In other districts where the revenue is farmed it is usual to take only the fractional parts of a rupee in copper coin in the payment of the Kist, but here, where the collection is from each ryot, it must be obvious that the Patghery cannot afford to pay for the difference of exchange in a depreciated currency or can the ryot afford to sell his produce for coin which will not be received as revenue.

5. I shall address letters to the collectors of Rungpore and Mymensingh and at the same time you will be able to supply me with information from Sylhet, and approve or amend my suggestion as may appear to you needful.

H. Rutherford, Lt in Civil Charge to A. Davidson, Offg Coll[ecto]r of NE Parts of Rungpore Gowalparah, Central Assame Collectorship, 19 June 1833

Sir,

I have to request you will favour me with the substance of the order respecting the receipt of the old pice for the payment of the revenue.

2. I am given to understand that the old are inferior rate in the Lower Provinces of Bengal and in order to protect the Government from the loss in consequence have forbid their receipt.

Should you have any of the now description I shall feel obliged by your favouring me with a supply to the value of 3000 Sica Rupees as early as practicable.

H. Rutherford, Lt in Civil Charge to the Accountant General Fort William, Central Assame Collectorship, 22 June 1833

Sir,

I beg to know whether I am authorized to receive the old pice as revenue and at what rate.

I have heard that this coin is now procurable in the Lower districts of Bengal at a very reduced rate and as it is natural to suppose that if received up here at its former value that it will become immediately an article of import into the country. I have deemed it my duty pending the approbation of the Commissioner to prohibit its receipt into this treasury.

It is customary I believe in other zillahs to allow only the fractional parts of the Kist to be paid in copper but this can be only applicable to the zamindary system, as in a rejotwary the coin once legalized must be received into the treasury, it being from the sale of his produce alone that the rejot is enabled to pay his dues to the state. The prohibition to the receipt into the treasury of the coin in question therefore amounts to its prohibition in retail trade and its place must be supplied by a new description or that trade must be materially affected. I therefore solicit information on this subject and request you will let me know from whence I can procure the new description of coin or whether you will give me credit for the old.

I shall forward a copy of this letter to the Commissioner for his information and orders he may have to give on this subject.

J.C. Robertson, Commissioner to Lieutt H. Rutherford, Asstt to the Governor-General Agent N.E. Frontier in-charge of Central Assam, Durrung, Coms Office, 17th Division Currapunjee, 8 July 1833

Sir,

In reply to your letter of the 22nd ultimo I regret to state my apprehension arising out of a communication from the Sudder Board of Revenue, which is herewith inclosed in original for your information that I am not competent to sanction the receipt of any copper money in payment of Revenue excepting for the fractional parts of rupee.

2. There can be no doubt therefore of your having done right in refusing to receive the old copper pice, but I fear that you must also reject the newly coined pice until the receipt of orders from Government to whom a reference on the subject shall immediately be made.

G.A. Bushby, Offg Secretary to the Govt. Accountant General to C. Morly, Accountant General, Council Chamber, 29 July 1833

Sir,

I am directed to transmit to you the accompanying letter from the Agent to the Govr Genl on the N.E. Frontier with the correspondence annexed hereto & request that you will report to Govr with reference to the opinion expressed by Mr. Robertson in the 2nd paragraph of his letter expecting the practical inconvenience which will be experienced from allowing the cultivators in Assam to pay in their revenue in copper pice.

C. Morly, Accountant General to G.A. Bushby, Officiating Secretary to Government Fin[ancia]l Dept, Fort William, 14 August 1833

Sir,

I have the honor to acknowledge the receipt of your letter of the 29th ultimo transmitting a letter in original from the Agent to the Governor-General in the North-East Frontier, with the correspondence annexed hereto and requesting that I will report to Government with reference to the opinion expressed by Mr. Robertson in the 2nd paragraph of his letter respecting the practical inconvenience which will be experienced from allowing the cultivators in Assam to pat in their Revenue in copper pyce.

2. Mr Robertson has stated that in his opinion the execution of Revenue in Assam in silver will for the reasons stated by Lieutenant Rutherford greatly obstruct the introduction of the village settlement upon which its future condition a great measure depends.

3. The reason assigned by Lieutt Rutherford, to which Mr. Robertson alludes appear to be that the Pathghery 'cannot afford to pay for the difference of exchange in a depreciated currency' or 'can the ryot afford to sell his produce for coin which will not be received as revenue'.

4. If it could be shown that the depreciation of pyce was limited to a comparison with silver, it would doubtless be a hardship on the ryot, who might be under the necessity of selling his small produce from time to time for the fractional parts of a rupee, expressed in copper money, to pay his rent in silver, and the same hardship would be experienced by the headman or native collector of the village revenue, if which he only exacted the authorized assessment in pyce he were held responsible for a payment in silver, but this is not the case, nor is it asserted to be so. On the contrary, the depreciation of pyce is general, or has relation to all commodities, and the ryot would be no less unwilling to sell his labour or his produce for remuneration [...?] in pyce, at the regulated rate of exchange with silver, than the money change would be, to exchange a rupee for 64 pyce when the market rate may be 70.

5. If then the petty wages of labour, and the pyce of small quantities of produce be regulated according to the market value of pyce, compared with silver, I know not how it can be said that the

demand for silver on the part of Government in satisfaction of the Revenue can be regarded as a hardship, although it would obviously be unjust on the part of payers of Revenue to desire to sell their labour or produce for pyce, at the depreciated rate of exchange and to pay Government in the same currency at the regulated rate.

6. It strikes me forcibly that with the fraudulent hope of blinding the Officers of Revenue to this view of the subject, interested parties have raised the clamour which effects to represent an abundant circulation of currency as a public evil.

7. If the amount for the periodical Kist for which parties engage be less than a Rupee, I would beg to suggest that arrangement be made for the consolidation of two or more Kists, so that the revenue may be demandable in silver, for any considerable amount of revenue received in pyce would be absolutely useless for the purpose of disbursement.

8. As stated in a former letter to Government* I am of opinion 'that copper should merely be employed as subsidiary to the operations of the main currency in the smaller or retail transactions of the poorer classes' but should be excluded from Government Treasuries, excepting in respecting to such payments as could not be expressed in silver without the use of an inconveniently minute silver coin. And I incline to think that the receipt of copper coin might more conveniently have been restricted by Regulation to the value of one fourth part of a rupee than to the highest fraction of the rupee.

9. Accordingly I beg to state my opinion no facility should be allowed for enlarged receipt of copper money in payment of Government revenue, nor is it apparent to me that the ryot or other party indebted to Government has any reasonable ground of grievance in being required to pay the Government dues in silver money.

10. The original papers which accompanied your letter are herewith returned.

Source: NAI, Finance, Mint Committee Proceedings, 26 August 1833, pp. 52-9.

* In the margin: Under date 9th January 1833 / 10 para / to the address of the Offg Sy to Govt in Reve Dept which I presume has been transferred to the Serial.

26

The Circulation of Copper Coins in the Lower and Western Provinces, 19 July 1833

[*The Mint of Saugor, taken over in 1818 by the British from the Marathas remained active until its closure in 1835. As the figures below demonstrate, Government took the lead in the coinage of pice, only later followed by individuals. One of the reasons to concentrate the production of the entire Presidency in Calcutta may have been the unpopularity of the Company's coppers who as fiduciary money were much overvalued according to the official exchange rates. Maybe because of the replacement of cowries by coins in this period, there was a greater demand in the Lower Provinces, i.e. Bengal.*

See Part II: Records, Nos. 18, 24 and 30.]

C. Morley, Acctt Genl to S[ecretar]y of Government in the Financial Department, Fort William, 19 July 1833

Sir,

With reference to the large amount of copper currency as per margin in store in the District Treasuries of the Lower and Western provinces including the Ceded Territory, ascertained from the last received cash balance reports.

TABLE R.26.1: SUPPLY OF COPPER COINS IN THE DISTRICT TREASURIES OF THE BENGAL PRESIDENCY, 1833

	Rs.
In Lower Provinces	306,842:10:0
In Western Provinces, including Ceded Territory	356,110:15:3

And to that of the copper pyce coined on account of Government and Individuals at the Saugor Mint during the past 4 years

TABLE R.26.2: COPPER COIN PRODUCTION OF THE SAUGOR MINT, 1829/30-1832/3

	Rs on account of Government	*Rs on account of Individuals*	*Total*
1829/30	82,700		
1830/1	40,828		
1831/2	39,657	33,550	
1832/3	10,500	69,255	
	173,685	102,805	276,490

I have the honor to recommend for the consideration of the Right Honorable the Governor-General in Council the propriety of immediately prohibiting the coinage of copper by that mint.

2. The measure seems called for by the fact of which His Lordship in Council is perhaps aware that the copper coinage throughout the country is depreciated in value and perhaps so much from the disproportion between the intrinsic value of the copper comprised in a rupees worth of pyce according to the legal rate of issue and the market value of copper for a great disproportion must more or less always occur owing to the great average cost attending the coinage of copper than that of the precious metals, but because of the market has been glutted with the copper currency and because of the scarcity of the legal silver currency.

3. The over circulation which is apparent has not been produced so far as I am aware by any forcing of the copper currency into the interior by any act of the public officers of Government for the issues from public treasuries in copper are restricted to payment of the fractional part of a rupee and to supplies to individuals (whether private or public) when applying for the same. The late mentioned indulgence will only be sought for when the pyce rise in value beyond the prescribed rate and must remain valueless so long as the market is overloaded or full of that currency, and therefore appears to me to have been produced in the Western

Provinces, particularly by the speculations in pyce of merchants who are allowed to bring copper to the Sagor Mint for coinage, and who can consequently traffic therein with profit even at rates lower than that prescribed by the regulations for public transactions.

There is reason also for believing that much of the pyce originally circulating in the Western has come down to the Lower Provinces for in exchanging a rupee in the markets of Calcutta for pyce I am informed that a portion of trisoolee pyce is almost invariably given and no reference to the Sub Treasurer for more authentic information on the subject that officer informs me that the proportion of trisooly pyce received at the General Treasury from the Post Office &ca is about 1/8 or 2 annas in the rupee.

4. It is proper to mention that about ten years ago a lac of rupees worth of Benares pyce was brought down to the General Treasury and put into circulation, but I am of opinion that additional supplies have at subsequent periods been brought hither on speculation.

Altho' I am of opinion that Government should not interfere with the rise and fall of the market rates of their copper currency, yet I think their interposition would be well directed to prevent an over circulation thro' the speculations of merchants which afford a plea to landholders, abkars &ca in their attempts to enforce the currency into the public coppers in lieu of silver in which they are under engagement to pay excepts for the fractional parts of a Rupee.

6. Such an interposition salutary in its effects in so far as it will cause the supplies of pyce in the markets to approximate to the wants of the people and consequently better regulate the rate of exchanging copper for silver currency will I receive be exercised by te prohibition it is the object of this address to suggest and recommend.

7. In conclusion I have the honor to state that the Mint Committee concur in the expediency of the proposed prohibition.

Source: NAI, Finance, Mint Committee Proceedings, 22 July 1833, pp. 247-9.

27

Petition by the Petty Shopkeepers of Calcutta, 14 August 1833

[*Apparently, the British authorities even in their own capital, were unable to enforce the official exchange rate of 64 pies per silver rupee. They implicitly conceded to have supplied too many new copper coins. By leaving it to the market forces, they told the complaining shopkeepers of Calcutta that the stipulated exchange rate between silver and copper would be restored automatically.*

See Part II: Records, Nos. 20-3 and 26.]

The Humble Petition by the Undersigned Bazar People, Petty Shopkeepers and Ejaurs of the Town of Calcutta

That in consequence of the unsettled price of the pice currency in the bazar of Calcutta your petitioners being the petty traders met with a great inconvenience and sustained a considerable loss in trade. It is stampt on every pice in three characters, Persian, Bengally and Nagree one pie sicca so that its usual rate was 64 per rupee, but it is so overrated that 72 and 74 are sold per rupee, and those that appear to be old and its marks a little effaced they are not taken by the Potdars, if ever 80 offered for a rupee. Consequently your petitioners suffer a loss at least 2 annas per rupee in converting the pice into rupees.

Your petitioners therefore pray that His Lordship in Council will be pleased to issue such an orders that the rate of the pice will be reestablished to its former price that is at 64 per rupee and thereby relieve your petitioners.

And your petitioners as in duty bound shall ever pray.

Ordered that the petitioner be informed that the depreciation of copper pice is the effect of a superabundant circulation which will in due time correct itself without the interference of the Government.

[22 signatures in Bangla script]

Source: NAI, Finance, Mint Committee Proceedings, 19 August 1833, pp. 25-6.

28

Bombay Government's Attempts to Suppress Mints, 17 September to 10 November 1834

[*After the submission of the Maratha State, ruled by the Peshwa (capital Pune) in 1819 most of its territory was incorporated in the Bombay Presidency, while other parts survived as British controlled semi-independent princely states: Baroda under the Gaekwad dynasty until 1949, Gwalior under the Shinde (Scindia / Sindhia) dynasty until 1948, Indore under the Holkar dynasty until 1950, Nagpur under the Bhonsle dynasty until 1853, and Satara until 1848. All these states eagerly preserved the right to mint coins. In the annexed territories the British provisionally maintained a number of Maratha mints, including that of Pune, striking copper coins (the latter called Shivajis after the founder of the Maratha Empire). The closure of the mint at Pune in 1830 turned out to have been too rash. This induced private minters under British Sovereignty, but claiming allegiance to some of the adjacent princely states, to fill the void by resuming copper coinage. In 1834 the Bombay government decided to stop these private semi-legal practices in places under its authority.*

See Part II: Records, No. 18.]

T.H. Baber, Principal Collector to L.R. Reis, Secretary to Government, Poona, 17 September 1834

Sir,

Having received information that mints for the coinage of copper pice had been established in some of the Enam villages of the Guickwar, Scindia, and Holkar, since the abolishment of the mint here, I ordered the acting Mamulutdar of this city to enquire what foundation there was for these reports. I have received his reply informing me that a mint was established about 2 years ago at Mowjee Darolee Nimbgoam in the Khaid Purgunna, belonging to the Guickwar, another at Ramudpoor, a village in the Meritch territory. When not said, another about four months ago at Korekgon belonging to Scindia in the Bhinturee Purgunna.

The Mamlutdar is making further enquiries, the result of which shall be reported to Government. In the meantime I have to request the orders of Government for my guidance, coining being generally considered the exclusive prerogative of the supreme authority, my opinion is that Government have the right of interference, and if there is no special provision in existing treaties with the Guickwar, Scindia or Holkar, to the contrary, I should certainly recommend that all these and any other mints within British territory be put down without delay.

2. It is proper I should mention here that in consequence of the fluctuating exchange of the 'Sheevaji' and other country coined pice of this place and throughout the district, the loss of Government in the copper coinage now in this Treasury and unavailable to the public exigencies amounting to Rupees 59,074:8:2 was on the 22nd May last (on which day a particular account was drawn out) Rupees 17,218:9:1. I herewith forward a copy of that statement for the fuller information of Government.

J.H. Baber, Principal Collector to Charles Norris,
Chief Secretary to Government Bombay, Poona,
10 November 1834

Sir,

I have the honor to acknowledge the receipt of your letter dated the 1st instant calling upon me to report with reference to my letter dated 17th September whether the Guickwar and Scindia hold their villages in Enam or Sovereignty.

2. Having been addressed by the Agent of Sirdars on nearly a similar question, namely the nature of the jurisdiction exercised by Scindia and Holkar in their villages within the British territories, I have the honor to submit for the information of the Right

Honble the Governor in Council copy of my reply to which I have merely to add that from every enquiry that I have been able to make, all these villages were originally held as hereditary fiefs from the former Government, in return for which vassalage or personal and military services were exacted, and over which the Supreme Authority was exercised, when occasions called for it, by The Peshwa.

3. I take this opportunity of referring for the consideration of the Right Honble the Governor in Council copy of a communication I recently had occasion to make to the Guickwar's vakeel with that person's answer, relative to the discovery and seizure of a quantity of newly coined Shewrai pice, in the very act of being transported from the Guickwar's copper mint in the village Dowdee in the Khair Mhal to Poona. It was entirely accidental my police extending their researches into this village, the information given to my late Assistant Mr. Lumsden being that a gang of Poona coiners were then at work in the Company's village of Nimba in Khair, which adjoins Dowdee. The discovery is not to be regretted as no doubt can exist now as to this being one of the sources of the false pice with which the Deccan has been inundated in defiance of the Proclamation of Government under date 12th October 1831.

J.H. Baber, Magistrate to S. Marriott,
Session Judge Poona, Poona, November 1834

Sir,

I have the honor to acknowledge the receipt of your letter dated the 4th September and 22nd October and herewith forward copies of two yads* from the vakeels of Scindia and Holkar to whom I thought it but fair to refer the question wherein they explain the extent of criminal jurisdiction in the villages of their Highness respectively distinctly admitting that the Supreme Authority is vested in the British Government, that is they both exercise jurisdiction in ordinary matters but in cases of great crimes and disorders they refer them to the Sirkar.

* Probably *yadasht* (memorial).

2. I have referred to the schedule A of Regulation XXIX of 1827 according to which the jurisdiction of the Established Court of Judicatory is to be determined and do not find either of these villages excepted, tho' the Turrufs in which they are situated are all mentioned. In solving however this question much must depend upon Subsisting Treaties and if by these neither Scindia or Holkar are recognized as possessing exclusive authority, they cannot, I conceive, be received in any other light than an ordinary Eenamdars, in which point of view, neither can legally exercise any power in criminal matters beyond what is conferred by Government on Patells of villages, or at most the extended penal jurisdiction of a Zilla Magistrate, as conferred upon the Sircar Jameedars Luxumun Rao, Mankeestwar and Deenkar Babowraw Lellee.

J.H. Baber to Jewan Rao, [Dominut?] Sircar Guicwar, 4 October 1834

During an investigation before the Assistant Magistrate it transferred that one Luximon Cassar of Poona, who was accused of fraud, had fled and taken up his abode at Nimbgaun Dowdee, where he had established a mint for coining pice. To apprehend this Cassar and all who were concerned with him, and also to seize his coining instruments, a party of police under Sowars were ordered to proceed to the Nimbgaum. They went there accordingly, and ascertained that in the adjoining village of Dowdee there was coining of pice going on, upon which they proceeded there, in expectation of discovering Luximon Cassar as above, but instead of finding him they discovered several persons from Poona, engaged in coining Rs. 150 worth pice, ready to transport to Poona. Concluding that these were the very persons the Sirkar was in quest of, they were taken up with their instruments and pice and brought to the Hoozoor, where after an examination they were discharged, and the pice they had coined are now forwarded to you, at the same time.

That I have to observe that formerly there were numerous rupee and copper mints in this country whereby the people were subjected to great loss from the circulation of a bad currency which induced the British Government to abolish them all. The Dowdee gaum is a village of your masters. It is within British territory, and under British Jurisdiction, consequently these new pice mints in the Company's districts is clearly in contravention of the above orders. As such it will be my [privilege] to bring the subject to the notion of my Government, and accordingly apprize you of this, that you may have an opportunity of justifying the practice and I will notice the same to my Government. It was quite accidental my police going into the Dowdee village, but having done so unintentionally, I have ordered the people they apprehended to be discharged and returned together with the pice they brought away with the request that you will send them back to Dowdee and in future like measures to prevent any more being circulated in the British territory.

Sewram Rao Malhar, Vakeel to the Guickwar Sircar,
dated First Rugub, Corresponding with 3 November 1834

Your letter of the 4th October duly come to hand and was to desire that the copper coinage carrying on at Dowdee, be not circulated in the Company's territories and if I had anything to represent so to do.

Considerable loss will be sustained by my Sircar by this order and in consequence I shall continue to coin pice there. To those merchants who bring copper &ca I must pay in pice. The neighbouring villagers also come to Dowdee for pice because there is no other equally convenient for them. All the transactions took place in my village. I have now sent order to my people, both merchants & mint people, not to take pice out of the village for sale. Still foreigners (persons from Mogalai) and others come to my village for Dubbo pice which I have in consequence ordered to be coined for their use. I have advised my Government of all the above and shall confirm to such orders as I may receive. During the interval I have interdicted consignments from my village to the Company.

Source: NAI, Foreign Department, Proceedings 31 December 1834, Nos. 12-13, P.C.

29

Remittance of Old Copper Pice from the Post Office to the Calcutta Mint, 10 September to 30 November 1841

[*Regularly officials of the governmental post services complained about the accumulation of copper coin, which they could not remit according to the official exchange rate to the Mint or Treasury, and as a consequence had to sell at a loss to the shroffs. It also entailed a lot of extra work to distinguish between pice of differing qualities. See Part II: Records, No. 7.*]

No. 670 Extract from the Proceedings of the Right Honorable the Governor of Bengal in the Financial Department under date the 29th September 1841

Calcutta Mint Committee to G.A. Bushby, Secretary to the Government of Bengal Financial Department, Calcutta, 20 September 1841

Sir,

We have the honor to forward, for the information and orders of the Right Honorable the Governor of Bengal the accompanying copy of a letter from the mintmaster of the 10th instant, soliciting orders in regard to a remittance of old copper pyce to the Mint by the Post Master General after arrangements had been made with the late Post Master General for discontinuing these remittances by causing the pyce to be reissued as change in rupees tendered in payment for postage.

2. We are satisfied that the practice of sending such remittances to the Mint entails much unnecessary expence, and we concur with the Mint Master in thinking that the reissue of the pyce in exchange for rupees could be conveniently effected by the several Departments receiving the pyce in the first instance. We therefore beg to suggest that a communication be made thro' Government to the respective Departments mentioned in the 2nd para of Major Forbes letter restricting them from receiving in payment more than a Rupees worth of pyce at one time and from the same party; with injunctions to endeavor to reissue the copper coin they may receive on such occasions, or to state any sufficient reason which may render them unable to do so. They should also be requested to report what checks have been observed by them to guard against an overreceipt or the purchase of pyce with silver, when a redundancy and consequent depreciation of copper coin exists by the subordinate officers of their respective Treasuries, delivering peons or such like servants.

3. The payers of pyce into Public Establishments ought not be allowed to pay the full rupees worth of copper, but we fear the check may not be quite perfect at present, and until a large supply of small silver coin is put into circulation we are not prepared to suggest any measure to make the legal copper tender proportionately less. The subject will however engage our attention and consideration hereafter.

No. 303 of 1841/2

W.N. Forbes, Mintmaster to Mint Committee of Calcutta, Calcutta Mint, 10 September 1841

Gentlemen,

With a view of obtaining your orders on the subject I have the honor to report that a remittance of old copper pyce has been this day made to the Mint by the Postmaster General, this after the late Postmaster General had made arrangements for discontinuing such remittances, partly I believe by reissuing the pyce as change on Rupees tendered in payment for postage.

2. As the practice of sending such remittances to the Mint entails upon the Government the unnecessary expence of shroffage on a constantly recurring series of them, as also that incident to reissuing the pyce to licensed potdars at 64½ (in place of 64) to the rupee and there is reason to believe their direct reissue could be effected by the several departments themselves in exchange for rupees, I would beg the expediency of instructions being issued to the General Post Office, to the Collector of Calcutta, to the Collector of the 24-Parganas, to the Police Office and to the Commissioners of the Court of Requests, prohibiting these departments from receiving in payment at one time and from one party, of a greater amount of copper coin than 63/64 of a rupee, and further directing htem to endeavor systematically to reissue such copper coin as under the above rule they may have occasion to receive.

Ordered

that a copy from the letter of the Mint Committee and its enclosure be communicated to the departments noted in the margin with a request that the officers therein named may be required to pay attention to the suggestions of the Mint Committee, and to report respecting the checks by which the receipt and disbursement of copper money in their respective treasuries is regulated.

G. Alexander, Postmaster General to G.A. Bushby, Secretary to the Government of India, General Deptt, Fort William, 30 November 1841

Sir,

I have the honor to advert to your letter No. 821 of the 13th ultimo to the address of the late officiating Postmaster General and to the papers therein transmitted which were received on the 23rd idem, and to state in reply for the information of the Right Honble the Governor-General of India in Council, that every possible effort has always been made for disposing of the copper pice received at this office by reissue in change, but, as probably not less than 7/10th of the letters both received and dispatched, are single letters, and the maximum rate of single postage is 14 annas, it will be readily credited that the postages paid varying from ½ an anna to 14 annas and are in a very large proportion made in copper money. Whenever the postage to be paid by one individual or party, amounts to a full rupee, our demand is for silver, and pice under such circumstances are never taken; and the same for larger sums, i.e. in other words, pice are only received in payment of the fractional parts of a rupee.

2. As respects the postages collected immediately in this office, the receivers have not the opportunity, even if so willed, to substitute pice for rupees, at least, they would be very open to detection in attempting to do so, since they are seated in the Public Dispatch room where many eyes are always upon them. At the close of the receipts, the amount collected by each receiver is counted, both silver and copper money, & a note of each is entered in a book kept for that purpose by the superintendent of the right duties. Their boxes are then locked up and are placed in a large strong chest in the Treasurer's room which remains under charge of the guard until the following morning when in the presence of the Office Cashier the boxes are opened & the money counted over. But as respects the outdoor collections made by the letter delivering peons, it is almost impossible to devise anything like a systematic check. The only possible proof obtainable would be the evidence of the individuals or parties which pay the postage, as to whether the amount was paid in copper money, the trouble & difficulty of procuring which will be sufficiently self-evident, to render further observations from me on that point unnecessary.

I may however add that several years since when pice were at a considerable discount, a partial check against the peons was established as respected the letters for houses of business whose daily postage mounted to a rupee or more, and they were made to account accordingly in silver. At present pice is only obtainable at a small premium that no advantage could accrue by the purchase of copper money to substitute for silver rupees, unless we can suppose that defaced pice might be cheaply purchased; but then it would be at the risk & responsibility of the cashier of this office should he receive such injured money from the receivers or peons.

Beyond the limited means afforded by giving change for rupees when tendered as payment for postage it would seem impossible to dispose of the large sums of copper money collected in this office unless they are received at the Mint, or unless sold in the bazar, in the latter case at a loss probably equal to 12 annas or a rupee per 100 rupees. Therefore, as it is quite out of the question to suppose that the present accumulation amounting to nearly 2,000 rupees can ever be reduced by the immediate re-issue at this office, but on the contrary must be expected to increase unless other channels for its disposal be provided, I would respectfully venture to solicit that the Right Honble the Governor-General in Council will be pleased to issue orders for the mintmaster to receive as heretofore all pice exchangeable in the bazar sent from this office at par, whilst the defaced coins taken by the servants of this office may be disposed of either by allowance at the Mint as metal, or in the bazar. His Lordship in Council will observe from the subjoined copy of a letter from the mintmaster dated the 26th instant that that officer in returning a remittance of Rs. 1,000 worth of copper altogether refuses to receive at present any pice into the Mint.

Source: NAI, Home Department, Public Original Consultation, 13 October 1841, Nos. 16 and 8 December 1841, No. 12, Genl. Dep. India.

30

Report Called for Regarding Operations of Mints in Native States, 6 February 1847

[*After half a century of attempts to set up their own coinage in the parts of India under their direct rule, the British became interested in the coin circulation in the states under their indirect rule (the so-called Princely States). One of their concerns was the possible reminting of Presidency coins by these states, in particular Presidency Rupees (called Kuldars). Therefore, a report was called for by the Court of Directors in London (21 October 1846, No. 28, paras 1 to 9) regarding operations of mints in the Native States in the North-West Provinces. This request for information was transmitted by the Governor-General to the secretary to government and the resident in the North-West Provinces, Agent Sindiah's Dominions, Agent Rajpootana, Resident Nagpore, Resident Lucknow, and Resident Hyderabad. A small selection, mainly regarding the minting of copper, from these extensive reports has been transcribed here.*

See Part II: Records, Nos. 18, 24, 26, and 31 to 33.]

No. 213

Lieutt Coll J. Sutherland, Agent Gov[ernor] General for the States of Rajpootana to W. Edwards Under Secy to the Govt of India with the Gov[ernor] General, Rajpootana Agency, Camp Jodpoor, 23 January 1847

[...]

2. The large export of opium from Malwa to the extent, I believe, of almost two crores of rupees per annum requires, I have always

understood an extensive importation of bullion from the Western Coast. But there is unfortunately no exports of this kind but salt from most of the states of Rajpootana except some portions of Meywar & Harowtee, where poppy is grown, altho' to no very great extent compared with the fertile regions of Malwa for generally throughout the desert and arid plains of Marwar, Jessulmere, Beekanere, Jyepore and Sheekawattee there is nothing produced to pay for the sugar, spices, and other things which they import.

3. I am not sensible, therefore, of any injurious effect produced on the circulating medium of those states by the abolition of our western mints or that at Saugor. All or mostly all these states have mints of their own and when the coin of our own mints has been introduced in large quantity for the payment of troops and establishments it has disappeared so rapidly that there was never any doubt but that it was recoined into the currency of the country as noticed in the 2nd para of the Honble Court's letter in the case of the Pertabgurh mint and for this I never saw any remedy.

4. The mints of the country appear to me to afford sufficient coins of their own denomination for all internal transactions and their payments of tributes to us are always made by the states through sarkars and bills of exchange. The time is yet far distant, I fear, when we can hope to make the Company's rupee the circulating medium of these countries, for the right of coinage is in the estimation of the Native States one of the emblems of sovereignty.

5, The agricultural classes in the Ajmere district pay their revenue according to our standard and are doubtless subject, like all the people of India, to 'the fraudulent schemes of native money dealers'. Altho' rupees have occasionally been sent in large quantity from the Agra Treasury to supply the wants of that of Ajmere.

No. 214

Lieutt Coll J. Sutherland, Agent Gov[ernor] General for the States of Rajpootana to W. Edwards Under Secy to the Govt of India with the Gov[ernor] General, Camp Erinpoorah, 25 March 1847

[...]

I have the honor to submit a copy of my letter no. 111 to Major Dixon, the Supdt of Ajmere and of my circular letter to Poll Agents and Supdts in Rajpootana on the subject.

2. I have also the honor to submit copies of the replies which I have received from Major Ludlow the Poll Agent at Jyepoor and Major Dixon, the only officers who have written on the subject [...].

No. 215

Major J. Ludlow, Poll Agent Jyepoor to Lieutt Coll J. Sutherland, Agent Gov[ernor] General for the States of Rajpootana, Jyepoor, 26 February 1847

[...]

2. I learn from the Treasurer of the Raj that in Sumbut 1902 the following rupees were melted at the Jyepoor mint for recoinage by a banking firm to meet some obligations connected with opium speculating.

TABLE R.30.1: MELTING OF GOVERNMENT RUPEES IN THE JEYPOOR MINT IN SUMBUT 1902 [AD 1845]

Straight-milled Kuldars	50,000
Diagonally milled Kuldars	400
	50,400

And that the straight milled bear a discount with reference to the Jyepoor currency of 7 per cent viz. Rs. 5:4:0 alloy & Rs. 1:12:0 expense in recoinage and duty.

3. The diagonally milled rupees bear a discount of Rs. 6:8:0 of which the expense in recoinage & duty is above stated.

4. It is asserted that within the past few years the above named rupees are the only coins of foreign currency which have undergone recoinage at this capital.

No. 216

Major C.G. Dixon, Supdt to Lieutt Coll J. Sutherland, Agent Gov[ernor] General for the States of Rajpootana, Ajmere Supdt Treasury Office, 16 March 1847

[...]

2. I have had conversations with various Sahookars of Ajmere and with the traders of Nya Nuggur on the subject of the currency of Rajwara. It appears there are fifteen coinages besides the Kuldar and Company's rupee, current in this part of the country. They may be thus enumerated:*

TABLE R.30.2: DIFFERENT TYPES OF RUPEES, CIRCULATING IN RAJPOOTANA, 1848

	Rupee	*Mint*	*Relation to kuldar*	*Where circulating and other observations*
1	Jyepoor	Jyepoor	equal	Throughout the whole of that principality; the silver is stated to be unalloyed
2	Jodhpoor	Jodhpoor	1 or 2 per cent premium or discount	In the west and south part of Marwar. In the northern portion of this principality dealings are more frequently made in the Kuchawun currency; no alloy is said to be mixed
3	Kotah	Kotah	equal	Chiefly restricted to the Harowtee Country; silver stated to be unalloyed
4	Boondee	Boondee	Old: 14 as New: equal	Circulation mainly restricted to the Boondee state
5	Kuchawun	Kuchawun in Marwar	12 as	Extensive in use in the northern portion of Marwar, at Ajmere and in our own villages bordering on the Marwar frontier

* Editor's note. The following information has been put by me in a tabular form and sometimes summarized.

6	Seree Shahee	Ceased since British conquest	14 as	Coined by the Mahrattas when they were sovereigns of Ajmere. The extent of this coinage does not exceed 2 ¼ lacks. It is alone current in Ajmere
7	Chittoree	Chittore in Meywar	12½ as	Commands a circulation over a large extent of the country. It is used in the Ketree Pergunnah of Ajmere, in the Mhairwara Hills, throughout the Meywar possessions and extends to various marts in Malwa. It is the currency in which opium and cotton dealings are made from Ketree in the north to Mundisor in the south
8	Oudey-poor	Oudeypoor	12 as	Restricted to Oudeypoor and its arrondissement
9	Shalum Shahee	Pertabgurh	14	It is most extensively used in Malwa for the purchase of opium
10	Bhilwaree	Ceased	15	It circulates at Pallee, Godwar, Serohee, and the Bheel Mugra. It is said this rupee was coined at Bhilwara in Meywar about 100 years ago. Since Palee became a commercial mart on the downfall of Bhilwara 80 years since, the mint at that place ceased
11	Soorut Shahee	Beekanere	equal	Its circulation is restricted to that country; said to be unalloyed
12	Guj Shahee	Jessulmere	equal	The same remark applies to this coin as to that of Bekanere
13	Shahpoora	Shahpoora	10½	The remarkable feature of this rupee is that as it is the smallest coin bearing the stamp of a rupee it is the most extensively used in gifts of charity – a cheap method of gaining a name for liberality at the lowest possible cost

14	Suwaee Madhaop-ore	Madhoopore in Jeypore	15	Current in the eastern portion of Dhoondhar and at Tonk
15	Kishngurh	Kishngur	14	Circulates through the small principality of Kishngur

3. The above detail embraces seventeen currencies of which, with the exception of the Seree Shahee and Bhilwara, all have their mints in operation. I have not mentioned the coins which are current at Bhurtpoor, Kurolee, Ulwur, Indore, Oojain and some places in Malwa, since my information as to their particulars is incomplete.

4. I have not been able to learn from any of the merchants with whom I have conversed on this subject that advantage has been taken of the bullion offices at Agra, for the supply of the mints. It is affirmed that the bullion for this purpose is brought from Bombay and consists of silver imported from China and sometimes of Spanish dollars. It is a rare occurrence to fuse kuldars for the coinage of Hindoostanee rupees. It is, however, observed that on extreme emergencies, a recourse has been had to this measure, the coin selected being the oblique or diagonal milled rupee coined under the Regulation XLV of 1803.

5. Putting aside the impolicy, if not the impracticability of closing the mints of our allies, the Princes of Rajwara, the question arises, does commerce suffer hindrance or inconvenience from having many, in place of one currency? Were all the coins detailed above to be current at one spot, no doubt their diversity and difference of value would cause confusion. Each distinct coinage may be said to have its separate duty to perform. Thus the Bijee Shahee Rupee of Jodhpoor is alone employed in a portion of Marwar or on its skirts in all dealings. It rarely finds its way to Malwa and Meywar. The Chittoree again is strictly restricted to its own beat and thus with the products of other mints. Merchants having occasion to purchase salt at Puchbuddra in Marwar arrange their accounts in Bijee Shahee Rupees. If making purchases of opium in Meywar they are well aware the currency is that of the Chittoree mint. In a word the different principalities have their own distinct

currencies and merchants being conversant with the monetary arrangements are always prepared to meet local usages.

6. [...] The merchants] allege that the different coinages in Rajwara are as much a marketable article as opium, cotton or any other staples of commerce. The value of each distinct coinage is as mutable as any ware in the market. The demand enhances the price as 'no enquiry' would in like manner deteriorate the value. One illustration will make its position intelligible. When there is no prepondering weight on either side, the batta, or difference between the Kuldar and Chittoree rupee may be taken at Rs. 25. That is 125 Chittoree rupees are exchanged for 100 Kuldars. On a demand for money arising to pay for opium on the close of the rubbee season, the batta of the Chittoree rupee has sometimes decreased to Rs. 19. Again, on sales being effected and no further calls for this currency it rises to Rs. 30. In the one case it became 6 per cent dearer and in the other 5 per cent cheaper than the general standard of 125 Chittoree to 100 Kuldars. Here then we have a variation, from the extremes 19 and 30, of 11 per cent. People commanding capital purchase Chittoree Rs when they are cheap to sell them at a gain during the season of demand. [...] To make the Kuldar or Company Rupees alone current would be to deprive thousands of the menial interests of their calling.

7. [...] It is the universal opinion of the whole of the Meehajun class. In Ajmere we have a large command of Companys and Kuldar Rupees. The troops at Nusseerabad, Moorad Munzil and [Berar?] are paid in that coin. [...] Of the 20 lakhs of Company's Rupees in circulation at Ajmere & in the different cantonments, it may be said they do not quit their locality, since they are taken in exchange for the tribute paid by the Native Princes of Rajwara and are from time to time lodged in our treasury, again to be issued as pay for the troops. So far from the natives considering their own coins debased, this is the very opinion they entertain of ours from the circumstance of the admixture of copper in the coinage. In the preparation of silver ornaments the Jyepoor rupee has a preference over that of other mints.

8. After giving the subject mature consideration, the impression on my mind is said that the inconvenience said to arise from

so varied a currency, has been overrated, if not misunderstood and that neither the establishment of Bullion Offices or an extra mint for the coining of Company's rupees would drive the present currency from the market unless a positive order be passed to abolish the native mints and buy up the various currencies, nor in my humble opinion does necessity exist for having recourse to the correctives that have been proposed.

No. 217

H.H. Greathed Poll Agent Jodhpoor to Lieutt Coll J. Sutherland Agent Gov General for the States of Rajpootana, Jodhpore 16 June 1847

2. There are three mints for the coinage of silver in the country: one at Jodhpoor another at Palee the great commercial mart, and a third at Koochawun. The latter belongs to the feudal chief of that place. The others are Govmt Estabts, superintended by the Hakim, the chief local officer or the kotwal, worked by the silver smiths hired for the occasion, and the materials are, with rare exceptions, furnished by individulas wishing to convert their silver into Bijee Shahee Rupees the local silver coinage.

[...]

8. There is a mint for copper coinage at Sojut, which supplies Marwar with the inferior currency. The Govmt charge is Rs. 2 per Rs. 100 worth. The value of copper coins is variable, and this fluctuation in the currency, in which the poorer classes chiefly deal, must press hard upon them. The money changers and retail traders might be expected to resist any innovation, which would close a large source of their profits, and I doubt whether the sufferers themselves would prefer a standard coin representing a certain value of copper to the present bulky pieces of metal, which are looked upon as equivalent to the quantity of copper, minus coining charges, purchasable in the market for the sum for which they are current.

No. 220

W.H. Sleeman, Agent Gov[ernor] Gen[era]l Bundlecund to M. Elliot, S[ecretar]y to the Govn[men]t of India with the Gov[ernor] General, Simla, Jhansi, 27 May 1847

[…]

13. As much loss and annoyance is felt by the mass of the people from the state of the copper as of the silver currency, & it was, I believe, of the copper coinage that the Saugor mint derived the chief part of its profits, at the same time that it prevented the very great inconvenience that is now felt at all times & in all the Saugor & Nerbudda districts from the attempt to supply them with copper coins from the Calcutta mint. They never reach the districts in the quantity & at the time they are required & the complaints I receive of the fluctuations in value & consequent loss & inconvenience are incessant. The cheap mints I have suggested would remedy this evil everywhere at the same time that they would pay a great part of their costs by a uniform copper coinage for all Central India.

No. 236

Minute on the Mint and on the Currency of the Nagpore State, 23 July 1847

A mint has long been established at Nagpore. During the reign of Moodhajee Bhonsla who died in 1788 the first coinage is supposed to have taken place. There are two distinct branches in the mint, one for the coinage of silver which is immediately controlled by the officers of the government, and one for the coinage of copper which is sometimes farmed for a certain sum to anyone who might be disposed to take the contract. The silver mint is in almost constant operation, the coinage of copper only takes place when the rate of exchange is so low that it is injuriously felt by the poor and an increased supply of pice is demanded.

About the year 1815 Rughojee Bhonsla attempted to establish a gold coinage and struck off about 800 gold mohurs but the expence so far exceeded the price for which the coin could be purchased in the bazars that the experiment was discontinued and no further attempts have since been made to establish a coinage of that metal.

[…]

13th I have before mentioned that copper is only coined when the rate of exchange rises so heigh (either owing to the scarcity of pice, or as I fear is more frequently the case, a combination of the Sowcars) that the evil is seriously felt in the bazars. There being no fixed rate of the copper currency the price of pice is therefore constantly fluctuating. In 1842 it rose to 14 gundas or nearly 56 pice to the rupee, when the Resident, on the representation of the Brigadr Comdg the subsidiary force, induced His Highness the Rajah to issue a new copper coinage. The Maharaja on the advice of the Resident, also at that time reduced the standard weight of each piece from 10 ½ to 9 mashas at which standard it has since been allowed to remain. The quantity of new copper then thrown into the market caused a material improvement in the exchange and the price of pice fell in a short time from 14 gundas to 18 gundas or 72 pice per rupee. For about four years the exchange has continued healthy, but during the latter part of 1846, and the early part of this year the price of pice again rose to 14½ gundas. The Brigadr Comdg the Subsidiary Force, twice called my attention to this circumstance [and] represented the distress the scarcity of copper caused to the sepoys and campfollowers and requested that I wd take some measures to remedy the evil. I accordingly suggested to the Durbar the advisability of putting the copper mint into active operation which they reluctantly consented to, as they said that the rise in the exchange would be but temporary. Their result however has proved that the measures was a necessary one for the exchange is still floating at about 15 gundas & were it not for the small daily supply furnished by the Raja for the use of the force the price of the pice would soon fall to 14½ or 14 gundas only. I fear however that no permanent improvement will take place for some time as there is but little copper now procurable at Nagpore and the season is unfavourable for its importation from other places.

14th Since the year 1842 the raja has given up farming the copper mint. It was formerly put up to auction. The privilege of coining sold for from Rs. 350 to 1650 for the year, the price chiefly depending upon the rate at which copper could be procured in the market, and the intentions of the speculator who took the lease.

15th The following table shows the number of pice coined during the past 10 years, or the sum at which the privilege of coining was farmed at the time that system obtained.

TABLE R.30.3: COPPER COIN PRODUCTION, NAGPORE
AH 1247-56 (1831/2-1840/1).

Nagpore Fusly year	*Number pice coined*	*Value in rupees*	*Mint farmed for*	*Remarks*
1247	Not known		750:0:0	
1248	Not known		1650:0:0	
1249	No coinage		0	
1250	Not known		342:7:3	
1251	111,760	5,735:00:0		The price of copper this year being 16 Rs only per maund 64 pice considered equal to one R
1252	5,531,415	28,809:07:3		
1253	8,930,485	46,512:15:1		The price of copper being 18:11:6 per maund 63 pice are calculated as equal to one rupee
1254	1,876,298	9,772:06:2		
1255	No coinage	0		
1256	210,024	1,093:14:0		
Total	16,659,982	91,923:10:6		

16th The standard weight of a Nagpore pice being 9 mashas only 63 pice or 15¾ gundas can be coined for a rupee as the average price of copper is R 18:11:6 per maund of 16 seers at 76 rupees to the seer or exactly 28 lbs 12 oz 8 drms avoir.

TABLE R.30.4: PRODUCTION COSTS OF THE NAGPORE PICE, 1848.

	Pice	*Pice*	*Rs*
In one maund of copper there are 12,616 mashas or nearly	1402		
Add of alloy (tin) 72 mashas equal to	9		
Total		1411	
Deduct consumed in melting etc 792 mashas equal to		88	
Balance (15¾ gundas, or at 63 pice to one rupee)		1323	21
One maund of copper costs			18:11:6
Add expenses of coining			1:12:0
Massool or extra sum to cover contingencies, writers, oil, paper, etc, etc			0:08:6
			21:00:0
The sum of 1 anna 3 pice for the crucible in which a maund of copper has been melted has not been taken into account			01:3

Source: NAI, Foreign Department, Foreign Political Proceedings, No. 1084 [*sic*], 7 April 1848, Nos. 207-37a.*

* With reference to earlier correspondence of 6 February 1847. - Ed.

31

Gold, Silver and Copper Coins, now or Formerly Current in Central India States 1865-1866

[Among all reports delivered by the Princely States to the authorities in the different presidencies, and most of all to the Bengal Presidency, and later to the Central Government of British India, only a few originals have been preserved, let alone illustrated ones. A rare example, written in Urdu, originates from the Princely State of Charkhari (now in the Mahoba district, UP), ca. 1860 in response to a request from the Central India Agency at Indore from 4 October 1865.

See Part II: Records, Nos. 30, 32, and 33.]

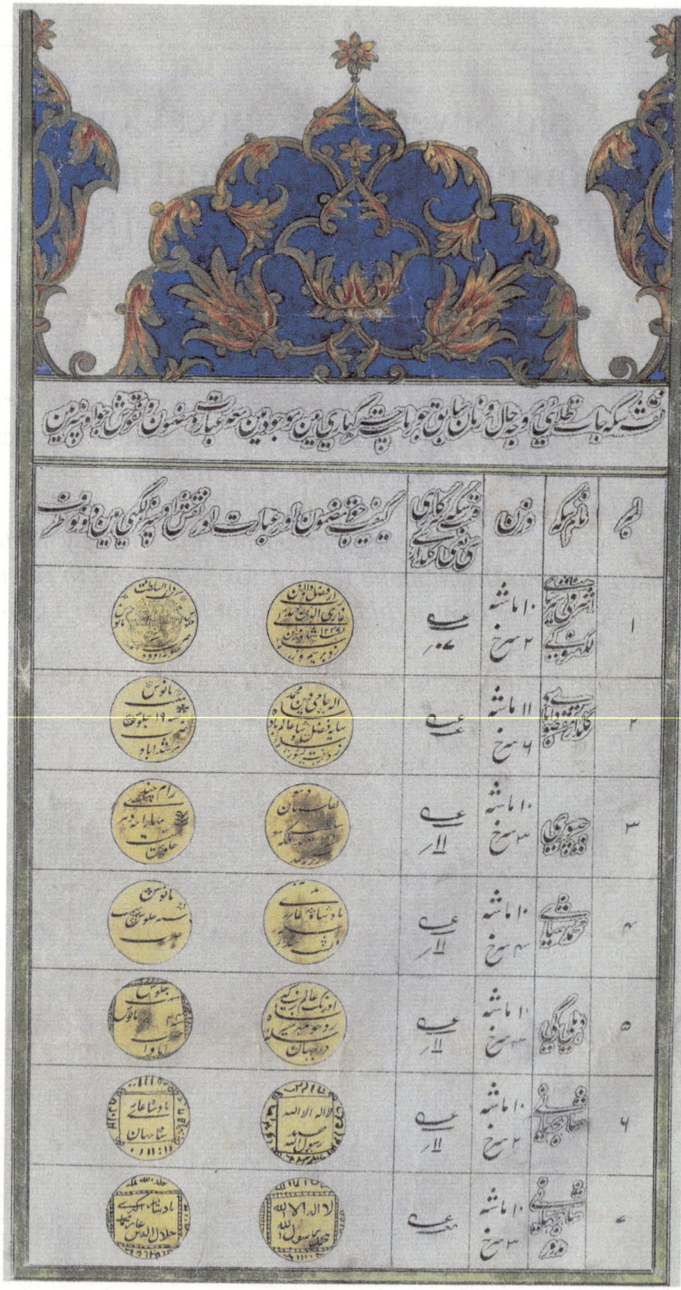

FIG. R.31.1

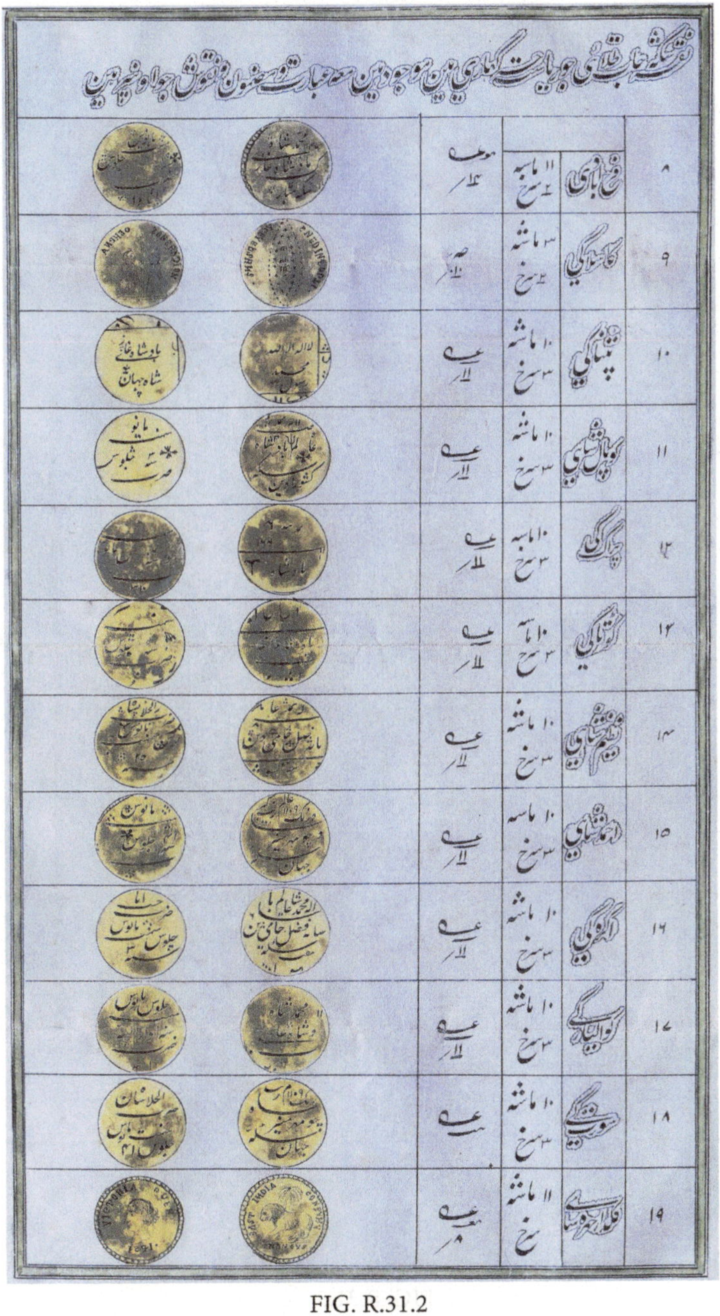

FIG. R.31.2

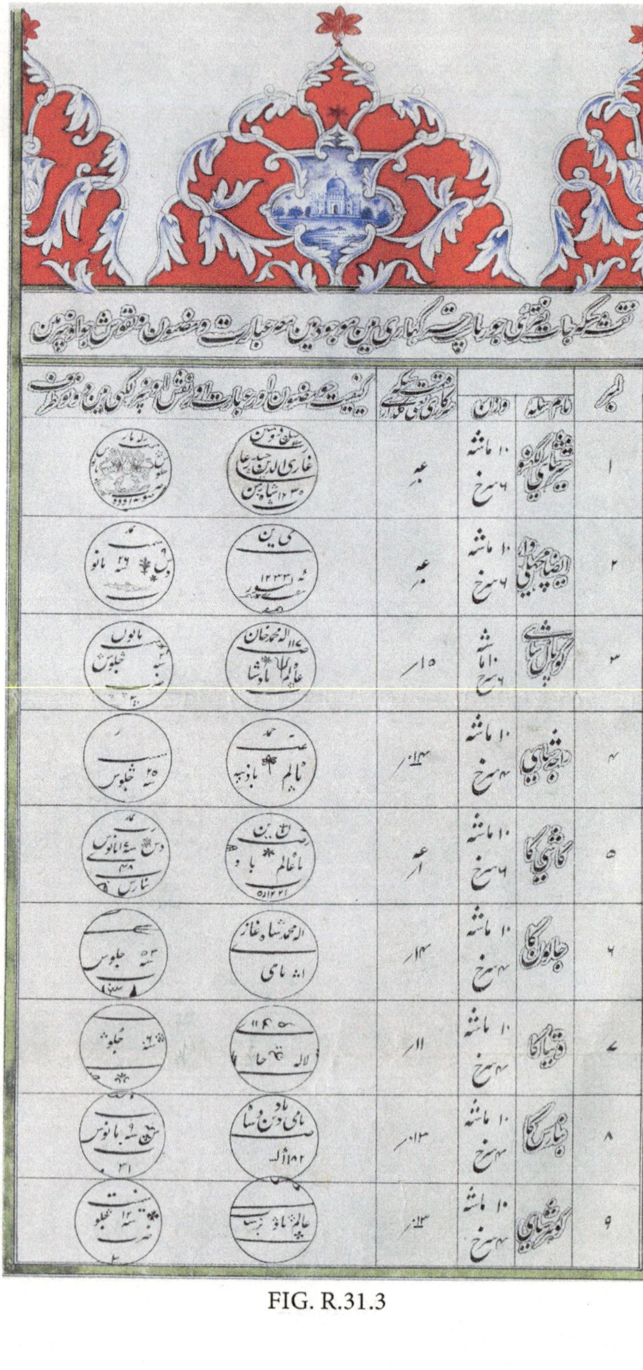

FIG. R.31.3

FIG. R.31.4

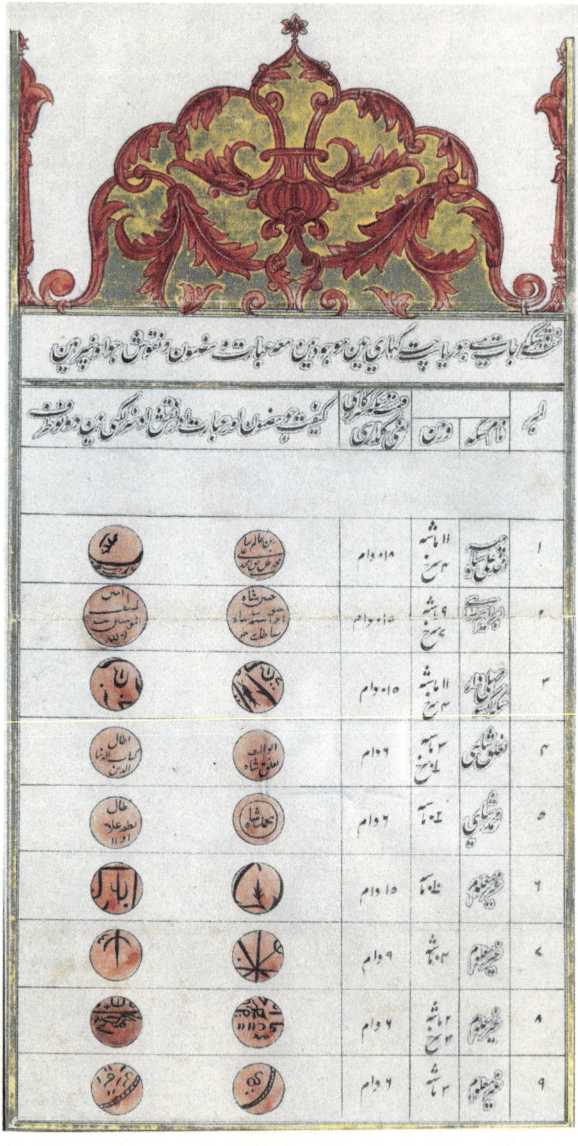

FIG. R.31.5

ILLUS. R.31.1–R.31.5: 5 COLOUR DRAWINGS OF GOLD, SILVER, AND COPPER COINS, NOW OR FORMERLY CURRENT IN CENTRAL INDIA STATES, 1865-6

Source: NAI, Residences, Central India Agency, Coins, Mints, No. 6: 814/ 1865-6.

32

Coinage in Native Territory of Various Native Currencies in Bundelkhand, 26 September 1870 to 4 June 1872

[*Also, after the end of the EIC, and in fact until the very end of British rule in India, a number of states continued its own currencies, which was followed by a suspicious eye from Calcutta via the various Agencies into which the Princely States were organized. One was the Central India Agency at Indore. The British interest was not only in the legal coinage by the Princely States, but also in the leniency of some to prosecute illegal fabrication by individuals.*

See Studies 12 and Part II: Records, Nos. 30, 31 and 33.]

J.P. Stratton, Political Agent for Bundelkhand to the Agent Governor General for Central India Indore, Nowgong, 31 October 1870

818 / 1870-5 Coinage in native Territory by Mahajan of Mhow Ranipoor of Various Native Currencies

Sir,

I have the honor to report the following case. Intimation was perceived of the seizure at Umraotee of a consignment of copper money, resembling, or identical with Nagpore pice, imported from Mow Raneepore in our Jhansi district, & said to be manufactured in Native Territory adjacent thereto.

2. In the investigation at Mow, large quantities of new pice, copper, and implements were seized, and above twenty persons were arrested as principals; while altogether about a couple of hundred

people of the same district were ascertained to have been engaged in the business in one way or another.

In the Native Territory, it was found that the Mow merchants and others had been manufacturing pice at several places, but as they had stopped work, and withdrawn establishments and stores, the enquiry here was of a more general nature than at Mow, where details of the business fell to be examined.

In the investigation there, it was established that sundry Mahajuns, Sonars and others of Mow were extensively engaged in the manufacture, sale, and export of dumpy copper pice of various native currencies.

The following appeared prominent as places of the manufacture, viz. Bumori in Orcha Territory, Tori of Tori Futtehpore, Kurara of Geroli, and Sursair of Alipora.

Inquiry in the Native Territory corresponded in its results with the foregoing, except as to the last named place, and except as to furnishing grounds of belief that the Mow Mahajuns confined the manufacture within Native limits.

The Mahajuns or Sonars had come into Native Territory, and obtained leave to manufacture pice, paying a few annas per maund for permission, for house rent, and for protection.

They appear in each case to have represented that their business was a legitimate one, and known to the authorities of our own district; but it is clear that the Native States ought to have reported the applications and inquired our opinion thereon.

The fact of the traders scattering their manufactories around Mow, instead of concentrating them there at their own homes might have suggested doubts as to the legitimacy of their business.

The traders selected places which, in the older times, had been used for the same purpose.

Apart from these older times, the present business appears to have risen into activity since the last famine, having been carried on for periods ranging, at the different places, from a few months upwards, and subject to intermissions from suspension of the supply of copper, pending sale of previous batches of pice.

3. The investigation at Mow led to charges being there prepared

against twenty-eight persons, under one or other of the following sections of the I.P. Code:

Manufacturing Counterfeit Coin, Sect. 231
Abetting therein, Section 109
Having possession thereof, Section 242
Exporting it, Section 237.

They however, maintained that they had committed no offence; that the manufacture and trade were old ones and openly carried on; that the pice were of pure metal and of full weight; that they were sold wholesale by weight at rates varying with that of copper, being of course, on account of the labor, somewhat higher; that the purchasers were fully acquainted with their source; that the pice circulate freely at their full value among people who know they are newly made, and who willingly receive them; that there is no deception or fraud; and that, within the last few years, pice have similarly been made at Cawnpore and Jhansi.

I enclose copies of the Report of the Deputy Commissioner of Jhansi No. 155 dated 26th ultimo; and of the Commrs Reply No. 397 dated 28th idem, which have been kindly furnished.

From these it will be seen that, while the traffic was of course considered highly objectionable, the accused were held to have committed no offence under the present wording of our law; that orders were consequently issued for their release, and for the restoration to them of the pice and copper &c seized; and that police procedure was directed to be limited to the suppression of any mints found within British Territory.

The trades had seemingly acquired a shrewd knowledge of the law; and believing their proceedings might be stopped by authority, but not punished by law, they scattered the manufacture as much as possible, so as not to attract too much attention.

The sheet copper is purchasable in open bazaar, the dies can be engraved by any good goldsmith or iron-smith, and the commonest workmen can do the rest. The manufacture, if conducted at a moderate scale, need not excite more notice than the ordinary work of a copper-smith's shop, where the ring of the hammer is heard, and there is, on sundry grounds, reason to believe the manufacture was diffused more widely and nearer home than the traders acknowledge.

Under the exposition above mentioned of the Law in our territory, which corresponds I believe with the view also held at Cawnpore and elsewhere, though it differs from what I had previously understood, and under that result of the case against the principals, including manufacturers, brokers, sellers, buyers, and workmen, there was no ground for judicial procedure in the Native Territory, where sundry workmen, laborers &c were employed, besides the numbers who came from the Mow district.

4. There remains the point of the permission given by the Native State Authorities to the Mow traders to manufacture copper pice in villages of their territory. The view I have taken, and impressed on them, is as follows:

> Orcha being the only one of them which has a Mint of its own, it appears clear that the other Petty Chiefships which have no authority to coin for themselves, can have no right to authorize others to coin within their limits.
>
> In respect to Orcha, it seems very inadvisable that, beyond its own mint, it should authorize strangers to carry on coinage in its territory, and still more highly objectionable when such persons manufacture pice, not merely for local use, but imitate the old native currencies of distant districts, and export large quantities thereto. There is a point mentioned by Orcha, in regard to its own copper mint, worthy of notice, viz. that as, besides its own Gujjasahi currency, the Balasahi pice, originally coined in Jaloun, are also largely current in its territory, it has been an understood custom, of old standing, to make from time to time Balasahi, as well as Gujjasahi pice.
>
> From the investigation at Mow, there is no reason to doubt the origin and old standing ascribed to the practice, or to suppose that it was formerly considered objectionable, as it would seem that when Jhansi and Jaloun were still Native States, and there was less British territory in the province, there can have been no very clear prohibition among the States themselves against copper coining in the way of a mercantile operation.

As however it seems to me objectionable that, at the present day, a Native State should coin any other than its own currency, I have communicated this opinion to Orcha. But the Balasahi pice will not die out of circulation by stoppage of manufacture at one place alone, which measure would merely stimulate the manufacture elsewhere, such as at Sindiah's town of Jhansi.

5. At the same time the case as a whole is not so clear for any summary order as might at first sight appear, and can scarcely be fully understood without noticing the ideas held by the natives about copper currency, differing as these do considerably from our own stricter views on everything connected with mints, which make our rules as rigid regarding copper, as regarding silver coinage.

It was found in the investigation at Mow that the trade had, though with frequent and considerable intervals of suspension, been an old established one; that, prior to the annexation* of Jhansi, various kinds of pice (i.e. of the currencies of various districts) had been manufactured commercially at Mow for export; that subsequently the Mow traders continued the manufacture in adjoining Native Territory (though whether or not solely there, as they represent, is another matter); that formerly even the Native States which had their own mints, did not seemingly hesitate to import pice if they could purchase elsewhere cheaper than they themselves could turn out; that large quantities of Balasahi pice were two or three years ago made at Jhansi; and that, within an equally recent period, Lucknow pice were, for a time, made at Cawnpore, where, though the manufacture was stopped on a presentation from Lucknow, no criminal proceedings were instituted, and where it was known that dumpy pice were imported from Mow, but considered that the law did not prohibit it.

It has been noticed in the Native States, that by the simple vernacular term for Mint, one for silver is alone generally understood, as if it alone was properly entitled to the name, while if one for copper is meant, it requires to be actually specified.

* In 1853. - Ed.

Sundry of the particulars ascertained at Mow and in the Native Territory illustrate a point which has been observed also in the west of India, and is ultimately connected with the subject of copper currency in this country.

It is that among natives, and a fortiori those of Native Territory, copper pice are looked on less as money or as furnishing a standard of value, than as a common market commodity, the value of which itself varies from day to day in the bazaar, and is expressed by the number (in bazaar language the number per rupee of 'Gundas' each of 4 pice, or as 'Tukas' each of two pice) procurable per rupee.

In fact native Narikhs or prices current usually contain the rate of pice just as they give that of any other articles, which is the more needful as, besides the market variation of every kind, some of the sorts vary among themselves in weight, so that it appears these native pice cannot all have been designed exactly to equal one quarter of an anna as in our currency.

The native pice, while of fair metal, are much heavier than ours, and their consequent greater intrinsic value doubtless partly aids their still holding their ground among the people.

The intrinsic value of ours is stated (in Govt. of India Resolution Financial Department No. 1577 dated 28 February 1862) to be only about half the nominal value, while the metal value of the native pice more nearly approaches its currency value, which latter depends jointly on the price of copper, and the supply of and the demand for the pice. At Mow it was found the manufacturers were lately supplying the following pice, at the advance on the cost of copper here noted:

TABLE R.32.1: PRODUCTION COSTS OF COPPER COINS, MOW, 1870

Price per seer of	*annas*
Copper	14½
Balasahi pice	15
Lucknow and Nawabi pice	16
Nagpore pice	18

Under the present market value respectively of copper and of pice, some of those kinds of pice could not just now be made at the rates above quoted. The varying cost of the different kinds appears connected with the amount of labor in their production. The Balasahi pice being the heaviest are fewer and involve less labour per seer and are the cheapest. The Nagpore pice are at the other side of the native scale and Govt pice are still lighter. The following weights, in the case of Balasahi and Govt. pice, are those of coins in bulk from the bazaar, more or less worn. The weights of the others are calculated from a small number. In all cases small fractions are omitted:

TABLE R.32.2: WEIGHTS OF DIFFERENT TYPES OF COPPER COINS, MOW, 1870

Pice	*Per 2 lbs avoirdupois = 14,000 grains*	*Per seer of 80 tolas of 180 grains = 14,400 grains*
Balashahi	59	61
Lucknow and Nawabi	79	81½
Nagpore	95	98
Government	143	147

These weights are nearly in the following proportion:

TABLE R.32.3: WEIGHT PROPORTIONS OF DIFFERENT TYPES OF COPPER COINS, MOW, 1870

Pice	
Government	4
Nagpore	6
Lucknow	7 ¼
Balashahi	9 ½

Since the mutinies, the retail bazaar rates per Govt rupee of the two kind of pice most used in these parts have ranged as follows at Chutturpore, which is the nearest large town to Nowgong. But rates vary considerably at different places:

TABLE R.32.4: EXCHANGE RATES OF COPPER COINS, CHUTTURPORE 1857/8-1869/70.

Average per year		*Pice*	
S[amba]t	AD	*Govt.*	*Balasahi*
1914	1857/8	65	51
1915	1858/9	69	45
1916	1859/60	66	41
1917	1860/1	65	42
1918	1861/2	65	40
1919	1862/3	65	41
1920	1863/4	65	39
1921	1864/5	65	42
1922	1865/6	65	43
1923	1866/7	65	48
1924	1867/8	65	57
1925	1868/9	65	66
1926	1869/70	65	65

These rates are doubtless correct enough for Balasahi, and during the last ten years for Govt. pice. But as regards the rates of the latter in the Mutiny years,* they are only the nominal rates, for it is known that in those times of unsettlement, when less regard was paid to stamp than to actual value, Govt. pice, both in our own and Native Territory, fell in value, till 100 or more were required to exchange for a rupee. At present at Nowgong and Chutturpore the rates of both pice, apart from small occasional variations, are the same and are here shown with the weights noted:

TABLE R.32.5: WEIGHTS OF GOVERNMENT AND BALASAHI PICE, NOWGONG AND CHUTTURPORE, 1870

Pice	*Number*	*Weight avoirdupois (oz.)*
Govt.	64, i.e. par, or one pice exactly equaling a quarter anna	14½
Balasahi	Do. Do.	34½

* For that reason, italicised by me. Ed.

Certain qualities of the Govt. copper currency are undoubtedly appreciated by the people, who find it less subject than Native pice to extreme variation of bazaar rate (e.g. in the last 10 years the variation of Govt. pice has only been from one or two pice below to the same above par, while Balasahi pice have ranged from 25 pice above par to 2 pice below), which quality to a poor man, whose dealings are mostly in pice, is very important; and less liable to have a deduction from its value made by the shopkeepers on account of wear, which is a fertile source of profit to the money changers, and of loss to the poor, in the use especially of the native currencies.

6. As other cases may any day arise, in which it will devolve in this office itself to deal with the legal aspect of the question, and as according to my understanding of the law it is really even at present applicable, I submit a separate letter No, 232 of this date on that subject.

Copy No. 155 of 1870

From P.J. White, Offg Deputy Commissioner Jhansie,
Jhansie, 26 September 1870

Sir,

On the 11th July last you addressed Mr. Lang with reference to a report, published in the newspapers, that the issue of a base coin had been traced to the town of Mow Raneepore in this district, Mr. Lang replied on the 12th idem that the matter was under inquiry and would be reported on hereafter.

2. I have now the honor to submit the English record of investigation. The case has been prosecuted by the Police before Mr. Sturtt Offg Asst Commissioner as one of counterfeiting coin under Section 231 and other branch sections of the Penal Code. The correspondence on the subject marginally noted is also herewith sent (from Dy Comr Jhansie to Poll Agent Nowgong No. 135, dated 17th August; reply No. 567 dated 20th August; from Poll Agent to Dy Comr No. 615 dated 5th September).

3. The case originated in a demi official (communication from

the Superintendent of Police, Nagpore dated 30th June, to the Superintendent of Police here. Other demi official letters and telegrams followed, all urging action on the Police [...]

4. The consequence was that 28 persons were apprehended, 213 maunds of pice of the descriptions specified in margin, and 442 maunds of copper seized, and sundry implements and account books impounded.

TABLE R.32.6: COPPER COINS AND COPPER, SEIZED FROM 28 PERSONS, UNAUTHORIZED TO MANUFACTURE COINS, JHANSI 1870

Pice	*Maunds*	*Seer*
Lucknow	115	0
Lucknow broken pieces	1	0
Nowabee	96	34
Total	212	34
		pice
Also (late) Nagparee		33
Balashahee		98
Munsooree		61

5. All particulars will be found in Mr. Sturt's abstract of the case [...]

No. 232 J.P. Stratton, Political Agent for Bundelkhand to the Agent Governor-General for Central India Indore, Nowgong, 31 October 1870

Sir,

With reference to paras 3 & 6 of my letter No. 231 of this date, regarding the continued coinage, or imitation of the coinage of certain Native Govts whose states now form part of the British Territory, I have the honor to remark that, as cases requiring the judicial action of this office may any day arise, it is very desirable that there should be no doubt of what the law on the subject really is.

[...]

3. The dumpy pice in the present case are not mere unstamped lumps of copper, which section 230(a) declares are not coin.

They are stamped with the device, or an imitation of the device, formerly used by the Native Govt. of Lucknow, or Nagpoor, or Jaloun, the currencies of which are still used by large populations throughout wide tracts of territory, both British and Native.

No. 395F, dated Simla, 4 June 1872 [Printed]

From C.U. Aitchison, Secy to the Govt of India, Foreign Dept with the GG to Major-General H.D. Daly, Agent to the Gov[erno]r-Gen[enera]l Central India

I am desired to communicate copy of papers which have been received by the Government of the North-Western Provinces regarding the manufacture of copper coin in the Native States and jageers around Mow Raneepoor in Jhansi.

2. Measures are being taken for amending the penal code so that penalties may attach to the unauthorized manufacture of any coin whether issued by the British or any foreign government; but as the correspondence which terminated with Resolution from this office No. 402F, dated 6th October 1870, paper sent by the Government of the North-Western Provinces, had been long closed, steps should, under the terms of that Resolution, be taken to prevent the issue of any coins by, or under the authority of, their Rulers. Even if they had the right of coining, it would extend only to their own currency. To manufacture the coins of other States or of extinct dynasties is a proceeding which ought not to be permitted.

Source: NAI, Residences, Central India Agency, Coins, Mints, No. 10.

33

Closing of Bhopal State Mints, 7 July 1897 and 11 February 1898

[*The final objective of the government in Calcutta was the closure of all Princely State mints. Before the end of British rule in India this objective has never been achieved, although the number of these mints diminished gradually. One example is the mint of Bhopal State, which minted copper anna pieces until* AH *1309 (1891/92).*

See Part II: Records, Nos. 30, 31, and 32.]

Printed Correspondence Regarding the Closing of Bhopal State Mints of the Currency Arrangements in Bhopal

Telegram from the Agent to the Governor-General in Central India, Indore, to the Revenue Secretary, Simla 7 July 1897

6299. The Political Agent, Bhopal, reports that a very significant grain riot occurred at Sehore on the night of the 5th July, owing to the bunnias demanding from coolies a sudden increase in number of State copper coins for one rupee. Riot easily suppressed. Arrangements have been made for coolies to be paid in British [Indian] copper coin and to obtain their grain from Kotwali.

Captain L.S. Newmarch, Political Agent in Bhopal, 11 February 1898 about the Conversion of the Bhopali Currency, now Nearly Finished:

Finding that small silver of the British Indian currency was very scarce throughout the Agency, I impressed upon the Bhopal Durbar the importance of providing a sufficient supply through the State Treasuries, and after some reluctance the Minister has at length asked me to obtain for him Rs. 45,000 worth of small silver coins.

The other states are making similar indents.

When these coins have been disseminated they will largely facilitate the currency, especially in the smaller and local markets, of the new [British Indian] rupees, which in many cases can now only be broken up into 30 or 35 (for the rate of exchange varies at different times and places) shapeless lumps of copper, known as gundas.

But the copper currency is a matter that will receive attention later on.

Source: NAI, Residences, Central India Agency 842, Pt. III / 1894-8.

Bibliography

A. ARCHIVAL MATERIAL AND MANUSCRIPTS

A.1 National Archives of India, New Delhi (NAI)

- Military Department, Military Board (NAI/MB), Proceedings
- Financial Department, Mint Committee
- Financial Department, Proceedings
- Home Department, Public Original Consultations
- Foreign Department, Finance

A.2 West Bengal State Archives, Kolkata (WBSA)

- Copy book of the Letters, issued by the Comptrolling Council (LC).

A.3 Department of Archives, Government of Goa, Panaji

- Feitorias #2316 Livro de registo

A.4. British Library, London

Asian and African Studies, OIOC, India Office Records (BL / IOR):

- Financial Department, Proceedings
- Foreign Department, Proceedings
- Home/Misc./420
- Bengal Despatches (BL/IOR/EIC/E/4)
- Madras Despatches (BL/IOR/EIC/E/4)
- Bombay Despatches (BL/IOR/EIC/E/4)
- India and Bengal Despatches (BL/IOR/EIC/E/4)
- Factory Records, Miscellaneous
- Factory Records, Surat
- Abul Fazl, *Akbarnama*, MS Add. 27247

- *Kaghzat-i Mutafarriqa* (Anonymous collection of administrative documents from eighteenth century Bengal).
- European Manuscripts, D 142, 144, 149 (BL/IOR/Eur. Mss/D/142; D/144; D/149).
- Ethé, Hermann, *Catalogue of Persian Manuscripts in the Library of the India Office*, Vol. I (Oxford: 1903, 211).

A.5 Royal Asiatic Society of Great Britain and Ireland, London

Akhbarat-i Darbar-i Mualla [Newsletters from the Mughal Court], MS 2361.

Papers of Francis Buchanan-Hamilton, GB 891 FBH/7.

A.6 Bodleian Library, Oxford

Barani, Zia-ud-din, *Tarikh-i Firuz-Shahi*. Ref. MS Elliot, 353.

A.7 Nationaal Archief/National Archives of the Netherlands, The Hague (NA)

- Verenigde Oost-Indische Compagnie (VOC).
- Voormalige Nederlandse Bezittingen in Voor-Indie (NBV-I).
- Geleynssen de Jongh Collection.

B. WEBSITES

a. https://iisg.amsterdam/en/research/projects/global-collaboratory-on-the-history-of-labour-relations-1500-2000
b. http://www.psindiancoins.com/
c. https://www.zeno.ru.

C. PRINTED MATERIAL

A Brief Sketch of the services of Sir G.H. Barlow, Bart. and K.B. Governor of Madras, founded on a series of authentic and interesting papers and correspondence (London, 1811).

Abdullah, *Tarikh-i Daudi*, ed. S.A. Rashid (Aligarh, 1954).

Abul Fazl, *Ain-i-Akbari*, ed. in the Original Persian by H. Blochmann, 2 vols. (Calcutta, 1872-7).

Abul Fazl, *Ain-i-Akbari*, translated and ed. H. Blochmann and H.S. Jarret, revised and enlarged by Jadunath Sarkar, 3 vols., 3rd rev. and enl. edn. (Delhi 1977).

Aelst, Arjan van, 'A South-Chinese Currency Zone between the Twelfth and Nineteen Centuries', in Jan Lucassen (ed.), 2007, 97-112.

Afif, Shams-i Siraj, *Tarikh-i Firozshahi*, ed. Wilayat Hussain (Calcutta, 1891).

Aktor, Mikael, 'Rules of Untouchability in Ancient and Medieval Law Books. Householders, Competence and Inauspiciousness', *International Journal of Hindu Studies* 6:3 (2002), 243-4.

________, *Ritualisation and Segregation: The Untouchability Complex in Indian Dharma Literature with special reference to Parasarasmriti and Parasaramadhaviya* (Turin, 2008).

________, (2018a). 'Social classes: varna', in Olivelle and Davis Jr. 2018, 60-77.

________, (2018b). 'Impurity and Purification: asauca, sauca', in Olivelle and Davis Jr. 2018, 220-35.

Alavi, Seema, *The Sepoys and the Company: Tradition and Transition in Northern India 1770-1830* (Delhi, 1995).

Algazi, Gadi, Valentin Groebner and Bernhard Jussen (eds.), *Negotiating the Gift. Pre-Modern Figurations of Exchange* (Göttingen, 2003).

Allen, Martin, 'The volume of the English currency, 1158-1470', *Economic History Review* 54: 4 (2001), 595-611.

________, *Mints and Money in Medieval England* (Cambridge, 2012).

________, (2015). 'Coin Finds and the English Money Supply, *c.* 973-1544', in Allen and Coffman (eds.), 2015, 7-23.

Allen, Martin and D'Maris Coffman (eds.), *Money, Prices and Wages: Essays in Honour of Professor Nicholas Mayhew* (Houndmills, Basingstoke, 2015).

Allen, Robert C., *The British Industrial Revolution in Global Perspective* (Cambridge, 2009).

Allen, Robert C., et al., 'Wages, Prices, and Living Standards in China, 1738-1925: In Comparison with Europe, Japan, and India', *The Economic History Review*, 64.1(2011), 8-38.

Ambedkar, B.R., *History of Indian Currency and Banking* (Bombay, 1947).

Amin, Shahid (ed.), *A Concise Encyclopaedia of North Indian Peasant Life. Being a compilation from the writings of William Crooke, J.R. Reid, G.A. Grierson* (New Delhi, 2005).

Anderson, B.L. and A.J.H. Latham (eds.), *The Market in History* (London, 1986).

Ansari, Tahir Hussain, *Mughal Administration and the Zamindars of Bihar* (London/ New York, 2019).

Appadurai, A., *Economic Conditions in Southern India (1000 to AD 1500)*, 2 vols. (Madras, 1936).

Appadurai, Arjun (ed.), *The Social Life of Things. Commodities in a Cultural Perspective* (Cambridge, 1986).

Arasaratnam, Sinappah, 'Trade and Political Dominion in South India 1750-1790. Changing British-Indian Relationships', *Modern Asian Studies* 13 (1979), 19-40.

———, 'Weavers, Merchants and Company: the handloom Industry in South-Eastern India 1750-1790', *IESHR* 17:3 (1980), 257-81.

———, 'Review symposium: I Chapters: II South India: Some General Considerations of the Region and its Early History; IV Vijayanagara *c.* 1350-1564; VII The State and the Economy *c.* 1500-1750. 3. The South; X Non-Agricultural Production; XI Indian Trade', *IESHR* 21: 1 (1984), 111-16.

———, *Merchants, Companies and Commerce on the Coromandel Coast, 1650-1740* (Delhi, 1986).

———, 'Merchants, commerce and the state in South India 1650-1700', *Revista de Cultura* 5: 1 (1991), 150-61.

Ashtor, E. *A Social and Economic History of the Near East in the Middle Ages* (London, 1976).

Athar Ali, M. (1981). 'Capital of the Sultans during the 13th and 14th Centuries', *Indian History Congress Session* (Cyclostyed Papers).

Atkinson, Fred. J., 'Silver Prices in India', *Journal of the Royal Statistical Society* 60: 1 (March 1897), 84-147.

Atkinson, Fred. J., 'Silver Prices in India for 1897', *Journal of the Royal Statistical Society* 61: 2 (June 1898), 387-403.

———, 'Rupee Prices in India, 1898-1901', *Journal of the Royal Statistical Society* 66: 1 (March 1903), 103-18.

Atwell, 'Notes on Silver, Foreign Trade, and the Late Ming Economy', *Ching-Shih Wen-t'i* 3: 8 (1977), 1-33.

Aubin, Jean, *Le latin et l'astrolabe : Recherches sur le Portugal de la Renaissance, son expansion en Asie et les relations internationales II* (Lisbon/ Paris: 2000).

Austin, Gareth and Kaoru Sugihara (eds.), *Local Suppliers of Credit in the Third World, 1750-1960* (London, 1993).

Babur, Zahiruddin Muhammad, *The Baburnama: Memoirs of Babur, Prince and Emperor*, tr. Wheeler M. Thackston (New York, 1996).

Bacharach, Jere, 'Monetary movements in medieval Egypt, 1171-1517', in Richards (ed.), 1983, 159-81.

Bacherikov, Pavel, 'Monety i zarplaty: vypusk monetykh denominatsii kak indikator rasprostranenii naemnogo truda v Rossii v XVII veke', Course Paper for Higher School of Economics and New Economic School (Moscow, 2013). Unpublished.

Bagchi, Amiya Kumar (ed.), *Money and Credit in Indian History. From Early Medieval Times* (New Delhi, 2002).

Bagchi, Amiya Kumar, 'Introduction: Money, Banking and Finance in India since early Medieval Times', in Bagchi (ed.), 2002, ix-xli.

________, 'Money and Credit as Areas of Conflict in Colonial India', *Reports of Section B6 of the 8th International Congress of Economic History* (Budapest 1982).

Baker, W.E., *Memoranda on the Western Jumna Canals in the North-Western Provinces of the Bengal Presidency* (London, 1849).

Ball, V., *A Manual of the Geology of India*, Part III *Economic Geology* (Calcutta, 1881).

Banerjee, Prathama, 'Debt, time and extravagance: Money and the making of 'primitives'in colonial Bengal', *IESHR* 37:4 (2000), 433-45.

Barani, Zia-ud-din, *Tarikh-i Firuz-shahi*, ed. Saiyid Ahmad Khan, W.N. Lees and Karibbudin (Calcutta, 1860-2).

Barbosa, Duarte, *The Book of Duarte Barbosa: An Account of the Countries Bordering on the Indian Ocean and their Inhabitants*, 2 vols. (New Delhi, 1989).

Barrett, Ward (1990). 'World Bullion Flows, 1450-1680', in Tracy (ed.) 1990, 224-54.

Bavel, Bas van, 'Rural wage labour in the sixteenth-century Low Countries: An assessment of the importance and nature of wage labour in the countryside of Holland, Guelders and Flanders', *Continuity and Change*, 21 (2006), 37-72.

________, *Manors and Markets: Economy and Society in the Low Countries, 500-1600* (Oxford, 2010).

Bavel, Bas van and Richard Hoyle (eds.), *Rural Economy and Society in North-Western Europe, 500-2000. Social Relations: Property and Power* (Turnhout, 2010).

Bayly, Christopher Alan, *Rulers, Townsmen and Bazaars: North Indian Society in the Age of British expansion, 1770-1870* (Cambridge, 1983).

———, 'State and Economy in India over seven hundred Years', *The Economic History Review*, 2nd Series, 37: 4 (1985), 583-96.

———, *Empire and Information: Intelligence gathering and social communication in India, 1780-1870* (Cambridge, 1996).

Bayly, Susan, *Caste, Society and Politics in India from the Eighteenth Century to the Modern Age* (Cambridge, 1999).

Béaur, Gérard, et al. (2010). 'Northern France, 1000-1750', in van Bavel and Hoyle (eds.) 2010, 111-66.

Bengal Secretariat (1884). *Alphabetical Index to the Proceedings of the Board of Revenue from January to June 1796* (Calcutta: Bengal Secretariat Press).

Bernier, Francois, *Travels in the Mogul Empire AD 1656-1668*. Translated by Archibald Constable, 2nd edn., revised by Vincent A. Smith (London, 1916).

Bertsch, Wolfgang, 'The Use of Maldivian Cowries as Money According to an 18th century Portuguese Dictionary on World Currencies', *ONS-NL*165 (2000), 16-19.

Bhandare, Shailendra, 'Jamgaon, Harda and Khachrod. Three new mints under under Sindhias of Gwalior', *JONS* 197 (2008), 32-7.

Bhandare, Shailendra and Sanjay Godbole, 'Maratha Seals from Konkan and Deccan', *ONS-NL*190 (Winter 2007), 32-6.

Bhatt, S.K., *The Coinage of the Native States of Central India*, Vol I: *The History of Coins and Seals of Jhabua State* (Indore, 1985).

Bhattacharya, Neeladri (1992). 'Agricultural Labour and Production: Central and South-East Punjab, 1870-1940', in Gyan Prakash (ed.), 1992, 146-204.

Bhattacharya, Sabyasachi (ed.), *Towards a New History of Work* (New Delhi, 2014).

Bhattacharya, Sabyasachi and Jan Lucassen, *Workers in the informal Sector: Studies in Labour History 1800-2000* (New Delhi, 2005).

Bhattacharya, Sukumar, *The East India Company and the Economy of Bengal from 1704 to 1740* (Calcutta, 1969).

Biernacki, Richard, *The Fabrication of Labor: Germany and Britain, 1640-1914* (Berkeley, 1995)

Bihari, Hidayatullah (1898), *Hidayat ul-Qawaid*, [NB: The section on mint with an English translation published by Irwine 1898].

Blake, Stephen P., 'The Structure of Money Exchange in North India: The Provinces of Agra, Delhi and Lahore in 1600', in Richards (ed.) 1987, 100-36.

Blanchard, Ian, *Mining, Metallurgy and Minting in the Middle Ages*, 3 vols. (Stuttgart 2001, 2001, 2005).

Blitz, Rudolph C., 'Mercantilist Policies and the Pattern of World Trade, 1500-1750', *Journal of Economic History* 27: 1 (1967), 39-55.

Bolton, J.L., *Money in the Medieval English Economy, 973-1489* (Manchester, 2012).

Boncan, Celestina P., 'Colonial Copper Coinage in the Tobacco Monopoly, 1769-1837', *Philippine Studies* 34 (1986), 518-27.

Bose, S.K. (1996), 'Tea Garden Tokens of Assam', in Maheshwari and Rath (eds.) 1996, 345-62.

Brant, J., 'Journey through a part of Armenia and Asia Minor in the year 1835', *Journal of the Royal Geographical Society of London* 6 (1836), 187-223.

Braudel, Fernand, *Capitalism and Material Life, 1400-1800* (London, 1973).

________, *The Structures of Everyday Life*, tr. Siân Reynolds (London, 1981).

Brennig, Joseph J., 'Silver in Seventeenth-Century Surat: Monetary Circulation and the Price Revolution in Mughal India', in Richards (ed.), 1983, 477-96.

Brewer John and John Styles (eds.), *An Ungovernable People: The English and their Law in the Seventeenth and Eighteenth Centuries* (London, 1980).

Bright, Richard K., *The Coinage of Kutch* (Dallas, 1975).

Britnell, Richard, 'Labour Turnover and Wage Rates on the Demesnes of Durham Priority', in Allen and Coffman (eds.), 2015, 158-79.

Bruce, Colin R. (ed.), *Standard Catalogue of World Coins, 1601-1700* (Iola, Wi, 2008).

Bruce, Colin R. (senior editor), *Standard Catalog of World Coins: Nineteenth Century*, 4th edn. (Iola, Wi, 2004).

Burger, Werner (2008). 'Coin production during the Qianlong and Jiaqing reigns (1736-1820): Issues in cash and silver supply', in Hirzel and Kim (eds.), 2008, 171-89.

Bruijn, Jaap R. and Femme S. Gaastra (eds.), *Ships, Sailors and Spices: East India Companies and their shipping in the 16th, 17th and 18th Centuries* (Amsterdam, 1993).

Burke, Peter and Halil Inalcik (eds.), *History of Humanity: Scientific and Cultural Developments, V, From the Sixteenth to the Eighteenth Century* (UNESCO, 1999).

Callataÿ, F. de (ed.), *Quantifying Monetary Supplies in Greco-Roman Times* (Bari, 2011).

Callataÿ, F. de, 'Quantifying monetary production in Greco-Roman times: a general frame', in Callataÿ (ed.), 2011, 7-29.

Cao, Jin and Hans Ulrich Vogel, 'Smoke on the Mountain. The Infamous Counterfeiting Case of Tongzi District, Guizhou Province, 1794', in Leonard and Theobald (eds.), 2015, 188-219.

Cardon, Thibault (2012), 'Les petites monnaies étrangères en Normandie au XIVe-XVe siècles: provenances, modalités d'introduction et circulation', in Chameroy and Guihard (eds.), 2012, 207-28.

Cardon, Thibault and Frédéric Lemaire (2004), 'Les sous des soldats de Napoléon au camp de Boulogne (1803-1805). Étude des monnaies issues des fouilles des camps napoléoniens d'Étaples-sur-Mer et Camiers (Pas-de-Calais, France)', *The Journal of Archaeological Numismatics*, 4, 67-176.

Carrier, James G. (ed.), *A Handbook of Economic Anthropology*, 3rd edn. (Cheltenham, 2022).

Carvalhal, Hélder and Jan Lucassen, 'Beyond the Great divergence: The household income and occupational mobility in the Indian subcontinent, 1500-1870', *International Review of Social History* 70, Special Issue S33: Wage Systems and Inequalities in Global History, 1500–1950 , April 2025, 135-59.

Carvalhal, Hélder, Jan Lucassen and Pim de Zwart, 'After Da Gama: Real Wages in West India, *c.* 1500-*c.* 1650, *European Review of Economic History* 28:3 (August 2024), 311-34; Online: https://doi.org/10.1093/ereh/head026.

Carvalhal, Hélder, Paulo Teodoro de Matos and Jan Lucassen, 'Wages, Income and Living Standards in Western India 1510-1570', in Lucassen and Seshan (eds.), 2022, 43-84.

Cautley, Proby T., *Report on the Ganges Canal Works*, Part 3 (London 1860).

Chakrabarti, Shubhra, 'Intransigent Shroffs and the English East India Company's Currency Reforms in Bengal, 1757-1800', *IESHR* 34: 1 (1997), 69-94.

Chakraborty, Titas, *Empire of Labor: How the East India Company Colonised Hired Work* (Oakland CA, 2025).

Challis, C.E. (ed.), *A New History of the Royal Mint* (Cambridge, 1992).

Chameroy, Jérémie and Pierre-Marie Guihard (eds.), *Circulations monétaires et réseaux d'échanges en Normandie et dans le Nord-Ouest européen (Antiquité - Moyen Âge)* (Caen, 2012).

Chandavarkar, A.G., 'Money and Credit, 1858-1947', in Dharma Kumar (ed.), 1983, 762-803.

Chandra, Satish (ed.), *Essays in Medieval Indian Economic History* (New Delhi, 1987).

———, 'Some aspects of the growth of a money economy in India during the seventeenth century', *IESHR* 3: 4 (1966), 321-33.

Chatterjee, Kumkum, 'Collaboration and Conflict. Bankers and Early Colonial Rule in India, 1757-1813', *IESHR* 30: 3 (1993), 283-310.

Chattopadhyay, Amal Kumar, *Slavery in the Bengal Presidency, 1772-1843* (London, 1977).

Chattopadhyaya, Brajadulal, *Coins and Currency Systems in South India, c.* AD *25-1300* (New Delhi, 1977).

———, *The Age of the Kushans. A Numismatic Study* (Calcutta, 1979).

———, 'Book Review of John Deyell, *Living without Silver: The Monetary History of Early Medieval North India* (Delhi, 1990)', *Studies in History*, n.s. 7:1 (1991), 168-73.

———, *The Making of Early Medieval India* (Delhi, 1994).

———, 'Trade and Urban Centres in Early Medieval North India', in Chattopadhyaya 1994, 130-54.

Chaudhuri, B., 'Agrarian Relations: Eastern India', in Dharma Kumar (ed.) 1983, 86-177.

Chaudhuri, K.N., *The Trading World of Asia and the English East India Company, 1660-1760* (Cambridge, 1978).

Chaudhury, Sushil, *Trade, Politics and Society: The Indian Milieu in the Early Modern Era* (New Delhi, 2015).

———, *Spinning Yarns: Bengal Textile Industry in the Backdrop of John Taylor's Report on 'Dacca Cloth Production' (1801)* (New Delhi, 2020).

Chevaleyre, Claude, 'Acting as master and bondservant: considerations on status, identities and the nature of "bond-servitude" in late Ming China', in Stanziani (ed.) 2012, 237-72.

Ciani, Louis, *Les monnaies royales françaises de Hugues Capet à Louis XVI* (Paris, 1926).

Colvin, [John], 'On the Restoration of the Ancient Canals in the Delhi Territory', *Journal of the Asiatic Society of Bengal* 2 (1833), 105-27.

Colvin, Auckland, *John Russell Colvin, the last Lieutenant-Governor of the North-West under the Company* (Oxford, 1895).

Cook, M.A. (ed.), *Studies in the Economic History of the Middle East* (Oxford, 1978).

Cooper, Randolf G.S., *The Anglo-Maratha Campaigns and the Contest for*

India: The Struggle for Control of the South Asian Military Economy (Cambridge, 2003).

Craig, John, *The Mint. A History of the London Mint from* AD *287 to 1948* (Cambridge, 2011).

Cribb, Joe, Barrie Cook and Ian Carradice, *The Coin Atlas: The world of Coinage from its Origins to the Present Day* (London, 1990).

Crooke, W., *Natives of Northern India* (London, 1907).

———, *The North-Western Provinces of India: Their History, Ethnology, and Administration* (London, 1897).

Cuhaj, George and Thomas Michael (eds.), *Standard Catalogue of World Coins 1701-1800*, 6th edn. (Iola, Wi, 2013).

Curley, D.L., 'Fair grain markets and Mughal famine policy in late eighteenth century Bengal', *Calcutta Historical Journal* 2 (1977), 1-27.

Dadachanji, B.E., *The Monetary System of India* (Bombay, 1948).

Dalton, George (ed.), *Primitive, Archaic and Modern Economies: Essays of Karl Polanyi* (Boston, 1971).

Dam, Pieter van, *Beschryvinge van de Oostindische Compagnie*, ed. F.W. Stapel and C.W.Th. van Boetzelaaar, 4 vols., 7 pts ('s Gravenhage, 1927-54).

Das Gupta, Ashin, *The World of Indian Ocean Merchant: Collected Essays of Ashin Das Gupta*, ed. Uma Das Gupta (New Delhi, 2000).

Datta, Kalikinkar, *Survey of India's Social Life and Economic Condition in the Eighteenth Century, 1707-1813* (New Delhi, 1978).

Datta, Rajat, *Economic Transition in Early Modern India: Production, Subsistence and the Market in Eighteenth-Century Bengal* (New Delhi, 2024).

———, *Society, Economy and the Market: Commercialization in Rural Bengal c. 1760-1800* (New Delhi, 2000).

Davis Jr., Donald R., 'Economics and Business as Vaisya-Dharma', in Olivelle and Davis Jr. (eds.) 2018, 496-505.

Davis, Donald R. Jr. (ed.), *The Oxford History of Hinduism: Hindu Law* (Oxford, 2018), 496-505.

Day, John, *The Medieval Market Economy* (Oxford, 1987)

———, 'The Great Bullion Famine of the Fifteenth Century', in Day 1987, 1-54.

De, Sushil Chandra, 'The cowrie currency in India', *The Orissa Historical Research Journal* 1: 1 (1952), 1-10 and 1: 2 (1952), 10-21.

Della Valle, Pietro, *The Travels of Pietro Della Valle in India*, ed. Edward Grey (London, 1882).

Deng, Kent Gang, 'Imperial China under the Song and late Qing', in Monson and Scheidel (eds.) 2015, 308-42.

Depeyrot, G. (ed.), *Documents and Studies on 19th c. Monetary History: When Orient and Occident Meet* (Wetteren, 2014).

________, *Three Conferences on International Monetary History* (Wetteren, 2013).

Derrett, J. Duncan M., 'The right to earn in ancient India: A conflict between expediency and authority', *JESHO*, Part 1 (1957), 66-97.

Desai, Ashok, 'Population and Standards of Living in Akbar's Time: A Second Look', *IESHR* 15: 1 (1978), 53-79.

Desan, Christine, *Making Money: Coin, Currency, and the Coming of Capitalism* (Oxford, 2015).

Desrousseaux, Stéphane, *La monnaie en circulation en France sous Napoléon*, Paris, 2012).

Deyell, John S., 'Numismatic Methodology in the Estimation of Mughal Currency Output', *IESHR*, 13.3 (1976), 393-401.

________, 'The China Connection: Problems of Silver Supply in Medieval Bengal', in Richards (ed.), 1983, 207-27.

________ (1987a). 'The Development of Akbar's Currency System and Monetary Integration of the Conquered Kingdoms', in Richards (ed.) 1987, 13-67.

________ (1987b). 'Long-Term Production Trends for Copper Coins in the Mughal Empire', in Richards (ed.), 1987, 160-4.

________, *Living Without Silver: The Monetary History of Early Medieval North India* (Delhi, 1990).

________, 'The China Connection: Problems of Silver Supply in Medieval Bengal', in Subrahmanyam (ed.), 1994, 186-218.

________, 'Cowries and coins: The dual monetary system of the Bengal Sultanate', *IESHR* 47, 1 (2010), 63-106.

________, *Treasure, Trade and Tradition: Post-Kidarite Coins of the Gangetic Plains and Punjab Foothills, 590-820* CE (Delhi, 2017).

Deyell, John and Rila Mukherjee, *From Mountain Fastness to Coastal Kingdoms: Hard Money and Cashless Economies in the Medieval Bay of Bengal World* (New Delhi, 2019).

Deyell, John S. and Robert E. Frykenberg, 'Sovereignty and the 'Sikka' under the Raj: Minting Prerogative and Imperial Legitimacy in India', *IESHR* 19 (1982), 1-25.

Deyell, John S., Nicholas Rhodes and William F. Spengler, *The Standard Guide to South Indian Coins and Paper Money since* AD *1556* (Iola, Wisc, 1981).

Dharma Kumar (ed.), *The Cambridge Economic History of India, II, c. 1757-c. 1970* (Cambridge, 1983).

Digby, Simon, 'Economic Conditions before 1200', in Raychaudhuri and Habib (eds.), 1982, 41-7.

———, 'The Currency System', in Raychaudhuri and Habib (eds.) 1982, 93-101.

———, *War-Horse and Elephant in the Delhi Sultanate: A Study of Military Supplies* (Oxford, 1971).

Doty, Richard, *The Soho Mint and the Industrialization of Money* (London, 1998).

Drèze, Jean and Amartya Sen, *An Uncertain Glory: India and its Contradictions* (Princeton, 2013).

Dyer, Christopher, 'A Golden Age Rediscovered: Labourers' Wages in the Fifteenth Century', in Allen and Coffman (eds.) 2015, 180-95.

Dyer, Graham P. and Peter P. Gaspar, 'Reform, the new technology and Tower Hill, 1700-1966', in Challis (ed.) 1992, 398-606.

Dyson, Tim (ed.), *India's Historical Demography* (London, 1989).

Dyson, Tim, *A Population History of India: From the First Modern People to the Present Day* (Oxford, 2018).

Ekama, Kate, Lisa Hellman and Matthias van Rossum, *Slavery and Bondage in Asia 1550-1850: Towards a Global History of Coerced Labour* (Berlin/Boston, 2022).

Ellis, Frank W., 'In What Way, and to What Degree, Did the Mughal State Inhibit Smithian Growth in India in the Seventeenth Century?', London School of Economics, Working Paper Nos. 14/05 (May 2005).

Ellstaetter, Karl, *Indiens Silberwährung: Eine wirtschaftsgeschichtliche Studie* (Stuttgart, 1894).

Encyclopedie van Munten en Bankbiltetten, ed. E.J.A. van Beek (Houten, 1986-2002; new edn.). Online: https://www.muntenenpapiergeld.nl/).

Fawa'id u'l Fu'dd, Conversations of Shaikh Nizamu'ddin of Delhi, recorded (1307-22) by Amir Hasan Sijzi, ed. Latif Malik, (Lahore, 1966).

Feinman, Gary M. and Christopher P. Garraty, 'Preindustrial markets and marketing: Archaeological perspectives', *Annual Review of Anthropology* 39 (2010), 167-91.

Fellman, Susanna et al. (eds.), *Creating Nordic Capitalism: The Business History of a Competitive Periphery* (New York, 2008).

Fengler, Heinz, Gerhard Gier and Willy Unger, *Lexikon der Numismatik*, 2nd edn. (Berlin, 1976).

Ferraro Vaz, J. and M. Correia de Souza, *Dinheiro Luso-Indiano: Indo-Portuguese Money* (Braga, 1980).

Firishta, *Gulshan-i Ibrahimi* or *Tarikh-i Firishta* (Kanpur, 1874).

Florén, Anders, 'Social organization of work and labour conflicts in proto-industrial iron production in Sweden, Belgium and Russia', *International Review of Social History* 39 (1994), Supplement, 83-113.

Fort William – India House Correspondence 1789-1792, ed. I.B. Banerjee (Delhi, 1974).

Foster, William (ed.), *A Supplementary Calendar of Documents in the India Office relating to India or the Home Affairs of the East India Company, 1600-1640* (London, 1928)

________, *English Factories in India, 1622-31*, Vol. 1 (Oxford, 1908).

________, *English Factories in India, 1622-31*, Vol. 2 (Oxford, 1908).

________, *English Factories in India, 1634-34*, Vol. 5 (Oxford, 1911).

________, *English Factories in India, 1661-64*, Vol. 11 (Oxford, 1927).

Fukazawa, Hiroshi, 'Agrarian Relations', in Raychaudhuri and Habib (eds.) 1982, 177-207.

________, *The Medieval Deccan: Peasants, Social Systems and States. Sixteenth to Eighteenth Centuries* (Delhi, 1991).

Further Reports from Her Majesty's Diplomatic and Consular Agents Abroad Respecting the Condition of the Industrial Classes and the Purchase Power of Money in Foreign Countries, 2 vols. (London, 1870-1).

Ganguli, B.N., *Indian Economic Thought* (New Delhi, 1977).

Garg, Sanjay, 'The Closure of the Delhi mint, AD 1818', in Macdowall, Sharma and Garg (eds.) 1992, II, 233-40.

________, '"Sikka" and the Crown: Genesis of the Native Coinage Act, 1876', *IESHR* 35 (1998) 359-380; substantially enlarged in *Princely States Report* (Fall 2001). Online: http://www.princelystates.com/CurrentIssue/fa-04-02a.shtml.

________, 'Dies and Minting Scenes from India', in Travaini and Bolis (eds.), *Conii e Scene di Coniazione* (Roma, 2007), 353-70.

________, 'Non-Metallic Currencies of India in Indian Ocean Trade and Economies', in Ray and Alpers (eds.), 2007, 245-62.

________, 'History of the Currency Legislations of the East India Company, 1772-1835' (unpublished PhD thesis JNU New Delhi, 2008).

________, *The Sikka and the Raj: A History of Currency Legislations of the East India Company, 1772-1835* (New Delhi, 2013).

Garg, Sanjay (ed.), *Monetary Foundations of the Raj* (Monetary History of India 1; New Delhi, 2019).

________, *The Raj and the Rajas: Money and Coinage in Colonial India* (Monetary History of India 2; New Delhi, 2022).

Gemmill, Elizabeth and Nicholas Mayhew, *Changing Values in Medieval Scotland: A Study of Prices, Money, and Weights and Measures* (Cambridge, 1995).

Gershenkron, Alexander, 'Mercator Gloriosus', *The Economic History Review*, 2nd Series 24:4 (1971), 653-66.

Gerson Da Cunha, J., *Contributions to the Study of Indo-Portuguese Numismatics* (Bombay, 1880).

________, *Notes on the History and Antiquities of Chaul and Bassein* (Bombay, 1876).

Glahn, Richard von, 'Monies of account and monetary transition in China, twelfth to fourteenth centuries', *JESHO*, 53 (2010), 463-505.

________, *Fountain of Fortune: Money and Monetary Policy in China, 1000-1700* (Berkeley, 1996).

Glamann, Kristof, 'The Dutch East India Company's Trade in Japanese Copper, 1645-1736', *The Scandinavian Economic History Review* 1 (1953), 41-79.

________, 'European Trade 1500-1750', in Carlo M. Cipolla (ed.), *The Fontana Economic History of Europe. The Sixteenth and Seventeenth centuries* (Glasgow, 1974), 427-526.

________, *Dutch-Asiatic Trade, 1620-1740* ('s-Gravenhage, 1981).

Gomes, Alberto, *Moedas Portuguesas e do Território que hoje é Portugal.* 5th edn. (Lisbon, 2007).

Gommans, Jos, 'Horse-traders, Mercenaries and Princes: The formation of the Indo-Afghan empire in the eighteenth century', Leiden: PhD dissertation 1993 (Abingdon, 2003).

Gopal, Lallanji, *Economic Life in Northern India, c. AD 700-1200* (Delhi, 1965).

Goron, Stan and J.P. Goenka, *The Coins of the Indian Sultanates, Covering the Area of Present-day India, Pakistan and Bangladesh* (New Delhi, 2001).

Goubert, Pierre, *Cent mille provinciaux au XVIIe siècle. Beauvais et le Beauvaisis de 1600 à 1730* (Paris, 1968).

Graeber, David, *Debt. The First 5,000 Years* (New York, 2011).

Gramlich-Oka, Bettina (2008), 'Shogunal administration of copper in the mid-Tokugawa period (1670-1720)', in Hirzel and Kim (eds.), 2008, 65-105.

Grout, Andrew, 'Geology and India 1775-1805: An Episode in Colonial Science', *South Asian Research* 10: 1 (1990), 1-18.

_______, *Geology and India, 1770-1851: A study in the methods and motivations of a colonial science* (PhD thesis, SOAS, London University, 1995).

Grover, B.R., 'An Integrated Pattern of Commercial life in the Rural Society of North India during the Seventeenth and Eighteenth Centuries', in Subrahmanyam (ed.) 1994), 219-55.

Growse, F.S., *Mathurá: A District Memoir*, rep. of the 3rd edn., 1883 revised (Bombay, 1978).

Grytten, Ola Honningdal, 'Economic growth and purchasing power parities in the Nordic countries, 1830-1910', in Heikkinen and van Zanden (eds.), 2004, 89-104.

Gupta, N.S., *Industrial Structure of India during Medieval Period* (Delhi, 1970).

Gupta, Parmeshwari Lal, *Coins* (Delhi, 1996).

Gupta, Ranjan Kumar, *The Economic Life of a Bengal District: Birbhum 1770-1857* (Burdwan, 1984).

Gupta, S.P., 'Prices and rural commerce in 17th century eastern Rajasthan', *Proceedings of the Indian History Congress* (Kurukshetra, 1982), 270-82.

Gupta, Satya Prakash, 'Jhain of the Delhi Sultanate', *Medieval India – A Miscellany*, 3 (1975), 209-15.

Gupta, S.P. and Shireen Moosvi, 'Weighted price and revenue rate indices of eastern Rajasthan (*c.* 1650-1750), *IESHR* 12: 2 (1975), 183-93.

Habib, Irfan, 'Banking in Mughal India', in Raychaudhuri (ed.), 1960, 1-20.

_______, 'The Currency System of the Mughal Empire', *Medieval India Quarterly* 4: 1/2 (1961), 1-21.

_______, 'The Mansab System, 1595-1637', *Proceedings of the Indian History Congress* (Patiala Session, 1967), 228-49.

_______, 'The System of Bills of Exchange (Hundis) in the Mughal Empire', *Proceedings of the Indian History Congress* 33 (1971), 290-303.

_______, 'Economic history of the Delhi Sultanate: An Essay in Interpretation', *Indian Historical Review* 4: 2 (1977), 287-303.

_______ (1982a), 'Agrarian Economy', in Raychaudhuri and Habib (eds.), 1982, 48-76.

_______ (1982b), 'Non-Agricultural Production', in Raychaudhuri and Habib (eds.),1982, 76-93.

———— (1982c), 'Population', in Raychaudhuri and Habib (eds.), 1982, 163-71.

———— (1982d), 'Monetary System and Prices', in Raychaudhuri and Habib (eds.), 1982, 360-81.

————, *An Atlas of the Mughal Empire: Political and Economic Maps with Detailed Notes, Bibliography and Index* (Delhi, 1986).

————, *Caste and Money in Indian History* (Bombay, 1987).

————, 'A System of Trimetallism in the Age of the "Price Revolution": Effects of the Silver Influx on the Mughal Monetary System', (with an appendix by John Deyell), in Richards (ed.), 1987, 137-70.

————, 'The Price Regulations of 'Ala'uddin Khalji. A Defence of Zia'Barani', in Subrahmanyam (ed.), 1994, 85-111 (Part I: Studies, No. 5 in this volume).

————, *Essays in Indian History: Towards a Marxist Perception* (New Delhi, 1995).

————. 'The Social Distribution of Landed Property in Pre-British India: A Historical Survey', in Habib 1995, 59-108.

————. 'The Peasant in Indian History', in Habib 1995, 109-60.

————. 'Caste in Indian History', in Habib 1995, 161-79.

————, *The Agrarian System of Mughal India*, 2nd edn. (New Delhi, 1999).

————, 'South Asia', in Burke and Inalcik (eds.) 1999, 277-301.

————, 'Exploring Medieval Gender History', *Indian Historical Congress, Symposia Papers* 23 (Calicut, 2000).

————, *The Indus Civilization* (Delhi, 2002).

Habib, Irfan (ed.), *India: Studies in the History of an Idea* (New Delhi, 2005).

————, *Economic History of Medieval India, 1200-1500* (New Delhi, 2011).

Habib, Irfan, *The Agrarian System of Mughal India (1556-1707)* (Bombay, 1963; 3rd edition Oxford, 2014).

Habib, Irfan and Vijay Kumar Thakur, *The Vedic Age* (Delhi, 2003).

Habib, Mohamed and K.A. Nizami (eds.), *A Comprehensive History of India*, Vol. V (Delhi, 1940).

Haddad, Eduardo A., and Inácio F. Araújo, *Regional Science Meets the Past: What Do Coin Finds Tell Us About the Ancient Spatial Economy?* (São Paulo, 2022).

Haider, Najaf, 'The Monetary Basis of Credit and Banking Instruments in the Mughal Empire', in Bagchi (ed.), 2002, 58-79.

————, 'Coinage and the silver crisis', in Habib (ed.) 2011, 149-62.

________, 'Fractional Pieces and Non-Metallic Monies in Medieval India (1200-1750)', in Leonard and Theobald (eds.), 2015, 86-107.

________, 'International Trade in Precious Metals and Monetary Systems of Medieval India 1200-1500', *Proceedings of the Indian History Congress* (Patiala Session, 1998), 237-54.

________, 'Mughals and Mahmudis: The Incorporation of Gujarat into the Imperial Monetary System', in Pati et al. (eds.), 2003, 134-52.

________, 'Precious Metal Flows and Currency Circulation in the Mughal Empire', *JESHO* 39 (1996), 298-364.

________, 'Structure and Movement of Wages in the Mughal Empire, 1500-1700', in Lucassen (ed.), (2007), 293-321.

________, 'The Quantity Theory and Mughal Monetary History', *Medieval History Journal* 2:2 (1999), 309-48.

________, 'The Monetary Integration of India under the Mughal Empire', in Habib (ed), 2005, 129-43.

Hall, Kenneth R., 'Coinage, trade and economy in early South India and its Southeast Asian neighbours', *IESHR* 36 (1999), 431-59.

________, 'Price-Making and Market Hierarchy in Early Medieval South India', in Subrahmanyam (ed.), 1994, 57-84.

Hanley, Susan B. and Kozo Yamamura, *Economic and Demographic Change in Preindustrial Japan, 1600-1868* (Princeton, 1977).

Hanumanthan, K.R., *Untouchability: A Historical Study up to 1500* AD: *with special reference to Tamil Nadu* (Madurai, 1979).

Hasan, Aziza, 'The Silver Output of the Mughal Empire and prices in India During the 16th and 17th Centuries, *IESHR* 6: 1 (1969), 85-116; revised in Subrahmanyam 1994, 156-218.

Haselgrove, Colin and Stefan Krmnicek, 'The archaeology of money', *Annual Review of Anthropology* 41 (2012), 235-50.

Haupt, Ottomar, *Arbitrages et parités: traité des opérations de banque: contenant les usages commerciaux, la théorie des changes et monnaies, les dettes publiques et la statistique monétaire de tous les pays du globe*, 8th edn. (Paris, 1894).

________, *L'histoire monétaire de notre temps* (Paris, 1886).

Hawkins, William, *Early Travels in India, 1583-1619*, ed. William Foster (London, 1921).

Headrick, Daniel R., *The Tentacles of progress: Technology Transfer in the Age of Imperialism, 1850-1940* (New York/Oxford, 1988).

Hegeland, Hugo, *The Quantity Theory of Money: A Critical Study of its Historical Development and Interpretation and a Restatement* (Göteborg, 1951).

Heikkinen, Sakari and Jan Luiten van Zanden (eds.), *Exploring Economic Growth: Essays in Measurement and Analysis: A Festschrift for Riitta Hjerppe on her 60th Birthday* (Amsterdam, 2004).

Heimann, J., 'Small Change and Ballast. Cowrie Trade and Usage as an Example of Indian Ocean Economic History', *South Asia*, n.s. 3 (1980), 48-69.

Herrli, Hans, 'Ways and by-ways of Indian numismatics: Aspects of money circulation in the Bengal and Madras Presidencies', *JONS* 214 (Winter 2013), 20-5.

________, *The Coins of the Sikhs* (Nagpur, 1993; 1st edn.; New Delhi, 2004; 2nd revised and augmented edition).

Hesselink, Reinier H., 'A Metal Dealer and Spy from Nagasaki in Manila in the First Quarter of the Seventeenth Century', in Leonard and Theobald (eds.), 2015, 489-510.

Heyne, Benjamin, *Tracts, Historical and Statistical, on India, with journals of several tours through various parts of the Peninsula, also an account of Sumatra in a series of letters* (London, 1814).

Hicks, John, *A Theory of Economic History* (Oxford, 1969).

Hirzel, Thomas and Nanny Kim (eds.), *Metals, Monies, and Markets in Early Modern Societies: East Asian and Global Perspectives* (Berlin, 2008).

Hodivala, S.H. *Historical Studies in Mughal Numismatics* (Calcutta, 1923).

________, *Historical Studies in Mughal Mint Towns and other Essays*, compiled and ed. by Sanjay Garg (New Delhi, 2014).

Hofmeester, Karin and Pim de Zwart (eds.), *Colonialism, Institutional Change, and Shifts in Global Labour Relations* (Amsterdam, 2018).

Hogendorn, Jan and Marion Johnson, *The Shell Money of the Slave Trade* (Cambridge, 1986).

Hossain, H., 'The Alienation of Weavers. Impact of the Conflict Between the Revenue and Commercial interests of the East India Company 1750-1800', *IESHR* 16 (1979), 323-45.

Hunter, William Wilson, *The Annals of Rural Bengal* (London, 1868).

________, *The Indian Empire. Its People, History, and Products*, 3rd edn. (London, 1893).

Hussain, Syed Ejaz, *Shiraz-i Hind: A History of the Jaunpur Sultanate* (New Delhi, 2017).

________, *The Bengal Sultanate: Politics, Economy and Coins (AD 1205-1576)*, (New Delhi, 2003).

Ibn Battuta, *Rihla Ibn batuta*, ed. Karam al-Bustani (Beirut, 1964).

________, *The Rihla of Ibn Battuta*, ed. Mehdi Husain (Baroda, 1976).

Ilahabadi, Khairuddin, *Jaunpurnama* (Jaunpur, 1878).

Iossif, Panos P., 'Who's wealthier? An estimation of the annual coin production of the Seleucids and the Ptolemies', *Revue Belge de Numismatique et de Sigillographie* 161 (2015), 233-72.

Irvine, William, 'Mint Rules in AH 1126 (1714-15 AD)', *Proceedings of the Asiatic Society in Bengal* (May 1898), 149-52.

Isami, *Futuh-us salatin*, ed. A.S. Usha (Madras, 1948).

Ismamoglu-Inan, Huri (ed.), *The Ottoman Empire and the World Economy* (Cambridge, 1987).

Iyer, S. Appadorai, 'The Cherumars of Malabar', *Calcutta Review* 110-11 (1900), 365-70

Izawa, Eiji, 'Developments in Japanese copper metallurgy for coinage and foreign trade in the early Edo period', in Nagase-Reimer (ed.), 2013, 11-24.

Jain, L.C., *Indigenous Banking in India* (London, 1929).

Jha, D.N., *Against the Grain: Notes on Identity, Intolerance and History* (New Delhi, 2020).

________, *Ancient India in Historical Outline*, 3rd edn. (New Delhi, 2018).

Johnson, Gordon (ed.), *The New Cambridge History of India*, Part II, Vol. 5 (Cambridge, 1998).

Jourdain, John, *The Journal of John Jourdain, 1608-1617*, ed. William Foster (Cambridge, 1905).

Kapoor, Mohit and Dinesh Master: *The Nawābs and Kings of Awadh and their Coinage* (Mumbai, 2018).

Karin, Lurvink, 'Strapped for Cash. Non-cash Payments on Louisiana Cotton Plantations, 1865-1908', *Tijdschrift voor Sociale en Economische Geschiedenis* 11: 3 (2014), 123-51.

Kaske, Christine, 'Silver, Copper, Rice, and Debt. Monetary Policy and Office Selling in China during the Taiping Rebellion', in Leonard and Theobald (eds.), 2015, 345-397.

Kathotia, Indra Kumar, 'A Newly Discovered Copper Ticket from Bengal', *ONS-NL* 181 (Summer 2006), 23.

Kelleher, Richard and Ian Leins, 'Roman, medieval and later coins from the Vintry, City of London', *The Numismatic Chronicle* 168 (2008), 167-233.

Kelleher, Richard Mark, 'Coins, monetisation and re-use in medieval England and Wales: New interpretations made possible by the Portable Antiquities Scheme', unpublished Ph.D. thesis, University of Durham (2013). Online: http://etheses.dur.ac.uk/7314.

Kellenbenz, Hermann, 'Final Remarks: Production and Trade of Gold,

Silver, Copper and Lead from 1450-1750', Papers of the XIVth International Congress of Historical Sciences (Stuttgart, 1981), 212-13.

Kerr-Cross, D., 'Ancient mines and miners of India', *Indian Minerals* 4 (1950), 5-10.

Khairu'l Majalis: Conversations of Shaikh Nasiru'ddin Mahmud, recorded (c. 1354) by Hamid Qalandar, ed. K.A. Nizami, (Aligarh, 1959).

Khan, Ali Muhammad, *Mirat-i Ahmadi*, ed. Syed Nawab Ali, 2 vols. and *Supplement* (Baroda, 1927-30).

Khan, Zahoor Ali, 'Railways and the Creation of a national market in Foodgrains', *Indian Historical Review*, 4: 2 (1978), 336-53.

Khanna, D.D. and and R.K. Tandon, 'Siege of the fort of Deeg 9th December to 26th December 1804', *Journal of the Society for Army Historical Research* 63 (1985), 31-52.

Khatun, M., 'Some Observations on Maratha Coins', *Journal of the Numismatic Society of India* 22 (1960), 221-4.

Khurd, Amir, *Siyar ul Auliya* (Lahore, 1885).

Khusrau, Amir, *Khaza'in al-Futuh*, ed. Mohammad Wahid Mirza (Calcutta, 1853).

King, W. and T.A. Pope, *Gold, Copper and Lead in Chota Nagpur and the Adjacent Country* (Calcutta, 1891).

Kling, Blair B. and M.N. Pearson (eds.), *The Age of Partnership: Europeans in Asia before Dominion* (Honolulu, 1979).

Kolchin, Peter, *Unfree Labor: American Slavery and Russian Serfdom* (Cambridge, MA, 1987).

Kolff, D.H.A. and H.W. van Santen (eds.), *De Geschriften van Francisco Pelsaert over Mughal Indië, 1627. Kroniek en Remonstrantie* ('s-Gravenhage, 1979).

Kolff, Dirk H.A., *Naukar, Rajput and Sepoy: The Ethnohistory of the Military Labour Market in Hindustan, 1450-1850* (Cambridge, 1990).

Kosambi, D.D., *Indian Numismatics* (Delhi, 1981).

Kostov, B., M. Gaydarska and M. Gurova (eds.), *Geoarchaeology and Archaeomineralogy* (Sofia, 2008), 248-52.

Kovalchuk, Marina and Georges Depeyrot (eds.), *Documents and Studies on 19th c. Monetary History: Japan. Selection of British and US Documents (1857-1898)* (Wetteren, 2012).

———, *Documents and Studies on Monetary History: India*, Wetteren, 2011).

Krause, Chester L., Clifford Mishler and Colin R. Bruce (eds.), *Standard Catalogue of World Coins*, 22nd edn. (Iola, Wi, 1995).

________, *Standard Catalogue of World Coins: World Coin Listings by Date and Mint, 1701-1800*, 3rd edn. (Iola, Wi, 2002).

Krishnamurty, J., 'The Occupational Structure', in Dharma Kumar (ed.), 1983, 533-50.

Kulkarni, G.T., 'Banking in the Eighteenth Century: A Case Study of a Poona Banker', *Artha Vijnana* 15 (1973), 180-200.

Kulkarni, Prashant P., 'Early Coins of Bharatpur State', in *ONS-NL* 167 (2003), 17.

________, *Coinage of the Bhonsla Rajas of Nagpur* (Nagpur/Bombay, 1990).

Kumar, Dharma, *Land and Caste in South India: Agricultural Labour in the Madras Presidency during the Nineteenth Century* (New Delhi, 1965, 1992).

Kumar, Mukesh, 'Slave Trade in Bihar and the British Responses in the 19th century', *Proceedings of the Indian History Congress* 65 (2004), 546-58.

Kuparadze, David M., Dimitri V. Pataridze and Thomas N. Kerestedjian, 'Ancient Georgian iron metallurgy and its ore base', in Kostov, Gaydarska and Gurova (eds.) 2008, 248-52.

Kostov, R.I., B. Gaydarska and M. Gurova (eds.), *Geoarchaeology and Archaeomineralogy* (Sofia, 2008).

Laere, Raf van, 'The Nieuwerkerken hoard and the circulation of copper coins in the Prince-Bishopric of Liege during the late 18th century', in Depeyrot (ed.), 2013, 179-229.

Lally, Jagjeet, *India and the Early Modern World* (London, 2024).

Lalman and Ritu, 'Numismatic Material from Sirmaur District, Himachal Pradesh', in: *Oriental Numismatic Studies* 2 (1999), 61-88.

Lane-Pool, S., *The Coins of the Mughal Emperors of Hindustan in the British Museum* (London, 1892).

Le Roy-Ladurie, Emmanuel, *Les paysans de Languedoc* (Paris, 1969).

Leeuwen, Bas van, *Human Capital and Economic Growth in India, Indonesia and Japan: A Quantitative Analysis, 1890-2000* (PhD, Utrecht University, 2007)

Leonard, Jane Kate and Ulrich Theobald (eds.). *Money in Asia (1200-1900): Small Currencies in Social and Political Contexts* (Leiden/Boston, 2015).

Liddle, Andrew, *Coinage of Akbar: The Connoisseur's Choice* (Gurgaon, 2005).

Linden, Marcel van der, *Workers of the World: Essays toward a Global Labor History* (Leiden/Boston, 2008).

Lingen, Jan and Jan Lucassen, 'Copper circulation in Northern India in 1830', *Numismatic Digest* 34-35 (2010-11), 148-83. (Part I: Studies No. 10 in this volume).

———, 'Pucka pice in Fatehpur District 1839: the wide and long-lasting circulation of Awadh's coppers', *JONS* 247 (Spring 2022), 9-15. (Part I: Studies No. 11 in this volume).

———, 'Two lacs of Bharatpur and Bindrabund rupees and 15 bags of copper pyce, captured at Dig on Christmas' eve 1804', *JONS* 218 (Winter 2014), 24-32; *Numismatic Digest*, vols. 36-7 (2012-13), 157-81 (Part I: Studies No. 9 in this volume).

———, 'The "mansuri" or "munsoori paisa" and its use: combining numismatic and social history of India, *c.* 1830-1900', *Numismatic Digest* 31 (2007), 187-220. (Part I: Studies No. 12 in this volume).

Lingen, Jan and Kenneth W. Wiggins, *Coins of the Sindhias* (London, 1978).

Lingen, Jan, *Marwar Jodhpur State: History and Coinage of the former Indian Princely State of Jodhpur* (Mumbai, 2012).

Little, J.H., *The House of Jagatseth* (Calcutta, 1967).

Liu, William Guanglin, *The Chinese Market Economy 1000-1500* (Albany, 2015).

Liverpool, Charles Jenkinson Earl of, *A Treatise on the Coins of the Realm; in a Letter to the King* (Oxford, 1805).

Lockyer, Charles, *An Account of the Trade in India* (London, 1711).

Lombard, Denys and Jean Aubin (eds.), *Asian Merchants and Businessmen in the Indian Ocean and the South China Sea* (Oxford, 2000).

Lombard, Denys, 'Introduction', in Lombard and Aubin (eds.) 2000, 1-15.

Lopez, Robert, Harry Miskimin and Abraham Udovitch, 'England to Egypt, 1300-1500: Long-term Trends and Long-distance Trade', in Cook (ed.) 1978, 93-128.

Lucas, Robert E. Jr., 'Nobel Lecture: Monetary Neutrality', *Journal of Political Economy* 104 (1996), 661-82.

Lucassen, Jan, 'Coin production, coin circulation, and the payment of wages in Europe and China 1200-1900', in Moll-Murata, Jianze, and Vogel (eds.), 2005, 423-46.

———, 'The Brickmakers' Strikes on the Ganges Canal in 1848-1849', *International Review of Social History* 51: Supplement 14 (2006), 47-83.

———, 'Brickmakers in Western Europe (1700-1900) and Northern

India (1800-2000): Some Comparisons', in Lucassen (ed.) 2006b, 513-71.

———, *Wages and Currency: Global Comparisons from Antiquity to the Twentieth Century* (Bern, 2007), 293-321 (Studies No. 6 in this volume).

———, 'Introduction: Wages and Currency, 500 BCE-2000 CE', in Lucassen (ed.) 2007b, 9-58.

———, 'The Logistics of Wage Payments: Changing Patterns in Northern India in the 1840s', in Lucassen (ed.), 2007b, 349-90. (Studies No. 13 in this volume).

———, 'Wage Payments and Currency Circulation in the Netherlands from 1200 to 2000', in Lucassen (ed.) 2007d, 221-63.

———, 'Working at the Ichapur Gunpowder Manufactury in the 1790s', *Indian Historical Review* 39 (2012), 19-56, 251-71.

———, 'Outlines of a History of Labour', *IISH Research Papers*, 51 (Amsterdam, 2013).

———, 'Deep Monetization, Commercialization and Proletarianization. Possible Links, India 1200-1900', in Bhattacharya (ed.), 2014a, 17-55. (Part I: Studies No. 2 in this volume).

———, 'Deep Monetisation: The Case of the Netherlands, 1200-1940', *Tijdschrift voor Sociale en Economische Geschiedenis*, 11:3 (2014b), 73-121.

———, 'Labour and Deep Monetization in Eurasia, 1000 to 1900', in Hofmeester and de Zwart (eds.) 2018a, 327-60 (Studies No. 3 in this volume).

———, 'Deep monetization in Eurasia in the long run', in Speck and van Leeuwen (eds.), 2018b, 55-101 (Studies No. 4 in this volume).

———, *The Story of Work: A New History of Humankind* (New Haven/London, 2021; New Delhi 2025).

———, 'Wages, Labour and Other forms of Remuneration in the Deccan in the 1820s', in Lucassen and Seshan (eds.), 2022, 166-240.

Lucassen, Jan (ed.), *Global Labour History. A State of the Art* (Bern, 2006).

Lucassen Jan and Radhika Seshan (eds.), *Wage Earners in India 1500-1900: Regional Approaches in an International Context* (Los Angeles, 2022).

Lucassen, Jan and Radhika Seshan, 'Introduction: The Study of Wages in India 1500-1900', in Lucassen and Seshan (eds.), 2022, 1-42.

Lucassen, Jan and Jaco Zuijderduijn, 'Coins, currencies, and credit instruments: Media of exchange in economic and social history',

Tijdschrift voor Sociale en Economische Geschiedenis, 11 (2014), 1-13.

Lucassen, Jan and Rombert Stapel, 'Shifts in Labour Relations in India 1800-2000', Paper for the *X International Conference on Labour History*, Noida (India) (22-4 March 2014).

———, 'Coin Prices in the Collectors' Market as a Proxy for Mint Production Figures: A Case Study of India (16th-20th Centuries)', Paper IISH, Amsterdam, 2026 (forthcoming).

Macdowall, D.W., Savita Sharma and Sanjay Garg (eds.), *Indian Numismatics, Art and Culture. Essays in Honour of Dr. P.L. Gupta*, 2 vols. (Delhi, 1992).

MacLeod, Henry Dunning, *Indian Currency* (London, 1898).

Magalhaes Godinho, Vitorino, *L' Economie de l' Empire Portugais au XVe et XVIe siècles* (Paris, 1969).

———, *Os descobrimentos e a economia mundial* (Lisbon, 1981-4).

———, 'The Portuguese and the 'Carreira da India' 1497-1810', in Bruijn and Gaastra (eds.), 1993, 1-47.

Maheshwari, K.K. and Biswajeet Rath (eds.), *Numismatic Panorama: Essays in the Memory of Late Shri S.M. Shukla* (New Delhi, 1996).

Maheshwari, K.K. and Kenneth W. Wiggins, *Maratha Mints and Coinage* (Bombay/Nashik, 1989).

Mahru, 'Ainu-l Mulk, *Insha-i Mahru*, ed. S.A. Rashid and M. Bashir Husain (Lahore, 1965).

Maity, S.K., *Early Indian Coins and Currency System* (New Delhi, 1970).

Malcolm, John, *Report on the Province of Malwa and adjoining districts* (Calcutta, 1822).

Manzar, Nishat, *Urban Wage Earners in Seventeenth Century India. Artisans, Labourers, Service Providers and Entertainers* (New Delhi, 2021).

Märcher, Michael, 'Bronze and copper coins in 19th century Denmark - and found at Koldekilde on Bornholm', in Depeyrot (ed.) 2013, 103-22.

Margariti, Roxani Eleni, 'Coins and commerce: Monetization and cross-cultural collaboration in the Western Indian Ocean (eleventh to thirteenth centuries)', in Trivellato, Halevi and Antunes (eds.), 2014, 192-215.

Martin, Marie H, 'The Reforms of the Sixteenth Century and Akbar's Administration: Metrological and Monetary Considerations', in Richards (ed.), 1987, 68-99.

———, *Bahmani Coinage, and Deccani and North Indian Metrological and Monetary Considerations, 1200-1600* (Ph.D. Dissertation University of Michigan, 1980; University Microfilms, Ann Arbor).)

Martiny, Jean-Claude, *Het Munthuis in Gent van de Karolingers tot de Calvinistische Republiek 768-1584*, 3 vols. (Ghent, 2014).

Mason, Shena, *Matthew Boulton. Selling What All the World Desires* (London, 2009).

Mathew, K.S., 'Calicut, the international emporium of maritime trade and the Portuguese during the sixteenth century', in Oliveira e Costa and Rodrigues (eds.) 2010, 280-99.

Matos, Paulo Teodoro de and Jan Lucassen, 'Early Portuguese Data for Wage developments in India: Kannur (Cananor) 1516-1517', *Ler História* 75 (2019), 13-131.

________, *Goa at Work around 1850: A source-based report on labour relations in Western India under the Portuguese* (IISH-Research Paper 54) (Amsterdam, 2020).

Matsukata, Masayoshi, 'Report on the adoption of the gold standard in Japan (1899),' republished by Georges Depeyrot and Marina Kovalchuk in *Documents and Studies on 19th c. Monetary History* (Wetteren, 2014).

Maurer, Bill. 'The anthropology of money' *Annual Review of Anthropology*, 35 (2006), 15-36.

Mayer, Peter, 'Trends of real income in Tiruchirapalli and the upper Kaveri Delta, 1819-1980: A footnote in honour of Dharma Kumar', *IESHR* 43: 3 (2006), 349-64.

Mayhew, Nicholas, 'Wages and currency. The Case in Britain up to *c.* 1600', in Lucassen (ed.), 2007, 211-20.

McCants, Anne, 'A Moral Measure of Capitalism? Pioneers of Capitalism: The Netherlands, 1000-1800', *The Low Countries Journal of Social and Economic History* 21: 2 (2024), 139-47.

Minutes of the Evidence taken at the trial of Warren Hastings Esquire, Late Governor General at the Bar of the House of Lords, Vol. 11 (London, 1788).

Mitchiner, Michael, *Oriental Coins and their Values: Non-Islamic States and Western Colonies A.D. 600-1979* (London, 1979).

________, *Oriental Coins and their Values: The Ancient and Classical World 600 BC-AD 650* (London, 1978).

________, *The Coinage and History of Southern India*, 2 vols. (London, 1998).

Mohsin, K.M., *A Bengal District in Transition. Murshidabad 1765-1793* (Dacca, 1973).

Moll-Murata, Christine, 'Maintenance and renovation of the Metropolitan City God Temple and the Peking City Wall during the Qing dynasty', in Moll-Murata, Jianze and Vogel (eds.), 2005, 233-62.

________, 'State and Crafts in the Qing Dynasty (1644-1911)' (Tübingen, 2008, unpublished Habilitationsschrift).

________, 'China, Taiwan, Japan 1500-2000', paper for the conference of the IISH Global Collaboratory on the History of Labour Relations, 1500-2000 (May 2012).

________, 'Legal conflicts concerning wage payments in eighteenth- and nineteenth-century China. The Baxian cases', in Leonard and Theobald (eds.), 2015, 265-308.

Moll-Murata, Christine, Song Jianze and Hans Ulrich Vogel (eds.), *Chinese Handicraft Regulations of the Qing Dynasty: Theory and Application* (München, 2005).

Monson, Andrew and Walter Scheidel (eds.), *Fiscal Regimes and the Political Economy of the Premodern States* (Cambridge, 2016).

Moosvi, Shireen, 'The Indian Economic Experience 1600-1900: A Quantitative Study', in Panikkar, Byers and Patnaik (eds.), 2000, 328-58.

________, 'The Silver influx, Money Supply, Prices and Revenue Extraction in Mughal India', *JESHO* 30 (1987), 47-94.

________, *The Economy of the Mughal Empire c. 1595: A Statistical Study* (Delhi, 1987).

Moreland, W.H., 'The Value of Money at the Court of Akbar', *Journal of the Royal Asiatic Society of Great Britain and Ireland* (1918), 375-85.

Moreland, W.H., *India at the Death of Akbar* (London 1920; reprinted ed. Delhi 1962).

________, 'Some Sidelights on Life in Agra, 1637-39', *Journal of the U.P. Historical Society* 3 (1923a), 146-61.

________, *From Akbar to Aurangzeb: A Study in Indian Economic History* (London, 1923b).

________, 'A Dutch Account of Mogul Administrative Methods', *Journal of Indian History* 4 (April 1925), 69-83.

________, *The Agrarian System of Moslem India: A Historical Essay with Appendices* (Cambridge, 1929).

Morris, Morris David, 'The Growth of Large Scale Industry to 1947', in Dharma Kumar (ed.), 1983, 553-676.

_______, 'The Population of all-India, 1800-1851', *IESHR* 11: 2-3 (1974), 309-13.

_______, *The Emergence of an Industrial Labour Force in India: A Study of the Bombay Cotton Mills, 1854-1947* (Berkeley, CA, 1965).

Mukherjee, Tilottama, 'Markets in Eighteenth-century Bengal Economy', *IESHR* 48:2 (2011), 143-76.

Mukhia, Harbans, 'Review symposium: II Chapters: III North India Under the Sultanate (sections 1-3) VII: The State and the Economy: The Mughal Empire; VIII: The Systems of Agricultural Production: Mughal India; IX: Non-Agricultural Production: Mughal India', *IESHR* 21: 1 (1984), 116-20.

Muldrew, Craig, 'Wages and the problem of monetary scarcity in early modern England', in Lucassen (ed.) 2007, 391-410.

Munro, John, 'Bullion Flow and Monetary Contraction in Late-Medieval England and the Low Countries' in Richards (ed.), 1983, 97-158.

Murton, Brian, 'Towns and Markets in Salem in the Eighteenth Century', in Raman et al. (eds.) 1983, 399-410.

Nadri, Ghulam A., *Eighteenth-Century Gujarat: The Dynamics of Its Political Economy, 1750-1800* (Leiden/Boston, 2009).

Nagase-Reimer, Keiko (ed.), *Copper in Early Modern Sino-Japanese Trade* (Leiden/Boston, 2016).

Nagaswamy, R., *Tamil Coins: A Study* (Madras, 1981).

Naismith, Rory, *Making Money in the Early Middle Ages* (Princeton/Oxford, 2023).

_______, *Money and Power in Anglo-Saxon England: The Southern English Kingdoms, 757-865* (Cambridge, 2012).

Nandram, Munshi, *Siyaqnama* [Accountancy Manual of Aurangzeb's Reign, 1694-6] (Lucknow, 1879).

Naqvi, Hamida Khatoon, *Urban Centres and Industries in Upper India, 1556-1803* (Bombay, 1968).

Naravane, M.S., *Battles of the Honourable East India Company: Making of the Raj* (New Delhi, 2006).

Neale, Walter C., 'Reciprocity and Redistribution in the Indian Village: Sequel to Some Notable Discussions', in Polanyi, Arensberg and Pearson (eds.), 1957a), 218-36.

_______, 'The Market in Theory and History', in Polanyi, Arensberg and Pearson (eds.), 1957b, 357-72.

Nelson Wright, H., *Coinage and Metrology of the Sultans of Delhi* (Delhi, 1936).

Neogy, Panchanan, *Copper in Ancient India* (Calcutta, 1918; rpt. Patna 1979).

Newbold, Thomas John, 'Mineral Resources of Southern India No. 1: Copper Districts of Ceded Districts, South Mahratta Country, and Nellore', *Journal of the Royal Asiatic Society* 7 (1843), 150-60.

Nolte, H.H., 'The Position of Eastern Europe in the International System in the Early Modern Times', *Review* 6 (1982), 25-84.

Noriko, Imai, 'Copper in Edo-period Japan', in Nagase-Reimer (ed.) 2016, 10-31.

O'Hanlon, Rosalind, Gergely Hidas and Csaba Kiss, 'Discourses of caste over the longue durée. Gopinatha and social classification in India, ca. 1400-1900', *South Asian History and Culture* 6: 1 (2015), 102-29.

O' Malley, L.S.S., *Bengal District Gazetteers: Saran* (Calcutta, 1908).

Oliveira e Costa, João Paulo and Vítor Luís Gaspar Rodrigues (eds.), *O Estado da Índia e os Desafios Europeus* (Lisbon, 2010)

Olivelle, Patrick and Donald R. Davis jr. (eds.), *Hindu Law: A New History of Dharmasastra* (Oxford, 2018).

Palairet, Michael, *The Balkan Economies c. 1800-1914: Evolution without Development* (Cambridge, 1997).

Palat, Ravi, *The Making of an Indian Ocean World-Economy, 1250-1650: Princes, Paddy Fields, and Bazaars* (Basingstoke/ New York, 2015).

Panchamukhi, R.S., 'The coinage of the Vijayanagara dynasties', in *Vijayanagara Sextenary Commemoration Volume* (Dharwar, 1936), 101-17.

Panikkar, K.N., Terence J. Byers and Utsa Patnaik (eds.), *The Making of History: Essays Presented to Irfan Habib* (Delhi, 2000).

Pannekeet, Kees and Anton Cruysheer, 'Holpenningen in Nederland (ca. 1460-1570)', *Jaarboek voor Munt- en Penningkunde* 100 (2013), 59-127.

Parker, Geoffrey, 'The Emergence of Modern Finance in Europe 1500-1730', in Carlo M. Cipolla (ed.), *The Fontana Economic History of Europe: The Sixteenth and Seventeenth Centuries* (Glasgow, 1974), 527-94.

Parry, Jonathan and Maurice Bloch (eds.), *Money and the Morality of Exchange* (Cambridge, 1989).

Parthasarathi, Prasannan, 'Rethinking Wages and Competitiveness in the Eighteenth Century: Britain and South India', *Past and Present* 158 (1998), 79-109.

———, *The Transition to a Colonial Economy: Weavers, Merchants and Kings in South India, 1720-1800* (Cambridge, 2001).

_______, *Why Europe Grew Rich and Asia Did Not: Global Economic Divergence, 1600-1850* (Cambridge, 2011).

_______, 'Money and Ritual in Eighteenth-Century South India', *The Medieval History Journal* 19:1 (2016), 1-20.

Passon, Tom, *Catalogus van de munten van de Nederlandse gebieden overzee vanaf 1601 tot heden* (Apeldoorn, 2022).

Pati, Biswamoy et al. (eds.), *Negotiating India's Past: Essays in memory of Partha Sarati Gupta* (Delhi, 2003).

Paul, Vinyl Baby, 'Local Networks of the Slave Trade in Colonial Kerala', in Ekama, Hellman and van Rossum, 2022, 199-212.

Paustovskij, Konstantin, *Onrustige jeugd: Prelude op de Russische revolutie*, translated from Russian *Bespokojnaja joenost* (Amsterdam, 1976).

Peebles, Gustav, 'The anthropology of credit and debt', *Annual Review of Anthropology*, 39 (2010), 225-40.

Pelsaert, Francisco, *Jahangir's India : The Remonstrantie*, translated by W.H. Moreland and P. Geyl (Cambridge, 1925).

Pelsdonk, Jan, 'Traces of Copper. The origin of copper and the approximate chemical compositions of some 1,500 Dutch coins and medals', *Jaarboek voor Munt- en Penningkunde* 110 (2023), 161-230.

Perlin, Frank, *Studies in Society and Economy in Late Pre-Colonial India* (PhD Leiden University 24 November 1983a).

_______, 'Proto-industrialization and pre-colonial south Asia', *Past and Present* 98 (1983b), 30-95.

_______, 'Growth of money economy and some questions of transition in late-colonial India', *Journal of Peasant Studies* 11: 3 (1984), 96-107.

_______, 'Monetary revolution and societal change in late medieval and early modern times', *The Journal of Asian Studies* 45 (1986), 1037-49.

_______, 'Money-use in Late Pre-colonial India and the International Trade in Currency Media', in Richards (ed.), 1987, 32-373.

_______, 'Disarticulation of the World: Writing India's Economic History', *Comparative Studies in Society and History* 30 (1988), 583-96.

_______, *The Invisible City. Monetary, Administrative and Popular Infrastructures in Asia and Europe, 1500-1900* (Aldershot, 1993), 131-281.

_______, 'Monetary revolution and societal change in late medieval and early modern times', in Perlin 1993.

________, *Unbroken Landscape: Commodity, Category, Sign and Identity; Their production as myth and Knowledge from 1500* (Aldershot, 1994a).

________, 'Changes in Production and Circulation of Money in Seventeenth and eighteenth Century India: An Essay on Monetization Before Colonial Occupation', in Subrahmanyam (ed.), 1994b, 276-308 (Studies, No. 1 in this volume).

Phelps Brown, Henry and Sheila V. Hopkins, *A Perspective of Wages and Prices* (London/New York, 1981).

Pheru, Thakkura, *Dravya Pariksha. Thakkura Pheru Virachita Ratnaparikkshadi Sapt Granth Samgraha,* ed. Agra Chand and Bahnwar Lal Nahta (Jodhpur, 1961).

Pieper, Wilfried, *Ancient Indian Coins: A Comprehensive Catalogue* (Mumbai, 2021).

Pires, Tomé, *The Suma Oriental of Tomé Pires: An Account of the East from the Red Sea to Japan, written in Malacca and India in 1512-1515 and the Book of Francisco Rodrigues.* Transl. by Armando Cortesao, 2 vols. (Lichtenstein, 1967).

Platts, John T., *A Dictionary of Urdu, Classical Hindi and English* (New Delhi, 1988).

Poggi, Gianfranco, *Money and the Modern Mind: Georg Simmel's Philosophy of Money* (Berkeley, 1993).

Polanyi, Karl, Conrad M. Arensberg and Harry W. Pearson, *Trade and Market in the Early Empires. Economies in History and Theory* (Glencoe ILL, 1957).

Polanyi, Karl, *The Great Transformation* (New York/Toronto, 1944).

Polder, Léon van de, 'Abridged history of the copper coins of Japan', *Transactions of the Asiatic Society of Japan* 19 (1891), 419-500.

Pope, G.U., *Text-book of Indian History: Geographical Notes, Genealogical Tables, Examination Questions* (London, 1880).

Prakash, Gyan (ed.), *The World of the Rural Labourer in Colonial India* (Delhi, 1992).

Prakash, Om, 'Bullion for Goods: International Trade and the Economy of Early Eighteenth Century Bengal', *IESHR* 13: 2 (1976), 159-87.

________, 'Asian Trade and European Impact. A Study of the Trade from Bengal, 1630-1720', in Kling and Pearson (eds.) 1979, 43-70.

________, 'Review symposium: III Chapters: III.4: The Currency System; V: The Maritime Trade of India; XII: Monetary System and Prices; XIII: Foreign Trade; XIV.1: Towns and Cities: Mughal India;

XV: Standard of Living: Mughal India Appendix The Medieval Economy of Assam', *IESHR* 21: 1 (1984), 120-7.

________, 'Foreign Merchants and Indian Mints in the Seventeenth and Early Eighteenth Century', in Richards (ed.), 1987, 171-92.

________, 'On coinage in Mughal India', *IESHR* 25:4 (1988), 475-91.

________, *Precious Metals and Commerce: The Dutch East India Company in the Indian Ocean Trade* (Aldershott, 1994).

________, *European Commercial Enterprise in Pre-Colonial India: The New Cambridge History of India*, Vol. II (5) (Cambridge, 1998).

________, *Bullion for Goods: European and Indian Merchants in the Indian Ocean Trade 1500-1800* (New Delhi, 2004).

________, 'Long Distance Trade, Coinage and Wages in India, 1600-1960', in Lucassen (ed.) 2007, 323-48 (See Studies, No. 1 in this volume).

Press List of Ancient Documents Vol. 1. Series II: *Comptrolling Council of Revenue, Patna* (Calcutta, 1917).

Price, J.C., *Notes on the History of Midnapore, as contained in records extent in the collector's office* (Calcutta, 1876).

Pridmore, F., *The Coins of the British Commonwealth of Nations to the End of the reign of George VI 1952*, Part 4: *India*, Volume 1: *East India Company Presidency series c 1642-1835* (London, 1975).

Prinsep, James, 'Analysis of Copper Ore from Nellore; with notice of the Copper Mines at Ajmír and Singhána', *Journal of Asiatic Society of Bengal* 4 (October 1835), 574-84.

Prinsep, James, *Essays on Indian Antiquities and historic, numismatic, and palaeographic, to which are added his Useful Tables*, ed. Edward Thomas, 2 vols. (London, 1858; rpt. New Delhi/Varanasi, 1971).

________, *Useful Tables forming an appendix to the Journal of the Asiatic Society. Part first: Coins, Weights and Measures of British India* (Calcutta, 1834).

Prunaux, Emmanuel, 'La question du cuivre-papier au début du 19ème siècle. Les banques de sols et la loi du 24 germinal an XI', in Depeyrot (ed.), 2013, 147-70.

Qaisar, Ahsan Jan, 'The role of brokers in medieval India', *Indian Historical Review* 1: 2 (1974), 220-246.

________, *Building Construction in Mughal India: The Evidence from Painting* (Bombay, 1988)

Rahman, Amanur, *Zahir-uddin Muhammad Babur: A Numismatic Study* (Karachi, 2005).

Raman, K.V. et al. (eds.), *Srinidhihi. Perspectives in Indian Archaeology, Art and Culture* (Madras, 1983).

Randeria, Shalini, 'Brahmans, Kings, Pariahs: Castes, Exchange and Untouchability in Western India Today', *Wissenschaftskolleg Jahrbuch* [Berlin] (1990/1), 294-312.

Ray, Himanshu Prabha (ed.), *Coins in India: Power and Communication*, (Mumbai, 2006).

Ray, Himanshu Prabha and Edward A. Alpers (eds.), *Cross Currencies and Community Networks: The History of the Indian Ocean World* (Oxford, 2007).

Ray, Himanshu Prabha, 'Inscribed Pots, Emerging Identities: The Social Milieu of Trade', in: Patrick Olivelle (ed.), 2006, 130-43.

Raychaudhuri, Tapan, 'Non-Agricultural Production', in Raychaudhuri and Habib (eds.), 1982, 279-81.

———, 'Non-Agricultural Production', in Raychaudhuri and Habib (eds.), 1982, 279-81.

———, *Bengal under Akbar and Jahangir. An Introductory Study in Social History*, 2nd edn. (Delhi, 1969).

Raychaudhuri, Tapan (ed.), *Contributions to Indian Economic History* (Calcutta, 1960-3).

Raychaudhuri, Tapan and Irfan Habib (eds.), *The Cambridge Economic History of India*, Vol. 1: *c. 1200-1750* (Cambridge 1982).

Reddy, William M., *Money and Liberty in Modern Europe: A Critique of Historical Understanding* (Cambridge, 1987).

Report of the Committee Appointed to Inquire into the India Currency (With Minutes of Evidence, Correspondence, Index, Further Papers (London 1894; rpt. in Kovalchuk and Dereyrot (eds.) 2011).

Rhodes, Nicholas G. et al., *The Coinage of Nepal* (London, 1989).

Rhodes, Nicholas, 'The First E.I.C. Copper Coins for Bengal', *ONS-NL* 159 (1999), 15-16.

Richards, John F., 'The Economic History of the Lodi Period', in Subrahmanyam (ed.) 1994), 137-55.

———, 'Mughal State Finance and the Pre-Modern World Economy', *Comparative Studies in Society and History* 23 (1981), 285-308.

———, 'Outflows of precious metals from early Islamic India', in Richards (ed.), 1983, 183-207.

Richards, John F. (ed.), *Precious Metals in the Late Medieval and Early Modern Worlds* (Durham NC, 1983).

———, *The Imperial Monetary System of Mughal India* (New Delhi, 1987).

Riello, Georgio and Prasannan Parthasarathi (eds.), *How India Clothed* the *World of South Asian Textiles, 1500-1850* (Leiden/Boston, 2009).

Robb, Peter, 'Intermediaries and change in eighteenth-century Gujarat. A note on G.D. Sharma's view of credit, revenue and commerce', in Austin and Sugihara (eds.) 1993, 29-35.

Robb, Peter, 'Çredit, work and race in 1790s Calcutta: Early colonialism through a contemporary European view', *IESHR* 37:1 (2000), 1-25.

———, *Empire, Identity and India. Peasants, Political Economy and Law* (New Delhi, 2007).

Rodgers, Charles J., *Coin-collecting in Northern India* (Allahabad, 1894; rpt.: New Delhi/Madras, 1997).

Romanos, The Manuel Romanos Collection: Coins of Portuguese India and Mozambique (Zürich: Hess-Divo Auction 269, 14 October 1996.

Roscher, Wilhelm, *System der Volkswirtschaft: Ein Hand-und Lesebuch für Geschäftsmänner und Studierende.* Dritter Band: *die Nationalökonomik des Handels und Gewerbefleisses* (Stuttgart, 1881).

Rössner, Philipp Robinson, 'Velocity! The speed of monetary circulation as a historical protagonist in European economic thought and practice, *c.* 1350-1800', Paper XLVIII Settimana di Studi Fondazione 'F. Datini', Prato, 8-11 May 2016. Unpublished.

Rossum, Matthias van et al., *Testimonies of Enslavement. Sources on Slavery from the Indian Ocean World* (London, 2020).

Roy, Tirthankar, *The Economic History of India, 1857-1947* (Delhi, 2000).

Sah, Srinath and Vivek Sah, Kashi ka Sah Gharana (History Past and Present of the Sah Family) (Varanasi, 2007).

Sahillioglu, Halil, 'The Role of International Monetary and Metal Movements in Ottoman Monetary History 1300-1750', in Richards (ed.) 1983, 269-304.

Santen, H.W. van, *De Verenigde Oost-Indische Compagnie in Gujarat and Hindustan, 1620-1660* (Leiden, 1982).

Sargent, Thomas J. and François R. Velde, *The Big Problem of Small Change* (Princeton, 2002).

Scheidel, Walter, 'Real Wages in Early Economies: Evidence for Living Standards from 1800 BCE to 1300 CE, *JESHO* 53 (2010), 425-62.

———, *Rome and China: Comparative Perspectives on Ancient World Empire* (Oxford, 2009).

Scholten, C., *De munten van de Nederlandsche gebi eds. deelen overzee* (Amsterdam, 1951).

Schwecke, Sebastian, Debt, *Trust, and Reputation: Extra-legal Finance in Northern India* (Cambridge, 2022).

Selgin, George, *Good Money: Birmingham Button Makers, the Royal Mint, and the Beginnings of Modern Coinage, 1775-1821: Private Enterprise and Popular Coinage* (Ann Arbor, 2008).

Sengupta, Kaustubh Mani, 'The New Fort William and the Dockyards: Constructing Company's Calcutta in the Late Eighteenth Century', *Studies in History* 32: 2 (2016), 231-56.

Seshan, Radhika, 'Wages and prices in Madras *c.* 1650-1720', in Lucassen and Seshan (eds.) 2022, 85-108.

________, *Empires of the Sea. The Human History of the Indian Ocean World* (New Delhi, 2024).

Sharma, G.D., *Rajput Policy: A Study of Politics and Administration of the State of Marwar 1638-1749* (New Delhi 1977, 2019).

Sharma, R.S. and D.N. Jha, 'The Economic History of India up to AD 1200: Trends and Prospects', *JESHO* 17: 1(1974), 48-80.

Sharma, R.S., *Indian Feudalism, c. 300-1200* (Calcutta, 1965).

________, *Urban Decay in India (c. 300-c. 1000)* (New Delhi, 1987).

Shikano, Yoshiaki (2007), 'Currency, wage payments, and large funds settlement in Japan, 1600-1868', in Lucassen (ed.) 2007, 113-37.

Shimada, Ryuto, *The Intra-Asian Trade in Japanese Copper by the Dutch East India Company During the Eighteenth Century* (Leiden/ Boston, 2006).

Shirras, G. Findlay, *Indian Finance and Banking* (London, 1920).

Shrimali, Krishna Mohan (2002), 'Money, Market and Indian Feudalism: AD 600-1200', in Bagchi (ed.) 2002, 1-39.

Siddiqi, Asiya, *Agrarian Change in a North Indian State: Uttar Pradesh 1819-1833* (Oxford, 1973).

Sijzi, Amir Hasan (1966). See *Fawa'id u'l Fu'dd.*

Simmel, Georg, *Philosophie des Geldes* (München/ Leipzig, 1900, 1907 2nd enlarged edn, 1922).

________, *Soziologie. Untersuchungen über die Formen der Vergesellschaftung* (Leipzig, 1908).

________, *The Philosophy of Money*, transl. Tom Bottomore and David Frisby; 3rd edn., ed. David Frisby (London/New York, 1978, 2009).

Singh, M.P., *Town, Market, Mint and Port in the Mughal Empire, 1556-1707: An Administrative-cum-Economic Study* (New Delhi, 1985).

Singhal, C.R., *Mint-Towns of the Mughal Emperors of India* (Bombay, 1953).

Sivramkrishna, Sashi (2009), 'Ascertaining Living Standards in Erstwhile

Mysore, Southern India, from Francis Buchanan's *Journey* of 1800-01: An Empirical Contribution to the Great Divergence Debate', *JESHO* 52.4, 695-733.

Smail, Daniel Lord, *Legal Plunder: Households and Debt Collection in Medieval Europe* (Cambridge MA/London, 2016).

Smith, Adam, *An Enquiry into the Nature and Causes of the Wealth of Nations*, vol. 2 ([1776] reprinted from the sixth edition, London, 1905).

Sonnenfels, Joseph von, *Grundsätze der Polizey, Handlung, und Finanzwissenschaft*, (München, 1787).

_______, *Grundsätze der Polizey, Handlung, und Finanz*, 2 vols. (Wien, 1804).

South Asian Coins and Paper Money (Iola, WI, 2013).

South Asian Coins and Paper Money, Indian edn. (Iola Wi, 2013).

Speck, Bert van der and Bas van Leeuwen (eds.), *Money, Currency and Crisis. In Search of Trust 2000 BC to AD 2000* (London, 2018).

Spengler, Joseph J., *Indian Economic Thought. A Preface to its History* (Durham, NC, 1971).

Sperling, J., 'The International Payments Mechanism in the Seventeenth and Eighteenth Centuries', *Economic History Review*, 2nd series 14: 3 (1962), 446-68.

Spooner, Frank, 'On the Road to Industrial Precision. The Case of Coinage in the Netherlands (1672-1791)', *Economisch- en Sociaal-Historisch Jaarboek* 43 (1980), 1-18.

Spufford, Peter, 'Scottish black money in the Low Countries *c.* 1484-1506', *The British Numismatic Journal* 84 (2014), 125-39.

_______, *How rarely did Medieval Merchants use Coin?* (Utrecht, 2010).

_______, *Money and its Use in Medieval Europe* (Cambridge, 1988)

_______, *Power and Profit. The Merchant in Medieval Europe* (New York, 2002).

Stahl, A.M., *Zecca. The Mint of Venice in the Middle Ages* (Baltimore, MD, 2000).

Stanziani, Alessandro (ed.), *Labour, Coercion, and Economic Growth in Eurasia, 17th-20th Centuries* (Leiden/Boston, 2012).

Steele, Mark, 'Movements of Exchange rates in the Second half of the Sixteenth Century', in Eddy van Cauwenberghe and Franz Irsigler (eds.), *Münzprägung, Geldumlauf und Wechselkurse: Minting, Monetary Circulation and Exchange Rates* (Trier, 1984), 291-312.

Stein, Burton, *A History of India*, 2nd edn., ed. David Arnold (Chichester, 2010).

———, *The New Cambridge History of India,* Vol. 1.2: *Vijayanagara* (Cambridge, 1989).

Steinfeld, Robert J., *The Invention of Free Labor: The Employment Relation in English and American Law and Culture, 1350-1870* (Chapel Hill, 1991).

Stephen, S. Jeyaseela, *The Coromandel Coast and its Hinterland. Economy, Society and Political System (A.D. 1500-1600)* (Delhi, 1997).

———, *Expanding Portuguese Empire and the Tamil Economy (Sixteenth-Eighteenth Centuries)* (New Delhi, 2009).

Stevens, Paul, 'The Coins of the Bombay Presidency: The Bankot Mint', *ONS-NL* 179 (2004a), 28-32.

———, 'The Coins of the Bombay Presidency: The Transitional Mints of the Deccan', *ONS-NL* 181 (2004b), 4-30.

———, 'The Coins of the Bombay Presidency', *ONS-NL* 180 (2004c), 27-31.

———, 'The Coins of the Bombay Presidency: The Mints of the Northern Districts', *ONS-NL* 182 (2005a), 25-32.

———, 'The Coins of the Bombay Presidency: The Transitional Mints of the Southern Maratha Country: Bagalkot, Belgaum-Shahpur and Dharwar', *ONS-NL*, 183 (2005b), 20-2.

———, 'Copper Pice of the Bombay Presidency, 1791-1794', *JONS* 187 (2006a), 37-43.

———, 'The Coins of the Ceded and Conquered Provinces of the Bengal Presidency', *JONS* 188 (2006b), 18-23.

———, 'The Introduction of the 1835 Quarter Annas (Pice) as Part of the Uniform Coinage of British India', *JONS* 189 (2006c), 22-9.

———, 'The Coins of the Ceded and Conquered Provinces of the Bengal Presidency – the Farrukhabad mint', *JONS* 190 (2007), 37-43.

———, 'Dr Stewart's copper patterns for Bombay 1820-1821', *JONS* 195 (2008a), 31-35.

———, 'The early years of the Calcutta mint, 1757 to 1765', *JONS* 197 (2008b), 37-47.

———, 'The Coins of the Ceded and Conquered Provinces of the Bengal Presidency- Saugor (later Sagar) and related mints', *JONS* 199 (2009), 29-36.

———, 'The Najibabad Mint. Information from the Records of the East India Company' (unpublished ms.).

———, *The Coins of the Bengal Presidency* (London, 2012).

_______, *The Coinage of the Bombay Presidency. A Study of the Records of the EIC* (London, 2019).

Styles, John, 'Our Traitorous Money Makers. The Yorkshire coiners and the law, 1760-1783', in Brewer and Styles (eds.) 1980, 172-249.

Subrahmanyam, Sanjay (ed.), *Merchants, Markets and the State in Early Modern India* (Delhi, 1990a).

_______, 'Rural industry and commercial agriculture in late seventeenth-century south-eastern Asia', *Past and Present* 126 (1990b), 76-114.

_______, *The Political Economy of Commerce. Southern India, 1500-1650* (Cambridge, 1990c).

_______, *Money and the Market in India 1100-1700* (Delhi, 1994).

_______, 'Introduction', in Subrahmanyam (ed.), 1994, 1-56.

_______, 'Precious Metal Flows and prices in Western and Southern Asia, 1500-1750: Some Comparative and Conjunctural Aspects', in Subrahmanyam (ed.), 1994, 186-218.

Svirina, Ekaterina (2014). 'Money circulation in the Siberian region of the Russian Empire', in G. Depeyrot (ed.), 2014, 319-22.

Sykes, William Henry, 'Special Report on the Statistics of the Four Collectorates of the Dukhun, under the British Government', *Report of the seventh meeting of the British Association for the Advancement of Science; held at Liverpool in September 1837*, Vol. 6 (London, 1838), 217-336.

Symons, David, '"Bringing to Perfection the Art of Coining": what did they make at the Soho Mint?', in Shena Mason (ed.), *Matthew Boulton. Selling what all the world desires* (Birmingham, 2009), 89-98.

Tabor, Bary (2010a), 'The "Kachcha Pice" of late 18th and 19th century Malwa', *JONS* 203 (2010a), 16-36.

_______, 'Theories of 'Kachcha-ness', *JONS* 205 (2010b), 33-35.

_______, 'Too Many Najibabads. (The History and Coinage of the "Najibabad" mints)', (unpublished ms., draft September 2008).

Tanabe, Akio, 'The System of Entitlements in Eighteenth-Century Khurda, Orissa: Reconsidering "Caste" and "Community" in Late Pre-colonial India', *South Asia: Journal of South Asian Studies*, n.s. 28: 3 (2005), 345-85.

Tann, Jennifer and John Aitken, 'The Diffusion of the Stationary Steam Engine from Britain to India 1790-1830', *IESHR* 29: 2 (1992), 109-214.

Tavernier, J.B., *Travels in India*. Translated by V. Ball, 2nd edn., rev. by W. Crooke, 2 vols. (London, 1925).

Tek Chand, Lala, *Bahar-i 'Ajam* (Delhi, 1866).

Temple, Richard, *Oriental Experience: A Selection of Essays and Addresses Delivered on Various Occasions* (London, 1883).

Tennant, William, *Indian Recreations, Consisting Chiefly of Strictures on the Domestic and Rural Economy of the Mahommedans and Hindoos*, 2 vols. (Edinburgh, 1803).

Thapar, Romila, *The Penguin History of Early India: From the Origins to AD 1300* (London, 2002).

The Imperial Gazetteer of India, 26 vols. (Oxford, 1908).

Thevenot, Jean de, *Indian Travels of Thevenot and Careri*, ed. Surendra Nath Sen (New Delhi, 1949).

Thomaz, Luíz Filipe F.R., *O Tesouro de Oranjemunde: Espólio da nau Bom Jesus, encalhada na costa da Namíbia à ida para a Índia em 1533. The Oranjemunde Hoard* (Lisbon/Windhoek, 2018).

Thue, Lars, 'Norway: a resource-based and democratic capitalism', in Fellman et al. (eds.), 2008, 394-493.

Thurston, Edgar (assisted by Kadambi Rangachari), *Castes and Tribes of Southern India*, 7 vols. (Madras, 1909).

Thurston, Edgar, *Ethnographic Notes in Southern India* (Madras, 1906).

———, *History of the Coinage of the Territories of the East India Company in the Indian Peninsula; and catalogue of the Coins in the Madras Museum* (Madras, 1890).

Touitou-Michon, Brigitte and Sylvain Michon (2013), 'Mémoire de Léonard de Martin Nadaud ou De l'usage de sou au XIXe siècle en France', in G. Depeyrot (ed.), 2013, 171-8.

Tracy, James D. (ed.), *The Rise of Merchant Empires: Long-distance Trade in the Early Modern World, 1350-1750* (Cambridge, 1990).

Trivellato, Francesca, Leor Halevi and Cátia Antunes (eds.), *Religion and Trade: Cross-Cultural Exchanges in World History, 1000-1900* (Oxford, 2014).

Twist, Johan van, *Generale Beschryvinge van Indien* (Amsterdam, 1648).

Tye, Robert and Monica Tye, *Jitals: A Catalogue and Account of the Coin Denomination of Daily Use in Medieval Afghanistan and North West India* (Lochboisdale, 1995).

Upadhyaya, Nirmala M., *The Administration of Jodhpur State (1800-1947 A.D.)* (Jodhpur, 1973).

Urquhart, David, *Turkey and its Resources* (London, 1833).

Valentine, W.H., *The Copper Coins of India,* 2 parts (London 1914, rpt. 1971).

Valenze, Deborah, *The Social Life of Money in the English Past* (Cambridge, 2006).

Vanhoudt, Hugo, *De munten van de Bourgondische, Spaanse en Oostenrijkse Nederlanden en van de Franse en Hollandse periode 1434-1830* (Heverlee, 2015).

van Cauwenberghe, E. (ed.), *Money, Coins and Commerce: Essays in the Monetary History of Asia and Europe (from Antiquity to Modern Times)* (Leuven, 1991).

Velde, François R., 'On the evolution of specie: circulation and weight loss in the 18th and 19th century coinage', *Document de Travail No. 422, Banque de France* (Paris, February 2013).

Verboven, Koenraad, 'Currency, billion and accounts: Monetary modes in the Roman world', *Revue Belge de Numismatique et de Sigillographie* 140 (2009), 91-124.

'Verhandeling der Munten, Maaten en Gewichten van Neerlandsch India', Verhandelingen van het Bataviaasch Genootschap der Konsten en Weetenschappen 6 (1786), 398-454.

Verma, Tripta, *Karkhanas under the Mughals: From Akbar to Aurangzeb* (Delhi, 1994).

Vieira, João Pedro, 'As amoedações de cobra do Estado da Índia: proveniências, fontes de aprovisionamento e fluxos de metal, *c.* 1510-1640', *Nummus*, 2nd series, 41 (2018), 109-67.

Vilar, Pierre, *A History of Gold and Money 1450-1920* (London 1976; rpt. 1991).

Visaria, L. and P. Visaria, 'Population (1757-1947)', in Dharma Kumar (ed.), 1984, 463-532.

Vogel, Hans Ulrich, 'Unrest and Strikes at the Metropolitan Mints in 1741 and 1816 and their Economic and Social Background', in Moll-Murata, Jianze and Vogel (eds.), 2005, 395-422.

Volckart, Oliver, 'The big problem of the petty coins', and how it could be solved in the late Middle Ages', London School of Economics, Working papers nos. 107/8 (2008).

Wagner-Hasel, Beate, 'Egoistic Exchange and Altruistic Gift', in Algazi, Groebner and Jussen (eds.), 2003, 141-71.

Wallerstein, Immanuel, *The Modern World-System*, 2 vols. (NewYork, 1973-4).

Wang, Helen, 'Official salaries and local wages at Juyan, North-West China, first century BCE to first century CE', in Lucassen (ed.) 2007, 59-76.

________, *Money on the Silk Road: The Evidence from Eastern Central*

Asia to c. AD 800. With a Catalogue of the Coins Collected by Sir Aurel Stein (London, 2004).

Wang, Helen et al. (eds.), *Metallurgical Analysis of Chinese Coins at the British Museum* (London, 2005).

Washbrook, David, 'Merchants, Markets and Commerce in Early Modern South India, *JESHO*, 53 (2010), 266-89.

Watson, Andrew M., 'Back to Gold and Silver', *The Economic History Review*, n.s. 20:1 (1967), 1-34.

Webb, William Wilfred, *The Currencies of the Hindu States of Rajputana* (Westminster, 1893).

Weber, Max, *General Economic History*, transl. by Frank H. Knight (New York, 1961).

Weirong, Zhou, 'Chinese coins: Alloy composition and metallurgical research', in Wang et al. (eds.), 2005, 95-7.

Welten, Joost, *Antihelden: Bijzondere levens van gewone mensen uit de tijd van Napoleon* (Leuven, 2015).

———, *Met klinkende munt betaald: Muntcirculatie in de beide Limburgen, 1770-1839* (Utrecht, 2010).

Whitcombe, Elizabeth, 'Irrigation', in Dharma Kumar (ed.) 1983, 676-737.

White, Jerry, *Mansions of Misery: A Biography of the Marshallsea Debtor's Prison*, (London, 2016).

Whitehead, R.B., *Catalogue of Coins in the Punjab Museum, Lahore*, Vol. 2: *Coins of the Mughal Emperors* (Lahore, 1914).

Whitmore, J.K., 'Vietnam and the monetary flow of eastern Asia, thirteenth to eighteenth centuries', in. Richards (ed.), 1983, 363-93.

Wicks, Robert S., *Money, Markets, and Trade in Early Southeast Asia: The Development of Indigenous Monetary Systems to AD* 1400 (Ithaca, NY, 1992).

Wiggins, K.W., 'The Acquisition of Indian Mints by the English East India Company' in Maheshwari and Rath (eds.), 1996, 327-44.

———, 'Tokens imitating coins of Awadh and other states', *Journal of the Numismatic Society of India* 40: 1-2 (1978), 53-79.

Willis, R.J., *The Weights of Mughal India* (New Delhi, 2024).

Wilson, H.H., 'A Sketch of the Religious Sects of the Hindus', *Asiatic Researches* 16 (1828), 1-136, & 17 (1832), 169-314.

Wilson, C.R., *The Early Annals of the English in Bengal*, 3 vols. (London, 1895-1917).

Wise, James, *Notes on the Races, Castes and Trades of Eastern Bengal.*

Edited with an introduction by Ananda Bhattacharya (New Delhi, 2016).

Wright, H. Nelson, *Catalogue of the Indian Museum, Calcutta*, Vol. 3 *Mughal Emperors of India* (Calcutta, 1907).

———, *The Coinage and Metrology of the Sultans of Delhi* (Oxford, 1936).

Yamamura, Kozo and Tetsuo Kamiki, 'Silver mines and Sung coins. A monetary history of medieval and modern Japan in international perspective', in Richards (ed.), 1983, 329-62.

Yang, Bin, *Cowrie Shells and Cowrie Money* (London/New York, 2019).

Zanden, Jan Luiten van, 'Linking Two Debates: Money Supply, Wage labour, and Economic Development in Java in the Nineteenth century', in Lucassen (ed.), 2007, 169-92.

———, 'The road to the Industrial Revolution: hypotheses and conjectures about the medieval origins of the "European Miracle"', *Journal of Global History* 3 (2008), 337-59.

Zanden, Jan Luiten van et al., *How was life? Global Well-Being since 1820* (Geneva/Amsterdam, 2014).

Zuijderduijn, Jaco, Rombert Stapel and Jan Lucassen, 'Dataset: Coin Production in the Low Countries: fourteenth century to the present', *The Low Countries Journal of Social and Economic History* 15: 2/3 (2018), 69-88.

Zwart, Pim de and Jan Lucassen, 'Poverty or prosperity in Bengal *c.* 1700-1785? New evidence, methods and perspectives', unpublished paper (WEHC Kyoto, August 2015).

———, 'Poverty or Prosperity in Northern India? New Evidence on real wages, 1590s-1870s', *Economic History Review* 73: 3 (2020), 644-67.

Contributors

HABIB, IRFAN (b. 1931), M.A. from Aligarh University, with D.Phil. from Oxford 1958. He taught from 1953 to 1994 at the Aligarh University where he is now Professor Emeritus. His works include *The Agrarian System of Mughal India, 1656–1707* (1963, revd. edn., 1999 & 2014); *An Atlas of the Mughal Empire* (1983); *Essays in Indian History: Towards a Marxist Perception* (1995); *Medieval India: The Study of a Civilization* (2008); *Economic History of Medieval India, 1200–1500* (2011); and *An Atlas of Ancient Indian History* (with Faiz Habib) (2012). He has published twelve monographs in the *People's History of India* series, two of these jointly authored. He has co-edited *Cambridge Economic History of India*, Vol. I (1982); UNESCO's *History of Humanity*, Vol. IV (1999) and Vol. V (2000); and UNESCO's *History of Central Asia*, Vol. V (2003).

HAIDER, NAJAF (b. 1966), is Professor of Medieval and Early Modern History at the Centre for Historical Studies, Jawaharlal Nehru University. He graduated from the Aligarh Muslim University and obtained a doctoral degree from the University of Oxford in Mughal monetary history. He was Samir Shamma Fellow at St Cross College, University of Oxford and Visiting Professor at the University of Vienna, University of Bonn and Erasmus Fellow at University of Göttingen. Haider is also on the editorial board of the *International Journal of Asian Studies*, Cambridge University Press, and he has published on monetary economy, communication and conflict, secretarial classes, the history of Delhi, and the intellectual history of Islam. His forthcoming book on *Money, Networks of Exchange and Prices and Wages in Medieval India* is being published by Primus.

LINGEN, JAN (b. 1942), educated in building engineering, in particular architectural design; he was posted in India from 1968 to 1972, where he got interested in numismatics, to become a leading expert in the field. From 1973 he has published profusely on mainly Indian numismatics, of which his *Coins of the Sindhias* (London: Seaby, 1978, together with Kenneth W. Wiggins) and his *Marwar, Jodhpur state: history and coinage of the former Indian princely state of Jodhpur* (Mumbai: IIRNS Publications, 2012) are best known. Besides being President of the Royal Dutch Numismatic Society, he functioned from 1994 to 2019 as Regional Secretary for Continental Europe of the Oriental Numismatic Society. He is also moderator and one of the most productive contributors to www.zeno.ru *Coins Database*.

LUCASSEN, JAN (b. 1947), the editor of the present volume, holds a Masters degree from Leiden University and he received his Ph.D. from Utrecht University, both in the Netherlands. In 1988 he was appointed at the International Institute of Social History (Amsterdam) to set up a research department. He also held a chair in international comparative labour history of the Free University of Amsterdam, and is a member of the Royal Netherlands Academy of Arts and Sciences. He retired in 2012. Most of his publications regard the history of work, labour, and labour migrations. His most recent major publication is *The Story of Work. A New History of Humankind* (New Haven / London: Yale University Press, 2021, and translated in a number of Asian and European languages).

PERLIN, FRANK (1939-2024), was a student at the School of Oriental and African Studies (SOAS). He did his BA from the University of London and a PhD from Leiden University in 1983 (supervisor J.C. Heesterman). He became a specialist in the monetary history of India, especially of Gujarat, and while joining the newly established section on Non-Western History of the Erasmus University of Rotterdam, he published a great number of books and articles on wide-ranging topics, culminating after his retirement in the *City Intelligible: A Philosophical and Historical*

Anthropology of Global Commodification Before Industrialization (Leiden: Brill, 2020).

PRAKASH, OM (b. 1940), is an economic historian working on the intercontinental trade in goods and precious metals in the early modern period. He completed his MA from the Delhi School of Economics in 1961, where he also defended his PhD. His doctoral thesis, *The Dutch East India Company and the Economy of Bengal, 1630-1720*, was published in 1985 by Princeton University Press. From 1965 to 2005 he joined the Economics Faculty of the Delhi School of Economics. He is a Foreign Member of the Royal Netherlands Academy of Arts and Sciences and the author of *European Commercial Enterprise in Pre-Colonial India* (1998), published under the *New Cambridge History of India* series (part II, vol. 5).

Index

Note: The bewildering spelling variety of Indian words and names in English sources make it impossible to include them all. Therefore, only the most confusing ones have been retained. Short explanations have only been given for mints, copper and other low value coins, and for persons. Gold coins, and the great variety of rupees have not been listed, nor have ubiquitous terms like pice / paisa.